Lecture Notes in Computer Science 9854

Commenced Publication in 1973
Founding and Former Series Editors:
Gerhard Goos, Juris Hartmanis, and Jan van Leeuwen

Editorial Board

David Hutchison
  Lancaster University, Lancaster, UK
Takeo Kanade
  Carnegie Mellon University, Pittsburgh, PA, USA
Josef Kittler
  University of Surrey, Guildford, UK
Jon M. Kleinberg
  Cornell University, Ithaca, NY, USA
Friedemann Mattern
  ETH Zurich, Zürich, Switzerland
John C. Mitchell
  Stanford University, Stanford, CA, USA
Moni Naor
  Weizmann Institute of Science, Rehovot, Israel
C. Pandu Rangan
  Indian Institute of Technology, Madras, India
Bernhard Steffen
  TU Dortmund University, Dortmund, Germany
Demetri Terzopoulos
  University of California, Los Angeles, CA, USA
Doug Tygar
  University of California, Berkeley, CA, USA
Gerhard Weikum
  Max Planck Institute for Informatics, Saarbrücken, Germany

More information about this series at http://www.springer.com/series/7410

Fabian Monrose · Marc Dacier
Gregory Blanc · Joaquin Garcia-Alfaro (Eds.)

Research in Attacks, Intrusions, and Defenses

19th International Symposium, RAID 2016
Paris, France, September 19–21, 2016
Proceedings

Editors
Fabian Monrose
University of North Carolina at Chapel Hill
Chapel-Hill, NC
USA

Marc Dacier
Qatar Computing Research Institute/HBKU
Doha
Qatar

Gregory Blanc
Télécom SudParis
Université Paris-Saclay
Evry
France

Joaquin Garcia-Alfaro
Télécom SudParis
Université Paris-Saclay
Evry
France

ISSN 0302-9743   ISSN 1611-3349 (electronic)
Lecture Notes in Computer Science
ISBN 978-3-319-45718-5   ISBN 978-3-319-45719-2 (eBook)
DOI 10.1007/978-3-319-45719-2

Library of Congress Control Number: 2016949121

LNCS Sublibrary: SL4 – Security and Cryptology

© Springer International Publishing Switzerland 2016
This work is subject to copyright. All rights are reserved by the Publisher, whether the whole or part of the material is concerned, specifically the rights of translation, reprinting, reuse of illustrations, recitation, broadcasting, reproduction on microfilms or in any other physical way, and transmission or information storage and retrieval, electronic adaptation, computer software, or by similar or dissimilar methodology now known or hereafter developed.
The use of general descriptive names, registered names, trademarks, service marks, etc. in this publication does not imply, even in the absence of a specific statement, that such names are exempt from the relevant protective laws and regulations and therefore free for general use.
The publisher, the authors and the editors are safe to assume that the advice and information in this book are believed to be true and accurate at the date of publication. Neither the publisher nor the authors or the editors give a warranty, express or implied, with respect to the material contained herein or for any errors or omissions that may have been made.

Printed on acid-free paper

This Springer imprint is published by Springer Nature
The registered company is Springer International Publishing AG Switzerland

Foreword

Welcome to the proceedings of the 19th International Symposium on Research in Attacks, Intrusions, and Defenses (RAID). Since its inception nearly 20 years ago, RAID has established itself as a highly influential venue with a strong focus on intrusion detection and prevention. Over the past four years, the conference has broadened to include a wider spectrum of research in computer and communications security. This year was no exception, and as a result, the conference offered a strong program covering papers in a multitude of important research areas in computer security. RAID 2016 received 85 submissions, 82 of which met the anonymity and formatting guidelines. The total number of submissions was down from the previous year, but the lower number of submissions could be attributed to a number of mitigating factors, most notably, the much earlier submission deadline of April (as opposed to June). From the submitted papers, the Program Committee (PC) selected 21 papers, representing an acceptance rate of 24.7 %. The papers were reviewed using a double-blind reviewing process, ensuring that the reviewers were unaware of the authors or their affiliations until after the selection was finalized. All papers that were on-topic and met the formatting requirements received at least three reviews and the final selection was made during an in-person meeting, co-located with the IEEE Security and Privacy Symposium, in San Jose, California in May. We thank the authors of both accepted and rejected papers for submitting their research to RAID.

Building on the model set forth last year, the bulk of the meeting was spent discussing papers where the reviews from the PC were not in agreement. The task at hand was not only to identify those papers that were ready for publication, but to also identify promising work that could be improved before the camera-ready deadline. To arrive at the best possible program, the vast majority of accepted papers were assigned a shepherd to ensure that the camera-ready version addressed all the reviewers' concerns and suggested improvements. In many cases, these papers received several rounds of feedback by their shepherds.

It is prudent to note that in selecting PC members, we strived to keep a balance by including experienced PC members while also introducing new talent to the RAID conference. Our goal was to form a PC that included researchers who had not served on the RAID PC more than once in the past three years, and also had a proven track record in terms of top-tier publications. With these limitations in mind, we also made a special effort to extend an invitation to PC members of the 2015 committee who had shown exceptional service. Our hope was that in infusing new talent with more seasoned PC members who had a tendency to offer positive, constructive criticism in the past, the younger researchers would gain invaluable experience by serving on the PC, and more importantly, could help shape the direction of future RAID conferences.

It goes without saying that we are indebted to the entire RAID 2016 PC for selflessly dedicating their time to the process of selecting papers and providing detailed feedback to authors. Serving as a PC member is no easy task, and we believe the recognition for these efforts is often overlooked. For that reason, and to encourage PC members to provide thorough, constructive, feedback to the authors, we adopted the idea introduced last year of awarding an *Outstanding Reviewer* prize. To help select the winner, each PC member was encouraged to rate the reviews of other members, especially on papers they reviewed in common. Additionally, the chairs provided input regarding the set of candidates who went beyond the call of duty, for example, by taking on a higher review load than others, submitting all their reviews on time, and working diligently to find the diamonds in the rough — even arguing for such papers in the face of significant opposition from other PC members! Many reviewers received positive ratings (a testament to the high quality of service we had on this year's PC) and after much deliberation, we are pleased to announce that the award goes to Roberto Perdisci (from the University of Georgia).

We are grateful to the general chair, Joaquin Garcia-Alfaro, and his assembled team for ensuring that the conference ran smoothly. Special thanks is also owed to Gregory Blanc and Françoise Abad for handling the local arrangements, to Christophe Kiennert for the job with the website, and to Yazan Boshmaf for widely publicizing the call for participation and related notices. We also express our gratitude to Murray Anderegg, for making sure that the submission server was almost always available, even during the numerous North Carolina thunderstorms that temporarily knocked out power. We are also indebted to Hervé Debar and Manos Antonakakis for their tireless efforts in securing sponsorship for RAID 2016. Indeed, an event of this caliber would be difficult to pull off were it not for the generous support of our sponsors: Sogeti, Comcast, Neustar, Nokia, Orange Labs, ANSSI, and IRT System X. We greatly appreciate their help and their continued commitment to a healthy research community in security.

We hope that all the participants enjoyed the conference as much as we enjoyed putting the event together.

September 2016

Fabian Monrose
Marc Dacier

Organization

Organizing Committee

General Chair
Joaquin Garcia-Alfaro   Télécom SudParis, France

Program Committee Chair
Fabian Monrose   University of North Carolina at Chapel Hill, USA

Program Committee Co-chair
Marc Dacier   Qatar Computing Research Institute/HBKU, Qatar

Publicity Chair

Yazan Boshmaf   Qatar Computing Research Institute/HBKU, Qatar

Sponsor Chair
Hervé Debar   Télécom SudParis, France

Local Arrangement Chair
Gregory Blanc   Télécom SudParis, France

Local Arrangement Co-chair
Françoise Abad   Télécom SudParis, France

Webmaster
Christophe Kiennert   Télécom SudParis, France

Program Committee

Magnus Almgren	Chalmers University, Sweden
Johanna Amann	International Computer Science Institute, USA
Manos Antonakakis	Georgia Institute of Technology, USA
Michael Bailey	University of Illinois at Urbana-Champaign, USA
Lucas Ballard	Google, USA
Leyla Bilge	Symantec, USA
Lucas Davi	Technische Universität Darmstadt, Germany

Hervé Debar   Télécom SudParis, France
Petros Efstathopoulos   Symantec, USA
Manuel Egele   Boston University, USA
William Enck   North Carolina State University, USA
Vasileios Kemerlis   Brown University, USA
Andrea Lanzi   University of Milan, Italy
Pavel Laskov   Huawei European Research Center, Germany
Zhiqiang Lin   University of Texas at Dallas, USA
Daniela Oliveira   University of Florida, USA
Roberto Perdisci   University of Georgia, USA
Michalis Polychronakis   Stony Brook University, USA
Konrad Rieck   TU Braunschweig, Germany
Christian Rossow   Saarland University, Germany
Stelios Sidiroglou-Douskos   Massachusetts Institute of Technology, USA
Kapil Singh   IBM T.J. Watson, USA
Kevin Snow   Zeropoint, USA
Cynthia Sturton   University of North Carolina at Chapel Hill, USA
Dongyan Xu   Purdue University, USA

External Reviewers

Matteo Dell'Amico   Symantec, USA
Anderson Nascimento   University of Washington, USA

Steering Committee

Marc Dacier (Chair)   Qatar Computing Research Institute/HBKU, Qatar
Davide Balzarotti   Eurécom, France
Hervé Debar   Télécom SudParis, France
Deborah Frincke   DoD Research, USA
Ming-Yuh Huang   Northwest Security Institute, USA
Somesh Jha   University of Wisconsin, USA
Erland Jonsson   Chalmers University of Technology, Sweden
Engin Kirda   Northeastern University, USA
Christopher Kruegel   UC Santa Barbara, USA
Wenke Lee   Georgia Institute of Technology, USA
Richard Lippmann   MIT Lincoln Laboratory, USA
Ludovic Mé   CentraleSupélec, France
Robin Sommer   ICSI/LBNL, USA
Angelos Stavrou   George Mason University, USA
Alfonso Valdes   SRI International, USA
Giovanni Vigna   UC Santa Barbara, USA
Andreas Wespi   IBM Research, Switzerland
S. Felix Wu   UC Davis, USA
Diego Zamboni   CFEngine AS, Mexico

Sponsors

Sogeti (Gold level)
Comcast Cable Communications (Gold level)
Neustar Inc. (Silver level)
Orange Labs (Bronze level)
Nokia (Bronze level)
IRT SystemX (Bronze level)
ANSSI (Bronze level)

Contents

Systems Security

GRIM: Leveraging GPUs for Kernel Integrity Monitoring 3
   Lazaros Koromilas, Giorgos Vasiliadis, Elias Athanasopoulos, and Sotiris Ioannidis

Taming Transactions: Towards Hardware-Assisted Control Flow Integrity
Using Transactional Memory 24
   Marius Muench, Fabio Pagani, Yan Shoshitaishvili, Christopher Kruegel, Giovanni Vigna, and Davide Balzarotti

Automatic Uncovering of Tap Points from Kernel Executions 49
   Junyuan Zeng, Yangchun Fu, and Zhiqiang Lin

Detecting Stack Layout Corruptions with Robust Stack Unwinding 71
   Yangchun Fu, Junghwan Rhee, Zhiqiang Lin, Zhichun Li, Hui Zhang, and Guofei Jiang

Low-Level Attacks and Defenses

APDU-Level Attacks in PKCS#11 Devices 97
   Claudio Bozzato, Riccardo Focardi, Francesco Palmarini, and Graham Steel

CloudRadar: A Real-Time Side-Channel Attack Detection System
in Clouds 118
   Tianwei Zhang, Yinqian Zhang, and Ruby B. Lee

Measurement Studies

The Abuse Sharing Economy: Understanding the Limits
of Threat Exchanges 143
   Kurt Thomas, Rony Amira, Adi Ben-Yoash, Ori Folger, Amir Hardon, Ari Berger, Elie Bursztein, and Michael Bailey

SandPrint: Fingerprinting Malware Sandboxes to Provide Intelligence
for Sandbox Evasion 165
   Akira Yokoyama, Kou Ishii, Rui Tanabe, Yinmin Papa, Katsunari Yoshioka, Tsutomu Matsumoto, Takahiro Kasama, Daisuke Inoue, Michael Brengel, Michael Backes, and Christian Rossow

Enabling Network Security Through Active DNS Datasets............. 188
  Athanasios Kountouras, Panagiotis Kintis, Chaz Lever, Yizheng Chen,
  Yacin Nadji, David Dagon, Manos Antonakakis, and Rodney Joffe

Malware Analysis

A Formal Framework for Environmentally Sensitive Malware 211
  Jeremy Blackthorne, Benjamin Kaiser, and Bülent Yener

AVCLASS: A Tool for Massive Malware Labeling 230
  Marcos Sebastián, Richard Rivera, Platon Kotzias, and Juan Caballero

Semantics-Preserving Dissection of JavaScript Exploits via Dynamic
JS-Binary Analysis 254
  Xunchao Hu, Aravind Prakash, Jinghan Wang, Rundong Zhou,
  Yao Cheng, and Heng Yin

Network Security

The Messenger Shoots Back: Network Operator Based IMSI
Catcher Detection 279
  Adrian Dabrowski, Georg Petzl, and Edgar R. Weippl

On the Feasibility of TTL-Based Filtering for DRDoS Mitigation 303
  Michael Backes, Thorsten Holz, Christian Rossow, Teemu Rytilahti,
  Milivoj Simeonovski, and Ben Stock

Systematization of Knowledge and Experience Reports

A Look into 30 Years of Malware Development from a Software
Metrics Perspective 325
  Alejandro Calleja, Juan Tapiador, and Juan Caballero

Small Changes, Big Changes: An Updated View on the Android
Permission System 346
  Yury Zhauniarovich and Olga Gadyatskaya

Who Gets the Boot? Analyzing Victimization by DDoS-as-a-Service........ 368
  Arman Noroozian, Maciej Korczyński, Carlos Hernandez Gañan,
  Daisuke Makita, Katsunari Yoshioka, and Michel van Eeten

Web and Mobile Security

Uses and Abuses of Server-Side Requests 393
  Giancarlo Pellegrino, Onur Catakoglu, Davide Balzarotti,
  and Christian Rossow

Identifying Extension-Based Ad Injection via Fine-Grained Web
Content Provenance.. 415
    Sajjad Arshad, Amin Kharraz, and William Robertson

Trellis: Privilege Separation for Multi-user Applications Made Easy 437
    *Andrea Mambretti, Kaan Onarlioglu, Collin Mulliner, William Robertson,
    Engin Kirda, Federico Maggi, and Stefano Zanero*

Blender: Self-randomizing Address Space Layout for Android Apps 457
    Mingshen Sun, John C.S. Lui, and Yajin Zhou

Author Index 481

Systems Security

GRIM: Leveraging GPUs for Kernel Integrity Monitoring

Lazaros Koromilas[1](✉), Giorgos Vasiliadis[2], Elias Athanasopoulos[3], and Sotiris Ioannidis[4]

[1] 45 Warren Close, Cambridge CB2 1LB, UK
koromilaz@gmail.com
[2] Qatar Computing Research Institute, HBKU, Ar Rayyan, Qatar
gvasileiadis@qf.org.qa
[3] Vrije Universiteit Amsterdam, Amsterdam, Netherlands
i.a.athanasopoulos@vu.nl
[4] FORTH, Heraklion, Greece
sotiris@ics.forth.gr

Abstract. Kernel rootkits can exploit an operating system and enable future accessibility and control, despite all recent advances in software protection. A promising defense mechanism against rootkits is Kernel Integrity Monitor (KIM) systems, which inspect the kernel text and data to discover any malicious changes. A KIM can be implemented either in software, using a hypervisor, or using extra hardware. The latter option is more attractive due to better performance and higher security, since the monitor is isolated from the potentially vulnerable host. To remain under the radar and avoid detection it is paramount for a rootkit to conceal its malicious activities. In order to detect self-hiding rootkits researchers have proposed *snooping* for inferring suspicious behaviour in kernel memory. This is accomplished by constantly monitoring all memory accesses on the bus and not the actual memory area where the kernel is mapped.

In this paper, we present GRIM, an external memory monitor that is built on commodity, off-the-shelf, graphics hardware, and is able to verify OS kernel integrity at a speed that outperforms all so-far published snapshot-based systems. GRIM allows for checking eight thousand 64-bit values simultaneously at a 10 KHz snapshot frequency, which is sufficient to accurately detect a self-hiding loadable kernel module insertion. According to the state-of-the-art, this detection can *only* happen using a snoop-based monitor. GRIM does not only demonstrate that snapshot-based monitors can be significantly improved, but it additionally offers a fully programmable platform that can be instantly deployed without requiring any modifications to the host it protects. Notice that *all* snoop-based monitors require substantial changes at the microprocessor level.

L. Koromilas—This work was performed while at FORTH, Greece.

1 Introduction

Despite the recent advances in software security, vulnerabilities can still be exploited if the adversary is really determined. No matter the protection enabled, there is always a path for successful exploitation, although admittedly, today, following this path is much harder than it was in the past. Since securing software is still under ongoing research, the community has investigated alternative methods for *protecting* software. One of the most promising is monitoring the Operating System (OS) for possible exploitation. Once an abnormality is detected then the monitor should be able to terminate the system's operation and alert the administrator.

This form of protection is commonly offered by tools known as *Kernel Integrity Monitors* (KIMs). The core operation of these tools is to inspect, as frequently as possible, both the kernel code and data for determining if something has been illegally modified. In principle, compromising an operating system is usually carried out using a kernel rootkit (i.e., a piece of malicious code that is installed in the OS), which usually subverts the legitimate operation of the system by injecting malicious functionality. For example, the simplest way for achieving this is by inserting a *new* (malicious) system call, which, obviously alters a fundamental structure in the kernel's code: the system-call table. In order to identify such a simple rootkit, it is enough to only monitor the memory region where the system-call table is mapped for possible changes.

Implementing KIMs may sound trivial, however the level of sophistication of modern kernel rootkits, gives space for many different choices. A straightforward approach is to implement the monitor solely in software, in the form of a hypervisor which runs and frequently introspects the OS for possible (malicious) changes [6,10,25,29]. This choice is really convenient, since there is no need for installing custom hardware, nevertheless it is implied that the monitor's code is non vulnerable itself. Unfortunately, it has been demonstrated that a hypervisor can be compromised by code running at the guest OS [24]. In addition, formally verifying the monitor's code may need significant effort [17]. A viable alternative is to offer monitors that are implemented in hardware. Copilot [13] is a representative architecture, implemented in a PCI card and it is basically a snapshot-based monitor. Essentially, a snapshot-based system monitors a particular memory region to identify possible malicious changes. As an example, consider the simple case of monitoring the region where the system-call table has been mapped, in order to detect if a new (malicious) system call has be injected. Copilot has a transparent operation, allowing the OS to be unaware of its existence, and thus it stands as a very attractive option, especially in terms of deployment. Still, modern rootkits have evolved and developed techniques that can evade detection, by exploiting the window of opportunity between two snapshots. As a matter of fact, a rootkit can simply perform a (malicious) change right after a snapshot is taken and subsequently remove it before the next snapshot is available.

To overcome this inherent limitation of snapshot-based detection systems, recent proposals have been focused on *snooping* based detection [18,22].

A snoop-based system monitors all the operations that are sent over the memory bus. In the context of the aforementioned example we used, the snoop-based detector would have achieved equivalent detection with the snapshot-based system by capturing the *write* operations that aim at modifying the region where the system-call table is mapped. It is evident, that the snoop-based approach performs a lighter check, since instead of monitoring a particular region, it monitors the bus for a particular operation. Nevertheless, snooping is possible *only* in custom processors, since the memory controller is integrated to the CPU, which poses critical deployment issues. The benefits of snoop-based systems were introduced by Vigilare [22] and have been demonstrated in KI-Mon [18] where, in short, the authors provide experimental evidence that a snapshot-based approach can only reach 70 % of detection rate, while their snoop-based system, KI-Mon, can reach 100 % of detection rate.

In this paper, we acknowledge the benefit of snoop-based systems, such as KI-Mon, but we stress that snapshot-based systems can essentially *do better*. We implement GRIM, a novel snapshot-based KIM based on a GPU architecture. Using GRIM we can easily reach 100 % of detection rate using a snapshot-based *only* architecture. GRIM does not aim to justify that excellent engineering can simply optimize a system. Instead, in this paper we promote the design of a novel architecture, which *does not only* demonstrate high detection rates in snapshot-based integrity monitors, but, also, provides a generic extensible platform for developing KIMs that can be instantly deployed. GRIM works transparently and requires no modifications such as re-compilation of the kernel and installing custom hardware on the system it protects. In addition, GRIM does not aim at simply promoting the usage of GPUs in a new domain. To the contrary, GRIM delivers a design that demonstrates many critical properties for KIMs. Beyond the dramatic speed gains in detection rates, the system is easily programmable and extensible, while it is not based on custom hardware but on commodity devices.

To summarize, we make the following contributions:

- We design, implement, and evaluate GRIM, a novel GPU-based kernel integrity monitor.
- GRIM demonstrates that snapshot-based monitors can do substantially better than it has been so far documented in current literature [18]. We are able to reach easily 100 % detection rate, surpassing substantially the reported detection rate (70 %) in the state of the art.
- GRIM is fully programmable and it provides a generic extensible platform for developing KIMs that can be instantly deployed using just commodity devices. It works transparently and requires no modifications such as re-compilation of the kernel and installing custom hardware on the system it protects.

2 Background

In this section, we describe the architecture of modern graphics cards, with an emphasis on their general-purpose computing functionalities that provide for non-graphics applications.

2.1 GPUs and CPUs

Graphics cards nowadays have significant more computing resources than they used to have a couple of decades ago. The processing speeds they achieve and their low cost makes them a good candidate for many applications beyond graphics rendering [26,27]. They contain hundreds of processor cores, which can be programmed by general-purpose programming frameworks such as OpenCL [3] and CUDA [23], and thus transformed to general-purpose computing platforms.

In general, GPUs execute programs organized in units called *kernels*. The main difference with programs that run on a CPU is that the execution model is optimized for data-parallel execution. The majority of its chip area is devoted to computation units, rather than data caching and flow control. As a result, maximum gains on GPUs are achieved when the same instructions run on all threads concurrently. In contrast, CPUs have big caches accounting for half of the chip and large control logic, since their main target is optimizing a single thread.

2.2 The GPU Memory Hierarchy

The NVIDIA CUDA architecture, which is used for the development of the prototype presented in this paper, offers different memory spaces, optimized for different usages. The host allocates memory for GPU kernels in *global* memory space which maps to off-chip DRAM memory. Furthermore, the *constant* memory space is optimized for read-only accesses, while the *texture* memory space for 2D spatial locality. Allocations to all these types of memory are visible to the host and persistent across kernel launches in the same process context. Individual threads have access to *local* memory, which could reside in global memory though, and is dedicated to a single thread as local storage for automatic variables. The GPU cores, called streaming processors (SP), are grouped together in multiprocessors. Depending on the device generation/model (CUDA compute capability) all different types of global (constant, texture, local) memory accesses are cached in possibly separate caches in each multiprocessor.

Threads are organized in blocks and each block runs on cores of the same multiprocessor. The *shared* memory space offers fast access to the whole thread block. The absolute sizes differ across architectures but some typical sizes are the following. Shared memory is 64 KB per group of 32 threads (warp) inside the thread block, but some of it is also used as a first-level cache by the hardware itself. Registers are not fully addressable, so they are not accessible from the host side. Values can, however, spill to global memory due to excessive allocation [23] which also makes accesses slower.

2.3 GPUs for Kernel Integrity Monitoring

In order to monitor the integrity of host memory, a coprocessor-based system, like GRIM, must meet, at a minimum, the following set of requirements [13]:

- **Independence.** GRIM has to operate in complete isolation, using a single dedicated GPU, and must not rely on the host for monitoring the system's integrity. The GPU must be used exclusively for memory monitoring, hence it cannot be used for other purposes. Any extra GPUs can be easily appended to serve other usages, if necessary, without affecting the proper usage of the kernel monitor. Moreover, GRIM must continue to operate correctly and report all malicious actions, regardless of the running state of the host machine, especially when it has been compromised.
- **Host-memory access.** GRIM must be able to access the physical memory of the host directly for periodically checking its integrity and detecting any suspicious or malicious actions.
- **Sufficient computational and memory resources.** GRIM must contain enough memory to keep a baseline of system state. Moreover, it must have sufficient on-chip memory that can be used for private calculations and ensure that secret data would not be leaked or held by an adversary that has compromised the protected system. In addition, GRIM should be able to process large amounts of data efficiently and perform any operation requested.
- **Out-of-band reporting.** GRIM must be able to report the state of the host system in a secure way. To do so, it needs to establish a secure communication channel and exchange valid reports, even in the case the host has been fully compromised.

In order to meet the above requirements, several characteristics of the GPU's execution model require careful consideration. For instance, GPU kernels typically run for a while, perform some computation and then terminate. While running, a GPU kernel can be terminated by the host or swapped with another one. This model is not secure, as the coprocessor needs to execute in isolation, without being influenced by the host it protects. Essentially we stress that leveraging GPUs for designing an independent environment with unrestricted memory access that will monitor the host's memory securely, is not straight forward, but rather challenging. Many GPU characteristics must be considered carefully and in a particular way. In the following sections we describe how we implement and enforce these requirements in a real system.

2.4 The GPU Execution Model

Execution on the GPU involves two sides, namely the host and the device. The host prepares the device and then signals execution. The basic steps are: *(i)* copying the compiled kernel code to the device, *(ii)* transferring the input buffers to device memory via DMA, *(iii)* running the kernel on the device, *(iv)* transferring the output buffers back to host memory via DMA.

The NVIDIA architectural details are not public but there is substantial work available on reversing the runtime and device drivers [14,21]. From what we already know, there is a host-side memory-mapped buffer that is used by the driver to control the device. API calls for data transfers and program execution translate to commands through this driver interface. Finally, there are alternative runtime libraries and drivers that offer CUDA support such as Gdev [5], Nouveau [1] and PSCNV [4].

2.5 Threat Model

We assume that the adversary has the capability to exploit vulnerabilities in any software running in the machine after bootup. This includes the OS and all of its privileged components. We also assume that the adversary does not have access to the hardware, and thus cannot replace the installed GPU with a malicious one using the same driver interface.

In-Scope Threats. Snapshot-based kernel integrity monitor techniques aim to ensure the integrity of the operating system of the already compromised host, and primarily to detect modifications on memory regions that are considered immutable after boot, such as the text of the kernel and any of the loaded LKMs, as well as the contents of their critical data structures.

Out-of-Scope Threats. Sophisticated rootkits [7,11,12,28] that evade snapshot-based kernel integrity monitors are out of scope. For example, there are CPU-controlled address translation methods that can be used to mount address space relocation attacks, by changing the page directory pointer of the kernel context [12]. So far, there is an arms race between building techniques that allow a rootkit to evade detection and bypass a KIM, and building detection methods that are able to capture these highly sophisticated attacks. To this aspect we contribute a new architectural paradigm for building fast snapshot-based KIMs that can potentially integrate the state-of-the-art detection algorithms.

3 Design

In this section we describe the design of GRIM at the hardware and software level, and we show how we can leverage modern GPUs as a monitoring mechanism that meets the requirements described in Sect. 2.3.

GRIM is an external, snapshot-based, integrity monitor, that can also provide programmability and easy deployment. The overall architecture is shown in Fig. 1. Essentially, the GPU reads the specified kernel memory regions over the PCI Express bus, via DMA. Each region is investigated in terms of integrity, and any abnormal or suspicious status is reported to an external admin station that is connected on the local network.

From a software perspective, GRIM has two counterparts that run concurrently: the device program (GPU code) and the host program (user process). The device program is responsible for checking the integrity of a requested list of memory regions, and raise any alerts. The host program periodically reads the status area and forwards it to the admin station in the form of a keep-alive

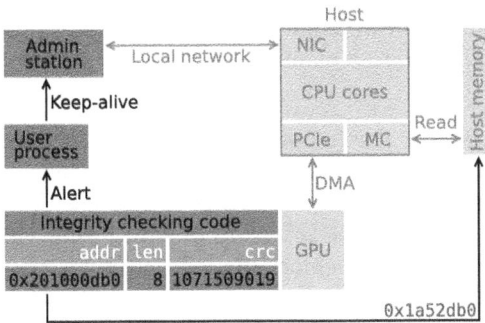

Fig. 1. Hardware/software architecture highlighting the monitor access path. The GPU is configured to periodically check a list of host memory regions against known checksums by reading the corresponding device virtual addresses (left). The user program periodically sends an encrypted sequence number together with a status code to a separate admin station. This mechanism defends against man-in-the-middle and replay attacks on the reporting channel.

message. The only trusted component is hosted on the GPU; the user process cannot be trusted, so there is an end-to-end encryption scheme between the GPU and the admin station to protect against attacks, as we explain in Sect. 3.

Autonomous GPU Execution. GRIM is designed to monitor the operating system's integrity isolated from the host, which may be vulnerable and could be compromised. For that reason, code and data used by GRIM must not be tampered with by an adversary. Modern GPU chips follow a cooperatively scheduled, non-preemptive execution style. That means that only a single kernel can run on the device at any single point in time. As we describe later on in Sect. 4.1 and also illustrated by previous work [26], we employ a bootstrapping method that forbids any external interaction with GRIM. Any attempt to kill, pause, or suspend the GPU component of GRIM results in system shutdown (as we will describe in Sect. 3), and the system can only resume its operation by repeating the bootstrap process. Some NVIDIA models conditionally support concurrent kernel execution, but those conditions can be configured. Therefore, even when running on those models, GRIM's kernel occupies all resources and no other, possibly malicious, code can run concurrently with it.

While these procedures ensure that GRIM can run safely once it has been initialized, current GPU programming frameworks such as CUDA and OpenCL have not been designed with isolation and independence in mind. Some drivers would even kill a context by default if its program appears to be unresponsive [2]. We configure the device to ignore these type of checks. Also, by default, only one queue, or stream in CUDA terminology, is active and the host cannot issue any data transfers before the previous kernel execution is finished. This can be addressed by creating a second stream dedicated to the GPU kernel of

GRIM. Therefore, all data communication with the host and the admin station is performed using a separate stream.

Host Memory Access. An important requirement for morphing the GPU into a kernel integrity monitor is to establish a mechanism to reference the corresponding memory pages that need to be monitored. Unfortunately, current GPGPU frameworks, such as CUDA and OpenCL, use a virtual address layer that is unified with the virtual memory of the host process that utilizes the GPU each time. Since GRIM must access the kernel's memory (and not userspace), the memory regions of the kernel that are monitored should be mapped to the user process.

Typically, modern OSes, including Linux and Windows, prohibit users to access memory regions that have not been assigned to them. An access to a page that is not mapped to a process' virtual address space is typically considered illegal, resulting in a segmentation violation. To access the memory regions where the OS kernel and data structures reside, the particular pages must be located and mapped to GRIM user-space (i.e., the host counterpart that runs on the CPU). This is needed as an intermediate step for finally mapping these regions to the GPU address space.

To overcome the protection added by the OS, we use a separate loadable kernel module that is able to selectively map memory regions to user-space. Then, we are able to register these memory regions to the device address space, through the CUDA programming API. Due to the fact that the GPU is a peripheral PCIe device, it only uses physical addressing to access the host memory. Hence, after the requested memory registration, the GPU is able to access the requested kernel memory regions directly, through the physical address space. This feature allows us to un-map the user-space mappings of the kernel memory regions during the bootstrap phase, that would otherwise pose significant security risks.

Integrity Monitoring. The memory regions to be monitored are specified by the user, and can include pages that contain kernel or LKM text, as well as arrays that contain kernel function pointers (i.e., jump tables). Hashing the static text parts of the kernel or the already loaded LKMs is straightforward. However, the OS kernel is fairly dynamic. Besides the static parts, there are additional parts that change frequently; for example, the VFS layer's data structures change every time new filesystems are mounted or removed. Also, every loaded kernel module can add function pointers.

Given the general-purpose programmability of modern GPUs, it is possible to implement checks that would detect malicious events, by performing several, multi-step, checks on different memory regions. These multi-step checks can become complex in cases where several memory pointers need to be dereferenced in order to acquire the proper kernel memory address. To support this kind of checks we need to walk the kernel page table and resolve the pointer's virtual address dynamically from the GPU. Assuming that we can already access the parts of the page table needed to follow a specific virtual address down to a leaf page table entry (PTE), we end up with a physical page number.

Accessing any physical page is not an inherent limitation of a peripheral PCIe device, such as the GPU. Ideally, the GPU can perform host page table walks, by reading the corresponding physical pages, and dereferencing any virtual page directly. However, the closed-source nature of the CUDA runtime and driver, on which we have based our current design, restrict us from accessing the requested physical page, if the latter has not been registered at the bootstrap phase, via the specialized API function call. For the time being, we do not support dynamic page table resolutions, instead we provide a static list of kernel memory regions, resolve their mappings, and create GPU-side mappings before entering the monitor phase, as we explain in Sect. 4.1. We note, however, that this is not a limitation of our proposed architecture, as the development of open-source frameworks (e.g. Gdev [5]) and drivers (e.g. Nouveau [1], PSCNV [4], etc.) would make a one-to-one mapping of all physical pages in the GPU address space practical. Exploring mapping of additional physical pages in the GPU's address space at run-time is part of our future work.

Sufficient Resources. Modern GPUs are equipped with ample memory (up to 12 GB) and hundreds (or even thousands) of cores. Having such a wide memory space, gives us the ability to store plenty of kernel-image snapshots and enough state for detecting complicated, multi-step, types of attacks. Obviously, these kind of checks can become quite complicated, mainly due to the lack of a generic language that will allow the modelling of such scenarios on top of our architecture. Even though we do not allow such sophisticated memory checks at the moment, the process of aggressively reading and hashing memory has been tested, and, as we show in Sect. 5, the GPU prevails the resources to support this. Implementing sophisticated attacks against GRIM and evaluating the system's effectiveness against them is part of our future work.

Out-of-Band Execution. In the context of GRIM, the GPU acts as a coprocessor with limited defenses against itself. For example, an adversary that has compromised the host system could easily disable or reset the GPU device, and block any potential defensive actions. To overcome this we deploy a completely separate admin station that is responsible for keeping track of the host's proper state.

In particular, the user program that is associated with the GPU context, periodically sends keep-alive messages to the admin station through a private connection. Obviously, simply sending a message to raise an alert can be unsafe, because it is hard for the admin station to distinguish normal operation from a network partition or other failure. Therefore, we use keep-alive messages that encapsulate a GPU-generated status. These messages are encrypted together with a sequence number, to prevent an attacker from imitating GRIM and send spoofed keep-alive messages or replay older ones. Subsequently, the admin station is involved in the bootstrapping process because the secure communication channel with the host is established at that point. The exact communication protocol is described in Sect. 4.

On the admin station, a program logs the reports and makes sure that the monitor is always responsive. The admin station is responsible to take any specified action, every time a message that contains an alert is received or in error cases. An error case can be an invalid message or a missed packet (initiated by a time-out).

4 Implementation

In this section we provide implementation details and discuss technical issues we encountered in the development of GRIM. The current prototype is built on the NVIDIA CUDA architecture, and is portable across all CUDA-enabled NVIDIA models.

4.1 Mapping Kernel Memory to GPU

During bootstrapping, GRIM needs to acquire the kernel memory regions that need to be monitored. These regions are located in the kernel virtual address space. Therefore, the first step is to map them to the address space the GPU driver requires them to live, which is the virtual address space of the user process that issues the execution of the kernel integrity monitoring GPU program.

Typically, a peripheral device bypasses virtual memory and accesses the system memory directly via physical addressing. To do so, the driver has to create a device-specific mapping of the device's address space that points to the corresponding host's physical pages. In order to create the corresponding OS kernel physical memory mappings to the GPU, a separate loadable kernel module is deployed which is responsible for providing the required page table mapping functionality. As shown in Fig. 2, given a kernel virtual address, the loadable kernel module resolves the physical mapping for this address in step 1. In step 2, the kernel module (i) allocates one page in the user context and saves its physical mapping, and (ii) makes the allocated page point to the same page as the kernel virtual address by duplicating the PTE in the user-page table. Then, in step 3, the kernel module maps this user page to the GPU and gets a device pointer[1]. Finally, in step 4 the kernel module restores the original physical mapping of the allocation and frees it[2]. By doing so, we are able to effectively map any OS kernel memory page to the GPU address space. Furthermore, the user-allocated page is unmapped right after the successful execution of the bootstrapping process, in order to destroy all intermediate mappings. We do the same for all kernel virtual memory ranges that we want to monitor with GRIM. The GPU driver populates a device-resident page table for the device to be able to resolve its virtual addresses and perform DMAs.

---

[1] cudaHostRegister() with the cudaHostRegisterMapped flag followed by a call to cudaHostGetDevicePointer().
[2] For memory regions that span multiple pages we need to allocate enough pages and point to them in a sequence, before registering the host-device mapping.

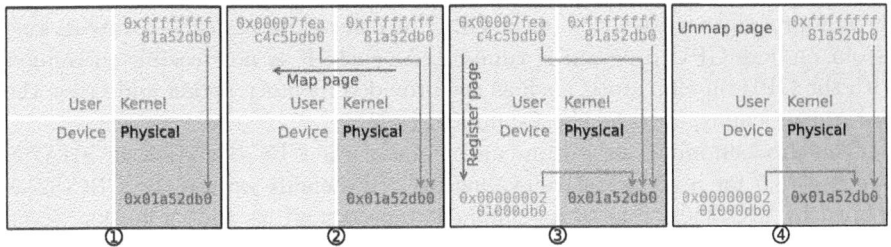

Fig. 2. Mapping OS kernel memory to the GPU. There are several address spaces involved in the operation of GRIM. Initially in step 1 we have a kernel virtual address pointing to a physical address. In step 2 we duplicate this mapping to user space using a kernel module that manipulates page tables. In step 3 we pass the user virtual address to a CUDA API call that pins the page into memory and creates the GPU-side page table entries. In step 4 we destroy the intermediate user space mapping, while the GPU continues to access the physical page.

Modern processor and chipset designs support IOMMUs between peripheral devices and the main memory. Similarly to normal memory management units they translate I/O accesses and provide an extra virtualization layer. Typical uses include contiguous virtual address spaces, extended addressing beyond an I/O device's physical limit, pass-through to virtual machine guests, and memory protection. In GRIM we don't support IOMMUs that perform anything different than 1:1 address re-mapping, at least for the memory address ranges we are interested in, because we don't want our DMA reads from the GPU to CPU-DRAM to go through an IOMMU and get diverted. Furthermore, the IOMMU mappings can be configured by the operating system. For these reasons, we run GRIM with generic CPU-side IOMMUs disabled and all our results are under this assumption.

In order to have unrestricted access to the /proc/kallsyms interface, we build Linux with the CONFIG_KALLSYMS=y and CONFIG_KALLSYMS_ALL=y flags. We note that this is not a requirement of our design, still it helps development and debugging considerably for two reasons: (i) it allows us to easily locate the address of the kernel page table instead of explicitly exporting the init_mm structure for use by loadable modules, and (ii) it saves us the coding of custom memory scanners for all the other data structures we need to locate for monitoring purposes. Obviously, the access to the kernel symbol lookup table might not be acceptable in certain environments. For these cases, we would locate our memory regions using an external symbol table or through memory pattern scanners for dynamic loadable parts, which is certainly feasible.

4.2 Kernel Integrity Monitoring on the GPU

After the successfully mapping of each requested memory region to the GPU, a daemon GPU program is started. The GPU program hashes all monitored regions and compares the checksums to find changes, in an infinite loop. Due to the non-preemptive execution of the GPU, no other program can execute as long as our endless GPU program is running. As such, it is not feasible to tamper with the GPU on-chip state, such as the provided memory region addresses, the known checksums, and the checksumming code.

The checksumming algorithm can be one of the CRC-32, MD5, or SHA256 (see Sect. 5.5 for a comparative evaluation). By default we use the CRC-32 as defined by ISO 3309, due to its simplicity, speed, and its wide adoption. Even though all these algorithms work on byte blocks in an incremental update loop, we have optimized to fetch 16-byte blocks from memory, by using uint4 typed reads (the widest native data type available). We have also tried to use wider user-defined structs, however it did not improve read performance, because the compiler deconstructs it to operations on the struct's members. To the best of our knowledge, there is no method of issuing larger DMAs from GPU code, using the cudaHostRegisterMapped technique.

Instead of maintaining a separate checksum for each memory region, we only keep a single master checksum for all individual checksums. The motivation behind this is to allow the checksum to be stored in registers and remain completely hidden from the host. Even if an attacker is able to stop the execution of the GPU program, the master checksum could not be extracted, due to the fact the GPU registers are automatically reset to zero every time a new program is loaded to the GPU for execution, as has been previously shown [26]. Similarly, the code for CRC32 is small enough to fit in the instruction cache of the GPU, hence an attacker cannot tamper with it [26].

4.3 Real-Time Notification

Even though the GPU kernel is scheduled to run forever, an adversary that has fully compromised the host, can force the GPU to stop its execution. In order to detect such incidents, we need an external offline host, the admin station, connected directly on the local network via a separate Ethernet port. The admin station monitors the rest of GRIM and is able to power off the host.

The two parties (i.e. the host and the admin station) run a simple protocol based on keep-alive messages. The controlling user process reads a predefined memory area from the GPU, sends the data to the admin station through an established connection, and sets a flag (for the GPU to see) to indicate that the data was sent. The data is a counter together with an alert flag encrypted with a symmetric key. The key is installed to both the GPU and the admin station, at bootstrap, before GRIM starts monitoring the host system. The monitored host has no knowledge of the key and in order to prevent from being leaked, it can be stored either in the GPU registers, which automatically reset to zero every time a new GPU program is loaded [26], or as opcodes in the GPU program's text, which also cannot be retrieved or tampered, as it is completely erased from global memory after bootup and resides only in the non-addressable instruction cache of the GPU. For convenience, we chose to use the former option in our current implementation.

The admin station, assumes that the machine is compromised if a message is missed or if it does not receive a valid message in twice the update period (i.e. 200 ms). Of course a valid message containing an alert also means that the host is compromised. The communication structure that is used between the GPU and the admin station is very simple, as shown in Fig. 3. The first two members are sent to the admin station (data[2]) and the third (sent) is used for communication between the GPU and its controlling program. When the master GPU thread sees that the sent flag is set it increments the counter and encrypts the message data with the key. In case the GPU discovers an illegal checksum, it sets the alert flag and re-encrypts the message. All messages are encrypted using the Extended Tiny Encryption Algorithm (XTEA).

The controlling user process, at the host side, is responsible to read the encrypted message of the integrity monitor and send it to the admin station. This process occurs periodically, every 100 ms, resulting to minimal CPU utilization (lower than 0.1 %). If a GPU thread discovers a corrupted region, it indicates it in this message for the admin station to be notified in the next iteration.

```
struct message {
    union {
        int data[2]; /* encrypted data */
        struct {
            int seq;
            int alert;
        };
    };
    int sent; /* plain sent flag */
};
```

Fig. 3. The message format used for synchronization between the GPU, host, and the admin station. When a GPU thread finds a corrupted memory region it sets the alert flag and encrypts it together with the sequence number. A master GPU thread is responsible for incrementing the sequence number when the sent flag is set. The host will send this message to the admin station in the next synchronization point and the alert will be handled there. The host sets the sent flag while the GPU unsets it.

4.4 Data-Parallel Execution

There are some implementation choices regarding the actual code execution on the GPU. For instance, the partitioning of checksumming work among GPU threads, how synchronization with the host is done, how to do the memory reads. We chose to have a master thread that, apart from being a normal worker, checks whether the host has sent the packet to the admin station and composes a new message with the incremented sequence number. Furthermore, memory regions are evenly distributed to all threads. During bootstrapping, GRIM finds the greatest common divisor among all region lengths and split larger regions to that size, ending up with equal sized regions. Because of the nature of the problem (checksum computation), we can divide and conquer as we wish. We configure the execution in blocks of 512 concurrent threads, which is the preferred block size. About the memory access pattern, we don't really have room to optimize much because all reads on monitored regions are serviced by the GPU's DMA copy engine(s) and are not local.

5 Evaluation

In this section we evaluate the performance and accuracy of GRIM. We measure the rate for detecting a self-hiding loadable kernel module, as well as the impact that GRIM has on the memory bandwidth of the base system. Furthermore, we show the memory coverage that GRIM can afford, without sacrificing accuracy.

Our experimental platform is based on an Intel Core i7-3770 CPU clocked at 3.4 GHz equipped with 8 GiB of DDR3 DRAM at 1333 MHz in a dual-channel configuration. The motherboard is the MSI Z77A-G45. The GPU we use for executing GRIM is an NVIDIA GeForce GTX 770 PCIe 3.0 card with 4 GiB of GDDR5 DRAM. We use a Linux 3.14.23 based system with NVIDIA driver version 343.22 and CUDA 6.5 for the GPU code.

5.1 Self-hiding LKM

Our basic test and case study for determining the accuracy of GRIM is the detection rate of a self-hiding loadable kernel module (LKM). Notice, that this case study is in-line with the evaluation methodology carried out in the state-of-the-art of similar works [18]. Also, the synthetic evaluation we present in this section can *stress* GRIM significantly more than an actual rootkit. The artificial LKM module, which resembles the operation of a rootkit, performs zero malicious operations; it only loads and unloads itself. On the other hand, an actual rootkit, once loaded, needs to perform malicious actions, and therefore it is exposed to the monitor for a longer time period.

Typically, a module is handled by a system utility which is responsible for loading it into memory and invoking a system call to initialize it. Specifically in Linux, the `insmod(8)` and friend tools open the kernel module object file and use the `finit_module(2)` system call with its file descriptor. The system relocates symbols, initializes any provided parameters, adds a handle to data structures (a modules list), and calls the module's `init()` function. A rootkit, implemented as a kernel module, is able to remove itself from that list—in order to increase its stealthiness—and this is typically performed in its `init()` function. Still, this transient change can be detected by carefully monitoring the head of the modules list with a large enough snapshot frequency. In the following experiment, we show the minimal snapshot frequency that is required to perceive such module list changes and thus achieve successful detection.

In order to measure the detection rate, a self-hiding kernel module is loaded, repeatedly, 100 times, using a different snapshot frequency. Figure 4 shows the

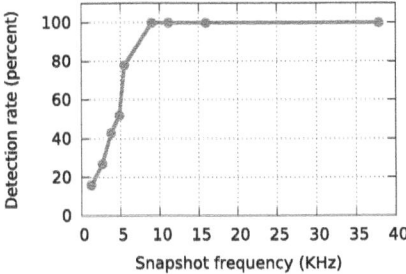
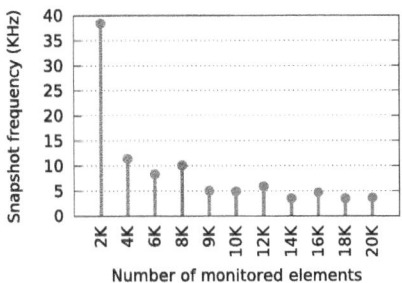

Fig. 4. Self-hiding LKM loading detection with different snapshot frequencies. For each configuration, we loaded a module that deletes itself from the kernel modules list 100 times, while monitoring the head of the list. We achieve 100 % detection rate with a snapshot frequency of 9 KHz or more.

Fig. 5. Maximum achieved frequency depending on the number of pointers being monitored. Increasing the number of (8-byte) memory regions we monitor, lowers the snapshot frequency. Staying above 9 KHz so that we can accurately detect a self-hiding LKM loading lets us monitor *another* 8K pointers.

detection rate achieved by GRIM under each configuration. We can see that GRIM can reliably detect that a new kernel module has been loaded before hiding itself with a snapshot frequency of 9 KHz or more, achieving 100 % detection rate. That means that GRIM detected all module insertions and generated exactly 100 alerts. Note that according to the state-of-the-art, a snapshot-based approach can deliver a 70 % detection rate at best [18].

The experiment we carry out in this paper for demonstrating the high levels of detection rate that can be achieved using GRIM is designed in analogy with the one presented in the evaluation of KI-Mon [18]. We have just omitted the verification part of the observed change. KI-Mon, once a change is detected, further verifies semantically if the change is meant to be malicious or not. This verification procedure happens *using snapshots* and in parallel with the detection algorithm, which is based on snooping. We argue that detection and verification are orthogonal. GRIM is fully programmable and can be easily extended with rich functionality for applying *in-parallel* semantic verification algorithms once a change is detected *without* decreasing its detection rate.

5.2 Address Space Coverage

Next we study the implications of requiring a snapshot frequency of at least 9 KHz for accurate detection, with respect to the amount of memory we can cover. The snapshot frequency is a function of the number and size of the monitored memory regions. Also, alignment plays a role in the read performance of the GPU, 16-byte aligned reads being the fastest. We don't, however, control the placement of the kernel data structures, and thus we assume that some of our monitored regions need one or two extra fetches. Given our specific implementation, the most efficient read width is 16 bytes (or one `uint4` in CUDA's device native data types). In the following experiment we focus on monitoring pointer values (8-byte regions). The results are shown in Fig. 5. Given our detection rate results, we see that we can monitor at most 8K pointers simultaneously without sacrificing accuracy, because we need to stay above the 9 KHz snapshot frequency. This limits the address space we can monitor using GRIM if we want to achieve 100 % detection rate, albeit 8K addresses spread out in memory could potentially safeguard many important kernel data structures. Moreover, this is not an inherent limitation that only GRIM suffers from. All hardware-based integrity monitors [13,18,22] can observe only a limited fraction of the host's memory. Even snoop-based systems need to filter out most of the memory traffic which targets memory that is not a potential target for a rootkit.

5.3 Impact on Memory Bandwidth

In this section we measure the overhead that GRIM adds to the memory subsystem. To do so, we ran the STREAM benchmark [20] while the system is under monitoring by GRIM and when the system is idle. We use all 8 CPU threads for the benchmark and we run our GPU snapshot loop with different throttling factors to obtain various frequency values. We count the total number of memory references by multiplying with the obtained snapshot frequency. We show the results in Fig. 6. At most 17 % of the available memory bandwidth is utilized by the GPU when GRIM is in place. Note, that the system consumes 17 % of the available memory bandwidth in the worst-case, in which GRIM is monitoring 8K of 8-byte memory elements. As we show in Fig. 7, monitoring of 512 8-byte memory elements (enough for safeguarding the system-call table) consume only 1 % of the memory bandwidth. For this particular experiment we throttled our snapshot loop to approximately get to the desired snapshot frequency of 9 KHz for different number of monitored regions (again of 8 bytes in size). We note that we can always limit the host memory bandwidth degradation by monitoring less pointers. Therefore, we stress that *(i)* our system is flexible and can adapt its configuration for consuming less memory bandwidth and safeguarding less memory if this is desirable, and *(ii)* even in the worst case, when GRIM is monitoring 8K 8-byte elements, it consumes 17 % of memory which is comparable with the memory consumption reported by similar systems [13].

5.4 Using a Low-End GPU

Given that the snapshot process is I/O bound on the DMA path, we also explore the behaviour of GRIM on low-end GPUs. To do so, we use a NVIDIA GT 630 PCIe 2.0 and measure the memory coverage that can afford while maintaining a detection rate of 100 %. The GT 630 is able to reliably monitor at most 2K 8-byte elements (without sacrificing detection accuracy). Even though this is 4 times lower than the detection rate sustained by the GTX 770, it comes with great benefits in terms of energy efficiency. Figure 8 shows the power consumption of each device while being idle and the active power consumption while executing

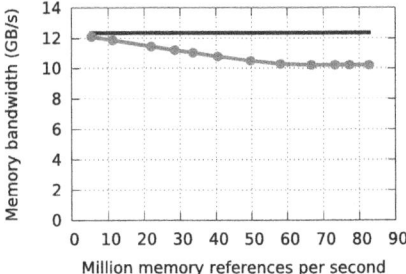 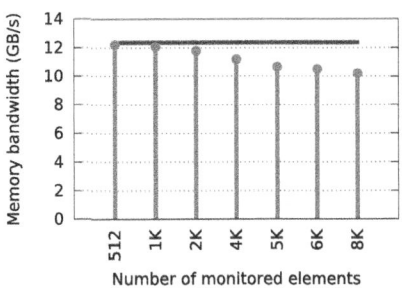

Fig. 6. Impact on memory bandwidth while the system is under monitoring. The GPU issues DMAs which contend with the CPU cores on the memory controller and/or the DRAM itself, limiting the memory bandwidth normally available to host. GRIM degrades STREAM performance by 17% in the worst case.

Fig. 7. Available memory bandwidth with respect to memory coverage. Snapshotting is throttled to approximately achieve the required snapshot frequency of 9 KHz. We see that monitoring 512 8-byte elements only consumes 1% of the memory bandwidth whereas with 8K we reach the 17% worst case.

	idle	active
GTX 770	67.84	148.87
GT 630	11.85	25.70

Fig. 8. Power consumption of each device in Watts while being idle, as well as including the additional power the device draws while GRIM is running ("active" column). We observe that the low-end GPU consumes almost 6 times less power both when idle and active.

the GPU component of GRIM. The low-end GPU draws almost 6 times less power both when running our code and in total when taking into account the idle power consumption. That creates an interesting trade-off and makes the low-end choice attractive for setups with low power budgets. Finally, the GT 630 can only affect STREAM performance by 6% in the worst case due to its host connectivity limitations.

5.5 Checksums and Message Digests

In the results we showed so far we have been using CRC32 to detect memory modifications. CRC32 has low complexity in terms of computation, while it is not considered cryptographically secure. Here we show the overheads involved in using MD5 or SHA256, and the impact it has to detection rate. We monitor different counts of 8-byte elements and show how accurately we can detect the LKM-hiding attack when one of the elements is the head pointer of the modules list. Figure 9 shows that MD5 performs a little worse than CRC32 sustaining 4K elements but losing accuracy at 8K elements. The same is true for SHA256. We

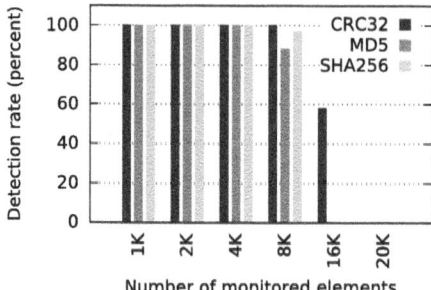

Fig. 9. Comparison of the LKM-hiding detection rate of the CRC32 checksum and the MD5/SHA256 digests for different number of monitored 8-byte elements. The CRC32 is faster and can cover a larger amount of memory without sacrificing accuracy. MD5/SHA256 on the other hand provide higher security.

expect MD5 to be faster than SHA256 but here we test with relatively small data blocks so read performance is more critical than actual computation. Both implementations of MD5 and SHA256 cannot detect the LKM memory-write when the monitor inspects 20K elements. This is a trade-off between memory coverage and collision resistance, which can be configured. Notice that for GRIM even a simple algorithm, like CRC32, can be quite effective in detecting kernel rootkits, unless the malicious code can perform operations on memory by preserving the CRC32 checksum of the particular modified memory page, which is not trivial.

6 Related Work

Integrity monitors have formed an attractive technology for protecting software against exploitation. Based on monitoring, they can *infer* about an attack and not *defend* against the attack. As an alternative method of protection, integrity monitors are considered promising, especially when even advanced defenses, such as preventing code-reuse in the operating system [19] can be bypassed by advanced attacks [15,16], and when it has been demonstrated that core protection principles, like Control-Flow Integrity (CFI) applied at the kernel [8], offer limited security [9].

Integrity monitors can be implemented in both software and hardware. Software integrity monitors [6,10,25,29] are based on hypervisors. The operating system runs as a guest and is occasionally checked by the hypervisor for possible (malicious) modifications. Although these monitors dramatically limit the code base that should be trusted and bug-free, there is always the possibility for the hypervisor to be exploited. The hypervisor and the operating system are not completely isolated and they are both written in untrusted languages. Of course, all these solutions are towards the right direction, and it is obviously easier to perform a security analysis in a significant smaller program (the monitor) compared to protecting the complete operating system. However, the community has been in parallel seeking for more solid monitors, which will be physically isolated from the rest of the system, they will be implemented using custom hardware, and won't run in the same code base with the kernel they protect.

As we have stressed throughout the paper, we offer an integrity monitor based on GPUs, which closely matches the work demonstrated by hardware monitors such as Copilot [13], Vigilare [22], and KI-Mon [18]. Copilot [13] is a snapshot-based monitor implemented on a custom FPGA. Essentially, GRIM offers all of the Copilot's functionality, in addition to better performance and extensibility, since GRIM is fully programmable. Vigilare [22], on the other hand, argues that it is hard to achieve good detection rates using snapshot-based monitors and thus it introduces snooping, i.e., monitoring the bus for particular memory operations that can affect the kernel structure. We believe that snooping is important, and certainly a lightweight check compared to the snapshot-based approach, however, in this paper, we argue that snapshot-based monitors can do significantly better. With GRIM we are able to achieve 100 % detection rate. Finally, KI-Mon [18] extends Vigilare by offering protection for mutable objects. In GRIM we can protect against mutable objects, however we have not implemented the *semantic verification check* for validating if a change of a mutable object in the kernel is the result of a legitimate operation or not. We omitted implementing this in GRIM, because the available API for programming the GPU is proprietary and limited. Nevertheless, as we have in detail discussed, our architecture can support this operation.

7 Conclusion

In this paper we revisited snapshot-based Kernel Integrity Monitors (KIMs) and we demonstrated that a novel GPU-based architecture can do substantially better than it has so far been reported in the state-of-the-art. GRIM builds on commodity GPUs and offers a fully extensible and programmable architecture for implementing complex KIMs. Our thorough evaluation of GRIM suggests that we can achieve 100 % detection rate of evolved rootkits that try to evade snapshot-based monitors. This detection rate outperforms the currently reported rate (70 %) of the state-of-the-art of hardware-based monitors.

GRIM offers an attractive option for instantly deploying a hardware-based KIM. It needs no modifications to the host it protects, no kernel recompilation or installation of custom hardware. This is particular important, because all so far proposed hardware monitors that base their operation on snooping require changes at the microprocessor level. In our case, GRIM acts as a secure co-processor that protects a vulnerable host from malicious rootkits. We believe our proposal will further promote research in the field of advanced KIMs that are snapshot-based, since there is clearly enough space for optimizations and many benefits to be considered when it comes to deployment.

Acknowledgements. We thank our shepherd Zhiqiang Lin and the anonymous reviewers for their invaluable feedback. This work was supported by European Commission through the H2020 ICT-32-2014 project SHARCS under Grant Agreement number 644571.

References

1. Nouveau driver for nVidia cards. http://nouveau.freedesktop.org/
2. NVIDIA Developer Forums - CUDA kernel timeout. https://devtalk.nvidia.com/default/topic/417276/cuda-kernel-timeout/
3. OpenCL. http://www.khronos.org/opencl/
4. PathScale NVIDIA graphics driver. https://github.com/pathscale/pscnv
5. shinpei0208/gdev. https://github.com/shinpei0208/gdev
6. Azab, A.M., Ning, P., Shah, J., Chen, Q., Bhutkar, R., Ganesh, G., Ma, J., Shen, W.: Hypervision across worlds: real-time kernel protection from the ARM TrustZone secure world. In: CCS (2014)
7. Chen, S., Xu, J., Sezer, E.C.: Non-control-data attacks are realistic threats. In: USENIX Security (2005)
8. Criswell, J., Dautenhahn, N., Adve, V.: KCoFI: complete control-flow integrity for commodity operating system kernels. In: Security and Privacy (2014)
9. Göktas, E., Athanasopoulos, E., Bos, H., Portokalidis, G.: Out of control: overcoming control-flow integrity. In: Security and Privacy (2014)
10. Hofmann, O.S., Dunn, A.M., Kim, S., Roy, I., Witchel, E.: Ensuring operating system kernel integrity with OSck. In: ASPLOS (2011)
11. Hund, R., Holz, T., Freiling, F.C.: Return-oriented rootkits: bypassing kernel code integrity protection mechanisms. In: USENIX Security (2009)
12. Jang, D., Lee, H., Kim, M., Kim, D., Kim, D., Kang, B.B.: ATRA address translation redirection attack against hardware-based external monitors. In: CCS (2014)
13. Petroni Jr., N.L., Fraser, T., Molina, J., Arbaugh, W.A.: Copilot - a coprocessor-based kernel runtime integrity monitor. In: USENIX Security (2004)
14. Kato, S.: Implementing Open-Source CUDA Runtime (2013)
15. Kemerlis, V.P., Polychronakis, M., Keromytis, A.D.: Ret2Dir: rethinking kernel isolation. In: USENIX Security (2014)
16. Kemerlis, V.P., Portokalidis, G., Keromytis, A.D.: kGuard: lightweight kernel protection against return-to-user attacks. In: USENIX Security (2012)
17. Klein, G., Derrin, P., Elphinstone, K.: Experience report: sel4: formally verifying a high-performance microkernel. In: ACM Sigplan Notices, vol. 44, pp. 91–96. ACM (2009)
18. Lee, H., Moon, H., Jang, D., Kim, K., Lee, J., Paek, Y., Kang, B.B.: KI-Mon: a hardware-assisted event-triggered monitoring platform for mutable kernel object. In: USENIX Security (2013)
19. Li, J., Wang, Z., Jiang, X., Grace, M., Bahram, S.: Defeating return-oriented rootkits with "return-less" kernels. In: EuroSys (2010)
20. McCalpin, J.: STREAM: sustainable memory bandwidth in high performance computers. https://www.cs.virginia.edu/stream/
21. Menychtas, K., Shen, K., Scott, M.L.: Enabling OS research by inferring interactions in the black-box GPU stack. In: USENIX ATC (2013)
22. Moon, H., Lee, H., Lee, J., Kim, K., Paek, Y., Kang, B.B.: Vigilare: toward snoop-based kernel integrity monitor. In: CCS (2012)

23. NVIDIA: CUDA Programming Guide, version 4.0. http://developer.download.nvidia.com/compute/cuda/4_0/toolkit/docs/CUDA_C_Programming_Guide.pdf
24. Rutkowska, J., Tereshkin, A.: Bluepilling the Xen hypervisor. In: Black Hat USA (2008)
25. Seshadri, A., Luk, M., Qu, N., Perrig, A.: SecVisor: a tiny hypervisor to provide lifetime kernel code integrity for commodity OSes. In: SOSP (2007)
26. Vasiliadis, G., Athanasopoulos, E., Polychronakis, M., Ioannidis, S.: PixelVault: using GPUs for securing cryptographic operations. In: CCS (2014)
27. Vasiliadis, G., Polychronakis, M., Ioannidis, S.: MIDeA: a multi-parallel intrusion detection architecture. In: CCS (2011)
28. Vogl, S., Gawlik, R., Garmany, B., Kittel, T., Pfoh, J., Eckert, C., Holz, T.: Dynamic hooks: hiding control flow changes within non-control data. In: USENIX Security (2014)
29. Wang, J., Stavrou, A., Ghosh, A.: HyperCheck: a hardware-assisted integrity monitor. In: Jha, S., Sommer, R., Kreibich, C. (eds.) RAID 2010. LNCS, vol. 6307, pp. 158–177. Springer, Heidelberg (2010)

Taming Transactions: Towards Hardware-Assisted Control Flow Integrity Using Transactional Memory

Marius Muench[1]([✉]), Fabio Pagani[1], Yan Shoshitaishvili[2],
Christopher Kruegel[2], Giovanni Vigna[2], and Davide Balzarotti[1]

[1] Eurecom, Sophia Antipolis, France
{marius.muench,fabio.pagani,davide.balzarotti}@eurecom.fr
[2] University of California, Santa Barbara, USA
{yans,chris,vigna}@cs.ucsb.edu

Abstract. Control Flow Integrity (CFI) is a promising defense technique against code-reuse attacks. While proposals to use hardware features to support CFI already exist, there is still a growing demand for an architectural CFI support on commodity hardware. To tackle this problem, in this paper we demonstrate that the Transactional Synchronization Extensions (TSX) recently introduced by Intel in the x86-64 instruction set can be used to support CFI.

The main idea of our approach is to map control flow transitions into transactions. This way, violations of the intended control flow graphs would then trigger transactional aborts, which constitutes the core of our TSX-based CFI solution. To prove the feasibility of our technique, we designed and implemented two coarse-grained CFI proof-of-concept implementations using the new TSX features. In particular, we show how hardware-supported transactions can be used to enforce both loose CFI (which does not need to extract the control flow graph in advance) and strict CFI (which requires pre-computed labels to achieve a better precision). All solutions are based on a compile-time instrumentation.

We evaluate the effectiveness and overhead of our implementations to demonstrate that a TSX-based implementation contains useful concepts for architectural control flow integrity support.

Keywords: Control flow integrity · Transactional memory · Intel[®] TSX · Binary hardening · Software security

1 Introduction

One serious security problem that continues to haunt security researchers and victims alike is the presence of memory corruption vulnerabilities, which can lead to the *arbitrary execution* of code specified by an attacker. Because these attacks can have serious consequences for the security of our lives and our society, countermeasures against classical stack- and heap based *code-injection attacks* are widely deployed together with general security mechanisms in modern computer systems. For instance, Operating Systems ship with Address Space Layout Randomization (ASLR) and executable space protection like Exec Shield [40] or Data Execution Prevention (DEP) [2]. Additionally, modern compilers are able to harden applications against specific classes of attacks. For example, stack canaries protect against buffer overflows, and Relocation Read-Only (RELRO) protects against Global Offset Table (GOT) overwrite attacks. In combination, these countermeasures have nearly eliminated code-injection attacks.

However, even with all of these mechanisms in place, *code-reuse attacks* are still feasible. Hereby, the attacker reuses parts of the existing codebase of an application to achieve his goal. Generally, attackers accomplish this by corrupting data within the program and overwriting the target of an indirect jump (for example, by creating a fake stack with fake return values), thus hijacking the program execution. Any *indirect control flow transfer* (that, unlike a direct control flow transfer, can be influenced by values in program memory and CPU registers) is potentially vulnerable to this hijacking.

One line of defense against this type of attacks consist of checking the correctness of indirect control flow transfers before they are executed, by using a technique called *Control Flow Integrity* (CFI) [1]. In essence, CFI prohibits malicious redirections of a program's control flow by white-listing the possible targets of indirect transfers. If a change of control flow resolves to anything but an allowed target, the system would assume that there is an ongoing attack and terminate the program. Therefore, the goal of CFI is to ensure that, even if an attacker can gain control of the target of an indirect jump, her possible targets for control flow redirection are very limited and confined to the expected behavior of the program. Many CFI implementations [1,4,28,41–43], countermeasures to CFI implementations [6,9,16,17,19], and defenses against these countermeasures [25,26,31,34,38,39] have been proposed in recent years. Most of these studies have focused on the recovery of accurate control flow graphs (to understand the valid targets for indirect control flow transfers), on the binary instrumentation (to add CFI to existing binaries), and on reducing the performance overhead of the solution. Despite the importance of a hardware-supported CFI was already envisioned its original proposal [1], not much work has focused on how control flow integrity can be enforced by using features available in commodity hardware.

In this paper we present an application of the *Transactional Memory*-enabling instruction set extension (*TSX*), recently released by Intel for their Haswell processors, to provide hardware support for the implementation of control flow integrity. In particular, we propose a novel design that uses TSX instructions to ensure control flow integrity and we present a novel CFI implementation that introduces several interesting challenges for attackers. TSX-based CFI can provide, in hardware, new constraints on the attacker capabilities and a set of interesting protection features. In fact, aside from ensuring control flow integrity, our solution prevents an attacker from executing any system call after a hijacked indirect control flow transfer and introduces the ability to "reset" a program to its state prior to the hijacked control flow when the presence of an attacker is detected. These are powerful, previously absent capabilities, that we believe can significantly raise the bar for attackers in terms of control flow hijacking attacks.

In summary, we make the following contributions:

Design. We design a novel approach to implement control flow integrity, using the TSX instruction set extension recently released by Intel. Aside from simply providing CFI, this approach also provides a level of protection against unwanted invocation of system calls.

Implementation. We present two proof-of-concept implementations to show how TSX can be used to enforce both loose and strict CFI solutions.

Evaluation. We perform a thorough evaluation of our TSX-based CFI implementations, detailing overhead, side-effects, and security gains.

2 Control Flow Integrity

In recent years, researchers have proposed several solutions to enhance programs with CFI policies. Control flow integrity policies comes in two main forms, depending on how *restrictive* they are in specifying and enforcing the possible control flow.

In strict, or "fine-grained" CFI, the minimum set for allowable targets for any indirect control flow transfer is identified. For example, a return from a function would only be allowed to return to callers that could (legitimately) call the function. Before the execution, the target of every indirect transfer must be determined, and at runtime, these targets are verified whenever a control flow transfer takes place. A common method to implement such a strict form of CFI is labeling. Labels are assigned to the edges of a control flow transfer and are checked whenever the transfer occurs. Before a transfer is allowed, a verification procedure ensures that this transfer resolves to a target with a valid label.

Strict CFI is difficult to implement correctly, since the targets of indirect control flow transfers must be determined statically. Thus, researchers proposed a weaker form of CFI, called loose or "coarse-grained" CFI. This approximate technique segregates indirect control flow transfers by category and enforces policies on each category. For instance, loose CFI mandates that a transfer initiated by a *ret* instruction should always resolve to a location directly after a *call* instruction. Likewise, a call instruction should always transfer the control flow to the beginning of a function. Recent CFI implementations improve loose CFI by segregating control flow transfers into less coarse categories. Typically, different types of control transfers are given a different label [42,43].

BinCFI [43], for instance, uses static disassembly techniques, code instrumentation, and binary rewriting to identify all indirect control flow transfers and then enhances the program with coarse-grained CFI. Likewise O-CFI [26] uses static binary rewriting to introduce coarse-grained CFI in combination with finegrained code randomization as protection against novel attacks. Another implementation requiring the relocation information of a binary, and thus slightly more knowledge, is CCFIR [42]. It introduces a springboard section and indirect control flow transfers are only allowed to target the springboard, which then redirects to the actual target. Contrary to these three implementations, which provide coarse-grained CFI and utilize static instrumentation, vfGuard [34] recovers C++ semantics of a given binary and uses Pin [3] to dynamically enforce strict CFI. Another example for dynamic CFI enforcement is Lockdown [33], which adds control flow guards for indirect calls and jumps and a shadow-stack to protect function returns via dynamic binary translation.

A completely different approach is to integrate CFI at compile time, which has the advantage of avoiding many complex issues related to resolving the targets of indirect control flow transfers (since static analysis of the source code before compilation can be used to provide this information) and removing the need to instrument or rewrite binaries. Niu et al. [28], for instance, introduced Monitor Integrity Protection, a coarse-grained form of CFI which aligns instruction to chunks and enforce that indirect jumps are targeting the beginning of a chunk with the goal to enforce low-level inlined reference monitor code integrity. Another example is SafeDispatch [24], a compiler based on Clang++/LLVM that adds protection for C++ dynamic dispatches.

All comprehensive compiler-based fine-grained CFI solutions need to deal with a common problem: shared libraries. Modern programs make often use of shared or dynamic loaded libraries. This problem is addressed by Niu et al. [29], who introduced modular CFI based on ID tables representing the actual CFG which is constructed during link-time. In between, production compilers could be enhanced to support compilation for binaries with fine-grained CFI policies. Tice et al. [38], for example, use vtable verification for virtual calls and indirect function-call checking to add practical CFI instrumentation to both GCC and LLVM.

A hybrid approach, combining both compile- and runtime instrumentation, is presented by πCFI [31]. In this case, programs are initialized with an empty CFG, which gets populated at runtime based on the provided input.

Recent research has expanded CFI beyond traditionally-compiled code on desktop systems. For example, just-in-time compilation can be enhanced with CFI policies, as shown in the case of RockJIT for JavaScript [30]. Furthermore, it has been shown that even entire commodity kernels can be instrumented to enforce CFI policies, as demonstrated in [12,18]. Moreover, MoCFI [13], a CFI framework for smartphones that uses static analysis to extract the CFG of binary files and utilizes library injection and in-memory patching to enforce CFI during runtime, shows that smartphones can also benefit from CFI.

Hardware support for CFI. The vast majority of CFI implementations employ software mechanisms for enforcing the integrity of control flow transfers [1,4,12,28,42,43]. However, a few attempts have been made to implement CFI using existing hardware features. CFIMon, for instance, utilizes Intel's Branch Trace Store, in combination with performance monitoring units, to detect control flow violations on-the-fly [41]. Likewise, kBouncer employs Intel's Last Branch Recording to mitigate ROP exploits without modification of the program [32] and PathArmor [39] uses the same hardware feature to enforce context-sensitive CFI. Unfortunately, those systems suffer from the fact that the Last Branch Record in its current implementation only records up to 16 branches. Our proposed method of using TSX to achieve CFI complements software-based CFI approaches by providing them with a mechanism to do the actual *enforcement* of CFI. Generally, it can work with any label-based CFI scheme, and replaces software-enforced control flow checking with a hardware-based solution.

Explicit architecture support of control flow integrity has been proposed by Budiu et al. [5]. In their proposal, new instructions are added for labeling targets of control flow transfer and for automated verification of these labels during a transfer. Davi et al. [15] have pointed out that this approach is likely to generate coarse-grained CFI policies and presented a different architecture for fine-grained CFI, based on two new instructions for function calls and returns as well as heuristics for validating indirect jumps.

Two recent approaches that proposed hardware-based, label-based CFI systems are HAFIX [14] and HCFI [7]. HAFIX enforces backward-edge CFI by extending the instruction set architecture of the Intel Siskiyou Peak and the LEON3 synthesizable processors. Similarly, HCFI extends the ISA of a SPARC SoC and utilizes an additional shadow stack to enforce both forward- and backward-edge CFI. Another hardware-based approach is presented by Clercq et al. [8], in which instructions reside encrypted in memory and are decrypted by the architectural CFI features in the instruction cache. This architectural features are implemented in a LEON3 processor and decryption errors occur when invalid branch targets are taken. While all these systems are good examples of hardware-based control flow integrity, they rely on custom hardware, rarely shipped in commodity computers. Our proposed approach, on the other hand, leverages a functionality that is *already* deployed in consumer CPUs.

An equivalent approach that uses recently introduced hardware features to enforce CFI was developed in parallel to our work by Mashtizadeh et al. in CCFI [25]. CCFI uses Intel's AES-NI extensions to construct, store and verify cryptographic MACs for pointers being used for control flow transfers, while the cryptographic key is held in compiler reserved registers, invisible to the attacker. This solution provides strong security guarantees, but it faces additional challenges not present in our approach, which result in an increased complexity. First, the introduced MACs for stack and heap addresses can suffer from replay attacks, in which an attacker leaks and uses a previous constructed MAC to change the control flow. To prevent this attack, additional heap- and stack-randomization need to be deployed. Furthermore, in certain corner cases, the compiler does not recognize function pointers which would lead to MAC failures and subsequent program termination. Although a static analyses pass for clang to detect these cases is provided, additional work by the developer of a software is required. Another minor problem is that the compiler reserved registers to store the cryptographic key are a subset of the registers introduced by Intel's SIMD extension. Thus, applications which are heavily using this extensions would experience additional overhead.

3 Transactional Memory

Transactional memory is a concept used in concurrent programming to describe a technique that allows synchronized and efficient access to data structures in a concurrent environment without the need of mutual exclusion [22]. Transactional memory introduces the concept of *transactions*, finite sequences of machine instruction that are *serializable* and *atomic*. Serializability means that different transactions appear as if they are executed serially, and therefore that different transactions do not interleave with each other. Atomicity, on the other hand, refers to the changes made to the shared memory: upon completion of a transaction, it either *commits* or it *aborts*. A commit makes all changes to the shared memory visible to other processors, while an abort discards the changes. Hence, the changes made to shared memory by one transaction are either fully represented in the memory space of the program or completely undone.

3.1 Transactional Synchronization Extensions

A selected subset of Intel's recent Haswell processors were manufactured with the Transactional Synchronization Extension (TSX) [36]. This extension enhances the x86-64 instruction set architecture by adding transactional memory features. Intel's TSX allows a programmer to specify code regions for transactional execution and provides two distinct interfaces, Hardware Lock Elision (HLE) and Restricted Transactional Memory (RTM) [10], that offer different functionality to users of transactional memory.

3.2 Hardware Lock Elision

HLE improves performance of concurrent code through the elision of hardware locks. Two new instruction prefixes are introduced to be used in front of instructions which normally would use software locks for synchronization:

XACQUIRE: The XACQUIRE prefix is used in front of an instruction which acquires a lock to a critical memory region. It marks the beginning of a transaction but instead of adding the shared memory to the processor's read or write set, the lock itself is added to the transaction's read set. For the acquiring processor, it appears as if it has acquired the lock, while for other processors the lock appears to be unchanged. Thus, other processors can read the lock without causing a conflict and, therefore, concurrently enter into the critical section. Although no data is *actually* written to the lock, the hardware ensures that conflicts on shared data will cause a transactional abort.

XRELEASE: The XRELEASE prefix is used in front of an instruction which releases a lock and ends a transaction. Normally, the release of a lock would involve a write to the lock. Instead, the system verifies that the instruction following the XRELEASE prefix restores the value of the lock to the value that it had before the XACQUIRE prefixed instruction. If this is the case, the processor tries to commit the transaction.

If a transaction fails due to a conflicting write in the shared data or the associated lock, all changes of the transaction are rolled back and the critical section is re-executed - this time using the lock in the classical manner. The advantage of HLE is that multiple threads can enter and execute critical sections protected by the same lock as long as no simultaneous operations on shared data are causing conflicts.

Additionally, HLE provides backward compatibility in the instruction set through a clever usage of instruction prefixes: processors without HLE support simply ignore the XACQUIRE and XRELEASE prefixes for all instructions which can be prefixed by XACQUIRE and XRELEASE and, thus, execute the critical code section with traditional locking.

3.3 Restricted Transactional Memory

RTM is a more flexible interface for marking code regions for transactional execution, without backward compatibility. This extension introduces three new instructions:

XBEGIN: The XBEGIN instruction is used to enter a transaction. Within a transaction, all accessed memory is added to the transaction's read set and all modified memory is added to the transaction's write set. The XBEGIN instruction must be followed by a 16- or 32-bit relative address to specify a fall-back path which gets executed when the transaction's commit fails or an explicit transactional abort occurs.

XEND: The XEND instruction ends a transaction and attempts to commit all changes. Should the commit fail, the fall-back path specified in the XBEGIN instruction is executed.

XABORT: The XABORT instruction is used to issue an abort for the transaction, rolling back all changes made by the transaction and executing the fall-back path. The XABORT instruction has to be followed by an 8-bit immediate as status code. This gives the programmer the possibility to specify a reason for issuing the abort.

The RAX register is used to indicate the reason for the execution of the fall-back path when a transaction abort occurs. The value of this register is not relevant for our purposes but, as we will see, the fact that it gets clobbered is inconvenient.

3.4 TSX Minutia

Intel's TSX provides another instruction, which can be used in both RTM and HLE based transactional execution paths:

XTEST: The XTEST instruction checks whether the processor is executing in a transactional state due to a HLE or RTM transaction. If XTEST is executed inside a transaction, the Zero Flag (ZF) is set to 0. Otherwise, it is set to 1.

Furthermore, both RTM and HLE are capable of transactional nesting and instruction-based aborts: While serializability of two distinct transactions is still ensured, both RTM and HLE allow the execution of transactions within transactions. The processor specific variables MAX_RTM_NEST_COUNT and MAX_HLE_NEST_COUNT are limiting this nesting. The nesting of a HLE transaction inside a RTM transaction or the nesting of RTM inside HLE remains undefined because both interfaces are accessing the same hardware capabilities.

Additionally, certain instructions cause a transaction to abort, regardless of how the transaction was initiated or what data has been written or read. Besides XABORT, the instructions CPUID and PAUSE cause a transactional abort in all situations. Depending on the TSX implementation, other instructions can trigger an abort as well. Among those are instructions for updating non-status parts of the EFLAGS register, interrupts, ring transitions, processor state saves, and instructions for updating the segment registers. A side-effect of the instruction-based aborts is context switch sensitivity. Several instructions, which can cause aborts depending on the specific implementation, are used by the kernel to perform context switches. As a consequence, transactions are aborted upon context switches.

3.5 Suitability for Software Security

TSX has already been analyzed for its possible application to software security. For example, Muttik et al. [27] pointed out that TSX can be used to detect malicious changes in memory by monitoring OS memory from a hypervisor and using transactional memory to automatically roll back these malicious changes. Furthermore, recent research by Guan et al. [21] proposes Mimosa, a system to protect private keys against memory disclosure attacks using hardware transactional memory features. Private keys are held in memory and decrypt or sign messages only within a transaction. Atomicity (as described in Sect. 3) causes the transaction to abort when a concurrent, malicious process tries to access the decrypted private key.

3.6 TSX Application for Control Flow Integrity

By studying the implementation of Intel's TSX, we realized that it can be leveraged as prototype for hardware-assisted CFI. Our intuition is that we can enter a transactional execution state before a control flow transfer and commit the transaction after the control flow transfer is done. In this manner, RTM can be used to implement loose CFI without checking labels in software. This is similar to the idea of *control flow locking* [4], which involves a write to a lock before an indirect control flow transfer and an unlock operation after the transfer.

Furthermore, HLE can be used to implement labels, allowing both loose CFI and strict CFI. This is based on the fact that the memory changed by a XACQUIRE instruction to enter a transaction has to be restored to its original value with the XRELEASE instruction in order to successful commit the transaction. By carefully choosing the memory location and value, we can ensure that redirected control flow will cause a transaction to abort, which will then be detected.

Besides basic CFI functionalities, the current implementation of TSX provides additional protection against current code-reuse attacks. Return Oriented Programming (ROP), for instance, relies on the fact that a set of so called Gadgets, each ending with a return instruction, can be chained together to form a more complex piece of code. In our TSX-based CFI, every return instruction is preceded by either a RTM or HLE instruction to begin a transaction. Thus, the number of gadgets that can be chained is limited by the corresponding MAX_NEST_COUNT for transactional nesting. Recent research has shown that restricting the maximum length of ROP gadget chains makes exploitation significantly harder, but attackers can still work around it [20]. However, TSX-based CFI adds another challenge for an attacker. In fact, many instructions that are typically used during an exploit (including system calls) trigger transactional aborts. Since for most exploits an interaction with the kernel is required, the attacker would need to find a way to escape from the transaction before the exploit can work.

4 Achieving CFI with TSX

Building up on the ideas described in Sect. 3.6, we designed an approach for providing control flow integrity using Intel's Transactional Memory Extensions (TSX). It is important to note that the techniques we discuss in this section can be adopted by any existing CFI techniques to ensure the integrity of control flow transfers, as well as to provide the additional protections afforded by TSX-CFI. Thus, we focus on the mechanism to detect the hijacking of the control flow, rather than on implementation details of CFI. Specifically, we expect that other techniques (such as [17,38,42,43]) can be leveraged to generate labels for strict CFI, which includes the computation of the valid targets for indirect control flow transfers.

In this section we discuss the implementation of both loose and strict CFI techniques. As with other loose CFI designs, our solution trades limited protection for simplicity in the implementation and deployment (i.e., the exact jump targets of every instruction do not have to be determined). On the other end, our reference strict CFI design provides stronger guarantees, with the requirement of a more complex analysis to identify jump targets.

An important difference between TSX CFI and traditional CFI is that TSX CFI *does not* prevent the attacker from hijacking the program's control flow. Instead, it simply ensures that any indirect control flow transfer in the program that can be hijacked by an attacker happens *inside* a TSX transaction. As a result, the control flow hijacking will eventually cause the transaction to abort, essentially *rewinding* the program to the clean state right before the control flow was hijacked and redirecting the execution into our fall-back path, which can use more sophisticated and time-consuming techniques to verify the presence of an attack and abort the program.

4.1 Transaction Protection

A core tenet of performing CFI with TSX is that many instructions, including system calls, cannot be performed inside a memory transaction. Thus, the underlying principle of our approach is that we enter into a transaction before attempting an indirect jump and exit from it at the jump target. These transactions are very short – in the normal case, the transaction starts, the indirect control flow occurs, and the transaction ends. If an attacker is able to manipulate the target of this instruction, and redirects it to an instruction that does not end the transaction, the transaction will fail for one of several reasons:

Context switch. The execution of the program is suspended by the kernel to run another process.

Instruction-based aborts. The execution of a transaction-aborting instructions (e.g., a system call).

TSX nesting limit. A transaction is nested in X other transactions, where X is the transaction nesting limit of the CPU.

Each TSX failure case presents a different challenge to an attacker. The context switch failure case limits the amount of code that an attacker can execute without closing the transaction, instruction based aborts makes it impossible to execute certain instructions like system calls while inside a transaction, and the TSX nesting limit puts a bound on the length of an attacker's ROP chain. This latter effect is very interesting: since we initiate a transaction before each indirect control flow transfer, an attacker that chains ROP gadgets in the traditional way will enter an extra nested transaction with each gadget. Since the nesting depth is limited (on most processors, this depth is 16), an attacker will quickly hit the transaction nesting limit, and, thus, cause a transactional abort. Furthermore, to be successful, an attacker must first *successfully exit* all entered transactions, in the reverse order of entering them, before operations such as system calls can be carried out. We want to emphasize that the nesting limit poses problems only for an attacker and not for benign applications. In fact, our implementation encloses only the control flow transfer instructions within transactions, and not the entire target function. For example, the transaction is opened just before a `call` instruction, and closed with the first instruction of the call destination.

When a transaction *aborts*, two things occur. First, the actions taken by the attacker while inside the transaction are *discarded* by the processor. Second, a *fall-back path* is triggered to check for the presence of an attacker (i.e., by verifying that the control flow transfer is going to a legal target). This is done because, aside from a control flow hijack, a context switch (for example, when the process is suspended to allow another process to run) will also abort a transaction. While this complicates our fall-back path, it introduces another challenge to the attacker: they must escape our transaction *quickly*, before the process is swapped out and the transaction is aborted.

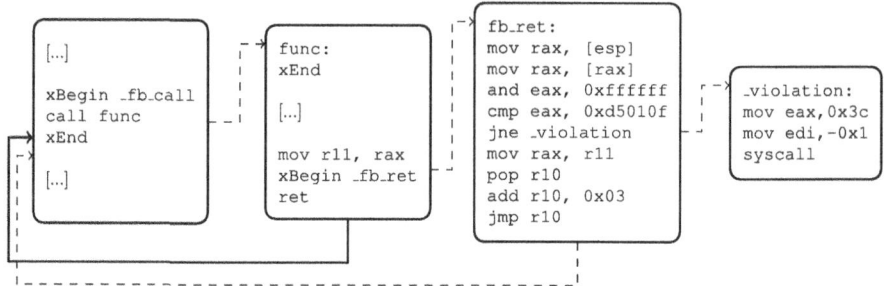

Fig. 1. Control flow of a function returning for RTM-based CFI

4.2 RTM and Loose CFI

We leverage Restricted Transactional Memory (RTM) to provide an implementation of loose CFI. To ensure that every indirect control flow transfer goes to a valid target, a transaction is started before each transfer and ended at the target site. For example, every function return is preceded by a XBEGIN instruction, while every function call is followed by a XEND instruction. Thus, a transaction will be started, the function will return, and the transaction will then be completed. As long the return address used by the return instruction is not manipulated, the transaction can only fail due to a context switch. The idea is visualized in Fig. 1, using the example of a function return.

In a failure case, the fall-back path specified in the XBEGIN transaction will be executed. Since RAX is used to indicate the reason for the fall-back path execution, we copy its value into an unused scratch register before entering a transaction. This enables us to restore the original function return value, which is also passed in RAX, in the case that the fall-back path gets executed due to a context switch during a benign control flow transfer. This can happen for two reasons: when the transaction is interrupted by chance because of a context switch initiated by the kernel, and when the control flow is hijacked by an attack. Thus, the fall-back path itself has to verify that the target of the control flow transfer is still pointing to a memory location containing the opcodes for an XEND instruction. Since different kinds of indirect control flow transfers determine the target of a transfer differently, several fall-back paths are required. In the case of function returns, the target (i.e., the return address) is on the stack, and can be dereferenced via RSP. Certain indirect jumps and calls, on the other hand, use a general purpose register to specify the target of the transaction. Thus, the fall-back path has to deference the content of the specific register. The only exception is provided by the CALL RAX and JMP RAX instructions because RAX gets overwritten upon entering the fall-back path. Naturally, instead of RAX, the local copy in the scratch register has to be dereferenced. Furthermore, if the control flow transfer is initiated by a call instruction, it is also necessary to save its origin inside another scratch-register. If the fall-back path can not detect the presence of an attacker, it can push the saved origin and jump to the target, effectively emulating the call. If the fall-back path does not detect the presence of a XEND instruction at the transfer's target, the presence of an attacker is assumed, and a CFI violation policy is triggered. This, naturally, terminates the program. If the presence of an attacker cannot be determined, the original value of RAX is restored, and the control flow is transferred to the target of the indirect jump.

Provided Protection. While the RTM implementation is very straightforward, it can only reason about a single set of *jump origins* and *jump targets*. That is, if an attacker hijacks the control flow, the presence of RTM CFI forces her to terminate the transaction at a valid jump target. However, with the exception of certain actions that are prohibited within a transaction (discussed in Sect. 4.1), an attacker can carry out any modification of memory (for example, by initiating a ROP chain) and then transfer the control flow back to a valid jump target, which will, in turn, terminate the transaction.

In essence, RTM provides weak security guarantees, but it is an important building block towards TSX CFI, and a useful tool to later measure the performance impact of our techniques. HLE, on the other hand, builds on these building blocks to provide security guarantees for TSX-assisted CFI.

4.3 HLE and Strict CFI

With strict CFI, every indirect control flow transfer is only allowed to proceed along strict well-defined paths. For example, functions may only return to their callers, and indirect jumps can only go to targets that were intended for them by the programmer. One way to implement such a policy is by using *labels*. With labels, every control flow transfer is assigned a label that it shares with the valid targets of that control flow transfer. When the transfer is triggered, the CFI policy ensures that the label at the source address matches the label at the destination address, terminating the program if this is not the case.

Intel's Hardware Lock Elision provides functionality that can be leveraged to implement such labeled CFI. Specifically, HLE elides a memory write to a memory location that represents the lock itself. We will term this location the *lock location*, and the value at the lock location the *unlock value*. A transaction is entered by performing a write to the lock location (termed a *locking write*), with the write instruction prepended by XACQUIRE, and is successfully terminated when the unlock value is restored by a write instruction prepended by XRELEASE (termed an *unlocking write*). We call the value that resides at the lock location during a transaction a *lock value*. For a transaction to commit successfully, the value written to the lock location during an XRELEASE *must* be the unlock value.

Our idea is to introduce labels by carefully choosing the (numeric) value used during the locking and unlocking write operations. The lock location is chosen as an offset on the stack, and we implement the locking write by simply adding the label value to that location. In turn, the unlocking write consists in subtracting the label, thus restoring the unlock value and successfully committing the transaction at the intended target of this control flow transfer. As with RTM,

Listing 1. HLE-based CFI

```
[...]
  call func
  xrelease lock sub [rsp], 0xcf1bee
[...]

func:
[...]
  xacquire lock add [rsp-0x8], 0xcf1bee
  xtest
  jnz __inside_transaction:
  mov r11, 0xcf1bee
  jmp __hle_cfi_fb_ret
__inside_transaction:
  ret
```

a transaction abort signals a potential attack. However, some additional details must be considered when enforcing HLE-based CFI. HLE has no mechanism to detect the *reason* why a transaction failed. While this has the benefit of not clobbering RAX (unlike RTM), it comes with a cost: HLE has no capability to execute a fall-back path on a transaction abort. Instead, HLE simply re-executes the critical section *without* eliding the lock write. Intel's intention is that, if the elided lock fails, a software-locking mechanism would simply take over. Thus, a *virtual fall-back path* has to be injected for HLE-protected control flow transfers. This can be done with the XTEST instruction, which identifies whether the process is currently in a transactional context. Therefore, a failed or aborted transaction can easily be detected by executing XTEST after entering the critical section. When an unsuccessful transaction is detected, a jump to the virtual fall-back path can be issued manually.

The fall-back path itself is similar to the fall-back path of RTM CFI. The only difference is that the fall-back path checks for a label in the code that would be executed after the indirect control flow completes. As with RTM, we cannot simply assume the presence of an attacker on transaction abort, because any context switch into the kernel would also trigger a transactional abort. Thus, the fall-back path is necessary.

An example showing an instrumented return using HLE is presented, for clarity, in Listing 1. A careful reader will notice that the lock location is actually different between the XACQUIRE and XRELEASE instructions. In reality, the lock location is the same: since the RET instruction itself modifies the stack pointer (by popping the 8-byte return address), the offset must be different by exactly 8 bytes after the RET executes.

Provided Protection. HLE extends the simple transactions provided by RTM with the ability to *label* indirect control flow transfers, allowing HLE CFI to ensure that indirect control flow transfers must proceed to a valid target and not just to *any* target. Likewise, the fact that indirect control flow transfers take place within a TSX transaction ensures that the execution flow cannot be hijacked and rerouted to system calls. Besides that, HLE introduces novel, interesting capabilities in control flow transfer protection: aside from ensuring that the transaction ends on a valid jump target, the use of HLE also mandates that, between the beginning and end of a transaction, the *value* of the stack pointer must be equal to itself plus the offset introduced by the instruction issuing the control flow transfer. This is implicit as part of its operation because a location on the stack is used as the lock location. To end a transaction successfully, this exact location must be written to, and the exact same value (the unlock value) that it had before the transaction began must be restored. If the stack pointer is unexpectedly modified during the transaction (for example, if the attacker hijacked the control flow and initiated a ROP chain), the unlock value will not be restored, since another location will be written to, instead. This, in turn, will cause the transaction to fail, the attacker's actions to be rewound, and the attacker to be detected.

Thus, HLE-supported CFI provides a formidable protection against control flow hijack attacks.

5 Implementation

We implemented our proposed TSX CFI design in a reference prototype to demonstrate that TSX-based CFI can be used to enforce CFI policies and to understand the overhead of such protection. This implementation is being released as open source, in the hope that it will be useful to other security researchers.

Because we did not possess a binary analysis system capable of constructing an accurate control flow graph from arbitrary binary applications, we implemented our approach at the source code level by instrumenting the compiler (specifically, we added a pass to the LLVM backend). While we consider binary analysis and rewriting outside of the scope of our work, existing tools have solved this problem [26,42,43], and their solutions could be reused directly to implement TSX-based CFI directly on binaries.

5.1 Integration Approach

We chose to implement our reference prototype as a backend compilation pass in LLVM. Our prototype combines a preprocessing-engine, the clang compiler with the TSX-CFI backend pass, and a postprocessing engine. The preprocessor performs a linear search over the provided source-code to detect and instrument

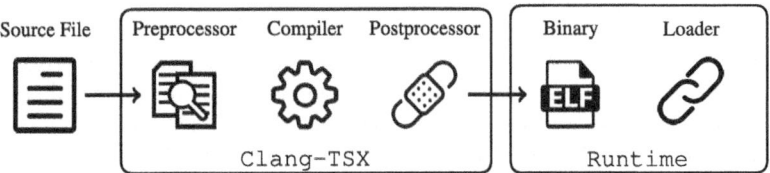

Fig. 2. Overview of the TSX CFI implementation

inline assembly, since it would be translated directly to binary code without being analyzed by the backend. The compiler produces an actual binary, where every function entry and every instruction issuing an *inter-functional control flow transfer* is instrumented (i.e. direct calls, indirect calls, function returns and tail-calls). During compilation, the TSX-CFI backend is unable to tell whether the targets of direct calls are located inside the binary or inside an external library, as this information is only visible at link time. However, since external calls are resolved via the *Procedure Linkage Table (PLT)*, these calls still require protection against control flow hijacks. Thus, the LLVM backend emits only no-op instructions for direct calls. These are fixed up by the postprocessor, which adds the protection for calls preformed via the PLT. Figure 2 shows the general overview of our implementation.

5.2 Implementation Details

As the implementation of our prototype is fairly intricate, we provide this section to introduce the interested reader with specific implementation aspects.

Selective Function Entry. Direct calls cannot be hijacked by attackers and, thus, do not need to be protected. However, this poses a problem: if a function is called by both direct *and* indirect calls throughout the binary, only the indirect calls should take place inside a transaction. To facilitate this, the post-processing engine modifies direct calls to a function to bypass the TSX transaction commit instruction. This does not reduce the security of the indirect jump because, even if the attacker redirects the jump to skip the transaction commit, he will still be stuck inside the transaction.

Lazy Binding and Full Relro. Our prototype supports the compilation of both binaries resolving external function during runtime (*Lazy Binding*) and binaries resolving all functions during load time. In *Full-Relro* the *Global Offset Table*, which stores the location of resolved functions, is marked as read-only. In this case, calls via PLT can only resolve to their intended target, which makes it impossible for an attacker to hijack those external function. Thus, these calls do not need protection. To optimize this case, we customized the dynamic loader to store pointers to the instruction *after* the commit instruction in the GOT, similar to the case of direct jumps to functions within the binary.

5.3 Limitations

Our prototype suffers from two classes of limitations, due to the fact that we lack kernel support and to our choice of using the clang compiler. While these problems are limiting the applicability of our current prototype for real-world applications, they do not pose any conceptual problem for TSX CFI. In the rest of this section, we address these limitations and describe how they could be solved in a future implementation.

Standard C Library. The standard C library for GNU/Linux systems, *glibc*, cannot be compiled with clang, since it requires functionality explicitly provided by *gcc*. In turn, it is not possible to create a TSX CFI instrumented *glibc* with our reference implementation. However, in order to provide a holistic TSX CFI solution, an instrumented standard C library is required. For this purpose, we instrumented musl, a free and lightweight standard C library. Obviously, this can be a problem for programs that are expecting the presence of `glibc`, for which we frequently observe crashes due to the different locale subsystems. We verified that these crashes are purely based on the incompatibility between the standard C libraries and are not introduced by our TSX CFI prototype. This issue can be solved by adding a `gcc` TSX CFI extension.

Virtual Dynamic Shared Object. Another interesting side-effect of our TSX CFI prototype is that we had to disable *Virtual Dynamic Shared Object (vDSO)* support. This object is provided by the kernel and mapped in the address space of every process, mainly to speed up syscalls, such as *gettimeofday()*, which are normally called via the standard library. Since vDSO is entered using a call instruction, an instrumented version of this object would be required for TSX CFI, which would require changes to the kernel and break the operation of uninstrumented programs. Therefore, the usage of vDSO in TSX-CFI instrumented programs is disabled for compatibility with unprotected programs. As solution, a holistic approach including kernel support for TSX CFI would be required.

Signal Handlers. Programs can register signal handlers that are executed upon the reception of given signals. However, in this case it is the OS kernel that redirects the control flow to the handler, and therefore a transaction is not entered when the signal handler is called. A possible solution would be to instrument the libc to alter the signal handlers pointers to use the un-instrumented function entry address. Another solution would be to instrument the kernel itself, similar to the case of vDSO.

Setjmp/Longjmp. The setjmp and longjmp interfaces are used to perform non-local gotos. While our implementation does not instrument non-local gotos, they still represent a class of indirect control-flow transfers. To cope with them, an advanced analysis engine for recovering the CFG would be required to retrieve the possible control flow targets. Nevertheless, the indirect transfer itself can easily be protected with transactions once the possible targets are known.

6 Evaluation

We evaluated our implementation to determine the practicality of TSX-based CFI. As we discuss in Sect. 4, we view our approach as a general way to implement the protection of indirect control flow transfers and expect that it will be leveraged by complete CFI approaches for that functionality. As such, the goal of this section is to provide an understanding of the overhead that TSX-protected control flow transfers induce in the runtime of actual application.

We performed our experiments on a diverse set of applications to evaluate the impact of TSX-CFI on different workflows. For this evaluation, we chose GNU coreutils (the collection of standard Linux binaries such ls), bzip2 (a common compression utility), lame (an audio encoder with the main purpose of encoding WAV audio files to MP3), and openssl (the general-purpose cryptography command line tool).

6.1 Experiments

We measured the performance of TSX-based CFI on a Intel Core i7 Haswell processor that supports TSX operations. To measure the overall performance overhead of our TSX CFI implementation, we selected tasks for the instrumented programs and calculated the average execution time over a series of 20 executions, using both HLE and RTM-provided indirect control flow protections. We chose the following programs and tasks:

coreutils: Execution of the 580 tests provided in the test-suite for the various utilities.
bzip2: Compression of a 200 megabyte file.
lame: Conversion of a 60 megabyte WAV file to a MP3 file with a bit rate of 128 Kbps.
openssl: Encryption of a 4 gigabyte file of random data with AES-256-CBC.

All of the experiments were executed with our instrumented version of musl, in which we also protected all indirect control flow transitions. The bzip2, lame, and openssl experiments ran without issue. However, of the 580 test cases provided by coreutils, 47 failed to run with our prototype, due to the differences of the locale subsystem of musl, and glibc, as described in Sect. 5.3. In the case of TSX-CFI implemented with RTM, three additional coreutils test cases failed with segmentation faults. Investigation into these segmentation faults revealed that they occurred due to program-defined signal handlers: some signal handlers would redirect the control flow of the process *without* entering a transaction, resulting in the execution of an XEND instruction outside of a transaction, which crashes the process.

6.2 Performance Overhead

We averaged the runtime of 20 executions on each experimental binary (in the case of the coreutils, we averaged the total time of 20 executions of all coreutils test cases). Due to the distinct workload carried out by the applications, we expected to see different overhead with our CFI implementation, and this was, indeed, the case as shown in Fig. 3. For example, lame, bzip2 and openssl, which spend most of their time in long-running loops for encoding, compression, or encryption, and call many helper functions in these loops, result in an overhead of up to 34 %. On the other hand, most tools inside coreutils spend much time

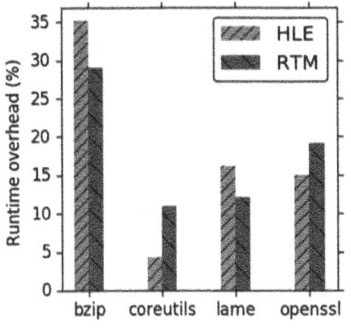 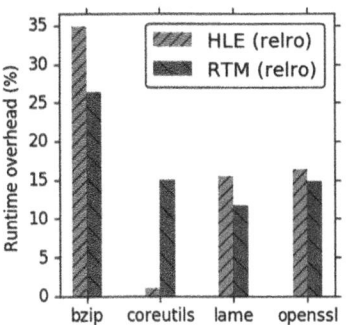

Fig. 3. Average runtime overhead

Table 1. Number of issued and aborted transactions.

Program	#Executed	#Aborted
bzip2	565711783	1781
lame	493580143	247
openssl	546743640	1088

Table 2. Size of instrumented programs, in Kilobytes.

Program	None	RTM	HLE	RTM-relro	HLE-relro
coreutils	85	101	117	90	99
bzip2	223	256	271	247	250
lame	401	459	523	422	450
openssl	2536	3362	4313	2817	3196
musl-libc	725	767	835	839	979

interacting with the host OS through system calls, resulting in a small overhead of up to 5 % in the case of HLE, which reflects our expectations.

In the coreutils case, the majority of the overhead from HLE came from the lazy binding of library functions. Again, this is consistent with what we expect: the coreutils binaries are a mostly short-running utilities and use many library functions, leading to the (CFI-protected) symbol resolution process to be called relatively frequently. Enabling RELRO (turning off lazy binding) for these binaries results in a drastic decrease of runtime overhead with HLE, to just 1 %. On the other binaries with less system interaction (lame, bzip2, and openssl), the difference is negligible.

6.3 Transaction Aborts

When a transaction fails, execution is diverted to the *fall-back* path, which checks whether the process has been exploited. However, as we discuss in Sect. 4.1, there are several reasons, other than exploitation, that can cause a transaction to abort.

To understand how frequently this occurs during normal operation, we evaluated the number of transactions that are attempted and the number that aborted. To do so, we utilized the capabilities of Intel's Software Development Emulator to measure the amount of executed transactions. Unfortunately, the emulator does not report aborted transactions caused by the environment (i.e., context switches).

Thus, we computed this number by instrumenting the aborted transaction fall-back path to track a counter of the number of times it was executed. The results of this measurement are presented in Table 1. From these results, we see that the rate of transaction failures is almost negligible. Thus, the most significant part of overhead that we experience with TSX-CFI is induced by continuously entering and leaving successful transactions. Ritson et Barnes [37] observed that invoking a transaction costs approximately 43 clock cycles, which, given the high number of executed transaction, results in the observed overhead.

6.4 Space Overhead

It is important to measure the space overhead of a program being protected by any CFI approach, both in terms of memory usage and program size.

While CFI, when implemented with TSX, suffers no additional memory usage overhead, the size of the program is increased due to the addition of both the TSX instructions themselves and also that of the fall-back paths. The size overhead, as shown in Table 2, depends on the TSX method that is used to enforce CFI and on the number of protected transitions inside the program. We calculated this overhead for the applications themselves (in the case of the coreutils, we used the arithmetic mean of the overhead for individual binaries) and the standard library.

We feel that, especially with modern systems, the low space overhead introduced by our implementation is quite acceptable for a CFI implementation.

7 Discussion

The use of TSX for control flow integrity brings interesting possibilities, but it also introduces several challenges. This section discusses the challenges, protections, and possible future research directions in the area of TSX-based CFI.

7.1 TSX Performance

As described in the evaluation section, the simple act of entering a TSX transaction incurs an immediate performance penalty. However, some different directions can be explored to reduce this overhead in the future:

Hardware improvements. TSX is a very young technology, and it is very likely that performance optimizations will be implemented in future Intel processors. While little can directly be done by security researchers to bring this about, the usefulness of TSX for things other than its actual intended application (i.e., this CFI approach or the protection of cryptographic keys in memory [21]) might make TSX a high-profile target for optimization.

Virtual Transactional Memory. TSX transactions are aborted whenever a context switch occurs. These transaction aborts have a strong impact on the performance, since they force our solution to use complex fall-back paths to check for the presence of an attack. These fall-back paths introduce runtime and space overhead, but are unavoidable with context-switch-based transaction aborts.

One approach toward eliminating this overhead is to allow a transaction to pause in the event of a process being paused, and resume when the process is resumed. In fact, designs for *virtual transactional memory* have been proposed [35] that would allow transactions to survive across context switches (specifically, pauses and resumes of a running process). If these techniques are adopted in the future, they could greatly improve the performance of TSX CFI.

Selective protection. Not every part of a program is equally vulnerable to a control flow hijack, and those functions that are not (and do not utilize any other functionality that must be protected) may not need CFI protection. A similar trade-off is seen in the application of *stack canaries* to prevent buffer overflows, where functions that lack any overflowable buffers do not receive stack canaries [11]. Performance could be greatly improved by leaving such "low-risk" functions similarly unprotected by TSX CFI. Similarly, protection could focus on specific types of control flow transfers. For example, function returns can be protected through the use of a shadow stack or a similar, less expensive approach, leaving the more expensive TSX protections for indirect calls and jumps, for which fewer alternative protection mechanisms exist.

While it is hard to speculate on the future of TSX, it is clear that it is an important capability, not only in the field of concurrent systems, but also in computer security. It seems quite likely that additional effort will be put into its optimization and the addressing of its limitations.

7.2 Protection Strength

As we discuss in Sect. 4.1, TSX-based CFI works by ensuring that, if an attacker manages to hijack the control flow of a program, he will find himself inside a TSX transaction. These transactions severely limit what an attacker can do, and if the attacker violates the restrictions the transaction is aborted and the process is rewound to the state *before* the control flow was hijacked. When this occurs, a fall-back path is triggered, checking for the presence of an attacker (by verifying whether the pending control flow transfer is targeting a legal location) and aborting the program if an attack is detected.

Thus, to perform useful actions, an attacker is forced to find a way to escape from the TSX transaction, using one of the following two options: (1) The attacker can jump to some previously-injected shellcode that commits the transactions and gives the attacker control or (2) the attacker can execute several ROP gadgets inside the transaction, influence the program state, then jump to the actual legal target of the initial protected control flow transfer.

Both options introduce challenges for the attacker. The first option is already mitigated by existing countermeasures against code-injection attacks, such as Data Execution Prevention or the *No-eXecute* bit, that are widely deployed in modern systems to prevent injected data from being executed. Attackers bypass these protections by diverting the control flow to execute a system call, such as mprotect(), that allows the injected data to be executed. However, this process involves the execution of a system call, which is not allowed inside a transaction. Thus, the attacker is presented with a chicken-and-egg problem: in order to commit the transaction, he must execute a system call, and in order to execute a system call, he must commit the transaction.

The second option is a possible, if seemingly infeasible way to escape a transaction. An attacker could hijack the control flow and, without aborting the transaction, utilize a small ROP chain to perform some action before jumping to the intended target of the hijacked control flow and letting the transaction commit happen. The attacker would then perform actions in this ROP chain, being careful not to violate the restrictions placed on him by the transaction. For example, these actions can include influencing sensitive data structures in the program. Although this certainly empowers the attacker in comparison to other CFI solutions, in practice, carrying out this attack is extremely difficult, especially for the HLE based CFI approach. Specifically, the stack pointer *and* the lock value must not unexpectedly change values during the control flow transfer. Thus, an attacker must execute this attack *without* altering the stack pointer or the lock value across the transaction. Additionally, this chain must be fairly short: a context switch during ROP chain execution will lead to an aborted transaction and the detection of the attacker. To make matters worse (for the attacker), using any protected indirect control flow transfer will cause the initiation of additional transactions, all of which the attacker must escape (in reverse order of initiation, and without modifying the stack pointer or lock value) before escaping the original transaction. We feel that, in practice, these restrictions make such an attack infeasible.

7.3 Comparison with Other Techniques

Our approach introduces a higher overhead when compared to other recent CFI enforcement schemes which do not require dedicated hardware features, such as [26,29,39,42]. While this is surely a drawback of the presented implementation, we believe that it is too early to disregard TSX CFI as unusable, since Hardware Transactional Memory itself is a new CPU feature and performance speed-ups are feasible in further iterations. However, our main goal is to explore the suitability of the new hardware transactional memory features for control flow integrity purposes. We hope that our study can provide useful insights on how hardware-assisted CFI could look like and that it can help other researchers in the field to design future CFI implementations.

Moreover, we were happy to see that Intel recently released its Control-flow Enforcement Technology Preview (CET) [23], in parallel to this paper, showing the demand of hardware manufacturers to provide architectural CFI support. CET is meant to advance the processor with features against ROP attacks. In more detail, a shadow stack is used to protect function returns and indirect branch tracking for protecting indirect control flow transfers. The latter technique introduces a new instruction, ENDBRANCH, which needs to be executed after the occurrence of an indirect control flow transfer. Since CET in its current state is only a preview and is not available for consumer hardware yet, we can not compare its performance to TSX CFI. However, it is notable that the CET's indirect branch tracking is similar to our RTM based approach: In both cases the processor is set to a state waiting for a certain instruction to specify the end of a control flow transfer; In TSX CFI this state is explicitly forced by opening a transaction, while CET introduces a new WAIT_FOR_ENDBRANCH state, which is implicitly imposed to the processor upon executing an indirect call or jump. While the shadow stack provides stronger security guarantees and could easily replace TSX CFI for backward-edges in a future implementation, the deployment of labels like presented in our HLE based CFI approach yields a finer granularity than CET's indirect branch tracking.

7.4 Additional Capabilities - Future Work

While not related directly to CFI, TSX has other potential applications that are interesting. A possible application is to ensure the integrity of certain sensitive memory regions or registers over the course of the execution of some functionality deemed to be "dangerous" (i.e., a strcpy known to contain user input). For example, a HLE transaction could be entered by subtracting 0 from the sensitive memory region, the functionality could be carried out, and the transaction would be committed by subtracting 0 again. If the contents of the sensitive memory region were different (i.e., due to an attack) at the end of the transaction from their value at the beginning, the transaction will abort. Registers can, likewise, be protected by XORing them to memory as part of initiating the transaction and XORing them to memory again to commit the transaction.

If virtual transactional memory is adopted, these approaches can be utilized to protect data in relatively complicated program functionality, as long as no system calls are performed.

8 Conclusion

In this paper, we proposed a technique to enhance control flow integrity by leveraging new hardware capabilities, intended to support transactional memory.

Our design provides two distinct levels of CFI protection: unlabeled CFI and labeled strict CFI. In a TSX-based CFI system, every indirect control flow transfer occurs inside a transactional memory transaction. If such a control flow transfer is hijacked by an attacker, the attacker will find himself inside the transaction, with severely limited capabilities. Eventually, this transaction will be aborted, which will roll back all of the changes to memory or registers made by the attacker and lead to the attacker's detection. As a side-effect, our technique can protect the values of the stack pointer as part of its operation. If an attacker modifies this register, for instance during a code-reuse attack, and attempts to commit the transaction, the transaction will fail.

We implemented a proof-of-concept prototype of TSX-supported CFI and used it to evaluate the runtime and size overhead of instrumented programs. The evaluation of our approach showed that induced overhead in performance is mediocre compared with other recent CFI solutions, with a very modest program size overhead and no other memory usage increase. While the overhead is higher in comparison to other CFI approaches, we discuss possibilities for speed-up, and the potential of future developments to enable faster TSX-supported CFI.

References

1. Abadi, M., Budiu, M., Erlingsson, U., Ligatti, J.: Control-flow integrity. In: Proceedings of the 12th ACM Conference on Computer and Communications Security. ACM (2005)
2. Andersen, S., Abella, V.: Data execution prevention. Changes to functionality in microsoft windows xp service pack 2, part 3: Memory protection technologies (2004)
3. Berkowits, S.: Pin-a dynamic binary instrumentation tool (2012)
4. Bletsch, T., Jiang, X., Freeh, V.: Mitigating code-reuse attacks with control-flow locking. In: Proceedings of the 27th Annual Computer Security Applications Conference. ACM (2011)
5. Budiu, M., Erlingsson, U., Abadi, M.: Architectural support for software-based protection. In: Proceedings of the 1st Workshop on Architectural and System Support for Improving Software Dependability. ACM (2006)
6. Carlini, N., Barresi, A., Payer, M., Wagner, D., Gross, T.R.: Control-flow bending: on the effectiveness of control-flow integrity. In: 24th USENIX Security Symposium (2015)
7. Christoulakis, N., Christou, G., Athanasopoulos, E., Ioannidis, S.: HCFI: hardware-enforced control-flow integrity. In: Proceedings of the Sixth ACM Conference on Data and Application Security and Privacy. ACM (2016)
8. de Clercq, R., De Keulenaer, R., Coppens, B., Yang, B., Maene, P., de Bosschere, K., Preneel, B., de Sutter, B., Verbauwhede, I.: SOFIA: software and control flow integrity architecture. In: Design, Automation & Test in Europe Conference & Exhibition (DATE) (2016)
9. Conti, M., Crane, S., Davi, L., Franz, M., Larsen, P., Negro, M., Liebchen, C., Qunaibit, M., Sadeghi, A.R.: Losing control: on the effectiveness of control-flow integrity under stack attacks. In: Proceedings of the 22nd ACM SIGSAC Conference on Computer and Communications Security. ACM (2015)
10. Intel Corporation: Intel Architecture Instruction Set Extensions Programming Reference (2012)
11. Cowan, C., Pu, C., Maier, D., Walpole, J., Bakke, P., Beattie, S., Grier, A., Wagle, P., Zhang, Q., Hinton, H.: Stackguard: automatic adaptive detection and prevention of buffer-overflow attacks. In: USENIX Security, vol. 98 (1998)
12. Criswell, J., Dautenhahn, N., Adve, V.: KCoFI: complete control-flow integrity for commodity operating system kernels. In: IEEE Symposium on Security and Privacy. IEEE (2014)
13. Davi, L., Dmitrienko, A., Egele, M., Fischer, T., Holz, T., Hund, R., Nürnberger, S., Sadeghi, A.R.: MoCFI: A framework to mitigate control-flow attacks on smartphones. In: NDSS (2012)

14. Davi, L., Hanreich, M., Paul, D., Sadeghi, A.R., Koeberl, P., Sullivan, D., Arias, O., Jin, Y.: HAFIX: hardware-assisted flow integrity extension. In: Proceedings of the 52nd Annual Design Automation Conference. ACM (2015)
15. Davi, L., Koeberl, P., Sadeghi, A.R.: Hardware-assisted fine-grained control-flow integrity: towards efficient protection of embedded systems against software exploitation. In: The 51st Annual Design Automation Conference on Design Automation Conference. ACM (2014)
16. Davi, L., Lehmann, D., Sadeghi, A.R., Monrose, F.: Stitching the gadgets: on the ineffectiveness of coarse-grained control-flow integrity protection. In: 23rd USENIX Security Symposium (2014)
17. Evans, I., Long, F., Otgonbaatar, U., Shrobe, H., Rinard, M., Okhravi, H., Sidiroglou-Douskos, S.: Control jujutsu: on the weaknesses of fine-grained control flow integrity. In: 22nd ACM SIGSAC Conference on Computer and Communications Security. ACM (2015)
18. Ge, X., Talele, N., Payer, M., Jaeger, T.: Fine-grained control-flow integrity for kernel software. In: 1st IEEE European Symposium on Security and Privacy. IEEE (2016)
19. Goktas, E., Athanasopoulos, E., Bos, H., Portokalidis, G.: Out of control: overcoming control-flow integrity. In: IEEE Symposium on Security and Privacy. IEEE (2014)
20. Göktaş, E., Athanasopoulos, E., Polychronakis, M., Bos, H., Portokalidis, G.: Size does matter: why using gadget-chain length to prevent code-reuse attacks is hard. In: 23rd USENIX Symposium (2014)
21. Guan, L., Lin, J., Luo, B., Jing, J., Wang, J.: Protecting private keys against memory disclosure attacks using hardware transactional memory. In: IEEE Symposium on Security and Privacy. IEEE (2015)
22. Herlihy, M., Moss, J.E.B.: Transactional memory: architectural support for lock-free data structures, vol. 21, pp. 289–300 (1993)
23. Intel: Control-Flow Enforcement Technology Review (Revision 1.0), June 2016
24. Jang, D., Tatlock, Z., Lerner, S.: Safedispatch: securing C++ virtual calls from memory corruption attacks. In: Symposium on Network and Distributed System Security (NDSS) (2014)
25. Mashtizadeh, A.J., Bittau, A., Boneh, D., Mazières, D.: CCFI: cryptographically enforced control flow integrity. In: Proceedings of the 22nd ACM SIGSAC Conference on Computer and Communications Security. ACM (2015)
26. Mohan, V., Larsen, P., Brunthaler, S., Hamlen, K., Franz, M.: Opaque control-flow integrity. In: NDSS (2015)
27. Muttik, I., Nazshtut, A., Dementiev, R.: Creating a spider goat: using transactional memory support for security (2014)
28. Niu, B., Tan, G.: Monitor integrity protection with space efficiency and separate compilation. In: Proceedings of the 2013 ACM SIGSAC Conference on Computer & Communications Security. ACM (2013)
29. Niu, B., Tan, G.: Modular control-flow integrity. In: Proceedings of the 35th ACM SIGPLAN Conference on Programming Language Design and Implementation. ACM (2014)
30. Niu, B., Tan, G.: RockJIT: securing just-in-time compilation using modular control-flow integrity. In: Proceedings of the 2014 ACM SIGSAC Conference on Computer and Communications Security. ACM (2014)
31. Niu, B., Tan, G.: Per-input control-flow integrity. In: Proceedings of the 22nd ACM SIGSAC Conference on Computer and Communications Security. ACM (2015)

32. Pappas, V., Polychronakis, M., Keromytis, A.D.: Transparent ROP exploit mitigation using indirect branch tracing. In: 22nd USENIX Security Symposium (2013)
33. Payer, M., Barresi, A., Gross, T.R.: Fine-grained control-flow integrity through binary hardening. In: Almgren, M., Gulisano, V., Maggi, F. (eds.) DIMVA 2015. LNCS, vol. 9148, pp. 144–164. Springer, Heidelberg (2015)
34. Prakash, A., Hu, X., Yin, H.: vfGuard: strict protection for virtual function calls in cots C++ binaries. In: NDSS (2015)
35. Rajwar, R., Herlihy, M., Lai, K.: Virtualizing transactional memory. In: 32nd International Symposium on Computer Architecture (ISCA 2005). IEEE (2005)
36. Reinders, J.: Transactional synchronization in Haswell, February 2012
37. Ritson, C.G., Barnes, F.: An evaluation of intels restricted transactional memory for CPAS. In: Communicating Process Architectures (2013)
38. Tice, C., Roeder, T., Collingbourne, P., Checkoway, S., Erlingsson, Ú., Lozano, L., Pike, G.: Enforcing forward-edge control-flow integrity in GCC & LLVM. In: 23rd USENIX Security Symposium (2014)
39. van der Veen, V., Andriesse, D., Göktaş, E., Gras, B., Sambuc, L., Slowinska, A., Bos, H., Giuffrida, C.: Practical context-sensitive CFI. In: Proceedings of the 22nd ACM SIGSAC Conference on Computer and Communications Security. ACM (2015)
40. van de Ven, A.: New security enhancements in red hat enterprise linux (2004)
41. Xia, Y., Liu, Y., Chen, H., Zang, B.: CFIMon: detecting violation of control flow integrity using performance counters. In: 42nd Annual IEEE/IFIP International Conference on Dependable Systems and Networks (DSN). IEEE (2012)
42. Zhang, C., Wei, T., Chen, Z., Duan, L., Szekeres, L., McCamant, S., Song, D., Zou, W.: Practical control flow integrity and randomization for binary executables. In: IEEE Symposium on Security and Privacy. IEEE (2013)
43. Zhang, M., Sekar, R.: Control flow integrity for cots binaries. In: 22nd USENIX Security Symposium (2013)

Automatic Uncovering of Tap Points from Kernel Executions

Junyuan Zeng, Yangchun Fu, and Zhiqiang Lin[(✉)]

The University of Texas at Dallas, 800 W. Campbell Rd, Richardson, TX 75080, USA
{jzeng,yangchun.fu,zhiqiang.lin}@utdallas.edu

Abstract. Automatic uncovering of tap points (i.e., places to deploy active monitoring) in an OS kernel is useful in many security applications such as virtual machine introspection, kernel malware detection, and kernel rootkit profiling. However, current practice to extract a tap point for an OS kernel is through either analyzing kernel source code or manually reverse engineering of kernel binary. This paper presents AUTOTAP, the first system that can automatically uncover the tap points directly from kernel binaries. Specifically, starting from the execution of system calls (i.e., the user level programing interface) and exported kernel APIs (i.e., the kernel module/driver development interface), AUTOTAP automatically tracks kernel objects, resolves their kernel execution context, and associates the accessed context with the objects, from which to derive the tap points based on how an object is accessed (e.g., whether the object is created, accessed, updated, traversed, or destroyed). The experimental results with a number of Linux kernels show that AUTOTAP is able to automatically uncover the tap points for many kernel objects, which would be very challenging to achieve with manual analysis. A case study of using the uncovered tap points shows that we can use them to build a robust hidden process detection tool at the hypervisor layer with very low overhead.

Keywords: Virtual machine introspection · Kernel function reverse engineering · Active kernel monitoring · (DKOM) rootkit detection

1 Introduction

A tap point [10] is an execution point where active monitoring can be performed. Uncovering tap points inside an OS kernel is important to many security applications such as virtual machine introspection (VMI) [15], kernel malware detection [17], and kernel rootkit profiling [19,25]. For example, by tapping the internal execution of the creation and deletion of process descriptors, it can enable a VMI tool to track the active running processes [4]. Prior systems mainly hook the execution of the public exported APIs (e.g., system calls such as `fork` in Linux) to track the kernel object creation (e.g., `task_struct`). However, attackers can actually use some of the internal functions to bypass the check and create the "hidden" objects. Therefore, it would be very useful if we can automatically identify these internal tap points and hook them for the detection.

Unfortunately, the large code base of an OS kernel makes the uncovering of tap points non-trivial. Specifically, an OS kernel tends to have tens of thousands of functions managing tens of thousands of kernel objects. Meanwhile, it has very complicated control flow due to the asynchronized events such as interrupts and exceptions. Finding which execution point can be tapped is daunting at binary level. In light of this, current practice is to merely rely on human beings to *manually* inspect kernel source code (if it is available), or reverse engineer the kernel binary to identify the tap points.

To advance the state-of-the-art, we present AUTOTAP, a system for AUTOmatic uncovering of TAP points directly from kernel binary. We focus on the tap points that are related to kernel objects since kernel malware often manipulates them. In particular, based on how an object is accessed, we classify the tap points into *creation, initialization, read, write, traversal,* and *destroy*. By observing which execution point is responsible for these object accesses, we derive the corresponding tap points.

The reason to derive tap points by associating kernel objects with the corresponding execution context is because different kernel objects are usually accessed in different kernel execution context. The context entails not only the instruction level access such as read or write to a particular field of an object, but also the calling context such as the current function, its call-chain, and its system call (syscall for brevity henceforth) if the execution is within a particular syscall, or other contexts such as interrupts. As to-be-demonstrated in this paper, such knowledge, along with the meaning of the available kernel data structures, is sufficient to derive the tap points for active kernel monitoring.

Having the capability of uncovering the tap points, AUTOTAP will be valuable in many security applications. One use case is we can apply AUTOTAP to detect the hidden kernel objects by tapping the internal kernel object access functions. Meanwhile, we can also use AUTOTAP to reverse engineer the semantics of kernel functions. For instance, with AUTOTAP we can now pinpoint the function that creates, deletes, initializes, updates, and traverses kernel objects. In addition, we can also identify common functions that operate with many different type of objects, which will be particularly useful to uncover the meanings of kernel functions especially for closed source OS.

In summary, we make the following contributions:

- We present AUTOTAP, the first system that is able to automatically uncover the tap points for introspection directly from kernel executions.
- We introduce a novel approach to classify the complicated kernel execution context into a hierarchical structure, from which to infer function semantics and derive tap points based on how an object is accessed.
- We have built a proof-of-concept prototype of AUTOTAP. Our evaluation results with 10 recent Linux kernels show that our system can directly recognize a large number of tap points for the observed kernel objects.
- We also show how to use our uncovered tap points to build a general hidden process detection tool, which has very small overhead.

2 System Overview

Since the goal of AUTOTAP is to uncover the tap points for the introspection of kernel object, we have to first track the kernel objects and their types. However, at binary code level, there is no type information associated with each object and we have to first recover them. Fortunately, our prior system ARGOS [30] has addressed this problem. ARGOS is a type inference system for OS kernels, and it is able to track the kernel object, assign syntactic types, and even point out the semantics for a limited number of important kernel objects but not all of them. Therefore, AUTOTAP has reused several components from ARGOS and also extended them for kernel object type inference.

Having inferred the types of kernel objects, we have to infer the tap points of our interest. A tap point is usually an instruction address (e.g., a function entry address) where active monitoring can be performed. Since tap points uncovering is essentially a reverse engineering problem, we have to start from known knowledge to infer the unknown one [10]. With respect to an OS kernel, the well-known knowledge would include its syscall interface (for user level programs), and all of its kernel module development interface (for kernel driver programs). Therefore, one of the key challenges would be how to leverage these knowledge to systematically infer the meaning of the accessed functions, from which to derive the corresponding tap points.

Key Insights. After analyzing how a typical OS kernel is designed and executed and also based on the experience from our prior systems including ARGOS and REWARDS [22], we have obtained the following insights to address the above challenges:

- **From data access to infer function semantics.** A program (with no exception to OS kernel) is composed of code and data, where code defines how to update data and data keeps the updated state. While there are a large number of kernel functions, from low level data access perspective, we can classify them into a number of primitive accesses including the basic data *read* and *write* according to how an instruction accesses it. We can also capture their lifetime based on their *allocation* and *deallocation* especially for heap and stack data. We can even differentiate further from the first time *write* (i.e., *initialization*) to the subsequent *write* according to the memory write operations. We can also conclude a piece of code is a *traversal* function if we observe it performs memory dereferences to reach other objects (either with the same type or different types).
- **From hardware level events to infer function semantics.** In addition to observing the instruction level data access behavior, we can also observe the hardware level events such as interrupts and exceptions to infer the function semantics. For example, if a function is always executed in a timer interrupt, we can conclude it is likely a periodic function (e.g., `schedule` function); if it is executed inside a keyboard response interrupt, we can conclude it is a keystroke interrupt handler.

– **From syscall level events to infer function semantics.** Another category of useful information is the system call events. If a function is executed inside fork, we know this function is likely kernel object creation related; if it is inside socket send, we know it must be network communication related. Meanwhile, we also know a fork syscall must create kernel objects such as task_struct, and a send syscall must access a socket object.
– **Inferring the semantics of objects from kernel APIs.** While kernel has a large number of kernel objects, not all of them are of attackers' interest. Consequently, we have to identify the type of the kernel objects such that we can pinpoint the tap points of our interest. To this end, we can leverage the types of the parameters and return values of kernel APIs, the public exported knowledge used when developing kernel modules, to resolve the object types (such as whether the object is a task_struct). Meanwhile, kernel developers often have access to a number of kernel header files (otherwise their modules may not be compiled). By combining the types resolved from the API arguments and the data structure definitions from the open header files, we can reach and resolve more kernel data structures.

Scope, Assumptions, and Threat Model. To make our discussion more focused, we target OS kernels executed atop a 32-bit ×86 architecture. To validate our experimental results with the ground truth, we use the open source Linux kernels as the testing software[1]. Regarding the scope of the tap points, we focus on those that are related to dynamically allocated kernel heap objects.

As alluded earlier, we assume the knowledge of kernel APIs, e.g., the kernel object allocation function (e.g., kmalloc, and kfree) such that AutoTap can hook and track the kernel object creation and deletion, and the types of the arguments of the kernel APIs, which will be used to resolve the kernel object types. Meanwhile, we assume the access of the header files related to kernel module development (this is also true for Microsoft Windows), and the data structure defined in the header files will also be used to type more kernel objects. AutoTap aims to discover the tap points for introspection in the existing kernel legal binary code. If there is any injected code, AutoTap cannot tap their executions.

Overview. We design AutoTap by using a binary code translation based virtual machine monitor (VMM) Pemu [29], which extends Qemu [2] with an enhanced dynamic binary instrumentation capability. There are three key components inside AutoTap: *kernel object tracking*, *object access resolution*, and *tap points uncovering*; they work in two phases: an online tracing phase, and an offline analysis phase (Fig. 1).

---

[1] Note that even though the kernel source code is open, it is still tedious to derive the tap points manually, and a systematic approach such as AutoTap is needed.

In the online phase, starting from the kernel object creation, *kernel object tracking* tracks the dynamically created kernel objects, their sizes, and their propagations and indexes them based on the calling context of the object creation for the monitoring. Whenever there is an access to these monitored objects, *object access resolution* captures the current execution context, resolves the types of the arguments, resolves the current access (e.g., whether it is a read, write, initialization, allocation, or deallocation), and keeps a record of the current object access with the captured execution context if this

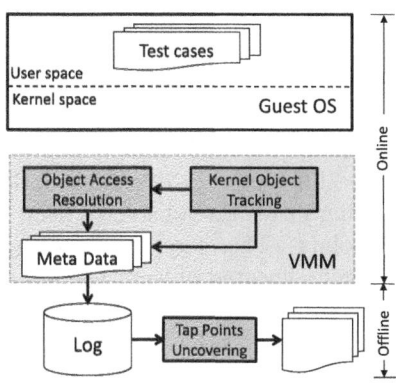

Fig. 1. An overview of AUTOTAP.

record has not been stored yet in the memory. Once we have finished the online tracing, we then dump the memory meta-data into a log file, and our *tap points uncovering* will analyze the log file to eventually derive the tap points. Next, we present the detailed design and implementation of these components.

3 Design and Implementation

3.1 Kernel Object Tracking

As the focus of AUTOTAP is to extract the tap points related to the dynamically allocated kernel objects, we have to first (i) track their life time, (ii) assign a unique type to each object, (iii) track the object propagation and its size such that we know to which object the address belongs when given a virtual address, and (iv) resolve the semantic types of kernel objects. Since our prior system ARGOS also need to perform these tasks for its type inference, we reused a lot of code base to handle kernel object tracking. However, there are still some differences between AUTOTAP and ARGOS on (ii) how we assign syntactic type to each object and (iv) how we resolve the semantic type of object. Next, we just describe these differences. More details on (i) how we track object life time and (iii) resolve the object size can be found in ARGOS [30].

Assigning a Syntactic Type to Each Object. In general, there are two standard approaches to convert dynamic object instances into syntactic forms: (1) using the callsite address of kmalloc, denoted as $PC_{kmalloc}$ to represent the syntactic object type, or (2) using the callsite-chain of kmalloc, denoted as $CC_{kmalloc}$ to represent the syntactic object type. The first approach is intuitive but it cannot capture the case where kmalloc is wrapped. While the second approach can capture all the distinctive object allocation, it may over classify the object types since the same type can be allocated in different calling context.

ARGOS used the first approach since it aims to uncover the general types (context-insensitive). In AUTOTAP, we adopt the second approach because we aim to identify the execution point for the tapping, and these points are usually context sensitive. For instance, a string is a general type but when it is used in different contexts (e.g., to represent a machine name or a process name), it means different type of strings and we may just need to tap a particular type of string instead of all strings (that is why sometimes we have context-sensitive tap points). Therefore, we use $CC_{kmalloc}$ to denote the syntactic type for each dynamic allocated object. The semantic meaning of $CC_{kmalloc}$ will be resolved later. Also, we use a calling context encoding technique [27] to encode $CC_{kmalloc}$ with an integer $E(CC_{kmalloc})$, and store this integer and its corresponding type with a hash table we call HT_{type} for easier lookup and decoding.

Resolving the Semantic Type of Object. The syntactic type ($CC_{kmalloc}$) assigned to each object is only used to differentiate objects, and it does not tell the semantics (i.e., the meaning) of the object. Since the tap points we aim to uncover are associated to each specific kernel object (e.g., task_struct), we need to resolve their semantic types. While ARGOS can recognize semantics for a number of kernel objects if there are unique rules to derive their meanings under certain syscall context, it cannot recognize all kernel objects. Therefore, we use a different approach, which is inspired by our another prior system REWARDS [22], a user level data structure type inference system. In particular, REWARDS infers the semantics of data structures through the use of well-known semantic type information from the argument and return value of system call and user level APIs. We adopt the RWEARDS approach to infer the kernel object semantic types from public known kernel APIs. However, not all objects can be typed from the argument and return value of these APIs, and therefore we also leverage the object types defined in the header files for kernel module development and track object point-to relations to infer more object types. To capture the point-to relation between objects, we use the same taint analysis approach as in ARGOS.

Summary. Our *kernel object tracking* will track the life time of the dynamically allocated objects with a red-black tree we call $RB_{instance}$ tree that is used to store $<v, s, T_i, E(CC_{kmalloc})>$, which is indexed by v, where v is the starting address, s is the corresponding size, T_i is the taint tag for O_i, and $E(CC_{kmalloc})$ is the encoded syntactic type of the allocated object. Also, it will maintain a hash table we call HT_{type} that uses $E(CC_{kmalloc})$ as the index key. This HT_{type} stores the decoded callsite chain, the resolved semantic type of the objects based on kernel APIs and available header files, as well as the captured point-to relations between them. Also, the resolved access context to each field of a particular type (described next) is also stored in our HT_{type}.

3.2 Object Access Resolution

Once we have captured each kernel object and its (field) propagations, the next step is to resolve the execution context when an instruction is accessing our monitored object. Note that the execution context *captures how and when a piece of data gets accessed.* In general, when a piece of data gets accessed, under dynamic binary code instrumentation based VMM, what we can observe includes: (i) which instruction is accessing the data, (ii) through what kind of access (read, or write). However, such information is still at too low level, and what we want is the high level semantic information that includes (i) which execution context (e.g., syscall, interrupt, kernel thread) is accessing the object and under what kind of calling context, and (ii) what the concrete operation is with respect to the accessed object (e.g., create, read, write, initialize, allocation, deallocation). Therefore, we have to bridge this gap.

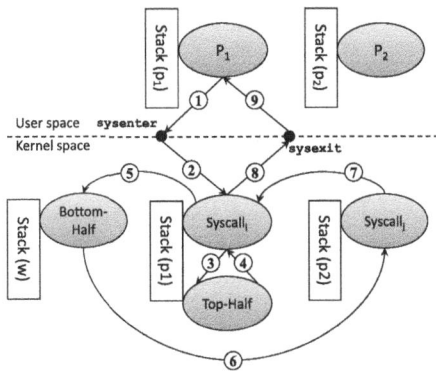

Fig. 2. An illustration of the three top level kernel execution contexts.

A kernel execution context in fact has a hierarchical structure and it can be classified into three layers. From top to bottom, there are syscall level context, function call level context, and instruction level context. In the following, we describe how we resolve these contexts and associate them to the accessed kernel objects.

Resolving Top Level Execution Context. When a given kernel object gets accessed, we need to determine under which highest level execution context it is accessed. As shown in Fig. 2, there are *three kinds of disjoint highest level execution contexts*:

- **(I) Syscall execution context.** When a user level program requests a kernel service, it has to invoke the syscalls. When a syscall gets executed, kernel control flow will start from the entry point of the syscall, and continue its execution until this syscall finishes. There is always a corresponding kernel stack for each process that tracks the return address of the functions called by this syscall. Therefore, we have to first identify to which process the current syscall belongs, and identify the entry point and exit point of this syscall.

  In x86, the entry point and exit point of a syscall for Linux platform can be easily captured by monitoring the syscall enter and exit instructions (e.g., `sysenter`, `sysexit`, `int 0x80`, `iret`). To identify a process context, we use the base address of kernel stack pointer, i.e., the 19 most significant bits of the kernel `esp`, denoted MSB19(`esp`), since kernel stack is unique to each process or kernel thread, as what we have done in ARGOS.

  Therefore, as shown in Fig. 2, when an instruction is executed between the syscall entry (Control Flow Transition ①, $CFT①$ for brevity) and exit point

($CFT⑧$), if it is not executed in an interrupt handler's context (discussed below), and if the context belongs to the running process, then it is classified the syscall execution context. We will resolve the corresponding syscall based on the `eax` value when the syscall traps to the kernel for this particular process. The corresponding process is indexed by the base address of each kernel stack, which is computed by monitoring the memory write to the kernel `esp`. We also use another RB-tree, and we call it RB_{sys} tree to dynamically keep the MSB19(`esp`) and the `eax` that is the syscall number, for each process such that we can quickly retrieve the syscall number when given a kernel `esp` if the execution is executed inside a syscall.

- **(II) Top-half of an interrupt handler execution context.** While most of the time kernel is executed under certain syscall context for a particular process, there are other asynchronous kernel events driven by the interrupts and exceptions, and they can occur at any time during the syscall execution. To respond them, modern OS such as Linux kernel usually splits the interrupt handlers into top-half that requires an immediate response and bottom-half that can be processed later [6].

  As illustrated in Fig. 2, top half of an interrupt can occur at anytime during a syscall execution (e.g., when a time slice is over, a key is stroke, or a packet is arrived). It starts from a hardware event ($CFT③$ which can be monitored by our VMM), and ends with an `iret` instruction ($CFT④$). The execution of a top-half is often very short, and it can use the kernel stack of the interrupted process to store the return address if there is any function call, or use a dedicated stack for this particular interrupt depending on how the interrupt handler is implemented. Meanwhile, an interrupt execution can be nested. Thus, we have to capture the pair of $CFT③$ and $CFT④$. This can be tracked by using a stack-like data structure. Through such, the top half of an interrupt handler can be precisely identified.

- **(III) Bottom-half of an interrupt handler execution context, or kernel thread execution.** When the response for an interrupt takes much longer time, kernel often leaves such an expensive execution to dedicated kernel threads (to execute the bottom half of an interrupt handler) such as `pdflush`, `ksoftirqd`. Therefore, *there must be a context switch event*, which can be observed by the kernel stack exchange. Note that $CFT⑤$, $CFT⑥$, and $CFT⑦$ all denotes the context switch event because of the stack exchange. In other words, as illustrated in Fig. 2, we can actually uniformly treat them as the syscall context of user level processes with the only difference that they do not have a syscall entry and syscall exit point.

Resolving Middle Level Execution Context. Having identified the highest level execution context, we also need to identify the middle level execution context at a function call level that includes which function is executing the current instruction and the callers of this function. Naturally it leads us to identify the function call chain. While we can get the call chain by traversing the stack frame pointer, it requires kernel to be compiled with this information. To make AUTO-TAP more general, we instrument `call/ret` instruction and use a shadow stack to track the callsite chain. Based on the above three high level disjoint execution contexts, we maintain the following three kinds of shadow stacks (SS):

- **(I) Syscall SS.** When a syscall execution (say s_i) starts, we will create a corresponding $SS(s_i)$. Then whenever there is a function call under the execution of s_i, we additionally push a tuple <f_entry_addr, f_return_addr, stack_ret_offset> into the corresponding $SS(s_i)$, and whenever there is a ret executed under this syscall context, we additionally pop the tuple whose f_return_addr matches the return address from the top of $SS(s_i)$. Note that without this matching check, there could exist cases that call and return are not strictly paired. Also, the push/ret of the return address when calling f will still use the original stack. The reason of tracking the stack_ret_offset in the original stack is for quickly retrieving of the entire calling context for context-sensitive tap points, when given just a kernel stack without instrumenting any call instructions. Then at any moment, the callsite chain for the current syscall context can be created by retrieving the value of f_return_addr in the corresponding kernel stack based on the location specified by stack_ret_offset.
- **(II) Top-half SS.** When a top half of an interrupt handler for interrupt i (say i_i) is executed, we also create a corresponding $SS(i_i)$ to track the call chain for this interrupt context. When the interrupt returns (observed by iret), we clear this shadow stack. At anytime during the execution of this interrupt, we similarly build its callsite chain from $SS(i_i)$ as what we do in the syscall context.
- **(III) Kernel Thread SS.** If the execution is neither in the syscall context, nor top half of the interrupt handler, then it must be in kernel thread execution context (or bottom half of an interrupt), say t_i. Similarly, we will create a corresponding $SS(t_i)$ for each of this context. As such, we can retrieve the callsite chain when a kernel object is accessed under this context.

It should be noted that at runtime there can be multiple instances of each of these SS, because there can be multiple processes, interrupts, and kernel threads. We will extract the callsite chain from the corresponding one based on the value of MSB19(esp).

Resolving Low Level Execution Context. Once we have resolved all these high level execution contexts, our final step is to resolve the low level context (e.g., read/write) of how an object is accessed and keep a record in the in-memory meta-data (i.e., our HT_{type}). Currently, we focus on seven categories of accesses as presented in Table 1.

Specifically, whenever there is an access to the monitored kernel object O_i (including its k-th field F_k and the propagations), we will insert an entry if this has not been inserted to the field F_k's access list that is stored in HT_{type}, which is indexed by the encoded syntactic type of O_i (i.e., $E(CC_{kmalloc})$), and this entry consists of $<AT, EX>$ where AT denotes the access types of the seven different categories, and EX denotes the current execution context.

To save both memory and disk space of our meta-data, we also encode EX. Basically, EX is composed with (1) the low level access behavior that includes the program counter (PC) of Read, Traversal, Write,

Table 1. Resolved access types based on the behavior.

Category	Behavior
Creation (O_i)	O_i is created by calling kmalloc
Deletion (O_i)	O_i is freed by calling kfree
Read (O_i, F_j)	A memory read field F_j of O_i
Traversal (O_i, F_j)	Read (O_i, F_j) $\wedge$ $F_j \in$ pointer field
Write (O_i, F_j)	A memory write to field j of O_i
Initialization (O_i, F_j)	Write (O_i, F_j) $\wedge$ first time write to F_j
Others	Other contexts, e.g., periodical access

Initialization of (O_i, F_k), or the entry address of kmalloc or kfree if it is object creation/deletion, as well as the encoding of these accesses; (2) middle level callsite chain and the corresponding offset in the running kernel stack to locate each function's return address; and (3) the top level context that is either a syscall number, or an interrupt number, or the value of MSB19(esp) of kernel thread. We also encode EX with an integer and use a hash table to store the mapping between the integer and the concrete execution context. Our *tap points uncovering* will scan the dumped meta-data to eventually uncover the tap points.

3.3 Tap Points Uncovering

Once collected the record describing how a particular type of monitored kernel object is accessed, the final step of AUTOTAP is to perform an offline analysis to further derive the tap points for each type of kernel object. At a high level, for a given syntactic type of a kernel object, we traverse our memory-dumped HT_{type} and locate its field access context $<AT, EX>$. For each EX, we rebuild a context-chain according to our encoding. The top of the chain is the highest level execution context (i.e., syscall, interrupt, or kernel thread), followed by the callsite chain. Examples of such context-chains are illustrated in Fig. 3. After having the context-chain, we are then ready to extract the tap points.

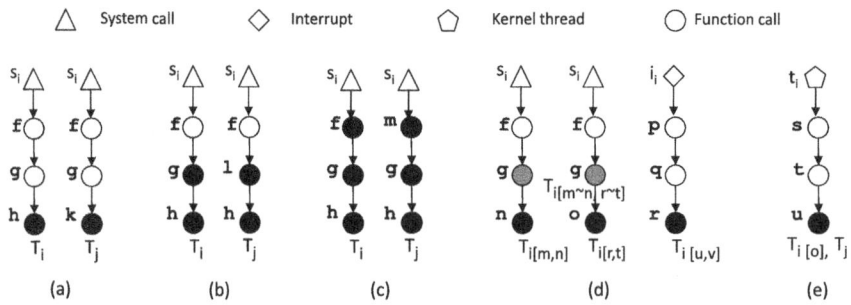

Fig. 3. Enumerated and simplified cases for tap points uncovering. Note that s_i denotes i_{th} syscall, i_i denotes i_{th} interrupt, t_i denotes i_{th} kernel thread, f, g, h etc. all denotes function calls, T_i represents the syntactic type, and $T_{i[m]}$ denotes the field m of T_i.

Introspection Related Tap Points. Among all the tap points, those related to object creation, deletion, traversal, and field read are of particular interest to introspection, especially for the detection of hidden kernel objects. In the following, we present how we uncover these tap points:

- **Object Creation and Deletion.** Given a specific syntactic type T_i (note that syntactic type is used to find the tap points, and semantic type is used to pinpoint the one we want) for a kernel object, we scan the context-chain, if the leaf node of the chain creates/deletes a kernel object with the matched type, then the tap points in this context chain will be included in the result. Ideally, if the leaf node is unique among all the types, we can directly output the PC that calls the leaf function as the corresponding tap points for this type. However, these functions might also create other types of object. Therefore, we will scan the context-chain again, and compare with other types to produce the final result.

  Specifically, there are at most three cases for the creation and deletion related tap points. One is the leaf node that is unique among all observed types (Fig. 3(a)), and as discussed we directly output the call-site PC of the leaf function as the tap points (function h and function k in this case) and these tap points are context-insensitive. Otherwise, we scan further and compare their parent functions (Fig. 3(b) and (c)). If they differ at their closest parent function, then we use the call-chain from the diffed parent function to the leaf node (Fig. 3(b)) and use the chained call-site PC as the tap points and these tap points are context-sensitive; otherwise we will scan until we reach their root node, and in this case we will use the entire context chain (Fig. 3(c)). Recall that there must exist a unique callchain for each syntactic object (Sect. 3.1). Therefore, we will not have a case in which we cannot find the unique context chain even though we have reached the root.

- **Object Traversal.** The tap points for object traversal are critical for introspection, especially if we aim to identify the hidden objects. To identify such tap points, we scan the context chain: if we observe there is a pointer field read from object O_i to reach object O_j, we conclude there is an object traversal in the observed function with the tap point of the PC that performs the read operation. If this PC only accesses this particular type of object, we just use this PC as the tap points; otherwise, we will use the call-chain as what we do in object creation/deletion tap points discovery. Also, we can identify recursive type traversal if both O_i and O_j share the same type, otherwise it will be a non-recursive traversal.

- **Object Field Read.** Pointer field read can allow us to identify the object traversal tap points. Non pointer field can also lead to certain interesting tap points. Similarly to how we identify object traversal tap points where we focus on the pointer field, we will also derive all the non pointer field read tap points.

Other Tap Points. In addition, there are also other types of tap points, such as object field initialization and object field (hot) write. Though these tap points may not be directly used in introspection, they could be useful for kernel function reverse engineering in general. AUTOTAP does support identify these tap points. For instance, it becomes straightforward to identify the initialization point (the first time memory write). The only issue is there may not exist a centralized function that initializes all the field of an object. For example, as shown in Fig. 3(d), the leaf node may just initialize partial fields of an object. Therefore, we need to hoist the field initialization information to their parent functions. Such hoist operation is a recursive procedure and we will use the lowest parent function that cannot expand the scope further of the fields of T_i as the initialization tap points for the observed field. We are also interested in several other particular interesting types of tap points, such as the periodic functions that are executed in the timer interrupts. We will demonstrate how to use these tap points in Sect. 5.

4 Evaluation

We have implemented AUTOTAP. The online analysis component is built atop PEMU [29] by reusing a large amount of code base from ARGOS [30], and the offline component is built using python. In this section, we present our evaluation result.

Experiment Setup. The input to AUTOTAP is the kernel API specification, the available kernel data structure definitions for kernel module developers, and the test cases to run the kernel. We acquired kernel API specification, namely, function name, the type of its arguments and return values from /lib/modules/KERNEL_VERSION/build. We extracted the kernel data structure definitions from the available kernel header files. In order to intercept the kernel APIs for object tracking and semantic type inference, we identified their function entry addresses from /proc/kallsyms.

To run the kernel, we used the test cases from the Linux-test-project [1], as what we have done in FPCK [14]. We took 10 recent released Linux kernels, presented in the first column of Table 2, as the guest OS for the test, and executed them inside our VMM. The testing host OS runs ubuntu-12.04 with kernel 3.5.0-51-generic. The evaluation was performed on a machine with a 64-bit Intel Core i-7 CPU with 8 GB physical memory.

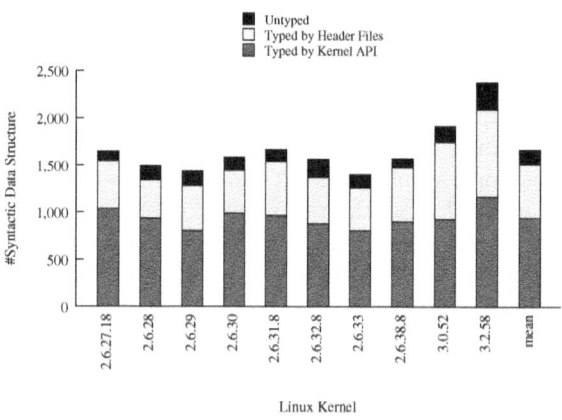

Fig. 4. Type resolution result for each kernel

To identify a tap point for a particular type of object, AUTOTAP first derives all the tap points for each syntactic type, and then us0es the resolved semantic type (e.g., task_struct) associated with the syntactic type to eventually pinpoint the tap points of introspection interest. Therefore, we first present the result regarding how AUTOTAP performed to identify the tap points for the syntactic type, and then the tap points for the semantic type.

Result for Syntactic Types. We first report how our *kernel object tracking* component performed in Fig. 4. As shown in this figure, our *kernel object tracking* component identifies on average 1.8 thousand unique syntactic types. We can see about 57 % of them can be semantically typed by using the kernel APIs. With the public open kernel module development header files, it can type additionally 35 % of them. In other words, close to 90 % of the data structures can be semantically typed.

Next, we report how our second and third components performed in Table 2. Specifically, the result of our *object access resolution* is reported from the 2nd column to the 7th column. The number of the top level context, namely syscall context, is reported in the 2nd column, interrupt in the 3th column, and kernel thread in the 4th column. We can notice that on average, AUTOTAP observed 219 system call contexts, 7 interrupt/exception contexts (e.g., page fault, timer, keyboard, device-not-available), and 29 kernel thread contexts. Regarding the middle level context, we report the total number of function call-site chain in the $|FC|$ column, and there are 104,971 unique call-site chains associated with these traced types. Finally, for the lowest level context, we report the total number of field read tap points in $|PC_R|$ and write tap points in $|PC_W|$ columns. We can notice that there is a significant large number of the unique field read/write access contexts. If we perform manual analysis, it is very challenging to systematically identify them all.

Finally, we report the statistics of the tap points uncovered for the introspection in the rest columns of Table 2. In total, we report five categories of introspection related to tap points: object creation, object deletion, object recursive type traversal ($R_{Traversal}$), object non-recursive type traversal ($N_{Traversal}$), and object field read (F_{Read}). For each category, we report the number of the tap points that are context-insensitive (i.e., we can directly use the corresponding PC as the tap points) in column $|PC|$, and context-sensitive (i.e., we need to inspect the call-chain in the corresponding stack frame when the PC is executed)

Table 2. Overall result of tap points uncovered for each tested kernel.

Kernel	Object Access Resolution						Tap Points Uncovered									
	$|Sys|$	$|Int|$	$|Thd|$	$|FC|$	$|PC_R|$	$|PC_W|$	Creation		Deletion		$R_{Traversal}$		$N_{Traversal}$		F_{Read}	
							PC	FC	PC	FC	PC	FC	PC	FC	PC	FC
2.6.27.18	219	7	23	77634	308643	136729	0	1646	47	1507	89	2408	1402	21585	4209	61632
2.6.28	218	7	22	73285	313488	134027	0	1492	61	1452	89	2313	1435	18460	4235	54706
2.6.29	216	7	29	69547	313442	132004	0	1436	59	1485	90	2375	1515	18251	4102	56866
2.6.30	217	7	28	40457	319834	136593	0	1585	62	1506	97	2341	1598	20303	4367	62927
2.6.31.8	217	7	28	74121	346884	147573	0	1666	66	1560	97	2497	1482	21679	4159	74504
2.6.32.8	218	7	31	92690	450004	194353	0	1566	54	1365	93	2322	1500	18192	3943	62115
2.6.33	217	7	31	85544	412563	176407	0	1402	64	1274	94	2208	1221	14084	4082	65531
2.6.38.8	217	7	33	91438	422170	185327	0	1573	56	1293	97	2479	1541	18881	3838	62361
3.0.52	222	7	36	205984	797643	238132	0	1915	68	1768	113	2695	1695	20538	4445	66432
3.2.58	227	7	35	239018	898387	270936	0	2377	71	2085	109	3967	1739	27619	4373	89204
Average	219	7	29	104971	458305	175207	0	1654	62	1545	97	2560	1672	19959	4175	65628

in column $|FC|$. We can notice that there are many context sensitive tap points because different syntactic types (which is from the same semantic type) use the same PC for the allocation, but in different calling context. We can also notice some tap points can be used to delete different type of object (e.g., in Linux kernel 2.6.32.8, there are 1566 syntactic types allocated, but it only requires 1365 deletion tap points), and there are too many object traversal tap points, which proves it will be extremely difficult to identify them with just purely manual analysis. Regarding how to use the derived tap points, we present a case study in Sect. 5.

Result for Semantic Types. As shown in Table 2, there are too many tap points. To really use them for introspection, we have to select the ones of our interest. Therefore, we have to get the tap points based on the semantic types. We take Linux-2.6.32.8 as an example, and describe in greater details how this is achieved.

For Linux-2.6.32.8, as our syntactic type is an over-split of the semantic types (i.e., multiple syntactic types can correspond to just one semantic type), our technique eventually resolved the semantic types of 87.6 % (1372/1566) of the syntactic types. Once we have resolved the semantic types, we have to iterate our tap points uncovering again for each semantic types using the same algorithm described in Sect. 3.3.

Take task_struct as an example, before applying the semantic types, we acquired 6 different syntactic types of task_struct, namely, each of these is created in a different call-chain. The (64-bit) integer encoding of these syntactic types are presented in the first column of Table 3. For object creation, each of these syntactic types has a context-sensitive tap point, and none of them is context-insensitive; similar result also applies to object deletion. For recursive traversal, we observed the 3rd syntactic type of task_struct has a heavy recursive traversal. Compared with other syntactic type, this one has many more task_struct instances. For non recursive type traversal, each syntactic type has a lot of context-sensitive pointer read. Finally, for the object field (i.e., non-pointer) read, we can notice most of their tap points are context sensitive.

Table 3. Tap points statistics for 6 different syntactic types of task_struct.

Syntactic type	Creation		Deletion		$R_{Traversal}$		$N_{Traversal}$		F_{READ}	
	$|PC|$	$|FC|$	$|PC|$	$|FC|$	$|PC|$	$|FC|$	$|PC|$	$|FC|$	$|PC|$	$|FC|$
4dd23b5e689e2ad7	0	1	0	1	0	9	3	102	1	299
536881ec388d6516	0	1	0	1	1	7	20	225	36	420
7554a8d7acf81704	0	1	0	1	41	131	403	402	435	563
8649536d24938b96	0	1	0	1	0	0	0	304	1	437
9ac37673946479aa	0	1	0	1	0	30	0	136	14	318
9d41a458fa47a47b	0	1	0	1	0	0	2	289	0	448

Table 4. The statistics for the uncovered tap points for the observed semantic types of linux-2.6.32.8 in slab/slub allocators

Category	Semantic Type	#Syntactic Type	Creation		Deletion		$R_{Traversal}$		$N_{Traversal}$		F_{Read}	
			PC	FC	PC	FC	PC	FC	PC	FC	PC	FC
Process	task_struct	6	1	0	1	0	98	93	725	6	1024	24
	pid	6	1	0	1	0	2	1	15	3	50	1
	task_delay_info	6	1	0	1	0	0	0	0	0	24	4
	task_xstate	7	2	0	1	0	0	0	0	0	38	1
	taskstats	2	1	0	1	0	0	0	0	0	27	0
Memory	anon_vma	7	1	0	1	0	0	0	5	1	8	1
	mm_struct	4	2	0	1	0	0	0	21	8	235	32
	vm_area_struct	44	7	0	2	0	84	94	113	1	395	1
Network	TCP	3	0	1	0	1	7	0	74	8	1023	137
	UDP	2	0	1	0	1	0	0	0	0	0	84
	UNIX	4	0	1	0	1	8	0	29	4	118	36
	neighbour	7	1	0	1	0	2	0	4	0	113	15
	inet_peer	1	1	0	1	0	0	0	0	0	23	1
	rtable	7	1	0	1	0	0	0	11	0	155	3
	nsproxy	1	1	0	1	0	0	0	1	0	6	0
	request_sock_TCP	2	1	0	1	0	0	0	1	0	70	8
	skbuff_fclone	7	0	1	0	1	0	0	76	78	89	161
	skbuff_head	53	1	1	0	1	1	0	152	78	148	161
	sock_alloc	4	1	0	1	0	0	4	64	2	59	34
File	bio-0	94	0	1	0	1	3	0	18	0	123	30
	biovec-16	5	0	1	0	1	0	0	0	0	0	26
	biovec-64	4	0	1	0	1	0	0	0	0	1	30
	io_context	17	1	0	1	0	0	0	7	2	15	7
	request	60	0	1	0	1	13	99	22	0	164	2
	dentry	85	1	0	1	0	80	4	321	4	197	10
	ext2_inode_info	4	1	0	1	0	6	17	74	12	136	262
	ext3_inode_info	21	1	0	1	0	6	19	38	35	580	348
	fasync_struct	1	1	0	1	0	0	0	1	0	1	1
	file_lock	10	1	0	1	0	11	6	17	0	113	3
	files_struct	4	1	0	1	0	0	3	25	10	41	41
	file	33	1	0	1	0	4	5	227	7	352	4
	fs_struct	4	1	0	1	0	0	0	9	2	44	3
	inode	5	1	0	1	0	2	5	5	8	15	113
	journal_handle	124	1	0	1	0	0	0	28	0	25	0
	journal_head	82	1	0	1	0	19	0	66	0	50	0
	proc_inode	9	1	0	1	0	0	0	6	3	33	95
	sysfs_dirent	36	1	0	1	0	12	0	7	0	31	0
	vfsmount	4	1	0	1	0	31	0	21	8	63	3
IPC	mqueue_inode_info	1	1	0	1	0	0	0	15	2	37	49
	shmem_inode_info	8	1	0	1	0	0	4	0	16	107	194
Signal	fsnotify_event	19	1	0	1	0	1	0	8	2	24	2
	inotify_event_private_data	19	2	0	1	0	0	0	3	0	2	0
	inotify_inode_mark_entry	1	1	0	1	0	1	0	7	1	25	1
	sighand_struct	6	1	0	1	0	0	0	0	0	66	4
	signal_struct	6	1	0	1	0	0	12	11	4	265	36
	sigqueue	17	1	0	1	0	4	2	8	2	8	0
Security	cred	41	2	0	1	0	0	3	28	3	352	1
	key	4	1	0	1	0	0	10	4	0	53	3
Other	buffer_head	61	1	0	1	0	20	0	21	0	423	0
	cfq_io_context	17	1	0	1	0	2	0	15	3	39	1
	cfq_queue	15	1	0	1	0	0	0	17	5	106	1
	idr_layer	12	1	0	3	0	5	5	1	3	19	3
	names_cache	58	2	0	3	0	0	0	0	0	16	10
	k_itimers	1	1	0	1	0	1	0	12	0	24	24
	radix_tree_node	56	1	0	1	0	10	3	2	3	22	9
	jbd_revoke_record_s	14	1	0	1	0	1	0	0	0	7	0

After we apply the resolved semantic type to each syntactic type and re-execute our tap points uncovering, many of the context-sensitive tap points become context-insensitive. For instance, for `task_struct`, as illustrated in the first row of Table 4, these 6 syntactic types get actually merged into one, and we then can directly use the PC for object creation and deletion without inspecting their call-stack. Due to space reason, we report the tap points uncovering statistics for some of the resolved semantic types in Table 4. In total, there are over 90 resolved semantics, and we only report 56 of them that are visible in the slab allocators.

Performance Result. Regarding the performance of AUTOTAP, for each tested kernel, our online analysis took around 12 h on average to finish the testing benchmark, and our offline analysis took just a few minutes to process the log files and produce the final tap points. The dumped log file size is around 500 MB (thanks to our encoding). The reason why our online analysis took so long is because we have one thousand test cases to execute and also we have to perform dynamic binary instrumentation to track object and field propagations in our instrumented VMM.

5 Security Application

In this section, we demonstrate how to use our tap points for a particular type of introspection application—hidden process detection. Typically when a system is compromised, it is often very common for attackers to hide the presence of their attack and also leave certain invisible services for future privileged access. To achieve this, one simple way is to keep running of a privileged process, and hide it from the system administrators through rootkit attacks.

At a high level, there are three different categories of rootkits for process hiding [18,25]. The first category directly modifies program binaries such as `ps`, `pslist`, etc. The second category hooks into the call path between a user application and the kernel by modifying system libraries (e.g., `glibc`), dynamic linker structures (`plt/got` table), system call tables, or corresponding operating system functions that report system status [28]. The third category manipulates kernel data structures using the so-called direct kernel object manipulation (DKOM) [12] attack, such as removing the process descriptor (e.g., `task_struct`) from the accounting list shown by `ps`.

Our Approach. Since AUTOTAP has extracted the tap points related to the `task _struct`, especially the creation/deletion and traversal tap points, it would enable the monitoring and detection of the hidden processes. One intuitive approach is to use the tap point that traverses all the elements in the accounting `task` list. However, we did not find such a tap point that iterates all the element of the `task` list. In fact, utility command such as `ps` will not traverse the accounting list to show all the running process, and instead it extracts the process list from the `/proc` file system [13].

While there are many traversal tap points for the `task_struct`, as shown in Table 3, there must be some traversal tap points executed by the `schedule` function. Note that `schedule` function is very easy to identify as it is always executed in the top half of the timer interrupt handler (though it can be called in various other places), and meanwhile there must be a stack exchange (a kernel esp write operation). Therefore, if we can identify the task_struct accessed by the schedule function, and if we can know to which task_struct instance the CPU switches, then we can identify the task_struct that is to-be-executed by the CPU.

However, we have to solve another challenge—how to identify the to-be-executed task_struct instance given that schedule function may access a number of other task_struct instances to pick up the next to-be-executed one (defined by the policy) for the execution. Fortunately, as we have noted, when performing a context switch, there must be a stack pointer exchange, and the new stack pointer must come from the to-be-executed process. Typically, this stack pointer is stored in task_struct. Therefore, by monitoring where the stack pointer comes from, we identify the to-be-executed task_struct instance. Recall that we have tracked all field (and its propagation) read, and we just need to identify this particular field.

More specifically, we found 123 Object Traversal tap points for task_struct in the context of schedule function. In particular, there are 76 recursive and 26 non-recursive traversal tap points. All of them are context insensitive. Part of the reason we believe is schedule function is very unique and other functions will not call it for other purposes other than scheduling. Among these 123 tap points, we know one of them must be of our interest since we aim to capture the task_struct traversal. Also, we found 121 task_struct Field Read, all of which are also context insensitive. By looking at these field read tap points, we found there is a particular field read tap point that uses the stack pointer (i.e., 0xc125e3b1:mov 0x254(%edi),%esp). Interestingly, the base register edi here actually holds the address of the to-be-executed task_struct. Therefore, we actually do not need the traversal tap points and we just need to hook this tap point, because we can directly identify the to-be-executed process from edi.

From the above analysis, we can notice that with AUTOTAP, we have significantly reduced the search space of the instruction of our interest from tens of thousands (4,422 instructions in the context of schedule function in which a manual analysis has to analyze) to only a few hundred (123 object traversal, and 121 field read). With insight of how context switch is performed, we further reduce the search space to only a few instructions (it is 0xc125e3b1:mov 0x254(%edi),%esp in our case). This is just one case we demonstrated for task_struct. Regarding many other kernel data structures, our system also applies even though we may have to consider certain data structure specific insight. For instance, if we want to detect hidden socket, we can use the insight that socket must be accessed at system call send/sendto/write or recv/recvfrom/read context.

The Detection Algorithm. We use a cross-view comparison approach that compares the CPU time execution from inside and outside to detect the hidden processes. Note that CPU time metric is

Table 5. Process hiding rootkits

Rootkits	Process hiding mechanism
ps_hide	Fake ps binary with process hiding function
libprocesshider	Override libc's readdir to hide process
LinuxFu	Hide the process by deleting its task_struct from task list

the most reliable source (tamper-proof) for rootkit detection. In particular, to detect rootkit, we first get an inside view by running `ps` command, and an outside view by counting the CPU TIME for the running process. In particular, the inside view will show the running process PID, TTY, TIME, and CMD. Among them, TIME is very critical and it is very challenging (nearly impossible) for attacker to forge a value that will be equivalent to the one counted at the hypervisor introspection layer.

To count the executed time for a particular process, we hook the tap points of task_struct creation at 0xc102c8be and deletion at 0xc102c7cc by replacing them with an "int 3" instruction to trap to the hypervisor layer. Then we hook the tap point "0xc125e3b1:mov 0x254(%edi),%esp" to get the task_struct of the to-be-executed process from edi and then we count its CPU execution time from this moment to the next context-switch point. We keep a hash table to store the accumulated CPU time for each process, and meanwhile we store their PID field. Then right after user running ps to get the inside view, we also print the list of the live process with the PID and their CPU TIME. If there is a discrepancy, it indicates there is a hidden process. We can notice while attacker can change/forge all the PID field, it is impossible for them to forge the correct CPU TIME to mislead the outside view. That is why we call TIME is a tamper-proof attribute for a particular process.

Experimental Result. We have implemented the above detection algorithm in KVM-2.6.37 and tested with a guest Linux kernel 2.6.32.8. We only need to hook 3 tap points: creation, deletion and field propagation read. We used three rootkits to test our detection capability. As show in Table 5, these rootkits cover all the three basic tricks to hide a particular process. Through our cross view comparison, we have successfully detected all of these hidden processes.

Regarding the performance impact of our rootkit detector, we used a set of benchmarks including SPEC2006, Apache, and 7zip to evaluate the performance overhead introduced by our detection at KVM hypervisor layer, and we compared the results on the Native-KVM and our Tapping-KVM. As expected, there is not noticeable performance overhead for these benchmarks due to our lightweight instrumentation at the hypervisor layer. We measured that the average overhead for them is about 2.7 %.

6 Limitations and Future Work

First and foremost, AUTOTAP uses dynamic analysis to uncover the tap points and its effectiveness relies on the coverage of the dynamic analysis. Therefore, any kernel path coverage techniques (e.g., guided-fuzzing) would improve AUTOTAP. On the other hand, we can also notice that sometimes an incomplete coverage can still lead to a complete uncovering of the tap points. For instance, as shown for the task_struct creation/deletion tap points, while we may not be able to exercise all the kernel path and find out all (context-sensitive) tap points, we can notice that these tap points all eventually become context-insensitive and we can just use the PC that creates and deletes the task_struct instance as the tap point.

Second, currently AUTOTAP only reveals the object creation and deletion, field read, and object traversal tap points and demonstrates their use cases. We believe in addition to these tap points, there will be also other useful ones. Another future effort is to uncover more tap points and investigate new applications. A possible immediate future work is to identify the hot (or cold) read/write field tap points, namely, frequently read/write field, which might be useful to identify the likely-invariants (e.g., a field never gets changed) of object field. The other possible use case is to detect the hidden socket by using our tap points.

Third, when kernel has address space layout randomization (ASLR) enabled (note that since kernel version 3.14, Linux began to randomize kernel address space), the tap points we discovered from dynamic execution might not work in other executions. An immediate fix for this problem is to integrate our recent kernel ASLR derandomization effort [16], which exploited using various signatures from kernel code and data to derandomize the kernel address space.

Finally, while we have demonstrated our techniques working for Linux kernel, we would like to validate the generality of our system with other kernels. We plan to extend our analysis to FreeBSD, since it is also open source and we can validate our results easily. Eventually, we also would like to test our system with the closed source OS kernel such as Microsoft Windows. These are other future works.

7 Related Work

Tap Points Uncovering. Recently, Dolan-Gavitt et al. [10] presented TZB, the first system that can mine (memgrep) the memory access points for user level applications, to identify the places for active monitoring. While TZB and AUTOTAP share similar goal (TZB directly inspires AUTOTAP), we focus on different applications and use different techniques. Specifically, TZB focused on the user level applications such as web browser, whereas AUTOTAP exclusively focused on OS kernel. TZB starts from visible strings (memgrep type of approach can apply here), whereas AUTOTAP faces diversified, many non-string data structures in OS kernel and it starts from syntactic type of kernel object and then semantic type and then execution context to eventually derive the tap points for introspection.

Data Structure Reverse Engineering. Over the past decade, there are significant efforts on data structure reverse engineering, or more broadly type inference with executables [7]. Earlier attempts include aggregate structure identification (ASI) [23], value set analysis (VSA) [3,24]. Recently, Laika [9], REWARDS [22], TIE [20], Howard [26], ARGOS [30], and PointerScope [31] all aim to infer the (certain) data structure types from binary code. To infer the semantic type of data structures, while AUTOTAP uses the basic approach proposed in REWARDS, it extends it to OS kernels. Also, it combines other knowledge such as the data structure definitions for kernel driver development to resolve more semantic types, because of the large amount of point-to related kernel data structures. However, REWARDS only uses the type of arguments and return values from standard libraries for the inference.

Virtual Machine Introspection. VMI [15] is a security analysis technique that pushes the traditional in-box analysis into the outside hypervisor layer. It has been proposed as an effective means for kernel rootkit detection (e.g., [8,11,12,17] and malware analysis (e.g.,. [19,25]). While there are a number of efforts of using VMI or memory analysis technique (e.g., [5,8,21]) for hidden process detection (e.g., [11, 17,18]), in this work we enrich these knowledge with a tamper-proof approach by applying the tap points related to process descriptor and build a robust hidden process detection tool.

8 Conclusion

We have presented AUTOTAP, the first system that can automatically uncover the tap points of kernel objects of introspection interest from kernel executions. Specifically, starting from the interface of system call, the exported kernel APIs, and the data structure definitions for kernel driver developers, AUTOTAP automatically tracks kernel objects, resolves their kernel execution context, and associates the accessed context with the objects, from which to derive the tap points based on how an object is accessed. The experimental results with a number of Linux kernel binaries show that AUTOTAP is able to automatically uncover all the possible observed tap points for a particular type of object, which would be very challenging to achieve with manual analysis. We have applied the tap points uncovered by AUTOTAP to build a novel hidden process detection tool that can capture all the existing attacks including the DKOM based with only 2.7 % overhead on our tested benchmarks.

Acknowledgement. We thank the anonymous reviewers for their invaluable feedback. This research was partially supported by AFOSR under grant FA9550-14-1-0119 and FA9550-14-1-0173, and NSF CAREER award 1453011. Any opinions, findings, conclusions, or recommendations expressed are those of the authors and not necessarily of the AFOSR and NSF.

References

1. Linux test project. https://github.com/linux-test-project
2. QEMU: an open source processor emulator. http://www.qemu.org/
3. Balakrishnan, G., Reps, T. Analyzing memory accesses in ×86 executables. In: CC, March 2004
4. Bauman, E., Ayoade, G., Lin, Z.: A survey on hypervisor based monitoring: approaches, applications, and evolutions. ACM Comput. Surv. **48**(1), 10:1–10:33 (2015)
5. Bianchi, A., Shoshitaishvili, Y., Kruegel, C., Vigna, G.: Blacksheep: detecting compromised hosts in homogeneous crowds. In: Proceedings of the 2012 ACM Conference on Computer and Communications Security (CCS 2012), Raleigh, North Carolina, USA, pp. 341–352 (2012)
6. Bovet, D., Cesati, M.: Understanding The Linux Kernel. Oreilly & Associates Inc., Sebastopol (2005)
7. Caballero, J., Lin, Z.: Type inference on executables. ACM Comput. Surv. **48**(4), 65:1–65:35 (2016)
8. Carbone, M., Cui, W., Lu, L., Lee, W., Peinado, M., Jiang, X.: Mapping kernel objects to enable systematic integrity checking. In: The 16th ACM Conference on Computer and Communications Security (CCS 2009), Chicago, IL, USA, pp. 555–565 (2009)
9. Cozzie, A., Stratton, F., Xue, H., King, S.T.: Digging for data structures. In: Proceeding of 8th Symposium on Operating System Design and Implementation (OSDI 2008), San Diego, CA, pp. 231–244, December 2008
10. Dolan-Gavitt, B., Leek, T., Hodosh, J., Lee, W.: Tappan zee (north) bridge: mining memory accesses for introspection. In: Proceedings of the ACM Conference on Computer and Communications Security (CCS) (2013)
11. Dolan-Gavitt, B., Leek, T., Zhivich, M., Giffin, J., Lee, W.: Virtuoso: narrowing the semantic gap in virtual machine introspection. In: Proceedings of the 32nd IEEE Symposium on Security and Privacy, Oakland, CA, USA, pp. 297–312 (2011)
12. Dolan-Gavitt, B., Srivastava, A., Traynor, P., Giffin, J.: Robust signatures for kernel data structures. In: Proceedings of the 16th ACM Conference on Computer and Communications Security (CCS 2009), Chicago, Illinois, USA, pp. 566–577. ACM (2009)
13. Fu, Y., Lin, Z.: Space traveling across VM: automatically bridging the semantic gap in virtual machine introspection via online kernel data redirection. In: Proceedings of 33rd IEEE Symposium on Security and Privacy, May 2012
14. Fu, Y., Lin, Z., Brumley, D.: Automatically deriving pointer reference expressions from executions for memory dump analysis. In: Proceedings of the 2015 ACM SIGSOFT International Symposium on Foundations of Software Engineering (FSE 2015), Bergamo, Italy, September 2015
15. Garfinkel, T., Rosenblum, M.: A virtual machine introspection based architecture for intrusion detection. In: Proceedings Network and Distributed Systems Security Symposium (NDSS 2003), February 2003
16. Gu, Y., Lin, Z.: Derandomizing kernel address space layout for introspection and forensics. In: Proceedings of the 6th ACM Conference on Data and Application Security and Privacy. ACM, New Orelans (2016)
17. Jiang, X., Wang, X., Xu, D.: Stealthy malware detection through VMM-based out-of-the-box semantic view reconstruction. In: Proceedings of the 14th ACM Conference on Computer and Communications Security (CCS 2007), Alexandria, Virginia, USA, pp. 128–138. ACM (2007)

18. Jones, S.T., Arpaci-Dusseau, A.C., Arpaci-Dusseau, R.H.: VMM-based hidden process detection and identification using lycosid. In: Proceedings of the Fourth ACM SIGPLAN/SIGOPS International Conference on Virtual Execution Environments (VEE 2008), Seattle, WA, USA, pp. 91–100. ACM (2008)
19. Lanzi, A., Sharif, M.I., Lee, W.: K-tracer: a system for extracting kernel malware behavior. In: Proceedings of the 2009 Network and Distributed System Security Symposium, San Diego, California, USA (2009)
20. Lee, J., Avgerinos, T., Brumley, D., TIE: principled reverse engineering of types in binary programs. In: NDSS, February 2011
21. Lin, Z., Rhee, J., Zhang, X., Xu, D., Jiang, X. SigGraph: Brute force scanning of kernel data structure instances using graph-based signatures. In: Proceedings of the 18th Annual Network and Distributed System Security Symposium (NDSS 2011), San Diego, CA, February 2011
22. Lin, Z., Zhang, X., Xu, D.: Automatic reverse engineering of data structures from binary execution. In: Proceedings of the 17th Annual Network and Distributed System Security Symposium (NDSS 2010), San Diego, CA, February 2010
23. Ramalingam, G., Field, J., Tip, F.: Aggregate structure identification and its application to program analysis. In: POPL, January 1999
24. Reps, T., Balakrishnan, G.: Improved memory-access analysis for ×86 executables. In: CC, March 2008
25. Riley, R., Jiang, X., Xu, D.: Multi-aspect profiling of kernel rootkit behavior. In: Proceedings of the 4th ACM European conference on Computer systems (EuroSys 2009), Nuremberg, Germany, pp. 47–60 (2009)
26. Slowinska, A., Stancescu, T., Bos, H.: Howard: a dynamic excavator for reverse engineering data structures. In: Proceedings of the 18th Annual Network and Distributed System Security Symposium (NDSS 2011), San Diego, CA, February 2011
27. Sumner, W.N., Zheng, Y., Weeratunge, D., Zhang, X.: Precise calling context encoding. In: Proceedings of the 32nd ACM/IEEE International Conference on Software Engineering, (ICSE 2010), Cape Town, South Africa, vol. 1, pp. 525–534. ACM (2010)
28. Wang, Z., Jiang, X., Cui, W., Ning, P.: Countering kernel rootkits with lightweight hook protection. In: Proceedings of the 16th ACM Conference on Computer and Communications Security (CCS 2009), Chicago, Illinois, USA, pp. 545–554 (2009)
29. Zeng, J., Fu, Y., Lin, Z. Pemu: a pin highly compatible out-of-VM dynamic binary instrumentation framework. In: The 11th ACM SIGPLAN/SIGOPS International Conference on Virtual Execution Environment (VEE 2015), Istanbul, Turkey, March 2015
30. Zeng, J., Lin, Z.: Towards automatic inference of kernel object semantics from binarycode. In: Proceedings of the 18th International Symposium on Research in Attacks, Intrusions and Defenses (RAID 2015), Kyoto, Japan, November 2015
31. Zhang, M., Prakash, A., Li, X., Liang, Z., Yin, H.: Identifying and analysing pointer misuses for sophisticated memory-corruption exploit diagnosis. In: NDSS, February 2012

Detecting Stack Layout Corruptions with Robust Stack Unwinding

Yangchun Fu[1,2], Junghwan Rhee[1(✉)], Zhiqiang Lin[2], Zhichun Li[1], Hui Zhang[1], and Guofei Jiang[1]

[1] NEC Laboratories America, Princeton, USA
{rhee,zhichun,huizhang,gfj}@nec-labs.com
[2] University of Texas at Dallas, Richardson, USA
{yangchun.fu,zhiqiang.lin}@utdallas.edu

Abstract. The stack is a critical memory structure to ensure the correct execution of programs because control flow changes through the data stored in it, such as return addresses and function pointers. Thus the stack has been a popular target by many attacks and exploits like stack smashing attacks and return-oriented programming (ROP). We present a novel system to detect the corruption of the stack layout using a robust stack unwinding technique and detailed stack layouts extracted from the stack unwinding information for exception handling widely available in off-the-shelf binaries. Our evaluation with real-world ROP exploits has demonstrated successful detection of them with performance overhead of only 3.93 % on average transparently without accessing any source code or debugging symbols of a protected binary.

Keywords: Stack layout corruption · Stack layout invariants · Stack unwinding information · Return oriented programming

1 Introduction

The stack is a critical memory structure to ensure the correct execution of programs since control flow changes through the values stored in it (e.g., return addresses and function pointers). Therefore, the stack has been a popular target of many attacks and exploits [9,33,36,46,48,51] in the security domain. For instance, the stack smashing attack [33,36,48,51] is a traditional technique that has been used to compromise programs. Recently return oriented programming (ROP) [9,46] has gained significant attention due to its strong capability of compromising vulnerable programs in spite of up-to-date defense mechanisms, such as canaries [17], data execution prevention (DEP) [32], and address space layout randomization (ASLR) [54] under certain conditions (e.g., memory disclosure vulnerabilities, and the low entropy of ASLR).

Such attacks manipulate one aspect of the stack regarding return addresses to hijack execution. However, the stack not only contains return addresses but

---

Y. Fu—Work done during an internship at NEC Laboratories America, Princeton.

also stores many other data, such as local variables and frame pointers, with specific rules on its layout for a correct execution state. These rules are statically constructed by a compiler precisely for each function. Unfortunately such constraints on the stack layout are not strictly checked by the CPU as evidenced by the aforementioned attacks allowed, but a correct program execution strictly follows such constraints and they are in fact parsed and checked when needed (e.g., exception handling, backtrace in debug). Our intuition is that the current ROP attacks are not aimed to follow these stack layout constraints. Thus the inspection of the stack layout could be an effective inspection method to detect ROP attacks based on the manipulation and the side-effects in the stack layout. Our method is applicable to multiple stack-based attacks that tamper with the stack layout (Sect. 3), but we focus on ROP attacks in this paper since it is one of the most sophisticated and challenging attacks to date.

While many approaches have been proposed to detect and prevent ROP attacks [16,19,38], they are not without limitations. In particular, many of them heavily rely on the patterns of ROP gadgets, e.g., the length of a gadget, and the number of consequent gadgets. As such, attacks violating these patterns keep emerging, as witnessed by the recent attacks [12,25].

An early exploration toward this direction, ROPGUARD [21], detects ROP attacks by unwinding stack frames using a heuristic approach, based on the stack frame pointer [3] (i.e., ebp-based stack unwinding in Windows). This is one way to check the sanity of the stack with an assumption on the compiler's practice. Unfortunately, its detection policy is not general in many operating systems causing a failure to protect the programs compiled without the stack frame pointers. For instance, from the version 4.6 of GCC (the GNU Compiler Collection), the frame pointer option (-fomit-frame-pointer) is omitted by default for the 32-bit Linux making this approach unreliable.

In this paper we present a novel systematic approach called SLICK[1] to verify the stack layout structure at runtime with accurate and detailed information, which is generated by a compiler for exception handling [1,2] and available inside the binaries. From this information, we extract stack layout invariants that must hold at all times. We show verifying these invariants is effective for detecting the stack manipulation caused by ROP attacks overcoming the limitations of previous approaches based on stack unwinding. For our approach to be practical, this information should not be optional during compilation, or require source code since in many environments a program is deployed in the binary format. A pleasant surprise is that the stack frame layout information is widely available in Linux ELF binaries stored in the .eh_frame section due to the support of exception handling (even for C code). Moreover, this binary section is required in the x86_64 application binary interface (ABI) [6].

The contribution of this paper is summarized as follows:

- We present two novel security invariants of the stack regarding *legitimate return address chains* and *legitimate code addresses* based on the data stored

---

[1] SLICK represents **S**tack **L**ayout **I**nvariants **C**hecker similar to fsck.

in the .eh_frame. While the .eh_frame provides the information regarding the stack layout, it is not directly applicable to ROP detection. The invariants proposed in this paper fill this gap.
- We present a novel ROP detection technique based on stack layout invariants and a robust stack unwinding. This mechanism improves the robustness of a prior heuristic-based stack unwinding (e.g., ebp-based [21]), which fails to inspect the binaries that are not compiled with frame pointer support.
- We propose flexible stack unwinding algorithm to overcome a general and practical challenge in stack unwinding approaches which fail to unwind the entire stack due to the incompleteness of stack frame information. Our evaluation shows this instance is quite often, which leads to frequent false negative cases of the stack inspections without addressing this issue.

2 Background

2.1 Return Oriented Programming

Return oriented programming (ROP) is an offensive technique that reuses pieces of existing code chained together to create malicious logic. An attacker identifies a set of instruction sequences called *gadgets* linked together using payloads, which traditionally are placed in the stack [46] transferring control flow via the return instructions. Recently the attack pattern became diverse involving the call or jump instructions, which can trigger an indirect control flow [13] and the payloads can be also placed in other places, such as the heap [49].

2.2 Stack Frame Information in Binaries for Exception Handling

When a program executes, many low level operations occur in the stack. Whenever a function is called, its execution context (e.g., a return address) is pushed to the stack. Also many operations, such as handling local variables, delivering function call parameters, the flush of registers, occur on the stack exactly as they are determined during the compilation time. The specific rules on how to use each byte of each stack frame are predetermined and embedded in the program.

Figure 1 illustrates an example of this stack layout information taken from a function (ngx_pcalloc) of nginx, a high-performance HTTP server and reverse proxy. The top of the figure shows a part of its disassembled code. The middle part of the figure shows an example of the stack layout information, which is organized with the reference to the head of each stack frame. The memory address of a stack frame is referred to as the Canonical Frame Address (CFA) [1,2], which is the stack pointer address at the function call site.

The decoded information at the bottom illustrates the detailed stack layout at each instruction. For instance, [40530c: cfa=32(rsp), rbx=-24(cfa), rbp=-16(cfa), ret=-8(cfa)] shows the exact locations of the top of the current stack frame (cfa=), the pushed register values (rbx=, rbp=), and the return address (ret=) described in terms of the stack pointer address and the offsets at

Disassembled code

```
00000000004052fb <ngx_pcalloc>:
  4052fb:   48 89 5c 24 f0          mov     %rbx,-0x10(%rsp)
  405300:   48 89 6c 24 f8          mov     %rbp,-0x8(%rsp)
  405305:   48 83 ec 18             sub     $0x18,%rsp
  405309:   48 89 f5                mov     %rsi,%rbp
  40530c:   e8 2d fe ff ff          callq   40513e <ngx_palloc>
  ...       ...                     ...
  405336:   48 83 c4 18             add     $0x18,%rsp
  40533a:   c3                      retq
```

Stack layout information from .eh_frame

```
00000530 000000000000001c 00000534 FDE cie=00000000
  pc=00000000004052fb..000000000040533b
  DW_CFA_advance_loc: 14 to 0000000000405309
  DW_CFA_def_cfa_offset: 32
  DW_CFA_offset: r6 (rbp) at cfa-16
  DW_CFA_offset: r3 (rbx) at cfa-24
  DW_CFA_advance_loc: 49 to 000000000040533a
  DW_CFA_def_cfa_offset: 8
  ...
```

Decoded stack layout information

```
4052fb: cfa=08(rsp),                                            ret=-8(cfa)
405300: cfa=08(rsp), rbx=-24(cfa),                              ret=-8(cfa)
405305: cfa=08(rsp), rbx=-24(cfa), rbp=-16(cfa),                ret=-8(cfa)
405309: cfa=32(rsp), rbx=-24(cfa), rbp=-16(cfa),                ret=-8(cfa)
40530c: cfa=32(rsp), rbx=-24(cfa), rbp=-16(cfa),                ret=-8(cfa)
...                                                             ...
405336: cfa=32(rsp), rbx=-24(cfa), rbp=-16(cfa),                ret=-8(cfa)
40533a: cfa=08(rsp), rbx=-24(cfa), rbp=-16(cfa),                ret=-8(cfa)
```

Fig. 1. A detailed view of the stack layout information of the Nginx binary.

the instruction at 0x40530c. This information shows the detailed rules on the stack usage which were not considered by the current ROP attacks to evade.

While we have found that the stack frame information is useful for the detection of ROP exploits, to be a practical solution, this information should be widely available in binaries. Modern programming languages mostly support exception handling. To do so, the runtime environment should be capable of interpreting and unwinding stack frames such that the exception handler can correctly respond to the exceptions. The ELF binary format, which is widely used in the Linux and BSD operating systems, stores it in the .eh_frame and .eh_framehdr sections [2]. Similar information is also available in other platforms to support exception handling. For instance, the Windows OS has an exception handling mechanism called Structured Exception Handling (SEH) [5,42]. The mach-O [4] binary format used by Apple Macintosh programs has similar binary sections (.eh_frame, .cfi_startproc, and .cfi_def_cfa_offset).

Our investigation shows that the .eh_frame section is included by default in the compilation using the gcc and g++ compilers for C and C++ programs. According to the definition of the application binary interface (ABI) for x86_64, it is a required section for a binary [6]. The strip utility with the most strict option (e.g., strip --strip-all) does not affect this section. In addition, most binaries deployed in modern Linux distributions include this section.

For instance, in Ubuntu 12.04 64 bit version all binaries in the /bin directory have a valid .eh_frame section. Among the entire set of the program binaries examined, over 97 % of around 1700 binaries have this information except special binaries: the Linux kernel image (e.g., kernel.img) and the binaries compiled with klibc, which is a special minimalistic version of the C library used for producing kernel drivers or the code executed in the early stage of a booting.

3 Overview of SLIck

We use the stack layout information available from the binary section for exception handling to detect ROP exploits. As a research prototype, we present SLIck, a robust stack unwinding based approach that does not rely on any gadget patterns, such as a gadget sequence, or behavior. Previous approaches (e.g., [16,19,38]) are based on the characteristics of ROP gadgets, such as call-precedence or the length of gadget sequences, which make them vulnerable to new attacks [12,25]. The overview of SLIck is illustrated in Fig. 2.

SLIck uses two invariants regarding the stack layout information (to be shortly described in Sect. 4 in details) to detect an ROP attack.

- **Stack Frame Chain Invariant (Sect. 4.1).** The stack frame information inside the binary describes how stack frames must be chained, and the unwinding of the runtime stack information should not be different from it.
- **Stack Frame Local Storage Invariant (Sect. 4.2).** The accumulated stack operations in a function are summarized as a constant because the memory usage in each stack frame should be cleaned up when the function returns.

SLIck inspects the runtime status of the monitored program's stack regarding these two invariants transparently and efficiently so that ROP attacks can be precisely detected. SLIck has two major system components.

- **Derivation of stack layout invariants (Sect. 4).** To achieve efficient runtime checks, the necessary information is derived in an offline binary analysis. Given a binary executable as an input, this component extracts the stack frame information from the .eh_frame section and constructs stack layout invariants. Also, the table of valid instructions of this binary is derived to verify the stack frame local storage invariant.

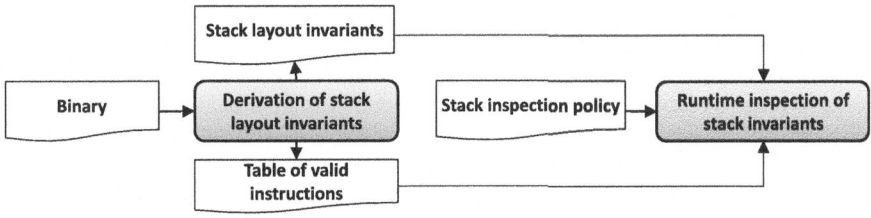

Fig. 2. System overview of SLIck.

– **Runtime inspection of stack invariants (Sect. 5).** This component verifies whether stack invariants hold at runtime and detects any violation caused. SLICK inspects the stack status when an OS event is triggered to avoid high overhead of fine-grained techniques [14,19]. Diverse OS events with different characteristics can be used to trigger the inspection as policies. For instance, the inspection on all system calls will catch the ROP behavior that uses any system services, such as a file access, and network usage. Using the timer interrupts, which trigger the context switches, enables non-deterministic inspection points that make it hard to accurately determine our inspection time and also enables frequent inspections in the CPU intensive workload.

Adversary Model and Assumptions. We consider an adversary who is able to launch a user-level stack-based return oriented programming (ROP) attack, which modifies the stack to inject its payload using a native program in the ELF format with the stack frame layout information widely available in the Linux platform. There is no assumption on the characteristics of gadget content (e.g., a sequence, a length, and the call-precedence of gadgets) which can be used in the attack.

The techniques in this paper are in the context of Linux and the ELF binary format because the mechanism and the implementation of the stack layout information is specific to each OS platform due to the distinct underlying structures of OSes. However, we believe a similar direction can be explored in other OS platforms which are described in the discussion section.

We assume that the integrity of the operating system kernel is not compromised and the ROP attack is not towards the vulnerability and the compromise of the kernel. While such attack scenarios of ROP exploits are realistic, in this paper we do not focus on the countermeasures for such attacks because of the existing detection and prevention mechanisms on OS kernel integrity [22,23,27,39–41,45]. We rely on such approaches to ensure the integrity of OS kernel and SLICK, which is designed to be a module of it.

Finally, we mainly focus on native programs for the detection of ROP exploits. The programs based on dynamically generated code running on virtual machines, interpreters, and dynamic binary translators have their own unique structures on their runtime and the stack layout. Currently, we do not focus on ROP defense for these binaries.

4 Derivation of Stack Layout Invariants

Rich stack layout information of the .eh_frame section can be used to derive potentially many invariants regarding the layout of the stack. In this paper, we focus on two invariants that are motivated by the following challenges.

First, ROP attacks can manipulate the valid chains of the function calls of the original program, and determining such manipulation robustly and transparently is a remaining challenge. Recent approaches on control-flow integrity have made substantial progress particularly when they can access or transform source code [18,56]. Some approaches attempted to achieve a practical control-flow integrity by relaxing strict control-flow [60,61]. However, they still introduce new attacks [24]. Second, ROP gadgets popularly utilize unintended instructions and it is non-trivial to detect such usage efficiently. We introduce two stack layout invariants to solve these challenges.

4.1 Stack Frame Chain Invariant (FCI)

Observation. The description regarding the head of a stack frame (CFA), can validate how far a previous stack frame should be apart from the current one. For instance, the information [40530c: cfa=32(rsp), ..., ret=-8(cfa)] in Fig. 1 shows that the CFA is at the address stored in the rsp register plus 32, and the return address is at $ret = -8(cfa)$ which is resolved as $rsp + 32 - 8$ using the location of the CFA. This information enables the validation of the linkage of stack frames.

Invariant. For an instruction c in a function, let us define the accumulation of stack operations between the function prologue and c in terms of a stack distance as $BL(c)$ (Backward stack frame Layout). This information generated by a compiler for the instruction c is retrieved from the CFA of .eh_frame. For instance, the return address at $B6$ in Fig. 3, $BL(B6)$ is $-12(SP)$ (i.e., stack pointer + 12 bytes) due to three decrements of the stack pointer (each by 4 bytes) for local variables. A runtime version, $BL'(c)$, is subject to manipulation under attacks requiring the verification whether it conforms to $BL(c)$ for all stack frames in a chain. This invariant is presented as $BL(c) = BL'(c)$ called the Stack Frame Chain Invariant (FCI).

Verification. SLICK checks this invariant using a stack unwinding algorithm (Sect. 5) iteratively over all stack frames validating the integrity of the BLs as a chain. Any inconsistency in one of the BLs in the chain causes cascading effects in the following stack frames, therefore, breaking the BL sequence in the unwinding

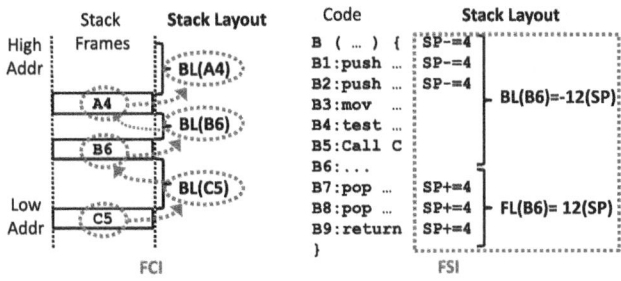

Fig. 3. Illustration of stack layout invariants.

procedure. SLICK determines this invariant is satisfied if the unwinding procedure over all stack frames is successful. To perform this runtime verification efficiently, we precompute the BLs using the CFAs from the .eh_frame section.

4.2 Stack Frame Local Storage Invariant (FSI)

Observation. Programs use the stack to store data (e.g., for local variables and register spills). To limit the impact across stack frames, the allocation and deallocation of local stack memory in a frame should be *paired up* so that the stack memory usage for a function could be cleaned up when the function returns.

Invariant. This observation regarding the gross sum of local stack operations is summarized as follows. Let us define the accumulated stack operations between the code c and the function epilogue in terms of a stack distance as $FL(c)$ (*F*orward stack frame *L*ayout). The observation on the stack local storage is represented as $BL(c) + FL(c) = k$, which we call the Stack *F*rame Local *S*torage *I*nvariant (*FSI*). In the right figure of Fig. 3, $BL(B6)$ is $-12(SP)$, and $FL(B6)$ is $12(SP)$ leading to $k = 0$. Typically k should be zero except the special corner cases where functions do not properly return such as the exit. This invariant allows to determine the usage of unintended code popularly used in ROP attacks because such code may not follow the original code's semantic.

Verification. To efficiently check whether the executed code conforms to this invariant, we precompute a table of instructions originally intended in the program, named as a *table of valid code addresses (TVC)*. Its rows show all possible code addresses (i.e., every byte offset of the code including unintended code in the program) and the column indicates a boolean state whether the code is valid (T) or invalid (F) depending on the $BL(c) + FL(c)$.

We use the .eh_frame and a binary analysis for the computation of this table. The instructions derived from the stack frame information are marked as valid. However, due to its compressed structure, which mainly describes the instructions involving stack operations, not every instruction is covered. For such cases, we use a binary analysis to simulate the instructions and determine the validity. SLICK applies this check as part of a stack unwinding algorithm.

SLICK considers that a program is compromised if either or both of these two invariants are violated. We present more specific details on how to check them at runtime in Sect. 5.

5 Runtime Inspection of Stack Invariants

In this section, we present how SLICK inspects stack invariants and robustly detects their violations.

5.1 Practical Challenges

After we use a traditional stack unwinding algorithm [3] to inspect the invariants, we have identified the cases that frustrate the current algorithm and limit the inspection of the full stack. There are two cases categorized.

Failure type	Description	Attributes of virtual memory pages		Binary exist exist	Unwind info exist
		Type	Page permission		
Type A	Incomplete unwinding info	Code	Executable	Yes	No
Type B	Invalid unwinding	Not found	Not executable	*	*

Type A: Incomplete Unwinding Information. We found that a rare portion of code in terms of coverage has incomplete unwinding information mainly in the low level libraries and the starting point of a program. It is important to address this issue because such code stays in the stack during execution and there is a high chance to face it during the unwinding. If this issue happens, the vanilla stack unwinding algorithm cannot proceed the unwinding procedure due to the missing location of the next stack frame.

Based on our experiments over 34 programs including widely used server applications and benchmark, the cases that we identified are summarized into mainly three cases. First, it is triggered by the entry point of ld, which is the dynamic linker and loader in Linux. Second, the first stack frame which is the start of the program can generate a type A error. The third case is the init section of the pthread library.

Type B: Invalid Unwinding Status. Unlike type A, this case should not occur in benign execution. However, this incorrect execution state is observed when the stack layout is manipulated by attacks. The stack unwinding algorithm strictly verifies the validity of the stack layout information formulated by the compiler across all stack frames. Any single discrepancy due to stack manipulation leads to invalid unwinding conditions. Specifically this case is characterized as the state shown in the table: the return code address obtained from the stack is not found from the executable memory area.

Type A failures can block the full inspection of all stack frames in stack unwinding-based approaches. Therefore, this issue must be addressed to achieve robust stack unwinding. We address it using *flexible stack unwinding*, which is a novel variant of the stack unwinding algorithm that enables robust detection of type B errors while addressing type A errors. Next, we present the details of our algorithm that inspects stack invariants based on the flexible stack unwinding.

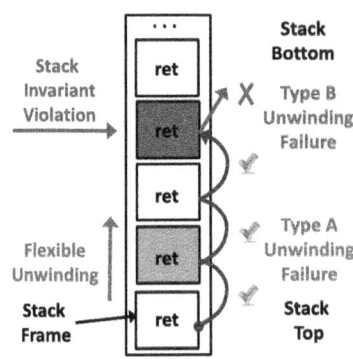
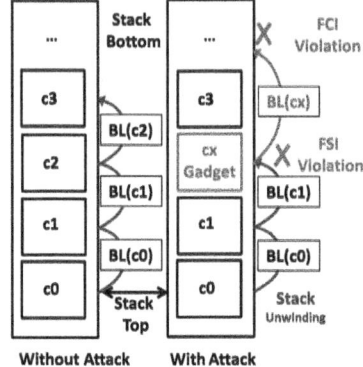

Fig. 4. Flexible unwinding.   Fig. 5. Stack invariant violation.

5.2 Stack Invariant Inspection Algorithm

Figures 4 and 5 presents a high level illustration of our algorithm to inspect stack invariants while addressing the practical stack unwinding challenges. When the inspection is triggered, Algorithm 1 inspects stack frames starting from the top to the bottom of the stack as shown in Fig. 4. The algorithm bypasses type A failures while detecting type B errors caused by the violation of stack invariants illustrated in Fig. 5. FCI and FSI violations are respectively caused by an illegitimate chain of stack frames and return addresses.

The Algorithm 1 is triggered by an operating system event (e.g., a system call, an interrupt) represented as the `OsEvent` function (Line 1). This function executes the `SIInspect` function (Line 2), the main logic for stack inspection. When this function detects either a type B error (FCI violation) or an invalid return code instruction (FSI violation) during stack unwinding, it returns `Fail`. Upon the detection of any violation, the `PostProcess` function is called (Line 4) to stop the current process and store the current context for a forensic analysis.

Unwinding Library Code. A program executes the code for multiple libraries as well as the main binary. Such libraries have separate stack frame information in their binaries which are loaded into distinct virtual memory areas (VMA). During the scan of the stack, our algorithm dynamically switches the VMA structure for the return address (Line 11), which is implemented as two nested loops in `SIInspect`; the outer `while` loop (Lines 10–38) switches different VMAs while the return addresses in the same binary are efficiently handled by the inner loop (Lines 17–27) without searching for another VMA.

For each VMA, the `.eh_frame` information is retrieved from the binary (Line 16). For each code address, the algorithm checks its validity (Line 20). If it is valid and the return code stays in the same VMA, the `GetNextRet` function is called to unwind one stack frame. Otherwise the algorithm returns a violation of FSI at Line 21. This loop is repeated to unwind following stack frames as

Algorithm 1. Stack Invariant Inspection Algorithm

```
     SZ = sizeof(UNSIGNED LONG)
 1:  function OSEVENT(REGS)
 2:      Ret = SIInspect(UserStack, REGS)
 3:      if Ret == Fail then
 4:          PostProcess(REGS, UserStack)
 5:      return
 6:  function SIINSPECT(UserStack, REGS)
 7:      CFA = REGS → SP; VMA = GetVMA(CFA); UnwindDepth = 0
 8:      StackTop = REGS → SP; StackBot = GetStackStart(VMA, CFA)
 9:      InvalidInstr = False
10:      while true do                                                      ▷ Outer loop
11:          VMA = GetVMA(REGS → IP)
12:          if VMA is invalid or not executable then
13:              return Fail                                                ▷ Type B, FCI violation
14:          if VMA → VM_FILE does not exist then                           ▷ Dynamic code
15:              Goto DoFlexibleSIInspect
16:          EH = GetEHSection(VMA)
17:          do                                                             ▷ Inner loop
18:              if REGS → SP < StackTop or REGS → SP >= StackBot then
19:                  return Fail                                            ▷ Type B, FCI violation, Stack Pivot Detection
20:              if TVC [REGS → IP] == False then                           ▷ FSI violation
21:                  return Fail
22:              if REGS → IP > VMA → VM_Start and REGS → IP < VMA → VM_End then
23:                  UnwindDepth += 1
24:              else
25:                  Ret = GotNext; break                                   ▷ Find another VMA
26:              Ret = GetNextRET(CFA, REGS, EH, StackBot, StackTop)
27:          while Ret == GotNext
28:          if Ret is NoUnwindingInfo then                                 ▷ Type A
29:          :DoFlexibleSIInspect
30:              offset = FlexibleSIInspect(REGS → SP, StackBot)
31:              if offset is EndOfStack then
32:                  return Success
33:              else
34:                  REGS → SP += offset; REGS → IP = *(REGS → SP) of UserStack,
35:                  REGS → BP = *(REGS → SP - SZ) of UserStack; REGS → SP += SZ
36:                  CFA = REGS → SP
37:          else if Ret is Invalid then
38:              return Fail                                                ▷ Type B, FCI violation
39:      return Success
40:  function FLEXIBLESIINSPECT(Start_SP, StackBot)
41:      for SP = Start_SP; SP < StackBot; SP += SZ do
42:          IP = *SP; VMA = GetVMA(IP)
43:          if VMA is valid and VMA → VM_FILE is available then
44:              return SP - Start_SP
45:      return EndOfStack
```

long as the function returns `GotNext`. For code c, its $BL(c)$ is returned by the `GetNextRet` function. If a return address is replaced by k, a manipulated value, the divergence $BL(k) = BL'(c) \neq BL(c)$ will cause cascading effects on unwinding of the following stack frames. Any mismatch of a single stack frame with its unwinding information causes a violation of FCI at Line 13, 19, or 38.

Stack Pivot Detection. During stack unwinding, Algorithm 1 performs various checks to ensure precise unwinding and detect anomaly cases. A popular technique in recent ROP attacks is stack pivoting [49,62] that changes the location of stack to the manipulated content (e.g., heap). This attack is trivially detected by our algorithm (Line 18) because SLICK can distinguish an invalid stack memory address.

Flexible Stack Unwinding. To handle type A failures, we provide *flexible stack unwinding* algorithm (Lines 40–45). When a type A case happens, the `FlexibleSIInspect` function advances the stack pointer in a brute force way and checks whether a legitimate stack frame appears next. If the return address found in this search belongs to a code section based on its memory address range and the corresponding file, this function returns the offset of the stack. And then the algorithm goes back to the outer loop (Line 10), and the stack layout information of the new stack frame is examined. If it is a type B case, the `GetNextRET` function will return `Invalid` in the next loop. If it turns out to be a type A case again, it will go back to the `FlexibleSIInspect` function by returning `NoUnwindingInfo`. Lastly, if it is a valid frame, it will be unwound and takes a following loop iteration.

5.3 Stack Inspection Policies

SLICK inspects the runtime status of a program stack based on the policies regarding which types of OS events trigger the inspection. Here we present two policies used for our evaluation (Sect. 6.3) and our framework allows user defined policies as well.

System Call Inspection (SYS). This policy checks the stack on all system calls which provide lower level services to the program, such as memory allocation, file operations, network operations, and a change of memory permission. They are the typical targets of ROP exploits to achieve functionality beyond the original program, and this policy provides a cost-effective inspection at the intermediary points of OS operations to observe high impact system activities.

System Call and Non-deterministic Inspection (SYS+INT). This policy achieves finer-grained inspection by narrowing down the gaps between the inspections and making inspection intervals non-deterministic by using non-deterministic OS events, such as interrupts. As an attack scenario against SLICK, an ROP exploit may attempt to predict SLICK's inspection time and clean up the stack manipulation to hide its evidence. Since this scheme uses non-deterministic OS events to perform inspections, this attack becomes significantly hard to be successful. This scheme can be further strengthened by increasing the randomness, e.g., by performing additional inspections with random intervals.

6 Evaluation

In this section, we present the evaluation of SLICK in the following perspectives.

- How effective is SLICK at detecting real-world ROP exploits?
- What is the impact of SLICK on benign programs?
- How efficient is SLICK for inspecting stack invariants?

We have implemented SLICK for 32 bit and 64 bit Ubuntu 12.04 LTS Linux systems as a kernel module and user level tools for offline analyses.

6.1 Detection of ROP Attacks

We applied SLICK on 7 real-world ROP exploits available in Linux of 32 bit and 64 bit architectures. Table 1 presents the details of the program's runtime status and the detection results by SLICK.

Table 1. Detection of stack invariant violations of ROP exploits. The number of unwinding failures (#F-unwind) is generally correlated with the number of events (# Events), but it can be higher if multiple stack frames have failures.

Program			Syscall inspection policy			Invariant violation		Attack description	
Name	Ver	Env	#Events	$\|\|S\|\|$	#F-unwind	Detection	Type	Exploit info	Syscall
Nginx	1.4	64 bit	100452	22	96895	✓	FSI	CVE-2013-2028	sys_write
Mysql	5.0.45	64 bit	2128	13	2156	✓	FCI & FSI	CVE-2008-0226	sys_execve
Nginx	1.4	32 bit	42937	22	40231	✓	FCI & FSI	CVE-2013-2028	sys_write
Mysql	5.0.45	32 bit	2027	12	1792	✓	FCI	CVE-2008-0226	sys_rt_sigaction
Unrar	4.0	32 bit	141	10	142	✓	FCI	CVE-2007-0855	sys_write
HT Editor	2.0.20	32 bit	292	13	326	✓	FCI	CVE-2012-5867	sys_lstat64
MiniUPnPd	1.0	32 bit	56	8	50	✓	FCI	CVE-2013-0230	sys_time

The first three columns show the description of the program, its name (Name), version (Ver.), and the architecture that it runs on (Env). For this experiment, we use the system call inspection policy. The 4th, 5th, and 6th columns show the runtime status: the number of system call events (# Events), the average stack depth ($\|\|S\|\|$) during the execution, and the number of type A stack unwinding errors (# F-unwind) that flexible stack unwinding algorithm successfully addressed. The next two columns show the detection of ROP exploits based on stack invariant inspection: the "Detection" column shows whether the violation of an invariant is detected. Our algorithm stops a program on the first violation of an invariant which could be either an FCI or an FSI. If both of them occur in the same iteration of algorithm, it is presented as FCI & FSI. The type of violation is presented in the "Type" column. Exploit information (Exploit Info) and the system call at the time of detection (Syscall) are presented in the next columns.

We experimented with real-world exploits against widely used server and desktop software: Nginx, Mysql, Unrar, HT Editor, and MiniUPnPd. These software and the ROP exploits have different characteristics shown as various numbers of system calls and the depths of the stack. All tested ROP exploits are successfully detected due to violations of stack invariants.

6.2 Impact on Benign Programs

For a practical usage of SLICK, it should have low false positives in benign programs. For this evaluation, we used total 34 programs from popular open source projects and benchmarks: 3 widely used server programs (Nginx, Apache, Mysql), a CPU benchmark for Linux (NBench), a data compression utility (7zip), and 29 programs from the SPEC 2006 benchmark. The stack invariants are inspected with two inspection policies: the system call inspection policy (SYS), and the system call and non-deterministic inspection policy (SYS+INT).

Table 2 summarizes our results. The first column describes the program name. We present the data for two inspection policies in different groups of columns. The next three columns describe the evaluation using the SYS inspection policy. The following three columns show the result using the SYS+INT policy. The SYS+INT inspection policy increases the number of inspection events in the CPU intensive benchmarks more significantly (e.g., 434.zeusmp has over 28 times higher events because of timer interrupts). I/O intensive programs get most timer interrupts from the kernel code, such as another interrupts or system calls. Such cases are not additionally inspected because the programs are already checked on the transition from the user mode to the kernel mode. This policy can harden the inspection of CPU intensive programs that have a low number of system calls. Timer interrupts capture a program call stack at arbitrary non-deterministic execution points. Therefore, the average call stack depth ($||S||$) is different between two experiments in many cases of the SPEC benchmark.

In general the number of type A failures that flexible unwinding addresses (#F-unwind) is highly correlated with the number of inspection events (# Events). One reason for this behavior is that the first stack frame created on the start of the program stays in the stack and triggers a type A failure on each system call. Another reason is the pthread library; large programs using multiple threads get additional type A errors due to this library.

While most of programs triggered non-trivial number of type A failures, in all cases, no violation of stack invariants is detected causing zero false positives of our approach.

6.3 Performance Analysis

We evaluate the runtime performance impact of SLICK on the protected programs in the prior evaluation. The overhead is related to the frequency of the inspections and the depth of stack unwinding. SLICK is configured to scan the full stack. We used the apache bench with the load of a thousand requests to generate the workload for Apache and Nginx webservers. The performance of the Mysql database and the 7zip tool are measured using the packaged benchmarking suites. The Nbench and SPEC 2006 benchmarks are executed using the standard setting. Performance numbers from different types of benchmarks are normalized in a relative way so that the performance of native execution becomes 1. Our measurement data are presented in Fig. 6. We present SLICK's performance in two inspection policies.

Table 2. Stack invariant inspection of benign applications. No violation is detected.

Program name	SYS			SYS+INT		
	#Events	$||S||$	#F-unwind	#Events	$||S||$	#F-unwind
Nginx	16164	16	16171	16183	16	16190
Apache	24466	15	24472	24481	15	24488
Mysql	40347778	12	40377139	40451780	12	40481318
Nbench	87371	7	87371	163973	7	163973
7zip	59922	8	74874	68516	8	82650
400.perlbench	35361	12	35361	35666	12	35666
401.bzip	450	7	450	4649	8	4649
403.gcc	714	15	714	1578	13	1568
410.bwaves	993	9	993	9048	9	9048
416.gamess	16848	17	16848	17057	17	17057
429.mcf	1023	8	1023	2945	7	2945
433.milc	19092	11	19092	26020	10	26020
434.zeusmp	258	8	258	7422	6	7422
435.gromacs	3009	15	3009	3651	14	3651
436.cactusADM	2115	16	2115	3869	14	3869
437.leslie3d	303	9	303	7646	5	7646
444.namd	6159	9	6159	14018	7	14018
445.gobmk	8799	12	8799	21492	23	21492
450.soplex	360	9	360	372	9	372
453.povray	5040	21	5040	5386	21	5386
454.calculix	537	9	537	568	9	568
456.hmmer	207	9	207	2168	5	2168
458.sjeng	1671	12	1671	4511	15	4511
459.GemsFDTD	1626	9	1626	2825	7	2825
462.libquantum	120	8	120	149	8	149
464.h264ref	1236	8	1236	9909	11	9909
465.tonto	6303	16	6303	6743	16	6743
470.lbm	2091	8	2091	3280	6	3280
471.omnetpp	570	12	570	829	11	829
473.astar	783	9	783	7371	6	7371
481.wrf	5598	17	5598	7666	15	7666
482.sphinx3	9213	12	9231	10510	11	10510
988.specrand	378	10	378	384	9	384
999.sperand	378	10	378	385	9	385

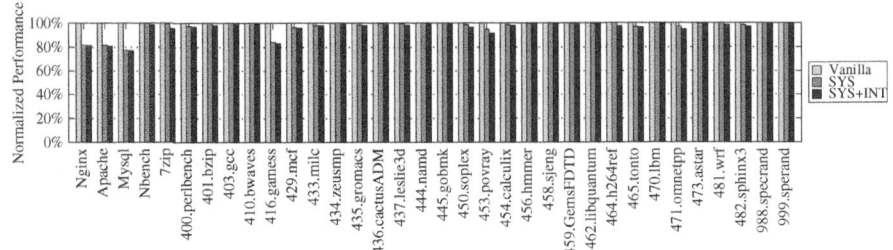

Fig. 6. Runtime performance of SLICK.

Runtime Impact for the SYS Policy. With this policy, the average overhead of SLICK in 34 evaluated programs is 3.09 % with the maximum overhead of 22.8 % in Mysql. High overhead of Mysql is due to very intensive stress tests for a database in I/O and low level services. As an evidence, the second column of Table 2 which is the system call count shows that Mysql benchmark generates a significantly higher number of system calls over 40 millions compared to other programs having under 164 thousands system calls.

Runtime Impact for the SYS+INT Policy. A finer-grained inspection based on system calls and timer interrupts is offered with a slightly higher performance cost of 3.93 % on average and with the maximum overhead of 22.8 % in Mysql. This policy causes increased overhead on CPU intensive workloads due to additional inspections introduced by timer interrupts.

7 Discussion

Comparison with ROPGuard/EMET. Our work is closely related to an early exploration based on stack unwinding, ROPGUARD/EMET [21]. However, there are several major differences that distinguish SLICK from ROPGUARD/EMET as follows.

- Our approach has a higher and reliable inspection coverage compared to ROPGUARD: SLICK inspects the user stack with the full depth on all system calls and timer interrupts. In contrast, ROPGUARD inspects the stack only on a selective set of critical user level APIs with a limited depth of the stack. Thus ROPGUARD/EMET cannot detect the attacks that directly trigger system calls without using the APIs. Also if the binary is built statically, ROPGUARD cannot be applied due to its base on the library interposition technique.
- ROPGUARD operates in the same user level as the monitored program. Therefore, it is subject to manipulation by the attacker. However, SLICK is isolated from the user space due to its implementation in the OS kernel.
- SLICK's inspections are performed with a higher frequency compared to ROPGUARD: SLICK inspects the stack on all system calls and non-deterministic

timer interrupts. ROPGUARD, however, only checks the stack on a set of critical API functions.
- SLICK achieves a reliable stack walking and improved ROP detection by using precise stack layout information extracted from the unwinding data while ROPGUARD uses a heuristic based on the frame pointer which is not reliable.
- This work proposes two stack layout invariants which are derived from the unwinding information, and these invariants are verified by using an improved and reliable stack walking mechanism.
- We discovered that a small number of binaries have incomplete unwinding information which affects the current stack walking mechanisms. We propose flexible stack unwinding algorithm to overcome this issue and enable a reliable and high quality inspection of the entire stack.

Stack Pivoting Attacks. A stack pivoting attack [49,62] manipulates the stack pointer to point to the data controlled by ROP gadgets. This attack is trivially detected by our approach because SLICK uses the valid stack memory address ranges assigned by the OS. When an unexpected memory area is used for the stack pointer, SLICK detects it as a FCI violation (Sect. 5.2). A related work [43] achieves this feature using a compiler approach and source code while SLICK can prevent this attack transparently for existing binaries.

Stack Manipulation Detection. Traditional buffer overflow attacks [36,48,51] attempting to overwrite the return addresses in the stack are likely to violate the invariants. Thus such attacks can be transparently detected by SLICK without any recompilation, or instrumentation of the program.

Support of Dynamic Code. Dynamically generated code is used by several platforms such as virtual machines, interpreters, dynamic binary translators, and emulators. While they are out of the scope of this paper, we believe our approach can be extended to support them with engineering efforts because these platforms also provide ways to unwind stack frames for dynamic code. For instance, Java has a tool called `jstack` that can dump the whole stack frames including both of the Java code and the underlying native code and libraries. If such a platform-specific logic is integrated into our stack unwinding algorithm, we should be able to support such dynamic code as well as native code.

Integrity of a Kernel Monitor. SLICK resides in the OS kernel. While the attack scenarios of ROP exploits against the kernel is certainly possible, in this paper we do not focus on the countermeasures for such attacks because of existing detection or prevention mechanisms on OS kernel integrity [22,23,27,39–41,45]. We rely on such approaches to ensure the integrity of SLICK.

Control-Flow Integrity. Our approach raises the bar for ROP exploits by introducing new security invariants on the layout of the stack. Essentially code and the stack status have correspondence generated by compilers, but it is not strictly enforced at runtime. SLICK verifies this loose correspondence by using a novel variant of a stack unwinding [3] inspecting stack layout invariants.

Control-flow integrity (CFI) [8] provides strong measures to defeat ROP attacks by strictly checking the control-flow of programs. Recent approaches made a significant progress in the compiler-based techniques [18,56] and achieved practical solutions by relaxing strict control-flows [60,61]. When only program binaries are available, the stack frame chain invariant of SLICK provides a practical and transparent alternative to verify the backward chain of control flow while providing a performance benefit and high applicability without requiring source code, program transformation, or a complete control flow.

User-Space-Only Self-hiding ROP Attacks. ROP gadgets are typically used to achieve a new logic which may not exist in the original program. Most real exploits typically make use of the OS level services [57], such as allocating memory and changing its permissions. Technically it is possible to execute ROP gadgets and recover the manipulation of the stack before the transition to the OS to hide the evidence from SLICK. Such user-space-only ROP attacks in practice would be non-trivial to keep track of the manipulated states and implement a clean up logic without stack pivoting which SLICK detects. The inspections on system calls will capture any such attempt on system related activities. Non-deterministic OS events, such as timer interrupts (varying between 4–20 ms in our experiments), and the inspection events with random intervals will make it further difficult for the exploit to precisely predict the inspection time. This advanced attack to hide itself is an aspect that needs further study which is our future work.

Integrity of Stack Frame Information. For a robust detection of ROP attacks, SLICK ensures the integrity of stack frame information as follows. The integrity of this information inside a binary is verified using a file integrity checker [30]. Given the file integrity, SLICK makes its own shadow copy of the .eh_frame section copied directly from the binary to prevent any manipulation. However, its copy loaded into the program's memory for exception handling is subject to potential attacks [34]. The OS kernel makes it read-only, but it is not immutable. Thus SLICK enforces the read-only permission on the program's copy to prevent the attack [34].

Attacks Using Binaries Without Stack Frame Information. Our study presented in Sect. 2 shows that most Linux ELF binaries except special binaries, such as a Linux kernel image and kernel drivers, have stack frame information. A typical compilation of programs includes stack frame information to support exceptions and debugging by default. Binaries without stack frame information are not supported by SLICK due to the lack of required information for stack walking. Such unusual binaries can be prevented from running using system wide program execution policies. For instance, SLICK can prevent the execution of such binaries when stack frame information is lacking.

Implementing SLIck on Other Platforms. This work focuses on the stack layout information in the ELF binary format, which is popular in Linux and BSD environments. However, other OS environments have similar information for exception handling and debugging. For instance, Windows has the RtlVirtualUnwind API that can unwind the stack by using the unwind descriptors of the structured exception handling (SEH) tables in the program images, which can be dumped using the dumpbin utility with the /UNWINDINFO option [7]. Mac OS' main binary format, Mach-O [4], has similar binary sections, such as .eh_frame, .cfi_startproc, .cfi_def_cfa_offset etc. These information can be used to implement a similar function as SLICK in those OS platforms.

Attacks Using Type A Cases for ROP Gadgets. Based on our study of diverse binaries, a very small number of common libraries have the missing unwinding information in a rare portion of their code: the entry point of the dynamic linker and loader, the first stack frame which is the start of the program, and the init section of the pthread library. Although the portion of code is small and its capability could be limited, it is possible for the attacker to use this code for gadgets. While we have not presented a specific mechanism to defeat this attack, it can be easily prevented by supplementing the incomplete unwinding information because the scope of such code is very limited. Similar to the technique that we used for constructing the TVC, the unwinding information can be generated by emulating the stack operations of the binary code.

8 Related Work

ROP and Related Attacks. Return oriented programming (ROP) [46] is an offensive technique that reuses pieces of existing program code to compromise a vulnerable program and bypass modern security mechanisms, such as DEP and some ASLR implementations [9] under certain conditions (e.g., memory disclosure vulnerabilities or low entropy ASLRs). It has also been applied in other attack vectors, such as rootkits [15,29]. In addition to the local application of this technique, Bittau et al. proposed the blind ROP (BROP) [9] which can remotely find ROP gadgets to fetch the vulnerable binary over network.

Similar to ROP, another type of control-flow transfer attack based on gadget-reuse is jump oriented programming (JOP) [10], which uses jumps instead of returns. Bosman et al. [11] proposed another type of ROP based on the signal handling function which is universal in UNIX systems. This technique called SigReturn Oriented Programming (SROP) is triggered by the manipulated signal frames stored on a user stack.

ROP Defense. Several mitigation techniques were proposed to defend against ROP attacks such as ASLR [26,28,37,44,53,59,60], compiler techniques [31,35], runtime instrumentation techniques [14,19], and hardware techniques [16,38].

ASLR has been used to block code reuse attacks by dynamically assigning the memory addresses of the code and data sections such that the predetermined memory addresses can be illegal. However, in practice some code may not be compatible with this scheme, thereby leaving attack vectors. Also several approaches have shown that it is possible to bypass this scheme based on information leakage or brute-force attacks [20,47,49,50,52,58].

When source code is available, it is possible to remove attack gadgets through a compiler transformation as shown in [31,35]. If source code is not available, dynamic binary instrumentation can be used to monitor the execution and detect ROP attacks. DROP [14] used the length of gadgets and the contiguous length of gadget chains to characterize and detect ROP attacks. ROPDEFENDER [19] uses binary instrumentation to manage a shadow stack which is not tampered by stack manipulation. These approaches in general have a low runtime efficiency due to a high cost of dynamic binary translation.

ROPECKER [16] and KBOUNCER [38] proposed to utilize the Last Branch Record (LBR) registers to efficiently inspect the runtime history. These approaches are established on the assumptions of gadget patterns, such as the short length of gadgets and a long sequence of consecutive gadgets. Unfortunately, new ROP attack techniques showed such gadget-pattern based schemes can be bypassed [12,25]. ROPGUARD [21] (later integrated into the Microsoft EMET [55]) performs stack inspections for a limited depth at selective critical Windows APIs. This inspection unwinds the user stack using the heuristic on the frame pointer which would be limited based on the build conditions; unless programs are compiled to use the frame pointers, they could not be reliably inspected. In contrast, the stack frame information in the .eh_frame enables a precise and reliable unwinding regardless of the requirement of the frame pointer.

The comparison between SLICK and related work in Table 3 highlights that SLICK does not have assumptions on the characterization of ROP gadgets. Hence it is not affected by recent attacks [12,25]. Also its stack unwinding technique

Table 3. Comparison of ROP detection approaches. CL: without using a chain length, GL: without using a gadget length. SC: without using source code. RW: without rewriting. RE: Runtime efficiency. RU: Reliable unwinding.

ROP detector	CL	GL	SC	RW	RE	RU	Main techniques
RETURNLESS [31]	✓	✓	✗	✗	✓	-	Gadget removal based on a compiler technique
GFREE [35]	✓	✓	✗	✗	✓	-	Gadget removal based on a compiler technique
DROP [14]	✗	✗	✓	✗	✗	-	ROP detection based on gadget characteristics
ROPDEFENDER [19]	✓	✓	✓	✗	✗	-	Shadow stack and dynamic instrumentation
KBOUNCER [38]	✗	✗	✓	✗	✓	-	Last branch recording and gadget characteristics
ROPECKER [16]	✗	✗	✓	✓	✓	-	Last branch recording and sliding window
ROPGUARD [21]	✓	✓	✓	✗	✓	✗	Stack unwinding based on the frame pointer
SLICK	✓	✓	✓	✓	✓	✓	Stack invariants verified by a reliable stack unwinding

is more reliable based on the precise stack frame information widely available in the binaries of mainstream Linux distributions. These unique properties enable SLICK to achieve a practical solution which does not require source code, or rewriting of the program binaries for ROP detection.

9 Conclusion

We have presented SLICK, a robust and practical detection mechanism of ROP exploits that is not affected by recent attacks based on the violation of previous assumptions on gadget patterns [12,25]. SLICK detects ROP exploits by using stack layout invariants derived from the stack unwinding information for exception handling widely available in Linux binaries. Our evaluation on real-world ROP exploits shows robust and effective detection without any requirements on source code or recompilation while it incurs low overhead.

Acknowledgments. We would like to thank our shepherd, Michalis Polychronakis, and the anonymous reviewers for their insightful comments and feedback. Yangchun Fu and Zhiqiang Lin were supported in part by the AFOSR grant no. FA9550-14-1-0173 and the NSF award no. 1453011. Any opinions, findings, conclusions, or recommendations expressed are those of the authors and do not necessarily reflect the views of any organization.

References

1. Dwarf debugging information format, version 4. http://www.dwarfstd.org/doc/DWARF4.pdf
2. Exception frames. https://refspecs.linuxfoundation.org/LSB_3.0.0/LSB-Core-generic/LSB-Core-generic/ehframechpt.html
3. Exceptions and stack unwinding in C++. http://msdn.microsoft.com/en-us/library/hh254939.aspx
4. Mach-o executables, issue 6 build tools. http://www.objc.io/issue-6/mach-o-executables.html
5. Structured exception handling. http://msdn.microsoft.com/en-us/library/windows/desktop/ms680657(v=vs.85).aspx
6. System V Application Binary Interface (ABI), AMD64 Architecture Processor Supplement, Draft Version 0.98
7. x64 manual stack reconstruction and stack walking. https://blogs.msdn.microsoft.com/ntdebugging/2010/05/12/x64-manual-stack-reconstruction-and-stack-walking/
8. Abadi, M., Budiu, M., Erlingsson, U., Ligatti, J.: Control-flow integrity. In: Proceedings of CCS (2005)
9. Bittau, A., Belay, A., Mashtizadeh, A., Mazieres, D., Boneh, D.: Hacking blind. In: Proceedings of IEEE Security and Privacy (2014)
10. Bletsch, T., Jiang, X., Freeh, V.W., Liang, Z.: Jump-oriented programming: a new class of code-reuse attack. In: Proceedings of ASIACCS (2011)
11. Bosman, E., Bos, H.: Framing signals - a return to portable shellcode. In: Proceedings of IEEE Security and Privacy (2014)

12. Carlini, N., Wagner, D.: ROP is still dangerous: breaking modern defenses. In: Proceedings of USENIX Security (2014)
13. Checkoway, S., Davi, L., Dmitrienko, A., Sadeghi, A.R., Shacham, H., Winandy, M.: Return-oriented programming without returns. In: Proceedings of CCS (2010)
14. Chen, P., Xiao, H., Shen, X., Yin, X., Mao, B., Xie, L.: DROP: detecting return-oriented programming malicious code. In: Prakash, A., Sen Gupta, I. (eds.) ICISS 2009. LNCS, vol. 5905, pp. 163–177. Springer, Heidelberg (2009)
15. Chen, P., Xing, X., Mao, B., Xie, L.: Return-oriented rootkit without returns (on the x86). In: Proceedings of ICICS (2010)
16. Cheng, Y., Zhou, Z., Yu, M., Ding, X., Deng, R.H.: ROPecker: a generic and practical approach for defending against ROP attacks. In: Proceedings of NDSS (2014)
17. Cowan, C., Pu, C., Maier, D., Hinton, H., Walpole, J., Bakke, P., Beattie, S., Grier, A., Wagle, P., Zhang, Q.: Stackguard: automatic adaptive detection and prevention of buffer-overflow attacks. In: Proceedings of USENIX Security (1998)
18. Criswell, J., Dautenhahn, N., Adve, V.: KCoFI: complete control-flow integrity for commodity operating system kernels. In: Proceedings of the IEEE Security and Privacy (2014)
19. Davi, L., Sadeghi, A.R., Winandy, M.: ROPdefender: a detection tool to defend against return-oriented programming attacks. In: Proceedings of ASIACCS (2011)
20. Durden, T.: Bypassing PaX ASLR protection. Phrack Mag. **59**(9), June 2002. http://www.phrack.org/phrack/59/p59-0x09
21. Fratric, I.: ROPGuard: runtime prevention of return-oriented programming attacks. https://code.google.com/p/ropguard/
22. Garfinkel, T., Pfaff, B., Chow, J., Rosenblum, M., Boneh, D.: Terra: a virtual machine-based platform for trusted computing. In: Proceedings of SOSP (2003)
23. Garfinkel, T., Rosenblum, M.: A virtual machine introspection based architecture for intrusion detection. In: Proceedings of NDSS (2003)
24. Goktas, E., Athanasopoulos, E., Bos, H., Portokalidis, G.: Out of control: overcoming control-flow integrity. In: Proceedings of IEEE Security and Privacy (2014)
25. Göktaş, E., Athanasopoulos, E., Polychronakis, M., Bos, H., Portokalidis, G.: Size does matter: why using gadget-chain length to prevent code-reuse attacks is hard. In: Proceedings of USENIX Security (2014)
26. Hiser, J., Nguyen-Tuong, A., Co, M., Hall, M., Davidson, J.W.: ILR: where'd my gadgets go? In: Proceedings of IEEE Security and Privacy (2012)
27. Hofmann, O.S., Dunn, A.M., Kim, S., Roy, I., Witchel, E.: Ensuring operating system kernel integrity with OSck. In: Proceedings of ASPLOS (2011)
28. Howard, M., Thomlinson, M.: Windows ISV software security defenses. http://msdn.microsoft.com/en-us/library/bb430720.aspx
29. Hund, R., Holz, T., Freiling, F.C.: Return-oriented rootkits: bypassing kernel code integrity protection mechanisms. In: Proceedings of USENIX Security (2009)
30. Kim, G.H., Spafford, E.H.: The design and implementation of tripwire: a file system integrity checker. In: Proceedings of CCS (1994)
31. Li, J., Wang, Z., Jiang, X., Grace, M., Bahram, S.: Defeating return-oriented rootkits with "return-less" kernels. In: Proceedings of EuroSys (2010)
32. Microsoft: A detailed description of the Data Execution Prevention (DEP) feature in Windows XP Service Pack 2 (2008). http://support.microsoft.com/kb/875352
33. Mudge: How to Write Buffer Overflows (1997). http://l0pht.com/advisories/bufero.html
34. Oakley, J., Bratus, S.: Exploiting the hard-working DWARF: trojan and exploit techniques with no native executable code. In: Proceedings of WOOT (2011)

35. Onarlioglu, K., Bilge, L., Lanzi, A., Balzarotti, D., Kirda, E.: G-free: defeating return-oriented programming through gadget-less binaries. In: Proceedings of ACSAC (2010)
36. Aleph One: Smashing the stack for fun and profit. Phrack 7(49), November 1996. http://www.phrack.com/issues.html?issue=49&id=14
37. Pappas, V., Polychronakis, M., Keromytis, A.D.: Smashing the gadgets: hindering return-oriented programming using in-place code randomization. In: Proceedings of IEEE Security and Privacy (2012)
38. Pappas, V., Polychronakis, M., Keromytis, A.D.: Transparent ROP exploit mitigation using indirect branch tracing. In: Proceedings of USENIX Security (2013)
39. Petroni Jr., N.L., Fraser, T., Molina, J., Arbaugh, W.A.: Copilot - a coprocessor-based kernel runtime integrity monitor. In: Proceedings of USENIX Security (2004)
40. Petroni Jr., N.L., Fraser, T., Walters, A., Arbaugh, W.A.: An architecture for specification-based detection of semantic integrity violations in kernel dynamic data. In: Proceedings of USENIX Security (2006)
41. Petroni Jr., N.L., Hicks, M.: Automated detection of persistent kernel control-flow attacks. In: Proceedings of CCS (2007)
42. Pietrek, M.: A crash course on the depths of win32 structured exception handling. Microsoft Syst. J. **12**(1), January 1997
43. Prakash, A., Yin, H.: Defeating ROP through denial of stack pivot. In: ACSAC (2015)
44. Roglia, G.F., Martignoni, L., Paleari, R., Bruschi, D.: Surgically returning to randomized lib(c). In: Proceedings of ACSAC (2009)
45. Seshadri, A., Luk, M., Qu, N., Perrig, A.: SecVisor: a tiny hypervisor to provide lifetime kernel code integrity for commodity OSes. In: Proceedings of SOSP (2007)
46. Shacham, H.: The geometry of innocent flesh on the bone: return-into-libc without function calls (on the x86). In: Proceedings of CCS (2007)
47. Shacham, H., Page, M., Pfaff, B., Goh, E.J., Modadugu, N., Boneh, D.: On the effectiveness of address-space randomization. In: Proceedings of CCS (2004)
48. Smith, N.P.: Stack Smashing Vulnerabilities in the UNIX Operating System (2000)
49. Snow, K.Z., Monrose, F., Davi, L., Dmitrienko, A., Liebchen, C., Sadeghi, A.R.: Just-in-time code reuse: on the effectiveness of fine-grained address space layout randomization. In: Proceedings of IEEE Security and Privacy (2013)
50. Sotirov, A., Dowd, M.: Bypassing browser memory protections in windows vista. http://www.phreedom.org/research/bypassing-browser-memory-protections/
51. Spafford, E.H.: The internet worm program: an analysis. SIGCOMM Comput. Commun. Rev. **19**, 17–57 (1989)
52. Strackx, R., Younan, Y., Philippaerts, P., Piessens, F., Lachmund, S., Walter, T.: Breaking the memory secrecy assumption. In: Proceedings of EuroSec (2009)
53. PaX Team: http://pax.grsecurity.net/
54. PaX Team: Pax address space layout randomization (ASLR) (2003). http://pax.grsecurity.net/docs/aslr.txt
55. The Enhanced Mitigation Experience Toolkit, Microsoft. http://technet.microsoft.com/en-us/security/
56. Tice, C., Roeder, T., Collingbourne, P., Checkoway, S., Erlingsson, Ú., Lozano, L., Pike, G.: Enforcing forward-edge control-flow integrity in GCC & LLVM. In: Proceedings of USENIX Security (2014)
57. Tran, M., Etheridge, M., Bletsch, T., Jiang, X., Freeh, V., Ning, P.: On the expressiveness of return-into-libc attacks. In: Proceedings of RAID (2011)
58. Vreugdenhil, P.: Pwn2own 2010: Windows 7 internet explorer 8 exploit. http://vreugdenhilresearch.nl/Pwn2Own-2010-Windows7-InternetExplorer8.pdf

59. Wartell, R., Mohan, V., Hamlen, K.W., Lin, Z.: Binary stirring: self-randomizing instruction addresses of legacy x86 binary code. In: Proceedings of CCS (2012)
60. Zhang, C., Wei, T., Chen, Z., Duan, L., Szekeres, L., McCamant, S., Song, D., Zou, W.: Practical control flow integrity and randomization for binary executables. In: Proceedings of IEEE Security and Privacy (2013)
61. Zhang, M., Sekar, R.: Control flow integrity for cots binaries. In: Proceedings of the USENIX Security (2013)
62. Zovi, D.A.D.: Return oriented exploitation. In: Blackhat (2010)

Low-Level Attacks and Defenses

APDU-Level Attacks in PKCS#11 Devices

Claudio Bozzato[1], Riccardo Focardi[1,2(✉)], Francesco Palmarini[1], and Graham Steel[2]

[1] Ca' Foscari University, Venice, Italy
cbozzato@dsi.unive.it, {focardi,palmarini}@unive.it
[2] Cryptosense, Paris, France
graham@cryptosense.com

Abstract. In this paper we describe attacks on PKCS#11 devices that we successfully mounted by interacting with the low-level APDU protocol, used to communicate with the device. They exploit proprietary implementation weaknesses which allow attackers to bypass the security enforced at the PKCS#11 level. Some of the attacks leak, as cleartext, sensitive cryptographic keys in devices that were previously considered secure. We present a new threat model for the PKCS#11 middleware and we discuss the new attacks with respect to various attackers and application configurations. All the attacks presented in this paper have been timely reported to manufacturers following a *responsible disclosure* process.

1 Introduction

Cryptographic hardware such as USB tokens, smartcards and Hardware Security Modules has become a standard component of any system that uses cryptography for critical activities. It allows cryptographic operations to be performed inside a protected, tamper-resistant environment, without the need for the application to access the (sensitive) cryptographic keys. In this way, if an application is compromised the cryptographic keys are not leaked, since their value is stored securely in the device.

Cryptographic hardware is accessed via a dedicated API. PKCS#11 defines the RSA standard interface for cryptographic tokens and is now administered by the Oasis PKCS11 Technical Committee [14,15]. In PKCS#11, fresh keys are directly generated inside devices and can be shared with other devices through special key *wrapping* and *unwrapping* operations, that allow for exporting and importing keys encrypted under other keys. For example, a fresh symmetric key k can be encrypted (wrapped) by device d_1 under the public key of device d_2 and then exported out of d_1 and imported (unwrapped) inside d_2 that will perform, internally, the decryption. In this way, key k will never appear as cleartext out of the devices. One of the fundamental properties of PKCS#11 is, in fact, that keys marked as *sensitive* should never appear out of a device unencrypted.

In the last 15 years, several API-level attacks on cryptographic keys have appeared in literature [1,3–6,9,12]. As pioneered by Clulow [6], the attributes of a PKCS#11 key might be set so to give the key conflicting roles, contradicting the standard *key separation* principle in cryptography. For example, to determine the value of a sensitive key k_1 given a second key k_2, an attacker simply wraps k_1 using k_2 and decrypts the resulting ciphertext using k_2 once again. The fact that a key should never be used to perform both the wrapping of other keys and the decryption of arbitrary data (including wrapped keys) is not explicitly stated in the specification of PKCS#11 and many commercial devices have been recently found vulnerable to Clulow's attack [5].

In this paper, we describe new, unpublished attacks that work at a different API-level. The PKCS#11 API is typically implemented in the form of a middleware which translates the high-level PKCS#11 commands into low-level ISO 7816 Application Protocol Data Units (APDUs) and exposes results of commands in the expected PKCS#11 format. In our experiments, we noticed that this translation is far from being a 1-to-1 mapping. Devices usually implement simple building blocks for key storage and cryptographic operations, but most of the logic and, in some cases, some of the sensitive operations are delegated to the middleware.

We have investigated how five commercially available devices implement various security-critical PKCS#11 operations, by analyzing in detail the APDU traces. Our findings show that APDU-level attacks are possible and that four out of the five analyzed devices leak symmetric sensitive keys in the clear, out of the device. We also show that, under a reasonable attacker model, the authentication phase can be broken, allowing for full access to cryptographic operations. Interestingly, we found that most of the logic of PKCS#11 is implemented at the library level. Key attributes that regulate the usage of keys do not have any importance at the APDU-level and can be easily bypassed. For example, we succeeded performing signatures under keys that do not have this functionality enabled at the PKCS#11 level. For one device, we also found that RSA session keys are managed directly by the library in the clear violating, once more, the PKCS#11 basic requirement that sensitive keys should never leave the token unencrypted.

The focus of this paper is primarily on USB tokens and smartcards, so our threat model refers to a typical single-user desktop/laptop configuration. In particular, we consider various application configurations in which the PKCS#11 layer and the authentication phase are run at different privileges with respect to the user application. Protecting the PKCS#11 middleware turns out to be the only effective way to prevent the APDU-level attacks that we discovered, assuming that the attacker does not have physical access to the token. In fact, physical access would enable USB sniffing, revealing any key communicated in the clear from/to the token. Separating authentication (for example using a dialog running at a different privilege) offers additional protection and makes it hard to use the device arbitrarily through the PKCS#11 API. However, an attacker might still attach to the process and mount a Man-In-The-Middle attack at the PKCS#11 layer, injecting or altering PKCS#11 calls.

Contributions. In this paper we present: (i) a new threat model for PKCS#11 middleware; (ii) new, unpublished APDU-level attacks on commercially available tokens and smartcards, some of which were considered secure; (iii) a security analysis of the vulnerabilities with respect to the threat model.

Related work. Many API-level attacks have been published in the last 15 years. The first one is due to Longley and Rigby [12] on a device that was later revealed to be a Hardware Security Module manufactured by Eracom and used in the cash machine network. In 2000, Anderson published an attack on key loading procedures on another similar module manufactured by Visa [1] and presented more attacks in two subsequent papers [3,4]. Clulow published the first attacks on PKCS#11 in [6]. All of these attacks had been found manually or through ad-hoc techniques. A first effort to apply general analysis tools appeared in [20], but the researchers were unable to discover any new attacks and could not conclude anything about the security of the device. The first automated analysis of PKCS#11 with a formal statement of the underlying assumptions was presented in [9]. When no attacks were found, the authors were able to derive precise security properties of the device. In [5], the model was generalized and provided with a reverse-engineering tool that automatically refined the model depending on the actual behaviour of the device. When new attacks were found, they were tested directly on the device to get rid of possible spurious attacks determined by the model abstraction. The automated tool of [5] successfully found attacks that leak the value of sensitive keys on real devices.

Low-level smartcard attacks have been studied before but no previous APDU-level attacks and threat models for PKCS#11 devices have been published in literature. In [2], the authors showed how to compromise the APDU buffer in Java Cards through a combined attack that exploits both hardware and software vulnerabilities. In [8], the authors presented a tool that gives control over the smart card communication channel for eavesdropping and man-in-the-middle attacks. In [13], the authors illustrated how a man-in-the-middle attack can enable payments without knowing the card PIN.

In [10] a subset of the authors investigated an automated method to systematically reverse-engineer the mapping between the PKCS#11 and the APDU layers. The idea is to provide abstract models in first-order logic of low level communication, on-card operations and possible implementations of PKCS#11 functions. The abstract models are then refined based on the actual APDU trace, in order to suggest the actual mapping between PKCS#11 commands and APDU traces. The two papers complement each other: the present one illustrates real attacks with a threat model and a security analysis, while [10] focuses on automating the manual, non-trivial reverse engineering task. All of the attacks presented here have been found manually and some of them have been used as test cases for the automated tool of [10].

Finally, for what concerns the threat model, in the literature we find a number of general methodologies (e.g., [17–19]) that do not directly apply to our setting. In [7] the authors discussed threat modelling for security tokens in the setting of web application while [16] described in details all the actors and threats for smart cards, but none of these papers considered threats at the PKCS#11 middleware layer. To the best of our knowledge, the threat model we propose in this work is the first one in the setting of PKCS#11 tokens and smartcards which takes into account the APDU layer as an attack entry point.

Structure of the paper. The paper is organized as follows: in Sect. 2 we give background about the PKCS#11 and APDU layers; in Sect. 3 we present the threat model; in Sect. 4 we illustrate in detail our findings on five commercially available devices; in Sect. 5 we analyze the attacks with respect to the threat model and in Sect. 6 we draw some concluding remarks.

2 Background

PKCS#11 defines the RSA standard interface for cryptographic tokens and is now developed by the Oasis PKCS11 Technical Committee [14,15].

The PKCS#11 API is typically implemented in the form of a middleware which translates the high-level PKCS#11 commands into low-level ISO 7816 Application Protocol Data Units (APDUs) and exposes results of commands in the expected PKCS#11 format. Thus, from an architectural perspective, the PKCS#11 middleware can be seen as the combination of two layers: the PKCS#11 API and the device API. All of the devices we have analyzed are based on the PC/SC specification for what concerns the low-level device API.[1] This layer is the one that makes devices operable from applications and allows for communication with the device reader, exposing both standard and proprietary commands, formatted as ISO 7816 APDUs. In the following, we will refer to this layer as the APDU layer.

The PKCS#11 and the APDU layer are usually implemented as separate libraries. As an example, in Windows systems PC/SC is implemented in the winscard.dll library. Then, a separate, device-specific PKCS#11 library links to winscard.dll in order to communicate with the device.

It is important to notice that, even if PC/SC provides a standard layer for low-level communication, different devices implement the PKCS#11 API in various, substantially different ways. As a consequence, each device requires its specific PKCS#11 library on top of the PC/SC one. Figure 1 gives an overview of a typical PKCS#11 middleware architecture with two cards requiring two different PKCS#11 libraries which communicates with the cards using the same PC/SC library.

In Subsects. 2.1 and 2.2 we illustrate the PKCS#11 and the APDU layers more in detail. Readers familiar with these layers can safely skip the following sections.

2.1 The PKCS#11 Layer

As well as providing access to cryptographic functions – such as encryption, decryption, sign and authentication – PKCS#11 is designed to provide a high degree of protection of cryptographic keys. Importing, exporting, creating and deleting keys stored in the token should always be performed in a secure way. In particular, the standard requires that even if the token is connected to an untrusted machine, in which the operating system, device drivers or software might be compromised, keys marked as sensitive should never be exported as cleartext out of the device.

---
[1] http://www.pcscworkgroup.com/.

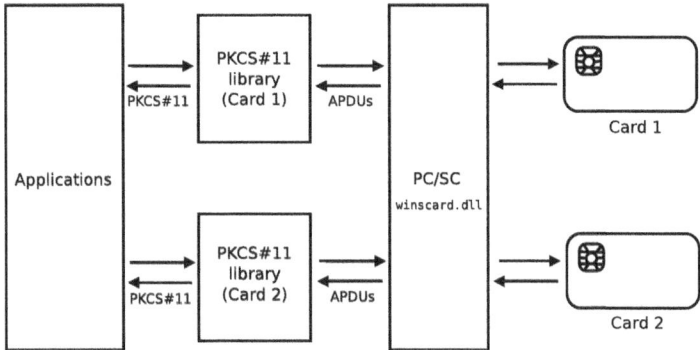

Fig. 1. PKCS#11 middleware for two PC/SC (`winscard.dll`) cards with different PKCS#11 libraries.

In order to access the token, an application must authenticate by supplying a PIN and initiate a session. Notice, however, that if the token is connected to an untrusted machine the PIN can be easily intercepted, e.g., through a keylogger. Thus, the PIN should only be considered as a second layer of protection and it should not be possible to export sensitive keys in the clear even for legitimate users, that know the PIN (cf. [15], Sect. 7).

PKCS#11 defines a number of *attributes* for keys that regulate the way keys should be used. We briefly summarize the most relevant ones from a security perspective (see [14,15] for more detail):

CKA_SENSITIVE the key cannot be revealed as plaintext out of the token. It should be impossible to unset this attribute once it has been set, to avoid trivial attacks;

CKA_EXTRACTABLE the key can be wrapped, i.e. encrypted, under other keys and extracted from the token as ciphertext; unextractable keys cannot be revelead out of the token even when encrypted. Similarly to CKA_SENSITIVE, it should not be possible to mark a key as extractable once it has been marked unextractable;

CKA_ENCRYPT, CKA_DECRYPT the key can be used to encrypt and decrypt arbitrary data;

CKA_WRAP, CKA_UNWRAP the key can be used to encrypt (wrap) and decrypt (unwrap) other CKA_EXTRACTABLE, possibly CKA_SENSITIVE keys. These two operations are used to export and import keys from and into the device;

CKA_SIGN, CKA_VERIFY the key can be used to sign and verify arbitrary data;

CKA_PRIVATE the key can be accessed even if the user is not authenticated to the token when it is set to false;

CKA_TOKEN the key is not stored permanently on the device (discarded at the end of the session) when it is set to false.

```
 0  /* Session initialization and loading of DESkey has been omitted ... */
 1
 2  CK_BYTE_PTR plaintext = "AAAAAAAA";                    /* plaintext */
 3  CK_BYTE iv[8] = {1, 2, 3, 4, 5, 6, 7, 8};              /* initialization vector */
 4  CK_BYTE ciphertext[8];                                 /* ciphertext output buffer */
 5  CK_ULONG ciphertext_len;                               /* ciphertext length */
 6  CK_MECHANISM mechanism = {CKM_DES_CBC, iv, sizeof(iv)}; /* DES CBC mode with given iv */
 7
 8  /* Initialize the encryption operation with mechanism and DESkey */
 9  C_EncryptInit(session, &mechanism, DESkey);
10
11  /* Encryption of the plaintext string into ciphertext buffer */
12  C_Encrypt(session, plaintext, strlen(plaintext), ciphertext, &ciphertext_len);
```

Listing 1.1. PKCS#11 DES/CBC encryption under key DESkey.

Example 1. (PKCS#11 symmetric key encryption). Listing 1.1 reports a fragment of C code performing symmetric DES/CBC encryption of plaintext "AAAAAAAA" with initialization vector 0x0102030405060708. PKCS#11 session has already been initiated and `session` contains a handle to the active session. We also assume that DESkey is a valid handle to a DES encryption key.

We can see that C_EncryptInit initializes the encryption operation by instantiating the DES/CBC cryptographic mechanism and the cryptographic key DESkey. Then, C_Encrypt performs the encryption of the string plaintext and stores the result and its length respectively in ciphertext and ciphertext_len. In order to keep the example simple, we skipped checks for errors that should be performed after every PKCS#11 API call (cf. [15], Sect. 11). In Subsect. 2.2 we will show how this example is mapped in APDUs on one token.

2.2 The APDU Layer

The ISO/IEC 7816 is a standard for identification, integrated circuit cards. Organization, security and commands for interchange are defined in part 4 of the standard [11]. The communication format between a smartcard and an off-card application is defined in terms of Application Protocol Data Units (APDUs). In particular, the half-duplex communication model is composed of APDU pairs: the reader sends a Command APDU (C-APDU) to the card which replies with a Response APDU (R-APDU). The standard contains a list of *inter-industry commands* whose behaviour is specified and standardized. Manufacturers can integrate these standard commands with their own *proprietary commands*.

A C-APDU is composed of a mandatory 4-byte header (CLA,INS,P1,P2), and an optional payload (Lc,data,Le), described below:

CLA one byte referring to the instruction class which specifies the degree of compliance to ISO/IEC 7816 and whether the command and the response are inter-industry or proprietary. Typical values are 0x00 and 0x80, respectively for inter-industry and proprietary commands;

INS one byte representing the actual command to be executed, *e.g.* READ RECORD;

```
 0  # The challenge-response authentication is omitted. For details see
       Subsect. 4.1
 1
 2  # ISO-7816 SELECT FILE command to select the folder (DF) where the
       key is stored
 3  APDU: 00 a4 04 0c 00 00 06 50 55 42 4c 49 43
 4  SW: 90 00
 5  # ISO-7816 SELECT FILE command to select the file (EF) containing the
       encryption key
 6  APDU: 00 a4 02 0c 00 00 02 83 01
 7  SW: 90 00
 8  # Encryption of the plaintext (red/italic) using the selected key and
       the given IV (green/overlined). The ciphertext is returned by
       the token (blue/underlined).
 9  APDU: 80 16 00 01 00 00 10 01 02 03 04 05 06 07 08
       41 41 41 41 41 41 41 41 00 00
10  SW: d2 ef a5 06 92 64 44 13 90 00
```

Listing 1.2. APDU session trace of the PKCS#11 symmetric key encryption.columns

P1,P2 two bytes containing the instruction parameters for the command, *e.g.* the record number/identifier;

Lc one or three bytes, depending on card capabilities, containing the length of the optional subsequent data field;

data the actual Lc bytes of data sent to the card;

Le one or three bytes, depending on card capabilities, containing the length (possibly zero) of the expected response.

The R-APDU is composed of an optional Le bytes data payload (absent when Le is 0), and a mandatory 2-bytes status word (SW1,SW2). The latter is the return status code after command execution (*e.g.* FILE NOT FOUND).

Example 2. (Symmetric Key Encryption in APDUs). We show how the PKCS#11 code of Example 1 is mapped into APDUs on the Athena ASEKey USB token. Notice that this token performs a challenge-response authentication before any privileged command is executed. For simplicity, we omit the authentication part in this example but will discuss it in detail in Sect. 4.1.

The encryption operation begins by selecting the encryption key from the right location in the token memory: at line 3, the token selects the directory (called *Dedicated File* in ISO-7816) and, at line 6, the file (*Elementary File*) containing the key. At line 9, the encryption is performed: the Initialization Vector and the plaintext are sent to the token which replies with the corresponding ciphertext.

We describe in detail the APDU format specification of SELECT FILE command at line 3:

CLA value 0x00 indicates that the command is ISO-7816 inter-industry;

INS value 0xA4 corresponds to inter-industry SELECT FILE (*cf.* [11], Sect. 6);
P1 value 0x04 codes a direct selection of a Dedicated File by name;
P2 value 0x0C selects the first record, returning no additional information about the file;
Lc the tokens is operating in extended APDU mode, thus this field is 3 bytes long. Value 0x000006 indicates the length 6 of the subsequent field;
data contains the actual ASCII-encoded name ("PUBLIC") of the DF to be selected;
SW1,SW2 the status word 0x90 0x00 returned by the token indicates that the command was successfully executed.

It is important to notice that the C_EncryptInit function call sends no APDU to the token: we can infer that the low level protocol of the encryption operation is stateless and the state is managed inside the PKCS#11 library. This example shows that the mapping between the PKCS#11 layer and the APDU layer is not 1-to-1 and the PKCS#11 library is in some cases delegated to implement critical operations, such as maintaining the state of encryption. We will see how this leads to attacks in Sect. 4.

3 Threat Model

In this section we analyze various threat scenarios and classify them based on the attacker capabilities.

We consider a typical scenario in which the target token is connected to a desktop or laptop computer running in a single-user configuration. We describe the threat model by focusing on the following sensitive targets:

PIN If the attacker discovers the PIN he might be able to perform cryptographic operations with the device when it is connected to the user's host or in case he has physical access to it;

Cryptographic operations The attacker might try to perform cryptographic operations with the token, independently of his knowledge of the PIN;

Cryptographic keys The attacker might try to learn sensitive keys either by exploiting PKCS#11 API-level attacks such as Clulow's wrap-and-decrypt [6] (cf. Subsect. 2.1) or by exploiting the new APDU-level vulnerabilities we will discuss in Sect. 4.

3.1 Administrator Privileges

If the attacker has administration privileges, he basically has complete control of the host. He can modify the driver, replace the libraries, intercept any input for the users and attach to any running process[2]. As such, he can easily learn the PIN when it is typed or when it is sent to the library, use the PIN to perform any cryptographic operations and exploit any PKCS#11 or APDU level attacks to extract cryptographic keys in the clear.

---
[2] This is typically done by using the operating system debug API to instrument or inspect the target process memory. Examples are the Event Tracing API for Windows and the Linux ptrace() syscall.

3.2 User Privileges

The most common situation is when the attacker has user privileges. In this case we have different scenarios:

Monolithic. The application is run by the same user as the attacker and directly links both the PKCS#11 and the APDU library. The attacker can easily sniff and alter data by attaching to the application process and by intercepting library calls. The attacker can easily learn the PIN when it is sent to the library, use the PIN to perform any cryptographic operations and exploit any PKCS#11 or APDU level attacks to extract cryptographic keys in the clear.

Separate Authentication Mechanism. The application is run by the same user as the attacker and directly links the PKCS#11 library but authentication is managed by a separate software or hardware which is not directly accessible with user privileges. Examples could be a separate dialog for entering the PIN running at different privileges or some biometric sensor integrated in a USB token. The attacker cannot directly log into the token but can still sniff and alter data by attaching to the application process and by intercepting library calls. If the attacker is able to place in the middle and alter data, he could additionally exploit PKCS#11 or APDU-level attacks to extract cryptographic keys in the clear. Notice that, knowing the PIN, this can be done by simply opening a new independent session. Without knowledge of the PIN, instead, the attacker needs a reliable Man-In-The-Middle (MITM) attack.

Separate Privileges. If the middleware layer is run as separate process at a different privilege level, the attacker cannot attach to it and observe or alter APDUs. The attacker can still try to access the token directly, so if there are ways

Table 1. Threats versus attackers and applications.

Attacker	Application	Attacker can access		Attacker can exploit			
		PKCS#11	APDU	PIN	PKCS#11	APDU passive	APDU active
Admin	Any	✓	✓	✓	✓	✓	✓
User	Monolithic	✓	✓	✓	✓	✓	✓
	Sep. Auth.	✓	✓	✗	✓[1]	✓	✓[1]
	Sep. Privileges	✓	✗	✓	✓	✗	✗
	Sep. Auth.&Priv.	✓	✗	✗	✓[1]	✗	✗
Physical	Any	✗	✓	✓[2]	✓[1]	✓[3]	✓[1,3]

[1] Requires MITM.
[2] Through a keylogger or a USB sniffer.
[3] Only APDU payloads, cannot access middleware memory.

to bypass authentication he might be able to perform cryptographic operations and exploit PKCS#11 or APDU-level attacks.

3.3 Physical Access

If the attacker has physical access to the user host he might install physical key-loggers and USB sniffers. This is not always feasible for example if the devices are integrated, as in laptops. In the case of a key-logger, the attacker can easily discover the PIN if it is typed through the keyboard. The case of directly sniffing APDUs passing, e.g., through USB, is interesting and more variegated since different sensitive data could be transmitted through the APDU layer, as we will illustrate in Sect. 4.

3.4 Summary of the Threat Model

Table 1 summarizes what the various attackers can access and exploit in different settings. We distinguish between passive APDU attacks, where the attacker just sniffs the APDU trace, and active APDU attacks, where APDUs are injected or altered by the attacker. In some cases active APDU attacks require mounting a MITM, e.g., when the PIN is now known or when the attacker does not have access to the middleware, as in physical attacks.

We point out that, if the application is monolithic, an attacker with user privileges is as powerful as one with administrative privileges. The maximum degree of protection is when the application offers separate authentication and the middleware runs with different privileges. We notice that the attacker can still perform PKCS#11-level attacks without knowing the PIN by mounting a MITM and altering or hijacking the API calls. Finally, physical attacker can in principle perform all the attacks, except the ones that are based on inspecting process (or middleware) memory and assuming, in some cases, MITM capabilities.

4 APDU-Level Attacks on Real Devices

We have tested the following five devices from different manufacturers for possible APDU-level vulnerabilities.

- Aladdin eToken PRO (USB)
- Athena ASEKey (USB)
- RSA SecurID 800 (USB)
- Safesite Classic TPC IS V1 (smartcard)
- Siemens CardOS V4.3b (smartcard)

For readability, in the following we will refer to the above tokens and smartcards as eToken PRO, ASEKey, SecurID, Safesite Classic and Siemens CardOS, respectively. These five devices are the ones tested in [5] for which we could find APDU-level attacks. It is worth noticing that we could not inspect the APDU traces of some other devices analyzed in [5] because they encrypt the APDU-level communication. We leave the study of the security of encrypted APDUs as a future work.

We have systematically performed various tests on selected sensitive operations and we have observed the corresponding APDU activity. We have found possible vulnerabilities concerning the login phase (Subsect. 4.1), symmetric sensitive keys (Subsect. 4.2), key attributes (Subsect. 4.3), private RSA session keys (Subsect. 4.4).

Quite surprisingly, we have found that, in some cases, cryptographic keys appear as cleartext in the library which performs cryptographic operations in software. Moreover, we have verified that the logic behind PKCS#11 key attributes is, in most of the cases, implemented in the library. We have also found that all devices are vulnerable to attacks that leak the PIN if the middleware is not property isolated and run with a different privilege (which is usually not the case). Moreover, attackers with physical access could sniff an authentication session through the USB port and brute-force the PIN once the authentication protocol has been reverse-engineered.

Our findings have been timely reported to manufacturers following a *responsible disclosure* process and are described in detail in the following subsections. Official answers from manufacturers, if any, will be made available at https://secgroup.dais.unive.it/projects/apduattacks/.

4.1 Authentication

In PKCS#11 the function C_Login allows a user to authenticate, in order to activate a session and perform cryptographic operations. For the five devices examined, we found that authentication is implemented in two different forms: plaintext and challenge-response.

Plain Authentication. This authentication method is used by Safesite Classic and Siemens CardOS. When the function C_Login is called, the PIN is sent as plaintext to the token to authenticate the session. This operation does not return any session handle at the APDU level, meaning that the low level protocol is stateless: a new login is transparently performed by the library before any privileged command is executed. The fact the PIN is sent as plaintext allows to easily sniff the PIN even without having control of the computer, for example using a hardware USB sniffer.

In Table 2 we report an excerpt of a real APDU session trace of the C_Login function. We can see that Safesite Classic and Siemens CardOS tokens use (line 4) the standard ISO-7816 VERIFY command to authenticate: the PIN, in red color/italic, is sent as a ASCII encoded string ("1234" and "12345", respectively).

Challenge-Response Authentication. In the eToken PRO, ASEKey and SecurID tokens the function C_Login executes a challenge-response protocol to

Table 2. APDU session trace of the PKCS#11 C_Login function for the five devices.

	C_Login session trace	Device
0	# Custom Get challenge:	
1	APDU: 80 17 00 00 08	
2	SW: df 89 61 34 62 05 13 36 90 00	Aladdin
3	# Custom External authenticate:	eToken PRO
4	APDU: 80 11 00 11 0a 10 08 64 d5 97 15 4a 44 eb 23	
5	SW: 90 00	
0	# Standard ISO-7816 Get challenge:	
1	APDU: 00 84 00 00 00 00 08	
2	SW: bb 8b ec f8 a3 a8 62 63 90 00	Athena ASEKey
3	# Standard ISO-7816 External authenticate:	USB
4	APDU: 00 82 02 00 00 00 18 00 00 11 12 8f e3 fa a6 a8 a8 07 10 47 e0	
	af 90 65 20 42 43 2d f0 47 16	
5	SW: 90 00	
0	# Send 8 random bytes:	
1	APDU: 80 50 81 01 08 c9 ff 3c d6 63 a2 13 b0	
2	SW: 61 1c	
3	# Standard ISO-7816 Get response:	
4	APDU: 00 c0 00 00 1c	RSA SecurID 800
5	SW: 35 34 95 09 14 02 1d 3a 03 2a 81 01 03 2a̅ ec a5 97 cc d0 ea 8a	
	cb 05 59 94 78 e1 04 90 00	
6	# Custom External authenticate:	
7	APDU: 84 82 03 00 10 fb bb dd 65 5f 0d 70 cc 41 a7 23 47 1d af b0 72	
8	SW: 90 00	
0	# Standard ISO-7816 Select file:	
1	APDU: 00 a4 04 00 0c a0 00 00 00 18 0a 00 00 01 63 42 00	
2	SW: 90 00	Safesite Classic
3	# Standard ISO-7816 Verify:	TPC IS V1
4	APDU: 00 20 00 01 08 31 32 33 34 00 00 00 00	
5	SW: 90 00	
0	# Standard ISO-7816 Select file:	
1	APDU: 00 a4 04 0c 0c a0 00 00 00 63 50 4b 43 53 2d 31 35	
2	SW: 90 00	Siemens CardOS
3	# Standard ISO-7816 Verify:	V4.3b
4	APDU: 00 20 00 81 05 31 32 33 34 35	
5	SW: 90 00	

authenticate the session: the middleware generates a response based on the challenge provided by the token and the PIN given by the user. At the APDU level, eToken PRO and ASEKey do not return any session handle thus, as for the previous devices, the low level protocol is stateless and a new login is transparently performed by the library before executing any privileged command. Instead, on the SecurID the challenge-response routine is executed only once for each session as it returns a session handle.

PKCS#11 standard allows PIN values to contain any valid UTF8 character, but the token may impose restrictions. Assuming that the PIN is numeric and short (4–6 digits), which is the most common scenario, an attacker is able to bruteforce the PIN offline, *i.e.* without having access to the device, as it is enough to have one APDU session trace containing one challenge and one response. As a proof of concept, we have reverse engineered the authentication protocol of eToken PRO and ASEKey implemented in the PKCS#11 library. This allowed us to try all possible PINs and check whether or not the response computed from the challenge and the PIN matches the one in the trace.

In Table 2 we can see that eToken PRO makes use of proprietary commands to request the challenge and provide the response, while ASEKey uses the standard ISO-7816 `GET CHALLENGE` and `EXTERNAL AUTHENTICATE` commands. We have not reverse engineered the challenge-response protocol of the SecurID token but, looking at the APDU session trace, we can identify a three-steps authentication protocol. At line 1 eight random bytes are sent to the token; then, a standard ISO-7816 `GET RESPONSE` command is issued to retrieve the challenge (highlighted in red and italic at line 5) and the identifier of the PKCS#11 session (highlighted in green and overlined). Line 7 contains the response generated by the middleware.

On both plain and challenge-response authentication, we have found that tokens implement no protection against MITM: if an attacker can place himself in the middle of the connection he could exploit an authentication exchange to alter user commands or inject his own ones.

4.2 Sensitive Symmetric Keys

We discovered that in Siemens CardOS, eToken PRO and SecurID encryption and decryption under a sensitive symmetric key is performed entirely by the middleware. As a consequence, the value of the sensitive key is sent out of the token as plaintext. This violates the basic PKCS#11 property stating that sensitive keys should never be exported in the clear. We also found that ASEKey surprisingly reuses the authentication challenge (sent in the clear) as the value of freshly generated DES keys.

In the following, we describe the four devices separately.

Siemens CardOS V4.3b. This smartcard does not allow to create symmetric keys with `CKA_TOKEN` set to true, meaning that symmetric keys will always be session keys. According to PKCS#11 documentation, session keys are keys that are not stored permanently in the device: once the session is closed these keys are destroyed. Notice that this does not mean that sensitive session keys should be exported in the clear out of the token. What distinguishes a session key from a token key is *persistence*: the former will be destroyed when the session is closed while the latter will persist in the token.

We observed that encryption under a sensitive key sends no APDUs to the token. This gives evidence that encryption takes place entirely in the middleware. Moreover, we verified that even `C_GenerateKey` function does not send any APDU: in fact, it just calls the library function `pkcs11_CryptGenerateRandom` to generate a random key value whose value is stored (and used) only inside the library.

Aladdin eToken PRO. In Table 3 (first row), we show that symmetric key generation in eToken PRO is performed by the middleware. We can see, in red and italic, a DES key value sent to the token in the clear.

The value of symmetric keys stored in the eToken PRO can be read by using the proprietary APDU command 0x18. No matter which attributes are set for the key, its value can be read. We tested it over a DES key with attributes CKA_TOKEN, CKA_PRIVATE, CKA_SENSITIVE set to true. In order to perform this attack a valid login is required. Since symmetric key operations are performed by the library, this APDU command is used to retrieve the key from the token before performing operations in software.

As an example, in Table 3 (second row) we see part of a C_WrapKey operation that retrieves a the DES cryptographic key from the token. We can see the value of the key in the clear.

RSA SecurID 800. In Table 3 (third row), we show that symmetric key generation in SecurID is also performed by the middleware. We can see, in red and italic, a 3DES key value sent to the token in the clear.

We were also able to retrieve the value of a sensitive key stored inside the SecurID by just issuing the correct APDU command. In fact, when trying to use the C_GetAttributeValue function, the library correctly returns the CKR_ATTRIBUTE_SENSITIVE error. However, what really happens is that the key

Table 3. Leakage of sensitive symmetric keys during PKCS#11 operations.

	APDU session trace	Token
0	# DES Key generation: red/italic = plain key value sent to the token	
1	APDU: 80 16 01 00 2b 01 01 02 02 02 40 01 03 02 00 18 04 04 11 11 11 11 10 18 17 3f ff ff ff ff 01 08 *3f 44 5f c4 eb 76 f1 86* 06 64 65 73 6b 65 79 00	C_GenerateKey sample on Aladdin eToken PRO
2	SW: 90 00	
0	# Fetch the key: green/overlined = attributes, red/italic = plain key value, blue/underlined = label	
1	APDU: 80 18 00 00 04 0e 02 00 00 18	C_WrapKey sample on Aladdin
2	SW: 17 3f ff ff ff ff 01 08 *3f 44 5f c4 eb 76 f1 86* 06 <u>64 65 73 6b 65 79 00</u> 90 00	eToken PRO
0	# 3DES Secret key generation	
1	APDU: 80 16 00 00 1a 72 35 *be 4e aa de 2d 47 72 b2 8b 47 5f de 63 4d 7e 30 a5 f0 ac 5f c0 56 c6 90*	C_GenerateKey sample on RSA SecurID 800
2	SW: 90 00	
0	# 3DES key is read in the clear even if CKA_SENSITIVE is set to true	
1	APDU: 00 c0 00 00 18	C_GetAttributeValue sample on RSA
2	SW: *36 90 fa c9 4e 82 55 b1 71 1d 81 e4 3c d1 bd fa 44 9c bb c3 b1 8b 1e 8d* 90 00	SecurID 800
0	# Get challenge (Standard ISO-7816):	
1	APDU: 00 84 00 00 00 00 08	
2	SW: *b7 c8 14 4b 4e 5f e6 3e* 90 00	
3	# External authenticate (Standard ISO-7816):	
4	APDU: 00 82 02 00 00 00 18 00 00 11 12 95 fa da de 0d 70 42 d9 21 c2 27 a4 8b af 7a 8b 90 47 ae 54	
5	SW: 90 00	C_GenerateKey
6	# Get an RSA modulus (in red/italic)	sample on Athena
7	SW: *79 23 57 33 9a be 2a dd ba ae 2e 09 4c d0 3d 57 8b d0 07 e4 cb* ... (omitted) ... *19 6d 15 ea b6 aa cc 2b e8 30 c3 e8 cf* 90 00	ASEKey
8	# Send the encrypted key to the token	
9	APDU: 80 24 00 80 00 00 a0 *20 5b f1 f9 cd 67 c8 3d e0 cf 9b 1b c7 ad* ... (omitted) ... *33 0b 85 1a 27 7e cd 69 95 71 ca 2e 88 33 a7 f6 4a 97 22 a0*	
10	SW: 90 00	

```
0  # Manage security environment
1  APDU: 00 22 41 b6 06 80 01 12 84 01 07
2  SW:     90 00
3  # Custom perform security operation
4  APDU: 80 2a 9e ac 16 90 14 59 b7 b5 0c 2e 69 4e 3f 7e 2f 06 7f 07 1d 8e dd de ba 8c c0
5  SW:     61 80
6  # Custom getData
7  APDU: 80 c0 00 00 80
8  SW:     9d 70 aa 8d c4 af 7a 88 ba e4 6c ab 47 3e 02 19 81 e5 85 53 8a 6a 1b 83 8c 73 39
        29 9e 49 bb 24 a7 27 4f 8e 38 60 b6 d1 71 c6 92 75 58 fe 33 78 d2 fe 99 5c 96 4e
        3e 43 15 9d 67 f9 db 7b 8b 3c 29 d4 97 d5 ec 2e 46 7e 2b c9 c4 92 0f 38 eb 65 11
        2b e1 ba 61 33 7c a1 03 62 f4 2c 2c f2 52 85 2a ee ab 77 ca 6e 37 8e 3b 5a 57 dd
        c1 64 ea d0 76 71 2a 46 0b bc d4 2a ef c0 6c 32 77 c3 5e 79 90 00
```

Listing 1.3. Forced signature sample

is read from the token but the library just avoids to return it. In Table 3 (fourth row) we can see (in red and italic) the value of the sensitive key leaked by the token.

Athena ASEKey. The most surprising behaviour is shown by the ASEKey: the value of token sensitive symmetric keys cannot be read arbitrarily via APDU commands, as they are stored in a separated Dedicated File (DF) which requires authentication. Nonetheless the key value is unnecessarily leaked when the key is generated.

In Table 3 (fifth row) we report an excerpt of APDU session for the C_GenerateKey function. We notice that C_GenerateKey sends (line 9) the key encrypted under RSA with a modulus (line 7), using the public exponent 0x010001. In fact, the library encrypts the whole Elementary File (EF) containing the key value, that is going to be written in the token. This means that special care was taken to avoid leaking the value as plaintext when importing it in the token. Unfortunately the key value already appeared in the clear: quite surprisingly, key generation re-uses the 8-bytes random string which is used by the authentication step (line 2) as the sensitive key value.

As a proof of concept, we encrypted a zero-filled 8-bytes buffer using the C_Encrypt function with the generated key and a null initialization vector. We then performed the same encryption using the 8-bytes challenge as the DES key value obtaining the same value.

4.3 Bypassing Attribute Values

In all five tokens examined, PKCS#11 attributes are interpreted by the middleware and do not have any import on the internal behaviour of the token. We performed a simple test by signing a text using an RSA key having the attribute CKA_SIGN set to false:

1. take a private RSA key with CKA_SIGN false;
2. verify that it cannot sign a message via the PKCS#11 API, as expected;

```
>>> signed = 0x9d70aa8dc4af7a88bae46cab473e021981e585538a6a1b838c7339299e49bb24a7274f8e3860b6
    d171c6927558fe3378d2fe995c964e3e43159d67f9db7b8b3c29d497d5ec2e467e2bc9c4920f38eb65112be1b
    a61337ca10362f42c2cf252852aeeab77ca6e378e3b5a57ddc164ead076712a460bbcd42aefc06c3277c35e79
>>> modulus =0xc1886b5f26ad5349426b8e8bfc9f73385d14f6cf2b2f1d95b080ae2df7a1db11b91d36db33f3b9
    8f16871774711c03b22d7d97939062031df2d15371173b468f9986701d144f315005ec99a71b226fc71b95660
    8c60747ceb4ac0c3725b7d04484ac286196975f18911361e28ec50b661273362131b4a4183e01667b090c96f9
>>> pubkey = 0x010001
>>> hex(pow(signed, pubkey, modulus))
'0x1ffffffffffffffffffffffffffffffffffffffffffffffffffffffffffffffffffffffffffffffffffffff
'ffffffffffffffffffffffffffffffffffffffffffffffffffffffffffffffffffffffffffffffffffffffff
'ffffffffffffffffffffffffffff0059b7b50c2e694e3f7e2f067f071d8edddeba8ccOL
```

Listing 1.4. Signature verification in Python

3. perform the sign operation manually, via APDU, using the private key and the message. Some tokens use the standard ISO-7816 command PERFORM SECURITY OPERATION and some others use a proprietary command but, in both cases after sniffing, it is easy to replicate any valid APDU trace for a signature.

This confirms that the low-level behaviour of the token is not compliant to PKCS#11 specification as it allows to perform signature under a key that has CKA_SIGN attribute set to false. Since the behaviour of all five tokens is similar, in Listing 1.3 we illustrate the case of Safesite Classic as a representative APDU example trace. At line 4 the message is sent to the token and, at line 8, the corresponding signature is returned.

We can verify that signature corresponds using Python shell, as shown in Listing 1.4. In particular, notice that the obtained message corresponds to the one we signed.

4.4 RSA Session Keys

When using session RSA keys on the eToken PRO, we discovered that key generation, encryption and decryption operations are performed inside the library. This means that the value of the private key is exposed in the clear out of the token.

Even if one might regard to session keys as less important than long-term keys, as we already discussed in Subsect. 4.2 for Siemens CardOS, PKCS#11 still requires that if such keys are sensitive they should not be exported out the token in the clear. For example we can generate a session key which, at some point before the end of the session, is persisted in the token's memory by calling the C_CopyObject function. Clearly this newly created object cannot be considered secure as the value of the private RSA key has already been leaked in the clear out of the token.

5 Security Analysis

In Table 4 we summarize the APDU-level attacks we found on the five devices. In the columns labelled PKCS#11 we also report the PKCS#11 attacks from [5],

Table 4. Summary of the vulnerabilities found.

Token	Auth.	Sensitive symmetric keys		Bypassing attribute values	RSA session keys	
		PKCS#11[1]	APDU		PKCS#11[1]	APDU
eToken PRO	✓[2]	✓	✓	✓	✗	✓[4]
ASEKey	✓[2]	✗	✓[3]	✓	✗	✗
SecurID	✓[2]	✓[5]	✓	✓	✗	✗
Safesite Classic	✓	✗	✗	✓	✗	✗
Siemens CardOS	✓	✗	✓[4]	✓	✗	✗

[1] PKCS#11-level attacks discovered in [5], for comparison.
[2] Requires reverse engineering of the authentication algorithm and bruteforcing.
[3] Leakage occurs only during generation.
[4] Requires access to middleware memory.
[5] Possible for RSA Authentication Client version $< 3.5.3$.

for comparison. In particular, the only token that allows for PKCS#11 Clulow-style attack extracting a sensitive key in the clear is eToken PRO. For SecurID we reported that it was possible to directly read the value of sensitive symmetric keys and RSA released a fix starting from RSA Authentication Client version $3.5.3$.[3] In the literature we found no known API-level attacks on sensitive keys for the remaining devices.

All devices are affected by attacks on the PIN, some of which requiring reverse engineering and brute forcing, and by attacks bypassing key attributes. For what concerns sensitive keys, only Safesite Classic is immune to attacks. For the remaining four tokens we have reported new attacks that compromise sensitive keys that are instead secure when accessed from the PKCS#11 API.

In order to clarify under which conditions the attacks are possible we cross-compare Table 1 with Table 4 producing table Table 5. In particular, for each device we take the vulnerabilities reported in Table 4 and we check from Table 1 if the combination attacker/application offers the necessary conditions for the attack. We omit the Admin attacker as it is in fact equivalent to the User attacker when the application is monolithic. In particular, we observe that:

User/Monolithic the attacker can attach to the process and eavesdrop the PIN at the PKCS#11 level. Knowing the PIN the attacker can perform any operation and inspect the process memory. So all attacks of Table 4 are enabled;

User/Separate authentication mechanism the attacker cannot eavesdrop the PIN directly. Interestingly PKCS#11-level attacks and attribute bypass are still possible through a MITM on the middleware. Moreover, APDU-level attacks on keys are still valid as they only require to eavesdrop the APDUs;

User/Separate privileges the attacker can still eavesdrop the PIN and work at the PKCS#11 level but all APDU-level attacks are prevented. In this setting the

---

[3] See https://secgroup.dais.unive.it/projects/tookan/.

Table 5. Summary of vulnerabilities with respect to attackers and applications.

Attacker	Application	Auth.	Sensitive symmetric keys		Bypass attribute values	RSA session keys	
			PKCS#11[4]	APDU		PKCS#11[4]	APDU
Aladdin eToken PRO							
User	Monolithic		✓	✓	✓	✓	✗	✓
User	Sep. Auth.		✗	✓[1]	✓	✓[1]	✗	✓
User	Sep. Privileges		✓	✓	✗	✗	✗	✗
User	Sep. Auth.&Priv.		✗	✓[1]	✗	✗	✗	✗
Physical	Any		✓[2,5]	✓[1]	✓	✓[1]	✗	✗
Athena ASEKey							
User	Monolithic		✓	✗	✓	✓	✗	✗
User	Sep. Auth.		✗	✗	✓[6]	✓[1]	✗	✗
User	Sep. Privileges		✓	✗	✗	✗	✗	✗
User	Sep. Auth.&Priv.		✗	✗	✗	✗	✗	✗
Physical	Any		✓[2,5]	✗	✓	✓[1]	✗	✗
RSA SecurID 800							
User	Monolithic		✓	✓[7]	✓	✓	✗	✗
User	Sep. Auth.		✗	✓[1,7]	✓	✓[1]	✗	✗
User	Sep. Privileges		✓	✓[7]	✗	✗	✗	✗
User	Sep. Auth.&Priv.		✗	✓[1,7]	✗	✗	✗	✗
Physical	Any		✓[2,5]	✓[1,7]	✓	✓[1]	✗	✗
Safesite Classic TPC IS V1							
User	Monolithic		✓	✗	✗	✓	✗	✗
User	Sep. Auth.		✗	✗	✗	✓[1]	✗	✗
User	Sep. Privileges		✓	✗	✗	✗	✗	✗
User	Sep. Auth.&Priv.		✗	✗	✗	✗	✗	✗
Physical	Any		✓[2]	✗	✗	✓[1]	✗	✗
Siemens CardOS V4.3b							
User	Monolithic		✓	✗	✓	✓	✗	✗
User	Sep. Auth.		✗	✗	✓	✓[1]	✗	✗
User	Sep. Privileges		✓	✗	✗	✗	✗	✗
User	Sep. Auth.&Priv.		✗	✗	✗	✗	✗	✗
Physical	Any		✓[2]	✗	✗	✓[1]	✗	✗

[1] Requires MITM.
[2] Through a keylogger or a USB sniffer.
[3] Only APDU payloads, cannot access middleware memory.
[4] PKCS#11-level attacks discovered in [5], for comparison.
[5] Requires reverse engineering of the authentication algorithm and bruteforcing.
[6] Leakage occurs only during generation.
[7] Possible for RSA Authentication Client version < 3.5.3.

only insecure token is eToken PRO since it allows for PKCS#11-level attacks on sensitive keys;

User/Separate authentication and privileges this is the more secure setting: the attacker con only perform PKCS#11-level attacks on eToken PRO through a MITM, since he cannot learn the PIN. All the other tokens are secure;

Physical/Any application through a keylogger or a USB sniffer the attacker can learn the PIN. In case of a USB sniffer, for the tokens adopting challange-response it is also necessary to reverse-engineer the protocol in the library and perform brute-forcing on the PIN. APDU-level attacks are possible only when the keys are transmitted from/to the device. So, for eToken PRO RSA session keys and Siemens CardOS symmetric keys the attacks are prevented, as keys are directly handled by the library and are never transmitted to the device. Other attacks can be performed only through a MITM at the USB level.

5.1 Fixes and Mitigations

Compliant PKCS#11 devices should implement all the cryptographic operations inside the hardware. This would prevent all of the attacks we have discussed so far, except for the ones on authentication. However, fixing this at the hardware level requires to redesign the device and is probably just not affordable, in general.

We have seen, however, that having separate authentication and privileges is a highly secure setting that fixes the problem of cryptographic operations implemented at the library level and, at the same time, protects PIN authentication. It is worth noticing that running the middleware with separate privileges can be done transparently to the application while having separate authentication requires to modify the application so that the login step is managed by separate software or hardware.

An alternative way to mitigate attacks on PIN, with no changes in applications, could exploit the OTP functionality of the devices with a display, such as SecurID. A one-time PIN might be generated by the token and shown on the display asking the user to combine it with the secret token PIN. In this way, offline brute-forcing would be slowed down by the longer, combined PIN and, even if successful, would require physical access to the token in order to re-authenticate since part of the PIN is freshly generated by the token each time the user authenticates.

6 Conclusion

We have presented a new threat model for the PKCS#11 middleware and we have analysed the APDU-level implementation of the PKCS#11 API for five commercially available devices. Our findings show that all devices present APDU-level attacks that, for four of them, make it possible to leak sensitive keys in the clear. The only smartcard immune to attacks to keys is Safesite Classic. We have also found that all devices are vulnerable to attacks that leak the PIN if the middleware is not property isolated and run with a different privilege (which is usually not the case). Moreover, attackers with physical access could sniff an authentication session through the USB port and brute-force the PIN once the authentication protocol has been reverse-engineered.

We have reported our finding to manufacturers following a responsible disclosure principle and we are interacting with some of them to provide further information and advices.

References

1. Anderson, R.: The correctness of crypto transaction sets. In: Christianson, B., Crispo, B., Malcolm, J.A., Roe, M. (eds.) Security Protocols 2000. LNCS, vol. 2133, pp. 128–141. Springer, Heidelberg (2001)
2. Barbu, G., Giraud, C., Guerin, V.: Embedded eavesdropping on Java card. In: Gritzalis, D., Furnell, S., Theoharidou, M. (eds.) SEC 2012. IFIP AICT, vol. 376, pp. 37–48. Springer, Heidelberg (2012)
3. Bond, M.: Attacks on cryptoprocessor transaction sets. In: Koç, Ç.K., Naccache, D., Paar, C. (eds.) CHES 2001. LNCS, vol. 2162, pp. 220–234. Springer, Heidelberg (2001)
4. Bond, M., Anderson, R.: API level attacks on embedded systems. IEEE Comput. Mag. **34**(10), 67–75 (2001)
5. Bortolozzo, M., Centenaro, M., Focardi, R., Steel, G.: Attacking and fixing PKCS#11 security tokens. In: Proceedings of the 17th ACM Conference on Computer and Communications Security (CCS 2010), pp. 260–269. ACM (2010)
6. Clulow, J.: On the Security of PKCS #11. In: Walter, C.D., Koç, Ç.K., Paar, C. (eds.) CHES 2003. LNCS, vol. 2779, pp. 411–425. Springer, Heidelberg (2003)
7. De Cock, D., Wouters, K., Schellekens, D., Singelee, D., Preneel, B.: Threat modelling for security tokens in web applications. In: Chadwick, D., Preneel, B. (eds.) Communications and Multimedia Security, pp. 183–193. Springer, Cham (2005)
8. de Koning, G., Gans, J., de Ruiter.: The smartlogic tool: analysing and testing smart card protocols. In: Fifth IEEE International Conference on Software Testing, Verification and Validation, ICST 2012, pp. 864–871 (2012)
9. Delaune, S., Kremer, S., Steel, G.: Formal analysis of PKCS#11 and proprietary extensions. J. Comput. Secur. **18**(6), 1211–1245 (2010)
10. Gkaniatsou, A., McNeill, F., Bundy, A., Steel, G., Focardi, R., Bozzato, C.: Getting to know your card: reverse-engineering the smart-card application protocol data unit. In: Proceedings of the 31st Annual Computer Security Applications Conference, ACSAC 2015, pp. 441–450. ACM (2015)
11. ISO, IEC 7816–4.: Identification cards - Integrated circuit cards - Part 4: Organization, security and commands for interchange (2013)
12. Longley, D., Rigby, S.: An automatic search for security flaws in key management schemes. Comput. Secur. **11**(1), 75–89 (1992)
13. Murdoch, S.J., Drimer, S., Anderson, R.J., Bond, M.: Chip and PIN is broken. In: 31st IEEE Symposium on Security and Privacy (S&P 2010), 16–19 May 2010, Berleley/Oakland, California, USA, pp. 433–446 (2010)
14. OASIS Standard: PKCS #11 Cryptographic Token Interface Base Specification Version 2.40. http://docs.oasis-open.org/pkcs11/pkcs11-base/v2.40/pkcs11-base-v2.40.html

15. RSA Laboratories: PKCS #11 v2.30: Cryptographic Token Interface Standard. http://www.emc.com/emc-plus/rsa-labs/standards-initiatives/pkcs-11-cryptographic-token-interface-standard.htm
16. Schneier, B., Shostack, A., et al.: Breaking up is hard to do: modeling security threats for smart cards. In: USENIX Workshop on Smart Card Technology, Chicago, Illinois, USA (1999). http://www.counterpane.com/smart-card-threats.html
17. Shostack, A.: Experiences threat modeling at microsoft. In: Modeling Security Workshop. Department of Computing, Lancaster University, UK (2008)
18. Swiderski, F., Snyder, W.: Threat Modeling. Microsoft Press, Redmond (2004)
19. Wang, L., Wong, E., Dianxiang, X.: A threat model driven approach for security testing. In: Proceedings of the Third International Workshop on Software Engineering for Secure Systems, SESS 2007, p. 10, Washington, D.C, USA. IEEE Computer Society (2007)
20. Youn, P., Adida, B., Bond, M., Clulow, J., Herzog, J., Lin, A., Rivest, R., Anderson, R.: Robbing the bank with a theorem prover. Technical Report UCAM-CL-TR-644, University of Cambridge, August 2005

CloudRadar: A Real-Time Side-Channel Attack Detection System in Clouds

Tianwei Zhang[1(✉)], Yinqian Zhang[2], and Ruby B. Lee[1]

[1] Princeton University, Princeton, NJ, USA
{tianweiz,rblee}@princeton.edu
[2] The Ohio State University, Columbus, OH, USA
yinqian@cse.ohio-state.edu

Abstract. We present *CloudRadar*, a system to detect, and hence mitigate, cache-based side-channel attacks in multi-tenant cloud systems. *CloudRadar* operates by correlating two events: first, it exploits signature-based detection to identify when the protected virtual machine (VM) executes a cryptographic application; at the same time, it uses anomaly-based detection techniques to monitor the co-located VMs to identify abnormal cache behaviors that are typical during cache-based side-channel attacks. We show that correlation in the occurrence of these two events offer strong evidence of side-channel attacks. Compared to other work on side-channel defenses, *CloudRadar* has the following advantages: first, *CloudRadar* focuses on the root causes of cache-based side-channel attacks and hence is hard to evade using metamorphic attack code, while maintaining a low false positive rate. Second, *CloudRadar* is designed as a lightweight patch to existing cloud systems, which does not require new hardware support, or any hypervisor, operating system, application modifications. Third, *CloudRadar* provides real-time protection and can detect side-channel attacks within the order of milliseconds. We demonstrate a prototype implementation of *CloudRadar* in the OpenStack cloud framework. Our evaluation suggests *CloudRadar* achieves negligible performance overhead with high detection accuracy.

Keywords: Attack detection · Side-channel attacks · Performance counters · Cloud computing · Mitigation

1 Introduction

Infrastructure-as-a-Service (IaaS) cloud systems usually adopt the multi-tenancy feature to maximize resource utilization by consolidating virtual machines (VMs) leased by different tenants on the same physical machine. Virtualization technology is used to provide strong resource isolation between different VMs so each VM's memory content is not accessible to other co-tenant VMs. However, confidentiality breaches due to cross-VM side-channel attacks become a major concern. These attacks often operate on shared hardware resources and extract sensitive information, such as cryptographic keys, by making inferences on the observed side-channel events due to resource sharing. CPU caches are popular attack surfaces that lead to cross-VM side-channel attacks. Several prior work have shown the possibilities of cross-VM secret leakage via different levels of CPU caches [10,14,15,21,42,45,46].

Mitigating side-channel attacks in clouds is challenging. Past work on defeating side-channel attacks have some practical drawbacks: they mostly require significant changes to the hardware [6,20,39,40], hypervisors [17,18,31,33,35,48] or guest OSes [48], making them impractical to be deployed in current cloud datacenters. Other work have proposed to mitigate these attacks in cloud contexts by periodic VM migrations to reduce the co-location possibility between victim VMs and potential malicious VMs [25,47]. These heavy-weight approaches cannot effectively prevent side-channel leakage unless performed very frequently, making them less practical as VM co-location takes on the order of minutes [34] while side-channel attacks can be done on the order of milliseconds [21,42].

In this paper, we propose to detect side-channel attacks as they occur and prevent information leakage by triggering VM migration upon attack detection. However, side-channel attack detection is non-trivial. To do so, we must overcome several technical challenges in the application of traditional detection techniques, like signature-based detection and anomaly-based detection, to side-channel attacks. Signature-based side-channel detection exploits pattern recognition to detect known attack methods [4,5,13]. While low in false negatives for existing attacks, it fails to recognize new attacks; anomaly-based detection flags behaviors that deviate significantly from the established normal behaviors as attacks, which can potentially identify new attacks in addition to known ones. However, differentiating side-channel attacks from normal applications is difficult as these attacks just perform normal memory accesses which resemble some memory intensive applications.

To overcome these challenges, we design *CloudRadar*, a real-time system to detect the existence of cross-VM side-channel attacks in clouds. There are two key ideas behind *CloudRadar*: first, *the victim has unique micro-architectural behaviors when executing cryptographic applications that need protection from side-channel attacks.* So the cloud provider is able to identify the occurrence of such events using a signature-based detection method. Second, *the attacker VM creates an anomalous cache behavior when it is stealing information from the victim.* Such anomaly is inherent in all side-channel attacks due to the intentional cache contention with the victim to induce side-channel observations. By correlating these two types of events, *CloudRadar* is able to detect the stealthy cache side-channel attacks with high fidelity.

We implement *CloudRadar* as a lightweight extension to the virtual machine monitors. Specially, it (1) utilizes the existing host system facilities to collect micro-architectural features from hardware performance counters that are available in all modern commodity processors, and (2) non-intrusively interacts with the existing virtualization framework to monitor the VM's cache activities while inducing little performance penalty. Our evaluations show that it effectively detects side-channel attacks with high true positives and low false positives.

Compared to past work, *CloudRadar* has several advantages. First, *CloudRadar* focuses on the root causes of cache-based side-channel attacks and hence is hard to evade using different attack code, while maintaining a low false positive rate. Our approach is able to detect different types of side-channel attacks and their variants with a simple method. Second, *CloudRadar* is designed as a lightweight patch to existing cloud systems, which does not require new hardware support or hypervisor/OS modifications. Therefore *CloudRadar* can be immediately integrated into modern cloud fabric without making drastic changes to the underlying infrastructure. Third, *CloudRadar* exploits hardware performance counters to monitor VM activities, which detects side-channel attacks within the order of milliseconds with negligible performance overhead. Finally, *CloudRadar* requires no changes to the guest VM or the applications running in it, and thus is transparent to cloud customers.

To summarize, *CloudRadar* achieves the following contributions:

- The first approach to detect cache side-channel attacks using techniques that combine both signature-based and anomaly-based detection techniques.
- A novel technique to identify the execution of cryptographic applications, which are of interest in its own right.
- A non-intrusive system design that requires no changes to the hardware, hypervisor and guest VM and applications, which shows potential of immediate adoption in modern clouds.
- Full prototype implementation and extensive evaluation of the proposed approach and detection techniques.

The rest of this paper is organized as follows: Sect. 2 presents the background of cache side-channel attacks and defenses, and other detection systems based on performance counters. Section 3 presents the design challenges and system overview. Section 4 discusses the signature-based methods to detect cryptographic applications. Section 5 shows the anomaly-based method to detect side-channel activities. Section 6 presents the architecture and implementation of *CloudRadar*. Section 7 evaluates its performance and security. We discuss the limitations of *CloudRadar* and potential evasive attacks against it in Sect. 8. Section 9 concludes.

2 Background and Related Work

2.1 Cache Side-Channel Attacks

In cache-based side-channel attacks, the adversary exfiltrates sensitive information from the victim via shared CPU caches. The sensitive information are usually associated with cryptographic operations (*e.g.*, signing or decryption), but may also be extended to other applications [46]. Such sensitive information are leaked through secret-dependent control flows or data flows that lead to attacker-observable cache use patterns. The adversary, on the other hand, may exploit several techniques to manipulate data in the shared cache to deduce the victim's cache use patterns, and thereby make inference on the sensitive information that dictates these patterns. Two cache manipulation techniques are well-known for side-channel attacks:

Prime-Probe Attacks: The adversary allocates an array of cacheline-sized, cacheline-aligned memory blocks so that these memory blocks can exactly fill up a set of targeted cache sets. Then the adversary repeatedly performs two attack stages: in the PRIME stage, the adversary reads each memory block in the array to evict all the victim's data in these cache sets. The adversary waits for some time interval before performing the PROBE stage, in which he reads each memory block in the array again, and measures the time of memory accesses. Longer access time indicates one or more cache misses, which means this cache set has been accessed by the victim between the PRIME and PROBE stages. The adversary will repeat these two steps for significant amount of times to collect traces that, hopefully, overlap with the victim's execution of cryptographic operations, for offline analysis. This technique was first proposed by Percival [27], and then applied to the cloud environment in [14,21,28,45].

Flush-Reload Attacks: This type of attacks assumes identical memory pages can be shared among different VMs, so that the adversary and victim VMs may share the same pages containing cryptographic code or data. The adversary carefully selects a set of cacheline-sized, -aligned memory blocks from these shared pages. Then he also conducts two stages repeatedly: in the FLUSH stage, the adversary flushes the selected blocks out of the entire cache hierarchy (*e.g.*, using the *clflush* instruction). Then it waits for a fixed interval in which the victim might issue the critical instructions and fetch them back to the caches. In the RELOAD stage, the adversary reloads these memory blocks into the caches and measures the access time. A short access time for one memory block indicates a cache hit, so this block has been accessed by the victim during the interval. By repeating these two stages the adversary can obtain traces of the victim's memory accesses and deduce the confidential data. This FLUSH-RELOAD technique was first proposed in [11], and further demonstrated in different virtualized platforms with different variants [9,10,15,46].

2.2 Defenses Against Side-Channel Attacks

Previous studies propose to defeat cache-based Side-channel attacks in one of these three ways:

- **Partitioning caches:** One straightforward approach is to prevent the cache sharing by dividing the cache into different zones by sers or ways for different VMs. This can be achieved by hardware [6,19,40] or software methods [17,31].

- **Randomization:** This idea is to add randomization to the attacker's measurements, making it hard for him to get accurate information based on his observations. This includes random memory-to-cache mappings [39,40], cache prefetches [20], timers [18,35] and cache states [48].
- **Avoiding co-location:** New VM placement policies were designed [1,12] to reduce the co-location probability between victim and attacker VMs. Zhang et al. [47] and Moon et al. [25] frequently migrated the VMs to add difficulty of VM co-location for the attackers.

These approaches, when applied in the cloud setting, require significant modification of computing infrastructure, and thus are less attractive to cloud providers for practical adoption. In our study, we aim to build atop existing cloud framework a lightweight side-channel attack detection system to detect, and then mitigate, the attacks as they take place, while doing so without modifying guest OS, hypervisor or hardware.

2.3 Intrusion Detection Using Hardware Performance Counters

Hardware performance counters are a set of special-purpose registers built into ×86 (*e.g.*, Intel and AMD) and ARM processors. They work along with event selectors which specify certain hardware events, and update a counter after a hardware event occurs. Most modern processors provide a Performance Monitor Unit (PMU) that enables applications to control performance counters. One of the basic working modes of PMUs is the interrupt-based mode. Under this working mode, an interrupt is generated when the occurrences of a given event exceed a predefined threshold or a predefined amount of time has elapsed. Therefore, it makes both event-based sampling and time-based sampling possible.

Performance counters were originally designed for software debugging and system performance tuning. Recently, researchers exploited performance counters to detect security breaches and vulnerabilities [2,5,23,32,36,37,41,43]. The intuition is that the performance counters can reveal programs' execution characteristics, which can further reflect the programs' security states. Besides, performance counter detection introduces negligible performance overhead to the programs. Related to ours were signature-based side-channel attack detection using performance counters [4,5,13], which, unfortunately, could be easily evaded by smarter attackers by slightly changing cache probing pattern.

3 Design Challenges and Overview

In this paper, we explore an oft-discussed, but never successfully implemented, idea: exploiting hardware performance counters available in commodity processors to detect side-channel attacks that abuse processor caches. We first systematically explore the design challenges and then sketch our design of *CloudRadar*.

Threat Model and Assumptions. We focus on cross-VM side-channel threats in public IaaS clouds based on Last Level Caches (LLC) that are shared between processor cores. We assume the adversary is a legitimate user of the cloud service who is able to launch VMs in the cloud and has complete control of his VMs. We further assume the attacker is able to co-locate one of his VMs on the same server as the victim VM, and the two VMs will share the same processor package, thus the LLC, with non-negligible probability. We consider both PRIME-PROBE side-channel attacks and FLUSH-RELOAD side-channel attacks, which represent all known LLC side channels in modern computer systems.

3.1 Design Challenges

Signature-Based Detection. Signature-based detection approaches are widely used techniques in detecting network intrusion and malware, by comparing monitored application or network characteristics with pre-identified attack signatures. Similarly, to detect side-channel attacks, signatures of side-channel attacks must be generated from all known side-channel attack techniques and used to compare with events collected from production systems. Prior work [4,5] has preliminarily explored such ideas. Particularly, Demme et al. demonstrated in a simplified experiment setting that classification algorithms could successfully differentiate normal programs from PRIME-PROBE attack programs. The advantage of this approach is that they have high true positive rate in detecting known attacks. However, such detection method is very fragile and easy to evade by clever attackers. It also fails to recognize unknown attacks even with only subtle changes from existing ones. For instance, the attacker can change the memory access pattern (*e.g.*, sequential order, access frequency) in a PRIME-PROBE attack to evade signature-based detection.

Anomaly-Based Detection. In anomaly-based detection, the normal behaviors of benign applications are modeled and any substantial deviation from such models are detected as attacks. To detect side-channel attacks using such techniques, one can build models for benign application behaviors. Then for each VM to be monitored, we check if its behaviors conform to the models in the database. Compared to signature-based detection, anomaly-based detection can potentially identify "zero-day" attacks in addition to known ones. However, the difficulty of applying the anomaly-based approach to side-channel attacks stems from the challenge of precisely modeling benign application activities using performance counters. Cache side-channel attacks resemble benign memory intensive applications (*e.g.*, memory streaming application [24]), and therefore they are difficult to be differentiated using only hardware performance counters. False positive or false negative rates can be extremely high due to imprecise application behavior modeling. We are not aware of successful side-channel detection methods that are based on anomaly detection.

3.2 Design Overview

We design a side-channel attack detection system, *CloudRadar*, that combines both anomaly-based and signature-based techniques. The only features used by *CloudRadar* are hardware event values read from the performance counters available in commercial processors. The key insight that motivates *CloudRadar* is derived from our prior research in side-channel attacks: in cache side-channel attacks, to effectively exfiltrate secret information from the victim's sensitive execution, the attacker needs to repeatedly conduct side-channel activities (*e.g.*, PRIME-PROBE or FLUSH-RELOAD) and deduce his own cache uses based on the execution time of his own memory activities. Then he can make inferences on the victim's cache use pattern by looking at the statistics of his use of caches (*e.g.*, cache hits and cache misses). As such, the attacker's cache use patterns must be different when the victim executes sensitive operations so that the attacker can differentiate them in his own analysis. Our intuition is that *if such distinction can be detected by the attacker using timing channels, it can be detected by the cloud provider using performance counters.*

We design *CloudRadar* to monitor all VMs running on a cloud server and collect their cache use patterns using hardware performance counters. Once anomaly in cache use patterns are detected by *CloudRadar*, these anomalies will be correlated with the sensitive operations (usually cryptographic operations) in the co-located protected VM (*i.e.*, VMs owned by customers paying for such services). Strong correlation will serve as a good indicator of cache-based side-channel attacks.

Two key *technical challenges* in our design are (1) identifying the execution of the protected VM's sensitive operations without asking the customers to modify their applications and (2) detecting untrusted VM's abnormal cache use patterns. We aim to achieve both by using only values read from performance counters. To do so, we *first* propose to use signature-based techniques to detect sensitive applications of the protected VM, because they are conducted by honest parties and will not attempt to evade detection intentionally—a perfect target of signature-based detection techniques. *Second*, we propose to use anomaly-based detection techniques to detect abnormal cache patterns due to side-channel activities, as they are expected to vary due to different attack techniques and intensity. As side-channel attack detection is done via correlation with sensitive operations, false positives that are common challenges to anomaly detection techniques can be ruled out. We will highlight our design of these two components in Sects. 4 and 5.

4 Signature Detection of Cryptographic Applications

As sensitive operations that are targeted by side-channel attacks are usually cryptographic operations, we consider detection of cryptographic applications in this paper. Our working hypothesis here is that all cryptographic applications have unique signatures that can be easily identified by performance counters. In this section, we validate our hypothesis by a set of preliminary experiments.

4.1 Cryptographic Signature Generation

To generate signatures for detecting cryptographic applications, we need to select a proper hardware performance feature that uniquely characterizes a certain execution phase [30] of such applications.

Feature Selection. Modern processors allow a large number of events to be measured and reported by performance counters. The signature generated from a proper hardware event should satisfy two requirements: (1) *uniqueness*: the signatures of different applications should be highly distinguishable; (2) *repeatability*: the signature of a cryptographic application should be identical each time it is generated, regardless of the platform's configurations and the inputs.

We consider different events from three main categories: CPU events, cache events and kernel software events. We use the Fisher Score [7] to test the *repeatability* and *uniqueness* of these events in identifying cryptographic applications. Fisher Score is one of the most widely used methods to select features quickly. It finds the optimal feature so that the distances between data points in the feature space of different classes are maximized, while the distances between data points in the same class are minimized.

To test the *uniqueness* of an event, we use performance counters to measure the number of this event every $100\,\mu s$ during the execution of six representative cryptographic applications (*i.e.*, asymmetric cryptography: ElGamal and DSA from GnuPG; symmetric cryptography: AES and 3DES from OpenSSL; hash: HMAC from OpenSSL and SHA512 from GnuPG). We select 10 consecutive counter values (collected from $10 \times 100\,\mu s$) from the beginning of each application to form a timing sequence as one training data point. We repeat this 100 times for each cryptographic application. For each hardware event we considered, we calculate the Fisher Score using 600 training data points from the six cryptographic applications to test the uniqueness of this event in distinguishing different applications. Table 1 (Inter-class F-Score column) shows the results. Note a larger inter-class F-Score indicates a better *uniqueness* of this event. We can see some CPU events (instructions, branches and mispredicted branch instructions) and cache events (L1I load misses) are better candidates for signature generation. They vary significantly for different cryptographic applications. The events that rarely happen during the cryptographic execution (*e.g.*, context switches and page faults), or remain identical for different cryptographic applications (*e.g.*, CPU cycles or clock) fail to satisfy the *uniqueness* requirement.

To test the *repeatability* of an event, we repeat the above experiments on three servers with different hardware and software configurations. For each cryptographic application, we calculate the Fisher Score from 300 training data points collected from three servers. Table 1 (Intra-class F-Score column) shows the average Fisher Score of the six cryptographic programs. A smaller Intra-class F-Score indicates the signature with this event is more repeatable. We are able to find some events with good repeatability (*e.g.*, instructions, branches and mispredicted branch instructions).

Table 1. Fisher scores for different events.

Category	Events	Inter-class F-Score	Intra-class F-Score
CPU events	Instructions	1.49	0.13
	Branch instructions	1.55	0.14
	Mispredicted branch instructions	1.11	0.15
	CPU cycles	0.01	0.30
Cache events	L1D load accesses	0.37	0.72
	L1D load misses	0.69	0.42
	L1I load misses	1.14	0.20
	LLC load accesses	0.79	0.31
	LLC load misses	0.05	0.36
	iTLB load accesses	0.55	0.27
	iTLB load misses	0.23	0.21
	dTLB load accesses	0.22	0.63
	dTLB load misses	0.36	0.62
Software events	Context switches	0.00	0.00
	Page faults	0.00	0.00
	CPU clock	0.01	0.50

Based on the inter-class and intra-class Fisher Scores, we can choose the features with both good uniqueness and repeatability for signature matching. For instance, we can use *instructions* and *branch instructions* to conduct multi-feature classification. Further evaluations in Sect. 7 show one single feature (*i.e.*, *branch instructions*) is already enough to give good accuracy. So we will collect the number of *branch instructions* as the feature to generate signatures in the following sections.

Phase Selection. It has been shown in prior studies that programs run in different phases [30]. Therefore, another question we need to solve is which phase of the cryptographic application we should use to generate the signature. The selected phase should be able to distinguish cryptographic applications from non-cryptographic applications. It should also be independent of the inputs.

We conducted the following experiments: we ran the same six cryptographic applications as above. For each cryptographic application, the cryptographic keys and input message (for signing or encryption) are randomly chosen each time the applications are executed. We exploit the performance counters to record the number of *branch instructions* taking place in the program within 100 μs windows. Figure 1 shows the profiling results for each cryptographic application. For comparison, we also show the profiling results for three non-cryptographic applications: Apache, Mysql and the Network File System (NFS).

We observe that the cryptographic applications have different behaviors from the non-cryptographic ones. Each cryptographic application exhibits three distinguishable stages, labeled in Fig. 1. (1) The first stage initializes the program

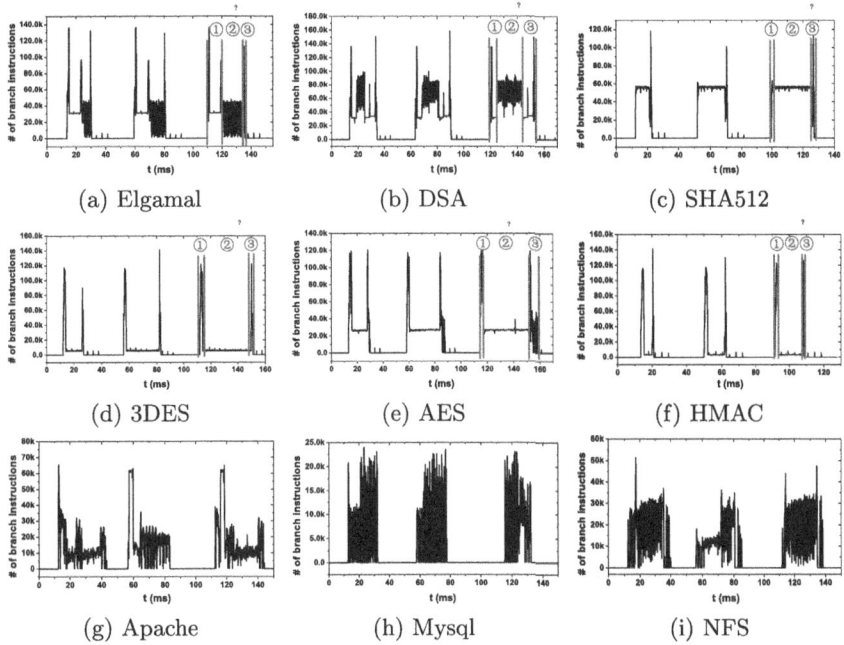

Fig. 1. Signatures of different applications based on the number of branches

and variables. Specifically, it analyzes the application's parameters, allocates buffers for the input and output messages, retrieves keys from passphrase or salts, and sets up the cipher context. This stage does not depend on the inputs. (2) The second stage computes the cryptographic operations (*e.g.*, multiply or square operations, checking lookup tables, *etc.*), the characteristics of which are input dependent: the duration of this stage is linearly related to the length of the plaintext/ciphertext, and the pattern depends on the values of the cryptographic key and the plaintext/ciphertext blocks. (3) The last stage ends the application, frees the memory buffer and reports the results. We chose the first stage as the signature to represent a crypto application, because it is input independent. The Fisher Score in Table 1 were also generated for this stage.

4.2 Cryptographic Application Detection

To detect the execution of the sensitive applications, *CloudRadar* only requires the customers to provide the signature generated offline using performance counters (not necessarily on the same hardware) or simply the executables for the service provider to generate the signature. At runtime, *CloudRadar* keeps monitoring the protected VM using the same set of performance counters. It then compares the data points collected at runtime with the signature of the cryptographic application. If a signature match is found, *CloudRadar* will assume the

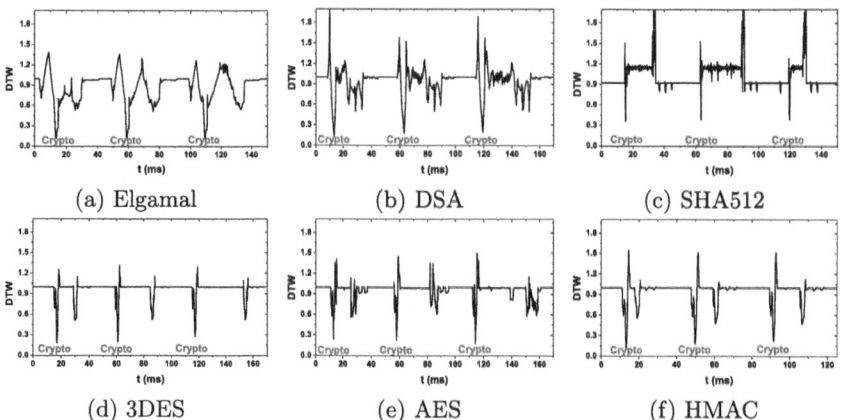

Fig. 2. DTW distances of different cryptographic programs. The lowest distance indicates a signature match.

cryptographic application is being executed by the protected VM (In fact, our evaluation in Sect. 7 shows high fidelity of this approach).

Because the cryptographic signatures and runtime measurements are temporal sequences of performance counter values, we cast the signature detection problem as a time series analysis problem: *i.e.*, measuring the similarity between the two sequences that represent the signature and the runtime measurement, respectively. We adopt the Dynamic Time Warping (DTW) algorithm [29] to calculate the distance between the two sequences. DTW is able to measure the similarity between temporal sequences which may vary in speed: it tries different alignments between these sequences and finds the optimal one that has the shortest distance. This distance is called the DTW distance. We chose the DTW algorithm because the runtime sequence may be slightly stretched or shrunk due to the difference of the computing environment (*e.g.*, CPU models, running speed, interruption, *etc.*). DTW is powerful enough to find the similarity between two temporal sequences even with distortion.

We normalize the DTW distance to the magnitude of the signature sequence, which is used as the metric for pattern matching. Figure 2 shows the normalized DTW distance of different cryptographic programs. We observe that occurrence of cryptographic programs yields very small DTW distances, which indicates a signature match. We defer a more systematic evaluation of the signature-based cryptographic program detection technique to Sect. 7.

5 Anomaly Detection of Side-Channel Activities

The cache use patterns that *CloudRadar* monitors for anomaly detection are characterized by the *cache hit* count and the *cache miss* count measured by the performance counters: In PRIME-PROBE side-channel attacks, the attacker

PROBEs certain cache sets and measures if there are cache miss via timing the accesses to this set after the victim executes. It is expected that cache misses will be higher than normal when the protected VM executes the cryptographic operations, since cache misses will be the tell-tale signal for the attacker to detect these operations in the first place. In FLUSH-RELOAD side-channel attacks, the attacker RELOADs certain cache lines and tries to detect a cache hit. Cache hits should occur more frequently during the protected VM's sensitive operations.

To validate this hypothesis, we conducted a set of experiments to show that abnormal cache activities in the untrusted VM can be correlated with the protected VM's sensitive operations. We first consider a PRIME-PROBE attack against the ElGamal cipher [21]. Figure 3 shows the DTW distance (low distance indicates a signature match) between the runtime sequence and the signature sequence observed on the protected VM (top figure), correlates with the attacker VM's high cache miss counts (bottom figure). We next consider a FLUSH-RELOAD attack against the RSA cipher [42]. Figure 4 shows the low DTW distance of the protected VM correlates with the high cache hit counts of the attacker VM. We align the top figures and the bottom figures according to timestamps. Strong correlation can be observed in both set of experiments, which suggest that this method can be used for side-channel attack detection.

To describe our detection algorithm more precisely, when *CloudRadar* detects that the victim VM starts executing crypto applications (a low DTW distance), two short sub-sequences are selected from the entire monitored runtime sequences in the untrusted VMs: $\mathbb{S}$, data points of size w before the DTW distance reaches its minimum, and $\mathbb{S}'$, data points of size w after the minimum points of DTW distance, where w is a parameter of the detection system. If *CloudRadar* detects that the difference between any value in $\mathbb{S}'$ and any value in $\mathbb{S}$ is larger than a pre-determined threshold T, *CloudRadar* will raise an alarm of a possible side-channel attack. This rule can be formally expressed in Eq. 1. We will further evaluate this side-channel detection method in Sect. 7.

$$\text{Alarm}: v' - v > T, \ \forall v \in \mathbb{S}, \ v' \in \mathbb{S}' \tag{1}$$

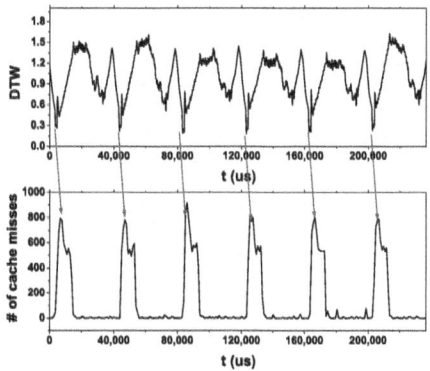

Fig. 3. PRIME-PROBE attack

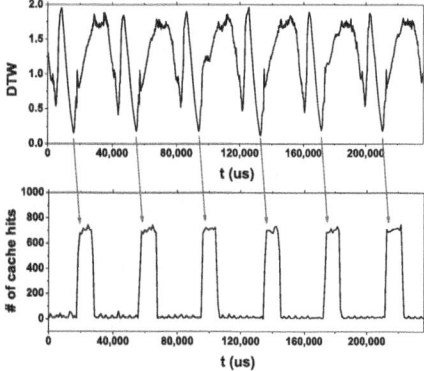

Fig. 4. FLUSH-RELOAD attack

6 Implementation

6.1 System Architecture Overview

CloudRadar is provided by the cloud operator as a security service to the customers who are willing to pay extra cost for better security, as in Security-on-Demand cloud frameworks [16,44]. Figure 5 shows the architecture of *CloudRadar*, and the workflow of detecting side-channel attacks. We implement *CloudRadar* in the opensource cloud software OpenStack platform. Two types of servers, the Cloud Controller and regular Cloud Servers, are relevant to our discussion.

The Cloud Controller is a dedicated server to manage the provided security services and coordinate the interaction between service users (cloud customers paying to use the side-channel detection service) and the Cloud Servers. The Signature Database is used to store signatures of crypto programs. The Controller Server is built upon the OpenStack Nova module. We modified the Nova API to enable the customers to request for the side-channel detection services.

CloudRadar's functionality within a Cloud Server is tightly integrated with the host OS. As shown in Fig. 5, *CloudRadar* consists of three modules, with each one running on a dedicated core. The Victim Monitor is responsible for collecting the protected VM's runtime events, which will be fed to Signature Detector to detect the cryptographic programs using our signature-based technique; The Attacker Monitor is responsible for collecting cache activities of the other VMs, using anomaly-based detection approach to identify side-channel attackers. We used the Linux *perf_event* kernel API for the PMU to manage the performance counters, therefore no change is needed to the hypervisor itself.

6.2 Operations

CloudRadar includes four steps, as shown in Fig. 5 with different paths. Each step is described below:

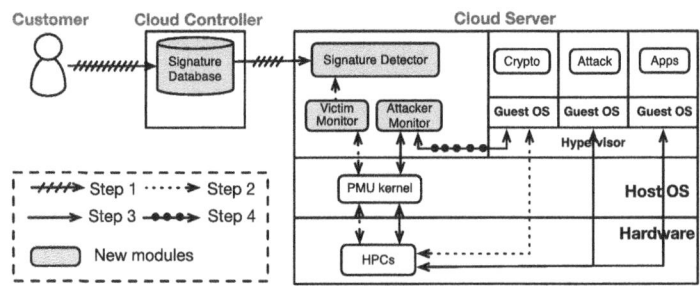

Fig. 5. Architecture overview of *CloudRadar*

Step 1: Generating Cryptographic Signature. In this step, the customer who seeks side-channel detection services for his protected VM can indicate to the Cloud Controller what sensitive applications to be protected, by providing the signatures generated offline using performance counters (not necessarily on the same hardware) or simply the executables. Then the Cloud Controller will run these crypto programs on a dedicated server with the same configuration as the Cloud Server that hosts the protected VM, and use performance counters to generate the signatures for the customer. The signatures will be stored in the `Signature Database` for future reference. They will also be sent to the Cloud Server that hosts this VM.

Step 2: Detecting Cryptographic Applications. This step takes place at runtime. In this step, the `Victim Monitor` monitors the protected VM using performance counters. It periodically (*e.g.*, every 100 μs) records the event counts (*e.g.*, branch instructions) as a time sequence, while the `Signature Detector` keeps comparing the most recent window of data points in the sequence with the signature. If a signature match is found, the `Signature Detector` can identify the protected VM is performing a cryptographic application, and signal this result to the `Attacker Monitor`.

Step 3: Monitoring Cache Activities. This step happens concurrently with Step 2. The `Attacker Monitor` exploits performance counters to monitor all untrusted VMs simultaneously. One challenge is that not enough performance counters are available on the servers to monitor all VMs, if this number is large: most of the Intel and AMD processors support up to six counters, and the number of counters does not scale with the number of cores. So when there are a lot of VMs on the server, the `Attacker Monitor` cannot monitor them concurrently.

To solve this problem, we use a time-domain multiplexing method: `Attacker Monitor` identifies active vCPUs that share LLC with the protected VM as the *monitored* vCPUs, and then measures each of them in turn. Specifically, in each period, the `Attacker Monitor` uses a kernel module to check the state and CPU affinity of each vCPU of each VM from its *task_struct* in the kernel. The `Attacker Monitor` marks the vCPUs in the *running* state that are sharing the same LLC with the protected VM as *monitored*. Then it sets up performance counters to measure each *monitored* vCPU's cache misses and hits in turn. When the `Attacker Monitor` is notified that a cryptographic application is happening in the protected VM, it will compare each *monitored* vCPU's cache misses and hits before and during the cryptographic application, as specified in Sect. 5. If one vCPU has an abrupt increase in the number of cache misses or hits during the cryptographic application, the `Attacker Monitor` will flag an alarm.

Step 4: Eliminating Side Channels. Once the `Attack Monitor` notices that one co-tenant VM has abnormal cache behavior exactly when the protected VM executes cryptographic applications, it will raise alarm for side-channel attacks.

It will migrate this malicious VM to a different processor socket which does not share the Last Level Cache (LLC), or another cloud server (*i.e.*, via VM migration [25,47], to cut off the cache side channels. In addition, the Cloud Controller will report this incident to the cloud provider for further processing, such as shut down the malicious VM or eventually block the attacker's account.

7 Evaluation

We used four servers to evaluate the security and performance of *CloudRadar*. A Dell R210II Server (equipped with one quad-core, 3.30 GHZ, Intel Xeon E3-1230v2 processor with 8 GB LLC) is configured as the Controller Server. Two Dell PowerEdge R720 Servers are deployed as the host cloud servers: one is equipped with one eight-core, 2.90 GHz Intel Xeon E5-2690 processor with 20 GB LLC; one is equipped with two six-core, 2.90 GHz Intel Xeon E5-2667 processors with 15 GB LLC. We also use another Dell 210II server as the client machine outside of the cloud system to communicate with cloud applications. Each VM in our experiments has one virtual CPU, 4 GB memory and 30 GB disk size. We choose Ubuntu 14.04 Linux, with 3.13 kernel as the guest OS.

7.1 Detection Accuracy

We measure the detection accuracy of cryptographic signature detection and cache anomaly detection.

Accuracy of Cryptographic Operation Detection. To detect a cryptographic operation, we used the branch instruction counts as the signature. We consider the detection of a cryptographic application as a binary classification, and measure its true positive rate and false positive rate. True positive happens when a cryptographic application is correctly identified as such. We used the same six cryptographic applications from Sect. 4.1. *CloudRadar* first generates a signature for each application. In the detection phase, the victim VM generates a random memory block and feeds it to the crypto application. We run the experiment 100 times, and measure the number of times *CloudRadar* can correctly identify the cryptographic under different thresholds. False positive is defined as non-cryptographic applications identified as cryptographic. We select 30 common linux commands and utilities [26] which do not contain cryptographic operations. In each experiment the victim VM run these commands in a random order. We repeated the experiment 100 times and measure the number of times false positives take place under different thresholds. We plot the ROC (Receiver Operating Characteristic) curves to show the relations between the true positive rate and false positive rate.

We explored the effect of changing performance counter sampling granularities (*i.e.*, period with which performance counter value is taken) on detection accuracy. We choose two different sampling granularities: 100 μs and 1 ms. Figure 6 shows the ROC curves of the six cryptographic applications under these two granularities. From this figure we can see 100 μs gives better accuracy than 1 ms: *CloudRadar* can achieve close to 100 % true positive rate with zero false positive rate when the DTW threshold is set between 0.3 and 0.4. For 1 ms, Elgamal and DSA application can be detected with less accuracy, while SHA512, AES, HMAC and 3DES cannot be differentiated from non-cryptographic applications with reasonable false positive and false negative at the same time.

The optimal sampling granularity depends on the length of the cryptographic application's initialization stage: if the sampling period is much shorter than the initialization stage, the signature will contain more data points, thus yielding more accurate results. In our experiments, the initialization stages of Elgamal, DSA, SHA512, AES, HMAC and 3DES last for 10 ms, 5 ms, 1.6 ms, 2 ms, 2 ms and 2 ms respectively. So a granularity of 100 μs can give good results for all the six applications, while 1 ms granularity performs worse, especially for SHA512, AES, HMAC and 3DES whose signatures only contain two data points.

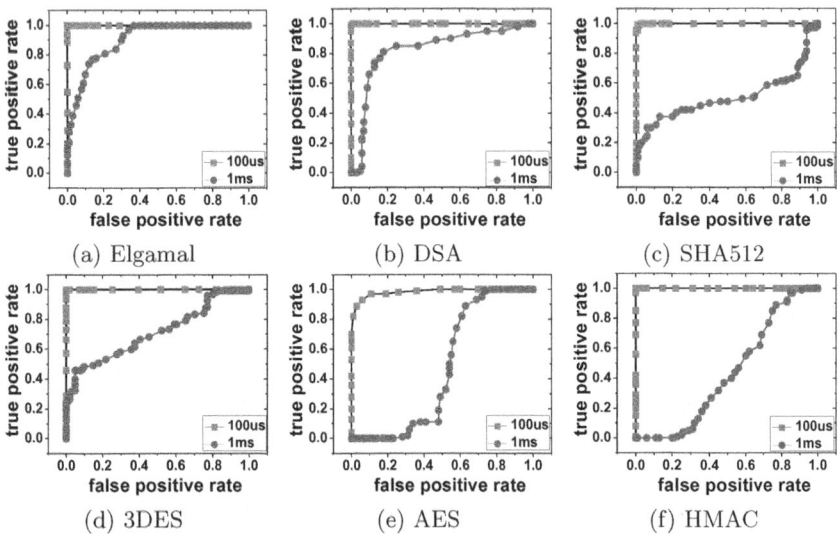

Fig. 6. ROC curve of crypto detection under two sampling intervals.

Accuracy of Cache Side-Channel Attack Detection. We measure the true positive rate and false positive rate of side-channel attack detection. True positive is the cases where side-channel attacks that are correctly identified. We test the PRIME-PROBE attack [21] and FLUSH-RELOAD attack [42]. False positive is defined as benign programs that are falsely identified as an attack. We select different common linux commands and utilities as benign applications. We change the threshold and draw the ROC curves to show the relations between true positive and false positive rate.

We first considered different window sizes w for $\mathbb{S}$ and $\mathbb{S}'$ (Sect. 5). Figure 7 shows the attack detection accuracy under three window size: $w = 1, 3$ and 5. In these experiments, we set the sampling granularity as 1 ms (this sampling rate is different from that of signature detection). From these results we see that *CloudRadar* has an excellent true positive rate: with appropriate thresholds (100–300 events per 1 ms), the true positive rate can be 100%. However, it also has false positives. When $w = 1$, the false positive rate can be as high as 20%–30%. False positives are caused by the coincidence that a benign application experiences a phase transition at exactly the same time as the victim application executes a crypto operation. *CloudRadar* will observe changes in the benign application's cache behavior and think it is due to interference with the victim. Then it will flag this benign VM as malicious. We can increase w to reduce the false positive rate without affecting the true positive rate: when $w = 5$, the false positive rate is close to 0 while true positive rate is 100%.

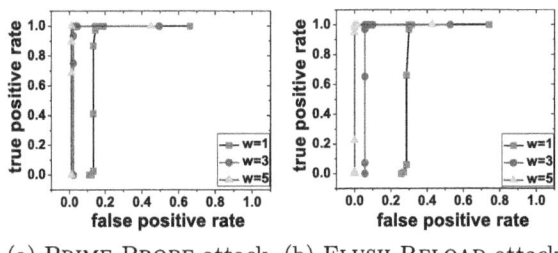

(a) PRIME-PROBE attack (b) FLUSH-RELOAD attack

Fig. 7. ROC curve of attack detection under different window lengths.

We also tested different sampling granularities. Figure 8 shows the ROC curves of detecting two attacks under two different sampling intervals: 1 ms and 100 μs. The window size is 5 data points. We can see the 1 ms interval is better than the 100 μs. This is because when the sampling interval is small, the number of cache events occurring within a sampling period is comparable to the measurement noise. So the measurements under this sampling granularity are not very accurate. It is interesting to note that we need different granularities to sample the victim's CPU events (100 μs) and attacker's LLC events (1 ms). This is because victim's CPU events occur more frequently than the attacker's LLC events. So at the granularity of 100 μs, sampling the victim can give finer information, while sampling the attacker will introduce large Signal-to-noise ratio (SNR), making the results less accurate.

7.2 Performance

Detection Latency. Table 2 reports the detection latency of *CloudRadar* under different window sizes w and sampling granularities. This detection latency is defined as the period from the time the victim VM starts to execute sensitive

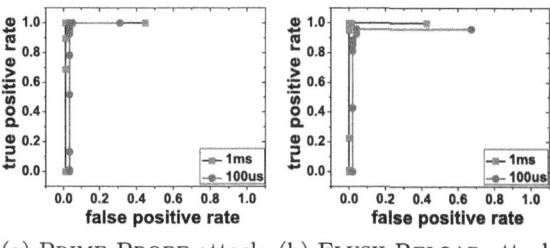

(a) PRIME-PROBE attack (b) FLUSH-RELOAD attack

Fig. 8. ROC curve of attack detection under different sampling intervals.

operations (*i.e.*, start of the second stage in Fig. 1) to the time an alarm for side-channel attacks is flagged. We see that *CloudRadar* can identify the attack on the order of milliseconds. Considering side-channel attackers usually need at least several cryptographic operations to steal the keys, this small latency can achieve our *real-time* design goal. We also observe that smaller window sizes and finer granularity can effectively reduce the detection latency, at the cost of slightly lower accuracy.

Table 2. Detection latency (μs) under different window sizes and sampling intervals

(μs)	granularity = 1 ms			granularity = 100 μs		
	$w=1$	$w=3$	$w=5$	$w=1$	$w=3$	$w=5$
PRIME-PROBE	1021.41	3065.86	5110.04	120.49	361.97	603.03
FLUSH-RELOAD	1021.50	3064.38	5107.57	122.48	363.27	605.30

Performance Overhead. We select a mix of benchmarks and real-world applications to evaluate the performance of *CloudRadar*. Our benchmarks can be categorized into three types: (1) crypto programs (AES, SHA, HMAC, BF and MD5 from OpenSSL; ElGamal, RSA and DSA from GnuPG); (2) CPU benchmarks (mcf, gobmk, omnetpp, astar, soplex and lbm from SPEC2006; canneal and streamcluster from PARSEC); (3) Cloud applications from CloudSuite [8] (data analytics, data caching, data serving, graph analytics, media streaming, software testing, web searching and web serving).

We test the performance penalty due to *CloudRadar* and show the normalized run time of each of the benchmark applications in Fig. 9 (results are average of 5 runs, error bars show one standard deviation). The results suggest *CloudRadar* has little impact on the performance of the monitored VM: even in the worst case, performance overhead is within 5 %.

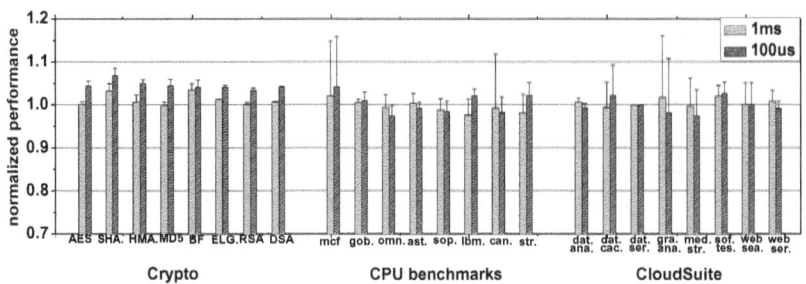

Fig. 9. Performance of different benchmarks under *CloudRadar*

8 Discussions

8.1 Detecting Other Side Channels

One can extend *CloudRadar* to detect cache-based side-channel attacks in other cloud models (*e.g.*, PaaS [46]), or in non-virtualization environments. The only change we need to make is to use performance counters to monitor the processes or threads instead of VMs. Besides, this method can be applied to other microarchitectural side-channel attacks that exploit resource contention. We can use performance counters to count the corresponding events that the attacker uses to retrieve information. For instance, we can monitor the DRAM bandwidth event to detect the DRAM side-channel attacks in [38]. Generalization of this method beyond cache-based side-channel attacks will be future work.

8.2 Potential Evasive Attacks

There can be potential evasive attacks against *CloudRadar*. To evade the detection of *CloudRadar*, a side-channel attacker can try to reduce the cache probing speed, so the abnormal increase in cache misses or hits may not be observed by *CloudRadar*. However, the attacker needs a much longer time to recover the keys, making side-channel attacks more difficult and less practical. An attacker can also try to evade the detection by adding noise to *CloudRadar*'s observations. However, such noise can also blur the attacker's observations, making it more difficult to extract side-channel information. How to design efficient evasive attacks and how to detect such attacks will be future work.

8.3 Limitations

CloudRadar may be limited in several aspects. First, each of its three modules (`Victim Monitor`, `Attacker Monitor` and `Signature Detector`) requires an exclusive use of one physical CPU core as they keep conducting data collection and analysis at full CPU speed. This can potentially reduce the server's capacity for hosting VMs. However, as many cloud servers today are equipped with dozens of CPU cores, the impact is not as big as one might imagine. Besides, public clouds usually have low server utilization (<20%) for preserving VMs' QoS [3,22]. So using three cores will not affect VMs' performance. Second, due to the limited number of performance counters available in modern processors, *CloudRadar* has to multiplex the monitoring for each VM using the same counter. When the number of *monitored* vCPUs scales up, *CloudRadar* may miss attacks. We expect future generations of processors will incorporate more performance counters and *CloudRadar* can make use of different counters to monitor different VMs at the same time.

9 Conclusions

This paper designs *CloudRadar*, a real-time detection system to detect cache-based side-channel attacks in clouds. *CloudRadar* leverages the existing hardware performance counter feature to both monitor a victim VM's cryptographic operations and capture a potential attacker VM's abnormal behavior during this time. *CloudRadar* is designed as a lightweight extension to the cloud system and does not require new hardware, hypervisor/OS or application modifications. The feasibility of *CloudRadar* is validated by our implementation on the open source OpenStack cloud system. Our evaluation shows *CloudRadar* can detect cache-based side-channel attacks with high fidelity, while introducing little overhead to the cloud applications.

Acknowledgements. We thank Fangfei Liu and Dr. Yuval Yarom for providing side-channel attack codes, and the anonymous reviewers for their feedback on this work. This work was supported in part by the National Science Foundation under grants NSF CNS-1218817 and NSF CNS-1566444. Any opinions, findings, and conclusions or recommendations expressed in this work are those of the authors and do not necessarily reflect the views of the NSF.

References

1. Azar, Y., Kamara, S., Menache, I., Raykova, M., Shepard, B.: Co-location-resistant clouds. In: ACM Workshop on Cloud Computing Security (2014)
2. Bahador, M., Abadi, M., Tajoddin, A.: HPCMalHunter: behavioral malware detection using hardware performance counters and singular value decomposition. In: IEEE International Conference on Computer and Knowledge Engineering (2014)
3. Barr, J.: Cloud computing, server utilization & the environment (2015). https://aws.amazon.com/blogs/aws/cloud-computing-server-utilization-the-environment/
4. Chiappetta, M., Savas, E., Yilmaz, C.: Real time detection of cache-based side-channel attacks using hardware performance counters. Cryptology ePrint Archive, Report 2015/1034 (2015). http://eprint.iacr.org/
5. Demme, J., Maycock, M., Schmitz, J., Tang, A., Waksman, A., Sethumadhavan, S., Stolfo, S.: On the feasibility of online malware detection with performance counters. In: ACM International Symposium on Computer Architecture (2013)

6. Domnitser, L., Jaleel, A., Loew, J., Abu-Ghazaleh, N., Ponomarev, D.: Non-monopolizable caches: low-complexity mitigation of cache side channel attacks. ACM Trans. Archit. Code Optim. **8**, 35:1–35:21 (2012)
7. Duda, R.O., Hart, P.E., Stork, D.G.: Pattern Classification, 2nd edn. Wiley-Interscience, Hoboken (2000)
8. EPFL: Cloudsuite. http://parsa.epfl.ch/cloudsuite/cloudsuite.html
9. Gruss, D., Maurice, C., Wagner, K., Mangard, S.: Flush+flush: a fast and stealthy cache attack. In: Detection of Intrusions and Malware and Vulnerability Assessment (2016)
10. Gruss, D., Spreitzer, R., Mangard, S.: Cache template attacks: automating attacks on inclusive last-level caches. In: USENIX Conference on Security Symposium (2015)
11. Gullasch, D., Bangerter, E., Krenn, S.: Cache games - bringing access-based cache attacks on aes to practice. In: IEEE Symposium on Security and Privacy (2011)
12. Han, Y., Alpcan, T., Chan, J., Leckie, C.: Security games for virtual machine allocation in cloud computing. In: Das, S.K., Nita-Rotaru, C., Kantarcioglu, M. (eds.) GameSec 2013. LNCS, vol. 8252, pp. 99–118. Springer, Heidelberg (2013)
13. Herath, N., Fogh, A.: These are not your grand daddys CPU performance counters: CPU hardware performance counters for security. In: Black Hat USA (2015)
14. Irazoqui, G., Eisenbarth, T., Sunar, B.: S$A: a shared cache attack that works across cores and defies VM sandboxing - and its application to AES. In: IEEE Symposium on Security and Privacy (2015)
15. Irazoqui, G., Inci, M.S., Eisenbarth, T., Sunar, B.: Wait a minute! A fast, cross-VM attack on AES. In: Stavrou, A., Bos, H., Portokalidis, G. (eds.) RAID 2014. LNCS, vol. 8688, pp. 299–319. Springer, Heidelberg (2014)
16. Jamkhedkar, P., Szefer, J., Perez-Botero, D., Zhang, T., Triolo, G., Lee, R.B.: A framework for realizing security on demand in cloud computing. In: IEEE Conference on Cloud Computing Technology and Science (2013)
17. Kim, T., Peinado, M., Mainar-Ruiz, G.: STEALTHMEM: system-level protection against cache-based side channel attacks in the cloud. In: USENIX Conference on Security Symposium (2012)
18. Li, P., Gao, D., Reiter, M.K.: Stopwatch: a cloud architecture for timing channel mitigation. ACM Trans. Inf. Syst. Secur. **17**, 8:1–8:28 (2014)
19. Liu, F., Ge, Q., Yarom, Y., Mckeen, F., Rozas, C., Heiser, G., Lee, R.B.: Catalyst: defeating last-level cache side channel attacks in cloud computing. In: IEEE International Symposium on High Performance Computer Architecture (2016)
20. Liu, F., Lee, R.B.: Random fill cache architecture. In: IEEE/ACM International Symposium on Microarchitecture (2014)
21. Liu, F., Yarom, Y., Ge, Q., Heiser, G., Lee, R.B.: Last-level cache side-channel attacks are practical. In: IEEE Symposium on Security and Privacy (2015)
22. Liu, H.: A measurement study of server utilization in public clouds. In: IEEE International Conference on Dependable, Autonomic and Secure Computing (2011)
23. Malone, C., Zahran, M., Karri, R.: Are hardware performance counters a cost effective way for integrity checking of programs. In: ACM Workshop on Scalable Trusted Computing (2011)
24. McCalpin, J.D.: Stream: sustainable memory bandwidth in high performance computers. http://www.cs.virginia.edu/stream/
25. Moon, S.-J., Sekar, V., Reiter, M.K.: Nomad: mitigating arbitrary cloud side channels via provider-assisted migration. In: ACM Conference on Computer and Communications Security (2015)

26. Natarajan, R.: 50 most frequently used unix/linux commands (with examples). http://www.thegeekstuff.com/2010/11/50-linux-commands/?utm_source=feedburner
27. Percival, C.: Cache missing for fun and profit. In: Proceedings of BSDCan (2005)
28. Ristenpart, T., Tromer, E., Shacham, H., Savage, S.: Hey, you, get off of my cloud: exploring information leakage in third-party compute clouds. In: ACM Conference on Computer and Communications Security (2009)
29. Sakoe, H., Chiba, S.: Dynamic programming algorithm optimization for spoken word recognition. IEEE Trans. Acoust. Speech Signal Process. **26**, 43–49 (1978)
30. Sherwood, T., Perelman, E., Hamerly, G., Sair, S., Calder, B.: Discovering and exploiting program phases. IEEE Micro **23**, 84–93 (2003)
31. Shi, J., Song, X., Chen, H., Zang, B.: Limiting cache-based side-channel in multi-tenant cloud using dynamic page coloring. In: IEEE/IFIP International Conference on Dependable Systems and Networks Workshops (2011)
32. Tang, A., Sethumadhavan, S., Stolfo, S.J.: Unsupervised anomaly-based malware detection using hardware features. In: Stavrou, A., Bos, H., Portokalidis, G. (eds.) RAID 2014. LNCS, vol. 8688, pp. 109–129. Springer, Heidelberg (2014)
33. Varadarajan, V., Ristenpart, T., Swift, M.: Scheduler-based defenses against cross-VM side-channels. In: USENIX Conference on Security Symposium (2014)
34. Varadarajan, V., Zhang, Y., Ristenpart, T., Swift, M.: A placement vulnerability study in multi-tenant public clouds. In: USENIX Security Symposium (2015)
35. Vattikonda, B.C., Das, S., Shacham, H.: Eliminating fine grained timers in Xen. In: ACM Workshop on Cloud Computing Security (2011)
36. Wang, X., Karri, R.: Numchecker: detecting kernel control-flow modifying rootkits by using hardware performance counters. In: ACM/EDAC/IEEE Design Automation Conference (2013)
37. Wang, X., Konstantinou, C., Maniatakos, M., Karri, R.: Confirm: detecting firmware modifications in embedded systems using hardware performance counters. In: IEEE/ACM International Conference on Computer-Aided Design (2015)
38. Wang, Y., Ferraiuolo, A., Suh, G.E.: Timing channel protection for a shared memory controller. In: IEEE International Symposium on High Performance Computer Architecture (2014)
39. Wang, Z., Lee, R.: A novel cache architecture with enhanced performance and security. In: IEEE/ACM International Symposium on Microarchitecture (2008)
40. Wang, Z., Lee, R.B.: New cache designs for thwarting software cache-based side channelattacks. In: ACM International Symposium on Computer Architecture (2007)
41. Xia, Y., Liu, Y., Chen, H., Zang, B.: CFIMon: detecting violation of control flow integrity using performance counters. In: IEEE/IFIP International Conference on Dependable Systems and Networks (2012)
42. Yarom, Y., Falkner, K.: Flush+reload: a high resolution, low noise, l3 cache side-channel attack. In: USENIX Conference on Security Symposium (2014)
43. Yuan, L., Xing, W., Chen, H., Zang, B.: Security breaches as PMU deviation: detecting and identifying security attacks using performance counters. In: Asia-Pacific Workshop on Systems (2011)
44. Zhang, T., Lee, R.B.: Cloudmonatt: an architecture for security health monitoring andattestation of virtual machines in cloud computing. In: ACM International Symposium on Computer Architecture (2015)
45. Zhang, Y., Juels, A., Reiter, M.K., Ristenpart, T.: Cross-VM side channels and their use to extract private keys. In: ACM Conference on Computer and Communications Security (2012)

46. Zhang, Y., Juels, A., Reiter, M.K., Ristenpart, T.: Cross-tenant side-channel attacks in PaaS clouds. In: ACM Conference on Computer and Communications Security (2014)
47. Zhang, Y., Li, M., Bai, K., Yu, M., Zang, W.: Incentive compatible moving target defense against VM-colocation attacks in clouds. In: Gritzalis, D., Furnell, S., Theoharidou, M. (eds.) SEC 2012. IFIP AICT, vol. 376, pp. 388–399. Springer, Heidelberg (2012)
48. Zhang, Y., Reiter, M.K.: Düppel: retrofitting commodity operating systems to mitigate cache side channels in the cloud. In: ACM Conference on Computer and Communications Security (2013)

Measurement Studies

The Abuse Sharing Economy: Understanding the Limits of Threat Exchanges

Kurt Thomas[1(✉)], Rony Amira[1], Adi Ben-Yoash[1], Ori Folger[1], Amir Hardon[1],
Ari Berger[1], Elie Bursztein[1], and Michael Bailey[2]

[1] Google, Inc., Mountain View, USA
kurtthomas@google.com
[2] University of Illinois, Urbana-Champaign, Champaign, USA

Abstract. The underground commoditization of compromised hosts suggests a tacit capability where miscreants leverage the same machine—subscribed by multiple criminal ventures—to simultaneously profit from spam, fake account registration, malicious hosting, and other forms of automated abuse. To expedite the detection of these commonly abusive hosts, there are now multiple industry-wide efforts that aggregate abuse reports into centralized *threat exchanges*. In this work, we investigate the potential benefit of global reputation tracking and the pitfalls therein. We develop our findings from a snapshot of 45 million IP addresses abusing six Google services including Gmail, YouTube, and ReCaptcha between April 7–April 21, 2015. We estimate the scale of end hosts controlled by attackers, expose underground biases that skew the abuse perspectives of individual web services, and examine the frequency that criminals re-use the same infrastructure to attack multiple, heterogeneous services. Our results indicate that an average Google service can block 14 % of abusive traffic based on threats aggregated from seemingly unrelated services, though we demonstrate that outright blacklisting incurs an untenable volume of false positives.

Keywords: Threat exchanges · Reputation systems · Underground specialization

1 Introduction

The underground commoditization of compromised hosts enables miscreants to purchase, rent, or repurpose a glut of machinery in order to relay abusive traffic [1,32]. This suggests a tacit capability where miscreants leverage the same machine—subscribed by multiple criminal ventures—to simultaneously profit from spam, denial of service, malicious hosting, and other forms of automated abuse. Evidence to this effect includes the Torpig botnet which acted as an information stealer, SOCKS proxy, and HTTP proxy [30]; and the ZeroAccess botnet involved in search hijacking, automated clickfraud, and bitcoin mining [21]. More broadly, the *pay-per-install* business model enables miscreants to pay $10–180 for a thousand installs of an arbitrary payload [4]. Prolific botnets such as ZeroAccess, Mariposa, and Torpig provided similar install capabilities [20,28,30]. As a consequence, a single infected client may host multiple malware families, such as 6–15 % of Confickr infections overlapping with Gameover Zeus [2], or 7–10 % of search bots overlapping with spamming hosts [35].

In the absence of coordinated action among affected Internet services, each target must redundantly detect and filter commonly abusive hosts. While longstanding domain and IP blacklists have proven effective at bridging the information divide between email providers [12,26,36], there is no similarly mature system for globally tracking reputation across heterogeneous services such as cloud providers, mail servers, and social networks. To address this gap, an industry-wide effort has emerged in recent years to collate intelligence on active attacks and abusive clients into centralized *threat exchanges* [9,19,25,27]. Under the mantra of "stronger together", these many-to-many exchanges have attracted participants across a spectrum of web services including Facebook, Bitly, Dropbox, Twitter, and Yahoo [9]. Despite momentum within industry, an important question remains for whether global threat intelligence will significantly improve current standalone anti-abuse pipelines, and if so, how best to reconcile, prioritize, and act upon warnings generated by algorithms and users rather than curated honeypots.

In this work, we design a threat exchange called Babel to explore the challenges and pitfalls inherent to any centralized reputation tracking of Internet devices. In particular, we measure: (1) the scale and network composition of infrastructure controlled by attackers; (2) the impact of network churn and evasion on long-term threat tracking; (3) the ratio of benign and abusive traffic originating from end hosts; and (4) ultimately whether commoditization has created a common substrate of abusive hosts that underpin multiple profit vectors. The answers to these questions serve to inform the nascent design of industry-lead threat exchanges and to illuminate any value in threat sharing between companies and government institutions.

To start, we develop an experimental threat exchange that collates hundreds of millions of real abuse incidents as reported by any of six federated Google services contending with spam, bulk account creation, fake engagement, and malware distribution over a 14 day period between April 7–April 21, 2015.[1] Each service relies on a specialized definition of abuse where incidents target semantically distinct entities (e.g., messages, accounts, domains) that are not immediately reconcilable—an inherent challenge for all threat exchanges. We decompose these application-specific, through context-rich abuse reports into a single repository of 45 million abusive IP addresses that serve as the launching point of attacks. We annotate each address with the volume of abuse per network, the services affected, and the duration of attacks.

---

[1] We opt for these reports over existing threat exchange data because the nascent (and invite-only) state of industry threat exchanges precludes a representative dataset for study.

We find that miscreants operate a vast apparatus of 8 million daily abusive hosts. Despite the sheer scale of infected devices in the wild, we find that the distribution of attacks across the Google services in our study is heavily skewed towards a small number of devices. The top 1 % of abusive IP addresses generate 48–82 % of abusive traffic per service, with email spam representing the most concentrated extreme. While this Zipf-like distribution holds for all abuse verticals, we also find evidence of regional specialization that biases the abuse perspective of individual Google services. In particular, we find the United States serves the majority of malware and drive-bys, Russian networks focus on fake YouTube engagement, and Indian networks create the most fake accounts. These non-uniform perspectives of abusive networks reduce the effectiveness of centralized threat exchanges, but as we will show does not render sharing inoperative.

Before actioning any network-based abuse intelligence, threat exchange consumers must contend with the possibility of coarse or stale abuse signals. To this end, we introduce a set of techniques to detect IP address re-assignment and quantify overlap between legitimate and abusive traffic on the same network. We find that a single device will cycle through an average of twenty IP addresses in two weeks. Translated into an abuse context, 66 % of abusive IP addresses remain active for a single day before the associated device acquires a new IP address due to DHCP churn. As such, we find that while abuse lasts long enough to justify reporting, threat exchanges must enforce explicit time frames after which stale IP reputation expires.

Ultimately, by accounting for IP dynamism and taking advantage of skew where a small number of hosts are responsible for the vast majority of abuse, we find that at most 13 % of Gmail spam and 43 % of fake accounts can be caught due to simultaneous attacks on other products. These results illustrate that underground commoditization has yet to manifest into the purported ideal of miscreants maximizing the value of an infected host by engaging in all possible profit-generating activities. Nevertheless, we argue there is a value to threat exchanges that unify the abuse perspectives of heterogeneous web services. However, acting on this intelligence remains a challenge: outright blacklisting results in an unacceptable level of collateral damage as 62 % of abusive IP addresses also relay legitimate content due to either NATing or simultaneous use by the device's owner. We discuss potential alternatives, such as incorporating centralized reputation signals into application-specific classifiers.

In summary, we highlight some of our key findings:

- **Exchanges must track millions of incidents:** We estimate miscreants control over 8 million daily IP addresses from a perspective of just six Google services.

- **Exchanges benefit even unrelated services:** Miscreants re-use underground infrastructure across abuse verticals. This allows an average service to catch 14 % of abuse even when comparing spamming to fake account creation.

- **Exchanges must prioritize threats:** An inherent skew in miscreant strategies results in 1 % of abusive devices generating 48–82 % of attacks across services.
- **Exchanges must contend with transient abuse:** We find 66 % of abusive IP addresses impact services for only a single day. Relying on stale incident reports results in unacceptable false positives.

2 Threat Exchanges: Design and Challenges

We begin by outlining current industry proposals for threat exchanges and potential challenges inherent to their design, the impact of which we evaluate throughout our work.

2.1 Existing Threat Exchanges

Threat exchanges are a community-driven, many-to-many broadcast platform for sharing abuse reports. This contrast with traditional domain and IP blacklists like Spamhaus or Safe Browsing that rely on a curated one-to-many model for reporting abuse. Examples include Microsoft's Interflow [25], Facebook's ThreatExchange [9], IBM's X-Force Exchange [27], and Alien Vault's Open Threat Exchange [19]—all launched between 2012–2015. More historical examples also exist such as DShield, dating back to 2001, which serves as a bulletin of network intrusion incidents [7]. In practice, exchanges serve as a platform for alerting other participants to malicious IP addresses, URLs, binaries, extensions, email addresses, and even phone numbers: the support infrastructure underpinning digital fraud and abuse. Early adopters include Twitter, Pinterest, Tumblr, Dropbox, Bitly, and Yahoo [9] while IBM reports over 1,000 business participants [27].

2.2 Challenges

While threat exchanges are invaluable in theory for improving anti-abuse pipelines and providing access to training data, it remains up to participants to sift through the data deluge to identify credible threats. We summarize the potential challenges that arise from community-driven reporting.

Translating Threats: The foremost challenge for threat exchange members is translating intelligence across abuse verticals. Email operates on messages, social networks on accounts and posts, URL shorteners on pages, and hosting providers on domains. Conveying threats between such web services requires decomposing abuse reports into universally recognizable subcomponents, potentially at the loss of rich contextual details such as collusion among accounts or domains all hosting the same spam template.

Competing Policies: Participants in threat exchanges each have competing definitions of abuse (e.g., Terms of Service). For example, one social network may flag a host for aggressive account creation due to registering five accounts in a short window, while a second network might consider that typical behavior for a mobile endpoint. Similarly, a search engine may de-list URLs flagged for blackhat SEO while a URL shortener's abuse policy may restrict penalties to drive-by and phishing domains. Due to the arbitrary nature of many policies, threat exchange participants must learn which other members most closely match their rule sets.

Implicit Bias: Abuse detection pipelines introduce an unmeasured bias due to the technology deployed, incomplete training data, and potentially skewed threats. Consequently, every reported (or unreported) entity carries an implicit false positive and negative rate that is unknown to all other participants absent longitudinal monitoring. While honeypots are highly curated to minimize false positives, any algorithm or user can report abuse to a threat exchange.

Stale Identifiers: Abuse indicators such as IP addresses and domains, unlike file hashes, suffer from an innate instability introduced by network management (e.g., DHCP churn), takedown, and compromise remediation after which a host should no longer be treated as malicious. Reported entities are potentially credible only for a short time window before they become stale.

Coarse Identifiers: Abuse indicators such as IP addresses and domains represent coarse identifiers for abusive hosts or pages. In particular, NATs, proxies, and middleboxes serve multiple simultaneous clients. Similarly, free hosting providers and URL shorteners serve content from a variety of owners all from the same domain. Blacklisting coarse identifiers inadvertently penalizes legitimate clients.

3 Building a Threat Exchange

With threat exchanges only recently launching, there is no agreed upon best practice for reconciling abuse incidents across web services. We present our approach for distilling application-specific abuse intelligence into a universal format. We apply this technique to hundreds of millions of abuse records collected by Google over a two week period ending on April 21, 2015. We note our limited collection window arises due to privacy restrictions.

3.1 Collating Abuse Reports

The greatest common divisor among services combating spam, malicious hosting, and account-related abuse is the IP address (and thus device) perpetrating the attack. Given a raw feed of labeled abusive and legitimate traffic belonging to a single web service, we aggregate threat intelligence into a tuple ⟨*service, IP, date, volume, badness*⟩ that contains a service identifier (e.g., Gmail), IP address, the date of abuse (restricted to 24 h granularity), the volume of traffic originating from the address over the 24 h period (e.g., email received), and the ratio of the traffic the service flagged as abusive. This approach allows us to identify which services are most impacted by mixed legitimate and abusive traffic and whether attacks persist for long periods. While other approaches exist, such as restricting analysis to domains or file hashes, we opt for IP addresses in our study because they are more expensive for miscreants to acquire and also universally applicable. We discuss limitations with this approach later in this section.

3.2 Abusive Traffic Dataset

In order to conduct our study, we rely on an abuse dataset that consists of 45 million IPv4 addresses reported by any of six Google services combating fraud and abuse. We detail each source of reports and highlight false positive and negative rates of respective feeds when previously published. A detailed breakdown of feeds is available in Table 1. As mentioned in Sect. 2, each of these datasets carries an implicit bias due to unknown accuracy, skewed threats, and orders of magnitude more traffic that are fundamental to threat exchanges.

Table 1. Summary of abusive IPv4 addresses and the service targeted. We use the abbreviated names of services for all figures throughout our study.

Abbr.	Reporting service	IP addresses	ASNs
–	Total abusive IPs	45,171,301	40,069
GML	Gmail spam	19,818,529	31,088
CAP	ReCaptcha failures	14,892,992	34,018
YTB	YouTube engagement	5,910,688	19,007
CMT	Comment spam	4,233,722	21,607
SIG	Bulk account creation	1,616,067	15,627
SAF	Safe browsing	49,117	3,348

Gmail Inbound Email [Spam]: Our Gmail dataset consists of SMTP relay IP addresses that sent an inbound spam email to a Gmail user, including messages blocked at the delivery layer and via content-based classification. Previous studies estimated this accuracy at above 99 % [3]. We annotate each IP address with the total number of emails sent and the fraction Gmail blocked as spam.

Bulk Account Registration [Fake Accounts]: Our bulk account dataset includes IP addresses tied to automated account registration attempts blocked at creation or retroactively disabled upon detection where our timestamp reflects the original creation time of the account. We annotate each IP address with the number of registration attempts and the fraction Google identified as fraudulent.

YouTube Likes, Subscribes [Fake Engagement]: Our YouTube dataset contains IP addresses belonging to Google accounts polluting videos with fake "likes" and "subscribes", a form of signed-in abuse. We annotate each IP address with the total volume of likes and subscribes and the fraction YouTube flagged as abusive.

Comments [Spam]: Our comment dataset contains IP addresses tied to Google accounts that post spam comments to Blogger, YouTube, and Google+. We annotate each IP address with the total number of comments posted via the address and the fraction Google blocked as spam.

ReCaptcha [Automation]: Our ReCaptcha dataset consists of IP addresses that fail to correctly solve a CAPTCHA challenge. Unlike our other datasets where blocked activity is a concrete abuse verdict, we caution that CAPTCHA failure is a soft measure of abuse. We annotate each IP address with the number of CAPTCHA attempts and the fraction failed. We set a minimum failure threshold of 50 %; we exclude IP addresses below this threshold from our dataset. We make no initial assumptions that unfiltered IP addresses are in fact abusive; instead, we rely on comparing CAPTCHA abuse to other verticals to draw conclusions.

Safe Browsing [Malicious Hosting]: Our final dataset consists of web server IP addresses reported by Safe Browsing for hosting malware and drive-by exploits [23]. We annotate each IP address with the number of web pages hosted on the IP and the fraction Safe Browsing flagged for distributing malware.

3.3 Inbound HTTP Requests Dataset

In order to contrast abuse with legitimate behavior, we rely on a second dataset that consists of de-identified HTTP logs restricted to signed-in users to the same subset of Google services we study for abuse. Log entries consist of $\langle PUID, User\text{-}Agent, service, IP, t\rangle$ containing a hashed, pseudo-anonymous account ID, User-Agent string, service identifier for what service the user interacted with, the user's IP address, and fine-grained microsecond timestamp of the event. The logs contain hundreds of millions de-identified users from the a 14 day window ending on April 21, 2015. We use this data solely to estimate a lower bound on the aggregate number of users and User-Agents per IP; gauge the stability of $\langle IP, PUID\rangle$ pairs over time; and estimate the volume of legitimate traffic that a service would erroneously block with IP blacklists. For ethical and privacy reasons, all user data was handled by exclusively by Google, covered by their Terms of Service, and approved by their internal privacy review board.

3.4 Limitations

Our study suffers from a number of limitations that we lay out herein. First, our coverage of abuse is limited to IPv4 addresses. Based on inbound HTTP requests to Google, we estimate this covers 94 % of signed-in traffic; the remaining 6 % originates from IPv6 clients. This is higher than previous findings by Czyz et al. which reported IPv6 adoption at less than 1 % of Internet traffic [6] or 4.8 % adoption reported by Kreibich et al. for a sample of clients operating Netalyzer [13]. We make no claims our study of IPv4 abuse translates to IPv6.

Second, we caution that each service reporting malicious IP addresses relies on a specialized definition of abuse that is likely biased towards threats facing

Google. We take such reports at face value—we cannot validate the precision or recall of the logic involved. This is identical to how participants in threat exchanges are blind to the accuracy of anti-abuse pipelines deployed by other members. As such, when we investigate the scale of abuse in Sect. 4 or examine the overlap of abusive IP addresses between services in Sect. 6 our results are biased towards the quality of abuse reports and their respective coverage.

4 Comparing Abuse Perspectives

Miscreants control a vast apparatus of hosts that, as a collective, encompasses 45 million IP addresses. We explore the scale of individual threats and the geographic specialization of attacks. We tie these into a broader understanding of bias introduced into threat exchanges due to participants with skewed abuse perspectives.

4.1 Scale of Abusive Networks

In aggregate, we estimate that miscreants control over eight million unique daily IP addresses as detailed in Fig. 1. The strata between abuse verticals provides a lens into the allocation of compromised hosts on the Internet. Our email spam dataset contains the largest volume of abuse totaling nearly five million daily IP addresses. This is an order of magnitude larger than the number of hosts involved in account-based abuse affecting Google such as fake engagement, comment spam, or fraudulent account creation. Even more, email spam represents a 200x increase over hosts serving drive-by downloads and malware. While we avoid characterizing the volume of IP addresses as a reflection of the most pressing abuse challenges (or the criminal profit involved), we argue (infected) hosts targeting Google during our collection period heavily skew towards email spam—a timeless staple of the underground monetization [15,17].

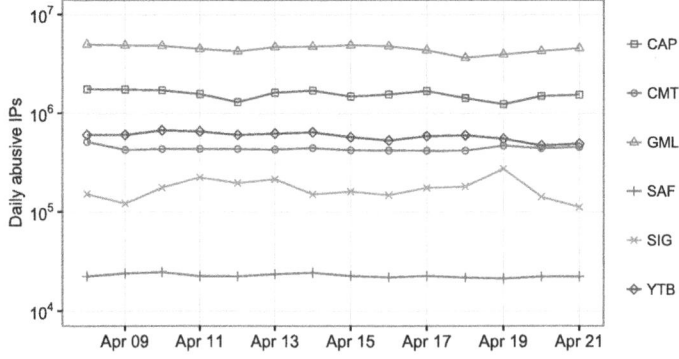

Fig. 1. Daily volume of IP addresses reported by various Google services for abuse. We observe an order of magnitude more spam bots than all other threats.

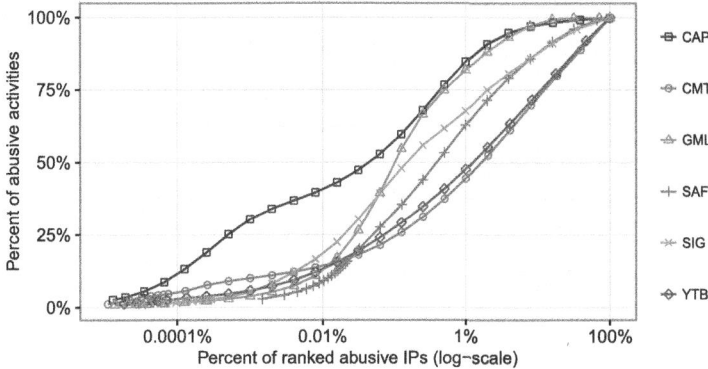

Fig. 2. Cumulative percentage of all abusive traffic relayed via unique IP addresses (ranked by contribution). The top 1% of abusive IP addresses contribute 48–82% of abusive activity.

Despite drastically different counts of abusive IP addresses between verticals, we find that the distribution of abusive traffic across IP addresses all follow a Zipf-like distribution as detailed in Fig. 2. At the most concentrated extreme we find the top 1% of abusive email IP addresses relay 82% of inbound Gmail spam. While email is biased towards large SMTP relays active for all 14 days of our collection, we nevertheless observe a similar pattern with IP addresses linked also to failed CAPTCHAs that appear more transiently throughout our collection (median of five days). At the most distributed end of the spectrum, we find 48% of fake YouTube engagement originates from the top 1% of abusive IP addresses. We find similar patterns for other signed-in fraud. We suspect that miscreants favor this more decentralized approach to avoid services that cluster abusive accounts based on IP addresses. Nevertheless, our results present an opportunity to systematically block a significant volume of abuse from only a few hundred thousand hosts—assuming the IP addresses do not also relay legitimate traffic due to either re-allocation or over subscription as we explore in Sect. 5.

4.2 Network Locality and Specialization

While we observe abuse from networks around the globe, six countries in particular host the largest volume of abusive IP addresses: the United States (12.5%), Brazil (5.9%), Germany (4.6%), Russia (3.7%), India (3.6%), and China (3%). Combined, these regions cover 27–64% of all abusive IP addresses per service. We find some attacks are niche to specific localities as illustrated in Fig. 3. For instance, networks in the United States serve the majority of malware and drive-bys (41%), followed by China (10%). With respect to bulk account, Indian networks create the most fake accounts (10%). This suggests that while miscreants rely on access to any compromised host possible, we find hints of bias potentially introduced by regional specialization within the underground or greater

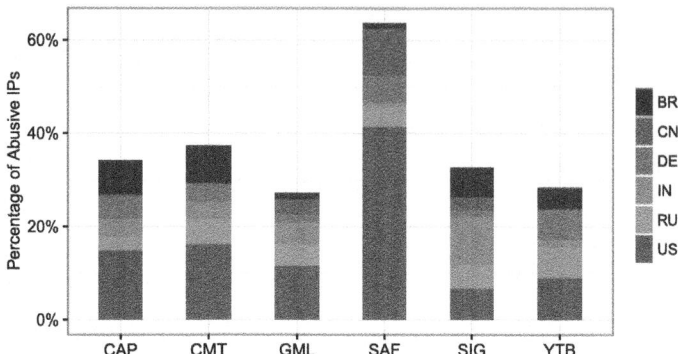

Fig. 3. Geolocation of abusive IP addresses for the top 6 offending regions. We observe a geographic bias in threats: malicious hosting in the United States; fake engagement from Russia; and bulk account creation in India.

geo-political threats. This observation is consistent with prior work that shows regional biases in other attack vectors [36]. One potential root cause is underground market dynamics: hosts outside of Europe and the United States are less expensive on the pay-per-install market and may be favored by miscreants for abuse with minimal bandwidth requirements [4].

5 Characterizing Abusive IP Addresses

We characterize the network-level behaviors of abusive IP addresses including the impact of DHCP churn and NAT on reconciling abuse reports. Given the diverse infrastructure and geographic distribution in each abuse vertical, we also examine whether any particular threat is more amenable to outright IP blacklisting.

5.1 Stability of IP-Device Pairs

One of the primary challenges of IP reputation is the stability of IP addresses as identifiers for abusive clients. While we observe a roughly constant daily volume of abusive hosts as previously discussed in Sect. 4, we, somewhat surprisingly, find 66 % of the hosts in our dataset actively relay abuse for only a single day over a two week period. One potential culprit for these observations is IP dynamism. We provide a more detailed breakdown of the duration of abuse per service in Fig. 4. Absent emails spam and malicious hosting, 75–80 % of abusive IP addresses persist for a single day. We find 14 % of spam SMTP relays persist for 7 days as well as 49 % of servers hosting malware, allowing for more stable IP reputation.

If we restrict our analysis to the top 1 % of abusive IP addresses, a different picture emerges as shown in Fig. 5. We find 52 % of the top abusive SMTP relays

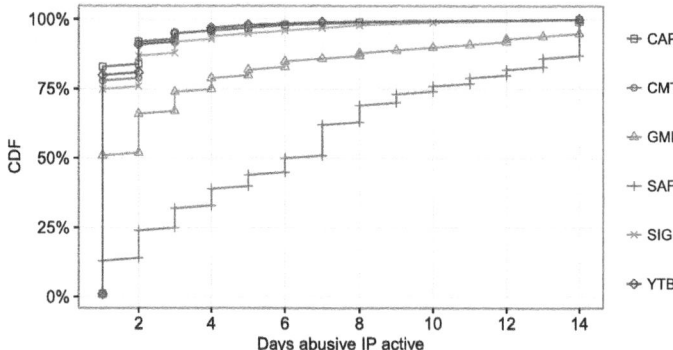

Fig. 4. CDF of the total number of days in the last two weeks a service reported an IP for abuse. We find 66 % of abusive hosts persist for only a single day and preclude long term reputation tracking.

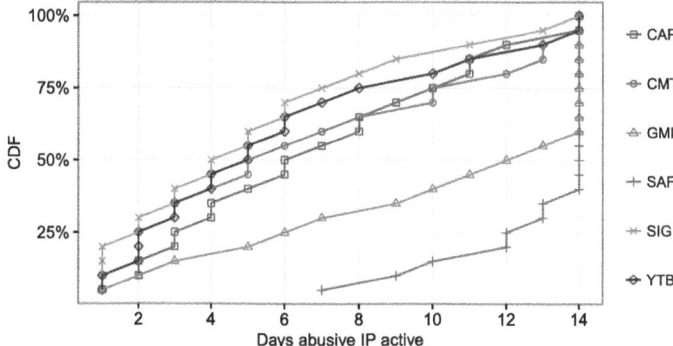

Fig. 5. CDF of the total number of days in the last two weeks a service reported an IP for abuse, restricted to the top 1 % most abusive IP addresses. The most abusive IP addresses remain stable for longer periods, enabling longer term reputation tracking.

actively send spam every day. Bulk account creation appears the least amenable to long-term IP reputation: 75 % of IP addresses appear for fewer than seven days and 50 % fewer than four days. We observe a similar pattern for the other top IP addresses involved in signed-in abuse.

The unsuitability of IP addresses as long-term stable identifiers is well documented. For example, Maier et al. observed that ISPs would re-assign 50 % of IP addresses to at least 2 different customers in the course of 24 h [16]. We re-visit this issue and estimate the duration that device, IP pairs remain stable. Using our HTTP request logs, we first approximate a unique device identifier as a ⟨*PUID, User-Agent*⟩ pair and then calculate the number of IP addresses per device for 24 h and one week.[2] Given the possibility that mobility rather than

---

[2] While clients may report spoofed User-Agents, we assume that the majority of non-abusive users accurately report their device information.

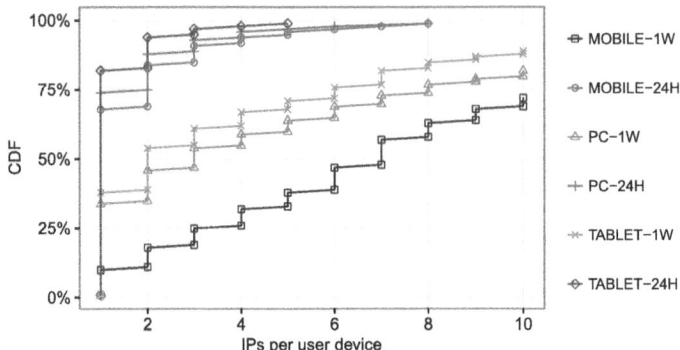

Fig. 6. Unique IP addresses per device for successively larger periods of time, broken down by device class. IP-device pairings rarely survive beyond 24 h.

reallocation explains short IP leases, we segment devices by class (e.g., mobile, tablet, personal computer) as gleaned from the OS family of a User-Agent.

We present our findings in Fig. 6. We observe that 74 % of PCs maintain the same IP over a 24 h period compared to 68 % of mobile phones and 82 % of tablets. After one week, only 10 % of mobile devices retain their original IP compared to 34 % of PCs and 38 % of tablets—clients likely behind static IP addresses. This is a strict underestimate as we may not observe clients during every DHCP lease window.

On average, we find devices that send at least one request for every day in our two week collection period cycle through 20 distinct IP addresses. Furthermore, we find that 50 % of all IP addresses remain active for the entirety of our collection period. As such, even though we observe short DHCP leases, ISPs quickly allocate the IP to a new set of devices. Our results differ drastically from previous measurements by Casado et al. who found that only 8 % of clients (identified by cookies) used more than three IP addresses over 2–4 weeks [5]. In summary, we argue that IP intelligence carries value for only a limited time frame, after which ISPs may re-allocate a previously abusive IP to a benign set of clients. For our own work, we restrict all subsequent IP analysis to 24 h windows.

5.2 Diverse Device Traffic

A second challenge of IP reputation is the coarse granularity of addresses compared to the diverse user populations they potentially service. Based on our HTTP request logs, we find 67 % of IP addresses service at least two unique ⟨PUID, User-Agent⟩ devices in a 24 h window and 21 % of IP addresses service at least 5 devices. We caution this is limited to signed-in users and thus likely underestimates the number of devices per IP. Our findings are higher than a prior report in 2011 by Ihm et al. who observed only a single User-Agent for 83–94 % of IP addresses depending on geographic region [11]. One explanation—matching the observations of Ihm et al.—is that networks have densified over time. The

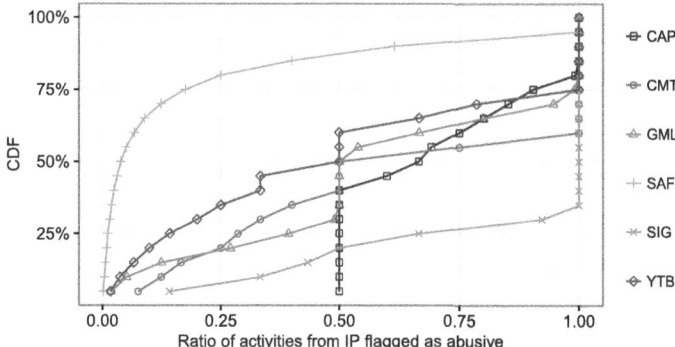

Fig. 7. CDF of the ratio of traffic from each IP flagged as abusive. Most IP addresses exhibit a mixture of legitimate and abusive activity.

consequence for IP reputation is that NATs are becoming increasingly coarse approximations of the devices served.

In the presence of large NATs or SMTP relays, exclusively abusive IP addresses will be a rarity. Indeed, most IP addresses in our dataset are unsuitable for outright blacklisting: only 38 % exclusively relay abusive content. However, in aggregate these exclusively abusive IP addresses carry 16–49 % of all malicious activity per service. We provide a more detailed breakdown of the fraction of traffic per IP flagged as abusive in a 24 h window in Fig. 7. Surprisingly, we find the top 1 % of abusive IP addresses exhibit a lower likelihood of exclusive abuse compared to all abusive IP addresses as shown in Fig. 8. This precludes the possibility of outright blacklisting many of the top offending IP addresses.

Malicious hosting represents one extreme where website content on 87 % of all abusive IP addresses is more likely to be innocuous than harmful. Only 5 % of malicious hosting IP addresses exclusively serve harmful content. This mirrors previous findings by Provos et al. who found drive-by downloads predominantly relied on compromised websites that otherwise serve legitimate content [24]. Bulk account registration presents an opposite extreme where 69 % of all IP addresses exclusively create fake accounts. Intuitively, account creation should be a rare event per IP with limited exceptions for mobile gateways. Other abuse verticals fall between these extremes and provide a less pristine signal for filtering, reinforcing our observation that the complex interplay between NATs and devices obstructs any path towards daily blacklist deployment.

5.3 Reputation Across IP Re-assignment

While DHCP churn impedes long-term reputation tracking, a significant question remains whether the same device continuously abuses services across days. In the absence of device-level identifiers, we instead examine a microcosm of the same problem: the number of days static IP addresses that remain abusive. We isolate static (or at least minimally churning) IP addresses by examining rare instances

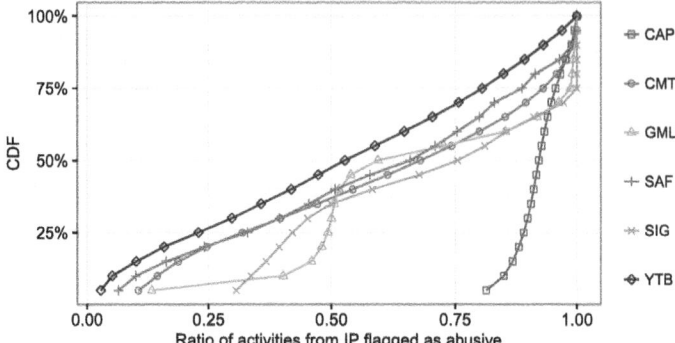

Fig. 8. CDF of the ratio of activity from each IP flagged as abusive for the top 1 % of harmful IP addresses. Even the worst offending hosts relay significant legitimate activity and cannot be blacklisted.

where we see at least one (legitimate) PUID make a HTTP request from the same IP for a minimum of seven days. This approach is aided in part by NATing: so long as one user behind the NAT remains active, we can approximate that ISPs never re-assigned the IP. We note this is a strict subset of static IP addresses as (1) not all static IP addresses will have user-traffic (e.g., web servers) and (2) not all users on static IP addresses will exhibit constant activity. In total, we identify between 26,000—530,000 static IP samples per abuse vertical with the exception of Safe Browsing where only 485 malicious hosts also carried consistent user traffic.

Even without DHCP churn we find that multi-day abusive IP addresses are in fact rare as shown in Fig. 9. With the exception of email spam and malicious hosting, miscreants use 72–80 % of static IP addresses for only a single day in the last 14 compared to 75–80 % of all IP addresses. Our results indicate that even were we able to track IP re-assignments, the likelihood of abuse in the next 24 h is only loosely predicted by previous abuse (20–28 % of IP addresses outside email and hosting). This leaves anti-abuse pipelines only a short window in which to detect abuse before miscreants migrate to entirely different devices and networks. However, we cannot rule out the possibility that miscreants continuously abuse dynamic IP addresses with full knowledge that churn provides greater anonymity to anti-abuse detection compared to static IP addresses. Furthermore, the rare exceptions matter: as we pointed out in previously in Fig. 5 the top 1 % of abusive IP addresses tend to be active for multiple days.

5.4 Subnet Abuse Affinity

We find that spatial qualities of networks provide a weak predictor of abusive IP addresses. For each /24 and /16 subnet containing at least one abusive IP, we calculate the likelihood miscreants abuse other IP addresses in the same subnet. Mechanistically, we calculate the ratio of observed IP addresses in HTTP request

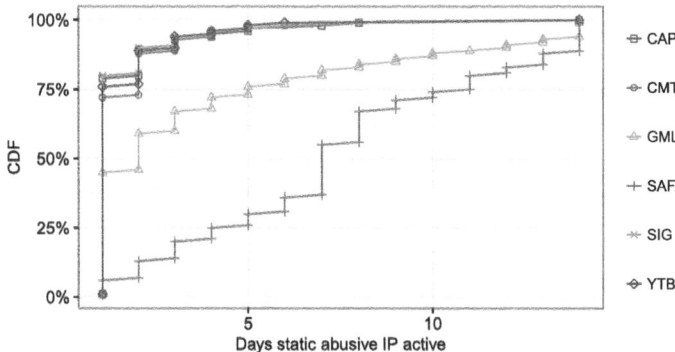

Fig. 9. CDF of the number of days exclusively static IP addresses remain abusive. Even without DHCP churn, attacks appear transient (potentially to avoid detection.)

logs versus IP addresses reported by any service for abuse over 2 weeks. We find a median of 15 % of observed IP addresses per /24 relay abuse. This increases to 24 % at the /16 subnet level. If we restrict ourselves to the top 1 % abusive IP addresses, this actually falls to 0.7 % for /24 networks and 0.08 % for /16 networks due to omitting more dynamic, short lived IP addresses and subnets.

The limited effectiveness of network topology in identifying abuse stems in part from devices migrating across subnet boundaries upon DHCP lease expiration. Using our HTTP request logs, if we compare a ⟨$PUID$, $User$-$Agent$⟩ device tuples' original and subsequent IP, we find 90 % of devices cross a /24 boundary and 70 % cross a /16 boundary. Only 6 % of clients cross an ASN boundary and 0.6 % appear in an entirely different geolocation after switching IP addresses.[3]

Translated into an abuse context, we observe 78–96 % of /24 subnets contain only a single abusive IP per service in a 14 day window and 91–100 % at most two abusive IP addresses. If we restrict our analysis to the top 1 % of abusive IP addresses, we still find 76–92 % of /24 subnets contain a single abusive IP. We note we cannot precisely identify where abusive clients migrate upon DHCP lease expiration as not all abuse verticals require account credentials and, more problematic, miscreants may access the same abusive account via multiple compromised devices and networks while reporting a spoofed User-Agent. Our findings illustrate that spatial properties of networks have little bearing on how ISPs re-assign devices to IP addresses. As a result, we advocate the most effective reputation system must operate on a per-IP rather than subnet granularity.

---

[3] ASN transitions may also occur due to a single network operator controlling multiple AS numbers, or alternatively, users may log in from duplicate devices (in terms of User-Agents) in different networks. Geolocation variations are within the predicted error of geolocation services.

6 Cross-Vertical Abuse

We now turn our attention to investigating the impact of sharing intelligence across heterogeneous web services. In terms of the absolute number of abusive IP addresses, we find that cross-vertical abuse is a rare event: miscreants use only 6 % IP addresses to attack at least two services in a 24 h window. However, in aggregate these IP addresses relay 5–43 % of all abuse per service. We examine which services benefit the most from sharing abuse intelligence due to miscreants re-using underground infrastructure as well as limitations of global IP reputation tracking.

6.1 Overlapping Abuse Verticals

To gauge the value of threat exchanges, we estimate the percentage of all abusive traffic per service S_1 that overlaps with malicious IP addresses reported by a second service S_2. We rely on an asymmetric calculation for the total volume of abuse caught:

$$\frac{|S_1 \cap S_2|}{|S_1|}$$

We present our results in Fig. 10a. As many abusive IP addresses relay a significant volume of legitimate traffic, we present a thresholded calculation restricted to IP addresses in S_2 with an abuse likelihood greater than 90 % in Fig. 10b. Even absent thresholding, we find the majority of abusive IP addresses exclusively target individual services. These findings are consistent with high-level observations in related work that identified little cross-abuse IP intersections between spam, phishing, and network scanning IP reputation lists [36]. However, those few IPs that do overlap generate a significant volume of abusive traffic. We discuss a few salient instances where abuse intelligence sharing has the strongest impact.

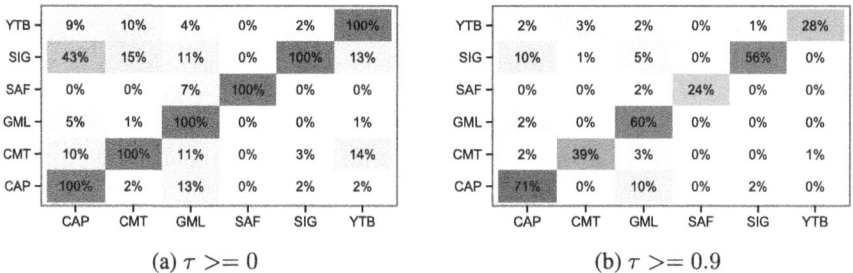

Fig. 10. Fraction of abusive traffic from a service (y-axis) overlapping with a list of abusive IP addresses from a second service (x-axis) with an abuse likelihood greater than τ.

Email Spam: Of all threats, IP addresses flagged for email spam provide the strongest predictor of abuse affecting other services. Coverage varies between 4–13 % of all abusive traffic, dropping to 2–10 % if we examine only SMTP relays where 90 % of all email sent is spam. Nevertheless, even with Gmail reporting five million daily IP addresses for spam, we find a significant fraction of abusive hosts engage solely in spam-based monetization rather than other forms of abuse.

Account-Based Abuse: We find that miscreants registering fake accounts nominally re-use the same infrastructure for comment spam (15 %) and YouTube fake engagement (13 %). This falls to 0–1 % if we examine thresholded abusive IP addresses. The weak correlation suggests that miscreants either stockpile accounts for more than 24 h prior to abuse, or that vertically integrated account creation and monetization may in fact be rare due to specialized account merchants [33]. Furthermore, even though comments and fake engagement both require Google accounts, we find infrastructure involved in either vertical rarely overlaps in a 24 h period: only 10–14 % of spam comments and fake likes and subscribes originate from the same IP address. Consequently, once a fake account evades initial detection upon registration, each service contending with account-based fraud must detect specialized threats even though other verticals may have more mature abuse prevention systems.

CAPTCHAs: The wide-spread adoption of CAPTCHAs across services including account creation and commenting creates a strong tendency where IP addresses that fail CAPTCHAs also tend to abuse other services. In particular, 43 % of all bulk registered accounts overlap with an IP that failed a CAPTCHA. However, as CAPTCHA failure is only a weak signal of abuse, if we restrict our analysis to IP addresses that fail over 90 % of CAPTCHA attempts (e.g., potentially automated solving), IP reputation catches only 10 % of abusive accounts.

Hosting Exclusivity: We observe a negligible overlap between web servers that miscreants compromise for malicious hosting and other forms of abuse. As a small exception, we find 7 % of malicious webpages overlap with IP addresses also serving as spam SMTP relays. Consequently, it appears that miscreants rarely re-use compromised web servers to proxy traffic for other abuse verticals. Our findings indicate that web security scanners for malware hosting cannot expedite their search coverage by scanning hosts also involved in email spam or other abuse.

6.2 Limitations of Intelligence Sharing

The coarse granularity of IP addresses as identifiers of abuse comes at a cost of false positives in the event of outright blacklisting. We estimate the volume of legitimate traffic in our signed-in HTTP request logs to a service S_1 that erroneously overlaps with abusive IP addresses reported by a service S_2. Given abuse appears in our request logs, we first optimistically filter all requests originating from IP addresses reported as abusive by S_1. Furthermore, as our request logs are limited to signed-in activity, we restrict our false positive estimates to

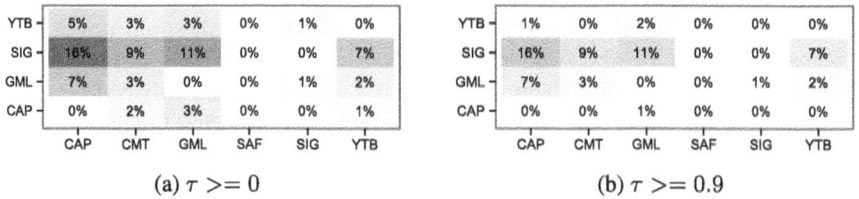

Fig. 11. Fraction of benign IP addresses from a service (y-axis) that erroneously overlap with abusive IP addresses reported by a secondary service (x-axis) with an abuse likelihood greater than τ.

YouTube engagement, account registration, outbound email, and CAPTCHAs solved by signed-in users.

We present our results for all abusive IP addresses in Fig. 11a and the same calculation restricted to IP addresses with an abuse likelihood greater than 90% in Fig. 11b. Without any threshold, IP blacklists would block 6–16% of all newly created, legitimate users and 0–5% of YouTube engagement. Even with thresholding, we find IP blacklists negatively impact account growth. We note our estimates are upper bounds on the volume of false positives as some erroneously blocked traffic may in fact reflect abuse currently unreported by an affected service. Similar trade-offs between blacklist false positives and false negatives with respect to the ratio of benign (so called ham) to spam traffic for email spam blacklists were demonstrated by Sinha et al. [29]. A key observation here is that individual organizations may have differing sensitivities to false positives, and that this sensitivity may even vary by abuse type.

Our findings indicate that while per-service, per-IP reputation captures a significant volume of abuse (as reported in Sect. 5), translating that abuse intelligence across services remains a challenge. This stems from the diverse user bases and devices served by a single IP address; while only a fraction of those devices may connect to one service, other services experience an entirely distinct user distribution. The end result is a limited utility for outright blacklisting based on cross-service intelligence.

7 Related Work

7.1 Characterizing IP Addresses

Research has spent a significant amount of effort to understand the network-level behaviors of (abusive) clients. This includes estimating the number of clients behind NATed IP addresses based on usage patterns [18], measuring the duration of DHCP leases and traffic patterns [16], examining the densification of networks over time [11], and understanding the behaviors of edge networks [5,13]. Within an abuse context, Xie et al. examined how to automatically detect dynamic IP addresses and the prevalence of abuse among such hosts [34], with an extension to automatically classify large NATed IP addresses as exclusively spam relays [10].

Ramachandran et al. examined the network behavior of spam bots and the confinement of abusive hosts to a subset of networks and autonomous systems [26]. We compared these prior estimates to our own findings and examined the impact of NAT and DHCP churn on the effectiveness of IP reputation tracking.

7.2 Blacklist Efficacy

IP blacklists enable web services to identify and penalize abusive hosts in the absence of overt user identifiers (e.g., authenticated session cookies). A number of studies previously examined the efficacy and global applicability of spam-based blacklists. The closest themes to our own work include estimating the coverage of various blacklists with respect to spamvertised abuse and affiliate programs [22], the performance of email spam blacklists when applied to alternative domains such as social network spam [8,31], the lack of overlap of abusive domains and IP addresses for blacklists targeting spam, phishing, and malware [36], instances where popular blacklists identify the same threats [12], and the efficacy of public versus commercial malware blacklists when applied to major malware families [14]. We provided a Google-centric view of abuse exclusivity across products which mirror these previous findings: abuse is an incredibly large and diverse space where miscreants are highly specialized. However, examining only the overlap of abusive IP addresses fails to capture skewed traffic emanating from rare co-occurrences.

8 Summary

In this work, we measured the effectiveness of centralized reputation tracking as a tool for identifying miscreants who leverage the same machine for spam, denial of service, malicious hosting, and other forms of automated abuse. We focused initially on the scale of these individuals threats and found they differ by two orders of magnitude, with email spam reigning as our top source of abusive hosts. Despite 8 million IP addresses reported every day by one of six Google services for abuse, blocking only 1 % of these sources can prevent 48–82 % of all harmful traffic. We found some of these threats exhibit a local specialization: malicious hosting in the United States; fake engagement in Russia; and bulk account registration in India.

Transforming this intelligence into actionable reputation data proved challenging: 66 % of abusive IP addresses remained active for only a single day, in part driven by dynamic reallocation where the average (compromised) device cycled through 20 IP addresses over the course of two weeks. Equally problematic, NATs representing large user populations polluted IP reputation to the point where only 38 % of abusive IP addresses exclusively relayed harmful traffic, while the rest shared some overlap with benign devices. Nevertheless, we found this minority of hosts delivered 16–49 % of all abuse per service. Ultimately, we found that hosts involved in cross-service abuse were in fact rare: only 6 % of abusive IP addresses negatively affected at least two services within a 24 h window. However, combined, these hosts generated 5–43 % of all abuse per service. In the end, we argued less mature anti-abuse pipelines for new products or Internet services could tap into such an intelligence feed to benefit from threat exchanges of seemingly unrelated attacks. However, these benefits must come from machine learning pipelines—outright blacklisting remains out of reach due to collateral damage to legitimate users.

Acknowledgments. This work was supported in part by the National Science Foundation under contracts CNS 1409758, CNS 1111699, and CNS 1518741. Any opinions, findings, and conclusions or recommendations expressed in this material are those of the authors and do not necessarily reflect the views of the sponsors.

References

1. Anderson, R., Barton, C., Böhme, R., Clayton, R., van Eeten, M.J.G., Levi, M., Moore, T., Savage, S.: Measuring the cost of cybercrime. In: Proceedings of the Workshop on Economics of Information Security (WEIS) (2012)
2. Asghari, H., Ciere, M., Van Eeten, M.J.: Post-mortem of a Zombie: conficker cleanup after six years. In: Proceedings of the USENIX Security Symposium (2015)
3. Taylor, B.: It's not about the spam (2007). http://goo.gl/zzAL4N
4. Caballero, J., Grier, C., Kreibich, C., Paxson, V.: Measuring pay-per-install: the commoditization of malware distribution. In: USENIX Security Symposium (2011)
5. Casado, M., Freedman, M.J.: Peering through the shroud: the effect of edge opacity on IP-based client identification. In: Proceedings of the Symposium on Networked Systems Design and Implementation (2007)
6. Czyz, J., Allman, M., Zhang, J., Iekel-Johnson, S., Osterweil, E., Bailey, M.: Measuring IPv6 adoption. In: Proceedings of the ACM Conference on SIGCOMM (2014)
7. DShield.: DShield (2015). https://www.dshield.org/
8. Grier, C., Thomas, K., Paxson, V., Zhang, M.: @spam: the underground on 140 characters or less. In: Proceedings of the ACM Conference on Computer and Communications Security (2010)
9. Hammell, M.: ThreatExchange: sharing for a safer internet (2015). http://on.fb.me/1zvuPdS
10. Hong, C.-Y., Fang, Y., Xie, Y.: Populated IP addresses: classification and applications. In: Proceedings of the Conference on Computer and Communications Security (2012)
11. Ihm, S., Pai, V.S.: Towards understanding modern web traffic. In: Proceedings of the ACM SIGCOMM Internet Measurement Conference (2011)
12. Jung, J., Sit, E.: An empirical study of spam traffic and the use of DNS black lists. In: Proceedings of the ACM SIGCOMM Internet Measurement Conference (2004)
13. Kreibich, C., Weaver, N., Nechaev, B., Paxson, V.: Netalyzr: illuminating the edge network. In: Proceedings of the ACM SIGCOMM Internet Measurement Conference (2010)
14. Kührer, M., Rossow, C., Holz, T.: Paint it black: evaluating the effectiveness of malware blacklists. In: Stavrou, A., Bos, H., Portokalidis, G. (eds.) RAID 2014. LNCS, vol. 8688, pp. 1–21. Springer, Heidelberg (2014)

15. Levchenko, K., Pitsillidis, A., Chachra, N., Enright, B., Félegyházi, M., Grier, C., Halvorson, T., Kanich, C., et al.: Click trajectories: end-to-end analysis of the spam value chain. In: Proceedings of the IEEE Symposium on Security and Privacy (2011)
16. Maier, G., Feldmann, A., Paxson, V., Allman, M.: On dominant characteristics of residential broadband internet traffic. In: Proceedings of the ACM SIGCOMM Internet Measurement Conference (2009)
17. McCoy, D., Pitsillidis, A., Jordan, G., Weaver, N., Kreibich, C., Krebs, B., Voelker, G.M., Savage, S., Levchenko, K.: Pharmaleaks: understanding the business of online pharmaceutical affiliate programs. In: Proceedings of the 21st USENIX Conference on Security Symposium (2012)
18. Metwally, A., Paduano, M.: Estimating the number of users behind IP addresses for combating abusive traffic. In: Proceedings of the SIGKDD International Conference on Knowledge Discovery and Data Mining (2011)
19. Miller, R.: AlienVault announces more social threat exchange (2015). http://tcrn.ch/1FL7E8A
20. Neville, A., Gibb, R.: ZeroAccess indepth (2013). http://goo.gl/j0eMHr
21. Pearce, P., Dave, V., Grier, C., Levchenko, K., Guha, S., McCoy, D., Paxson, V., Savage, S., Voelker, G.M.: Characterizing large-scale click fraud in zeroaccess. In: Proceedings of the Conference on Computer and Communications Security (2014)
22. Pitsillidis, A., Kanich, C., Voelker, G.M., Levchenko, K., Savage, S.: Taster's choice: a comparative analysis of spam feeds. In: Proceedings of the ACM SIGCOMM Internet Measurement Conference (2012)
23. Provos, N.: Safe browsing - protecting web users for 5 years and counting (2012). http://goo.gl/psdXkP
24. Provos, N., Mavrommatis, P., Rajab, M.A., Monrose, F.: All your iFRAMEs point to us. In: Proceedings of the USENIX Security Symposium (2008)
25. Rains, T.: Microsoft interflow: a new security and threat information exchange platform (2015). http://bit.ly/1SKpcs2
26. Ramachandran, A., Feamster, N.: Understanding the network-level behavior of spammers. In: Proceedings of the ACM Conference on SIGCOMM (2006)
27. Rowinski, M.: More than 1,000 organizations join IBM to battle cybercrime (2015). https://www-03.ibm.com/press/us/en/pressrelease/46856.wss
28. Sinha, P., Boukhtouta, A., Belarde, V.H., Debbabi, M.: Insights from the analysis of the Mariposa botnet. In: Proceedings of the International Conference on Risks and Security of Internet and Systems (CRiSIS) (2010)
29. Sinha, S., Bailey, M., Jahanian, F.: Improving spam blacklisting through dynamic thresholding and speculative aggregation. In: Proceedings of the Network & Distributed System Security Symposium (2010)
30. Stone-Gross, B., Cova, M., Cavallaro, L., Gilbert, B., Szydlowski, M., Kemmerer, R., Kruegel, C., Vigna, G.: Your botnet is my botnet: analysis of a botnet takeover. In: Proceedings of the ACM Conference on Computer and Communications Security (2009)
31. Thomas, K., Grier, C., Song, D., Paxson, V.: Suspended accounts in retrospect: an analysis of Twitter spam. In: Proceedings of the Internet Measurement Conference (2011)
32. Thomas, K., Huang, D.Y., Wang, D., Bursztein, E., Grier, C., Holt, T.J., et al.: Framing dependencies introduced by underground commoditization. In: Proceedings of the Workshop on the Economics of Information Security (2015)

33. Thomas, K., McCoy, D., Grier, C., Kolcz, A., Paxson, V.: Trafficking fraudulent accounts: the role of the underground market in Twitter spam and abuse. In: Proceedings of the USENIX Security Symposium (2013)
34. Xie, Y., Fang, Y., Achan, K., Gillum, E., Goldszmidt, M., Wobber, T.: How dynamic are IP addresses? In: Proceedings of the ACM Conference on SIGCOMM (2007)
35. Fang, Y., Xie, Y., Ke, Q.: Sbotminer: large scale search bot detection. In: Proceedings of the ACM International Conference on Web Search and Data Mining (2010)
36. Zhang, J., Chivukula, A., Bailey, M., Karir, M., Liu, M.: Characterization of blacklists and tainted network traffic. In: Roughan, M., Chang, R. (eds.) PAM 2013. LNCS, vol. 7799, pp. 218–228. Springer, Heidelberg (2013)

SandPrint: Fingerprinting Malware Sandboxes to Provide Intelligence for Sandbox Evasion

Akira Yokoyama[1], Kou Ishii[1], Rui Tanabe[1], Yinmin Papa[1],
Katsunari Yoshioka[1], Tsutomu Matsumoto[1], Takahiro Kasama[2],
Daisuke Inoue[2], Michael Brengel[3], Michael Backes[3],
and Christian Rossow[1,3(✉)]

[1] Yokohama National University, Yokohama, Japan
{yokoyama-akira-bs,ishii-kou-yf,tanabe-rui-nv}@ynu.jp,
yinminpapa@gmail.com, yoshioka@ynu.ac.jp,
tsutomu@mlab.jks.ynu.ac.jp
[2] National Institute of Information and Communications Technology,
Koganei, Japan
{kasama,dai}@nict.go.jp
[3] Center for IT-Security, Privacy, and Accountability, CISPA,
Saarland University, Saarbrücken, Germany
{mbrengel,crossow}@mmci.uni-saarland.de,
backes@cs.uni-saarland.de

Abstract. To cope with the ever-increasing volume of malware samples, automated program analysis techniques are inevitable. Malware sandboxes in particular have become the *de facto* standard to extract a program's behavior. However, the strong need to automate program analysis also bears the risk that anyone that can submit programs to learn and leak the characteristics of a particular sandbox.

We introduce SANDPRINT, a program that measures and leaks characteristics of Windows-targeted sandboxes. We submit our tool to 20 malware analysis services and collect 2666 analysis reports that cluster to 76 sandboxes. We then systemically assess whether an attacker can possibly find a subset of characteristics that are *inherent* to all sandboxes, and not just characteristic of a single sandbox. In fact, using supervised learning techniques, we show that adversaries can automatically generate a classifier that can reliably tell a sandbox and a real system apart. Finally, we show that we can use similar techniques to stealthily detect commercial malware security appliances of three popular vendors.

1 Introduction

Malicious software poses one of the major security challenges nowadays. In its various forms, malware is equally a threat to consumers (e.g., banking trojans, ransomware), businesses (e.g., targeted attacks, denial-of-service bots), and society in general (e.g., spambots). In 2014, Symantec faced 65 million previously-unseen malicious files targeting Windows [51]. Similarly, PandaLabs reports on a daily flood of over 200,000 new unknown, potentially malicious programs [49].

This trend of increasing malware samples is a consequence of polymorphism, but is also caused by new threats that are discovered almost on a daily basis.

To cope with the volume of malware, defenders started to improve technology and their organization within the community. On the technological side, researchers introduced several complementary approaches to analyze unknown programs in an automated way. Windows-based malware sandboxes in particular have become the *de facto* standard for automated malware analysis [24], equally for academia and industry. Sandboxes are excessively leveraged to obtain threat information, such as previously-unseen malware, inputs for supervised detection mechanisms, malware C&C servers, targets of banking trojans, intelligence on spreading campaigns, or simply to assist in the manual process of reverse engineering. Finally, sandboxes are also used as part of commercial malware security appliances that aim to protect organizations by dynamic malware analysis.

The requirement to automate the analysis of unknown programs ("samples") also bears the risk that the analysis is unattended. That is, oftentimes the entire process from receiving a sample, scheduling it for analysis, executing it, and possibly even returning an analysis result to the sample submitter is embedded in a fully-automated processing chain. Anyone that can submit samples to the input feed of a sandbox can possibly learn and leak the characteristics of a particular sandbox. While it may seem non-trivial to send programs to any sandbox, as we will show, it is typically sufficient to submit a sample to automated malware analysis services, which then redistribute the samples for other sandboxes, easily generating a massive source of insights about the internals of global sandboxes.

In this paper, we follow this general idea and introduce SANDPRINT, a Windows-based program that measures and leaks characteristics of the sandbox, such as precise OS information, network configuration or installed (or emulated) hardware. Over a period of 2 weeks, we continuously submit our tool to 20 malware analysis services [1–3, 5–8, 11–14, 20, 25, 28, 35, 38, 48, 50, 52, 55] and collect 2666 analysis reports from eleven of these services. In an attempt to fingerprint sandboxes, we use unsupervised learning mechanisms to cluster the SANDPRINT reports and their various features into groups to identify sandboxes. This process exposes 76 sandboxes, many of which presumably obtain their samples via automated sample exchanges with malware analysis services.

We then turn to our next research question: Is it possible to *detect* a sandbox from the perspective of a (potentially malicious) program? By now, many malware families already follow ad-hoc procedures to identify individual sandbox artefacts, such as detecting virtualization or avoiding specific sandbox configurations. Instead, we assess a more systematic approach and explore whether an attacker can possibly find characteristics (e.g., using a tool like SANDPRINT) that are *inherent* to all sandboxes, and not just characteristic of a single sandbox. We leverage supervised learning based on the collected features to train an automated classifier that can reliably tell sandboxes apart from normal systems.

Finally, we turn our attention to the possibility of detecting malware appliances of popular vendors. We follow the intuition that these appliances internally also use sandboxing technology and are thus likely susceptible to similar evasion attacks. In fact, by training a classifier just on the aforementioned sandboxes, we show that adversaries can even evade appliances—undermining the entire security concept of such installations.

Summarizing, the contributions of this paper are:

- We present SANDPRINT, a tool to exfiltrate characteristics of malware sandboxes. We submit it to 20 public malware analysis services and use unsupervised learning techniques to identify the characteristics of 76 sandboxes.
- We leverage the resulting SANDPRINT reports to train an automated classifier that can reliably distinguish between a sandbox and a user system.
- We show that we can use characteristics that we learned from public sandboxes to detect malware security appliances, even without *a priori* insights on the internals of the appliance's sandbox.

2 Background

We first describe the terminology that we use throughout the paper. We use the term *sandbox* to refer to a dynamic analysis environment that executes unknown programs (called *samples*). Sandboxes are widely used to gain insights on malicious software (*malware*), such as its current campaigns [19], recent C&C servers and traffic patterns [36,44,46] or attack targets [26]. Similarly, sandboxes can be used to group behavior into malware families [16,45], or to identify suspicious behavioral patterns [32]. Egele et al. give a comprehensive overview of known sandbox implementations [24].

By now, malware sandboxes are not used only by academics. In contrast to manual analysis, sandboxes are highly automated. As a consequence, the antivirus industry and security companies that offer anti-malware appliances heavily rely on sandboxes as part of their daily business. In fact, sandboxes have become the industry standard to cope with the daily feed of hundreds of thousands of previously-unseen malware samples. In times where manually analyzing each malware does not scale anymore, sandboxes are a vital component in the fight against malware.

Virtualization: To scale the analysis, most sandboxes rely on some form of virtualization (with the notable exception of bare-metal sandboxes [30,31]). To this end, sandboxes rely on various virtualization techniques such as VMWare [15] and VirtualBox [10] or CPU emulators [4,17]. Cuckoo Sandbox [8] is a popular open-source sandbox. However, as we will see, many security organizations operate other sandboxes, either choosing from commercial sandboxes or designing their own solution. Virtualization offers the benefit that many virtual machines (VMs) can run in parallel on a single system, each analyzing one sample. In addition, virtualization software makes it possible to take so called *snapshots* of VMs, which freeze the state of a VM and allow reversion back to this state. Snapshots help to reset the system state once a piece of malware was executed, so that future executions do not suffer from side effects.

Operating System: Regardless of precise sandbox implementations, the most common and popular sandboxes execute samples on commodity operating systems, such as MS Windows. Due to the prevalence of Windows-based malware, we focus on Windows-based sandboxes, although our results likely also apply to Android-based [37] or Linux-based [39] sandboxes.

Malware Analysis Services: In contrast to a sandbox, a *malware analysis service* (or simply "service" hereafter) receives submissions of samples (e.g., via a web interface), analyzes the submitted samples in various ways, and normally provides analysis results to the users. As we will show, these services typically use one or more sandboxes to analyze the sample. In addition, services such as VirusTotal [14] and Jotti's malware scan [28] provide anti-virus scans. Also, it is quite common that services share samples with other sandbox operators. In fact, some services offer to search for submissions of other users with various key words, such as the hash value of the sample or anti-virus labels, and parties can use paid APIs to automate searches and downloads. Table 2 summarizes the analysis results provided by each service. There are nine services that accept the submission of samples but do not provide any analysis results to the users. Following the feedback by the vendors, the submitted samples were manually analyzed in an isolated environment without Internet access.

Malware Security Appliances: Sandboxes have become an integral part of commercial malware security appliances (or simply "appliances" hereafter). Such appliances protect endpoints by dynamically analyzing an unknown program and inspecting its behavior for suspicious actions. Appliances are frequently deployed at the network layer and are used orthogonally to anti-virus scanners, e.g., to protect endpoints from opening malicious email attachments or malicious file downloads. Internally, appliances also use sandbox technologies to analyze the program behavior.

3 Sandbox Fingerprinting

Sandboxes are a vital tool for malware analysis, which highlights the importance of having a thorough understanding of their live deployment and characteristics. In this section, we will *fingerprint* sandboxes to investigate the landscape of Internet-connected sandboxes. In our context, a fingerprint reveals artifacts that are specific to individual sandboxes. In Sect. 3.1, we will describe 24 features, i.e., attributes that reveal certain characteristics of a sandbox. We will then present SANDPRINT, a tool that exfiltrates characteristics from any sandbox. In Sect. 3.2, we will use the tool to collect fingerprints by submitting it to 20 public malware analysis services, and describe the dataset obtained.

3.1 Sandbox Fingerprinting Features

We first introduce fingerprinting features that we use to discriminate sandboxes from each other, or put differently, to describe characteristics of individual sandboxes. We propose a (non-exhaustive) list of 24 features, as shown in Table 1. We group these characteristics into the following five categories:

Table 1. Sandbox fingerprinting features (Clustering distance metrics: ED = Edit Distance, EU = Euclidean Distance, EQ = Equality Distance, JD = Jaccard Distance)

Category	Feature	Clustering	Category	Feature	Clustering
System installation	Host name	✓ ED	Network config	Default gateway	✓ EQ
	Installation date	✓ EQ		External IP address	✓ EQ
	OS information			ARP list	
	Organization name	✓ EQ		MAC address	
	Owner name	✓ EQ		DNS servers	✓ EQ
	Windows product ID	✓ EQ	Activity	Clipboard	
	System manufacturer			Desktop icons	
Hardware	Disk space	✓ EU		Event log	
	Display resolution			Recent files	✓ JD
	Mouse devices		Execution start	Sample name	✓ EQ
	RAM	✓ EQ		Sample path	✓ EQ
	Processor			Time from boot to start	

1. **System Installation:** Sandboxes require an operating system (OS) to run samples. Typically, to minimize manual effort, sandbox operators install and configure the OS only once, and then take a snapshot of the system. Assuming that all parallel instances of the sandbox (e.g., VMs) use the same system snapshot, this results in many features that are persistent across executions.
2. **Hardware:** The underlying hardware, whether emulated or physical, can also reveal unique characteristics of a sandbox. All features are agnostic to whether the hardware is emulated or actually physically present.
3. **Network Configuration:** Sandboxes are typically configured such that the sample can communicate with the Internet, e.g., with C&C servers. We thus collect network features and also local configurations.
4. **Activity:** The system snapshot reveals certain events that have taken place in the past (i.e., during installation time). In general, these features can measure whether the system is close to default settings.
5. **Execution Start:** Once the fresh, non-infected sandbox has been started, it needs to obtain a sample that the analyst wants to analyze. There are multiple different ways to automate this process.

This list can easily be extended with further features. We favor features that potentially show a high entropy and are specific to a certain sandbox—the more a feature can differentiate a sandbox from others, the better. In addition, most of the selected features are deterministic and their values discrete and reliable. Note that a stealthy sandbox could try to diversify the feature values.

3.2 Extracting Sandbox Fingerprints with SandPrint

We implemented SANDPRINT, a tool to exfiltrate all above-mentioned features from a system. SANDPRINT is a Windows 32-bit PE binary written in C, which uses the Windows API and custom functions to reveal the features. Once SAND-PRINT is executed, it uses HTTP to communicate with the SANDPRINT server. A unique identifier is assigned to each SANDPRINT sample and after the HTTP session is established, this ID, embedded in an HTTP POST request, is sent

Table 2. Malware analysis services and summary of SANDPRINT submissions

Malware analysis service	Dyn.	Stat.	AV Scan	Report/submission	Reports	Sandboxes
Service #1	✓	✓		0/20	0	0
Service #2	✓			14/20	14	1
Service #3			✓	0/20	0	0
Service #4	✓			0/20	0	0
Service #5			✓	0/20	0	0
Service #6				6/20	85	25
Service #7		✓	✓	2/20	8	6
Service #8			✓	20/20	21	1
Service #9			✓	0/20	0	0
Service #10			✓	20/20	378	36
Service #11	✓	✓	✓	20/20	134	28
Service #12				19/20	25	1
Service #13	✓	✓		20/20	427	36
Service #13 (win7 64 bit)	✓	✓		20/20	399	49
Service #13 (win7 32 bit stealthy)	✓	✓		20/20	424	35
Service #14	✓			0/20	0	0
Service #15				0/20	0	0
Service #16	✓	✓	✓	20/20	268	26
Service #17	✓			0/20	0	0
Service #18			✓	20/20	162	20
Service #19		✓		0/20	0	0
Service #20	✓	✓	✓	20/20	321	31

to the server. In this way we can track which sample is executed in which system. After the ID is sent, a challenge-response authentication is done in order to detect replayed requests.

After this initial handshake, SANDPRINT starts collecting features of the system. For the implementation of feature collection, we avoided using commands like `systeminfo`, `netstat`, and `ipconfig`, as they are often used by adversaries to collect system features, and indeed we have confirmed that some sandboxes restrict them. Moreover, to avoid potential deadlocks caused by collecting individual features (due to e.g., slow disk I/O), we balanced all feature collection functions across multiple threads. In addition, to estimate the overall execution time, a heartbeat thread periodically notifies the server that SANDPRINT is still executing. Each thread sends features to the server after the feature collection process is completed. Note that all SANDPRINT traffic imitates HTTP protocol and so it seems as if it is communicating with a Web server.

We submitted SANDPRINT to 20 malware analysis services to collect fingerprints. Table 2 summarizes the public services and includes both popular academic and non-academic services. We periodically submitted SANDPRINT from January 5, 2016 to January 18, 2016.

For each service, we created a unique SANDPRINT instance so that we could map which file was uploaded where. That is, while the semantic functionality is unaltered, the resulting file hashes are distinct. In addition, we use a unique identifier that is computed during runtime, report this identifier to our server, and aim to expose it in the public analysis report that the service generates. This way, we can later match the identifier in a report with the corresponding identifier of the analysis report, revealing that a report was generated by a particular service. In total, we collected 2666 SANDPRINT reports from 221 of our 440 submissions. Thus, on average, we received 6 reports per submission. The reports came from 395 IP address including 33 countries. As we will discuss later, this already indicates that there is a strong tendency to (i) re-execute the same sample multiple times (on the same or a slightly different sandbox) and (ii) share samples across sandboxes/services. We will now study this observation in more detail and group similar SANDPRINT reports for further analyses.

4 Clustering Sandboxes

The fingerprint collection revealed over 2500 reports. But are there really that many sandboxes, or are some sandboxes responsible for multiple reports? To answer this question, in this section, we introduce a clustering technique to group similar reports and identify which reports were sent to us by which sandboxes.

4.1 Clustering

Initial observations have shown that subsets of the entire list of reports actually share similar characteristics. As soon as a sandbox sends multiple reports, this is intuitive, as there are likely features that remain unchanged across two sample executions. Naïvely, one could even check which reports contain equal features. However, we found that sandboxes indeed (intentionally or not) diversify parts of the features. Instead, we thus propose to use unsupervised learning techniques to group *similar* reports together. Lacking any labels and ground truth for sandboxes, we face a classical unsupervised problem here. We chose to use agglomerative hierarchical clustering to group reports. Hierarchical clustering has the advantage that it allows specifying a custom distance function and does not require determining the number of expected clusters in beforehand. The *distance function* determines how different two reports are. We define a distance function that spans all "clustering" features in Table 1 (see checkmark). That is, for a pair of reports R1 and R2, we sum the distances of all pairwise features and divide by the number of features to achieve the average distance. More formally, the distance function between $R1$ and $R2$ is: $dist(R1, R2) = \frac{1}{N} * \sum_{k=0}^{N} dist_k(R1, R2)$ where $dist_k$ is the distance between the values of a particular feature k. When comparing a feature between two reports, we expect equality (EQ), and otherwise assume maximum dissimilarity. That is, $dist_k(R1, R2)$ is zero if the feature k is equal in both reports, or 1 otherwise. For selected features which we observed to vary in individual sandboxes, we do not expect equality. That is, we compare the host name using a normalized edit distance (ED), deploy the Euclidean distance (EU) to compare the disk space and length of the sample name, and use the Jaccard distance (JD) to compare the recently opened files. Table 1 categorizes the features accordingly. All distance functions have been normalized in the range [0, 1] so that a single feature does not introduce bias.

In some cases, features are not present in one of the reports to compare. SANDPRINT may have failed to collect some features, e.g., if the sandbox analysis time was too short to complete all measurements (e.g., tracking all files in the Programs directory may take a long time). To tackle sparse features, we focus on those features that are included in the majority of the reports, as indicated by the checkmark in Table 1. If a report does not have characteristics for a remaining feature, we still cannot judge if two features are similar. To tackle this problem, we ignore features that are not present in both reports and decrement N (the number of features) accordingly to avoid biases in the average.

We then compute the distance between all reports and group the most similar ones together, using agglomerative single linkage clustering. This process results in a dendrogram, a tree-like structure that represents how the reports are clustered together. After the clustering, we consider groups that have a distance less than 0.5 as clusters. The intuition for this threshold is that we expect that at least half of the features are similar for reports of a single sandbox.

4.2 Clustering Results and Validation

Clustering helped to reduce the 2666 reports down to 76 clusters. Of these, 16 are singleton clusters, i.e., sandboxes that only contributed one report to our dataset. The largest cluster spans 233 reports, while the average cluster consists of 35 reports, or 44 reports if we exclude the singleton clusters.

To verify the clustering output, we divided our research team in two disjoint groups. While one group independently designed and performed the automated clustering, the other group validated the clustering output. To this end, we manually grouped similar sandboxes based on unique characteristics that we identified for a particular sandbox, explicitly also those that slightly varied information across different executions. For each such outstanding feature, we defined a regular expression that matches all reports of the sandbox. We only selected features whose entropy was large enough to avoid coincidental collisions and define at least two characteristic features per sandbox.

We then compared the clustering result with the outcome of the manual "clustering" done by the validation group. The outcome of the manual assignments was equal to the clustering result, except in one case where our clustering merged two sandboxes that we did not group manually. In this case, while the user name, working group name, and host name were similar, the OS installation date was more than three years apart. Other than that, we did not find any further inconsistencies, which shows that our clustering methodology can accurately map SANDPRINT reports (and their features) to a smaller number of sandboxes.

4.3 Sandbox vs. Service

Table 2 summarizes the results of SANDPRINT submissions to the 20 malware analysis services. At a glance, the number of SANDPRINT reports received from these services varies widely. We did not receive any reports from nine services, which implies that sandboxes deployed by these services do not have Internet connectivity, or the services simply did not conduct any dynamic analysis on the submitted samples. Note that SANDPRINT is implemented such that it first reports back to our server before collecting any features. As we also did not see the initial connection for the nine services, we argue that the lack of reports is not caused by sandboxes that are trying to avoid being fingerprinted. Due to the lack of data, we exclude these nine services and will focus on the remaining eleven services in the following.

4.4 Mapping Malware Analysis Services to Sandboxes

Next, we aim to map the SANDPRINT reports to malware analysis services. In other words, did our fingerprinting help to expose internals of the sandbox(es) used by a service? To map sandboxes to services, we followed a two-fold approach.

First, we studied the analysis reports (i.e., those provided by the services, and not by SANDPRINT) that were returned by a service. These reports include the behavior of the submitted samples. Recall that we encoded a unique identifier in each SANDPRINT submission, which became visible in the analysis reports. We found this identifier in the analysis reports of services #2, #11, #13, and #20.

Second, to map the remaining services, we analyzed whether some sandboxes were exclusively used when submitting a sample to a particular service. That is, we identify sandboxes that are seemingly attached to a certain service. Figure 3 (see Appendix) depicts the mapping between all samples submitted to eleven malware analysis services (y-axis) and 76 sandboxes according to the report clustering (x-axis). Some mappings could be confirmed by the analysis reports. Next to these confirmed mappings, we find that some sandboxes are frequently and exclusively used by the same service. For example, Sandbox 69 is constantly used by Service #11 and no other services. In such a case, we can with some likelihood conclude that the sandbox is exclusively used by the service. In total, we revealed the dedicated sandboxes for four of the eleven services in this way.

After we mapped services to sandboxes, we were left with 71 sandboxes that do not directly belong to one of the services. This is also shown in Fig. 3, which lists many sandboxes that are commonly used to analyze samples from various services. The degree of activity per sandboxes is an indicator for the coverage, i.e., how many samples a sandbox receives and executes. But foremost, it highlights that samples are actively shared among the services.

4.5 Empirical Sandbox Analysis

After determining the sandboxes, we will highlight some insights obtained from the collected features. First, we inspected the system installation features. We found that the most popular OS for these sandboxes is still Windows XP, counting 37 out of 71 sandboxes for which we could identify the OS. 29 sandboxes were Windows 7. The other 5 sandboxes run Windows 8. The installation date can approximate the age of a sandbox. Assuming the other installation dates are not faked, we can see that all of the obtained OS installation dates are between the years 2008 and 2016. We also see that more than half of the sandboxes are at least three years old. As of 2014, 10 sandboxes were installed and already 18 sandboxes in 2015 or 2016. It is notable that the Windows product ID of 41 sandboxes is static, while 18 sandboxes vary the value. We presume this serves for diversification purposes, as malware has been observed to use the Windows product ID as a feature for sandbox identification.

The distribution of sandbox host names and owner names falls into two extreme cases, namely, they are either highly diversified or completely static. We deduce that some sandbox developers take countermeasures against being fingerprinted, while many others do not. Among the sandboxes that diversify host and owner names, the randomized names of most sandboxes still exhibit common patterns, such as common prefixes and/or fixed length of the strings.

In some cases, we can infer sandbox implementations. Namely, Cuckoo Sandbox includes a particular file named *agent.py*, which must be running upon the analysis of a sample. We can infer that Cuckoo Sandbox is installed and running by checking if the recent files list includes *agent.py*. We infer that five sandboxes are implemented with Cuckoo Sandbox. Note that the sandboxes are not clustered together, although they use the same technology. This is mainly due to the fact that sandbox operators have to set up their own VM image, regardless of whether they use common frameworks like Cuckoo. Although some sandboxes use the same virtualization technology, these sandboxes can still be distinguished based on their installation features (such as OS installation date or product ID).

Next, we inspected the Internet uplinks used by the sandboxes. 64 sandboxes use external IP addresses of a single country according to GeoIP. Among them, the US comes first with 22 sandboxes, Germany ranks second with six sandboxes, China ranks third with five sandboxes, and Ireland ranks fourth with four sandboxes. Three sandboxes each are in Sweden, Russia, and Korea, and Romania, Japan, and Britain host two sandboxes. We note that there are two sandboxes that we cannot geolocate due to their high diversity of external IP addresses. These sandboxes use Tor to diversify the IP address. We also note that 29 sandboxes use a single fixed IP address, which makes them trivially detectable from the server side. For instance, if a malware sample sends a command to a C&C server, the IP address could be checked against a black list on that server, which then tells the client to stop executing.

The MAC addresses show the highest diversity in all features we collected. Only 12 sandboxes use a single fixed MAC address, as confirmed by multiple SANDPRINT reports. The majority of MAC addresses are at least partly diversified (e.g., the first three octets, namely the vendor ID, are often fixed but the rest are diversified). We speculate this is due to the fact that the sandboxes actually consist of multiple VMs running in parallel, sharing the same VM image, but all having unique MAC addresses to avoid collisions on the Ethernet layer. Of those sandboxes that did not hide the vendor prefix, we could reveal 6 VMware-based (prefix: 00-50-56) and 21 VirtualBox-based (prefix: 08-00-27) sandboxes.

Table 3. Sandbox classifier features.

	Feature	Observation	Transf.
Hardware	Display resolution	Uncommon	id
	Display width	Small	id
	RAM size	Small/Uncommon	id
	PS/2 mouse	Uncommon	{0,1}
	#Cores	Small	id
	Disk size	Small	id
History	System uptime	small	id
	Last login	Long ago	id
	Last file access	Long ago	id
Execution	Image name	Uncommon	{0,1}
	Clipboard	Empty	len
	System manufacturer	Uncommon	len

5 Sandbox Classification

We have shown that the fingerprints can be used to discover that certain reports belong to the same sandboxes. We now explore whether we can leverage the extracted features to judge if a system is a sandbox. Intuitively, we explore features that are *inherent* to sandboxes due to hardware constraints, their snapshot-based operations, or lack of user interactions. We will show how we can use those inherent features to detect sandboxes using supervised machine learning techniques. We will first describe the feature selection for this task and then outline how we design and evaluate a classifier for sandboxes with those features using Support Vector Machines (SVMs) [21].

5.1 Feature Selection

The key idea behind the feature selection is to find patterns which are characteristic for a sandbox operation but unlikely for a machine under human control. Instead of identifying specific fingerprints for particular sandboxes, we strive to find sandbox-inherent features that are common to all sandboxes.

Feature Selection Process. To establish a ground truth for user PCs, we execute SANDPRINT on 50 commodity Windows workstations which are not used as sandboxes and are under the control of human operators. We then manually examined the reports to identify inherent and meaningful patterns which we observed in the sandbox reports but which were not as characteristic for the user reports. Table 3 summarizes the selected features, which we divide in the three categories hardware, history and execution. The second column contains the feature name, the third one describes our observations from the sandbox reports, and the last column shows how we transform the feature value to an integer before we pass it to the SVM (as we will discuss in Sect. 5.2).

The observations mentioned in Table 3 are a vague description of the feature characteristic. A naïve approach would be to derive sandbox signatures for concrete values, such as searching for reports with a display resolution of 4:3. This observation was made for the vast majority of sandboxes, but was uncommon for a real user. However, there are several problems when choosing such *concrete* values. First, the feature value is not necessarily so precise that such a solution would make sense. The screen resolution, for example, was not 4:3 for all sandbox reports, but 5:4 or some other suspicious value which we did not observe in the user reports. Thus, instead of figuring out concrete values and checks for each feature, we leave this task to the training process of our SVM classifier.

Similarly, we also refrain from detecting *virtualization* techniques, and rather focus on inherent sandbox techniques. Technically, we could check for artifacts that indicate the presence of a virtualization solution such as VMWare or Virtual Box, which is frequently used by sandboxes. However, we would bias our classifier towards detecting virtual machines, which is not the objective. While virtualization is definitely a hint toward the presence of a sandbox, it is also definitely not a guarantee. For instance, we found one user report which indicated that the execution was taking place in a VMWare virtual machine. Our classifier should be able to classify this machine as a user machine and not as a sandbox. Conversely, a sandbox does not necessarily use virtualization as, for example, in the case of bare-metal sandboxes. Our classifier should be able to classify those systems as sandboxes despite the absence of virtualization, as our features are based on the observation that sandboxes use snapshots, have restricted resources, and uncommon user interaction.

Feature Description. We now describe the features in more detail. The *hardware* features are motivated by the fact that sandbox operators restrict resources in order to leverage parallel computation. Therefore, it is quite common that sandboxes are single core, use little RAM, and have small disk sizes, whereas these quantities are much larger on the average user PCs. Second, since sandboxes are usually not interactively used by a human, the operators often do not customize the hardware configurations. We argue that a small display size and uncommon display resolution as well as a PS/2 mouse are all indicators for a sandbox. It is worth mentioning that this is not equivalent to virtualization detection, where these configurations are usually the default as well. A user interactively using her VM likely customizes its screen resolution and increases its computation power by using more cores and more RAM. The *history* features mainly originate from the observation that sandboxes leverage snapshot technology. Prior to a malware sample being analyzed, the sandbox usually restores the system state to a previously captured clean state, which is called a snapshot. A snapshot is typically taken once when the sandbox is set up and is then used for the rest of the operation time of the sandbox (unless it is occasionally updated). As a consequence, it is likely to show history artifacts. For example, if a snapshot was taken months ago, every time the snapshot is restored, the login history would reveal that the last login was at that time. Similarly, the file access history would reveal that the last file access happened suspiciously long ago. In addition, we observed that many sandboxes had just been started, whereas user PCs usually have a longer uptime. Sandbox reports frequently show system uptimes on the order of seconds, whereas a vulnerable system that is about to be infected (e.g., via a drive-by download) likely has a significantly higher uptime.

The *execution* features stem from the sandbox showing uncommon execution patterns. We noticed, for example, that sandboxes tend to change the image executable name to something which is easier to handle in terms of automation. It is quite common that sandboxes uses MD5 hashes or generic names such as `virus.exe`, whereas the user reports indicate that such renaming is unlikely. We also found that the clipboard of the sandboxes was empty or contained seemingly-random strings, whereas users' clipboards tended to contain more meaningful values such as links, text, or file objects. Finally, we observed that sandboxes returned suspicious values for the system manufacturer, such as empty or random strings, possibly to hide real names—which we did not observe in the user reports.

5.2 Classification

We use the previously-described features to train a classifier that can automatically learn a model to predict if an unknown feature report was taken on a sandbox or a user PC. To this end, we build up a training data set that consists of all 50 user reports and up to three random samples from each sandbox cluster. In total this gives us a training set of 202 reports, 50 of which are user reports and 152 of which are sandbox reports.

For building the classifier, we use an SVM with a radial basis function kernel. To normalize the feature vector that we pass to the SVM, we need to transform the feature values into numerical values. This is done according to the last column in Table 3. Here, `id` means that we simply take the number as is, `len` means that we consider the length of the string feature, and {0,1} is a boolean value (in our case, to show if the report indicates a PS/2 mouse or not). Similarly, for the image name feature we check if the file image name has been altered. Since not every feature is available for every report, for reasons explained in Sect. 4, we decided to use mean imputation to estimate missing values. Finally, we normalize values to the [0, 1] range using Min-Max Scaling.

To build a classifier, we need to specify an effective combination of the SVM regularization constant C and the kernel parameter γ. For this purpose, we use hyperparameter tuning with grid search and 10-fold cross validation to compute the accuracy of our classifier. We use 10-fold cross validation on top of this methodology to ensure that we get unbiased results. In an initial step, to evaluate the strength of each individual feature, we built a classifier for each single feature. The results of this experiment are depicted in Fig. 1. As we can see, even a single feature can be used to detect sandboxes with high accuracy, with the RAM feature being the best, at an accuracy of 98.06 %. However, a single feature is easier to fix for a sandbox operator than multiple features. We thus also created a classifier that trains on all features. The rightmost bar in Fig. 1 shows that this classifier has a perfect accuracy of 100 % (i.e. 0 false positives and 0 false negatives), illustrating the strength of combining multiple detection features.

5.3 Comparison to Existing Solutions

In order to evaluate how well our classifier performs, we decided to compare our methodology to existing work. For this purpose, we use Paranoid Fish (PAFISH), a popular framework consisting of a collection of several well-known sandbox detection techniques used by malware in the wild. We encoded 45 detection techniques used by PAFISH in SANDPRINT and performed them during each run. Using those 45 detection results, we then built a classifier in the same fashion as before. We consider each detection a feature for which we build a single classifier, and we also build a classifier for the combination of all 45 features. The accuracy results for these classifiers are depicted in Fig. 2. Again, each light colored bar shows the accuracy for a single feature, and the black bar shows the accuracy for the classifier which combines all the features. As we can see, the majority of the single-feature classifiers are not much better than guessing. Two features are above 80 % accuracy, with the best individual feature (rdtsc time measurements to detect virtualization [18]) having 93 % accuracy. The combined version has an accuracy of 97.8 %.

Besides having a better accuracy, we argue that our methodology is superior to PAFISH for two additional reasons. First, PAFISH mainly checks for virtualization artifacts, from which we refrain for reasons explained before. Second, the majority of the checks performed by PAFISH are not stealthy by any means, since it heavily queries information from the registry, network adapters, and other sources which are likely to be monitored by the sandbox. By doing so, PAFISH

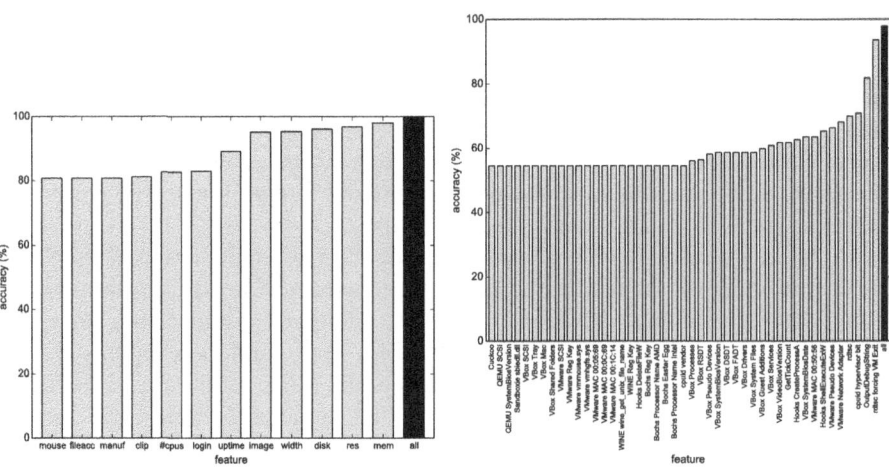

Fig. 1. Classifier accuracy (larger is better).

Fig. 2. PAFISH classifier accuracy.

risks being detected as an environment-sensitive malware. In contrast, we argue our method's information extraction is stealthier. In fact, as we will see in Sect. 6 our approach is not even detected by state-of-the-art security appliances, which highlights the stealthiness of our approach.

5.4 Summary

As we have shown, we can reliably distinguish between a sandbox and a user machine based on sandbox-inherent features. Although the number of features seems quite small, we argue that hiding those features takes a lot of effort for the sandbox operator. While changing the screen size and switching to a USB emulated mouse is configurable, removing the parallel computation artifacts is not as simple. Increasing the number of cores and the amount of memory is likely not to be an option for the operator, as this would decrease the productivity of the sandbox. This could be solved through a solution which gives the running programs the impression of more resources. Similarly, avoiding history artifacts introduced by snapshots also requires engineering effort. For example, the sandbox operator could make sure that all the relevant history information on the system appears to be normal. A solution could be to customize sandbox snapshots and keep them up-to-date like non-sandbox systems. Unfortunately, such customization it is high effort, might be prone to errors, and likely needs to be reimplemented for every operating system under analysis. For other countermeasures which could be applied by sandbox operators, we refer to Sect. 7.1, where we combine this aspect with an ethical discussion of our work.

6 Malware Appliance Detection

Seeing that one can detect publicly-exposed sandboxes, we wondered if we could use the classifier trained on public knowledge to evade closed malware analysis appliances. Appliances are different from sandboxes in that their main objective is not to *analyze* the complete behavior of malware, but rather to *detect* malware in order to protect a sensitive infrastructure against cyber attacks. An advanced attacker may thus have strong incentives to detect an appliance in order to fly under the radar. That is, if an attacker can detect an appliance, she could hide her program's malicious behavior to avoid triggering any alert in the appliance.

Looking at the feature selection in Sect. 5, we realized that we can possibly assume that appliances could share the same feature characteristics as sandboxes. To verify this, we run SANDPRINT on three popular appliances from well-known vendors[1]. For this purpose, we gained access to various instances (Windows 7, Windows XP, 32/64 bit, different service packs, etc.) of the appliances. We ran SANDPRINT four times on each instance and collected 40 reports. Obtaining the features was not as trivial as in the case of publicly available sandboxes, since the appliances did not allow for network communication. To overcome this issue,

---

[1] We omit the vendor names not to pinpoint to weaknesses of individual appliances.

we encoded the extracted features in the analysis report which was produced by the appliance after executing SANDPRINT.

When manually inspecting the feature reports, we found out that our assumption about the feature characteristics was correct. Similar to sandboxes, appliances also exhibit hardware, history and execution characteristics that indicate non-human and non-interactive usage. To our surprise, some features were even stronger than in the sandbox case. For example, all 40 reports contained a small screen width and a 4:3 screen resolution.

For each appliance, we then measure how accurately the classifier that we trained on the sandboxes and user report performs on the appliance reports. With an accuracy of 100 %, the classifier detected all appliances as non-user machines. However, the main priority in this setting is not evasion *per se*, but rather *stealth evasion*. That is, while an attacker aims to detect an appliance, she does not want her detection method to be unveiled. We thus had a look at the reports produced by the appliances and found out that SANDPRINT created many security alerts by reading information such as motherboard information, BIOS information, or serial numbers. We then checked if the features used for the classifier were also on the list of alerts, which would essentially negate the stealthiness of the detection. For example, many PAFISH checks were detected by the appliances. Although the majority of the sandbox-inherent features did not trigger an alert by any appliance, we discovered that one appliance considers reading the disk information as suspicious behavior. To counter this, we removed the disk feature from the feature vector and evaluated the classifier again on the appliance reports, resulting again in 100 % accuracy—even for stealth evasion.

To summarize, an attacker can reveal characteristics of publicly available sandboxes and use the gathered information to build a classifier that can perfectly distinguish between a user PC and an appliance. With insider knowledge on security appliances, an advanced attacker could tweak her classifier such that the evasion is stealthy and remains undetected by the appliance.

7 Discussion and Limitations

This section discusses ethical aspects and potential limitations of our work. As part of the ethical discussion, we also describe a responsible disclosure process in which we informed the sandbox and appliance operators about our findings.

7.1 Ethical Considerations

Our research may seem offensive in the sense that we reveal fingerprints of malware sandboxes that adversaries can use to evade them. Note, however, that the information we presented can be gathered by any other person reproducing our (conceptually simple) fingerprinting method. We thus consider the information shown in this paper as public knowledge. Still, we present data only in aggregated form and refrain from revealing any internals of particular sandboxes.

Using our insights, sandbox operators can aim to implement stealthier analysis systems. For example, we have shown that one should periodically update features that are inherent to the snapshot of a sandbox. While it will always be possible to find artifacts that can identify an individual sandbox, it is significantly harder to build a classifier that works for *all* sandboxes, especially if more people randomize characteristics. We have shown which features are particularly characteristic of sandboxes, giving sandbox operators hints on where to significantly improve the stealthiness of their systems.

7.2 Responsible Disclosure

Organizations developing sandboxes and/or appliances are immediately affected by our research results and we thus considered them as the main target of our responsible disclosure process. To notify these organizations, we contacted them 90 days prior to the publishing date of this paper, detailing the proposed attack and including hints on how to protect against potential adversaries in the future. We used direct contacts whenever possible and available. Alternatively, we resorted to contact details stated on the organization's websites, notably including Web-based contact forms. If we did not receive a response after 2 weeks, we retried to contact the organization, if possible using alternative communication channels (e.g., using generic email addresses like info@organization.com or email addresses found in the WHOIS database for the organization's website domain). If we did not hear back from the organization after 4 weeks, we contacted the national CERT(s) that are in the same country as the affected organization in order to notify the party via the CERT as trusted intermediary.

We handed to each organization an executive summary of our research results as well as a full description of our research methodology (i.e., a copy of this paper in the pre-print version). We made sure to highlight the implications of our work with respect to future operations of the sandbox and/or appliance. We also specified our contact details of both research institutions, including physical address, phone number, and the email address of a representative for the research activities. We allowed the organizations to download the latest version of SANDPRINT and its source code. Such auxiliary data is helpful to build protection mechanisms against sandbox-evasive programs similar to SANDPRINT. We also remove all organizations' names when referring to individual sandboxes/services.

7.3 Isolated Sandboxes

Most sandboxes allowed the program under analysis to communicate over the Internet, whereas nine services and all three appliances did not do so. To some extent we could also extract features of isolated sandboxes (the appliances) by encoding the features into events of the analysis report. However, this requires access to the isolated sandboxes, which may be hard to obtain for an attacker. Note that our sandbox classification did not use features that depend on the network configuration. In principle, our classification results should also generalize to non-connected sandboxes. Although we cannot rule out the possibility that there are non-connected sandboxes for which our classifier would perform poorly, we argue that the successful detection of appliances supports this claim.

Due to our assumption of Internet-connected sandboxes, the number of in-the-wild sandboxes is likely higher than our findings in the clustering results suggest. We argue, though, that our analyses are based on a statistically significant set of sandboxes, including those of the most popular analysis services.

8 Related Work

Evasion Techniques: Seeing the increasing popularity of sandboxes, malware authors try to find a way to evade sandbox analysis. Egele et al. give an overview of sandbox implementations [24]. Most sandboxes use virtual machine (VM) technology or CPU emulators. Such virtualization eases the process of analyzing multiple samples in parallel. Accordingly, studies show how to distinguish between a real machine and virtual environment. RedPill [47] determines whether it is executed on VMware using the `sidt` instruction. Many other detection methods have also been developed for not only VMware [29,43], but also for famous system emulators such as QEMU [22,29,40,43] and BOCHS [34,40]. There are also some detection methods for emulation-based Android sandboxes [27,42,54]. The fundamental difference between our approach and the above techniques is that we do not aim to detect virtualization or emulation, as VMs and sandboxes are not equivalent. In addition, as shown with PAFISH, most of these checks are not stealthy, whereas our approach even managed to detect security appliances without triggering alerts. It is also likely that our approach could work for bare metal sandboxes. We argue that bare metal sandboxes conceptually share many sandbox-inherent features with traditional sandboxes as the major difference is only the absence of virtualization and emulation—not the snapshot mechanism.

The work closest to our approach has been done by Maier et al. [33]. They gathered several features about Android sandboxes and showed that Android malware can bypass the existing sandboxes by using the fingerprints. However, they do neither perform automated clustering and classification of *sandbox-inherent* features, nor do they test their approach against security appliances. Furthermore, the feature selection of Maier et al. is very specific to smartphones. Features such as "the device needs at least n saved WiFi-networks" or "the device must have a paired Bluetooth device" cannot be used in our (non-mobile) context in a meaningful way. However, we also use some similar features like special hardware artifacts or system uptime. Regarding sandboxes for Windows malware, Yoshioka et al. [56] clustered and detected sandboxes by their external IP addresses. We were inspired by these works and performed a study in greater detail, collecting 25 features and identifying 76 sandboxes with an unsupervised machine learning technique.

Transparent Sandboxes: Seeing the threat of VM evasion, researchers started to explore transparent sandboxes that are stealthy against detection. Vasudevan et al. proposed Cobra [53], which was the first analysis system countering anti-analysis techniques. Dinaburg et al. proposed Ether [23], a transparent sandbox using hardware virtualization extensions such as Intel VT. Those systems focus on how to conceal the existence of analysis mechanisms from malware. Pek et al. introduced a timing-based detection mechanism to detect Ether [41]. In addition, as we have shown, the majority of sandboxes, including VT-based sandboxes, are susceptible to evasion due to sandbox-inherent features.

Kirat et al. proposed to use actual hardware to analyze malware [9,31]. The proposed system, called BareBox, is based on a fast and rebootless system restore technique. Since the system executes malware on real hardware, it is not vulnerable to any type of VM/emulation-based detection attacks. Still, as it is snapshot-based, it falls for the methods described in Sect. 5.

9 Conclusion

Our real-world malware sandbox investigations have shown it is quite straightforward to fingerprint malware sandboxes. We identified 76 sandboxes by uploading a measurement binary to 20 services, all of which can be rather trivially detected and evaded just based on sandbox-inherent characteristics. Our findings also suggest detecting and evading malware appliances is similarly possible. This calls into question how we can protect against the threat of sandbox evasion in the future, and should serve as a heads-up for sandbox operators to inform them about threats that may actually be already silently misused by malware.

Acknowledgements. We would like to thank the anonymous reviewers for their valuable comments. Special thanks goes to our shepherd Michael Bailey, who supported us during the process of finalizing the paper. This work was supported by the MEXT Program for Promoting Reform of National Universities and by the German Federal Ministry of Education and Research (BMBF) through funding for the Center for IT-Security, Privacy and Accountability (CISPA) and for the BMBF project 13N13250.

Appendix

See Fig. 3.

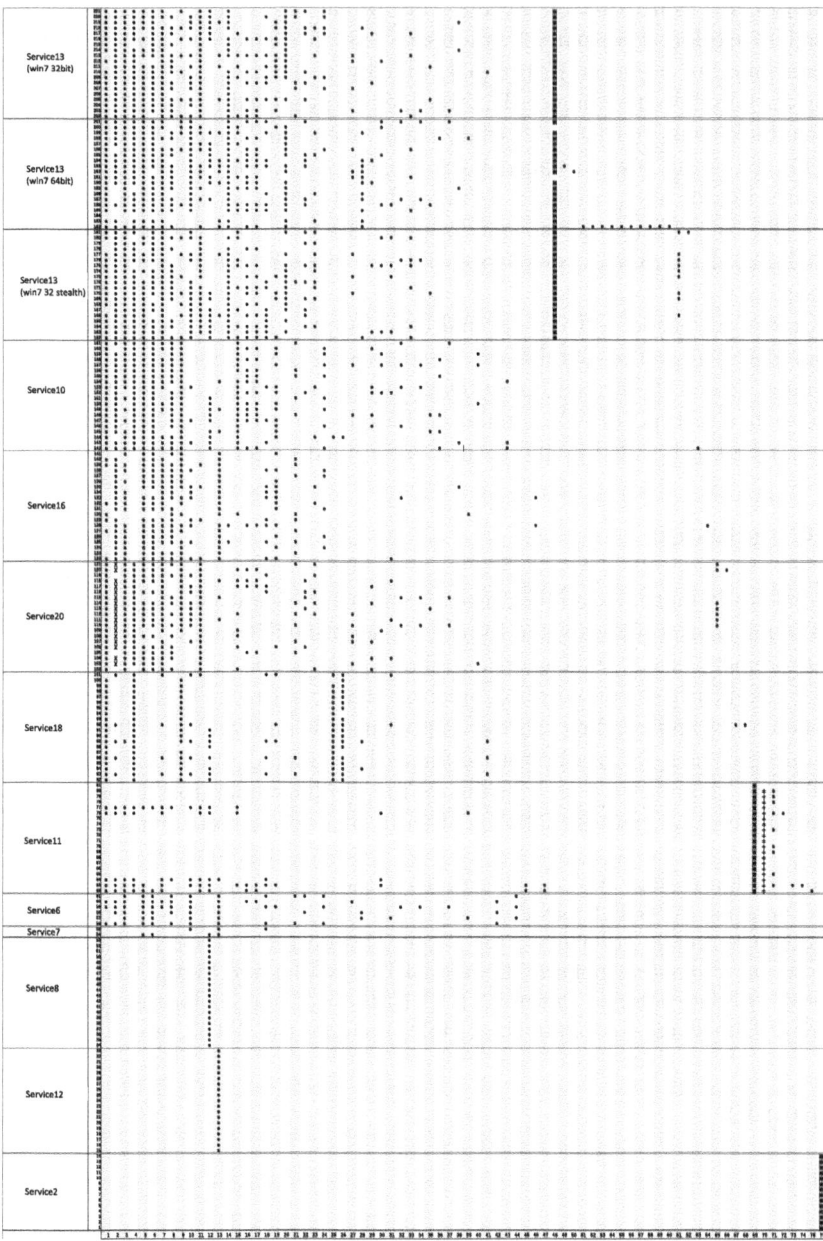

Fig. 3. Mapping between submitted SANDPRINT instances and sandboxes. The noncircle shapes indicate constant and exclusive use of a sandbox by a particular service and thus are inferred as being a sandbox attached to the service. A cross indicates that the mapping is confirmed by mapping the SANDPRINT report to the dynamic analysis report provided by the service.

References

1. Amnpardaz Sandbox - File Analyzer. http://jevereg.amnpardaz.com/
2. Anubis: Malware Analysis for Unknown Binaries. https://anubis.iseclab.org/
3. Bkav - Scan virus online. http://quetvirus.vn/default.aspx?lang=en
4. bochs: The Open Source IA-32 Emulation Project. http://bochs.sourceforge.net
5. Dr. Web Online Check. http://online.drweb.com/?lng=en
6. FortiGuard Center. Online Virus Scanner. http://www.fortiguard.com/virusscanner
7. Gary's Hood. Online Virus Scanner. http://www.garyshood.com/virus/
8. Malwr - Malware Analysis by Cuckoo Sandbox. https://malwr.com/
9. NVMTrace: Proof-of-concept Automated Baremetal Malware Analysis Framework. https://code.google.com/p/nvmtrace/
10. Oracle VM VirtualBox. https://www.virtualbox.org
11. #totalhash. https://totalhash.cymru.com/upload/
12. http://www.Vicheck.ca
13. Virusblokada. http://anti-virus.by/en/index.shtml
14. VirusTotal - Free Online Virus, Malware and URL Scanner. https://www.virustotal.com/en/
15. VMware. http://www.vmware.com/
16. Bayer, U., Milani Comparetti, P., Hlauschek, C., Kruegel, C., Kirda, E.: Scalable, behavior-based malware clustering. In: Network and Distributed System Security Symposium (NDSS) (2009)
17. Bellard, F.: QEMU, a fast and portable dynamic translator. In: Proceedings of the Annual Conference on USENIX Annual Technical Conference, ATEC 2005 (2005)
18. Brengel, M., Backes, M., Rossow, C.: Detecting hardware-assisted virtualization. In: Caballero, J., Zurutuza, U., Rodríguez, R.J. (eds.) DIMVA 2016. LNCS, vol. 9721, pp. 207–227. Springer, Heidelberg (2016). doi:10.1007/978-3-319-40667-1_11
19. Caballero, J., Grier, C., Kreibich, C., Paxson, V.: Measuring pay-per-install: the commoditization of malware distribution. In: USENIX Security (2011)
20. Comodo. Comodo Instant Malware Analysis. http://camas.comodo.com/
21. Cristianini, N., Shawe-Taylor, J.: An Introduction to Support Vector Machines and Other Kernel-based Learning Methods. Cambridge University Press, Cambridge (2000)
22. DEXLabs. Detecting Android Sandboxes (2012). http://www.dexlabs.org/blog/btdetect
23. Dinaburg, A., Royal, P., Sharif, M., Ether, L.W.: Malware analysis via hardware virtualization extensions. In: Proceedings of the 15th ACM Conference on Computer and Communications Security, CCS 2008 (2008)
24. Egele, M., Scholte, T., Kirda, E., Kruegel, C.: A survey on automated dynamic malware-analysis techniques and tools. ACM Comput. Surv. **44**, 2 (2008)
25. F-Secure. Sample Analysis System. https://analysis.f-secure.com/portal/login.html
26. Freiling, F.C., Holz, T., Wicherski, G.: Botnet tracking: exploring a root-cause methodology to prevent distributed denial-of-service attacks. In: di Vimercati, S.C., Syverson, P.F., Gollmann, D. (eds.) ESORICS 2005. LNCS, vol. 3679, pp. 319–335. Springer, Heidelberg (2005)
27. Jing, Y., Zhao, Z., Ahn, G.-J., Hu, H.: Morpheus: automatically generating heuristics to detect android emulators. In: Proceedings of the 30th Annual Computer Security Applications Conference, ACSAC 2014 (2014)

28. Jotti. Jotti's Malware Scan. http://virusscan.jotti.org/en
29. Jung, P.: Bypassing Sandboxes for Fun. https://www.botconf.eu/wp-content/uploads/2014/12/2014-2.7-Bypassing-Sandboxes-for-Fun.pdf
30. Kirat, D., Vigna, G., Kruegel, C.: Barecloud: bare-metal analysis-based evasive malware detection. In: Proceedings of the 23rd USENIX Conference on Security Symposium, SEC 2014 (2014)
31. Kirati, D., Vigna, G., Kruegel, C.: BareBox: efficient malware analysis on bare-metal. In: Proceedings of the 27th Annual Computer Security Applications Conference, ACSAC 2011 (2011)
32. Lanzi, A., Balzarotti, D., Kruegel, C., Christodorescu, M., Kirda, E.: AccessMiner: using system-centric models for malware protection. In: Proceedings of the 17th ACM Conference on Computer and Communications Security, CCS 2010 (2010)
33. Maier, D., Müller, T., Protsenko, M.: Divide-and-Conquer: why android malware cannot be stopped. In: Proceedings of the 2014 Ninth International Conference on Availability, Reliability and Security, ARES 2014 (2014)
34. Martignoni, L., Paleari, R., Roglia, G.F., Bruschi, D.: Testing CPU emulators. In: Proceedings of the Eighteenth International Symposium on Software Testing and Analysis, ISSTA 2009 (2009)
35. Microsoft. Submit a sample - Microsoft Malware Protection Center. https://www.microsoft.com/security/portal/submission/submit.aspx
36. Neugschwandtner, M., Comparetti, P. M., Platzer, C.: Detecting malware's failover C&C strategies with squeeze. In: Proceedings of the 27th Annual Computer Security Applications Conference, ACSAC 2011 (2011)
37. Neuner, S., van der Veen, V., Lindorfer, M., Huber, M., Merzdovnik, G., Mulazzani, M., Weippl, E.: Enter Sandbox: Android Sandbox Comparison (2015). http://arxiv.org/ftp/arxiv/papers/1410/1410.7749.pdf
38. OPSWAT. Metascan Online: Free File Scanning with Multiple Antivirus Engines. https://www.metascan-online.com/#!/scan-file
39. Pa, Y.M.P., Suzuki, S., Yoshioka, K., Matsumoto, T., Kasama, T., Rossow, C.: IoT-POT: analysing the rise of IoT compromises. In: Proceedings of the 9th USENIX Workshop on Offensive Technologies, WOOT (2015)
40. Paleari, R., Martignoni, L., Roglia, G.F., Bruschi, D.A.: Fistful of red-pills: how to automatically generate procedures to detect CPU emulators. In: Proceedings of the 3rd USENIX Conference on Offensive Technologies, WOOT 2009 (2009)
41. Pék, G., Bencsáth, B., Buttyán, L.: nEther: in-guest detection of out-of-the-guest malware analyzers. In: Proceedings of the Fourth European Workshop on System Security, EUROSEC 2011 (2011)
42. Petsas, T., Voyatzis, G., Athanasopoulos, E., Polychronakis, M., Ioannidis, S.: Rage against the virtual machine: hindering dynamic analysis of android malware. In: Proceedings of the Seventh European Workshop on System Security, EuroSec 2014 (2014)
43. Raffetseder, T., Kruegel, C., Kirda, E.: Detecting system emulators. In: Garay, J.A., Lenstra, A.K., Mambo, M., Peralta, R. (eds.) ISC 2007. LNCS, vol. 4779, pp. 1–18. Springer, Heidelberg (2007)
44. Rieck, K., Schwenk, G., Limmer, T., Holz, T., Laskov, P.: Botzilla: detecting the phoning home of malicious software. In: Proceedings of the 2010 ACM Symposium on Applied Computing (ACSAC 2010) (2010)
45. Rieck, K., Trinius, P., Willems, C., Holz, T.: Automatic analysis of malware behavior using machine learning. J. Comput. Secur. **19**(4), 639–668 (2009)

46. Rossow, C., Dietrich, C., Bos, H.: Large-scale analysis of malware downloaders. In: Flegel, U., Markatos, E., Robertson, W. (eds.) DIMVA 2012. LNCS, vol. 7591, pp. 42–61. Springer, Heidelberg (2013)
47. Rutkowska, J.: Red Pill... Or How To Detect VMM Using (Almost) One CPU Instruction (2004). http://www.securiteam.com/securityreviews/6Z00H20BQS.html
48. Payload Security: Free Automated Malware Analysis Service. https://www.hyblid-analysis.com/
49. Payload Security: Blog article (2015). http://www.pandasecurity.com/mediacenter/press-releases/pandalabs-neutralized-75-million-new-malware-samples-2014-twice-many-2013/
50. ThreatTrack Security. Free Online Malware Analysis. http://www.threattracksecurity.com/resources/sandbox-malware-analysis.aspx
51. Symantec. Internet Security Threat Report 04/2015 (2015). http://www.symantec.com/de/de/security_response/publications/threatreport.jsp
52. ThreatExpert. http://www.threatexpert.com/submit.aspx
53. Vasudevan, A., Yerraballi, R.: Cobra: fine-grained malware analysis using stealth localized-executions. In: Proceedings of the 2006 IEEE Symposium on Security and Privacy, S&P 2006 (2006)
54. Vidas, T., Christin, N.: Evading android runtime analysis via sandbox detection. In: Proceedings of the 9th ACM Symposium on Information, Computer and Communications Security, ASIA CCS 2014 (2014)
55. VirSCAN.org. Free Multi-Engine Online Virus Scanner. http://www.virscan.org/
56. Yoshioka, K., Hosobuchi, Y., Orii, T., Matsumoto, T.: Your sandbox is blinded: impact of decoy injection to public malware analysis systems. J. Inf. Process. **52**, 3 (2011)

Enabling Network Security Through Active DNS Datasets

Athanasios Kountouras[1](✉), Panagiotis Kintis[2], Chaz Lever[2], Yizheng Chen[2], Yacin Nadji[2], David Dagon[1], Manos Antonakakis[1], and Rodney Joffe[3]

[1] School of Electrical and Computer Engineering,
Georgia Institute of Technology, Atlanta, USA
{kountouras,manos}@gatech.edu, dagon@sudo.sh
[2] School of Computer Science, Georgia Institute of Technology, Atlanta, USA
{kintis,chazlever,yzchen,yacin}@gatech.edu
[3] Neustar, Sterling, USA
rjoffe@centergate.com

Abstract. Most modern cyber crime leverages the Domain Name System (DNS) to attain high levels of network agility and make detection of Internet abuse challenging. The majority of malware, which represent a key component of illicit Internet operations, are programmed to locate the IP address of their command-and-control (C&C) server through DNS lookups. To make the malicious infrastructure both agile and resilient, malware authors often use sophisticated communication methods that utilize DNS (i.e., domain generation algorithms) for their campaigns. In general, Internet miscreants make extensive use of *short-lived disposable domains* to promote a large variety of threats and support their criminal network operations.

To effectively combat Internet abuse, the security community needs access to freely available and open datasets. Such datasets will enable the development of new algorithms that can enable the early detection, tracking, and overall lifetime of modern Internet threats. To that end, we have created a system, Thales, that actively queries and collects records for massive amounts of domain names from various seeds. These seeds are collected from multiple public sources and, therefore, free of privacy concerns. The results of this effort will be opened and made freely available to the research community. With three case studies we demonstrate the detection merit that the collected active DNS datasets contain. We show that (i) more than 75 % of the domain names in public black lists (PBLs) appear in our datasets several weeks (and some cases months) in advance, (ii) existing DNS research can be implemented using only active DNS, and (iii) malicious campaigns can be identified with the signal provided by active DNS.

1 Introduction

The Domain Name System (DNS) is a fundamental component of the Internet. Most network communication on the Internet starts with a DNS lookup that maps a domain name to a corresponding set of IP addresses. Cyber criminals frequently leverage DNS to provide high levels of network *agility* for their illicit operations. For example, most malware relies on DNS to locate its command-and-control (C&C) servers. Such servers are used to send commands from the attacker, exfiltrate secret information, and send malware updates.

DNS abuse is an enduring, if not permanent, feature of the Internet, which might at best be managed through various policies, remediation technologies and defenses. Traditionally, network operators have relied on *static blacklists* to detect and block DNS queries to malware domains. Unfortunately, static blacklists, which are often manually compiled, cannot keep pace with the quantity of network agility of modern threats. This results in blacklists that are incomplete and become outdated quickly.

To overcome the limitations of static blacklists, new analytical systems have been proposed [12–15, 26, 29] to shorten the response time necessary to react to new threats and secure networks. Those systems rely on the efficient collection and presentation of passive DNS datasets. However, such datasets are difficult to find, challenging to collect, and often require restrictive legal agreements. These obstacles make further innovation difficult and are an impediment to repeatability of research.

The lack of open and freely available DNS datasets puts the security community at a disadvantage because they lack access to datasets describing a critical component used by adversaries on the Internet. Clearly, the security community is in need of open, freely available DNS datasets than can help increase the situational awareness around modern threats. This is illustrated by the fact that most modern threats rely on DNS for their illicit activities.

This paper provides a solution aimed at filling this gap. We introduce the concept of active DNS and discuss a new large scale system, Thales, which is able to systematically query and collect large volumes of active DNS data. The output of this system is a distilled dataset that can be easily used by the security community. Thales has been reliably active for more than six months and collected many terabytes of DNS data, while causing only a handful of abuse complaints. Access to this dataset is currently available to the community from the following project website: http://www.activednsproject.org/[1].

In summary, our paper makes the following contributions:

1. We present a system, Thales, that can reliably query, collect, and distill active DNS datasets. Due to the public nature of our seed data, our active DNS datasets do not contain any potentially sensitive information that preclude their use by the security community. Thales has been collecting active DNS data for more than six months with almost zero down time (only three days). During this time, the system has generated more than a terabyte of unprocessed DNS PCAPs along with tens of gigabytes of de-duplicated DNS records per day. Thus, the active DNS datasets represent a significant portion of the world's daily DNS delegation hierarchy.

---

[1] In order to not violate the double blind nature of the submission, we kept the web site in the simplest possible format.

2. We provide in-depth comparison between the newly collected active DNS datasets and passive DNS collected from a large university network. We show that the active DNS datasets provide greater breadth (i.e., reaches out to a larger portion of the IPv4, IPv6, and DNS space). Conversely, passive DNS yields a denser graph between the queried domain names and the remaining IP and DNS infrastructure.
3. We practically explore how active DNS can be used to improve the security of modern networks through several case studies. We show that the active DNS datasets can be use for early detection of financial and other Internet threats. Our analysis shows that more than 75 % of malicious domain names appear in the active DNS datasets months before they get listed in a public blacklist. We demonstrate how active DNS can be used to implement and extend existing DNS related research, specifically, by implementing an algorithm used to detected potential domain ownership changes. Finally, we show how active DNS can be used as a signal to identify malicious campaigns on the Internet.

2 Active DNS Data Collection

With this section we introduce Thales. We will begin by discussing the network and system infrastructure necessary to systematically and reliably collect the active DNS datasets. Then, we will discuss the details of the domain names that compile the daily seed for Thales. The section will be concluded by discussing the long term measurement behind the collected active DNS datasets.

2.1 Infrastructure

The reliable collection of DNS data is far from easy. Thales was designed to retain high levels of availability, efficiency and scalability. The goal of Thales is clear; the generation of active DNS datasets that will provide systematic snapshots of the DNS infrastructure, several times per day. These datasets will enable the security community to construct a timeline of the evolution of threats in the broader Internet.

Our system, Thales, is composed of two main modules as seen in Fig. 1: (a) the traffic generator and (b) the data collector. The first is responsible for generating large numbers of DNS queries using a list of seed domain names as an input to the system. The second module is responsible for collecting the network traffic and guiding these raw DNS datasets for further processing (i.e., data deduplication).

Traffic Generation. In order to achieve high availability, redundant systems are used to generate traffic. Linux containers (LXC) [7] are setup across several physical systems, creating a DNS scanning cluster of 30 LXC containers. Each

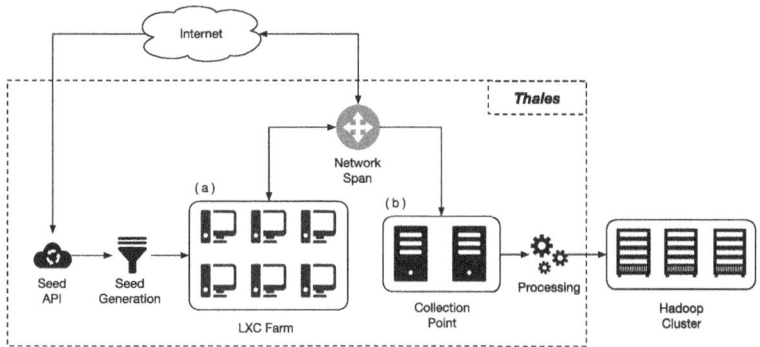

Fig. 1. The Seed API is responsible for collecting the seed domains from various sources and the Seed Generation reduces them to a list of unique domains. The LXC Farm corresponds to the query generator which is connected to the internet through a Network Span. That in turn is sending traffic to the Collection Point from where data is being reduced and stored for long term on our Hadoop Cluster.

LXC contains its own local recursive software[2] and is assigned a job, where a subset of the overall daily seed domain names will have to be resolved by a particular container. High efficiency is achieved by increasing the rate of DNS resolution requests (a.k.a. queries per second) that can be handled by the recursive in the LXC container. However, just increasing the resources of the LXC container will not suffice for the container to handle a large enough number of DNS requests. This is because the local recursive in the LXC is bounded by the maximum number of ports that can be used for UDP sockets. This means that the number of requests that can be sent by a host have to be limited to the number of available concurrent ports that the local recursive (in the LXC container) can handle.

At any given point in time, a container could theoretically handle up to 64,512 ($2^{15} - 1024$) sockets per IP address – and therefore 64,512 UDP query packets in transit. The LXC containers support custom network interfaces, which support assigning a different IP address to each container. More specifically, we use 30 contiguous IPs out of an assigned IP block of 63 available addresses (/26). Thus, they are able to send and receive up to $30 \times 64,512 \approx 2^{21}$ simultaneous DNS resolution requests from the infrastructure. These results are achieved by deploying the containers on two physical systems. Each of these two systems has 64 processing cores and 164 GB of RAM. It is worth pointing out that using LXC containers allows us to scale the infrastructure horizontally by simply adding more systems to our scanning cluster.

Data Collection. The requests submitted by Thales are collected at two vantage points. The first one is on the LXC container that has submitted the reso-

---

[2] We used the Unbound (https://www.unbound.net/) recursive software in every LXC container.

lution request for a given domain name, whereas the second one is at the SPAN of a switch that routes traffic for all our containers. As mentioned earlier, we are utilizing several IP addresses from several local virtual LANs (VLAN). These VLANs have been "trunked" to a single 1Gbit interface on a host that collects all port 53 UDP traffic. We are collecting traffic at both points for redundancy and verification of correctness for the daily active DNS datasets.

```
{
    "date": "20160303",
    "qname": "0746jiaoyou.com.",
    "qtype": 1,
    "rdata": "61.151.239.202",
    "ttl": 3600,
    "authority_ips": "58.216.26.232,120.52.19.142",
    "count": 5,
    "hours": 32778,
    "sensor": "active-dns"
}
```

Fig. 2. A sample record from our dataset that shows the data fields that are stored. The `authority ips` field represents the authoritative nameservers that replied for this domain name and the `hours` variable captures the hour of the day that this record was seen in a 24 bit integer.

Capturing network traffic results (on average) in a massive 1.67TB of raw data in *packet capture* format (pcap). This data is transferred in a local Hadoop cluster composed of 22 data nodes. The Hadoop cluster is responsible for parsing the pcap files, deduplicating the resource records (RRs) and converting the RRs into meaningful DNS tuples of following format: (date, QNAME, QTYPE, RDATA, TTL, authorities, count) as seen in Fig. 2. Deduplication is a critical step, since many responses we collect remain the same throughout a day. Thus, after removing duplicate RRs, we are left (on average) with approximately 85 GB of data per day. Detailed measurements for both daily raw and deduplicated RRs will be discussed in Sect. 2.3.

2.2 Domain Seed

Before Thales can begin scanning the domain name system, it has to be provided with a list of domain names that will act as candidates for resolutions. We will refer to these domain names as the *seed* for Thales. The seed is an aggregation of publicly accessible sources of domain names and URLs that we have been collecting for several years. These include but are not limited to Public Blacklists, the Alexa list, the Common Crawl project, and various Top Level Domain (TLD) zone files.

More specifically, we are using the zone files that are published daily by the administrators of the zones for com, net, biz and org. In Fig. 3 we present the number of domains obtained by each zone file. Because of the relative number

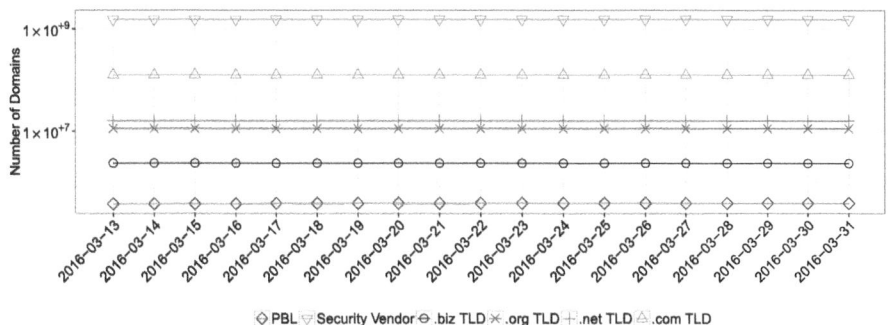

Fig. 3. Number of domains over time per seed input. The security vendor list contains about 1.5 billion domains and from the TLDs com is obviously the largest one with about 127 million domains.

of small daily changes, compared to the size of the zone files, the daily changes are not that apparent in Fig. 3. We note that the number of domains obtained by zone files changes as new domains get registered and old ones expire (and get removed from the zone). In Thales we input these zone files that we collect daily to our domain seed. This way our seed includes the current state of each zone every day.

We also add the entire Alexa [3] list of popular domains to the domain seed. This provides us with a large number of domains that would most likely be queried in a network by users.

In order to capture domains that might not be available in one of the zone files, we built a crawler that collects and parses domains seen in the Common-Crawl dataset [4]. The Common-Crawl dataset is an open repository of web crawl data that offers large volumes of crawled pages to anyone. We used components (i.e., URLs, HTML code) from the common crawl dataset to extract only the domains of the pages visited. Due to the size of even the Common-Crawl "metadata section" from the common crawl, we are still using the data published for last September 2015 and will start updating that list regularly. Because the common crawl data is published in monthly releases, the domain list that we extract from it and use in our seed list remains the same between updates.

A different list of data that we utilize in our domain seed is a feed of interesting domains that have been provided to us by a security company. This feed provides us with domains that have been observed to engage in forms of potentially malicious Internet activity. Because the feed provides us with new domain names constantly, we gather all new information and append it to the already existing list of interesting domains. We push the updated list to our collection infrastructure daily. The feed provides us with tens of thousands of new domains each day, making this list one of the fastest growing lists we use.

Finally we use a collection of public blacklist data in order to provide our data with interesting hand curated domains that originate from malicious activity.

More specifically the public blacklists we employ are: Abuse.ch [2], Malware DL [9], Blackhole DNS [8], sagadc [10], hphosts [6], SANS [11] and itmate [1]. We aggregate these lists daily and we input them into our domain seed by replacing the old list.

2.3 Measurements

Thales has been collecting data for a little less than six months. For the purpose of this paper we are focusing on analyzing all data in this section and then limit in depth analysis to the last 12 days of March (the last full week forth) for more specific measurements, unless a different window is explicitly stated. Over six months, Thales identified approximately 10,714,784 unique IP addresses, 199,110,841 unique domain names and 662,319,389 unique RRs per day. Figure 4 shows the distribution of IP addresses, domain names and RRs on average per day from October 5th to March 3rd 2016.

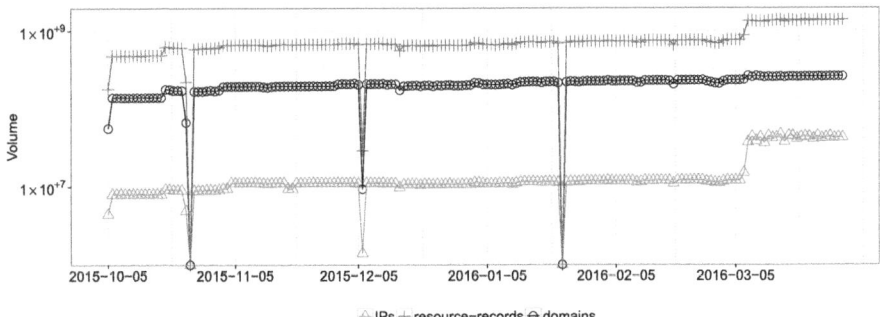

Fig. 4. Volumes of IPs, resource records and domains observed with Thales. March 7th was the day when we started querying for the QTYPEs: SOA, AAAA, TXT and MX. There have been two full outages on October 25, 2015 and January 23, 2016. On December 6, 2015 we had an outage that lasted for most of the day but we were able to recover the system later in the day.

During these months, we experienced two outages. The first was when the system was initially setup because of an update which was not rolled out correctly and caused the system to go off-line. Therefore, there is no data available for October 25, 2015, and policy has been updated to avoid future interruption since then. On January 23, 2016, our campus data center was undergoing maintenance for the cooling infrastructure, which caused a temporary shutdown of all our systems. Such cases can now be mitigated by Thales. We have made the system portable, which gives us the ability to move it to another location within a day's prior notice. Also on December 6, 2015 early in the day we had a hardware failure on our system that was detected early in the morning. We were able to recover the system and perform a check of the system by the same afternoon.

After the system check, we immediately restarted the collection, but there was not enough time in the day to go through the entirety of data in our seed list. This is depicted by the significant dip in the data. This incident was not a full outage since we were able to collect some data for the day.

3 Comparing Active and Passive DNS Datasets

Passive DNS has been an invaluable weapon in the community's arsenal for research combatting malware, botnets, and malicious actors [12–14,22,28]. Passive DNS, though, is rare, difficult to obtain, and often comes with restrictive legal clauses (i.e., Non Disclosure Agreements). At the same time, laws and regulations against personal identifiable information (PII), the significant financial cost of the passive collection, and storage infrastructure are some of several reasons **that make passive DNS cumbersome**. The primary goal for the active DNS dataset is to reduce the barrier for (repeatable) security research on DNS. In this section, we show how active DNS relates and contrasts to passive DNS. We will see that, while not a true replacement for passive DNS, Thales is able to create active DNS datasets that in many cases contain an order of magnitude more domain names and IP addresses.

3.1 Datasets

We first discuss how we obtain our passive DNS datasets. Our passive DNS dataset consists of traffic collected at our university network. The collection point is both *below* and *above the recursive*. This means that we collect the responses on the both paths; (1) between the (anonymized) clients and the local recursives and (2) between the local recursives and the upper layers of the DNS hierarchy (i.e., name servers, top level domains, etc.). For the active and passive DNS comparison, we decided to utilize datasets collected during the entire month of March 2016.

Figures 5 and 6 show eight detailed plots of the distribution of records in both our active and passive DNS datasets. Note that all plots are log-scale for the y-axis. As we can see, the active DNS dataset does not fluctuate a lot, compared to the passive DNS one. This is primarily an artifact of the collection technique, since the daily changes in the domain name seed we are using is minimal. On the other hand, the passive DNS dataset, is primarily driven by the behavior of the users on the local network, which may fluctuate on weekends, holidays, and during certain periods such as exams. This also explains the sudden increase in traffic for passive DNS, since our campus network experienced a reduction in traffic from March 21st until March 25th during spring break. Therefore, Fig. 6c shows an increase to more than double the unique resource records (RRs) identified per day after Monday, March 28th, when the spring break ended. Table 1 shows a breakdown of the datasets over the last 12 days of March, in much greater detail.

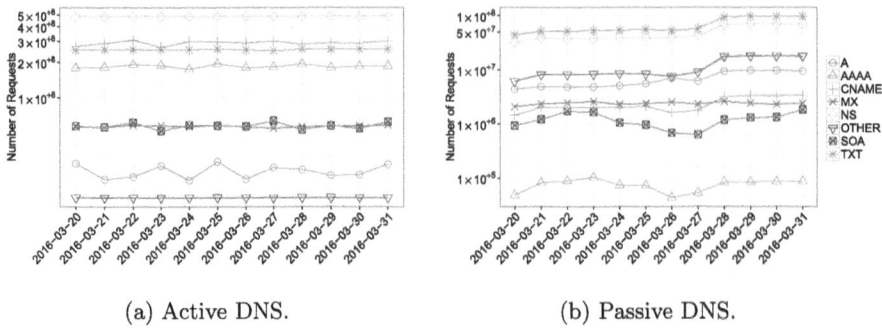

(a) Active DNS.   (b) Passive DNS.

Fig. 5. The distribution of different query types (QTYPE) in the active (left) and passive (right) DNS datasets. The active DNS dataset is almost sustaining the same volume of records per day, whereas the passive DNS dataset is fluctuating more over time. Note the growth after March 28, when the Spring Break was over and the Institute was operating at full capacity again.

It is worth noting that Thales is able to generate an order of magnitude more unique domain names, IP addresses and RDATA in the active DNS dataset (see Fig. 6, subfigures a to e), in comparison to the passive DNS data collected in a large university. This means that in actual DNS records, the active DNS dataset is more than comparable to the passive DNS that someone can collect in a large university. Now, as we can see from Fig. 6(f), active DNS is not able to create as dense graphs of resource records, as someone would expect to find in passive DNS data. This is somewhat to be expected, as in active DNS, Thales is scanning all possible domain names that can be seen in our public sources. This inevitably will include domain names that are rare, and in the context of a graph compiled by RRs, they will form islands. While not necessarily bad, we would advise researchers to take cautionary sanity steps when they utilize the active DNS data for spectral processes.

The diversity of the different query record types (QTYPEs) we are able to identify, in the two different datasets compared can been seen in Figs. 5a and b. Although there is a big difference regarding the volume of the records available, on average the visibility is very similar, since we are collecting the most popular QTYPEs when querying for the active DNS datasets Table 2.

4 Case Studies

To this point, we exposed several of the data properties from the active DNS datasets. In this section, we demonstrate the security value of these new active DNS datasets. We should clarify that our goal is not to claim as a contribution any of the following abuse detection processes. All of them have been discussed by previous work in the field. Rather, our goal is to practically demonstrate, using the actual active DNS datasets, the security merit that active DNS data can offer to the research and operational communities.

Enabling Network Security Through Active DNS Datasets   197

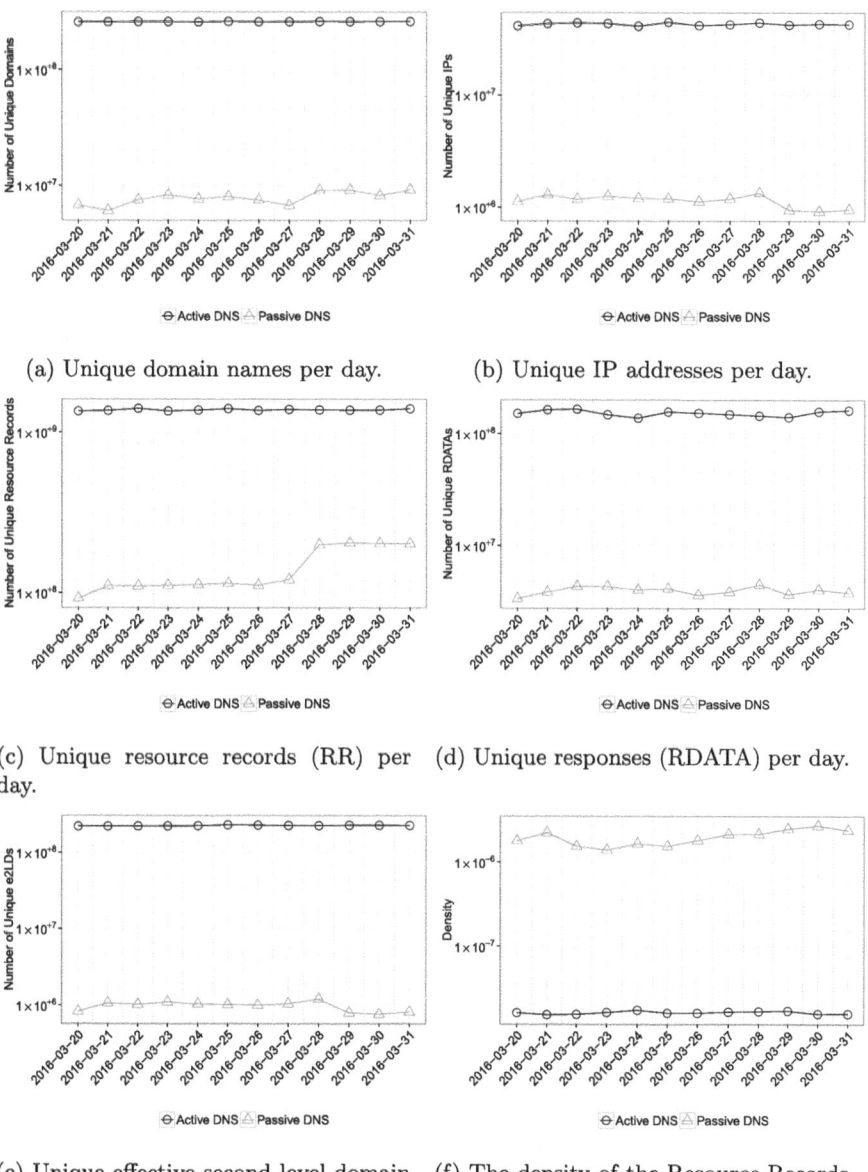

(a) Unique domain names per day.

(b) Unique IP addresses per day.

(c) Unique resource records (RR) per day.

(d) Unique responses (RDATA) per day.

(e) Unique effective second level domain names per day.

(f) The density of the Resource Records graph in the active and passive DNS dataset.

Fig. 6. The distribution of different records in our active and passive DNS datasets. The plots show that Thales is able to generate orders of magnitude more data than the passive DNS collection engine (Figures a to e) and much more diverse (Figure f).

Table 1. Number of data points collected over the last 12 days of March 2016. Values are in thousands ($\times 10^3$).

Date	Domains		IPv4/IPv6		RDATA		RR		e2LD	
	Active	Passive	Active	Passive	Active	Passive	Active	Passive	Active	Passive
3/20	258,702	6,759	41,360	1,130	150,629	3,356	1,350,118	92,218	219,009	831
3/21	259,305	6,056	43,333	1,292	162,366	3,845	1,360,660	110,379	219,009	1,072
3/22	260,676	7,535	44,090	1,180	164,685	4,364	1,400,427	109,896	219,985	1,028
3/23	260,420	8,267	43,538	1,255	147,190	4,338	1,352,019	111,247	221,466	1,105
3/24	259,389	7,635	41,273	1,206	137,491	4,024	1,367,554	112,513	222,464	1,037
3/25	261,883	8,008	44,769	1,197	155,830	4,125	1,399,724	114,518	228,119	1,024
3/26	260,011	7,479	41,830	1,127	152,918	3,616	1,362,978	111,646	226,030	1,009
3/27	260,506	6,727	42,556	1,190	148,728	3,871	1,382,096	120,624	223,313	1,043
3/28	261,551	9,100	44,216	1,340	144,365	4,499	1,375,399	199,023	223,345	1,208
3/29	261,171	9,145	42,189	948	140,225	3,658	1,369,100	204,017	225,513	789
3/30	261,513	8,200	42,992	921	157,477	4,030	1,370,090	202,702	225,642	754
3/31	261,766	9,195	42,651	956	161,387	3,798	1,399,218	202,511	225,128	809

Table 2. The distribution of QTYPEs for the active and passive DNS in our datasets.

QTYPE	Aggregate ($\times 10^3$)		Mean		Median	
	Active	Passive	Active	Passive	Active	Passive
A	3,082,960	813,485	256,913,375.92	67,790,485.33	257,181,439.5	54,989,441.0
AAAA	292,278	81,992	24,356,555.67	6,832,692.33	23,918,026.5	5,920,971.5
CNAME	174,881	136,901	14,573,484.5	11,408,450.0	14,582,732.0	8,495,216.5
MX	2,222,465	908	185,205,470.67	75,690.83	184,075,003.5	83,309.0
NS	5,822,874	586,695	485,239,507	48,891,296.25	485,117,732.0	39,316,201.5
SOA	3,498,172	28,162	291,514,366.5	2,346,885.75	291,172,940.5	2,022,850.0
TXT	701,689	14,499	58,474,102.67	1,208,253.83	58,304,209.5	1,205,094.5
Other	694,067	28,655	57,838,938.5	2,387,929.75	57,693,964	2,380,550

4.1 Enhancing Public Blacklists

Due to the nature of Thales we can make use of the collected data in ways that can reveal abuse signal about domains before they are identified as actual malicious use. Blacklisted domains, for example, are an interesting category of candidate indicators of abuse that can be registered, set-up, and pointed to an IP location well before they are actually used in malicious activities. Thus, active DNS could be used as a potential source of raw datasets that can be used for timely domain abuse detection.

As we have already discussed, alongside the active DNS data collection, we were also able to gather a plethora of public domain name blacklists. As expected, domain names in these blacklists also appeared in the active DNS traces we collected using the active DNS project. For all domain names seen in both the public blacklists and active DNS data, we identified two important dates. The first denotes the first day the domain name was probed by Thales. This behavior is driven by the addition of the domain in our seed list that can be caused by a change in any of the zone files collected daily from the top level domain authorities. The second important date we identified is the first day one of the many blacklists we collect (on a daily basis) actually listed this domain name as part of a particular abusive activity.

We compared the first seen dates of blacklisted domains and the first seen date of a domain resolved by Thales and we plotted the results in a cumulative distribution function (CDF) that depicts the time difference in days between a resolution in our passive or active DNS data and the appearance of the domain in a public blacklist. Negative values represent the number of domains that have first appeared in our active or passive DNS data before getting eventually blacklisted. On the other hand, positive values represent domains that had been blacklisted before they had a resolution in our data.

It is worth pointing out that not all the public domain names blacklists were used as a seed domain source for Thales, rather the ones that are described in Sect. 2.2. That is, we should expect a fair amount of both positive and negative values in these CDFs. Positive values indicate that a domain name was first seen in a blacklist and then in either the active or passive DNS data that we present in Fig. 7, while negative values indicate that the domain was first seen in DNS before being blacklisted.

Thales resolves domains that came in part from zonefiles for major top-level domains. It queries any domain registered in that zone within a day after it was registered and added in the zonefile. This creates a temporal history of the DNS activity capable of describing the IP infrastructure history that supported the domain name, before blacklisting, at the time, and after it was blacklisted. This is a new property that active DNS datasets will freely offer to the security community, and it is a property that is rarely seen in passive DNS data. The reason for this behaviour that active DNS exhibits compared to passive DNS is simple; infections get remediated and hosts are mobile, thus making it hard for the network operator to passively observe the network evolution of the infrastructure that supports a domain. Thus, Thales should be able to offer a strong signal augmenting existing passive DNS data to which researchers and network operators have access.

Figure 7 shows the CDF plots for different classes of malicious domain names (Figs. 7a to d). The values plotted include the domains in our active and passive DNS datasets that have been blacklisted. Several instances of these domains are found in our dataset long before they are blacklisted; for example 50 % of domain names associated with spam were queried approximately 2.5 months before they were blacklisted. On the other hand, we do not have the same visibility for ephemeral types of attacks, like phishing and exploit kits. In the latter two cases, approximately 75 % of the domain names are queried by Thales at least one day earlier, with the 50 % mark being at around 50 days earlier.

In total 42,000 domain names have been blacklisted and also appeared in our active DNS dataset. From this set, 30 % were queried and data have been collected for approximately 100 days before the blacklisting instance (Fig. 7(e)). For 75 % of the blacklisted domain names, we have collected data for more than a week before they appeared on a PBL. Considering that PBLs have been used

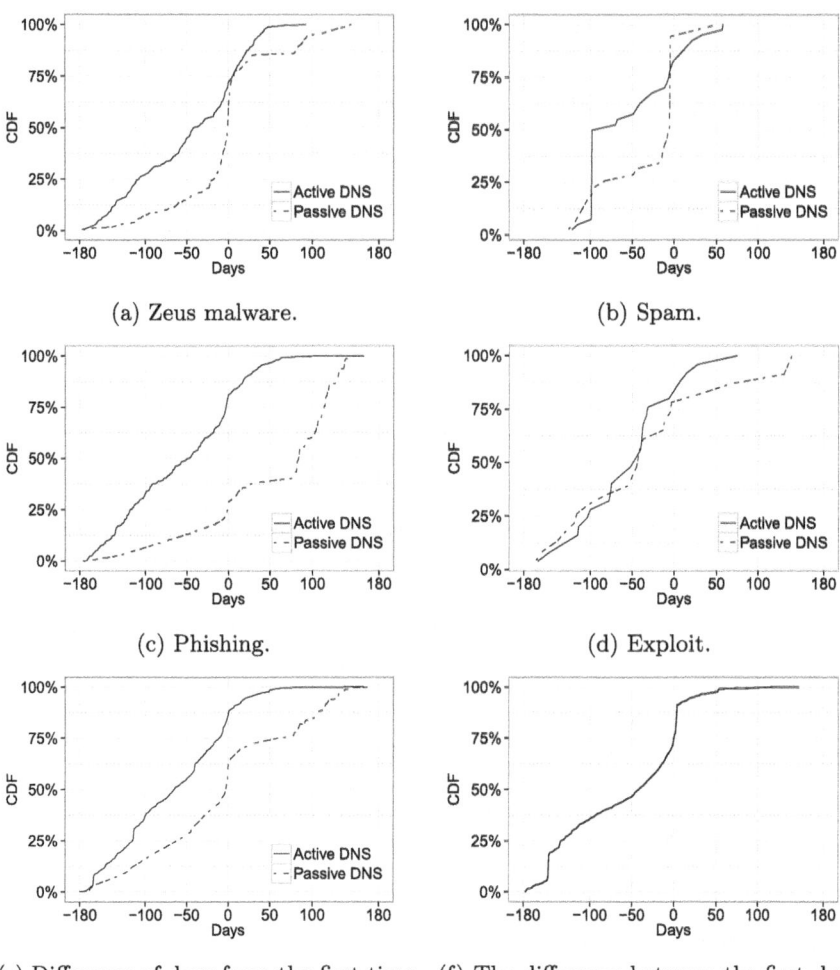

(a) Zeus malware.

(b) Spam.

(c) Phishing.

(d) Exploit.

(e) Difference of days from the first time a domain name was seen in active and passive DNS before it appeared in a PBL.

(f) The difference between the first date a blacklisted domain was seen in active DNS versus the passive DNS dataset, for the domains that were seen before they were blacklisted. Approximately 70% of the 17,000 domains that exist in both datasets and were blacklisted, were first seen in active DNS.

Fig. 7. Cumulative distribution of the first seen date in active and passive DNS, subtracting the first seen date of the same domain in a PBL for Zeus, Spam, Phishing, and Exploit domains.

as ground truth for various security systems [21,23,26,30], we are planning to utilize this data over time to model the behavior of these domains and identify the threats long before current systems, or even before they are utilized by the adversaries.

On the other hand, we were able to identify 20,000 domain names in the passive DNS dataset that also appear in blacklists. The dashed line in Fig. 7 plots represents these domain names. Approximately 50 % of the domain names that are blacklisted appear in the passive DNS data feed, with only 25 % revealing themselves 50 days earlier than the blacklisting event, as shown in Fig. 7e. In this case, there are only 20,000 domain names that have been blacklisted and the visibility that we have is approximately 15 % for the 100 days mark. About 50 % of all the domain names were seen roughly two days before they were blacklisted. This clearly supports our claim about the merit of active DNS datasets, and how well they complement existing passive DNS repositories. The early linkage between domain names and IP infrastructure witnessed by the active DNS data will be able to enrich the signal that passive DNS data contains, potentially making local DNS modeling efforts easier for researchers and operators.

In most cases, the active DNS dataset contains domain names far before they appear in either the passive DNS or the blacklist dataset. Note that the intersection between active and passive DNS records that have been blacklisted is approximately 19,000. This is almost half of the domains in the active DNS dataset and 95 % of the domain names in the passive DNS dataset. Passive DNS seems to show better results in early days for the spam domain names case (Fig. 7b), but active DNS catches up very fast (within 15 days) and then loses the advantage again at the time of the blacklisting events (0 point in the plot).

Lastly, Fig. 7f depicts the difference between the day a blacklisted domain name was first seen in our active DNS dataset and the day it was seen in our passive DNS dataset. This includes only the domain names that were seen before the PBLs included them. Approximately 17,000 domain names have been found in both active and passive DNS before they were blacklisted. The vast majority of them were first resolved by Thales, at least one day before it was visited by a system in our university. Approximately 40 % of the domain names were already being resolved by Thales for more than 100 days before they appeared in the passive DNS dataset.

4.2 Enhancing the Detection of Domain's Residual Trust Change

On the Internet, domain names serve as trust anchors for numerous systems and services, and for many, ownership of a domain is enough to prove one's identity. Work by Lever et al. [25] discussed the problems caused by the use of domains as trust anchors and showed that residual trust, implicitly inherited by domains after an ownership change, is a root cause of many seemingly disparate security problems. Therefore, identifying changes in ownership, due to expiration or some other cause, is an important problem in protecting against the abuse of residual trust. WHOIS [19] is typically used to discover more information about the owner of a particular domain, and thus, it would a appear to be a natural fit for creating a remedy to this problem. However, collecting WHOIS at scale is outside the grasp of most organizations due to rate limiting imposed on automated collection of WHOIS records. To make matters worse, these limits frequently vary by registrar, further adding to the complexity of collecting WHOIS data at scale. To circumvent this problem, Lever et al., proposed Alembic, a lightweight algorithm for locating potential ownership changes that relies solely on passive DNS. This algorithm relied upon three different components: changes in infrastructure, changes in lookup volume distribution, and change in SOA records.

While passive DNS is much easier collect, it is also very sparse, and this results in two limitations with respect to Alembic. Scores can only be computed for domains observed in passive DNS and that have sufficient historical resolutions. Active DNS can help improve upon these limitations. First, Fig. 6e shows that active DNS captures many more effective second level domains than passive DNS. Given that the passive DNS dataset used for comparison was generated from a large university network, this result is particularly important. It demonstrates that even large networks have difficulty matching the breadth of domains that can be collected using active DNS querying. Next, active DNS querying can consistently gather specified DNS record types over time. In particular, Figs. 5a and b show that active DNS results in substantially more SOA records than passive DNS each day. Since one of the key components of the Alembic scoring is SOA records, active DNS should be able to enhance the performance of the Alembic scoring algorithm. While active DNS provides many benefits, it is important to note that the one component Active DNS cannot enhance is the lookup volume distribution of domains. This component is derived by user behavior observed in passive DNS, and therefore, there is no analog in the active DNS dataset.

To evaluate whether Alembic could work using only active DNS, we implemented a modified version of the algorithm that excluded lookup volume distribution as a component and used a fixed window size of two weeks. Then we computed scores for March 27, 2016 using our modified algorithm. In total, this resulted in 63,332,836 domains with non-zero scores, where larger scores indicate a higher confidence in an ownership change. The distribution of those scores can be seen in Fig. 8. The majority fell in the range between 0.4 and 0.5, and further inspection revealed that the SOA component contributed the most to these scores. In short, most of the scores in this range were a result of changes in the SOA record for the domains. Since we saw very little change in hosting infrastructure, it is possible these scores could simply be the result of minor changes within the SOA record. The next largest range was between 0.9 and 1.0 and consisted of 5,652,910 domains. According to the

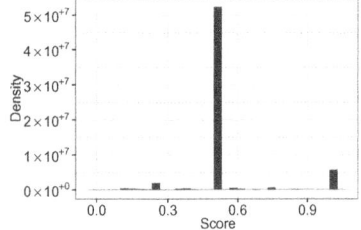

Fig. 8. Histogram showing the distribution of Alembic scores for March 27, 2016.

algorithm, domains with a score in this range are most likely to have undergone a change in ownership. 5,625,397 (99.5%) of these domains had a score of 1.0, indicating that both infrastructure and SOA records had undergone complete changes. Indeed, we found 10,885 of these domains on a public service's list [5] of expired domains for March 27, 2016. The remainder of these domains provide interesting cases for further study.

Our modified version of the Alembic algorithm, originally proposed by Lever et al., provides an interesting example of how active DNS can be used to enhance or extend existing research. Without active DNS, deploying an algorithm like Alembic would require access to a large scale passive DNS dataset (e.g., university, enterprise, Internet service provider). However, using openly available active DNS data, as offered by this research, can help remove the barriers to using or deploying existing DNS research.

4.3 Tracking Malicious Domain Names in Non-routable IP Space

Bogons are private, reserved, or otherwise unallocated network blocks [18,32,34]. Bogons should be boring since by definition they should not be hosting anything in the context of the global Internet. But occasionally, a domain name, like messisux.bix, resolves to a bogon like 0.0.0.0 despite the fact this IP can not host anything. The presence of a domain name, however, indicates a service that should be globally reachable exists. These "nonsense" resolutions are at times caused by misconfigurations, brand protection services, and occasionally, malicious actors. To investigate further, we don our threat researcher hats and analyze domain names that resolved to bogon IP space during our analysis. Here we focus on malicious infrastructure as it is a primary interest of the security community. However, we also note that active DNS data that resolves to bogons would be useful in other contexts such as identifying potential trademark infringements.

We identified two known malicious campaigns in the subset of bogon data: "Operation Hangover" and "CopyKittens." The former is infrastructure of a cyber espionage threat targeting government, military, and private sector networks with some ties to India [17]. Domain names seen in active DNS data for this threat are shown on the left hand side in Table 3. The latter is infrastructure for threats targeting "high ranking diplomats at Israel's Ministry of Foreign Affairs and some well-known Israeli academic researchers specializing in Middle East Studies" [33] and its active DNS domains are shown on the right column in Table 3.

These are useful indicators despite the fact these attacks are known and likely inactive. Neutered, yet unidentified, infections are likely still operating in networks today, which should lead to incidence responses and damage assessments. For example, knowing the specific internal machine that was infected with targeted malware is useful even after an attack has taken place. An end-user machine on a company's corporate network has different implications than a locked down server in a data center, or the CEO's personal laptop. Interestingly, some targeted threats do resolve to bogon space, while active, to reduce

Table 3. Operation Hangover and CopyKittens attack group infrastructure and domain names.

Operation Hangover	CopyKittens
alertmymailsnotify[dot]com	alhadath[dot]mobi
cloudone-opsource[dot]com	big-windowss[dot]com
download-mgrwin[dot]com	cacheupdate14[dot]com
necessaries-documentation[dot]com	fbstatic-akamaihd[dot]com
newsfairprocessing[dot]com	fbstatic-a[dot]space
onestop-shops[dot]com	fbstatic-a[dot]xyz
servicesloginmail-process[dot]com	gmailtagmanager[dot]com
servicesprocessing[dot]com	haaretz[dot]link
websourceing[dot]com	haaretz-news[dot]com
worldvoicetrip[dot]com	mswordupdate15[dot]com
	mswordupdate16[dot]com
	mswordupdate17[dot]com
	patch7-windows[dot]com
	patch8-windows[dot]com
	patchthiswindows[dot]com
	walla[dot]link
	wethearservice[dot]com
	wheatherserviceapi[dot]info
	windowkernel[dot]com
	windows-drive20[dot]com
	windowskernel14[dot]com
	windows-my50[dot]com
	windowsupup[dot]com

their network footprint [27]. This suggests signal for malicious detection in active DNS's non-routable IPs.

5 Related Work

The collection of passive DNS data has been proposed by Weimer et al. [35] over a decade ago as a method that network operators could use to investigate security events in their environments. Zdrnja et al. [36] was the first to discuss how passive DNS data can be used for spotting security incidents using domain names. Notos [12] and Exposure [15] used the idea of building passive DNS reputation by statistically modeling various properties of the successfully resolved passive DNS traffic. Plonka et al. [29] introduced Treetop, a scalable way to manage a growing collection of passive DNS data and at the same time correlate zone and network properties. Since then, several researchers were able to use proprietary passive DNS data to build systems that can detect abuse in the Internet [13,14,16,24,26,31]. Clearly, passive DNS is considered to be a very valuable tool that network operators and security researchers use in the fight against Internet abuse. As already discussed, our active DNS project can provide researchers open access to DNS datasets, comparable to the very useful passive DNS, but without any concerns on personally identifiable information (PII) or other legal barriers to repeatable DNS research.

There have been many commercial and nation efforts to create passive DNS repositories. The costs for the commercial offerings[3] often pose a barrier for researchers and network operators. Now, some of the national efforts are hindered by DNS policy, and thus have yet to be widely adapted by the community. Perhaps the most successful has been `passiveDNS.cn`, which was quickly dismissed as an unreliable source of DNS information. The reason behind this development is very simple. The Chinese operators[4] passively collected DNS records that have been already censored by their egress sensors. In our project, we do not censor the views of the recursive DNS servers that Thales uses to resolve the seed domain names on a daily basis.

With the respect of active scanning efforts, most of the efforts have been conducted from the side of the industry. In the last year, however, new work surfaced from the academic community [20] that provides the ability to researchers to scan the entire IPv4 space and use the results for open security research. This is the work that is closest to the proposed system. The key difference, however, is that Censys was not designed to scan the domain name space, rather, IPv4. Thus, while researchers could find some DNS logs into this great public project, our work both complements Censys and also is designed to deal with DNS scanning.

6 Conclusion

DNS is vital to the operation of the Internet. Users, systems, and services rely on its operation for most network communication—often without even realizing it. Malware is no different. It makes use of DNS to locate C&C servers and provide network agility. Despite all its uses, it is incredibly difficult to gain access to large, open, and freely available DNS datasets, and even when possible, such data is often encumbered with privacy regulations or access restrictions. This severely limits the pool of security researchers than can leverage DNS in their work. Furthermore, it limits the repeatability of existing DNS based research. Clearly, there is a need in the research community for access to large, open, and freely available DNS data. To that end, this work built a new system, Thales, to query and collect massive quantities of DNS data starting from publicly available lists of domains (e.g., zone files, Alexa, Common Crawl, etc.). We are releasing the resulting active DNS data from this system to the public, and since this data is derived from public sources, it can be easily incorporated into new or

---
[3] For example, https://www.farsightsecurity.com/.
[4] http://www1.cnnic.cn/ScientificResearch/LeadingEdge/fymly1/.

existing research without having to worry about privacy regulations or access restrictions.

To prove its merit, we provide an in-depth comparison between active DNS and a passive DNS dataset collected on a large university network. This analysis showed that active DNS data provides a greater breadth of coverage (i.e., greater quantity and greater variety of records), but passive DNS data provides a denser, more tightly connected graph. Due to these differences, we provided case studies demonstrating how active DNS can be used to facilitate new research or even re-implement existing DNS related research. It is our sincere hope that by opening up active DNS to the security community we can spur more and better research around DNS.

Acknowledgment. This material is based upon work supported in part by the US Department of Commerce grant no. 2106DEK, National Science Foundation (NSF) grant no. 2106DGX and Sandia National Laboratories grant no. 2106DMU. Any opinions, findings, and conclusions or recommendations expressed in this material are those of the authors and do not necessarily reflect the views of the US Department of Commerce, National Science Foundation, nor Sandia National Laboratories.

References

1. I.T. Mate List (2016). http://vurldissect.co.uk/daily.asp/
2. Abuse.ch domain blacklist (2016). http://www.abuse.ch/
3. Actionable analytics (2016). https://www.alexa.com
4. Common Crawl (2016). https://commoncrawl.org/
5. Domain Graveyard (2016). http://domaingraveyard.com/
6. Hphosts feed (2016). http://hosts-file.net/?s=Download
7. LinuxContainers.org (2016). http://hosts-file.net/?s=Download
8. Malc0de Database (2016). http://malc0de.com/bl/BOOT
9. Malware Domain List (2016). https://www.malwaredomainlist.com/
10. Sagadc.org list (2016). http://dns-bh.sagadc.org/
11. SANS ISC Feeds (2016). https://isc.sans.edu/feeds/
12. Antonakakis, M., Dagon, D., Luo, X., Perdisci, R., Lee, W., Bellmor, J.: A centralized monitoring infrastructure for improving DNS security. In: Jha, S., Sommer, R., Kreibich, C. (eds.) RAID 2010. LNCS, vol. 6307, pp. 18–37. Springer, Heidelberg (2010)
13. Antonakakis, M., Perdisci, R., Lee, W., Vasiloglou, N., Dagon, D.: Detecting malware domains in the upper DNS hierarchy. In: Proceedings of the 20th USENIX Conference on Security (USENIX Security), August 2011
14. Antonakakis, M., Perdisci, R., Nadji, Y., Vasiloglou, N., Abu-Nimeh, S., Lee, W., Dagon, D.: From throw-away traffic to bots: detecting the rise of DGA-based malware. In: Proceedings of the 21st USENIX Conference on Security Symposium, Security 2012, Berkeley, CA, USA, pp. 24–24. USENIX Association (2012)
15. Bilge, L., Kirda, E., Kruegel, C., Balduzzi, M.: EXPOSURE: finding malicious domains using passive DNS analysis. In: Proceedings of NDSS (2011)
16. Chen, Y., Antonakakis, M., Perdisci, R., Nadji, Y., Dagon, D., Lee, W.: DNS noise: measuring the pervasiveness of disposable domains in modern DNS traffic. In: 2014 44th Annual IEEE/IFIP International Conference on Dependable Systems and Networks (DSN), pp. 598–609, June 2014

17. Coat, B.: Snake in the grass: Python-based malware used for targeted attacks (2014). https://www2.bluecoat.com/security-blog/2014-06-10/snake-grass-python-based-malware-used-targeted-attacks
18. Cotton, M., Vegoda, L.: Special Use IPv4 Addresses. RFC 5735 (Best Current Practice), Obsoleted by RFC 6890, updated by RFC 6598, January 2010
19. Daigle, L.: WHOIS Protocol Specification. RFC 3912 (Draft Standard), September 2004
20. Durumeric, Z., Adrian, D., Mirian, A., Bailey, M., Halderman, J.A.: A search engine backed by Internet-wide scanning. In: Proceedings of the 22nd ACM Conference on Computer and Communications Security, October 2015
21. Felegyhazi, M., Kreibich, C., Paxson, V.: On the potential of proactive domain blacklisting. In: Proceedings of the 3rd USENIX Conference on Large-Scale Exploits, Emergent Threats (2011). Observation of strains. Infect Dis Ther. **3**(1), 35–43: Botnets, Spyware, Worms, and More (LEET), April 2010
22. Holz, T., Gorecki, C., Rieck, K., Freiling, F.C.: Measuring and detecting fast-flux service networks. In: NDSS (2008)
23. Ishibashi, K., Toyono, T., Hasegawa, H., Yoshino, H.: Extending black domain name list by using co-occurrence relation between DNS queries. IEICE Trans. Commun. **95**(3), 794–802 (2012)
24. Krishnan, S., Monrose, F.: An empirical study of the performance, security and privacy implications of domain name prefetching. In: 2011 IEEE/IFIP 41st International Conference on Dependable Systems Networks (DSN), pp. 61–72, June 2011
25. Lever, C., Walls, R., Nadji, Y., Dagon, D., McDaniel, P., Antonakakis, M.: Domain-Z: 28 registrations later measuring the exploitation of residual trust in domains. In: 37th IEEE International Symposium on Security and Privacy, May 2016
26. Ma, J., Saul, L.K., Savage, S., Voelker, G.M.: Beyond blacklists: learning to detect malicious web sites from suspicious URLs. In: Proceedings of the 15th ACM SIGKDD International Conference on Knowledge Discovery and Data Mining (KDD), June 2009
27. Mandiant. APT1. Technical report (2013). http://intelreport.mandiant.com/Mandiant_APT1_Report.pdf
28. Nadji, Y., Antonakakis, M., Perdisci, R., Lee, W.: Connected colors: unveiling the structure of criminal networks. In: Stolfo, S.J., Stavrou, A., Wright, C.V. (eds.) RAID 2013. LNCS, vol. 8145, pp. 390–410. Springer, Heidelberg (2013)
29. Plonka, D., Barford, P.: Context-aware clustering of DNS query traffic. In: Proceedings of the 8th ACM SIGCOMM Conference on Internet Measurement, IMC 2008, pp. 217–230. ACM, New York (2008)
30. Prakash, P., Kumar, M., Kompella, R.R., Gupta, M.: Phishnet: predictive blacklisting to detect phishing attacks. In: Proceedings of IEEE INFOCOM, 2010, pp. 1–5. IEEE (2010)
31. Rahbarinia, B., Perdisci, R., Antonakakis, M.: Segugio: efficient behavior-based tracking of malware-control domains in large ISP networks. In: 2015 45th Annual IEEE/IFIP International Conference on Dependable Systems and Networks (DSN), pp. 403–414, June 2015
32. Rekhter, Y., Moskowitz, B., Karrenberg, D., de Groot, G.J., Lear, E.: Address Allocation for Private Internets. RFC 1918 (Best Current Practice), Updated by RFC 6761, February 1996
33. Minerva Labs & ClearSky Cyber Security: CopyKittens Attack Group (2015). https://eforensicsmag.com/copykittens/

34. Weil, J., Kuarsingh, V., Donley, C., Liljenstolpe, C., Azinger, M.: IANA-Reserved IPv4 Prefix for Shared Address Space. RFC 6598 (Best Current Practice), April 2012
35. Weimer, F.: Passive DNS replication. In: Proceedings of the 17th First Conference on Computer Security Incident Handling, June 2005
36. Zdrnja, B., Brownlee, N., Wessels, D.: Passive monitoring of DNS anomalies. In: Hämmerli, B.M., Sommer, R. (eds.) DIMVA 2007. LNCS, vol. 4579, pp. 129–139. Springer, Heidelberg (2007)

Malware Analysis

A Formal Framework for Environmentally Sensitive Malware

Jeremy Blackthorne[✉], Benjamin Kaiser, and Bülent Yener

Rensselaer Polytechnic Institute, Troy, USA
{whitej12,byener}@rpi.edu, benjamin.h.kaiser@gmail.com

Abstract. Theoretical investigations of obfuscation have been built around a model of a single Turing machine which interacts with a user. A drawback of this model is that it cannot account for the most common approach to obfuscation used by malware: the observer effect. The observer effect describes the situation in which the act of observing something changes it. Malware implements the observer effect by detecting and acting on changes in its environment caused by user observation. Malware that leverages the observer effect is considered to be environmentally sensitive.

To account for environmental sensitivity, we initiate a theoretical study of obfuscation with regards to programs that interact with a user and an environment. We define the System-Interaction model to formally represent this additional dimension of interaction. We also define a *semantically obfuscated* program within our model as one that hides all semantic predicates from a computationally bounded adversary. This is possible while still remaining useful because semantically obfuscated programs can interact with an environment while showing nothing to the user. In this paper, we analyze the necessary and sufficient conditions of achieving this standard of obfuscation and show how these conditions relate to real-world programs.

Keywords: Malware · Tamper-resistance · Obfuscation · Formalization · Framework · Environmental sensitivity · Environmental keying

1 Introduction

Program obfuscation is defined as the transformation of code with the intent of making it "hard" to understand while maintaining functionality. Authors of commercial software obfuscate their products to protect their intellectual property, criminals obfuscate their malware to protect against detection by anti-virus software, and nations obfuscate cyber-weapons to prevent repurposing. But no obfuscation technique thus far has been able to guarantee any provable security for everyday programs. This is partly due to the large divide in the theoretical and systems approaches. Each approach has its strengths and weaknesses. It is the goal of this work to combine the strengths of both theoretical and systems approaches in order to shed additional light on the subject of obfuscation.

Theoretical Approach. Theoretical work in obfuscation focuses on simplified models, well-defined properties, and provable results. The most famous of these properties is the virtual black-box (VBB) property, defined by Barak et al. [4]. Informally, the property states that an adversary should gain no more information from the obfuscated source code than they would gain through black-box access to the original program. This is seen as the ultimate goal of formalized obfuscation because no more information could possibly be hidden without also hindering functionality. Recently, VBB obfuscation schemes have actually been constructed [3,12].

Another standard of obfuscation is defined by the indistinguishability property, also first established by Barak et al. [4]. It concerns functionally equivalent programs that have multiple distinct circuit implementations. The property states that such a program could be run without the adversary knowing which of the possible circuits was actually used. Garg et al. provided a construction that was proven secure under a very restricted model which only allows adversaries to perform computations on matrices in a specific order [20].

There are many other well-defined obfuscation types, such as extractability [10], virtual grey-box [9], tau [7], and best-possible [21]. All of these obfuscation types are weaker than VBB, so all comparisons to our own definitions will be with VBB.

Limitations. A common theme among theoretical obfuscation is the use of a single Turing machine (TM) as a model. The representation of the complex interactions between users, software, and hardware as a single TM that interacts with a user leads to limitations on what can be achieved by obfuscation. For instance, if the program is to be useful in any way, it must allow access to its input and output. This limits the goal of obfuscation to protect only the transformation from input to output. Consider the case of malware, in which a program needs to interact with a system and simultaneously not show any information to the user. The single TM model does not account for interactions other than with the user, and hence cannot properly represent this case.

Another limitation implicit in the single TM model is the lack of security possible for learnable functions. A function is learnable if an adversary can determine the definition of the function through only its inputs and outputs. Consider a program that implements the function $f(x) = x^2$. Even without access to the program itself, an adversary can guess the definition by querying the function at a few locations. Because programs obfuscated in the single TM model must allow access to inputs and outputs to be useful, the obfuscated program cannot be both learnable and meaningfully obfuscated.

Systems Approach. The systems approach relies on the concept that observation *requires* modification. This modification can be either of the program itself or the environment. Because observation requires modification, and modification can be detected, observation can be detected. Authors can design programs that detect observation and create deviations in execution, which ultimately impedes observation. This allows obfuscated software to behave in different ways depending on whether or not it is being observed.

The practical set of techniques that leverage the observer effect are known most commonly by their anti-X names, where X is the observation environment. Examples are anti-debugging [14,18,30], anti-virtual machine (VM) [17,30], and anti-emulator [22,26]. There are even special-purpose commercial and malicious programs called packers or protectors which combine many of these techniques with obfuscation in an easy to use package [23]. Packers allow users to protect their binaries without needing to modify the source code.

The anti-X techniques look for artifacts of observation during execution and change the behavior of the program when found. Obviously, one of goals of these analysis environments is to not create artifacts. The result is an arms race between detecting new artifacts and building environments that do not have them. This is in contrast to the large body of research regarding theoretical obfuscation, in which the adversary is allowed to observe without cost. In the theoretical approach, there are no artifacts and there is no effect on the running program when it is being observed. After all, Turing machines are mathematical objects that can be described at any time-step without actually affecting them.

Limitations. Many obfuscation schemes have been proposed and implemented using the methods in the systems approach, but they are ultimately heuristic in nature with no provable security [11,15,28]. Security standards cannot be proven because the concepts are not sufficiently formalized.

1.1 Results

System-Interaction Model. We introduce a model that accounts for the hardware, operating system (OS), program, and user. We define a new type of obfuscation within this model called semantic obfuscation. This obfuscation hides all semantic predicates about a program from a user while allowing the program to remain useful. This is possible within the System-Interaction model because a program can still give output to the OS while showing nothing to the user.

Existing Sensors. Two common ways a program can measure itself and its environment are memory hashing and timing checks. Memory hashing describes the process of a program running a hash over sections of memory. Timing checks are the recording of the time it takes to execute batches of instructions. Both techniques can be used to check the integrity of a program or its environment. We formalize these sensors and strengthen them by allowing them access to a random oracle based on the hardware of the computer. We show the impossibility of achieving semantic obfuscation with either of these sensors – individually or combined.

Ideal Sensor. The ideal sensor approximates a random oracle by returning a random number based on the state of the OS and program. In this way, no bit can be changed in either without it registering with the sensor. We show that with access to an ideal sensor, there exists a semantically obfuscated program that runs in polynomial time and which guarantees exponential time to deobfuscate. The catch is that it also takes exponential time to construct. We show that a semantically obfuscated program which uses an ideal sensor actually can take no less than exponential time to construct. This obfuscator must create the obfuscated program using the hardware on which the obfuscated program is intended to run because each hardware has its own unique randomness. This naturally places the obfuscator at a practical disadvantage because the adversary can try to deobfuscate the program with the hardware of their choice, including much faster hardware than what was intended (or many separate hardware configurations running in parallel).

Piece-Wise Sensor. We propose a sensor constructed from a piece-wise function. This function has asymmetric properties which allow environmentally sensitive software to achieve semantic obfuscation within the System-Interaction model. We believe this sensor can be practically implemented.

1.2 Related Work

In addition to the field of obfuscation, our work relates to tamper-resistance. Canetti and Varia formally define nonmalleable obfuscation, another term for tamper-resistance, and show how existing point functions can achieve their security standard in the random oracle and common reference string models [13]. Another formalization of tamper-resistance is provided by Basile et al. [6], for which they define tamper protection techniques in terms of attacker goals, capabilities, and limitations.

A hardware approach to tamper-resistance is physically unclonable functions (PUFs). These are hardware devices that are unique, hard to replicate, and produce random output. The concept of program sensors within the System-Interaction model is closely related to work done in PUFs. Recent work in PUFs has explored the idea of using intrinsic properties of commercial off-the-shelf systems [24,25]. Plaga and Koob [27] formally describe PUFs and their limitations.

There have been a few cases of formalization for transparent analysis, i.e. analysis that does not induce an observer effect, but nothing yet reaching a rigorous treatment of the subject. Dinaburg et al. present a formalization of transparent malware analysis and describe its requirements [16]. Their requirements are higher privilege, the absence of side-channels, transparent exception handling, and identical timings. Kang et al. also briefly formulate the problem of transparent malware analysis within emulators [22], but do not offer any further investigation.

2 Preliminaries

2.1 Notation

TM is short for Turing machine. UTM is short for universal Turing machine. PPT is short for probabilistic polynomial-time Turing machine. A TM can also be encoded as a bitstring $b \in \{0,1\}^n$, for some natural number n, and used as input to other TM's. Oracle access is input–output only access. A TM A running on input string x with oracle access to a TM B is represented as $A^B(x)$. A function $\alpha : \mathbb{N} \to \mathbb{N}$ is called negligible if it grows slower than any other polynomial.

2.2 Properties of Turing Machines

A property of a TM can be expressed as a yes-no question, sometimes called a predicate. An individual predicate of a TM is denoted by $\pi(M)$, where M is any TM. There are two types of TM properties, *semantic* and *syntactic* [2]. Semantic properties are those that are dependent on the input–output relationship of the function the TM implements. In other words, a semantic property of a TM is also a property of the language which the TM recognizes. Syntactic properties are not necessarily dependent on the language which a TM recognizes, but rather the encoding of that TM.

Obfuscation is the syntactic transformation of a program while maintaining its semantic properties. In other words, the obfuscated program and original program should be input–output equivalent, yet appear different. It is the relationship between the syntax and semantics that is being obfuscated.

2.3 Definitions

Definition 1. *(Instantaneous Description). The instantaneous description (ID) of a TM is defined as*

$$ID \colon TM \to \Gamma^*$$
$$M \mapsto \gamma,$$

where

1. Γ is the tape alphabet,
2. $M \in TM$,
3. and $\gamma \in \Gamma^*$, which is the specific string of characters which represent the total contents of the tape at the time-step in which the ID function is called. The contents of the tape include M and any input to M. This string is the state vector of the entire machine.

Definition 2. *Learnable Function [29]*
A function f, computed by a TM M, is learnable if there exists a PPT L such that

$$Pr[X \leftarrow L^M(1^{|M|}) : X = M] > \alpha(|M|)$$

Informally, a function is learnable if an adversary can query that function at a finite number of locations and with high probability, correctly guess the definition of that function.

Definition 3 *(Virtual Black-Box Obfuscation) [5]. A PPT $\mathcal{O}$ is a virtual black-box obfuscator if the following conditions hold:*

1. Functionality: $\mathcal{O}(M)$ and M are input–output equivalent.
2. Polynomial Slowdown: $\mathcal{O}(M)$ is at most polynomial longer in running time and polynomially larger in description length than M. Specifically there exist a polynomial p such that for every TM M, $|\mathcal{O}(M)| \leq p(|M|)$ and if M halts in t steps on input x, then $\mathcal{O}(M)$ halts in at most $p(t)$ steps on x.
3. Virtual Black-Box Property: For all semantic predicates π:

$$|Pr[A(\mathcal{O}(M)) = \pi(M)] - Pr[S^M(1^{|M|}) = \pi(M)]| \leq \alpha(|M|)$$

3 System-Interaction Model

The model we outline in this chapter is conceptually simple, but allows us to explore an obfuscation that is regularly used in practice but has yet to be formalized. We begin by explaining the fundamental assumptions of our model.

To decide properties of a TM M, we must first observe M. We know that in real software, program states are mostly hidden. For every line of text or single animation shown, a program may be executing thousands of instructions with many variables. To gain information about these hidden program states, we have two options. First, we can try to infer the internal state of M based on its visible output. Second, we can directly observe the internal state of M by simulating M in an analysis environment such as a debugger, virtual machine, or emulator. We state this assumption formally as follows:

Assumption 1 *(Observation). Given any two TMs M_1 and M_2, the only ways for M_1 to view M_2's current configuration are by simulating M_2 and viewing M_2's configuration directly, or by viewing M_2's output and inferring M_2's configuration.*

Although directly viewing a program's configuration through simulation is tempting, it comes at a cost. Simulation changes the program's environment. These changes can be detected by a program and reacted to.

The second method of observation in Assumption 1 is to infer the program's configuration through the program input and output. To increase observation through this method, an observer can modify the program itself, as opposed to the program's environment. An example of modifying the program to increase observation is inserting print statements into the program. This will leak internal configuration data about the program, but as mentioned before, these changes can be detected by the program.

This idea, that increased observation requires modification, is central to our model and accurately reflects real programs. We highlight this concept in our assumption below:

Assumption 2 *(Modification). The only ways to change a TM's output is by modifying the UTM simulating it or by modifying the TM itself.*

When a real program is running on a computer, we know that the program can take its environment as input. An example of this is a program checking for how many other programs are currently running in the same environment. We use the term *sensor* to refer to any mechanism that allows a program to read in its environment.

Assumption 3 *(Sensation). A TM M_1 has the ability to read information about a TM M_2 when M_2 is simulating M_1.*

We combine these simple ideas into a single model called the System-Interaction model.

3.1 Definitions

Definition 4 *(System-Interaction Model). The hardware H is a unique physically implemented two-tape UTM with access to a unique random oracle R based on physical phenomena. H is a black-box that takes input from the user which we represent by a PPT A. The user gives input in the form of an operating system U, program M, and any input x_1 to M. U is an encoding of a UTM and M is an encoding of a TM. H then simulates $U(M(x_1))$ and produces two outputs: (y_1, y_2). The first output y_1, will be returned to the user via being written to the user-tape. The second output y_2, is the output to the operating system U via the system-tape. The user can only see the output that is returned to it via the user-tape. In addition to user-input, H can give an input to M, labeled x_2. H would then simulate $U(M(x_1, x_2))$ (Fig. 1).*

Definition 5 *(Program). A program M is a two-tape TM that implements the following function:*

$$M : \Sigma^* \times \Sigma^* \to \Gamma^* \times \Gamma^*$$
$$x_1, x_2 \mapsto y_1, y_2$$

where

1. *x_1 is the user input string to M,*
2. *x_2 is the system input string to M,*
3. *y_1 is output from M written to the user-tape,*
4. *and y_2 is the output from M written to the system-tape.*

3.2 Adversaries

To more accurately represent the obfuscation of real programs, we have expanded the single TM model into the System-Interaction model. But in order to gain any insights from our work, we must limit the scope. We have chosen to not consider the hardware-based adversary that can perform circuit-level instrumentation.

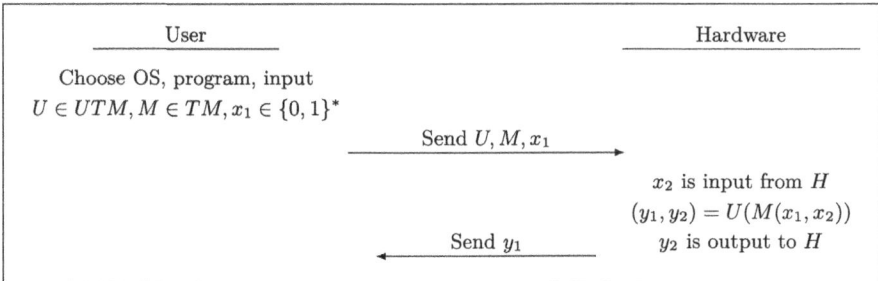

Fig. 1. This illustrates basic interaction between user, program, OS, and hardware.

We have also chosen not to address the problem of information leakage through permanent changes to the system. An example of this would be the adversary that inspects the state of the system after the program runs. For this work, we assume that after the program has completed execution, the system U resets back to the state it held upon being loaded onto the hardware. A practical example of this would be a program that removes all traces of itself after it has completed computation. We do allow the adversary to make any changes to U and then load it onto the hardware. This is akin to loading a custom operating system or hypervisor onto the hardware.

Given the limitations above, there are three natural approaches to determining a property of a program M: statically extracting information from M alone, emulating the hardware H, and changing U or M to leak information. We consider each in turn.

Static Analysis. Static analysis is the technique of analyzing a program without running it. This means that a system is not needed to simulate it. VBB obfuscation prevents any information leaking other than through the inputs and outputs of a program. This is half of the solution to the problem of M leaking information; the other half involves protecting M's inputs and outputs. Throughout this paper, we will utilize VBB obfuscation to address the static adversary. As of this writing, no efficient implementation of a VBB obfuscator exists. There has been an attempt at implementation, with source code released, by Apon et al. [1]. They even provided a obfuscated challenge binary to the community which was quickly broken by Berstein et al. [8]. It is clear there is a long way to go on practical implementations.

Emulation. We consider the possibility of the hardware H being simulated by another software or hardware UTM H'. This would be akin to placing an operating system in a hypervisor or hardware emulator. Empirical results show that any H' could simulate H, but not with exact similarity to that of the original hardware H [19].

Assumption 4. *The hardware H can be simulated on any UTM $H' \neq H$, but it is infeasible to do so with perfect accuracy.*

Modification. The third approach is the modification of the operating system U and is the one on which we focus in this paper. When we discuss modifying the operating system, we are referring to techniques such as attaching a debugger to the program under analysis. Although a debugger is not part of the OS proper, as thought of in the software community, it is how we choose to model changes made to the environment of the program. A much more detailed model would account for the differences between the OS proper, debuggers, programs, and hardware. We have chosen to simplify the system into a simple delineation between the program, OS, and hardware in order to better highlight the relationships between observation of programs and their functionality. We think that the relationships highlighted within our simplified model are representative of those seen in real computer systems.

3.3 Semantic Obfuscation

This new model of obfuscation calls for an exploration of obfuscation ideals. In the single TM model, virtual black-box obfuscation was the absolute ideal because no more information could be hidden without also hindering functionality. In our model with multiple observers, namely the user and the system, a program can hide all semantic information from the user while still remaining useful through interaction with the system.

Definition 6 *(Semantic Obfuscation).* *A TM $\mathcal{O}$ is a semantic obfuscator if the following conditions hold for the obfuscated program $M_o = \mathcal{O}(M)$:*

1. Functionality: M_o and M are input–output equivalent.
2. Polynomial Slowdown: M_o is at most polynomial longer in running time and polynomially larger in description length than M. Specifically there exist a polynomial p such that for every TM M, $|M_o| \leq p(|M|)$ and if M halts in t steps on input x, then M_o halts in at most $p(t)$ steps on x.
3. Semantic Security: M_o hides all semantic properties from an adversary bounded polynomially in time and space.

The property of semantic security is so strong that a program cannot allow for any input–output access to the adversary. In the traditional single TM model, this would cause the obfuscated program to be non-functional.

The idea of semantic security existing simultaneously with functionality is predicated on two concepts: the distinction between user tape and system tape and the ability to distinguish between a normal system and an adversarial one.

The first requirement is that a program model must have a user tape and system tape. Any input–output relationship exposed to the adversary via either tape would violate the property of semantic security. Within the System-Interaction model, the adversary has access to the user tape by default, so this restricts our discussion of semantically obfuscated programs to those with no user input–output. This leaves us with programs which only have system input–output. This corresponds neatly with our chosen practical reference: malware, which often does not accept user input or produce user output.

In addition to eschewing user interaction, a program must distinguish between a normal system and an adversary. It is easy to see that any program that cannot distinguish a system H from an adversary A can be simulated by A, allowing the adversary to watch all of the program's system input and output. Even just poorly approximating the system would allow the adversary to see some system inputs and outputs. Semantic security is violated if any input–output relationships are learned by the adversary. To prevent an adversary from any input–output access to an obfuscated program, we can wrap the obfuscated program in another program. This wrapper program will only run the obfuscated program if the system has not been changed by the adversary. This requires the wrapper program to be able to measure the system; this is achieved through a type of function called a sensor, which we explore in the following sections.

4 Sensors

Programs can distinguish normal systems from adversaries by measuring properties of themselves and the system on which they run. We call these types of measurement functions sensors. Using sensors to distinguish between the system and the adversary is necessary for any program to achieve semantic obfuscation.

All of our constructions follow a similar pattern. We construct a program M_k which distinguishes a normal system from an adversarial one. This program calls another program M_o as a subroutine. We only make claims about the security properties of M_o and not the distinguisher program M_k. The ability for M_k to measure the system is what allows the subroutine M_o to fulfill the properties of semantic obfuscation.

Recall that the system input is labeled $x_2 = H()$. When that value is dependent on the environment, we refer to the machine as a sensor. An example of this is $x_2 = sensor(U, M)$. This would return different values based on the values of U and M. In the following sections, we explore sensors with varying properties to show what is necessary and sufficient to achieve semantic obfuscation.

4.1 Learnable Sensor

It is trivial to show that semantic obfuscation cannot be achieved in the System-Interaction model when the sensor is a learnable function. A polynomial number of queries by the adversary is enough to forge the sensor, making the hardware unnecessary to run the program correctly.

Theorem 1. *A semantically obfuscated program cannot exist within the System-Interaction model when the sensor is learnable.*

Proof. Let M_o be any semantically obfuscated program wrapped by M_k, such that $M_k(x)$ calls M_o on the input $x = k$ and halts otherwise. Let $k = sensor(U, M_k)$, where $sensor : U \times M \to \mathbb{N}$ and $sensor$ is learnable.

To defeat the obfuscation, the adversary first creates an instrumented environment $U' = A(U)$. In U', any system output from an executed program is copied to the user tape. The adversary then repeats this process n times, where n is polynomial with respect to the size of M_o, creating the set $(U'_1 \ldots U'_n)$. Now the adversary executes M_k on each instrumented environment U'_i, computing n different sensor readings $k'_i = sensor(U'_i, M_k)$. Since $sensor()$ is learnable via a polynomial number of input-output pairs, the adversary can determine the definition of $sensor$ based on the information it has computed. The adversary can now simulate $sensor()$ on any input, including the original $k = sensor(U, M_k)$, even without access to the intended hardware H. Given this capability, the adversary can now execute $M_k(k)$, which calls M_o. Now that the adversary has full input-output access to M_o, they can compute semantic properties of M, thus violating the property of semantic security guaranteed by semantic obfuscation.

4.2 Random Oracle Sensor

The opposite of a learnable function is an unlearnable function, in which the definition of the function cannot be determined through inputs and outputs alone. An example of an unlearnable function is a random oracle: a function which returns a unique, perfectly random value for every input. Given the same input, a random oracle will return the same random value. A random oracle can be thought of as the most unlearnable function because an infinite number of inputs and outputs will not give any information about any other input–output pairs.

We now model a sensor that is a random oracle. This sensor allows a program to detect any differences made in the program or its environment. With access to this ideal sensor, we can now achieve semantic obfuscation.

Theorem 2. *There exists a semantic obfuscator within the System-Interaction model when the sensor is a random oracle.*

Proof. We will construct an obfuscator $\mathcal{O}$ in the System-Interaction model with a sensor that acts as a random oracle such that $M_o = \mathcal{O}(U, M)$ with wrapper M_k such that $M_k(k)$ calls M_o when $k = sensor(U, M)$. We assume M has no user input or output and that M_k is VBB obfuscated. The program M_k has no user output when receiving an input of k, otherwise M_k outputs a 0 to the user tape and halts. We will now provide a construction of M_k and M_o such that M_o is semantically obfuscated.

We design M_k such that M_k will call M_o when $x = k$ and at all other points M_k just outputs 0 to the user tape and halts. For $i = 0$ to $i = n$, we construct M_i, with the goal of $i = sensor(U, M_i) \bmod 2^n$, where n is our security parameter. This gives us the ability to increase or decrease the codomain of the random oracle. We construct 2^n different VBB obfuscated M_i's, and submit them to

H. The single M_i that returns no user output will be the program for which $i = sensor(U, M_i)$. Now that we have constructed M_k which calls M_o as a subroutine, we will show that M_o is semantically secure. To do so we employ a semantic security game.

We allow a PPT adversary A to pick any two programs of equal size M_1, M_2, such that neither have user input or output, and send them to the challenger. The challenger will flip a fair coin to choose a bit b. The challenger then computes $M_o = \mathcal{O}(U, M_b)$ with wrapper M_k and sends back M_k to the adversary. The adversary must determine whether M_o is the obfuscated version of M_1 or M_2.

The adversary has three sources from which to extract information about the subroutine M_o: the user output, source code, and the system output. By definition there is no user output from the program. Our obfuscator is a VBB obfuscator, so the source code does not leak any information. This leaves the system output as the only source of information. In the System-Interaction model, the user cannot see the system output without modifying U. If the adversary runs M_k with a modified U', the reading from $sensor(U', M_k)$ returns some x not equal to and independent of k, which is needed by M_k to call M_o. The program M_k is a point function with a domain of 2^n, which means it is computationally infeasible for a PPT adversary to guess k.

Discussion. We have shown that we can create a semantically obfuscated program M_o with a wrapper M_k, but the obvious drawback is that it was done in exponential time. In the world of cryptography, exponential time is intended for the adversary, not the legitimate user. In the case of obfuscation, it could still be considered useful. This is because even though the creation time is exponential, the deobfuscation time would be exponential, while the running time of the obfuscated program would remain polynomial.

Theorem 3. *No polynomial time semantic obfuscator $\mathcal{O}$ exists within the System-Interaction model when the sensor is a random oracle.*

Proof. Assume by way of contradiction that $\mathcal{O}$ is a polynomial time obfuscator in the System-Interaction model using a random oracle sensor such that $M_o = \mathcal{O}(U, M)$ with wrapper M_k, where $k = sensor(U, M_k)$. The program M_k is VBB obfuscated and only calls M_o when receiving an input of k, otherwise M_k outputs a 0 to the user and halts.

If PPT $\mathcal{O}$ can construct M_o with wrapper M_k, then there exists a dependent relationship between M and M_k by way of the algorithm $\mathcal{O}$, which implies a dependent relationship between $x = sensor(U, M)$ and $k = sensor(U, M_k)$. This is a contradiction because $sensor()$ is a random oracle, guaranteeing total independence of outputs given any two different inputs.

Discussion. We have highlighted the essential limitation of using the observer effect. The strongest observer effect possible, formalized here in the random oracle sensor dependent on the system and program, necessarily limits the creation of the program as much as the deobfuscation.

Theorem 4. *A semantic obfuscator $\mathcal{O}$ cannot obfuscate a program M in less time than an adversary can deobfuscate $\mathcal{O}(M)$ within the System-Interaction model when the sensor is a random oracle.*

Proof. As proven in Theorem 3, any semantically obfuscated program M_o in the System-Interaction model wrapped by M_k with a random oracle sensor can at best be created in exponential time. This computational effort is restricted by the speed at which H runs. This is because the System-Interaction model assumes that H is unique and independent for all $H' \neq H$. This forces the author to generate 2^n programs and test each on H and only H.

By default, the adversary will not see any output from M_k when running on H with U. Thus, the adversary must change U to U' to see the system input and output. This necessarily changes the value of $sensor(U', M_k)$ and forces the adversary to brute-force all possible $U' \neq U$ such that $sensor(U', M_k)$ mod $2^n = sensor(U, M_k)$ mod 2^n, where n is the security parameter. The adversary can parallelize these brute-force attempts over any number of H's, thus not being subject to the bottleneck of running on H and H alone, as the author does. This gives the adversary a large computational time advantage.

Discussion. Theorem 3 showed that the observer effect guarantees a computational symmetry between obfuscation and deobfuscation within the System-Interaction model. But Theorem 4 highlights an additional consideration in the real world: hardware speed and parallel computing. The obfuscator extracts secret information from H and embeds it in the program. But this new representation of the secret knowledge has an innate vulnerability: it allows itself to be computed on by the adversary with hardware superior to what the original obfuscator could use to perform the obfuscation. This demonstrates that not only can the observer effect not be used to any advantage by the obfuscator, but it is actually to the obfuscator's disadvantage.

4.3 Piecewise Learnable Sensor

We established in Theorem 1 that a learnable sensor cannot be used to build a semantically obfuscated program. We proved in Theorem 3 that a sensor that functions as a random oracle cannot be used to create a semantically obfuscated program in polynomial time. We are now left with unlearnable functions which are not random oracles as possible candidates for a semantic obfuscator that runs in polynomial time.

We now model a sensor as an unlearnable function which is a hybrid of both learnable functions and a random oracle. The sensor is *piecewise learnable*. This means the sensor function as a whole is not learnable, but each sub-function by itself is learnable.

The total state space of the system is $S = U \times M$, with the system being in any given state $S_t \in S$ at time t. The state of the system S_t is a binary encoding of a TM and so can be sectioned off by S_i, where $S_i + 1$ is some arbitrary number, and $i \in \{0, 1, \ldots, n-1, n\}$. There are $n = 2^\lambda$ number of different learnable sub-functions, where λ is a security parameter. The assignment of each sub-function to a subset of the state space is unknown a priori, but is itself measurable. We model this by assigning each sub-function to a subset of the state space by a random oracle R.

$$Sensor(S_t) = \begin{cases} f_{R(0)}(S_t): & S_0 \leq S_t < S_1 \\ f_{R(1)}(S_t): & S_1 + 1 \leq S_t < S_2 \\ \ldots & \\ f_{R(n)}(S_t): & S_{n-1} \leq S_t \leq S_n \end{cases}$$

With this sensor, it is not clear how it can be used to create a semantically obfuscated program. We need to be able to make changes to the program to embed the correct k such that $k = sensor(U, M_k)$. Simultaneously, we need the adversary to not be able to make changes to the system U and still generate the correct k. These two conditions can be summarized with the following two properties of our piece-wise learnable sensor:

1. $S'_t = (U, M_{k'})$ and $S_t = (U, M_k)$ fall under the same sub-function. And because each sub-function is learnable, there exists a PPT A such that given $x_2 = sensor(U, M'_k)$, A can derive $x_2 = sensor(U, M_k)$.
2. $S'_t = (U', M_k)$ and $S_t = (U, M_k)$ do NOT fall under the same sub-function. This means there does NOT exist a PPT A such that given access to $x_2 = sensor(U', M_{k'})$ can derive $x_2 = sensor(U, M_k)$.

If the sensor is learnable then condition 1 is true and 2 is false. If the sensor is a random oracle then 1 is false and 2 is true. It clear we need both 1 and 2 to be true. Let us now prove that having both conditions true is sufficient to create a semantic obfuscator in the System-Interaction model.

Theorem 5. *Given a sensor which can be represented by a piecewise learnable function, there exists a PPT $\mathcal{O}$ that transforms a TM M into a semantically obfuscated program by wrapping it in M_k, within the System-Interaction model.*

Proof. Let M be a program with no user input or output. We construct a program M_o wrapped by M_k such that M_o is semantically obfuscated. The program M_k calls M_o as a subroutine when $x = k$ and $k = sensor(U, M_k)$. We do this construction in constant time through public-key encryption. This is achieved by creating M_i from $i = 0$ to $i = p$, where p is polynomial with regards to the size of M_o. Each M_i writes out $x_2 = sensor(U, M_i)$ to the user tape encrypted with the author's public key. Only the author can decrypt these readings with the private key. Given access to p sensor readings, all from the same sub-function, the author learns the sub-function and constructs M_k such that $k = sensor(U, M_k)$.

The adversary is required to modify U to determine the input–output of the program because they do not possess the private key. And due to property two of our piece-wise learnable sensor, changing U to U' will cause the sensor to jump sub-functions. The new sub-function and its sensor values will be independent of the original sub-function the program was in when it was being run with U, thus giving the adversary no information.

Discussion. Given the hefty assumptions we made, it does not come as a surprise that we can achieve semantic obfuscation. It does help illustrate a point though: there must exist an asymmetry in the observer effect for it to be useful. Quite like in cryptography, we need a one-way function. One-way functions in cryptography are typically over the domains of integers or lattices. Our one-way function is over the domain of TMs in the System-Interaction model. This comes in the form of the assumptions that changing keys in our point function does not change the sub-function, but changing the environment does change the sub-function. This is much like a noise threshold within an error correction scheme.

5 Existing Sensors

So far we have considered properties of functions that act as sensors. We have shown that it is necessary that a function be unlearnable but not a random oracle in order to achieve semantic obfuscation. Then we showed that a piecewise learnable function is sufficient to achieve semantic obfuscation within the System-Interaction model.

In this section we will consider existing sensors within real programs and show what relation they have to the sensors we have discussed within our model.

5.1 Static Sensor

One of the simplest types of sensors in real programs is the self-memory check. A program can compute a hash of its own memory and compare it against a stored value in order to determine if anything has been changed. We represent this capability in our model with the following definition:

Definition 7 *(Static Sensor). Any program M has oracle access to a $Sensor(S)$, where $Sensor(S) = R(S)$, R is the random oracle from the hardware H, and $S \subseteq ID(U(M))$.*

We show why this simple type of sensor cannot be used to ensure integrity for obfuscation.

Lemma 1. *An adversary can leak the return value of $Sensor(S)$ in the System-Interaction model.*

Proof. We begin by changing U to write out the entire contents of the system tape to the user-tape just before any call to Sensor(S). The tape contents D are then modified to remove the changes made to U. The modified version of D will be denoted D'. Then a new program M' is constructed with the old tape contents appended as data D'. The new program M' contains D', and makes a call to $Sensor(S')$, where S' is now equal to subset of the tape that contains D'. The call to this sensor will return the same value as the sensor call in the original program M. This shows that the return value of the static sensor, even when measuring any subset of the system, will not remain hidden.

5.2 Dynamic Sensor

Programs can also measure properties that change over time. A practical example is the use of the RDTSC x86 assembly instruction which measures an internal hardware clock. Pairs of these instructions can be used to measure the time it takes for code to execute between them. We formalize the idea of measurement over time by first introducing the notion of a trace.

Definition 8 *(Trace). The trace (Tr) of a TM M is defined as the ordered set of IDs of M from timestep= $0 \ldots t-1$, where t is the current timestep.*

To represent simple dynamic sensor like RDTSC, we formalize a sensor which sums all the values in a trace.

Definition 9 *(Dynamic Sensor). Any program M has oracle access to Sensor(Tr), defined as Sensor(Tr) = $\sum_{i=0}^{t-1} R(ID_i)) \mid ID_i \in Tr(U(M))$, and t is the current time-step.*

This sensor is also inadequate for use in ensuring integrity for obfuscation purposes.

Lemma 2. *An adversary can leak the return value of any call to Sensor(Tr) in a program M in the System-Interaction model.*

Proof. Leaking the value of Sensor(Tr) in a program M is trivial, simply because Sensor(Tr) does not measure any instructions that occur after the call to the sensor. To leak the value, modify the part of U that occurs after the call to $Sensor(Tr)$ to write the result of the sensor call to the user-tape. Multiple calls to the sensor could be leaked in turn. For each call to Sensor(Tr), generate a new program which writes the return value of that call to Sensor(Tr) to the user-tape.

5.3 Static and Dynamic Sensors

Real programs often combine static and dynamic sensors. A practical example is a program that both computes hashes over its memory and checks the time it takes to compute those hashes. Even this combination of sensors cannot ensure integrity for obfuscation.

Theorem 6. *Semantic obfuscation is not possible with combined static and dynamic sensors when the dynamic sensor is learnable.*

Proof. The following is a simple algorithm to extract all of the sensor readings: First apply Lemma 1 to all calls to Sensor(S). Next we must extract the calls to Sensor(Tr). There are two possible cases.

Case 1: We can modify U to write the result of Sensor(Tr) to the user-tape without any call to Sensor(S) being affected. If this is true, we can apply Lemma 2 and are finished.

Case 2: There exists a call to Sensor(S) that will measure any modification of U needed to write the value of Sensor(Tr) to the user-tape. In this case, Sensor(Tr) will be affected by the modified return value of Sensor(S). But because Sensor(Tr) is linear and thus learnable, we can determine what the return value of Sensor(Tr) should be through summing a series of calls to Sensor(S), where S is set to areas of the tape that contain the intended ID(U(M)) for that timestep.

Discussion. The underlying reason of this impossibility is the same as why a learnable sensor in general cannot be used. It is easy to see that this same impossibility applies when the dynamic sensor is a random oracle. Both cases reduce to the cases discussed in Sect. 4.

Now we will consider a construction of combined static and dynamic sensors, but this time we will assume the dynamic sensor is the piece-wise learnable sensor described in Sect. 4.

Theorem 7. *Given a static sensor and piece-wise learnable dynamic sensor, there exists a semantic obfuscator within the System-Interaction model.*

Proof. Let M be a program with no user input or output in the System-Interaction model. Let M have access to $Sensor(S)$, which is a random oracle. Let M have access to $Sensor(Tr)$ which is piece-wise learnable. We construct the program $M_o = \mathcal{O}(M, U)$ wrapped by M_k, such that M_k is VBB obfuscated and calls M_o on input k. We construct M_k in the same method as Theorem 5, but this time so that it first calls $Sensor(S)$ where $S = U(M_k)$ and then calls $x_2 = Sensor(Tr)$. The program M_k then checks to see if x_2 is equal to k.

The program M_k, upon receiving k, calls M_o. This M_o and original M are input–output equivalent. The wrapper M_k calls M_o in constant time, so we may say that there is at most polynomial slowdown. Finally, we must establish the semantic security property.

The adversary can extract a semantic predicate from the source of M_k – which includes M_o – or modify U to print out additional information about M_k or M_o. We know that M_k is VBB obfuscated so no information can be attained from the source that can not also be attained from running M_k. The adversary can modify U to print out the value of x_2 by copying it to the user tape. If any modifications are made to U, then the value x_2 will change and become independent of the original value, thus leaking no information. The program M_k will halt upon running $M_k(x_2')$, thus not allowing the adversary to determine any semantic predicates about M.

6 Conclusion

We have provided a formal framework for which to describe environmental sensitivity in programs. We constructed a well-defined standard of obfuscation within that framework, and we have shown the necessary and sufficient conditions of achieving that standard. We believe our research has formed a basis for which to construct practical, semantically obfuscated programs. The clear next step, is to now construct prototypes that fulfill the requirements of semantic obfuscation.

References

1. Apon, D., Huang, Y., Katz, J., Malozemoff, A.J.: Implementing cryptographic program obfuscation (2014)
2. Arora, S., Barak, B.: Randomized computation. In: Computational Complexity: A Modern Approach, pp. 121–122. Cambridge University Press, New York (2012). Chap. 7, Sect. 7.5.3
3. Barak, B., Garg, S., Kalai, Y.T., Paneth, O., Sahai, A.: Protecting obfuscation against algebraic attacks. Cryptology ePrint Archive, Report 2013/631 (2013). http://eprint.iacr.org/2013/631.pdf. Accessed 6 Apr 2015
4. Barak, B., Goldreich, O., Impagliazzo, R., Rudich, S., Sahai, A., Vadhan, S., Yang, K.: On the (im)possibility of obfuscating programs. Cryptology ePrint Archive, Report 2001/069 (2001). http://eprint.iacr.org/
5. Barak, B., Goldreich, O., Impagliazzo, R., Rudich, S., Sahai, A., Vadhan, S.P., Yang, K.: On the (im)possibility of obfuscating programs. In: Kilian, J. (ed.) CRYPTO 2001. LNCS, vol. 2139, p. 1. Springer, Heidelberg (2001)
6. Basile, C., et al.: Towards a formal model for software tamper resistance. COSIC, University of Leuven, Flanders, Belgium (2009). https://www.cosic.esat.kuleuven.be/publications/article-1280.pdf. Accessed 6 Apr 2015
7. Beaucamps, P., Filiol, E.: On the possibility of practically obfuscating programs towards a unified perspective of code protection. J. Comput. Virol. **3**(1), 3–21 (2007)
8. Bernstein, D.J., Hülsing, A., Lange, T., Niederhagen, R.: Bad directions in cryptographic hash functions. In: Foo, E., Stebila, D. (eds.) ACISP 2015. LNCS, vol. 9144, pp. 488–508. Springer, Heidelberg (2015)
9. Bitansky, N., Canetti, R.: On strong simulation and composable point obfuscation. In: Rabin, T. (ed.) CRYPTO 2010. LNCS, vol. 6223, pp. 520–537. Springer, Heidelberg (2010)
10. Bitansky, N., Canetti, R., Kalai, Y.T., Paneth, O.: On virtual grey box obfuscation for general circuits. In: Garay, J.A., Gennaro, R. (eds.) CRYPTO 2014, Part II. LNCS, vol. 8617, pp. 108–125. Springer, Heidelberg (2014)
11. Borello, J.M., Mé, L.: Code obfuscation techniques for metamorphic viruses. J. Comput. Virol. **4**(3), 211–220 (2008)
12. Brakerski, Z., Rothblum, G.N.: Virtual black-box obfuscation for all circuits via generic graded encoding. Cryptology ePrint Archive, Report 2013/563 (2013). http://eprint.iacr.org/2013-563.pdf, http://eprint.iacr.org/2013-563.pdf. Accessed 6 Apr 2015
13. Canetti, R., Varia, M.: Non-malleable obfuscation. In: Reingold, O. (ed.) TCC 2009. LNCS, vol. 5444, pp. 73–90. Springer, Heidelberg (2009)
14. Chen, X., Andersen, J., Mao, Z., Bailey, M., Nazario, J.: Towards an understanding of anti-virtualization and anti-debugging behavior in modern malware. In: IEEE International Conference on Dependable Systems and Networks with FTCS and DCC, DSN 2008, pp. 177–186, June 2008
15. Collberg, C., Thomborson, C., Low, D.: A taxonomy of obfuscating transformations. Technical report 148. Department of Computer Science University of Auckland, 36 p., July 1997. http://scholar.google.com/scholar?hl=en&btnG=Search&q=intitle:A+Taxonomy+of+Obfuscating+Transformations#0
16. Dinaburg, A., Royal, P., Sharif, M., Lee, W.: Ether: malware analysis via hardware virtualization extensions. In: Proceedings of the 15th ACM Conference on Computer and Communications Security, CCS 2008, pp. 51–62 (2008). http://dl.acm.org/citation.cfm?id=1455779

17. Ferrie, P.: Attacks on more virtual machine emulators. Technical report. Symantec Advanced Threat Research (2007)
18. Ferrie, P.: The Ultimate Anti-Debugging Reference, May 2011. http://pferrie.host22.com/papers/antidebug.pdf. Accessed 6 Apr 2015
19. Garfinkel, T., Adams, K., Warfield, A., Franklin, J.: Compatibility is not transparency: VMM detection myths and realities. In: Proceedings of 11th USENIX Workshop on Hot Topics in Operating Systems, pp. 6:1–6:6 (2007). http://dl.acm.org/citation.cfm?id=1361397.1361403
20. Garg, S., et al.: Candidate indistinguishability obfuscation and functional encryption for all circuits. In: FOCS 2013, pp. 40–49 (2013)
21. Goldwasser, S., Rothblum, G.N.: On best-possible obfuscation. In: Proceedings of 4th Theory Cryptography Conference, pp. 194–213 (2007)
22. Kang, M.G., Yin, H., Hanna, S., McCamant, S., Song, D.: Emulating emulation-resistant malware. In: Proceedings of the 1st ACM Workshop on Virtual Machine Security, VMSec 2009, pp. 11–22. ACM, New York (2009). http://doi.acm.org/10.1145/1655148.1655151
23. Moon, P.: The use of packers, obfuscators and encryptors in modern malware the use of packers, obfuscators and encryptors in modern malware. Technical report, Royal Holloway University of London, March 2015
24. Nithyanand, R., Solis, J.: A theoretical analysis: physical unclonable functions and the software protection problem. In: Proceedings of 2012 IEEE Symposium Security and Privacy Workshop, pp. 1–11 (2012)
25. Nithyanand, R., Sion, R., Solis, J.: Solving the software protection problem with intrinsic personal physical unclonable functions. Sandia National Laboratories, Livermore, CA, USA. Report SAND2011-6603 (2011)
26. Paleari, R., Martignoni, L., Roglia, G.F., Bruschi, D.: A fistful of red-pills: how to automatically generate procedures to detect CPU emulators. In: Proceedings of the 3rd USENIX Conference on Offensive Technologies, WOOT 2009, p. 2. USENIX Association, Berkeley (2009). http://dl.acm.org/citation.cfm?id=1855876.1855878
27. Plaga, R., Koob, F.: A formal definition and a new security mechanism of physical unclonable functions. In: Proceedings 16th International GI/ITG Conference Measurement, Modeling, and Evaluation of Computing Systems and Dependability and Fault Tolerance, pp. 228–301 (2012). http://arxiv.org/abs/1204.0987
28. Popov, I.V., Debray, S.K., Andrews, G.R.: Binary obfuscation using signals. In: Proceedings of 16th USENIX Security Symposium on USENIX Security Symposium, SS 2007, pp. 19:1–19:16. USENIX Association, Berkeley (2007). http://dl.acm.org/citation.cfm?id=1362903.1362922
29. Saxena, A., Wyseur, B., Preneel, B.: Towards security notions for white-box cryptography. In: Samarati, P., Yung, M., Martinelli, F., Ardagna, C.A. (eds.) ISC 2009. LNCS, vol. 5735, pp. 49–58. Springer, Heidelberg (2009)
30. Sikorski, M., Honig, A.: Practical Malware Analysis: The Hands-On Guide to Dissecting Malicious Software, 1st edn. No Starch Press, San Francisco (2012)

AVCLASS: A Tool for Massive Malware Labeling

Marcos Sebastián[1], Richard Rivera[1,2(✉)], Platon Kotzias[1,2], and Juan Caballero[1]

[1] IMDEA Software Institute, Madrid, Spain
richard.rivera@imdea.org
[2] Universidad Politécnica de Madrid, Madrid, Spain

Abstract. Labeling a malicious executable as a variant of a known family is important for security applications such as triage, lineage, and for building reference datasets in turn used for evaluating malware clustering and training malware classification approaches. Oftentimes, such labeling is based on labels output by antivirus engines. While AV labels are well-known to be inconsistent, there is often no other information available for labeling, thus security analysts keep relying on them. However, current approaches for extracting family information from AV labels are manual and inaccurate. In this work, we describe AVCLASS, an automatic labeling tool that given the AV labels for a, potentially massive, number of samples outputs the most likely family names for each sample. AVCLASS implements novel automatic techniques to address 3 key challenges: normalization, removal of generic tokens, and alias detection. We have evaluated AVCLASS on 10 datasets comprising 8.9 M samples, larger than any dataset used by malware clustering and classification works. AVCLASS leverages labels from any AV engine, e.g., all 99 AV engines seen in VirusTotal, the largest engine set in the literature. AVCLASS's clustering achieves F1 measures up to 93.9 on labeled datasets and clusters are labeled with fine-grained family names commonly used by the AV vendors. We release AVCLASS to the community.

Keywords: Malware labeling · AV labels · Classification · Clustering

1 Introduction

Labeling a malicious executable as a variant of a known family is important for multiple security applications such as identifying new threats (by filtering known ones), selecting disinfection mechanisms, attribution, and malware lineage. Such labeling can be done manually by analysts, or automatically by malware classification approaches using supervised machine learning [8,28,29] (assuming the sample belongs to a family in the training set), and also through malware clustering approaches [2,3,24,26] followed by a manual labeling process to assign a known family name to each cluster.

Labeling executables is also important for building reference datasets that are used by researchers for training those malware classification supervised approaches and for evaluating malware clustering results. This creates a bit of a chicken-and-egg problem, which prior work resolves by building reference datasets using AV labels [2,3,24,28,29]. However, AV labels are well-known to be inconsistent [2,6,18,20]. In particular, AV engines often disagree on whether the same sample is malicious or not, and the family name that the label encodes may differ, among others, because of lack of a standard naming convention (conventions such as CARO [7] and CME [4] are not widely used), lack of interest (the main goal of an AV is detection rather than classification [5,10]), using heuristic or behavioral detections not specific to a family, and vendors assigning different names (i.e., *aliases*) to the same family.

Still, despite their known inconsistencies, AV labels are arguably the most common source for extracting malware labels. This likely happens because in many occasions no other ground truth is available, and because, despite its noisy nature, AV labels often contain the family name the analyst wants. Thus, extracting as accurate family information as possible from AV labels is an important problem.

Several limitations affect the process in which prior work builds family name ground truth from AV labels. First, some approaches use the full AV labels, which is inaccurate because the family name comprises only a fraction of the full label. For example, an AV engine may use different labels for samples in the same family, but still assign the same family name in those labels, e.g., when using two different detection rules for the family. Other works extract the family name in the labels through a manual process that is not detailed, does not handle aliases between family names, and does not scale to hundreds of thousands, or millions, of samples.

Second, it has been shown that no single AV engine detects all samples and that the number of AV engines needed to achieve high correctness in the family name is higher than for detection [20]. To address these issues, it is common to resort to majority voting among a fixed set of selected AV vendors. But, this requires selecting some AV vendors considered better at labeling, when prior work shows that some AV vendors may be good at labeling one family, but poor with others [20]. In addition, a majority cannot be reached in many cases, which means a family name cannot be chosen for those samples and they cannot be added into the evaluation or training data [25]. And, focusing on the samples where the majority agrees may bias results towards the easy cases [16]. Furthermore, prior work assumes the results of this process correspond to the ground truth, without quantitatively evaluating their quality.

In this work, we describe AVCLASS, an automatic labeling tool that given the AV labels for a, potentially massive, number of samples outputs the most likely family names for each sample, ranking each candidate family name by the number of AV engines assigning it to the sample. Selecting the top ranked family corresponds to a plurality vote, i.e., family with most votes wins. AVCLASS implements novel automatic techniques to address 3 main challenges: normalization, removal of generic tokens, and alias detection. Using those techniques

AVCLASS automatically extracts as precise family information as possible from the input AV labels.

We envision AVCLASS being used in two main scenarios. In the first scenario, an analyst does not have access to a state-of-the-art malware clustering system (e.g., [2,3,24,26]). When faced with labeling a large amount of samples, the analyst uses AVCLASS to efficiently obtain the most likely families for each sample. Here, AVCLASS acts as an efficient replacement for both clustering and labeling the resulting clusters.

In the second scenario, the analyst has access to an state-of-the-art malware clustering system and can use AVCLASS for 3 tasks. First, it can use AVCLASS to automatically label the output clusters with the most likely family name used by AV vendors. Second, AVCLASS's output can be used to implement a feature based on AV labels (e.g., whether two samples have the same family name) that can be added to the existing clustering. Thus, rather than assuming that the AV labels constitute the ground truth, the analysts incorporates the AV labels knowledge into the clustering system. Third, AVCLASS's output can be used to build a reference clustering to evaluate the clustering results. Since AVCLASS tags each candidate family name with a confidence factor based on the number of AV engines using the name, the analyst can select a threshold on the confidence factor for building the reference dataset, e.g., replacing the default plurality vote with a more conservative (majority or else) vote.

The salient characteristics of AVCLASS are:

- **Automatic.** AVCLASS removes manual analysis limitations on the size of the input dataset. We have evaluated AVCLASS on 8.9 M malicious samples, larger than any dataset previously used by malware clustering and classification approaches.
- **Vendor-agnostic.** Prior work operates on the labels of a fixed subset of 1–48 AV engines. In contrast, AVCLASS operates on the labels of any available set of AV engines, which can vary from sample to sample. All labels are used towards the output family name. AVCLASS has been tested on all 99 AV engines we observe in VirusTotal [31], the largest AV engine set considered so far.
- **Plurality vote.** AVCLASS performs a plurality vote on the normalized family names used by all input engines. A plurality vote outputs a family name more often than a majority vote, since it is rare for more than half of the AV engines to agree.
- **Cross-platform.** AVCLASS can cluster samples for any platforms supported by the AV engines. We evaluate AVCLASS on Windows and Android samples.
- **Does not require executables.** AV labels can be obtained from online services like VirusTotal using a sample's hash, even when the executable is not available.
- **Quantified accuracy.** The accuracy of AVCLASS has been evaluated on 5 publicly available malware datasets with ground truth, showing that it can achieve an F1 score of up to 93.9.
- **Reproducible.** We describe AVCLASS in detail and release its source code.[1]

---

[1] https://github.com/malicialab/avclass.

2 Related Work

Table 1 summarizes relevant works that have used AV labels. For each work, it first presents the year of publication and the goal of the work, which can be malware detection, clustering, classification, combinations of those, cluster validity evaluation, as well as the development of metrics to evaluate AV labels. Then, it describes the granularity of the information extracted from the AV labels, which can be Boolean detection (i.e., existence or absence of the label), coarse-grained classification in particular if a sample is a potentially unwanted program (PUP) or malware, and extracting the family name. Next, it shows the number of labeled samples used in the evaluation and the number of vendors those labels come from. For supervised approaches, the samples column includes only malicious samples in the training set. As far as we know the largest dataset used previously for malware clustering or classification is by Huang and Stokes [11], which comprises 6.5 M samples: 2.8 M malicious and 3.7 M benign. In contrast, we evaluate AVCLASS on 8.9 M malicious samples, making it the largest so far. The next two columns capture whether the AV labels are used to evaluate the results and for training machine learning supervised approaches. Finally, the last column captures if normalization is applied to the AV labels (✓), or alternatively the full label is used (✗).

Table 1. Related work that uses AV labels. The number of samples includes only those labeled using AV results and for classification approaches only malicious samples.

Work	Year	Goal	Granularity			Samples	AV	Eval	Train	Norm
			Det.	PUP	Fam.					
Bailey et al. [2]	2007	Cluster	✓	✗	✓	8.2 K	5	✓	✗	✗
Rieck et al. [28]	2008	Classify	✓	✗	✓	10 K	1	✓	✓	✗
McBoost [23]	2008	Detect	✓	✗	✗	5.5 K	3	✓	✓	✗
Bayer et al. [3]	2009	Cluster	✓	✗	✓	75.7 K	6	✓	✗	✗
Perdisci et al. [24]	2010	Cluster+Detection	✓	✗	✓	25.7 K	3	✓	✗	✓
Malheur [29]	2011	Cluster+Classify	✓	✗	✓	3.1 K	6	✓	✓	✗
BitShred [13]	2011	Cluster	✓	✗	✓	3.9 K	40	✓	✗	✓
Maggi et al. [18]	2011	Metrics	✓	✗	✓	98.8 K	4	✗	✗	✓
VAMO [25]	2012	Cluster Validity	✓	✗	✓	1.1 M	4	✓	✗	✓
Rajab et al. [27]	2013	Detect	✓	✗	✗	2.2 K	45	✓	✗	✗
Dahl et al. [8]	2013	Detect+Classify	✓	✗	✓	1.8 M	1	✓	✓	✗
Drebin [1]	2014	Detect	✓	✓	✓	5.5 K	10	✓	✓	✓
AV-Meter [20]	2014	Metrics	✓	✗	✓	12 K	48	✗	✗	✗
Malsign [15]	2015	Cluster	✓	✓	✗	142 K	11	✓	✗	✗
Kantchelian et al. [14]	2015	Detect	✓	✗	✗	279 K	34	✓	✓	✗
Miller et al. [19]	2016	Detect	✓	✗	✗	1.1 M	32	✓	✓	✗
MtNet [11]	2016	Detect+Classify	✓	✗	✓	2.8 M	1	✓	✓	✗
Hurier et al. [12]	2016	Metrics	✓	✓	✓	2.1 M	66	✗	✗	✗
AVCLASS	2016	Cluster+Label	✓	✓	✓	8.9 M	99	✓	✗	✓

Most works consider a sample malicious if at least a threshold of AV engines detects it (i.e., returns a label) and weigh each AV engine equally in the decision. There is no agreement in the threshold value, which can be a single AV engine [25,32], two [1], four [15,19], or twenty [13]. Some works evaluate different thresholds [20,22] showing that small threshold increases, quickly reduce the number of samples considered malicious. Recently, Kantchelian et al. [14] propose techniques for weighing AV engines differently. However, they assume AV labels are independent of each other, despite prior work having found clusters of AV engines that copy the label of a leader [20], which we also observe. In addition, an AV engine with poor overall labels may have highly accurate signatures for some malware families. In our work we adjust the influence of AV engines that copy labels and then weigh remaining labels equally.

Other works show that AVs may change their signatures over time, refining their labels [9,14]. Recently, Miller et al. [19] argue that detection systems should be trained not with the labels available at evaluation time (e.g., latest VT reports), but with the labels available at training time. Otherwise, detection rate can be inflated by almost 20% points. However, for evaluating clustering results, it makes sense to use the most recent (and refined) labels.

AV Label Inconsistencies. Prior work has identified the problem of different AV engines disagreeing on labels for the same sample [2,6,18,20]. While such discrepancies are problematic, security analysts keep coming back to AV labels for ground truth. Thus, we believe the key question is how to automatically extract as much family information as possible from those labels and to quantitatively evaluate the resulting reference dataset. We propose an automatic labeling approach that addresses the most important causes for discrepancies, namely different naming schemes, generic tokens, and aliases.

Li et al. [16] analyze the use of a reference clustering extracted from AV labels to evaluate clustering results. They argue that using only a subset of samples, for which the majority of AV engines agrees, biases the evaluation towards easy-to-cluster samples. AVCLASS automatically extracts the most likely family names for a sample (even if no majority agrees on it), helping to address this concern by enlarging the reference dataset. Mohaisen and Alrawi [20] propose metrics for evaluating AV detections and their labels. They show how multiple AVs are complementary in their detection and also that engines with better detection rate do not necessarily have higher correctness in their family names. Recently, Hurier et al. [12] propose further metrics to evaluate ground truth datasets built using AV labels. One limitation of proposed metrics is that they operate on the full AV labels without normalization.

Most related to our work is VAMO [25], which proposes an automated approach for evaluating clustering results. VAMO normalizes the labels of 4 AV vendors to build an AV graph (introduced in [24]) that captures the fraction of samples where labels, possibly from different engines, appear together. Our alias detection approach is related, although VAMO does not output aliases as AVCLASS does. Furthermore, VAMO finds the set of reference clusters from the

AV labels that best agrees with a third-party clustering, while AVCLASS labels samples without requiring third-party clustering results.

Naming Conventions. There have been attempts at reducing confusion in malware labels through naming conventions, but they have not gained much traction. A pioneering effort was the 1991 CARO Virus Naming Convention [7]. More recently, the Common Malware Enumeration (CME) Initiative [4] provides unique identifiers for referencing the same malware across different names.

3 Approach

Figure 1 shows the architecture of AVCLASS. It comprises two phases: *preparation* and *labeling*. During the preparation phase, an analyst runs the *generic token detection* and *alias detection* modules on the AV labels of a large number of samples to produce lists of generic tokens and aliases, which become inputs to the labeling phase. In particular, the generic token detection takes as input the AV labels of samples for which their family is known (e.g., from publicly available labeled datasets [1,21,29,33]) and outputs a list of generic tokens, i.e., tokens that appear in labels of samples from different families. The alias detection module takes as input AV labels of a large number of unlabeled samples and outputs pairs of family names that alias to each other.

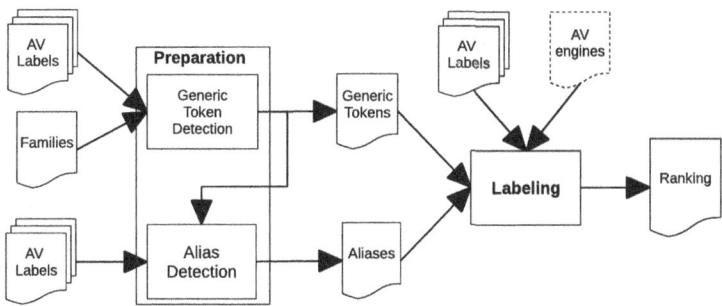

Fig. 1. AVCLASS architecture.

The labeling phase is the core of AVCLASS and implements the label normalization process. It takes as input the AV labels of a large number of samples to be labeled, a list of generic tokens, a list of aliases, and optionally a list of AV engines to use. For each sample to be labeled, it outputs a ranking of its most likely family names. The list of generic tokens and aliases are the outputs of the preparation phase. By default, AVCLASS uses all AV engines in the set of AV labels for a sample. However, by providing an AV engine list, the analyst can restrict the processing to labels from those engines.

AVCLASS implements both the preparation and labeling phases. But, we expect that many analysts may not have large numbers of samples used for preparation. Thus, AVCLASS also includes default lists of generic tokens and aliases obtained in this work, so that an analyst can skip the preparation phase.

The remainder of this section first details the labeling phase (Sect. 3.1), and then the generic token detection (Sect. 3.2) and alias detection (Sect. 3.3) preparation modules. To illustrate the approach, we use the running example in Fig. 2.

3.1 Labeling

The labeling phase takes as input the AV labels of a, potentially massive, number of samples. For each sample, it returns a ranking of its most likely family names. This Section describes the 8 steps used in labeling each sample.

AV Selection (Optional). By default, AVCLASS processes the labels of all AV engines in the input set of a sample. The labels of each sample may come from a different set of AV engines. This design decision was taken because selecting a fixed set of AV engines (as done in prior work) is difficult since there is no real information about which engines are better, and some engines may be good in a family but poor with others. Furthermore, a fixed set of AV engines throws away information as certain AV vendors may have been analyzed only by certain AV vendors. In particular, it is common to obtain AV labels from VT, which has used different AV engines to scan uploaded files over time. Overall, we observe 99 different AV engines in our VT reports, which are detailed in Table 11 in the Appendix. Some engines are only seen for a few days, while others have been continually used by VT for nearly a decade.

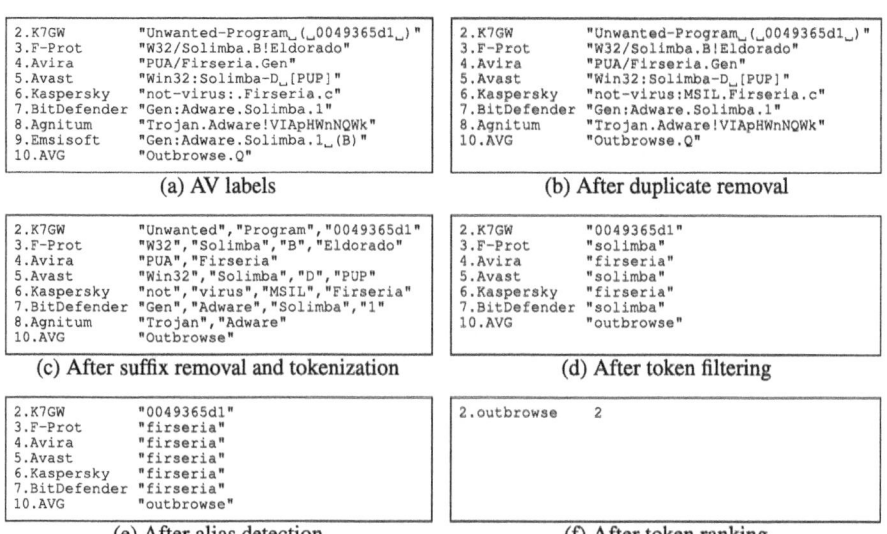

Fig. 2. Running example.

Still, an analyst can optionally provide an input list of engines to AVCLASS. If provided, labels from engines not in the input list are removed at this step and only labels from the input set of AV engines are used for every sample. For brevity, our running example in Fig. 2 assumes the analyst provided an input list with 10 engines. Figure 2a shows the input AV labels from the selected 10 engines for the same sample.

Duplicate Removal. The same AV vendor may have multiple engines such as McAffee and McAffee-GW-Edition, or TrendMicro and TrendMicro-HouseCall. Those engines often copy labels from each other. While we could include only one engine per vendor, the reality is that their detections often differ. In addition, we observe groups of AV vendors that copy labels from each other, something also observed in prior work [20]. In both situations, the detection from these groups of engines are not independent (an assumption of some prior works [14]).

To avoid giving too much weight on the selected family name to vendors with multiple engines, or whose labels are often copied, we leverage the observation that when two AV engines output exactly the same label for a sample this very likely corresponds to one of those two situations. This happens because each vendor structures its labels differently and also uses slightly different keywords in their labels, so that two engines producing exactly the same label is rare unless they are copying each other. Thus, at this step, AVCLASS remove all duplicate labels. A special case is a vendor (*Emsisoft*) that when copying labels adds to them the suffix "(B)". For this vendor, we first remove this suffix from its labels, and then check for duplicates. We have not observed any other such cases. Figure 2b shows how the *Emsisoft* label is removed at this step as a duplicate of the *BitDefender* label.

Suffix Removal. We have empirically observed that most noise in AV labels is introduced in the suffix, i.e., the part of the AV label after the family name, where AV vendors may encode information such as rule numbers and hexadecimal strings that may be hashes. In general, it is difficult to remove those suffixes for all engines as vendors use different label structures, which may even change over time. Still, we have found 3 simple rules to truncate useless suffixes: (1) for 17 AV engines, truncate label after last dot; (2) for *AVG*, truncate after last dot if the suffix only contains digits or uppercase chars; and (3) for *Agnitum*, truncate after the last '!' character. Suffix removal is the only engine-specific step in AVCLASS.

Tokenization. The next step is to split each label into tokens. We use a simple tokenization rule that splits the label on any sequence of consecutive non-alphanumeric characters. Figure 2c shows the results of the suffix removal and tokenization steps. Labels 4, 6, 8, and 10 have been truncated by the suffix removal rules, and all labels have been tokenized.

Token Filtering. The goal of this step is to remove tokens that are not family names. Each token goes through five substeps: (1) convert to lowercase; (2) remove digits at the end of the token; (3) remove token if short, i.e., less than 4 characters; (4) remove token if present in the input list of generic tokens; and

(5) remove token if it is a prefix of the sample's hash[2]. Figure 2d shows the results of token filtering where label 8 was removed as a result of not having any tokens left.

Alias Replacement. Different vendors may use different names for the same family, i.e., aliases. If a token shows in the input list of aliases as being an alias for another family name, the token is replaced by the family name it aliases. The alias detection process is detailed in Sect. 3.3. Figure 2d shows the results after alias replacement, where token *solimba* has been identified as an alias for the *firseria* family.

Token Ranking. Next, tokens are ranked by decreasing number of engines that include the token in their label. Tokens that appear in at most one AV engine are removed. This allows removing random tokens that earlier steps may have missed, as the likelihood is low that a random token appears in labels from multiple AV engines that did not copy their labels. At this point, the ranking captures the candidate family names for the sample and the number of AV engines that use each token can be seen as a confidence score. Figure 2f shows the final token ranking for our running example where token *0049365d1* have been removed because it appears in only one label.

Family Selection. AVCLASS chooses the most common token (top of the ranking) as the family name for the sample. This corresponds to a plurality vote on the candidate family names. AVCLASS also has a verbose option to output the complete ranking, which is useful to identify samples with multiple candidate family names with close scores, which may deserve detailed attention by the analyst. In our running example, the selected family is *firseria*, which outscores 5 to 2 the other possible family name.

3.2 Generic Token Detection

AV labels typically contain multiple generic tokens not specific to a family. For example, the labels in Fig. 2 include generic tokens indicating, among others, the sample's architecture (e.g., *Win32*, *Android*), that a sample is unwanted (e.g., *Unwanted*, *Adware*, *PUP*), generic malware classes (e.g., *Trojan*), and generic families used with heuristic rules (e.g., *Eldorado*, *Artemis*). The generic token detection module is used during the preparation phase to automatically build a list of generic tokens used as input to the labeling phase in Sect. 3.1.

The intuition behind our technique for identifying generic tokens is that tokens appearing in the labels of samples known to be of different families cannot be specific to a family, and thus are generic. For example, an AV engine may output the label *Gen:Adware.Firseria.1* for a sample known to be of the Firseria adware family and the label *Gen:Adware.Outbrowse.2* for a sample known to be of the Outbrowse adware family. Here, tokens *Gen* and *Adware* are likely generic because they are used with samples of different families, and thus are not specific to the Firseria or Outbrowse families.

---

[2] We check the sample's MD5, SHA1, and SHA256 hashes.

Table 2. Categories in the manual generic token list.

Category	Tokens	Example tokens
Architecture	14	android, linux, unix
Behavior: download	29	download, downware, dropped
Behavior: homepage modification	2	homepage, startpage
Behavior: injection	5	inject, injected, injector
Behavior: kill	5	antifw, avkill, blocker
Behavior: signed	2	fakems, signed
Behavior: other	3	autorun, proxy, servstart
Corrupted	2	corrupt, damaged
Exploit	2	expl, exploit
File types	15	html, text, script
Generic families	13	agent, artemis, eldorado
Heuristic detection	12	generic, genmalicius, heuristic
Macro	11	badmacro, macro, x2km
Malicious software	5	malagent, malicious, malware
Malware classes	53	spyware, trojan, virus
Misc	9	access, hack, password
Packed	17	malpack, obfuscated, packed
Packer	6	cryptor, encoder, obfuscator
Patch	3	patched, patchfile, pepatch
Program	5	application, program, software
PUP	29	adware, pup, unwanted
Suspicious	13	suspected, suspicious, variant
Test	2	test, testvirus
Tools	8	fraudtool, tool, virtool
Unclassified	3	unclassifiedmalware, undef, unknown

The generic token detection module takes as input samples for which their family name is known. It iterates on the list of input samples. For each sample, it builds a *sample token list*, by iterating on the set of AV labels for the sample. For each label, it tokenizes the label on non-alphanumeric characters, converts tokens to lowercase, removes digits at the end of the token, removes tokens less than 4 characters, and appends the remaining tokens to the sample token list. Once all labels are processed, it removes duplicate tokens from the sample token list. The sample token list for the sample in Fig. 2 would be: *outbrowse, unwanted, program, 0049365d1, solimba, eldorado, firseria, virus, msil, adware,* and *trojan*. Then, it iterates on the tokens in the sample token list updating a *token family map*, which maps each unique token to the list of families of the samples where the token appears in their labels.

After all samples have been processed, it iterates on the token family map. Each token that does not match a family name and has a count larger than T_{gen} is considered generic. The default $T_{gen} > 8$ threshold is chosen empirically in Sect. 4.3. For example, tokens *firseria* and *solimba* may have appeared only in labels of samples from the *Firseria* family and thus are not generic, but token *eldorado* may have appeared in labels from samples of 9 different families and is identified as generic.

We have applied this approach to automatically generate a list of generic tokens. One author has also manually generated a list of generic tokens. Our experiments in Sect. 4.3 show that the automatically generated generic token list performs similarly in most cases, and even outperforms the manually generated lists in some cases, while scaling and being independent of an analyst's expertise.

Table 2 shows the 15 categories of generic tokens in the manually built generic token list. For each category, it shows the number of tokens in the category and some example tokens. The categories show the wealth of information that AV vendors encode in their labels. They include, among others, architectures; behaviors like homepage modification, code injection, downloading, and disabling security measures; file types; heuristic detections; macro types; malware classes; encrypted code; and keywords for potentially unwanted programs. The categories with more generic tokens are malware classes with 53 tokens (e.g., *trojan, virus, worm, spyware*), download behavior with 29 (e.g., *download, dload, downl, downware*), and potentially unwanted programs with 29 (e.g., *pup, adware, unwanted*).

3.3 Alias Detection

Different vendors may assign different names (i.e., aliases) for the same family. For example, some vendors may use *zeus* and others *zbot* as aliases for the same malware family. The alias detection module is used during the preparation phase to automatically build a list of aliases used as input to the labeling phase in Sect. 3.1.

The intuition behind our technique for automatically detecting aliases is that if two family names are aliases, they will consistently appear in the labels of the same samples. Alias detection takes as input the AV labels of a large set of samples, for which their family does not need to be known, and a generic token list. Thus, alias detection runs after the generic token detection, which prevents generic tokens to be detected as aliases. Alias detection outputs a list of (t_i, t_j) token pairs where t_i is an alias for t_j. This indicates that t_i can be replaced with t_j in the alias detection step in Sect. 3.1.

Alias detection iterates on the list of input samples. For each sample, it builds the sample token list in the same manner as described in the generic token detection in Sect. 3.2, except that tokens in the generic token list are also removed. Then, it iterates on the tokens in the sample token list updating two maps. It first increases the *token count map*, which stores for each unique token the number of samples where the token has been observed in at least one label. Then, for each pair of tokens in the sample token list it increases the *pair count*

Table 3. Top 10 families by number of aliases.

Family	Aliases	Example aliases
wapomi	12	pikor, otwycal, protil
firseria	10	firser, popeler, solimba
vobfus	9	changeup, meredrop, vbobfus
virut	8	angryangel, madangel, virtob
gamarue	7	debris, lilu, wauchos
hotbar	7	clickpotato, rugo, zango
bandoo	6	ilivid, seasuite, searchsuite,
gamevance	6	arcadeweb, gvance, rivalgame
loadmoney	6	ldmon, odyssey, plocust
zeroaccess	6	maxplus, sirefef, zaccess

map that stores for each token pair the number of samples in which those two tokens have been observed in their labels.

We define the function $alias(t_i, t_j) = \frac{|(t_i, t_j)|}{|t_i|}$, which captures the fraction of times that the pair of tokens (t_i, t_j) appears in the same samples. The numerator can be obtained from the pair count map and the denominator from the token count map. Note that $alias(t_i, t_j) \neq alias(t_j, t_i)$.

Once all samples have been processed, the alias detection iterates on the pair count map. For each pair that has a count larger than n_{alias}, it computes both $alias(t_i, t_j)$ and $alias(t_j, t_i)$. If $alias(t_i, t_j) > T_{alias}$ then t_i is an alias for t_j. If $alias(t_j, t_i) > T_{alias}$ then t_j is an alias for t_i. If both $alias(t_i, t_j) > T_{alias}$ and $alias(t_j, t_i) > T_{alias}$ then the less common token is an alias for the most common one.

The two parameters are empirically selected in Sect. 4.4 to have default values $n_{alias} = 20$ and $T_{alias} = 0.94$. n_{alias} is used to remove pairs of tokens that have not been seen enough times, so that a decision on whether they are aliases would have low confidence. T_{alias} controls the percentage of times the two tokens appear together. For t_j to be an alias for t_i, t_j should appear in almost the same samples where t_i appears, but T_{alias} is less than one to account for naming errors.

Table 3 shows the Top 10 families by number of aliases. For each alias, it shows the chosen family name, the total number of aliases for that family, and some example aliases that appear both in the automatically and manually generated alias lists.

Table 4. Datasets used in evaluation.

Dataset	Platform	Lab.	Samples	EXE	Collection period
University	Windows	✗	7,252,810	✗	01/2011 - 08/2015
Miller et al. [19]	Windows	✗	1,079,783	✗	01/2012 - 06/2014
Andrubis [17]	Android	✗	422,826	✗	06/2012 - 06/2014
Malsign [15]	Windows	✓	142,513	✗	06/2012 - 02/2015
VirusShare_20140324 [30]	Android	✗	24,317	✓	05/2013 - 05/2014
VirusShare_20130506 [30]	Android	✗	11,080	✓	06/2012 - 05/2013
Malicia [21]	Windows	✓	9,908	✓	03/2012 - 02/2013
Drebin [1]	Android	✓	5,560	✓	08/2010 - 10/2012
Malheur Reference [29]	Windows	✓	3,131	✗	08/2009 - 08/2009
MalGenome [33]	Android	✓	1,260	✓	08/2008 - 10/2010

4 Evaluation

4.1 Datasets

We evaluate AVCLASS using 10 datasets summarized in Table 4. The table shows the architecture (5 Windows, 5 Android), whether the samples are labeled with their known family name, the number of samples in the dataset, whether the binaries are publicly available (otherwise we only have their hashes), and the collection period. In total, the datasets contain 8.9 M distinct samples collected during 7 years (08/2008 - 08/2015). Some of the datasets overlap, most notably the Drebin [1] dataset is a superset of MalGenome [33]. We do not remove duplicate samples because this way it is easier for readers to map our results to publicly available datasets.

Labeled Datasets. All 5 labeled datasets come from prior works [1,15,21,29, 33]. Among the 3 labeled Windows datasets, Malheur and Malicia contain only malware samples. In contrast, the Malsign dataset [15] contains majoritarily PUP. Each of the labeled datasets went through 2 processes: clustering and labeling. Samples may have been clustered manually (MalGenome), using AV labels (Drebin), or with automatic approaches (Malheur, Malicia, Malsign). For labeling the output clusters, the authors may have used AV labels (Drebin), manual work (MalGenome), the most common feature value in the cluster (Malsign), or a combination of popular features values and information from public sources (Malicia). Drebin [1] is a detection approach and the family classification was done separately using AV labels. Because of this we later observe best results of AVCLASS on this dataset.

Drebin, MalGenome, Malheur, and Malicia datasets are publicly available. Thus, AV vendors could have refined their detection labels using the dataset clustering results after they became public. In contrast, the Malsign dataset and thus its clustering results (i.e., labels) are not publicly available.

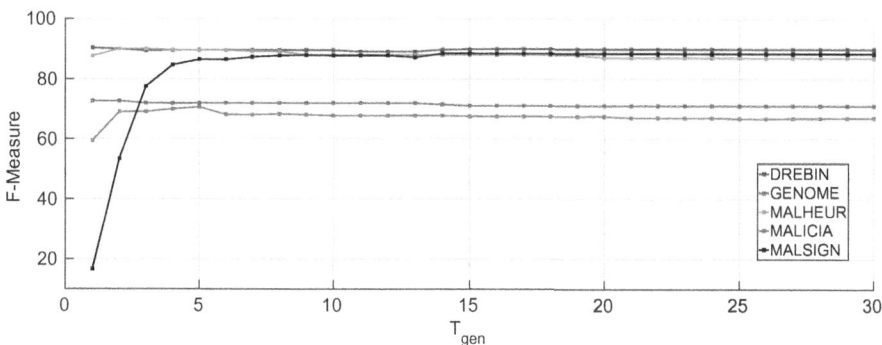

Fig. 3. Parameter selection for generic token detection.

Unlabeled Datasets. For the unlabeled datasets, we do not know the family of the samples and in some cases we only have access to the hashes of the samples, but not their binaries. The University dataset contains malware hashes collected from different sources including a commercial feed. It is our largest dataset with 7.2 M samples. The Andrubis dataset [17] contains hashes of samples submitted by users to be analyzed by the Andrubis online service. The two VirusShare [30] and the Miller et al. [19] datasets are publicly available.

For all samples in the 10 datasets we were able to collect a VT report. The VT report collection started on September 2015 and took several months. Overall, we observe 99 AV engines in the VT reports.

4.2 Metrics

To evaluate the accuracy of AVCLASS, we use an external clustering validation approach that compares AVCLASS's clustering results with a reference clustering from one of the datasets in Table 4 for which we have ground truth. Note that the external validation evaluates if both clusterings group the samples similarly. It does not matter if the family names assigned to the equivalent cluster in both clustering differ. If AVCLASS is not able to find a family name for a sample (e.g., because all its labels are generic), the sample is placed in a singleton cluster. Similar to prior work [3,15,21,25,29] we use the precision, recall, and F1 measure metrics, which we define next.

Let M be a malware dataset, $R = \{R_1, ..., R_s\}$ be the set of s *reference clusters* from the dataset's ground truth, and $C = \{C_1, ..., C_n\}$ be the set of n clusters output by AVCLASS over M. In this setting, precision, recall, and F1 measure are defined as

- **Precision.** $Prec = 1/n \cdot \sum_{j=1}^{n} max_{k=1,...,s}(|C_j \bigcap R_k|)$
- **Recall.** $Rec = 1/s \sum_{k=1}^{s} max_{j=1,...,n}(|C_j \bigcap R_k|)$
- **F-measure Index.** $F1 = 2\frac{Prec \cdot Rec}{Prec + Rec}$

4.3 Generic Token Detection

The generic token detection, detailed in Sect. 3.2, takes as input the AV labels for samples with family name and counts the number of families associated to each remaining token after normalization. Tokens that appear in more than T_{gen} families are considered generic. To select the default threshold, we produce generic token lists for different T_{gen} values and evaluate the accuracy of the labeling phase using those generic token lists. Figure 3 shows the F1 measure as T_{gen} increases for datasets with ground truth. Based on Fig. 3 results, we select $T_{gen} > 8$ as the default threshold. The rest of experiments use, unless otherwise noted, the automatically generated generic token list with this default threshold, which contains 288 generic tokens. In comparison the generic token list manually generated by one author contains 240 generic tokens.

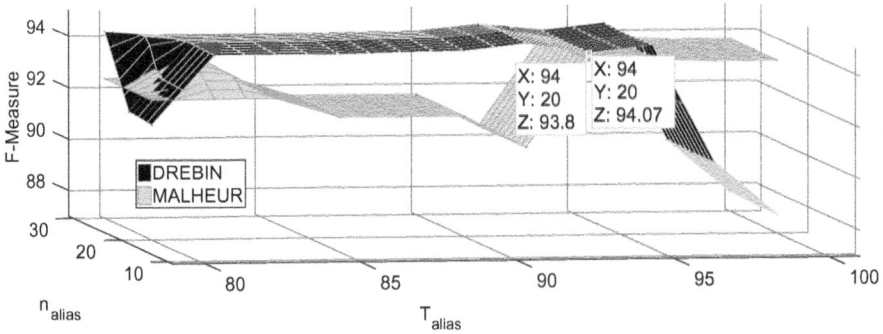

Fig. 4. Parameter selection for alias detection.

4.4 Alias Detection

The alias detection module, detailed in Sect. 3.3, requires two parameters: n_{alias} and T_{alias}. To select their default values, we first produce alias lists for different combinations of those parameters using as input the 5 datasets with unlabeled samples. Then, we evaluate the accuracy of the labeling phase using those alias lists. Figure 4 shows the F_1 measure for different combinations of parameter values on the Drebin and Malheur datasets. The parameter values that maximize the mean value in both surfaces are $n_{alias} = 20$ and $T_{alias} = 0.94$. The rest of experiments use, unless otherwise noted, the automatically generated alias list with these default values, which contains 4,332 alias pairs. In comparison, the alias list manually generated by one author contains 133 alias pairs.

Table 5. Accuracy evaluation. *Full Label* corresponds to using a plurality vote on all labels without normalization. *Manual* corresponds to running AVCLASS with manually generated generic token and alias lists. AVCLASS corresponds to running AVCLASS with automatically generated generic token and alias lists. The MalGenome* row corresponds to grouping the 6 DroidKungFu variants in MalGenome into a single family.

Dataset	AVCLASS			Manual			Full Label		
	Prec	Rec	F1	Prec	Rec	F1	Prec	Rec	F1
Drebin	95.2	92.5	93.9	95.4	88.4	91.8	92.9	40.7	56.6
Malicia	95.3	46.3	62.3	94.9	68.0	79.2	98.6	2.4	4.6
Malsign	96.3	67.0	79.0	90.4	90.7	90.5	88.7	15.9	26.9
MalGenome	67.5	98.8	80.2	68.3	93.3	78.8	99.5	79.4	88.3
MalGenome*	87.2	98.8	92.6	87.9	93.3	90.5	99.7	63.3	77.5
Malheur	89.3	93.8	91.5	90.4	98.3	94.2	96.3	74.8	84.2

4.5 Evaluation on Labeled Datasets

In this section we evaluate the accuracy of AVCLASS on the labeled datasets. We first compare the reference clustering provided by the dataset labels with the clustering output by AVCLASS (i.e., samples assigned the same label by AVCLASS are in the same cluster) using the precision, recall, and F1 measure metrics introduced in Sect. 4.2. Then, we examine the quality of the output labels.

Clustering Accuracy. Table 5 summarizes the clustering accuracy results for 3 scenarios. *Full Label* corresponds to not using AVCLASS but simply doing a plurality vote on the full AV labels without normalization. *Manual* corresponds to running AVCLASS with manually generated generic token and alias lists. AVCLASS corresponds to running AVCLASS with automatically generated generic token and alias lists.

The results show that using AVCLASS increases the F1 measure compared to using the full label in 4 datasets (Drebin, Malicia, Malsign, and Malheur). The median F1 measure improvement is 37 F1 measure percentual points and can reach 13 times higher (Malicia). The exception is the MalGenome dataset, whose F1 measure decreases. Manual examination shows that the main problem is that the MalGenome dataset differentiates 6 variants of the DroidKungFu family (DroidKungFu1, DroidKungFu2, DroidKungFu3, DroidKungFu4, DroidKungFuSapp, DroidKungFuUpdate). However, AV labels do not capture version granularity and label all versions as the same family. If we group all 6 DroidKungFu variants into a single family (MalGenome* row in Table 5), the F1 measure using AVCLASS increases 12 points (from 80.2 to 92.6) and the full label results decreases 11 points (from 88.3 to 77.5). This shows that AV labels are not granular enough to identify specific family versions.

Table 6. Labels for the top 5 clusters identified by AVCLASS in the Miller et al. dataset and the most common full labels on the same dataset.

(a) AVCLASS.

#	Label	Samples
1	vobfus	58,385
2	domaiq	38,648
3	installrex	37,698
4	firseria	28,898
5	multiplug	26,927

(b) Full labels.

#	Label	Samples
1	Trojan.Win32.Generic!BT	42,944
2	Win32.Worm.Allaple.Gen	12,090
3	Gen:Variant.Adware.Graftor.30458	10,844
4	Gen:Adware.MPlug.1	10,332
5	Trojan.Generic.6761191	8,986

Table 7. Clustering results on unlabeled datasets.

Dataset	Samples	Clusters	Singletons	Unlab.	Largest	Runtime
University	7,252,810	1,465,901	1,456,375	19.2 %	701,775	235 min. 33 s
Miller et al.	1,079,783	187,733	183,804	16.6 %	56,044	35 min. 42 s
Andrubis	422,826	7,015	6,294	1.3 %	102,176	12 min. 47 s
VirusShare_20140324	24,317	2,068	1,844	6.9 %	7,350	48 s
VirusShare_20130506	11,080	568	446	3.3 %	3,203	17 s

Comparing the *Manual* section of Table 5 with the AVCLASS section shows that the automatically generated lists of generic tokens and aliases work better in 2 datasets (MalGenome and Drebin) and worse in 3 (Malicia, Malsign, Malheur). For Malheur the difference is small (2.7 F1 points), but for Malicia and Malsign it reaches 11–17 F1 points. Overall, the automatically generated lists have comparable accuracy to the manual ones, although an analyst can improve results in some datasets. While the manual list raises the worst F1 measure from 62.3 to 79.2, the automatic generation is faster, more convenient, and does not depend on the analyst's skill. To combine scalability with accuracy, an analyst could first produce automatically the lists and then refine them manually based on his expertise.

The final F1 measure for AVCLASS with automatically generated lists of generic tokens and aliases ranges from 93.9 for Drebin down to 62.3 for Malicia. The higher accuracy for Drebin is due to that dataset having been manually clustered using AV labels. The lower accuracy for Malicia is largely due to *smartfortress* likely being an (undetected) alias for the *winwebsec* family. Manually adding this alias improves the F1 measure by 18 points. The reason for the large impact of this alias is that the Malicia dataset is strongly biased towards this family (59 % of samples are in family *winwebsec*).

Label Quality. The clustering evaluation above focuses on whether samples are grouped by AVCLASS similarly to the ground truth, but it does not evaluate the quality of the family names AVCLASS outputs. Quantifying the quality of

Table 8. Top 10 clusters on unlabeled datasets.

(a) University.

#	Label	Samples
1	vobfus	701,775
2	multiplug	669,596
3	softpulse	473,872
4	loadmoney	211,056
5	virut	206,526
6	toggle	108,356
7	flooder	96,571
8	zango	89,929
9	upatre	82,413
10	ibryte	80,923

(b) Miller.

#	Label	Samples
1	vobfus	58,385
2	domaiq	38,648
3	installrex	37,698
4	firseria	28,898
5	multiplug	26,927
6	sality	23,278
7	zango	21,910
8	solimba	21,305
9	ibryte	20,058
10	expiro	16,685

(c) Andrubis.

#	Label	Samples
1	opfake	88,723
2	fakeinst	84,485
3	smsagent	24,121
4	plankton	22,329
5	kuguo	19,497
6	smsreg	15,965
7	waps	12,055
8	utchi	7,949
9	droidkungfu	7,675
10	ginmaster	6,365

Table 9. University dataset clustering with 4, 10, 48, and all AVs.

AVs	Clusters	Singletons	Unlabeled	Largest
All	1,465,901	1,456,375	1,394,168 (19.2%)	vobfus (701,775)
48	1,543,510	1,534,483	1,472,406 (20.3%)	vobfus (701,719)
10	3,732,626	3,730,304	3,728,945 (51.4%)	multiplug (637,787)
4	5,655,991	5,655,243	5,654,819 (77.9%)	vobfus (539,306)

the family names output by AVCLASS is challenging because the ground truth may contain manually selected labels that do not exactly match the AV family names. Table 6 shows on the left the labels assigned to the top 5 clusters in the Miller dataset by AVCLASS and on the right, the labels for the top 5 clusters when the full AV labels are used. The table shows that the cluster labels automatically produced by AVCLASS are more fine-grained thanks to the generic token detection, and also assigned to a larger number of samples thanks to the normalization and alias detection techniques. More examples of the final labels output by AVCLASS are shown in Table 8, which is discussed in the next section.

4.6 Evaluation on Unlabeled Datasets

In this section we apply AVCLASS to label samples in datasets without ground truth. Table 7 summarizes the clustering results of using AVCLASS with automatically generated lists on the 5 unlabeled datasets. For each dataset it shows: the number of samples being clustered, the number of clusters created, the number of singleton clusters with only one sample, the percentage of all samples that did not get any label, the size of the largest cluster, and the labeling runtime. The results show that 78%–99% of the clusters are singletons. However, these only represent 1.4 %–20 % of the samples. Thus, the vast majority of samples are grouped with other samples. Singleton clusters can be samples for which no label can be extracted as well as samples assigned a label not seen in other samples. Overall, the percentage of unlabeled samples varies from 1.3 % (Andrubis) up to 19.2 % (University). All AV labels for these samples are generic and AVCLASS could not identify a family name in them.

Table 8 presents the top 10 clusters in the 3 largest unlabeled datasets (University, Miller, Andrubis). The most common family in both Windows datasets is *vobfus*. Top families in these two datasets are well known except perhaps *flooder*, which the author building the manual lists thought it was generic, but the automatic generic token detection does not identify as such. This is an example of tokens that may sound generic to an analyst, but may be consistently used by AV vendors for the same family. In the University dataset 6 of the top 10 families are malware (vobfus, multiplug, virut, toggle, flooder, upatre) and 4 are PUP (softpulse, loadmoney, zango, ibryte). In the Miller dataset 3 are malware (vobfus, zbot, sality) and 7 PUP (firseria, installerex, domaiq, installcore, loadmoney, hotbar, ibryte). This matches observations in Malsign [15] that large "malware" datasets actually do contain significant amounts of PUP. The Andrubis top 10 contains 4 families that also sound generic (opfake, fakeinst, smsagent, smsreg). However, these families are included as such in the ground truth of the labeled Android datasets (MalGenome, Drebin). While these labels may be used specifically for a family, we believe AV vendors should try choosing more specific family names to avoid one vendor using a label for a family and another using it generically for a class of malware.

Number of AV Vendors Used. To evaluate the effect of using an increasing number of AV vendors into the labeling process, we repeat the clustering of the University dataset using the same fixed sets of AV vendors used in some prior work: VAMO (4 vendors), Drebin (10), and AV-meter (48). The results in Table 9 show that increasing the number of AV vendors reduces the fraction of samples for which a label cannot be obtained (Unlabeled column). This motivates the design choice of AVCLASS to include AV labels from any available vendor.

5 Discussion

This section discusses AVCLASS limitations, usage, and areas for future work.

As Good as the AV Labels Are. AVCLASS extracts family information AV vendors place in their labels, despite noise in those labels. But, it cannot identify families not in the labels. More specifically, it cannot label samples if at least 2 AV engines do not agree on a non-generic family name. Results on our largest unlabeled dataset show that AVCLASS cannot label 19 % of the samples, typically because those labels only contain generic tokens. Thus, AVCLASS is not a panacea for malware labeling. If AV vendors do not have a name for the sample, it cannot be named.

Clustering Accuracy. AVCLASS is a malware labeling tool. While it can be used for malware clustering, its evaluated precision is 87.2%–95.3%. This is below state-of-the-art malware clustering tools using static and dynamic features, which can reach 98%–99% precision. As shown in Appendix Table 10, when comparing F1 measure, tools like Malheur [29] (F1= 95%), BitShred [13] (F1=93.2%), and FIRMA [26] (F1=98.8%) outperform AVCLASS. Thus, AVCLASS should only be used for clustering when a state-of-the-art clustering system is not available and implementing one is not worth the effort (despite improved accuracy).

Building Reference Datasets. When using AVCLASS to build reference datasets, there will be a fraction of samples (up to 19% in our evaluation) for which AVCLASS cannot extract a label and others for which the confidence (i.e., number of AV engines using the chosen family name) is low. While those can be removed from the reference dataset, this introduces selection bias by removing the harder to label samples [16].

AV Label Granularity. Our evaluation shows that AV labels are not granular enough to differentiate family versions, e.g., DroidKungFu1 from DroidKungFu2. Thus, when releasing labeled datasets, researchers should clearly differentiate the family name from the family version (if available), enabling users to decide which granularity to use.

Validation with Real Ground Truth. To evaluate AVCLASS, we have assumed that the labels of publicly available datasets are perfectly accurate and have compared accuracy to those. However, those labels may contain inaccuracies, which would affect our results either positively or negatively. This can only be resolved by using real ground truth datasets. How to obtain such real ground truth is an important area for future work.

Generic Token Detection. Our generic token detection requires labeled samples. This creates a bit of a chicken-and-egg problem, which we resolve by using publicly available labeled datasets. We also release a file with the generic tokens we identified so that users can skip this step. We leave the development of techniques to identify generic tokens that do not require ground truth for future work.

6 Conclusion

In this work we have described AVCLASS, an automatic labeling tool that given the AV labels for a potentially massive number of malware samples, outputs the most likely family names for each sample. AVCLASS implements novel techniques to address 3 key challenges: normalization, removal of generic tokens, and alias detection.

We have evaluated AVCLASS over 10 datasets, comprising 8.9 M samples, larger than any previous dataset used for malware clustering or classification.

The results show that the fully automated approach used by AVCLASS can achieve clustering accuracy between 93.9 and 62.3 depending on the dataset. We have compared the generic token and aliases lists automatically produced by AVCLASS with the manual ones produced by an analysts observing that the achieve comparable accuracy in most datasets. We have shown that an increasing number of AV vendors reduces the percentage of samples for which a (non-generic) family name cannot be extracted, thus validating the design choice of using all AV engines. We have also observed that AV labels are not fine-grained enough to distinguish different versions of the same family.

Finally, we have released AVCLASS's source code to the community, along with precompiled lists of alias and generic tokens.

Acknowledgments. We specially thank Manos Antonakakis and Martina Lindorfer for providing us with the University and Andrubis datasets, respectively. We also thank the authors of the Drebin, MalGenome, Malheur, Malicia, and the Malicious Content Detection Platform datasets for making them publicly available. We are grateful to Srdjan Matic for his assistance with the plots, Davide Balzarotti and Chaz Lever for useful discussions, VirusTotal for their support, and Pavel Laskov for his help to improve this manuscript.

This research was partially supported by the Regional Government of Madrid through the N-GREENS Software-CM project S2013/ICE-2731 and by the Spanish Government through the Dedetis Grant TIN2015-7013-R. All opinions, findings and conclusions, or recommendations expressed herein are those of the authors and do not necessarily reflect the views of the sponsors.

A Additional Results

Table 10. Accuracy numbers reported by prior clustering works.

Work	Metrics
Bailey et al. [2]	Consistency=100 %
Rieck et al. [28]	Labels prediction=70 %
McBoost [23]	Accuracy=87.3 %, AUC=0.977.
Bayer et al. [3]	Quality(Prec*Rec)=95.9
Malheur [29]	F1= 95 %
BitShred [13]	Prec=94.2 %, Rec=92.2 %
VAMO [25]	F1=85.1 %
Malsign [15]	Prec=98.6 %, Rec=33.2 %, F1=49.7 %
AVCLASS	Prec=95.2 %, Rec=92.5 %, F1=93.9 %

Table 11. AV engines found in our datasets and their lifetime in days.

Engine	First Scan	Last Scan	Days	Engine	First Scan	Last Scan	Days
Ikarus	22/05/2006	29/03/2016	3599	Malwarebytes	30/11/2012	29/03/2016	1215
TheHacker	22/05/2006	29/03/2016	3599	K7GW	15/04/2013	29/03/2016	1079
F-Prot	22/05/2006	29/03/2016	3599	Prevx	13/05/2009	23/04/2012	1076
Fortinet	22/05/2006	29/03/2016	3599	NOD32v2	22/05/2006	19/01/2009	973
BitDefender	22/05/2006	29/03/2016	3599	Ewido	22/05/2006	20/01/2009	973
CAT-QuickHeal	22/05/2006	29/03/2016	3599	eTrust-InoculateIT	22/05/2006	15/01/2009	968
AVG	22/05/2006	29/03/2016	3599	UNA	22/05/2006	15/01/2009	968
Microsoft	22/05/2006	29/03/2016	3599	Baidu	02/09/2013	29/03/2016	939
ClamAV	22/05/2006	29/03/2016	3599	Baidu-International	03/09/2013	29/03/2016	938
Avast	22/05/2006	29/03/2016	3599	F-Prot4	30/06/2006	15/01/2009	929
McAfee	22/05/2006	29/03/2016	3599	Bkav	13/09/2013	29/03/2016	928
TrendMicro	22/05/2006	29/03/2016	3599	Antivir7	22/06/2006	05/01/2009	928
VBA32	22/05/2006	29/03/2016	3599	CMC	13/09/2013	29/03/2016	928
Symantec	22/05/2006	29/03/2016	3599	T3	14/07/2006	15/01/2009	915
Kaspersky	22/05/2006	29/03/2016	3599	Prevx1	15/11/2006	12/05/2009	909
Panda	22/05/2006	29/03/2016	3599	Ad-Aware	26/11/2013	29/03/2016	854
DrWeb	22/05/2006	29/03/2016	3599	SAVMail	03/10/2006	18/01/2009	838
Sophos	22/05/2006	29/03/2016	3599	Qihoo-360	21/01/2014	29/03/2016	798
F-Secure	07/02/2007	29/03/2016	3338	AegisLab	29/01/2014	29/03/2016	790
AhnLab-V3	14/03/2007	29/03/2016	3303	McAfee+Artemis	21/11/2008	18/01/2011	787
Norman	22/05/2006	30/05/2015	3294	PandaBeta	12/02/2007	10/02/2009	729
Rising	26/07/2007	29/03/2016	3169	Zillya	29/04/2014	29/03/2016	700
AntiVir	22/05/2006	03/09/2014	3025	FileAdvisor	19/02/2007	18/01/2009	699
GData	12/05/2008	29/03/2016	2878	Tencent	13/05/2014	29/03/2016	686
ViRobot	24/07/2008	29/03/2016	2805	Zoner	22/05/2014	29/03/2016	677
K7AntiVirus	01/08/2008	29/03/2016	2797	Cyren	22/05/2014	29/03/2016	677
Comodo	05/12/2008	29/03/2016	2671	Avira	22/05/2014	29/03/2016	677
nProtect	14/01/2009	29/03/2016	2631	Webwasher-Gateway	20/03/2007	19/01/2009	671
McAfee-GW-Edition	19/03/2009	29/03/2016	2567	AVware	28/07/2014	29/03/2016	610
Antiy-AVL	24/03/2009	29/03/2016	2562	a-squared	24/12/2008	28/07/2010	581
eSafe	16/11/2006	16/09/2013	2496	Avast5	03/03/2010	28/09/2011	573
Jiangmin	16/06/2009	29/03/2016	2478	McAfeeBeta	04/07/2007	18/01/2009	564
VirusBuster	13/06/2006	18/09/2012	2288	FortinetBeta	01/08/2007	18/01/2009	535
eTrust-Vet	22/05/2006	22/05/2012	2191	PandaBeta2	07/09/2007	16/01/2009	496
TrendMicro-HouseCall	04/05/2010	29/03/2016	2156	ALYac	26/11/2014	29/03/2016	489
SUPERAntiSpyware	12/07/2010	29/03/2016	2087	AhnLab	14/03/2007	03/07/2008	477
Emsisoft	20/07/2010	29/03/2016	2079	Alibaba	12/01/2015	29/03/2016	442
VIPRE	17/11/2010	29/03/2016	1959	NOD32Beta	24/09/2008	16/08/2009	325
PCTools	21/07/2008	23/10/2013	1919	Arcabit	02/06/2015	29/03/2016	301
Authentium	22/05/2006	29/04/2011	1803	SecureWeb-Gateway	26/09/2008	14/04/2009	200
ByteHero	20/08/2011	29/03/2016	1683	VIRobot	23/07/2008	17/01/2009	177
Sunbelt	30/11/2006	29/04/2011	1611	Command	17/11/2010	29/04/2011	163
TotalDefense	15/05/2012	29/03/2016	1414	PandaB3	04/09/2008	19/01/2009	136
NOD32	24/09/2008	19/07/2012	1394	eScan	25/09/2012	15/10/2012	19
ESET-NOD32	11/07/2012	29/03/2016	1357	DrWebSE	18/01/2015	03/02/2015	15
Commtouch	18/01/2011	28/08/2014	1317	ESET NOD32	26/06/2012	26/06/2012	0
Agnitum	18/09/2012	29/03/2016	1288	Yandex	29/03/2016	29/03/2016	0
Kingsoft	18/09/2012	29/03/2016	1288	TotalDefense2	16/04/2015	16/04/2015	0
MicroWorld-eScan	02/10/2012	29/03/2016	1274	SymCloud	11/08/2015	11/08/2015	0
NANO-Antivirus	28/11/2012	29/03/2016	1217				

References

1. Arp, D., Spreitzenbarth, M., Huebner, M., Gascon, H., Rieck, K.: Drebin: efficient and explainable detection of android malware in your pocket. In: Network and Distributed System Security (2014)
2. Bailey, M., Oberheide, J., Andersen, J., Mao, Z.M., Jahanian, F., Nazario, J.: Automated classification and analysis of internet malware. In: International Symposium on Recent Advances in Intrusion Detection (2007)

3. Bayer, U., Comparetti, P.M., Hlauschek, C., Kruegel, C., Kirda, E.: Scalable, behavior-based malware clustering. In: Network and Distributed System Security (2009)
4. Beck, D., Connolly, J.: The common malware enumeration initiative. In: Virus Bulletin Conference (2006)
5. Bureau, P.-M., Harley, D.: A dose by any other name. In: Virus Bulletin Conference (2008)
6. Canto, J., Dacier, M., Kirda, E., Leita, C.: Large scale malware collection: lessons learned. In: IEEE SRDS Workshop on Sharing Field Data and Experiment Measurements on Resilience of Distributed Computing Systems (2008)
7. CARO Virus Naming Convention. http://www.caro.org/articles/naming.html
8. Dahl, G.E., Stokes, J.W., Deng, L., Yu, D.: Large-scale malware classification using random projections and neural networks. In: IEEE International Conference on Acoustics, Speech and Signal Processing (2013)
9. Gashi, I., Sobesto, B., Mason, S., Stankovic, V., Cukier, M.: A study of the relationship between antivirus regressions and label changes. In: International Symposium on Software Reliability Engineering (2013)
10. Harley, D.: The game of the name: malware naming, shape shifters and sympathetic magic. In: International Conference on Cybercrime Forensics Education & Training (2009)
11. Huang, W., Stokes, J.W.: MtNet: a multi-task neural network for dynamic malware classification. In: Detection of Intrusions and Malware, and Vulnerability Assessment (2016)
12. Hurier, M., Allix, K., Bissyandé, T., Klein, J., Traon, Y.L.: On the lack of consensus in anti-virus decisions: metrics and insights on building ground truths of android malware. In: Detection of Intrusions and Malware, and Vulnerability Assessment (2016)
13. Jang, J., Brumley, D., Venkataraman, S.: BitShred: feature hashing malware for scalable triage and semantic analysis. In: ACM Conference on Computer and Communications Security (2011)
14. Kantchelian, A., Tschantz, M.C., Afroz, S., Miller, B., Shankar, V., Bachwani, R., Joseph, A.D., Tygar, J.: Better malware ground truth: techniques for weighting anti-virus vendor labels. In: ACM Workshop on Artificial Intelligence and Security (2015)
15. Kotzias, P., Matic, S., Rivera, R., Caballero, J.: Certified PUP: abuse in authenticode code signing. In: ACM Conference on Computer and Communication Security (2015)
16. Li, P., Liu, L., Gao, D., Reiter, M.K.: On challenges in evaluating malware clustering. In: Jha, S., Sommer, R., Kreibich, C. (eds.) RAID 2010. LNCS, vol. 6307, pp. 238–255. Springer, Heidelberg (2010)
17. Lindorfer, M., Neugschwandtner, M., Weichselbaum, L., Fratantonio, Y., van der Veen, V., Platzer, C.: ANDRUBIS-1,000,000 apps later: a view on current android malware behaviors. In: International Workshop on Building Analysis Datasets and Gathering Experience Returns for Security (2014)
18. Maggi, F., Bellini, A., Salvaneschi, G., Zanero, S.: Finding non-trivial malware naming inconsistencies. In: International Conference on Information Systems Security (2011)

19. Miller, B., Kantchelian, A., Tschantz, M.C., Afroz, S., Bachwani, R., Faizullabhoy, R., Huang, L., Shankar, V., Wu, T., Yiu, G., Joseph, A.D., Tygar, J.D.: Reviewer integration and performance measurement for malware detection. In: Caballero, J., Zurutuza, U., Rodríguez, R.J. (eds.) DIMVA 2016. LNCS, vol. 9721, pp. 122–141. Springer, Heidelberg (2016). doi:10.1007/978-3-319-40667-1_7
20. Mohaisen, A., Alrawi, O.: AV-Meter: an evaluation of antivirus scans and labels. In: Detection of Intrusions and Malware, and Vulnerability Assessment (2014)
21. Nappa, A., Rafique, M.Z., Caballero, J.: The MALICIA dataset: identification and analysis of drive-by download operations. Int. J. Inf. Secur. **14**(1), 15–33 (2015)
22. Oberheide, J., Cooke, E., Jahanian, F.: CloudAV: N-version antivirus in the network cloud. In: USENIX Security Symposium (2008)
23. Perdisci, R., Lanzi, A., Lee, W.: McBoost: boosting scalability in malware collection and analysis using statistical classification of executables. In: Annual Computer Security Applications Conference (2008)
24. Perdisci, R., Lee, W., Feamster, N.: Behavioral clustering of HTTP-based malware and signature generation using malicious network traces. In: USENIX Symposium on Networked Systems Design and Implementation (2010)
25. Perdisci, R., ManChon, U.: VAMO: towards a fully automated malware clustering validity analysis. In: Annual Computer Security Applications Conference (2012)
26. Rafique, M.Z., Caballero, J.: FIRMA: malware clustering and network signature generation with mixed network behaviors. In: Stolfo, S.J., Stavrou, A., Wright, C.V. (eds.) RAID 2013. LNCS, vol. 8145, pp. 144–163. Springer, Heidelberg (2013)
27. Rajab, M.A., Ballard, L., Lutz, N., Mavrommatis, P., Provos, N., CAMP: content-agnostic malware protection. In: Network and Distributed System Security (2013)
28. Rieck, K., Holz, T., Willems, C., Düssel, P., Laskov, P.: Learning and classification of malware behavior. In: Detection of Intrusions and Malware, and Vulnerability Assessment (2008)
29. Rieck, K., Trinius, P., Willems, C., Holz, T.: Automatic analysis of malware behavior using machine learning. J. Comput. Secur. **19**(4), 639–668 (2011)
30. Virusshare. http://virusshare.com/
31. Virustotal. https://virustotal.com/
32. Yang, C., Xu, Z., Gu, G., Yegneswaran, V., Porras, P.: DroidMiner: automated mining and characterization of fine-grained malicious behaviors in android applications. In: European Symposium on Research in Computer Security (2014)
33. Zhou, Y., Jiang, X.: Dissecting android malware: characterization and evolution. In: IEEE Symposium on Security and Privacy (2012)

Semantics-Preserving Dissection of JavaScript Exploits via Dynamic JS-Binary Analysis

Xunchao Hu[1], Aravind Prakash[2], Jinghan Wang[1], Rundong Zhou[1], Yao Cheng[1], and Heng Yin[1(✉)]

[1] Department of EECS, Syracuse University, Syracuse, USA
{xhu31,jwang153,rzhou02,ycheng,heyin}@syr.edu
[2] Computer Science Department, Binghamton University, Binghamton, USA
aravind@cs.binghamton.edu

Abstract. JavaScript exploits impose a severe threat to computer security. Once a zero-day exploit is captured, it is critical to quickly pinpoint the JavaScript statements that uniquely characterize the exploit and the payload location in the exploit. However, the current diagnosis techniques are inadequate because they approach the problem either from a JavaScript perspective and fail to account for "implicit" data flow invisible at JavaScript level, or from a binary execution perspective and fail to present the JavaScript level view of exploit. In this paper, we propose JSCALPEL, a framework to automatically bridge the semantic gap between the JavaScript level and binary level for dynamic JS-binary analysis. With this new technique, JSCALPEL can automatically pinpoint exploitation or payload injection component of JavaScript exploits and generate minimized exploit code and a Proof-of-Vulnerability (PoV). Using JSCALPEL, we analyze 15 JavaScript exploits, 9 memory corruption exploits from Metasploit, 4 exploits from 3 different exploit kits and 2 wild exploits and successfully recover the payload and a minimized exploit for each of the exploits.

Keywords: Exploit analysis · Malicious JavaScript

1 Introduction

Malicious JavaScript has become an important attack vector for software exploitation attacks. Attacks in browsers, as well as JavaScript embedded within malicious PDFs and Flash documents, are common examples of how attackers launch attacks using JavaScript. Interactive nature of JavaScript allows malicious JavaScript to take advantage of binary vulnerabilities (e.g., use-after-free, heap/buffer overflow) that are otherwise difficult to exploit. In 2014, 639 browser vulnerabilities were discovered and the number was increased by 8 % over 2013 reported by Symantec [5]. This provides the attacker a broad attack space.

Previously unknown, or "zero-day", exploits are of particular interest to the security community. Once a malicious JavaScript attack is captured, it must be analyzed and its inner-workings understood quickly so that proper defenses can be deployed to protect against it or similar attacks in the future. Unfortunately, this analysis process is tedious, painstaking, and time-consuming. From the analysis perspective, an analyst seeks to answer two key questions: (1) Which JavaScript statements uniquely characterize the exploit? and (2) Where is the payload located within the exploit? The answer to the first question results in the generation of an exploit signature, which can then be deployed via an intrusion detection system (IDS) to discover and prevent the exploit. The answer to the second question allows an analyst to replace the malicious payload with an amicable payload and use the modified exploit as a proof-of-vulnerability (PoV) to perform penetration testing.

Program slicing [34] is a key technique in exploit analysis. This technique begins with a source location of interest, known as slicing source, such as a statement or instruction that causes a crash, and identifies any statements or instructions that this source location depends on. Prior exploit analysis solutions have attempted to analyze exploits at either the JavaScript level [11,12,18,20,26,27] or the underlying binary level [23,24,31,36,38].

While binary level solutions execute an exploit and analyze the underlying binary execution for anomalies, they are unaware of any JavaScript level semantics and fail to present the JavaScript level view of the exploit. JavaScript level analysis fails to account for implicit data flows between statements because any DOM/BOM APIs invoked at the binary level are invisible at the JavaScript level. Unfortunately, implicit flows are quite common in attacks and are often comprised of seemingly random and irregular operations in the JavaScript that achieve a precise precondition or a specific trigger which exploits a vulnerability in the binary. The semantic gap between JavaScript level and binary level during the analysis makes it challenging to automatically answer the 2 key questions.

In this paper, we present JSCALPEL with password: "artifacts", a system that creatively combines JavaScript and binary level analyses to analyze exploits. It stems from the observation that seemingly complex and irregular JavaScript statements in an exploit often exhibit strong data dependencies in the binary. JSCALPEL utilizes the JavaScript context information from the JavaScript level to perform *context-aware* binary analysis. Further, it leverages binary analysis to account for implicit JavaScript level dependencies arising due to side effects at the binary level. In essence, it performs JavaScript and binary, or *JS-Binary* analysis. Given a functional JavaScript exploit, JSCALPEL performs JS-Binary analysis to: (1) generate a minimized exploit script, which in turn helps to generate a signature for the exploit, and (2) precisely locate the payload within the exploit. It replaces the malicious payload with a friendly payload and generates a PoV for the exploit.

We evaluated JSCALPEL on a corpus of 15 exploits, 9 from Metasploit[1], 4 exploits from 3 different exploit kits and 2 wild exploits. On average, we were able to reduce the number of unique JavaScript statements by 49.8 %, and precisely identify the payload, in a semantics-preserving manner, meaning that

---

[1] Metasploit Framework – http://www.metasploit.com/, a popular penetration testing framework.

the minimized exploits are still functional. In addition, we were able to replace the payload with amicable payload to perform penetration testing. JSCALPEL showed an average reduction of 75.5 % in trace size and 16x improvement in time taken to trace. Finally, we presented the wild exploit CVE-2011-1255 as a case study. We demonstrate how the exploit is minimized and payload is located.

Contributions. We make the following contributions:

- We make a key observation that semantics-preserving JavaScript exploit analysis must bridge the gap between JavaScript and binary level.
- We propose a technique to bridge the semantic gap and tackle several challenges (e.g. dependency explosion and script engine code filtering) and incorporate our techniques into the JSCALPEL analysis framework.
- Using JSCALPEL, we analyze 15 JavaScript exploits, 9 memory corruption exploits from Metasploit, 4 exploits from 3 different exploit kits and two exploits from the wild and successfully recover the payload and a minimized exploit for each of the exploits.

2 Background and Overview

2.1 Components of JavaScript Attack

Modern JavaScript attacks can be divided into four general components. Figures 1(a) and (b) show these four components within the Aurora exploit.

Obfuscation: To avoid detection, obfuscation techniques are widely deployed in JavaScript attacks. For example, in Fig. 1(a) JavaScript obfuscation is used to perform a document.write(``Get payload'') operation. Simple static analysis-based scanners cannot identify that "i[x][y]" is actually a document.write() operation.

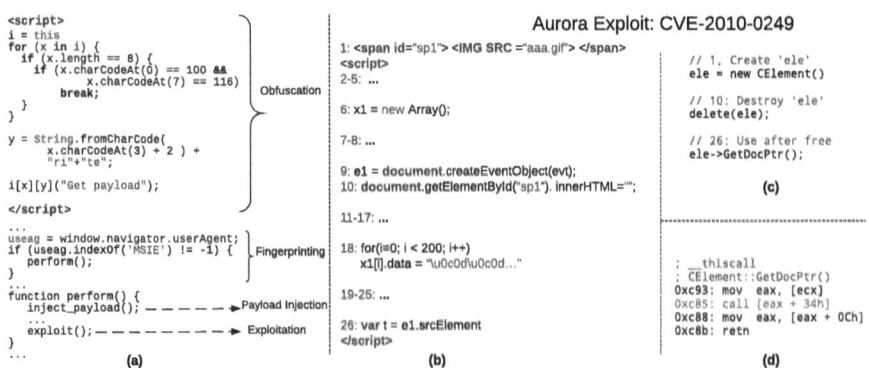

Fig. 1. (a) describes the components of a modern exploit, (b) presents the relevant JavaScript code involved in Aurora Exploit and (c) presents the underlying code execution that results in use-after-free, (d) presents the assembly code for function GetDocPtr.

Fingerprinting: An exploit uses fingerprinting to glean information about victim's environment. With such information, exploits specific to vulnerable components are launched to compromise the victim process. For example, in Fig. 1(a), the Aurora exploit is only performed if the type of the browser is identified as being Microsoft Internet Explorer ("MSIE").

Payload Injection: The exploit injects a malicious payload into the victim process. Payloads can be broadly categorized as executable or non-executable payloads. presents the payloads and the flow of execution in modern exploits. The goal of exploits is to execute a malicious payload, but since the wide deployment of data execution prevention (DEP), the page containing the executable payload cannot be directly executed. First, return-oriented programming (ROP) is used to make a page executable by invoking `VirtualProtect()` on Windows or `mprotect()` on Linux. Then, control is transferred to the malicious executable code.

Exploitation: In this step, using one or more carefully crafted JavaScript statements, the vulnerability in the victim process is exploited. The statements may seem random and may lack data-dependencies, but they often involve a combination of explicit and implicit data dependency. Consider the exploit statements for the Aurora exploit presented in Fig. 1(b, c and d). (b) presents the HTML (statement 1) and JavaScript (2–26) statements that exploit a use-after-free vulnerability in `mshtml.dll` of Internet Explorer browser. Figures 1(c and d) present the underlying C++ and assembly code that is executed as a part of the exploit. Statement 18 corrupts the memory that was freed in statement 10. The corrupted memory is utilized in a `call` instruction arising from statement 26. All the statements in Fig. 1(c) are pertinent to the exploit.

2.2 Problem Statement

We aim to develop JSCALPEL– a framework to combine JavaScript and binary analyses to aid in analysis of JavaScript-launched memory corruption exploits. It is motivated by two key observations.

First, analysis performed at only the JavaScript level is insufficient. In Fig. 1(b), JavaScript level analysis of Aurora captures the explicit data dependencies between statements 9 and 26 and statements 6 and 18. However, because no explicit dependency exists between statements 18 and 26, the two groups of statements will be incorrectly deemed to be independent of each other. Second, while complete, analysis performed at only the binary level is also insufficient. In Fig. 1(d), binary level analysis can expose the manipulation of pointers, however it can not expose exploit-related JavaScript statements in Fig. 1(c) due to the lack of JavaScript context. A binary-level analysis will show the memory written by the binary instructions of statement 18 is utilized through reads performed by binary instructions of statement 26, revealing a straight-forward data dependency between statements 18 and 26.

Input: JSCALPEL accepts a raw functional exploit and a vulnerable program as input. The vulnerable program can be any program like (PDF reader, web browser, etc.) as long as it can be exploited through JavaScript. The exploit consists of HTML and malicious JavaScript components. The exploit can be obfuscated or encrypted. JSCALPEL makes no assumptions about the nature of payloads. That is, the payload could be ROP-only, executable-only or combined.

Output: JSCALPEL performs JS-Binary tracing and slicing and generates 3 specific outputs. (1) A simplified exploit HTML that contains the key JavaScript statements that are required to accomplish the exploit, and (2) the precise JavaScript statements that inject the payload into the vulnerable process' memory along with the exact payload string – both non-executable and executable – within the JavaScript. Finally, (3) an HTML page, where the malicious payload is replaced by a benign payload is generated as a Proof-of-Vulnerability (PoV).

Delta debugging [37] is firstly proposed to generate the minimized C programs that crash the compiler and might be a feasible approach to minimize the exploit JavaScript to cause a crash. However, the effectiveness of this approach is unknown, because of the complex and sophisticated nature of JavaScript. Attackers can insert arbitrary junk code to make delta debugging ineffective. In contrast, JSCALPEL can precisely pinpoint the JavaScript statements that cause a crash and locate the malicious payload and our experiment has proven its effectiveness.

2.3 JSCALPEL– Overview

Figure 2 presents the architecture of JSCALPEL, which leverages Virtual Machine Monitor (VMM) based analysis. It consists of multiple components. A multi-level tracer is used to gather JavaScript and binary traces. A CFI module is used to determine the binary level "slicing sources", which are the violations that cause the exploit along with the various payload components. The multi-level slicer augments JavaScript level slicing with information from binary level slicing to obtain the relevant exploit and payload statements. Finally, JSCALPEL packages the relevant exploit statements within an HTML page to generate the minimized script. It also replaces the malicious payload with a benign payload to generate a PoV.

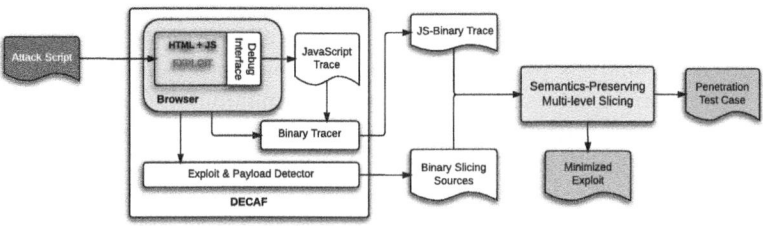

Fig. 2. Architecture of JSCALPEL

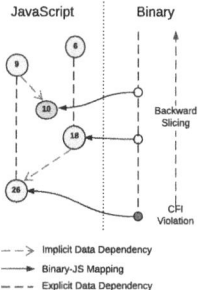

Fig. 3. Performance index of 2-relays system

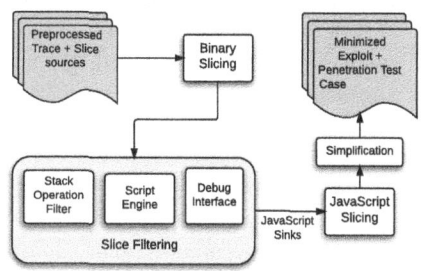

Fig. 4. Semantics-preserving multi-level slicing.

3 Multi-level Tracing and Slicing-Source Identification

We implement JSCALPEL on top of DECAF [19], a whole-system dynamic analysis framework. The tracing consists of two parts, JavaScript and binary tracers. JavaScript tracing is performed using a helper module that is injected into the browser address space. It interacts with the JavaScript debug interface within the browser to gather the JavaScript-level trace. The binary tracer and the exploit detection module are implemented as 2 plugins of DECAF. Below, we detail each of the components.

3.1 Context-Aware Multi-level Tracing

JavaScript Tracer. Prior approaches that gather JavaScript trace [11,21] modify JavaScript engine or the browser to identify the precise statements being executed, however such an approach requires access to JavaScript engine (and/or browser) source code which is not available for close sourced browsers like IE.

We take a JavaScript debugger-based approach. Our approach has two key advantages. (1) Most browsers – open-sourced or otherwise – support a debugging interface to debug the JavaScript statements being executed, and (2) Because the debugger runs within the browser context, it readily provides the JavaScript-level semantics. That is, we can not only gather the exact statements being executed, but also retrieve the values of variables and arguments at various statements. From within the VMM, we hook the JavaScript debugger at specific APIs to retrieve the various JavaScript statements and the corresponding contexts. The accumulation of the JavaScript statements yields the JavaScript trace.

JavaScript tracer runs as an injected module within Internet Explorer. It implements the "active script debugger" [1] interface and performs three specific actions:

1. *Establish Context*: Through the script-debugger interface, the tracer is notified when execution reaches JavaScript code. Specifically, if a SCRIPT tag is

encountered within an existing script or the script generated through `eval` statement, the tracer is activated with the information regarding the statement being executed. Until the next statement executes, the tracer associates the context to the current JavaScript statement.
2. *Record Trace*: At the beginning of every JavaScript statement, the tracer records the exact statement semantics along with the variable values and arguments to APIs (if any).
3. *Drive Binary Tracer*: A stub function is defined to coordinate the JavaScript tracer and the binary tracer. Before the statement executes, the binary tracer is activated along with the context information passed as the arguments of stub function such that the binary trace is associated with the particular JavaScript statement.

Binary Tracer. Binary tracer is triggered by the JavaScript tracer with the context information pertaining to a particular JavaScript statement. One way to gather a binary trace would be to monitor and capture the entire execution of the browser process at an instruction level. However, such a solution is resource intensive and inefficient. In order to be practical, our solution is selective about *what* is traced and *when* it is traced. Our goals towards an effective binary trace are to: (1) include all the relevant binary instructions that contribute to the attack, and (2) minimize the trace footprint as much as possible.

Firstly, since binary tracer is driven by JavaScript tracer, it has the precise JavaScript context. Tracing is limited and selectively turned on only when the execution is within a JavaScript statement. It is likely that the multithreading of the browser will introduce unrelated execution trace. But it does not jeopardize the analysis since all the binary instructions that contribute to the attack are included. Secondly, the effects of statements at a JavaScript-level manifest as memory reads and writes at a binary-level. Therefore, we implement a lightweight tracing mechanism. Instead of logging every binary instruction, we only log the memory read or write operations. We leverage memory IO specific callbacks supported by DECAF to record the values of *eip*, memory address, memory size, value in the memory and *esp* for each memory IO instruction. We also record the addresses of basic blocks that are executed and dump their raw bytes from virtual memory space of the monitored process at the end of every JavaScript statement. Furthermore, the binary tracer maintains information about active allocations made by the victim process. This information is used to identify self-modifying (or JIT) code. When such code is encountered, the code is dumped to the disk. When needed, the raw bytes are decoded to retrieve the actual instructions. The propagation of the slicing sources between registers and memory is identified by the memory IO logs and the binary instruction logic. While preserving the completed information as full instruction trace does for slicing process, this lightweight trace minimizes the trace size and also speeds up the slicing process.

Binary tracer is implemented as a plugin to DECAF. In the plugin, the stub function of JavaScript tracer is hooked to coordinate the binary tracing and JavaScript tracing. When the stub function is invoked by JavaScript tracer, the Binary tracer first reads the parameters of stub function from the stack where JavaScript Tracer passes the JavaScript statement and debugger information, then starts the logging of binary trace and generates a combined JS-Binary trace which contains the JavaScript and binary traces for each of the JavaScript statements. Meanwhile, a JS-binary map is built to keep track of corresponding JavaScript statement for every binary instruction.

Obfuscation and Encryption Resistance. The nature of JavaScript tracing provides inherent resistance to obfuscation and encryption because it captures each statement that is executed along with the runtime information like variable values, arguments, etc. Therefore, the intermediate statements (like the ones in Fig. 1(a)) that are used to calculate a value are each captured with their concrete values. Similarly, encrypted statements must be decrypted before they are executed, and the decrypted statements execute. Therefore, JSCALPEL encounters and records the decrypted statements that execute.

In fact, JSCALPEL performs preliminary preprocessing by performing constant folding with the help of the script execution trace. This simple optimization will not cause over simplification and generates a functionally equivalent de-obfuscated and decrypted version of the script. Then JSCALPEL executes the de-obfuscated version to perform the analysis. This preprocessing reduces the amount of analyzed JavaScript statements.

3.2 Identifying Slicing Sources

JSCALPEL makes use of a CFI module to identify slicing sources. Several solutions have been proposed to implement CFI [7]. Since JSCALPEL already relies on a VMM for trace gathering, it can leverage a VMM based CFI defense. We opt the techniques presented in Total-CFI [24] because (1) it is a recent and practical solution, (2) it has been demonstrated to work on recent real-world exploits and finally (3) it imposes low overhead.

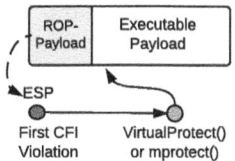

Fig. 5. Non-executable (ROP) and executable payloads used in an exploit.

It monitors the program execution at an instruction level and each point where the CFI is violated is noted as a slicing source. Albeit the recent advancement of exploitation techniques [28] can bypass the coarse-grained CFI techniques like Total-CFI, JSCALPEL's CFI module can be enhanced to include more policies to adapt the development of exploitation techniques.

Specifically, the first violation is the slicing source for the exploit-related code, whereas the subsequent violations (if any) arise from the executable payload or ROP-payload. In Fig. 5, the first violation is caused by the exploiting code, then the violations that occur up to the execution of executable payload serve as sources for ROP-payload. Moreover, the CFI module continues execution to check for executable payloads. If after the first violation, the execution ever reaches a region that within the list of allocated regions, the address is noted and it serves as the binary slicing source for the executable payload.

4 Multi-level Slicing

Multi-level slicing employed by JSCALPEL is based on the following hypothesis.

Hypothesis. *Implicit data dependencies at JavaScript level often manifest as direct data dependencies at binary level.*

Memory corruption exploits typically corrupt the memory by causing precise memory writes to key locations that are read by the program and result in corruption of program counter. Chen et al., show that a common characteristic of many classes of vulnerabilities is pointer taintedness [9], where a pointer is said to be tainted if the attacker input can directly or indirectly reach the program counter. In essence taint propagation reflects runtime data-flow within the program. Therefore, at a binary level, memory corruption exploits such as use-after-free, heap overflow, buffer overflow, etc. often exhibit simple data-flow, which can be captured through data-dependency analysis.

Figure 4 presents the overview of slicing employed by JSCALPEL. In order for the simplified exploit to be functional, it is necessary that the simplification preserves the semantics between the original and simplified scripts. Given the slicing sources and the JS-binary trace, JSCALPEL first performs a binary backward slice from the slice source provided by CFI violation and generates sources for JavaScript-level slicing. Slicing at the binary level ensures that no required statement is missed. Then, slicing is performed at a JavaScript level to include all the statements that sources are either data- or control-dependent on.

4.1 Binary-Level Slicing

The goal of binary slicing is to identify all the JavaScript statements that are instrumental in coercing the control flow (i.e., statements that modify the program counter) or injecting the payload into memory.

Algorithm 1 describes the backward slicing method using the lightweight binary trace. For every JavaScript statement $J[i]$, the corresponding binary instruction trace B_i is extracted. A map called "JS-Binary map" M – a mapping between the JavaScript statements and the binary instructions that execute within the statement context – is used. Then for every binary instruction $b_{ik} \in B_i$, if all of the elements in the slicing source S belong to memory locations, then the slicer checks if the current binary instruction b_{ik} has memory write operations $M_w \subseteq S$ and if it is false, the slicer jumps to the next instruction $b_{i(k+1)}$. Otherwise, the slicer does as traditional slicer to disassemble the binary instruction b_{ik} and updates the slicing source S and determine if b_{ik} should be added in the binary slice L based on the propagation rules for every X86 instruction. If L is not empty when the slicing on B_i is finished, $J[i]$ is added to the JavaScript slice O as the hidden dependency slice which may be ignored by pure JavaScript-level slicing.

In theory, a binary backward slice from the slicing sources must include all the JavaScript statements that are pertinent to the attack. However, in practice we found a key problem with such an approach. It is too permissive and ends up including *all* the JavaScript statements in the script. The main reason is the binary-level amalgamation of JavaScript and browser code along with JavaScript code. In order to track the exploit-specific information-flow, the flow through pointers must be considered. However, at a binary level, due to the complex nature of a JavaScript engine, dependencies are propagated to all the statements thereby leading to dependency explosion.

We exclude data propagation arising from code corresponding to the script engine and debug interface. Particularly, we apply the following filters to minimize the dependency explosion problem.

Algorithm 1. Binary level backward slicer

Input: binray trace B, slicing source S and JS-Binary map M and JavaScript trace list J
Output: JavaScript slice O
1: $S \leftarrow \{slicing\ source\ (exploit\ point\ or\ payload\ location)\}$
2: $O \leftarrow \emptyset$
3: **for** $i = len(J); i > 0; i -- $ **do**
4:   $B_i \leftarrow getBinInsTraceForJS(M, J[i], B)$
5:   **for** $k = len(B_i); k > 0; k -- $ **do**
6:     $b_{ik} \leftarrow B_i[k]$
7:     $L \leftarrow \emptyset$
8:     **if** S is all memory locations **then**
9:       $M_w \leftarrow GetMemWriteRec(b_{ik})$
10:      **if** $S \cap M_w == \emptyset$ **then**
11:        $continue$
12:      **end if**
13:    **end if**
14:    **if** $getDestOperand(b_{ik}) \in S$ **then**
15:      $S \leftarrow S \cup updateSliceSource(b_{ik}, S)$
16:      $L \leftarrow L \cup \{b_{ik}\}$
17:    **end if**
18:   **end for**
19:   **if** $L! = \emptyset$ **then**
20:     $O \leftarrow O \cup \{J[i]\}$
21:     $L \leftarrow \emptyset$
22:   **end if**
23: **end for**

Stack Filtering. Once the dependency propagates to stack pointer esp or stack frame ebp, all data on the stack becomes dependent [30]. To avoid this, dependencies arising due to esp or ebp are removed during slicing. In certain cases, the stack data could be marked dependent, but when the callee returns, the dependency is discarded if it exists on a stack variable. So JSCALPEL records the current stack pointer for every read/write, and during backward slicing, when `call` instruction is encountered in the trace, the slicer checks the current stack pointer and clears the dependencies propagating from the callee's stack.

Module Filtering. During the slicing process, the propagation to or from the JavaScript engine module or script debugger is stopped. In principle, every Javascript statement executed by the same Javascript engine instance shares the data and control dependency introduced by the Javascript engine and debugger module. This kind of dependency is *outside* of "exploit specific" dependency and should be excluded from slicing.

Other Filters. Between two consecutive JavaScript statements, we found that sometimes there are data flows via CPU registers because of the deep call stack incurred by JavaScript engine and script debugger. To avoid unintended dependencies, the slicer clears the register sinks at the end of the slicing for every JavaScript statement. During our experiments (Sect. 5), we found the above filters good enough to reduce the dependency-explosion problem without missing any required statements.

4.2 JavaScript Slicing

The output of binary tracer provides the slicing sources for the JavaScript slicer. Suppose binary slice S contains n instructions. For each instruction S_i, let J_i be the JavaScript statement that represents the context under which S_i executes. Then, the JavaScript slicing sources are $\mathcal{O} = \bigcup_{i=0}^{n} J_i$. For every JavaScript statement in the slicing sources, we add the object used by this JavaScript statement to the slicing sources and include this JavaScript statement in the slice. Given the JavaScript trace, the slicer uses WALA's [4] slicing algorithm to include all the related JavaScript statement in the slice.

4.3 Minimized Exploit Script and PoV Generation

The statements are first simplified and then embedded into the exploit HTML page to obtain the minimized exploit. Also, the identified executable payload is replaced by an amicable payload to obtain a PoV in the form of a test case for the Metasploit framework.

Simplification. As a final step, JSCALPEL performs constant folding and dead-code elimination at JavaScript level to simplify the slice. It is focused on strings and constants. Specifically, for each variable v, the definitions are propagated to the uses. This is repeated for all the variables in all the statements until no more propagations are possible. Finally, if a definition of a variable has no more uses, the definition is considered dead-code and is removed only if the statement is not a source for the JavaScript slicing. This distinction is important because, the need for slice sources is already established from binary slicing. The resulting processed script is used to exploit the browser and is accepted only if the exploitation succeeds. Finally, all the statements in the script that are not a part of the slice are removed. During our experiments, we found that the simplicity of simplification incorporated by JSCALPEL is sufficient to bring about significant reduction in the sizes of the scripts as highlighted in Sect. 5.

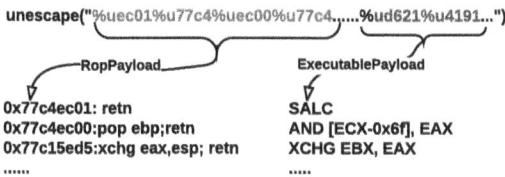

Fig. 6. CVE-2012-1876: ROP- and executable-payloads within the same string.

Collocated ROP and Executable Payloads. In some exploits, the payload and the ROP-gadgets are contained within the same string or array. For example in Fig. 6 the same string contains both ROP-payload and the executable shellcode. In such cases, JS-Binary analysis identifies the statement as both exploit and payload statement. This is an expected behavior. However, in order to replace the payload to generate the PoV, we must precisely identify the location of the start of the payload within the string. First, the JavaScript string that contains the payload is located in the memory. Then, from the payload-slice source we obtain the address of the entry point of the payload. Binary slicing from the payload-slice source leads us to the offset within the JavaScript string that corresponds to the payload. The substring beginning from the offset is replaced for PoV generation.

ROP-Only Payload. Shacham [29] showed that a set of Turing complete gadgets can be created using program text of libc. Though we cannot find any instances of *ROP-only* payload during our experiments, it is possible to compose the entire payload using only ROP-gadgets without any executable payload. Since JSCALPEL can locate the ROP-only payload precisely, a straightforward way is to replace malicious ROP-only payload with benign ROP-only payload.

JSCALPEL can generate dependent JavaScript statements in the script for any given binary-level source and the JS-Binary trace. Along with the exploit point and the payload entry point, CFI component of JSCALPEL captures multiple violations caused due to the ROP-gadget chain as separate binary-level slicing sources. The sources are then subject to multi-level tracing the slicing to extract the payload in JavaScript.

Disjoint Payload. Detecting the entry point of executable payload is sufficient to replace the payload and generate the PoV. However, sometimes an analyst may want to locate the *entire* executable payload. This is not a problem if the payload is allocated by the same string in the JavaScript. However, it is not necessary to be so.

JSCALPEL can only detect an executable payload when it executes. Therefore, it is unaware of *all* the various fragments of payload that may be injected into the memory. As a result, JSCALPEL will only be able to detect the JavaScript statement (and all its dependencies) that injects the entry point of the payload. It may miss some JavaScript statements that inject non-entry point payload if such statements are disjoint with the JavaScript statements that inject the entry point, and the sources for those statements are missing. Note that this is not quite a limitation for JSCALPEL, because the payload entry point is sufficient to generate a PoV. One way to increase the amount of payload recovered is for the CFI module to allow the payload to execute longer and capture more binary-level sources for the payload.

5 Evaluation

We evaluate JSCALPEL on a corpus of 15 exploits. These samples exploit the vulnerabilities discovered from 2009 to 2013 and target at Internet Explorer 6/7/8. In contrast to the large number of browser vulnerabilities discovered every year, this sample set is relatively old and small. The reasons are twofold. First, DECAF leveraged by JSCALPEL is based on emulator QEMU and only supports 32-bit operating system. Not all of the exploits can function correctly on DECAF. Second, it is difficult to collect working exploits although many vulnerabilities are discovered every year. We went over Internet Explorer related exploits in Metasploit, and tried to set up a working environment for each of them. We were able to set up 15 exploits on the real hardware. The remaining exploits either require specific browser/plugin versions that we were unable to find, or do not use JavaScript to launch the attacks. We then tested these 15 exploits on DECAF and 9 of them worked correctly. The 6 exploits failed to work on DECAF, because they exhibited heavy heap spray behavior, which could not finish within a reasonable amount of time in DECAF. Based on a whole-system emulator QEMU, DECAF translates a virtual memory address into its corresponding physical address completely in software implementation, and thus is much slower than the MMU (Memory Management Unit) in a real CPU. In the future, we will replace DECAF with Pin to avoid this expensive memory address translation overhead. We also crawled the Virustotal with the keyword "exploit type:html", and finally found 2 functional exploits on DECAF. In addition, from 16 exploit kits used in EkHunter [14], we managed to get 4 functional exploits from exploitkit, Siberia and Crimepack. As a result, our testset includes 9 exploits from Metasploit framework, 4 exploits from 3 different exploit kits and 2 wild exploits.

To identify the CVE number of exploits from exploit kits and wild, we ran JSCALPEL to extract exploitation component first and then manually searched Metasploit database and National Vulnerability Database [3] for a match. While CVE-2012-1889 exploits the vulnerability in `msxml.dll`, all the remaining samples exploit `mshtml.dll`.

Though we evaluated JSCALPEL on Internet Explorer only, potentially it can work on other browsers or any other programs (e.g., Adobe Reader) that have JavaScript debug interface. The experiments were performed on a server running

Ubuntu 12.04 on 32 core Intel Xeon(R) 2 GHz CPU and 128 GB memory. The code comprises of 890 lines of Python, 2300 lines of Java and 4000 lines of C++.

5.1 Minimizing Exploits

Table 1 presents the results for exploit analysis. Given one exploit, we first ran JSCALPEL to get the multi-level trace and CFI violation point. Then multi-level slicing was conducted to yield exploitation component and payload injection component. Based on this knowledge, our experiments demonstrate that for each exploit, JSCALPEL was able to generate a simplified exploit and PoV which were able to successfully exploit the vulnerability and launch the payload.

Exploitation Analysis. The binary-level slicing was conducted on the multi-level trace starting from the CFI violation point. It mapped binary level slicing results to JavaScript statements with the help of JS-binary map. The number of JavaScript statements identified by binary-level analysis is listed in Column I.

Table 1. Exploit analysis results

Source	CVE	Exploitation component					Payload injection	Simplified exploit			
		I	II	III	IV	V	VI	VII	VIII	IX	X
Metasploit	2009-0075	9	6	✓	17	✓	14	30	30	0.00	
	2010-0249	3	6	✗	19	✓	10	45	22	0.51	b c
	2010-0806	2	10	✓	10	✓	14	803	13	0.98	a c b
	2010-3962	1	1	✓	1	✓	15	105	17	0.83	a c b
	2012-1876	32	1	✗	30	✓	14	67	47	0.30	a c b
	2012-1889	1	2	✓	2	✓	67	77	77	0.00	
	2012-4969	16	1	✗	8	✓	53	117	70	0.40	b c
	2013-3163	9	1	✗	13	✓	32	43	42	0.02	a b d
	2013-3897	26	1	✗	41	✓	23	187	63	0.66	d
Wild	2011-1255	40	1	✗	16	✓	26	97	44	0.55	a b e
	2012-1889	1	2	✓	2	✓	27	53	12	0.77	a b e
exploitkit	2010-0806	2	6	✓	6	✓	13	109	29	0.73	b c
Siberia	2010-0806	2	6	✓	6	✓	12	103	22	0.79	a b c
Crimepack	2010-0806	2	1	✗	6	✓	11	198	30	0.85	a b c
	2009-0075	4	6	✗	12	✓	12	36	33	0.08	a b c

I. # of JS slicing sources.
II. # of stmts from JS analysis only.
III. Can stmts from JS-only analysis cause crash?
IV. # of stmts from JS-Bin analysis
V. Can stmts from JS-Bin analysis cause crash?
VI. # of stmts from JS-Bin analysis
VII. # of unique JS stmts of original exploit.
VIII. # of unique JS stmts of simplified exploit.
IX. potency of minimization.
X. Obfuscation & fingerprinting Techniques. ([a]: Randomization Obf. [b]: Data Obf. [c]: Encoding Obf. [d]: Logic Structure Obf. [e]: Fingerprinting tech)

They were used as the slicing sources for JavaScript level slicing. This multi-level slicing extracted the exploitation related statements the number of which were listed in Column IV. Column V shows if the extracted statements can crash the browser. For the exploits with the same CVE number like CVE-2009-0075 and CVE-2010-0806, the results of Column IV can be different due to the different implementation of exploitation. But we can see that for all of the exploits, the extracted statements can crash the browser, meaning that the semantics of exploitation component are preserved.

In comparison, the JavaScript-level only analysis cannot achieve this as presented in Column II and III. Column II lists the number of JavaScript statements obtained from backward slicing only at the JavaScript level starting from the statement that causes the first CFI violation. Column III indicates if the statements extracted from JavaScript-level slicing can cause the browser to crash. We can see that for 8 out of 15 exploits, the extracted statements do not cause a crash, which means these exploits are overly simplified in these cases. For the exploits with the same CVE number like CVE-2010-0806 and CVE-2009-0075, the JavaScript-level only analysis results were different, because the different obfuscation techniques used in these exploits introduced or eliminated unexpected dependency at JavaScript level.

Payload Injection. The CFI violation information provides the exact location of the payload in memory. The multi-level slicing yields the payload injection statements of which the number is listed in Column VI of Table 1. Column 3 in Table 2 lists the payload definition statements. For each of the exploit, our JS-Binary analysis was able to precisely pinpoint the payload injection statements for PoV generation. By contrast, solutions like JSGuard [16] or NOZZLE [26] cannot do the same, because they lack the JavaScript context and can only pinpoint the payload in the memory. Solutions by scanning the exploit code directly cannot always identify the correct payload injection statements since the payload is often obfuscated.

Minimized Exploit. For each of the exploits, we combined the payload injection statements (Column VI) with the exploitation component (Column IV) to generate a minimized working exploit. In the experiment, we observed that each minimized exploit was indeed functional, meaning that it can exploit the vulnerability and launch the payload successfully. The Column VII lists the number of unique JavaScript statements observed at the execution of the original exploit. Column VIII lists the number of unique JavaScript statements observed in the execution of the minimized exploit.

The minimized exploit excludes the JavaScript statements that belong to obfuscation code or fingerprinting code. We characterize those codes in Column X of Table 1. They cover different obfuscation or fingerprinting techniques. These techniques are designed to bypass the detection tool and make the analysis challenging. So the minimized exploit can ease the manual analysis process by removing these JavaScript statements. To quantify the degree of code complexity reduction in these minimized exploits, we adopt a metric called "potency of minimization" from an existing work [10]. A minimization is potent if it makes the

Table 2. Payload analysis results. All exploits provide a single JavaScript statement from the binary perspective, which is the context in which the exploiting instruction executes.

Source	CVE	Payload definition stmt	I	II
Metasploit	2009-0075	var shellcode = unescape("%u1c35%u90a8%u3abf...")	3024	✗
	2010-0249	var LLVc = unescape("%u1c35%u90a8%u3abf%u..")	3024	✗
	2010-0806	var wd$ = unescape((function(){return "%u4772%u9314%u9815..."}))	3072	✗
	2010-3962	var shellcode = unescape("%u0c74%ud513%uf...")	3072	✗
	2012-1876	for (var a3d = unescape("%uec01%u77c4%u..."),...)	3072	✓
	2012-1889	var code = unescape("%uba92%u91b5%ub0b1...")	3072	✗
	2012-4969	var GBvB = unescape("%uc481%uf254%uffff...")	618	✗
	2013-3163	p += unescape("%ub860%u77c3%ud038...")	36696	✓
	2013-3897	sprayHeap({shellcode:unescape("%u868a%u77c3..."})	696	✓
Wild	2011-1255	var sc = unescape("%u9090%u9090%u9090%u1c3...")	3024	✗
	2012-1889	var mmmbc=("Data5756Data3352Data64c9...)	2880	✗
Exploitkit	2010-0806	var qq = unescape("%ucddb%u74d9%uf424%u...")	649	✗
Siberia	2010-0806	var qq = unescape("!5350!5251!..".replace(...")	1750	✗
Crimepack	2010-0806	var rktchpv= unescape("%u06b8%u5c67%udae4...")	648	✗
	2009-0075	var ysazuzbwzdqlr=unescape("%u06b8%u5c67%u...")	648	✗

I. Payload Length II. Collocated payload?

minimized program P' less obscure (or complex or unreadable) than the original program P. we choose the number of unique JavaScript statements observed in the execution as the metric because it represents the number of inspected statements by an analyst. This is formalized in the following definition:

Definition 1 (Potency of Minimization). Let $U(P)$ be the number of unique JavaScript statements observed at the execution of P. τ_{pot}, the minimization potency with respect to program P, is a measure of the extent to which the minimization reduces the obscurity of P. It is defined as

$$\tau_{pot} \stackrel{\text{def}}{=} 1 - \frac{U(P')}{U(P)}.$$

On average, the minimization potency was 0.498, which means we were able to eliminate 49.8 % of statements in the trace, whereas the maximum is 0.98. The potency of minimization of CVE-2009-0075 and CVE-2012-1889 from Metasploit are both 0, because no obfuscation techniques are applied to them. We did observe that for the exploits from the wild and exploit kits, the average potency of minimization (0.63) was higher than that (0.41) for the exploits from Metasploit. This means that it is generally more difficult to analyze the real world exploits.

5.2 PoV Generation

PoV generation is an end result of payload analysis. By replacing the payload in the minimized exploit with a benign one, a PoV is generated for penetration test. Column 3 in Table 2 lists the payload definition statements, where the payload content is first introduced or defined in the JavaScript code. The definition statement is usually accompanied with other statements required to inject the

Table 3. Effects of filtering on exploit analysis.

Source	CVE	Unique # JS stmts	# JS after pre-processing	No filter	Stack filter	Module filter	All filters
Metasploit	2009-0075	30	30	30	14	28	9
	2010-0249	45	32	32	4	32	3
	2010-0806	803	27	27	13	27	2
	2010-3962	105	17	16	16	16	1
	2012-1876	67	51	50	41	50	32
	2012-1889	77	78	78	2	77	1
	2012-4969	117	77	77	16	75	16
	2013-3163	43	43	41	4	41	9
	2013-3897	187	64	64	26	64	26
Wild	2011-1255	97	66	66	45	66	40
	2012-1889	53	53	51	1	1	1
Exploitkit	2010-0806	109	32	31	31	31	2
Siberia	2010-0806	103	27	26	26	26	2
Crimepack	2010-0806	198	195	194	22	194	2
	2009-0075	36	35	25	5	5	4

payload. Payload length (Column 4 in Table 2) is the size of the payload that was identified. In one of the samples (CVE-2013–3163), the encoder was embedded within the payload and therefore, the size of the payload was much larger than other exploits. In 3 out of 15 exploits, we found the ROP and executable payloads to be collocated within the same string. In each exploit, the payload was replaced with a benign payload and a PoV was generated.

5.3 Effects of Filtering

The filters help to exclude the unexpected dependencies. In Table 3, we evaluated the effects of filtering on minimizing exploits. We found that preprocessing is effective in cases where the scripts are obfuscated because, during obfuscation, multiple statements are used to accomplish the tasks of a single statement like eval. Column 3–4 lists the number of the unique JavaScript statements in the slicing results under different filter configurations. With no filters, we did not find any significant reduction in the slicing results. This emphasizes the need for filtering. Stack Filter and Module Filter individually produced varying amount of size reduction depending on the exploit, but in general, the combination proved to be most effective. For example, for CVE-2010-3962, the combination of all the filters reduced the number of statements to a single statement, while none of the filters were individually effective.

5.4 Case Study – CVE-2011-1255

In order to highlight the advantages of JSCALPEL, we perform a study of the wild exploit, CVE-2011-1255 [2], which exploits a "Time Element Memory Corruption Vulnerability" of the Timed Interactive Multimedia Extension implementation in Microsoft Internet Explorer 6 through 8. The exploit (MD5:016c280b8f1f155 80f89d058dc5102bb) targets Internet Explorer 6 on Windows XP SP3. Given the exploit sample, JSCALPEL successfully generated the minimized exploit code, payload injection code and penetration test template for Metasploit. We would like to highlight that a sample for CVE-2011-1255 was previously unavailable on Metasploit DB and JSCALPEL was able to generate one.

Simplified Exploit Statements JSCALPEL loads the simplified page and logs the JS-Binary trace until the CFI violation-point (detailed in Fig. 7) is reached. The violation point ① represents the hijacked control flow transfer from 0x7ddd44a1 to the payload location 0x0c0c0c0c through an indirect call instruction – call DWORD[ecx+0X8]. Note that the exploit does not contain any ROP-gadgets and that the entire payload is executable. From the violation, either ecx or [ecx + 0x8] may be manipulated by the attacker and therefore both will have to be considered as possible slicing sources. From the memory IO log (point ②), the location of [ecx+0x8] is extracted as 0x0c0c0c14. Both ecx and the memory location 0x0c0c0c14 are provided as the slicing sources for the binary-level slicer to uncover the implicit data dependency pertaining to the exploit.

The binary level slicer identified 40 JavaScript level sources. JavaScript slicer included an additional 64 statements to generate the simplified exploit. Using the simplified exploit), we were able to trigger the vulnerability in IE 6.

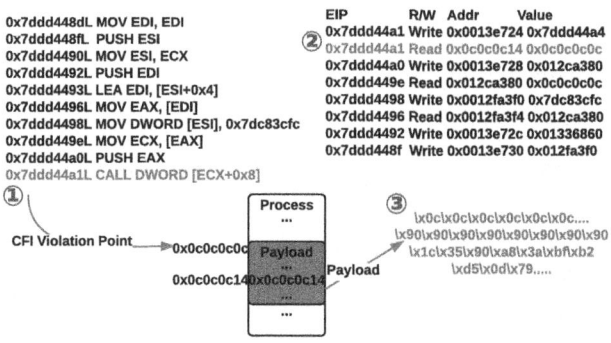

Fig. 7. CFI violation point

Simplified Payload-Injection Statements and Payload Location Similar to simplifying the exploit statements, JSCALPEL uses payload location *0x0c0c0c0c* as the slicing source for identifying the payload-injection statements, and gathers the simplified statements. The binary-level slicer confirmed the statement 36: a[i] = lh.substr(0, lh.length) as the JavaScript statement that injects payload into memory. Then, this statement was used as the slicing source for JavaScript-level slicer. Finally, JSCALPEL identified all the payload injection JavaScript statements.)

The payload is located at 0x0c0c0c0c. Therefore, JSCALPEL extracts the page at 0x0c0c0c0c to analyze the payload. JSCALPEL first trims the padding instruction like nop from the payload. Next, JSCALPEL compares it with the constant strings in the payload injection JavaScript statements to identify the exact payload string. JSCALPEL identified (var sc = unescape(''%u9090%u9090%u9090%u9090%u1c35%u90a8%u3abf%ub2d5....'')) as the JavaScript statement containing the payload. Since the entire payload is executable, JSCALPEL replaced the entire payload to generate the Metasploit test case. We generate a Ruby template script) for Metasploit framework, and we were able to successfully test it on Internet Explorer 6 on Windows XP SP3.

6 Discussion

Vulnerabilities Within Filtered Modules. If the vulnerability exploited exists within the filtered modules, the slicer produces the incomplete slice. Current implementation of JSCALPEL can not detect exploits that target the filtered modules. In the future, fine-grained analysis can be applied on these modules to determine which part of the code introduces the dependency and then limit the filter from whole module to some specific code range. This will reduce the number of vulnerabilities that JSCALPEL cannot handle.

Debug-Resistant JavaScript. In order for JSCALPEL to be able to analyze a script, it is important that JSCALPEL executes the program and monitors from the debugger. Though we did not find any samples that can detect debuggers, it is possible that exploits could use techniques (e.g., timing-based) to determine if a debugger is running and hide the malicious behavior. Currently, JSCALPEL is vulnerable to such attacks. It would be an interesting future work to reconstruct JavaScript-level semantics directly from the Virtual Machine Monitor, similar to how DroidScope [35]) recovers Java/Dalvik level semantic view.

Impact of JIT-Enabled JavaScript Engine on JSCALPEL. When JIT is enabled on JavaScript engine, the data flow within JavaScript engine becomes more complex because of the mixture of code and data. JScalpel may not work in this case. Since JScalpel is designed as an analysis tool and is not performance sensitive, the analyst can simply disable the JIT engine. However, this workaround would sacrifice the capability of analyzing attacks that perform JIT spray, as these attacks rely on the side-effects of the JIT compiler. We leave it as future work to address this issue.

7 Related Work

Drive-by-download Attacks. The drive-by-download attacks drive the emergence of "Exploit-as-a-Service" paradigm on the malware ecosystem [15]. Machine learning based approaches [6,11,13,25,32] and honeypot based approach [33] for large scale analysis have been explored to detect the malicious web pages. JShield [8] proposed a vulnerability-based approach, which uses opcode vulnerability signature to match drive-by-download attacks. NOZZLE [26] detects the existence of shellcode to identify heap spray attacks launched by malicious web pages. ZOZZLE [12] uses Bayesian classification of hierarchical features of the JavaScript abstract syntax tree to identify syntax elements that are highly predictive of malware. BLADE [22] focuses on the client side approach by preventing unconsented content execution, which is the ultimate goal of drive-by-download attacks.

Exploit Diagnosis. PointerScope [38] uses type inference on binary execution to detect the pointer misuses induced by an exploit. ShellOS [31] built a hardware virtualization based platform for fast detection and forensic analysis of code injection attacks. Dynamic taint analysis [23] keeps track of the data dependency originated from untrusted user input at the instruction level, and detects an exploit on a dangerous use of a tainted input. explored whole system taint tracking for malware analysis. Chen et al., [9] showed that pointer taintedness analysis can expose different classes of security vulnerabilities, such as format string, heap corruption, and buffer overflow vulnerabilities. pinpoints the guilty bytes in polymorphic buffer overflows on heap or stack by tagging data from network with an age stamp. However, it is not feasible for complex attacks launched using JavaScript code.

Malicious JavaScript Analysis. To deobfuscate malicious JavaScript, Kolbitsch et al., [20] uncover environment-specific malware by exploring multiple execution paths within a single execution. Previous work [11,17,21] execute JavaScript using an emulated JavaScript running environment and acquire deobfuscated JavaScript. Our solution adopts the real browser environment and can defend most of the obfuscation techniques. JSGuard [16] proposed a methodology to detect JS shellcode that fully uses JS code execution environment information with low false negative and false positive. [21] simplify the obfuscated JavaScript code by preserving the semantics of the observational equivalence. However, the simplified JavaScript code may not exploit the vulnerability of web browser due to oversimplification. Our combined analysis can identify the JavaScript code contributing to exploit and avoid over simplification.

8 Conclusion

We presented JSCALPEL, a framework that combines JavaScript and binary analyses to analyze JavaScript exploits. Our multi-level tracing bridges the semantic gap between the JavaScript level and binary level to perform dynamic

JS-Binary analysis. We analyzed 15 JavaScript exploits, 9 memory corruption exploits from Metasploit , 4 exploits from 3 exploit kits and 2 exploits from the wild and successfully recover the payload and a minimized exploit for each of the exploits.

Acknowledgments. We would like to thank anonymous reviewers and our shepherd Dr. Manuel Egele for their insightful feedback. This research was supported in part by National Science Foundation Grant #1054605, Air Force Research Lab Grant #FA8750-15-2-0106, and DARPA CGC Grant #FA8750-14-C-0118. Any opinions, findings, and conclusions in this paper are those of the authors and do not necessarily reflect the views of the funding agencies.

References

1. Active script debugging overview. http://msdn.microsoft.com/en-us/library/z537xb90(v=vs.94).aspx
2. Detailed analysis exp/20111255-a. http://www.sophos.com/en-us/threat-center/threat-analyses/viruses-and-spyware/Exp~20111255-A/detailed-analysis.aspx
3. National vulnerability database. https://nvd.nist.gov/
4. The T.J. Watson Libraries for Analysis (WALA). http://wala.sourceforge.net/
5. Internet security threat report. https://www4.symantec.com/mktginfo/whitepaper/ISTR/21347932_GA-internet-security-threat-report-volume-20-2015-social_v2.pdf, April 2015
6. Borgolte, K., Kruegel, C., Vigna, G.: Delta: automatic identification of unknown web-based infection campaigns. In: Proceedings of the 2013 ACM SIGSAC Conference on Computer & Communications Security (2013)
7. Burow, N., Carr, S.A., Brunthaler, S., Payer, M., Nash, J., Larsen, P., Franz, M.: Control-flow integrity: precision, security, and performance. arXiv preprint (2016). arXiv:1602.04056
8. Cao, Y., Pan, X., Chen, Y., Zhuge, J.: Jshield: towards real-time and vulnerability-based detection of polluted drive-by download attacks. In: Proceedings of Annual Computer Security Applications Conference (ACSAC) (2014)
9. Chen, S., Pattabiraman, K., Kalbarczyk, Z., Iyer, R.K.: Formal reasoning of various categories of widely exploited security vulnerabilities using pointer taintedness semantics. In: Security and Protection in Information Processing Systems (2004)
10. Collberg, C., Thomborson, C., Low, D.: A taxonomy of obfuscating transformations. Technical report, Department of Computer Science, The University of Auckland, New Zealand (1997)
11. Cova, M., Kruegel, C., Vigna, G.: Detection and analysis of drive-by-download attacks and malicious JavaScript code. In: Proceedings of the 19th International Conference on World Wide Web (2010)
12. Curtsinger, C., Livshits, B., Zorn, B.G., Seifert, C.: Zozzle: fast and precise in-browser JavaScript malware detection. In: USENIX Security Symposium (2011)
13. Eshete, B.: Effective analysis, characterization, and detection of malicious web pages. In: Proceedings of the 22nd International Conference on World Wide Web Companion, International World Wide Web Conferences Steering Committee (2013)
14. Eshete, B., Alhuzhali, A., Monshizadeh, M., Porras, P., Yegneswaran, V.: Ekhunter: a counter-offensive toolkit for exploit kit infiltration. In: Proceedings of the 22nd Annual Network and Distributed System Security Symposium, February 2015

15. Grier, C., Ballard, L., Caballero, J., Chachra, N., Dietrich, C.J., Levchenko, K., Mavrommatis, P., McCoy, D., Nappa, A., Pitsillidis, A., Provos, N., Rafique, M.Z., Rajab, M.A., Rossow, C., Thomas, K., Paxson, V., Savage, S., Voelker, G.M.: Manufacturing compromise: the emergence of exploit-as-a-service. In: Proceedings of the 2012 ACM Conference on Computer and Communications Security (2012)
16. Gu, B., Zhang, W., Bai, X., Champion, A.C., Qin, F., Xuan, D.: Jsguard: shellcode detection in JavaScript. In: Security and Privacy in Communication Networks (2013)
17. Hartstein, B.: Jsunpack: an automatic JavaScript unpacker. In: ShmooCon Convention (2009)
18. Hedin, D., Birgisson, A., Bello, L., Sabelfeld, A.: JSFlow: tracking information flow in JavaScript and its APIs. In: Proceedings 29th ACM Symposium on Applied Computing (2014)
19. Henderson, A., Prakash, A., Yan, L.K., Hu, X., Wang, X., Zhou, R., Yin, H.: Make it work, make it right, make it fast: building a platform-neutral whole-system dynamic binary analysis platform. In: Proceedings of the 2014 International Symposium on Software Testing and Analysis (2014)
20. Kolbitsch, C., Livshits, B., Zorn, B., Seifert, C.: Rozzle: de-cloaking internet malware. In: 2012 IEEE Symposium on Security and Privacy (SP) (2012)
21. Lu, G., Debray, S.: Automatic simplification of obfuscated JavaScript code: a semantics-based approach. In: Proceedings of the 2012 IEEE Sixth International Conference on Software Security and Reliability (2012)
22. Lu, L., Yegneswaran, V., Porras, P., Lee, W.: Blade: an attack-agnostic approach for preventing drive-by malware infections. In: Proceedings of the 17th ACM Conference on Computer and Communications Security (2010)
23. Newsome, J., Song, D.: Dynamic taint analysis: automatic detection, analysis, and signature generation of exploit attacks on commodity software. In: Proceedings of the Network and Distributed Systems Security Symposium, February 2005
24. Prakash, A., Yin, H., Liang, Z.: Enforcing system-wide control flow integrity for exploit detection and diagnosis. In: Proceedings of the 8th ACM SIGSAC Symposium on Information, Computer and Communications Security (2013)
25. Provos, N., McNamee, D., Mavrommatis, P., Wang, K., Modadugu, N., et al.: The ghost in the browser analysis of web-based malware. In: Proceedings of the First Conference on First Workshop on Hot Topics in Understanding Botnets (2007)
26. Ratanaworabhan, P., Livshits, B., Zorn, B.: Nozzle: a defense against heap-spraying code injection attacks. In: Proceedings of the Usenix Security Symposium (2009)
27. Saxena, P., Akhawe, D., Hanna, S., Mao, F., McCamant, S., Song, D.: A symbolic execution framework for JavaScript. In: 2010 IEEE Symposium on Security and Privacy (SP) (2010)
28. Schuster, F., Tendyck, T., Liebchen, C., Davi, L., Sadeghi, A.-R., Holz, T.: Counterfeit object-oriented programming: on the difficulty of preventing code reuse attacks in C++ applications. In: 2015 IEEE Symposium on Security and Privacy (SP). IEEE (2015)
29. Shacham, H.: The geometry of innocent flesh on the bone: return-into-libc without function calls (on the X86). In: Proceedings of the 14th ACM Conference on Computer and Communications Security (2007)
30. Slowinska, A., Bos, H.: Pointless tainting? evaluating the practicality of pointer tainting. In: Proceedings of the 4th ACM European Conference on Computer systems. ACM (2009)

31. Snow, K.Z., Krishnan, S., Monrose, F., Provos, N.: Shellos: enabling fast detection and forensic analysis of code injection attacks. In: USENIX Security Symposium (2011)
32. Stringhini, G., Kruegel, C., Vigna, G.: Shady paths: leveraging surfing crowds to detect malicious web pages. In: Proceedings of the 2013 ACM SIGSAC Conference on Computer & Communications Security (2013)
33. Wang, Y.-M., Beck, D., Jiang, X., Roussev, R., Verbowski, C., Chen, S., King, S.: Automated web patrol with strider honeymonkeys: finding web sites that exploit browser vulnerabilities. In: Proceedings of the 2006 Network and Distributed System Security Symposium (2006)
34. Weiser, M.: Program slicing. In: Proceedings of the 5th International Conference on Software Engineering. IEEE Press (1981)
35. Yan, L.K., Yin, H.: Droidscope: seamlessly reconstructing the OS and Dalvik semantic views for dynamic Android malware analysis. In: Proceedings of the 21st USENIX Conference on Security Symposium (2012)
36. Yin, H., Song, D., Egele, M., Kruegel, C., Kirda, E.: Panorama: capturing system-wide information flow for malware detection and analysis. In: Proceedings of the 14th ACM Conference on Computer and Communications Security, New York, NY, USA (2007)
37. Zeller, A., Hildebrandt, R.: Simplifying and isolating failure-inducing input. IEEE Trans. Softw. Eng. **28**(2), 183–200 (2002)
38. Zhang, M., Prakash, A., Li, X., Liang, Z., Yin, H.: Identifying and analyzing pointer misuses for sophisticated memory-corruption exploit diagnosis. In: Proceedings of 19th Annual Network & Distributed System Security Symposium (2012)

Network Security

The Messenger Shoots Back: Network Operator Based IMSI Catcher Detection

Adrian Dabrowski[1(✉)], Georg Petzl[2], and Edgar R. Weippl[1]

[1] SBA Research, Vienna, Austria
{adabrowski,eweippl}@sba-research.org
[2] T-Mobile Austria, Vienna, Austria
Georg.Petzl@t-mobile.at

Abstract. An IMSI Catcher, also known as *Stingray* or *rogue cell*, is a device that can be used to not only locate cellular phones, but also to intercept communication content like phone calls, SMS or data transmission unbeknown to the user. They are readily available as commercial products as well as do-it-yourself projects running open-source software, and are obtained and used by law enforcement agencies and criminals alike. Multiple countermeasures have been proposed recently to detect such devices from the user's point of view, but they are limited to the nearby vicinity of the user.

In this paper we are the first to present and discuss multiple detection capabilities from the network operator's point of view, and evaluate them on a real-world cellular network in cooperation with an European mobile network operator with over four million subscribers. Moreover, we draw a comprehensive picture on current threats against mobile phone devices and networks, including 2G, 3G and 4G IMSI Catchers and present detection and mitigation strategies under the unique large-scale circumstances of a real European carrier. One of the major challenges from the operator's point of view is that cellular networks were specifically designed to reduce global signaling traffic and to manage as many transactions regionally as possible. Hence, contrary to popular belief, network operators by default do not have a global view or their network. Our proposed solution can be readily added to existing network monitoring infrastructures and includes among other things plausibility checks of location update trails, monitoring of device-specific round trip times and an offline detection scheme to detect cipher downgrade attacks, as commonly used by commercial IMSI Catchers.

1 Introduction

IMSI Catchers are MITM (Man-in-The-Middle) devices for cellular networks [28]. Originally developed to steal IMSI (International Mobile Subscriber Identity) numbers from nearby phones, later versions offered call- and message interception. Today, IMSI Catchers are used to (i) track handsets, (ii) deliver geo-target spam [32], (iii) send operator messages that reconfigure the phone (e.g., installing a permanent MITM by setting a new APN, http-proxy, or attack the management interface [39]), (iv) directly attack SIM cards with encrypted SMS [33] that are filtered by most operators by now, and (v) also can potentially intercept mobile two-factor authentication schemes (mTAN). IMSI Catchers have become affordable, and can be build for less then USD 1,500 [14]. Pell and Soghoian [36] argue that we are currently on the brink of age where almost everyone is able to eavesdrop phone calls, similar to the 1990ies when cheap analog scanners were used to listen to mobile phones in the US and Europe.

In brief, these devices exploit the phone's behavior of preferring the strongest cell phone tower signal in the vicinity to maximize the signal quality and minimize its own power consumption. Additionally, on GSM networks (2G), only the phone (via the SIM - Subscriber Identification Module) needs to authenticate to the network, but not vice versa and can therefore be easily deluded to disable content data encryption. This enables an attacker to answer a phone's requests as if the phone was communicating with a legitimate cell phone network.

In contrast, the Universal Mobile Telecommunication System (UMTS, 3G) and Long Term Evolution (LTE, 4G) require mutual two-way authentication, but are still not completely immune to IMSI Catchers. Tracking and identifying IMSI Catchers are build on the weakness that a network has to be able to identify its subscriber before it can authenticate him/her. Additionally, unauthenticated commands can be used to downgrade a phone into using 3G or the less secure 2G (GSM) only, eventually giving way to a full Man-in-the-Middle attack. Additionally, some phones execute unauthenticated commands, even though the standard demands prior authentication [35].

This issue gains additional momentum as commercial networks increasingly surpass dedicated administrative and governmental networks in coverage and data rates and thus carry more and more increasingly sensitive data. Additionally, today, many economic sectors critically depend on a reliable and secure mobile communication infrastructure (e.g., logistics).

While previous work [15,31,34,37,40] mainly focused on the detection of rouge base stations on the consumer side, this paper takes the approach from the network operator's perspective and discusses novel detection capabilities from an academic as well as practical point of view.

The cooperation with a mobile phone network operator with over four million subscribers enabled us to test theories, identify detection artifacts and generate statistics out of core network data. We focused on passive detection methods, readily available data in today's monitoring solutions and the identification of changes that promise better detectability and scalability.

The scope of this paper is the detection of attacks on the radio access network (RAN) in 2G (GE/RAN), 3G (UTRAN), and LTE networks (E-UTRAN). While there are attacks on the backbone and interconnection interface, or within a mobile network provider, we focus on the last-mile radio link between the cell tower and the terminal device. The traditional telecommunication network model centers all the intelligence in the network and attaches (dumb) end devices that have to obey the network. Thus, these types of attacks give an attacker a lot of control over the end user device.

The pivotal sections of the paper are as follows:

- Evaluation of 22 phones on (i) how they interact with the genuine network once released from an IMSI Catcher (Sect. 5.1) and (ii) which artifacts are produced.
- Development and implementation of detection strategies based on the artifacts and test of their fitness including their limitations on real-world data of a network operator (Sects. 5 and 6)

2 Background

Previous work [15,31,34,37,40] focused on the subscriber (customer) side; this paper shifts perspectives and addresses the detection of such attacks from the operator side. The particular challenge lies in the structure of digital mobile networks: They where drafted in a time of low bandwidth connections, when signaling traffic occupied a significant amount of the network infrastructure. Therefore, these networks were designed in a highly hierarchical and geographically distributed fashion with as much signaling traffic as possible being handled locally or regionally, thus, offloading the backbone. This poses unique challenges when acquiring and correlating the necessary data in order to detect anomalies in the network. Additionally, the legacy of having a GSM network being upgraded to UMTS and later again upgraded to LTE implies that the structure and the used data formats are not as clean and neat as one would expect from a freshly built LTE network with additional 2G and 3G radio front-ends.

Compared to the time when 2G networks were designed, today the ratio between user data and signaling data has completely changed. With LTE, users are offered 100 MBit or more.

The lowered backbone bandwidth costs and the (now) relatively low volume of signaling data allows mobile phone operators to en-bloc collect and monitor more data parameters than before. Many cellular network operators routinely collect data on different network levels and elements (e.g., from switches, servers, and via network probes) to detect, track and debug malfunctions and optimize their network. The strength of such Network Intelligence systems is to correlate transactions over different levels and protocols in the network structure, extract important values, and build an extensive index of the latter. This is done for several million signaling packets per minute. The limitation is that these indices are primarily built to search for traffic based on simple identifiers such as a specific customer, network element, protocol, or transaction type. Our goal is to use this monitoring systems to find far more complex symptom patterns that are typically produced by IMSI Catchers.

2.1 Working Principles of a Mobile Phone Network

Mobile phone networks became much more complex over the years. Each new generation or access technology (e.g., 2G GSM, 3G UMTS, 4G LTE) introduced a new terminology which complicates the description in an access-technology-neutral fashion.

For example, the base station (the radio front end of the network) with roughly the same functionality is called *Base Transceiver Station* (BTS) in GSM, *Node B* in UMTS, and *evolved Node B* (eNodeB or eNB) in LTE. Likewise, a mobile phone is called *Mobile Station* (MS) in GSM and *User Equipment* (UE) in UMTS as well as LTE. However, apart from the radio layer and some distinct organizational differences, they have many similarities on higher (more abstract) levels. Regardless of the access technology, the network needs to know how and (roughly) where to reach every subscriber, even when they are idle. This is solved by grouping radio cells into *Location Areas* (GSM, UMTS), *Routing Areas* (GPRS, UMTS; a subdivision of a Location Area), or *Tracking Areas* (LTE). In the phone's idle state, the network only knows the Location/Routing/Tracking Area where the subscriber is located, but not the exact cell. The phone (MS, UE) can listen to the broadcast channel of any cell as an incoming phone call, message, or data triggers a paging of the subscriber in all cells of a Location/Routing/Tracking Area. Upon a received page, the phone will contact the network and request a dedicated (logical) channel for further communication, thus giving away its position on cell level.

Only if the UE/MS switches to another Location/Tracking Area, it will tell the network about it, using a *Location Update Request* (GSM, UMTS) or *Tracking Area Update* (LTE). This method substantially reduces the signaling traffic caused by the subscribers' mobility.

In general, all subscribers are not identified by their phone ID (the 14-digit *International Mobile Equipment Identity*, IMEI), but by their *Subscriber Identity Module* (SIM) on GSM, or *Universal Subscriber Identity Module* (USIM) on UMTS and LTE which provides a 15-digit unique *International Mobile Subscriber Identity* (IMSI). However, sending the IMSI over the air would make subscribers easily trackable. Therefore, the network frequently (re)assigns a *Temporary Mobile Subscriber Identity* (TMSI) that is used instead[1] of the IMSI on 2G and 3G. 4G extends the TMSI by multiple *Radio Network Temporary Identifiers* (RNTI) for different use cases (e.g., paging, random access). TMSIs are meant to be reassigned on Location/Tracking Area changes, and some networks even reassign them on every interaction (e.g., call, text message) between the phone (MS, UE) and the network.

On a Location/Tracking Area Update message the phone will (usually) transmit its current TMSI and the old Location Area Identity (LAI, consisting of the *Mobile Country Code* MCC, *Mobile Network Code* MNC, and the *Location Area Code* LAC on GSM and UMTS) or *Tracking Area Identity* (TAI, comprising MCC, MNC, and the *Tracking Area Code* TAC). The *Mobile Switching Center* (MSC) for a Location/Tracking Area can now fetch all the data about the subscriber from the old Location/Tracking Area and inform the central user database (*Home Location Register* HLR on GSM and UMTS, *Home Subscriber Server* HSS on LTE) about where to reach that subscriber from now on.

---

[1] Except for the very first initial registration.

Location/Tracking Area Update Messages are the Swiss army knife of the *Mobility Management* (MM) in mobile networks: A phone freshly turned on will first try to make a *Location/Tracking Area Update Request* (LUR, TAUR) using its last known (cached) values. If its TMSI hasn't expired and is valid in this Location/Tracking Area, the network will accept the phone. Otherwise it will trigger a re-authentication. Therefore, even a phone arriving on a plane from another continent will first try to perform an LUR/TAUR providing the LAI/TAI data from another network. This is intended, as it allows for national roaming and seamless handover of active calls across an international border. (In LTE, the network can additionally provide an individual set of Tracking Areas for each UE, so that a group of subscribers – e.g., on a train – do not perform a Tracking Area Update all at once.)

Additionally, a ME/UE will perform periodic Location/Tracking updates, even when not moved in an interval configured by the network (e.g., 24 h) to assure the network of its continued presence.

Periodically during operation and at shutdown, parts of the baseband state are stored on the SIM card and the phone itself. For example, instead of performing a full frequency scan for all receivable base stations at power on, the phone will first try the frequency range where it received signals from its mobile phone network before. Also, it will retry its old TMSI in an attempt to speed up the procedure. (After all, if the phone has not been offline for too long, it still could be valid.)

3 Capabilities of IMSI Catchers

In general, IMSI Catchers come in two variants: (i) a tracking or identifying IMSI Catcher and (ii) capturing or Man-in-the-Middle IMSI Catchers. The first read out specific data from a phone or launch a specific attack before releasing the phone back into the genuine network. This is useful for enumerating phones in the vicinity or check for a specific device in radio range. The latter holds the phone captured in its fake cell and can relay traffic to the outside world.

While IMSI Catchers originally exploit a specific vulnerability in 2G networks, they are still a relevant threat in 3G and LTE networks, for several reasons: First, the weakest-link principle applies. As long as users can be deliberately downgraded to a less secure system, the weakest link sets the limit. Additionally, it has been recently shown that IMSI Catchers are possible on 3G and 4G in either a tracking-only setup or for full traffic interception in combination with backbone attacks (SS7, Diameter). These protocols are often used for interconnection and roaming of phone calls, but also of cryptographic material such as keys. In the roaming case the remote network has to be able to fulfill the same cryptographic operations as the home network. Engel [19] also presented sole backbone attacks, but they are out of this paper's scope.

3.1 Access Technology

2G/GSM. The original IMSI Catcher was build for GSM. Originally used only for identifying users (tracking), later devices allowed full man-in-the-middle attacks. GSM networks are specifically easy to impersonate, as the standard does not require encryption nor support mutual authentication.

3G/UMTS. Recent datasheets [22] show (limited) 3G capabilities of commercial available IMSI Catchers. For man-in-the-middle attacks they often downgrade users to 2G and capture them there. Osipov and Zaitsev [35] presented a de-facto 3G IMSI Catcher by using a reverse engineered femtocell. They also discovered that contrary to the standard, many phones accept unauthenticated SMS messages or time synchronization.

4G/LTE. Similar to UMTS, tracking IMSI Catchers are possible and phones tend to ignore integrity for many messages [38].

3.2 Catching Capability

Tracking or Identification Mode (Catch and Release). In this mode, the IMSI Catcher is luring phones into its fake cell, reading out IMSI and IMEI and pushing them back into the real network. For a target with known IMSI or IMEI this method can be used to check his/her presence in vicinity (omnidirectional antenna) or position (directional antenna). When used with a directional antenna, this can also be used to (visually) correlate a person to his/her IMSI and IMEI (see Sect. 5).

Capturing or MITM Mode (Catch and Hold). In this case the MS/UE is held in the cell and not pushed back into the real network. There exist several methods to decrypt, relay, and/or modify the traffic (see Sect. 6).

Passive Monitoring. This mode can be used e.g., after a target has been identified. Since the attacker does not have control over the phone it can switch to different cells and Location/Tracking Areas anytime. It has to follow the target across different frequencies and cells.

3.3 Cryptographic Capabilities

On GSM an attacker can choose between several methods. The easiest one, is to downgrade the client side and the network side to A5/0 (i.e. no encryption). However, many networks started prohibiting clients using A5/0. This can be problematic if legacy clients do not support any encryption. The GSM export-grade cypher A5/2 has been broken by Goldberg et al. in 1999 [23] and phased out by GSMA (GSM Association) by 2006 [25]. Barkham et al. presented a

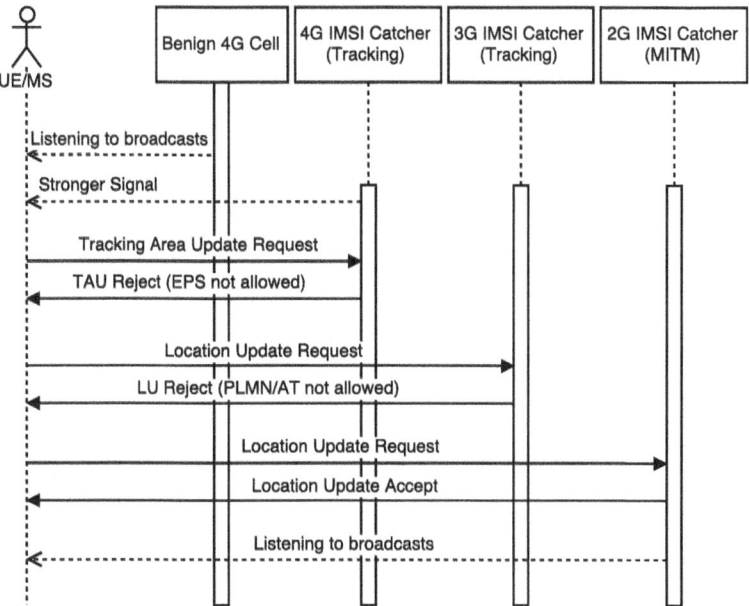

Fig. 1. Downgrade attack from 4G to 2G using *Access Technology not allowed* messages (simplified)

realtime ciphertext-only attack on A5/2 [10] in 2008. However, the GSM standard cipher A5/1 is also not secure; a number on publications [10,18,26] showed severe weaknesses and later 2 TB rainbow tables for decryption within seconds became freely available [29]. Thus, we must assume [3], that reasonable new IMSI Catcher are able to decrypt A5/1 and A5/2. Recently, many operators implemented A5/3 – a backport of the KATSUMI based UMTS cipher – for which no practical attacks are known. However, only newer handsets support this mode (cf. Fig. 4), and are easily downgrade-able by a fake cell (Sect. 3.4 below).

For UMTS and LTE encryption no practical cryptanalytic attacks are known, and mutual authentication is needed for (most) transactions. However, vulnerabilities in the SS7/Diameter exchange between providers allow the recovery of sessions keys [19,34] and therefore either decrypting traffic or impersonating a network.

3.4 Access Technology Downgrade Capability

For UMTS and LTE a downgrade to a less secure access technology (such as GSM) is also an option.

Jamming. A simple but brutal way is to jam the frequency band. In an attempt to restore connection to the network, the phone will try other (potentially less secure) access technology: e.g., jamming the UMTS band will encourage phones to connect via GSM. Longer jamming sessions will show up in the operator's network quality metrics and allow radio technicians to pin-point the source. Therefore, this method is only suitable for short term operations. In general, an attacker might strive for more subtle and less detectable ways.

Spoofing No-Authorization for a Specific Access Technology. A BTS, NodeB and eNodeB has the ability to deny access to a specific cell, location/tracking area or access technology for a number of reasons (e.g., no resources left, no subscription for a specific service, no authorization, etc.). Depending on the error code from the network, the phone will not retry and revert to other methods (e.g., another access technology) [8,9,24]. An error code for a permanent error will be cached by the MS/UE until next reboot. 3GPP defined rules on how to allow a network operator to expel a mobile from one access technology e.g., for LTE [9,38, c.f. reject cause #7] or 3G [24]. Therefore, a chain of tracking IMSI Catchers denying access and forcing a cell re-selection with another access technology can downgrade a client step by step (Fig. 1). Once arrived at 2G/GSM without mutual authentication the attacker can capture the phone and hold it in the fake cell.

These Location/Tracking Update Reject messages are intentionally not covered by the mutual authentication in UMTS and LTE, as a (foreign) network must be able to reject a user that has no subscription or no roaming agreement with the home network.

4 Design and Data Sources

For the development of our detection methods, we tested the interaction of 22 phones between an IMSI Catcher based on an USRP [20] and a mobile phone network. After that, we ware able to retrieve log and PCAP files from the mobile phone network's monitoring system for analysis. Based on that we developed detection strategies and implemented them. We tested them on real monitoring data and counter checked them with statistics from the real network.

Based on our NDA and the secrecy of telecommunications laws we had to work on site and where not allowed to take any actual data outside of the building. Additionally, the limitations of the current monitoring systems only allowed us to retrieve data based on simple queries and a specific buffer size. For example, we could either retrieve data for a specific IMSI (e.g. our test SIM card) or a specific cell for longer periods of time, or a specific transaction type nationwide but only for a short time period (e.g. minutes), but not both.

The problem lies in the scattered transactions in mobile phone networks that forbid a natural global view on the status of a network. Thus, state-of-the-art mobile network monitoring put probes next to the MSCs which preselect and extract key values out of the signaling traffic. This signaling traffic is heavily depended on the access technology. A database cluster collects this data and makes it available based on simple queries on the extracted features. This system has to deal with high loads: e.g. just the Location Updates for 2G and 3G peak at roughly 150,000 transaction per minute during daytime, whereas the 3G transaction are more complex and consist of more packets than on 2G.

The number of returned transactions on a query is limited by a (rather small) return buffer. However, data can be retrieved and reassembled to complete transactions which include everything from the initial mobile request, its way through the network instances up to the database access at the HLR and back to the mobile. This data can be exported to text and PCAP files for further analysis. Basically, any data extraction has to be reimplemented for each access technology. Even if the hight level behavior (e.g. Location Updates) are quite similar, the signaling traffic is completely different on a technical level.

This setup sets limits in the ability to analyze data for complex anomalies such as finding network areas with higher than usual non-adjacent neighbor location updates (see Sect. 6.3). Therefore, we tested our programs and made our statistics on data sets consisting of several thousands up to 47,000 transactions, based on the type of transaction. With small changes in the monitoring system (e.g. extraction and indexing of additional values by the probes) our solutions below can work on much larger data sets or on real-time data (e.g. they can request a much more focused selection of packets, and don't have to filter them themselves).

5 Tracking IMSI Catcher

A tracking (or identifying) IMSI Catcher does not hold a mobile device in the fake cell, but drops it back into the real network immediately. For an attacker it is advantageous to simulate a new Cell-ID as well as a new LAC as this will always trigger an active communication (Location/Tracking Update) from the attracted mobile device.

Simulation of a new Cell without a LAC leaves the attacker without knowledge which phones are currently listening to the broadcast channel. He/she could only page previously known subscribers (based on IMSI) to verify their existence. Additionally, it will disturb the availability of the attracted phones for the complete operating time of the IMSI Catcher.

Unless for very specific operations, for the above mentioned reasons, an attacker will most likely choose a fake Location/Tracking Area Code (LAC) (or one that is unused in the geographical area) so that every mobile phone attaching to this cell initiates a Location/Tracking Update procedure. This informs the attacker of every phone entering the cell, gives him/her the ability to download identification data and then reject the Location/Tracking Update. Depending on the error cause used, the phone might return later (temporary error), or put the LAC or MNC on a blacklist (permanent error). An attacker wishing to enumerate all phones again simply chooses another LAC. This procedure disturbs each phone for less than a second per scan and has no major implications on availability.

Figure 2 (upper part) presents the message flow. Known IMSI Catchers download the IMSI and IMEI since both are easily retrievable. The IMEI is also

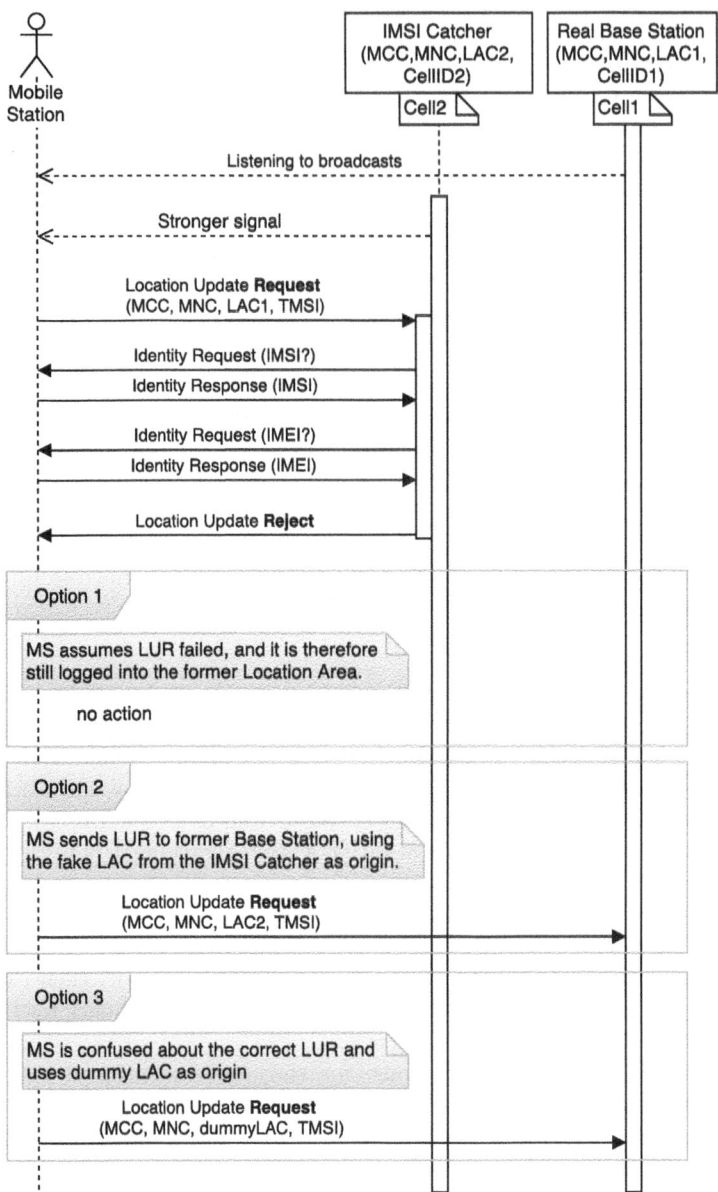

Fig. 2. A tracking IMSI Catcher identifies a phone and drops it back into the real network.

commonly downloaded by genuine networks in order to apply the correct protocol (workaround) policy based on the phone model.

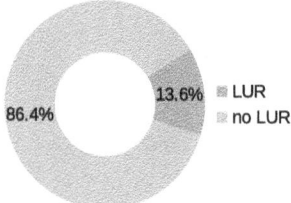
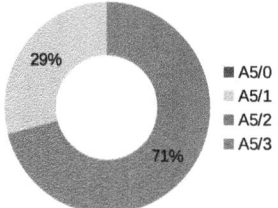

Fig. 3. Phone models that produce a new LUR after a Location Update Reject (n = 22 test phones)

Fig. 4. Cipher usage on 2G nationwide (n = 7402 call setups)

5.1 Detecting Phones When Reattaching to the Original Network

From the operator's point of view, a phone leaving the network for a fake cell is invisible. If there should be a page request in the mean time, the phone will not receive it. However, since the phone is away for only a short period of time, it will likely receive a retransmit of that page request.

Once the phone receives a *Location Update Reject* message, it has three options (cf. Fig. 2):

1. Assume that it is still known by the network at its old location. Therefore, no new message is needed.
2. A new Location Update Request is sent to the network using the IMSI Catcher's Location Area Code as origin (see also Sect. 6).
3. A new Location Update Request is sent using a dummy Location Area Code, since the last LAC value isn't valid.

We tested 22 different phone models[2] for their behavior after they dropped back into the genuine network in 2G (Fig. 3). 86 % produced no Location Update (Option 1) and 14 % generated[3] a Location Update Request with a dummy origin-LAC 0xFFFE (65534). The special values 0 and 0xFFFE are reserved when no valid LAC is available by the MS/UE [1,7]. Additionally, on GSM many phones also use 0×8001 (32769).

However, these dummy LACs are no direct indicator for an IMSI Catcher even for this minority of phones, as they are used quite regularly. In a dataset containing all nationwide 2G Location Update Requests within one minute (daytime) we found 9.1 % of all transactions using a dummy LAC and 11.1 % using no LAC at all (see Fig. 5a) without any geographical pattern. The numbers for 3G (Fig. 5b) are smaller: 4 % of Location Update Requests contained a dummy LAC ($0 \times FFFE$ or 0×0000) from the same network. 1 % contained also dummy values for the Mobile Country Code (MCC) and Mobile Network Code (MNC).

---

[2] Nokia Lumia 920.1, E71, 6310, 6150, 3210, 3710A-1, LG Nexus 4, Nexus 5, Apple IPhone 4, IPhone 6, Nexus One, Motorola Moto G2, Moto G XT1032, Samsung Galaxy Nexus, Galaxy S3, Galaxy Xcover2, Galaxy S5, Sony Xperia Z2-SCR10, BG Aquaris E4.5 Ubuntu Phone, Kyocera Torque KS-701, Sony Ericsson ST17I.

[3] All Nokia models introduced before 2000.

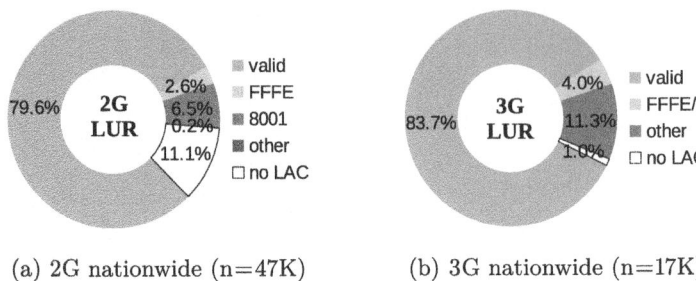

(a) 2G nationwide (n=47K)   (b) 3G nationwide (n=17K)

Fig. 5. Origin LAC provided at Location Update Requests. *Valid* means that the LAC is within the local LAC plan. *0, 0x8001*, and *0xFFFE* are literal (dummy) values. *Other* are LACs from outside the network (e.g. international or national roaming, accepted and rejected). *No LAC* describes the requests that do not provide a valid LAC or that provide dummy Values for MNC and MCC as well (such as 0×00 or $0 \times FF$)

64 % of our test phones generated a *GPRS Attach*[4] request within the next two minutes, if and only if it had a data connection before and did not have an additional WiFi connection. This is due to the fact that our test setup did not indicate GPRS support for the fake cell. Such a GRPS Attach request is nothing extraordinary and happens regularly (42 % of all Location Updates on a real network contain such a header) for example if a phone drops out of WiFi and needs an Internet connection.

18 % of this *GPRS Attach* messages had the *No Valid TMSI available* flag set. However, on a real network 4.5 % of LUR messages have this flag set.

6 Capturing IMSI Catcher

An IMSI Catcher of this type holds the mobile in the cell and can therefore man-in-the-middle any transaction, and has control over the mobile phone by means of any network management commands (Fig. 6).

6.1 Detection of Cipher Downgrades

A man-in-the-middle IMSI Catcher has to forward the traffic to the network. An easy way, is to tap into the cipher negotiation sequence and change the set of supported ciphers. The easiest choice for attackers is A5/0 (no encryption) and A5/2 (the weakened export-variant of A5/1), as described in Sect. 3.3. However, many networks (incl. T-Mobile Austria) banned these ciphers for years.

Instead, they started to support the A5/3 cipher [2]. On GSM this is the only cipher without (publicly) available rainbow tables or other decryption methods.

---

[4] Technically, this is an Location Update Request with *Origin LAC* set to the current LAC and an optional GRPS header with the Attach-Bit set.

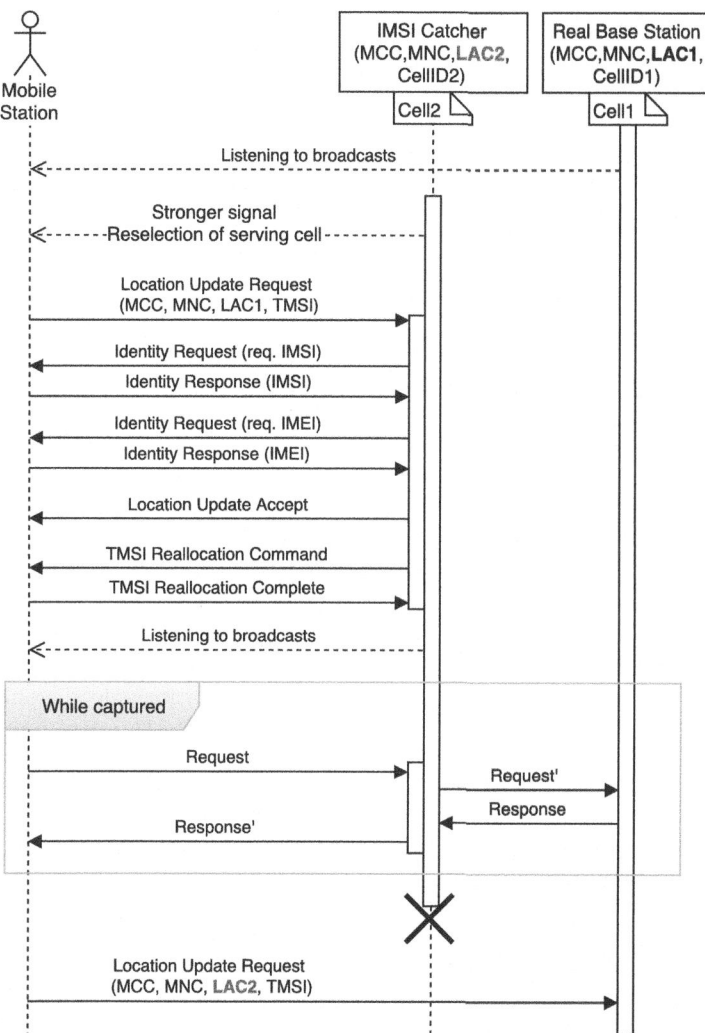

Fig. 6. A man-in-the-middle IMSI Catcher identifies a phone and withholding it from the real network. During fall-back into the real network, the captures phone gives away the LAC of the IMSI Catcher.

However, many MS still do not support this mode. On our network, in September 2015, 29 % used A5/1 and 71 % A5/3 (Fig. 4, n = 7402). Other cipher modes where prohibited in this network.

An operator-run database of {IMEI, highest-used-cipher}-tuples provides the basis to detect cipher downgrades. This database is updated on first contact with the network and whenever a device uses a higher ranked[5] encryption than the

---

[5] $A5/0 < A5/2 < A5/1 < A5/3$.

one stored. As long as there is no SS7/Diameter standard on exchanging this form of information, every operator has to run their own database (or include it into the HLR/HSS). Once the highest available cipher of a device is established, the network should not accept a lower one, or at least generate a warning. Thus, making a downgrade attack visible to the operator except when the user is attacked on the very first contact with a new network. Except for a firmware bug, there is no reason why a device should stop supporting higher cipher levels.

6.2 Detection of Relayed Traffic

The most compatible and least interfering way for a capturing IMSI Catcher to operate is to relay all traffic. If it is encrypted with A5/1 or A5/2 the decryption can be done separately, otherwise it has to be downgraded. Based on enough traces, the session key K_c can be reconstructed [27,29]. In conjunction with another vulnerabilities (e.g., weak COMP128), also the secret authentication key K_i can be read and the SIM card cloned [12]. Once K_c is known, this allows an IMSI Catcher to decrypt A5/3 as well, since the K_c is used for all ciphers. For SIM cards with only a 64 bit key, the K_c is doubled $K = \{K_c||K_c\}$ to 128 bit and therefore allows decryption of UMTS as well[6].

We tested if the analysis of the round-trip times can be a good measure to uncover traffic relay. Therefore, we analyzed authorization round trips in the wild of 4165 random transactions within one minute, nationwide. The histogram in Fig. 7 shows a high deviation ($\bar{x} = 0.586$ sec, $\delta = 0.334$) of response times

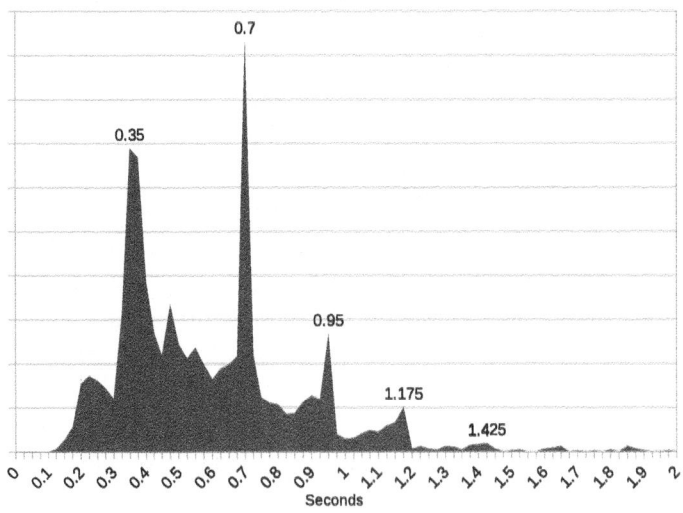

Fig. 7. Authorization round trip time: distribution of time between *Authentication Request* and *Authentication Response* on a real network.

---

[6] The attacker has to brute-force the 48-bit sequence number, though.

with a notable retransmission interval of about 0.25 s. We estimate that a well-designed traffic-forwarding IMSI catcher could relay the traffic in 100 ms or less, thus being far from statistically significant in single instances.

Further analysis presented vast differences between manufacturers as well as handset types. Based on the *Type Allocation Code* (TAC)[7] we run independent nationwide collections. Figure 8 shows 12 diverse popular handset types and highlights three different iPhones to illustrate their different behavior (based on an average of 3,400 transactions per phone type). Since this values have a much smaller standard deviation (e.g., $\sigma_{GalaxyS4} = 0.198$, $\sigma_{IPhone3gs} = 0.200$, $\sigma_{IPhone4s} = 0.206$), they are a better basis to detect relay delays (i.e. average authorization round trip time increases on multiple occasions for a single user). Additionally, a provider side detection can correlate such changes geographically (i.e. average authorization round trip time increases in a geographical area).

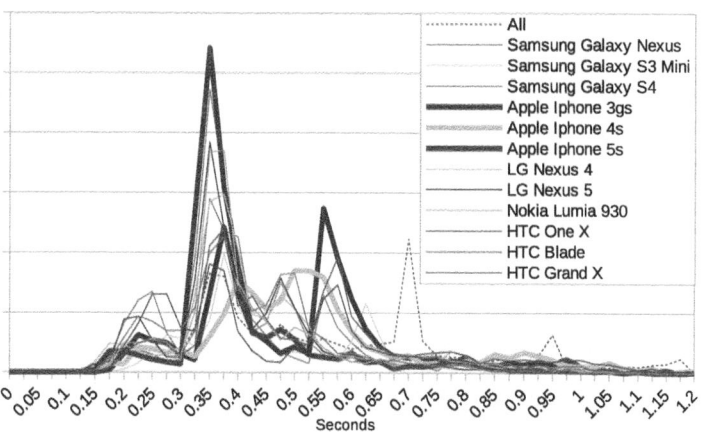

Fig. 8. Normalized distribution of authorization round trip time broken up by phone models. Three Apple phones highlighted to show the distinct differences in their authorization response time. ($n \approx 3400$ for each phone type)

6.3 Detection of Unknown, Unusual or Implausible Origin-LAI/TAI in Location Update Requests

Eventually, every IMSI Catcher victim falls back into the genuine network (Fig. 6). During this step, the LAC of the attacker is leaked back into the real network[8]. As stated above, it is favorable for an attacker to choose an unused LAC as this forces

---

[7] TAC are the first 8 digits of an IMEI that encode the manufacturer and phone model. Popular models might end up with multiple assigned TACs. This is somewhat similar to the assigned OUI prefix in Ethernet MAC addresses: they encode the manufacturer.

[8] See Sects. 7.3 and 7.4 for further discussion and possible mitigations.

every victim to actively contact the fake base station on entrance and therefore inform the attacker about its capture. This LAC is either completely unknown in the genuine network or far away.

We investigated the possibility of creating shadow instances that follow every location area update and reject implausible location changes. While the current monitoring infrastructure does not allow to monitor all location updates nationwide for all mobile phones (Sect. 7.3), we scaled down and implemented a prototype that is able to follow individual UE/MS through different access technologies based on PCAP files from the core network. The two main investigated properties are (i) the correctness and completeness of location update trails and (ii) the geographical plausibility of location updates (i.e. only adjacent locations).

The *correctness and completeness of location update trails* means that location trails form an uninterrupted chain. A gap would be a strong hint for a visited LAC to not be under the control of the operator. The *geographical plausibility* checks if updates only occur between geographically neighboring locations. This neighbor property does not have to be derived geographically, but can be established statistically (i.e. recording frequent location updates between Location Areas). Unless operators agreed on national roaming, the phone stays on the home network, so no operator collaboration is necessary.

In the following evaluation we discovered a number of corner cases that complicate the interpretation of the results.

Power on at a New Location. UE/MS not always correctly detach from a network when turned off (e.g. battery loss, temporary reception loss during power off). At the next power on, the UE/MS will use the previous LAC as origin for a location update. Imagine this plausible case as depicted in Fig. 9: A flight passenger turns off the phone at takeoff in one city, but the *IMSI deattach* message was not produced or did not arrive at the network. After landing, the passenger turns the phone back on during the train ride from the airport to the city. In most cases, the phone will send a location update to the network as if it just passed the border between the two location areas. This even happens after intercontinental flights. Airport cells could be whitelisted to some extent, but they will not catch all cases (such as in the example above).

Because such (tunneled) location update are indistinguishable from a direct location changes, they are not immediately a red flag.

Additionally, road and railway tunnels also offer geographical shortcuts, but – unlike plane routes – the ends of the tunnel only connect two points and will be statistically assigned as neighbors, since a large number of passengers traverse without turning off their phones.

Old Baseband State Restoration. Phones regularly and at certain events save parts of the baseband state information to non-volatile memory. For faster boot

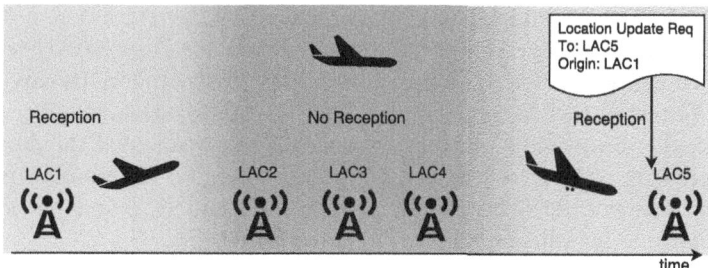

Fig. 9. Location update tunneling effect: Because a detach message is not guaranteed, location/tracking area updates happen between non-adjacent cells.

times, the phone can facilitate this information (e.g. already knows the frequency range of the preferred operator and does not has to scan the whole frequency range). This includes the last known LAC.

One of our test phones had a defective power button which lead to random reboots. In the traces we discovered that the phone sometimes used obsolete LAC information as origin (i.e. reused a LAC as origin a second time, because another location change was not recorded properly before reboot).

6.4 Detection of a Access Technology Downgrade

As described in Sect. 3.4 and Fig. 1, access technology downgrades are easy to perform and included in todays commercially available IMSI Catchers [22]. A phone camping on 2G even though 3G or 4G should be available in the area is not a strong indicator. In some cases, structural properties can lead to better reception of certain frequency ranges (e.g., 2G on lower frequencies is usually better receivable underground). On the other hand, a MS/UE can be set intentionally to use 2G only for power conservation. A provider could install an application on the SIM to monitor the access technology and location updates; however, this is out of scope for this paper.

7 Discussion

We identified strong and weak indicators based on the statistics of certain features in real-world data. Strong indicators have low potential for false positives.

A **per device (IMEI) database of the highest-used cipher** can reliably detect cipher downgrades or deactivation of ciphering. Additionally, we have shown that mobile phones **leak the (fake) LAC of the capturing IMSI Catcher to the real network**. This case can trivially be detected based the on analysis of Location Update Requests. If the attacker misuses a genuine LAC, it can still be detected by a **consistence check of the Location Update trail**. Based on certain corner cases, the latter has the potential for false positives

(LUR tunnel effect, restoration of old baseband states) and therefore needs to be backed up by additional geographical, temporal and subscriber based correlation.

Another method is the **transmission delay introduced by an MITM attack**. We tested this technique based on the authorization round trip times. In general, the deviation is quite large, but can be narrowed if the device type is considered as well. Every device has a very specific distribution of round trip times. However, for a statistically significant result (e.g. for a device under attack), multiple measurements have to be collected.

From the provider point of view, the hardest attack to detect is that of a tracking-only IMSI Catcher. Except for a few very old phones, this particular attack does not produce any messages in the core network. It has still to be explored if certain frequency-monitoring functions on BTS, NodeBs, and eNodeBs can be repurposed to detect such rouge base stations.

7.1 Ethical Considerations

As described in the research set up (Sect. 4) we have used real data only under very strict conditions to comply with ethical and legislative requirements. We have only worked on signaling data and never had access to user data or personal subscriber information.

7.2 Comparison with Client Detection Methods

Operator detection of IMSI Catchers does not supersede client detection (c.f. Sect. 8.1). It complements it and gives the operator the opportunity to monitor such attacks in its network regardless of precautions by individual subscribers. However, since the detection schemes can only find phones that are either under the control of an attacker - or just switched back to the genuine network - the operator can only warn the user in question post-attack.

On the other hand, client based techniques give the user the ability to detect a current attack against his/her very device. On tracking IMSI Catchers this technique provides better detection rates.

7.3 Limitations

The current implementation of our detection methods is based on the old somewhat limited monitoring system deployed in the network. It can filter some pre-extracted of each packet and transaction against a query containing a limited set of operators and literal values (i.e. filter by a specific cell, IMSI, IMEI, protocol type, etc.). It can not compare between cells or apply more complex filters. Additionally, the return buffer size is limited to 10 K–30 K results, depending on the search mode. This limits our current implementations to single users (or single cells) at a time. This is the reason we could not run a nation wide search so far.

7.4 Future Work

Our results show that detection from the operator side is possible and tested its usefulness within the limitations of the current monitoring system. We suggest that parameters such as ciphering and origin LAC in Location Area Updates should be extracted directly at the probes and made available. This pre-selection step will eliminate current limitations. For example, it will allow to search for inconsistencies in used ciphers, based on the IMEI (or TAC). Additionally, a new monitoring system based on Apache Hadoop is currently in development that is expected to remove most limitations of the current system.

With the large number of dummy LACs used by phones, one can wonder if an attacker could use dummy LACs such as 0xFFFE for masking their existence. Another way, to mask the fake LAC of an IMSI Catcher is, to announce a neighbor frequency occupied by a second IMSI Catcher with a reasonable LAC. While doubling the hardware costs for an attacker, this might whitewash the *Origin LAC* field used in Sect. 6.3. Both ideas need further testing with end devices to confirm or deny their practical feasibility. As discussed before (Sect. 6.4), a SIM card application can monitor and report certain network parameters back to the network (e.g., keep a local copy of a CellID/LAC trail) and detect both cases. However, over time, many different cards from different vendors have been acquired so developing and maintaining such an application poses a financial burden and an operational risk.

Furthermore, we plan to refine the timing models used in Sect. 6.2 to become more accurate and create better models for timing delays introduced by traffic relaying.

8 Related Work

8.1 IMSI Catcher Detection

So far, IMSI Catcher detection has almost exclusively been tackled from the clients' point of view. Malete and Nohl first developed a solution for OsmocomBB phones, and later on for rooted Android phones with a very specific Qualcomm chipset [31,40]. Other applications replicated similar client side detection without the need for a rooted phone [15,37].

Van den Broek et al. proposed a pseudo-random IMSI that will not allow others than the home operator to distinguish particular users [13]. However, this will introduce a higher overhead in the roaming case and needs to be extended to cover cases where IMSI Catchers use additional identification numbers (such as IMEI).

Van Do et al. are so far the only ones to look at the provider side [16]. Their solution is based on encryption elimination detection and anomalies such as disappearance of a large group of phones in a geographical area, fed into a machine learning system. However, their approach has limited applicability, for real world networks: Disabling encryption is only found in older capturing IMSI catchers and disappearance detection has a latency up to 24 h – the time scale of periodic location updates (i.e. the mobile phone's periodic reassurance to the network). This will only detect IMSI Catchers operating for an extended amount of time.

8.2 Working Principle of IMSI Catchers

Osipov and Zaitsev reverse-engineered a Huawei Femtocell and were able to create a 3G IMSI Catcher and test phone implementations for messages where integrity is ignored [35]. Shaik et al. researched 4G IMSI Catchers and their possibilities [38]. Dunkelman et al. did research on the KATSUMI algorithm on which A5/3 is based, but the attack is not practical in real-world networks [17].

8.3 Related Attacks on Cellular Devices

There are many attacks that are relevant as they are performed directly or in conjunction with an IMSI Catcher.

SS7 MSISDN Lookup. IMSI Catching does not reveal the telephone number (known as *Mobile Station International Subscriber Directory Number*, MSISDN) of the subscriber. If not blocked by a firewall, an attacker with access to the international interconnect network using Signaling System 7 (SS7) can request subscriber information based on the IMSI (or the TMSI), just as any roaming network would do [19].

SS7 Session Keys. An attacker with access to the international interconnect network based on SS7 is able to retrieve RAN session keys [19,34]. The key retrieval is a legitimate function required for roaming support: The roaming network needs to authenticate on behalf of the home network. SS7 stateful firewalls (e.g., keep track if and where a user is roaming) can block such requests.

SIM Card Rooting. Several SIM card attacks described by Nohl et al. [33] have been blocked by the network operators worldwide. However, an IMSI Catcher is directly communicating with the UE/MS. This gives the attacker the ability to perform attacks such as the retrieval of SIM card application keys, eventually giving him/her the control over the installation of new SIM card applications on the victims device.

SIM Card Cloning. In 1998, Briceno, Goldberg, and Wagner reverse engineered and broke the COMP128 [11] key derivation algorithm which enabled cloning of GSM SIM cards of many network operators [12]. In 2015, Liu et al. [30] found that AES-based MILENAGE algorithm on some USIM implementations is prone to power-based side-channel analysis and thus giving way to clone these cards as well. Unfortunately, they never named the manufacturers of the USIMs.

Unauthenticated SMS. 2G as well as some 3G devices [35] allow the reception of SMS messages while captured by the rouge base station. The results for 3G are somewhat surprising, since this is actually prohibited by current standards. However, many phones do accept these messages nonetheless. SMS in 4G works entirely differently and is therefore not affected by this vulnerability, although recent results [41] show that vulnerabilities exist in other constellations.

Presidential Alert Cell Broadcast. A feature dubbed *presidential alert messages* [6] is a special form of short messages that cannot be suppressed and interrupt the phone in whichever state it is to be shown to the user. A fake base station can send out this kind of messages.

GPS Lookup Initialized by Network. The *Radio Resource Location Services (LCS) protocol* (RRLP) is an extension [4] to GSM and UMTS that allows the network (real or fake) to trigger a GPS localization on the phone and submitting the location back to the network. Harald Welte [42] demonstrated that this happens without any authentication.

Measurement Triangulation. The network has the ability to request measurement reports to other cells in the vicinity. A fake base station can use these reports to estimate the position of the phone based on signal levels and known positions of the cells. This is also possible on 4G [38].

Disable GPS. Because of (former) Egyptian regulations prohibiting the usage of GPS, some older phones (iPhone [21], Nokia [5]) are known to disable the GPS receiver when either associated or just in the vicinity of a network using the Egyptian Mobile Country Code. An attacker can use this to disable the GPS receiver on certain phones.

9 Conclusion

IMSI Catchers are still a major problem for todays networks: (i) Tracking IMSI Catchers work directly on GSM, UMTS, and LTE networks as Location/Tracking Update Rejects are excluded from cryptographic message integrity checks. Mutual authentication only prevent plain capturing IMSI Catchers. (ii) These reject messages can be used to downgrade a phone until the next reboot to a lower access technology (e.g. GSM) without mutual authentication. Therefore, the weakest-link principle applies.

In this paper we analyzed the different types of IMSI Catchers and their working principles as well as if and how they can be detected from the network operator's side. Due to our cooperation with an European carrier we have been able to systematically perform real-world experiments and test our detection methods on real world-data.

Strong indicators we identified are for example the usage of invalid LACs (which are transmitted by the phones when they fall back to the genuine network after an attack), or the usage of weak ciphers to detect downgrade attacks for devices that were previously able to use strong ones. Additionally we showed that a number of weak indicators can be correlated geographically, temporally, and on subscriber basis e.g., for detecting targeted attacks, similar to current fraud detection schemes used by credit card companies. This includes fingerprinting devices based on profiles, unusual movements, and implausible location update trails. We also addressed corner cases and how to deal with them.

As mobile networks where initially designed with the reduction of signaling traffic in mind, not all of the necessary information is readily available for analysis, or even not collected centrally and in a scalable fashion. Some of the indicators we identified therefore demand changes in the monitoring systems currently used in such networks. However, based on already available data from a real-world mobile network, we were able to show the practical applicability for multiple of our methods.

Acknowledgments. We want to thank the whole crew of the core network security team and radio access network team at T-Mobile. They have been a great help. We are very grateful for the reviewers' comments and help to improve the quality of the paper and point to new interesting future work opportunities. This research was partially funded by the COMET K1 program through the Austrian Research Promotion Agency (FFG).

References

1. Digital cellular telecommunications system (Phase 2+); Interworking between Phase 1 infrastructure and Phase 2 Mobile Stations (MS). http://www.etsi.org/deliver/etsi_ts/101600_101699/101644/05.01.00_60/ts_101644v050100p.pdf
2. GSM security map. http://gsmmap.org/
3. How the NSA pinpoints a mobile device. http://apps.washingtonpost.com/g/page/world/how-the-nsa-pinpoints-a-mobile-device/645/. Accessed 30 Oct 2015
4. Digital cellular telecommunications system (Phase 2+); Location Services (LCS); Mobile Station (MS) - Serving Mobile Location Centre (SMLC) Radio Resource LCS Protocol (RRLP), 3GPP TS 04.31 version 8.18.0 (2007). http://www.etsi.org/deliver/etsi_ts/101500_101599/101527/08.18.00_60/ts_101527v081800p.pdf
5. Egypt tries to control the use of GPS by banning except with individual licences (2008). http://www.balancingact-africa.com/news/en/issue-no-429/top-story/egypt-tries-to-contr/en
6. Emergency Communications (EMTEL); European Public Warning System (EU-ALERT) using the Cell Broadcast Service (2012). http://www.etsi.org/deliver/etsi_ts/102900_102999/102900/01.01.01_60/ts_102900v010101p.pdf
7. Digital cellular telecommunications system (Phase 2+); Universal Mobile Telecommunications System (UMTS); Numbering, addressing and identification (2014). http://www.etsi.org/deliver/etsi_ts/123000_123099/123003/12.04.01_60/ts_123003v120401p.pdf
8. 3rd Generation Partnership Project: Non-Access-Stratum (NAS) Functions related to Mobile Station (MS) in Idle Mode, 3GPP TS 23.122 v8.2.0

9. 3rd Generation Partnership Project: Technical Specification Group Core Network and Terminals; Non-Access-Stratum (NAS) protocol for Evolved Packet System (EPS), 3GPP TS 24.301
10. Barkan, E., Biham, E., Keller, N.: Instant ciphertext-only cryptanalysis of GSM encrypted communication. J. Cryptol. **21**(3), 392–429 (2008)
11. Briceno, M., Goldberg, I., Wagner, D.: An implementation of the GSM A3A8 algorithm. (Specifically, COMP128.). http://www.scard.org/gsm/a3a8.txt. Accessed 24 Jun 2016
12. Briceno, M., Goldberg, I., Wagner, D.: GSM Cloning. http://www.isaac.cs.berkeley.edu/isaac/gsm.html. Accessed 24 Jun 2016
13. van den Broek, F., Verdult, R., de Ruiter, J.: Defeating IMSI catchers. In: 22nd ACM Conference on Computer and Communications Security (CCS 2015), pp. 340–351. ACM (2015)
14. Paget, C. (Kristin Paget): Practical Cellphone Spying. In: DEFCON 19 (2010)
15. Dabrowski, A., Pianta, N., Klepp, T., Mulazzani, M., Weippl, E.: IMSI-Catch me if you can: IMSI-catcher-catchers. In: Proceedings of the Annual Computer Security Applications Conference (ACSAC 2014). ACM, December 2014
16. van Do, T., Nguyen, H.T., Momchil, N., et al.: Detecting IMSI-catcher using soft computing. In: Berry, M.W., Mohamed, A.H., Yap, B.W. (eds.) Soft Computing in Data Science. CCIS, vol. 545, pp. 129–140. Springer, Heidelberg (2015)
17. Dunkelman, O., Keller, N., Shamir, A.: A practical-time attack on the A5/3 cryptosystem used in third generation GSM telephony. IACR Cryptology ePrint Archive 2010, 13 (2010)
18. Ekdahl, P., Johansson, T.: Another attack on A5/1. IEEE Trans. Inf. Theor. **49**(1), 284–289 (2003)
19. Engel, T.: SS7: Locate. Track. Manipulate, at 31C3 (2014). https://events.ccc.de/congress/2014/Fahrplan/events/6249.html. Accessed 30 Oct 2015
20. Ettus Research: Universal Software Radio Peripheral. https://www.ettus.com/product
21. Farivar, C.: Apple removes GPS functionality from Egyptian iPhones (2008). http://www.macworld.com/article/1137410/Apple_removes_GPS_func.html
22. Gamma Group: 3G-GSM Interctiopn and Target Location. Sales brochure. https://info.publicintelligence.net/Gamma-GSM.pdf. Accessed 2 Nov 2015
23. Goldberg, I., Wagner, D., Green, L.: The (Real-Time) Cryptanalysis of A5/2. In: Rump Session of Crypto 1999 (1999)
24. GSM Association: IR.50 2G 2.5G 3G Roaming v4.0 (2008). http://www.gsma.com/newsroom/all-documents/ir-50-2g2-5g3g-roaming/. Accessed 25 Sep 2015
25. Prohibiting A5/2 in mobile stations and other clarifications regarding A5 algorithm support. http://www.3gpp.org/ftp/tsg_sa/TSG_SA/TSGS_37/Docs/SP-070671.zip
26. Güneysu, T., Kasper, T., Novotny, M., Paar, C., Rupp, A.: Cryptanalysis with COPACOBANA. IEEE Trans. Comput. **57**(11), 1498–1513 (2008)
27. Steve, H.D.: Cracking GSM. In: Black Hat DC, March 2008 (2008)
28. Joachim, F., Rainer, B.: Method for identifying a mobile phone user or for eavesdropping on outgoing calls, patent, Rohde & Schwarz, EP1051053 (2000)
29. SR Labs: Kraken: A5/1 Decryption Rainbow Tables. via Bittorent (2010). https://opensource.srlabs.de/projects/a51-decrypt. Accessed 12 Nov 2015
30. Liu, J., Yu, Y., Standaert, F.X., Guo, Z., Gu, D., Sun, W., Ge, Y., Xie, X.: Small tweaks do not help: differential power analysis of MILENAGE implementations in 3G/4G USIM cards. In: Pernul, G., Ryan, P.Y.A., Weippl, E. (eds.) ESORICS 2015. LNCS, vol. 9326, pp. 468–480. Springer, Heidelberg (2015)

31. Malette, L.: Catcher Catcher. https://opensource.srlabs.de/projects/mobile-network-assessment-tools/wiki/CatcherCatcher. Accessed 12 Nov 2015
32. Muncaster, P.: Chinese cops cuff 1,500 in fake base station spam raid. The Register, 26 March 2014. http://www.theregister.co.uk/2014/03/26/spam_text_china_clampdown_police/
33. Nohl, K.: Rooting SIM cards. In: Blackhat (2013)
34. Nohl, K.: Mobile self-defense, 31C3 (2014). https://events.ccc.de/congress/2014/Fahrplan/events/6122.html. Accessed 30 Oct 2015
35. Osipov, A., Zaitsev, A.: Adventures in Femtoland: 350 Yuan for invaluable fun. In: Black Hat USA 2015, August 2015
36. Pell, S.K., Soghoian, C.: Your secret stingray's no secret anymore: the vanishing government monopoly over cell phone surveillance and its impact on national security and consumer privacy. Harvard J. Law Technol. **28**(1) (2014)
37. SecUpwN (Pseudonym, Maintainer): Android IMSI-Catcher Detector. https://secupwn.github.io/Android-IMSI-Catcher-Detector/. Accessed 12 Nov 2015
38. Shaik, A., Borgaonkar, R., Asokan, N., Niemi, V., Seifert, J.: Practical attacks against privacy and availability in 4G/LTE mobile communication systems (2015). http://arxiv.org/abs/1510.07563
39. Solnik, M., Blanchou, M.: Cellular exploitation on a global scale: the rise and fall of the control protocol. In: Blackhat 2014, Las Vegas (2014)
40. SR Labs: Snoopsnitch, December 2014. https://opensource.srlabs.de/projects/snoopsnitch. Accessed 12 Nov 2015
41. Tu, G., Li, Y., Peng, C., Li, C., Raza, M.T., Tseng, H., Lu, S.: New threats to sms-assisted mobile internet services from 4G LTE networks (2015). http://arxiv.org/abs/1510.08531
42. Welte, H.: OpenBSC - running your own GSM network, talk at Hacking at Random, August 2009. https://openbsc.osmocom.org/trac/raw-attachment/wiki/FieldTests/HAR2009/har2009-gsm-report.pdf

On the Feasibility of TTL-Based Filtering for DRDoS Mitigation

Michael Backes[1], Thorsten Holz[2], Christian Rossow[3], Teemu Rytilahti[2(✉)], Milivoj Simeonovski[3(✉)], and Ben Stock[3(✉)]

[1] CISPA, MPI-SWS, Saarland University, Saarland Informatics Campus, Saarbrücken, Germany
[2] Horst Görtz Institute for IT-Security, Ruhr University Bochum, Bochum, Germany
teemu.rytilahti@rub.de
[3] CISPA, Saarland University, Saarland Informatics Campus, Saarbrücken, Germany
stock@cs.uni-saarland.de, simeonovski@cs.uni-saarland.com

Abstract. A major disturbance for network providers in recent years have been *Distributed Reflective Denial-of-Service* (DRDoS) attacks. In such an attack, the adversary spoofs the IP address of a victim and sends a flood of tiny packets to vulnerable services. The services then respond to spoofed the IP, flooding the victim with large replies. Led by the idea that an attacker cannot fabricate the number of hops a packet travels between amplifier and victim, *Hop Count Filtering* (HCF) mechanisms that analyze the Time-to-Live (TTL) of incoming packets have been proposed as a solution.

In this paper, we evaluate the feasibility of using HCF to mitigate DRDoS attacks. To that end, we detail how a server can use active probing to learn TTLs of alleged packet senders. Based on data sets of benign and spoofed NTP requests, we find that a TTL-based defense could block over 75 % of spoofed traffic, while allowing 85 % of benign traffic to pass. To achieve this performance, however, such an approach must allow for a tolerance of ±2 hops.

Motivated by this, we investigate the tacit assumption that an attacker cannot learn the correct TTL value. By using a combination of tracerouting and BGP data, we build statistical models which allow to estimate the TTL within that tolerance level. We observe that by wisely choosing the used amplifiers, the attacker is able to circumvent such TTL-based defenses. Finally, we argue that any (current or future) defensive system based on TTL values can be bypassed in a similar fashion, and find that future research must be steered towards more fundamental solutions to thwart any kind of IP spoofing attacks.

Keywords: IP spoofing · Hop count filtering · Reflective Denial-of-Service

1 Introduction

One of the major hassles for network provides in recent years have been so-called *Distributed Reflective Denial-of-Service* (DRDoS) attacks [5]. In these attacks, an attacker poses as its victim and sends a flood of tiny packets to vulnerable services which then respond with much larger replies to the victim. This is possible because the Internet Protocol (IP) does not have means to protect against forgery of source addresses in its packets, so-called *IP spoofing*. A variety of different UDP-based protocols have been known to be vulnerable for this category of attacks for long [22], but despite the efforts to locate and shut down vulnerable services, they remain a problem even today.

To ensure that a server does not become unwilling participant in a DRDoS attack, an appealing defense is to detect spoofed packets *at the recipient*. One such technique is to validate certain IP header fields and drop packets that seem unsound. Most promising, Cheng et al. [10] propose a technique called Hop Count Filtering (HCF) to leverage the Time-to-Live (TTL) field encoded in the IP header. The intuition behind a TTL-based filtering approach is that the route of the *actual* source of the traffic and the *claimed* source is likely different, i.e., the spoofing source is in a different network than the spoofed IP address. This is then also reflected in the TTL value, as the attacker's route to the server differs from the one of the spoofed system, and hence the number of hops is different. Thus, it is seemingly possible to filter most spoofed traffic by dropping any traffic which does not correspond to the expected TTL.

In this paper, we evaluate the feasibility of using HCF to defend against DRDoS attacks. To do so, we analyze several means of probing for the TTL of an alleged sender, using different types of probes towards a host in question as well as horizontal probing of its neighbors. We show that this process is prone to errors and frequently tedious in practice, raising the need for a certain tolerance in TTL-based defenses. More precisely, we show that an error margin of ± 2 must be allowed to enable 85 % of benign traffic to pass, while dropping more than 75 % of spoofed traffic.

Any TTL-based defense relies on the tacit assumption that an attacker cannot learn the correct TTL when spoofing a packet. We, however, show that a spoofing attacker can subvert TTL-based filters by predicting the TTL value—without having access to the system or network of either server or impersonated victim. Our idea is to leverage publicly available traceroute data to learn subpaths that an IP packet from IP_A to IP_B will take. We follow the intuition that subpaths from IP_A to any other host on the Internet are quite constant and can be learned by the attacker. Similarly, we show that the attacker can observe that any packet to IP_B traverses a certain subpath. We augment such subpath information with an approximation of how the packet is routed on the higher-tier Internet layers. Given the tolerance required in TTL-based defenses, we can estimate the initial TTL value that the attacker has to set to enable bypassing of such defenses.

These "negative" results prove that TTL-based spoofing filters are unreliable and (if at all) a short-sighted solution only. Rather than attacking existing defense systems, our findings conceptually show that TTL-based defenses cannot work to thwart the outlined attacks. Hence, we see this paper as a valuable contribution to steer future research towards more fundamental solutions, be it alternative defenses against spoofing, or conceptual redesigns of the Internet and its protocols.

To summarize, we make the following contributions:

- We discuss how a server can use active probing to measure the hops to hosts which connect to its services (Sect. 3).
- We re-evaluate the concept of HCF to determine the necessary level of tolerance required for it to work in practice (Sect. 4).
- We describe a methodology which leverages previous knowledge about routing and statistical models to estimate the number of hops between an arbitrary victim and an amplifier of the attacker's choosing (Sect. 5).
- In doing so, we show that TTL-based defenses can be circumvented by an attacker with as little as 40 globally distributed probes (Sect. 6).

2 Background

In this section, we discuss the background information on routing on the Internet, Distributed Denial of Service attacks, and Hop Count Filtering as a countermeasure against such attacks.

2.1 Relevant Internet Technologies

The Internet is a network of interconnected sub-networks, which route packets between them based on the established routes. These smaller networks are also referred to as *Autonomous Systems* (*AS*). For a host in network A to connect to a host in network B, a route must be found through potentially several different ASes. Traffic between different autonomous systems is routed based on the Border Gateway Protocol, in which routers exchange information about accessible IP ranges and the corresponding AS paths, i.e., routes to these ranges.

To ensure that a packet is not stuck in a routing loop, the Internet Protocol (IP) header contains a field dubbed Time-to-Live (*TTL*). When handling a packet, "[...] every module that processes a datagram must decrease the TTL" and whenever a packet's TTL value reached zero, the packet must be discarded by the routing device [19]. In practice, the TTL is implemented as a decreasing hop count. The value is initially set by the sending host and depends on the operating system, e.g., Mac OS X uses 64, Windows 128, and while Linux distributions nowadays mostly use 64, some even use 255 [1]. When receiving a packet, analysis of the TTL values therefore allows to approximate the number of routing devices the packet has passed.

The concept of TTLs can also be used to learn the exact route of a packet (*tracerouting*). To that end, the initiator of the tracerouting sends an IP packet towards the intended destination, initially setting the TTL value to 1. When this packet reaches the first hop, the TTL is decreased. According to the RFC, the router must now drop the packet. In such a case, most routers will also send an Internet Control Message Protocol (*ICMP*) error message to the original sender, indicating that the timeout of the packet has been exceeded. This response can be used by the tracerouting machine to learn the IP address of the first hop. By repeating this process with increasing TTL values, this method can be used to learn all IP addresses of routers on the packet's way to its destination.

2.2 Source Spoofing and DRDoS

In its original design, the Internet Protocol does not feature a means of verifying the source of a packet. Since IP packets are only directed based on the *destination*, an attacker may generate an IP packet with a fabricated (or *spoofed*) source address. This design flaw can be abused by an adversary towards several ends. One example are Denial of Service (DoS) attacks, where an attacker tries to either saturate the network link to a server or exhaust resources on the target machine by, e.g., initiating a large number of TCP handshakes. To defend against this, a network administrator may configure a firewall to drop packets from the attacker. The attacker, however, can spoof IP packets from other machines to bypass this defense mechanism.

Moreover, recent years have seen an increase in Distributed Reflective Denial of Service (DRDoS) attacks. These attacks rely on spoofing packets in conjunction with services which respond to requests with significantly larger responses. There are a variety of vulnerable protocols (described in [22,23]), but recently, the most nefarious attacks have been misusing protocols such as DNS, NTP, SSDP, or chargen. As an example, the Network Time Protocol's (NTP) *monlist* feature may generate a response that is more than 4,500 times larger than the request. To abuse this, an attacker generates a flood of *monlist* requests to vulnerable servers while spoofing the source IP address to be that of the victim. Subsequently, a vulnerable NTP server will send the response to the victim's IP. In doing so, the attacker can massively amplify his own bandwidth, while also not revealing his real IP address in the process.

Although this kind of attack has been well-known for long [14,24] and attempts have been made to shut down vulnerable systems used in such attacks (e.g., [12]), they still pose a threat to online services. In order to fight such attacks, several countermeasures dating back to 2001 [17] have been proposed. One obvious defense strategy would be to limit the number of requests a client may issue. However, while such mechanisms may help to protect against excessive abuse of a single amplifier, Rossow's [22] analysis shows that even with rate limiting the aggregated attack bandwidth of some protocols is still an issue. This and many other countermeasures have been evaluated and analyzed by Beitollahi and Deconinck [7], hence we omit to discuss them further and refer the reader to their paper. Instead, we discuss the hop count filtering mechanisms relevant for our work in the following.

2.3 Hop Count Filtering

When a packet is received, its TTL depends on (i) the initial TTL value and (ii) the number of hops the packet has traversed. While it is easy to forge an

IP header as such, Cheng et al. [10] propose to use the TTL to detect nefarious packets. More precisely, they assume that an attacker trying to impersonate a specific host cannot ascertain the hop count between the spoofed host and the recipient of the packet. Based on this assumption, they present a reactive defense against DDoS attacks. To detect an attack in which the sender spoofs IP addresses to conceal his true location, they first require a period of observing the legitimate upcoming traffic (learning state), where the victim builds a mapping between the legitimate clients (IP addresses) and their respective hop count. Once an attack is detected, the victim rejects all packets where the TTL values do not match the recorded hop count. This way, the victim does not have to allocate resources for handling incoming spoofed traffic.

To increase the accuracy of the hop count filtering (HCF), Mukaddam et al. [15] proposed a modified version of HCF that aims to improve the learning phase. Instead of recording only one hop count value per IP, they record a list of all possible hop count values seen in the past. They justify the need for such an extension by arguing that the hop count may change due to the use of different routes. Indeed, such a system decreases the collateral damage by correctly classifying legitimate traffic. On the other hand, however, this mechanism allows an attacker more guesses in evasion attempts by ascertaining the correct TTL value.

3 Re-evaluating the Feasibility of Hop-Count Filtering

As the previous work by Mukaddam et al. has shown, the original HCF approach may be impaired by routing on the Internet. In addition, such an approach requires a prior learning phase, e.g., through passive TCP handshake analysis, to facilitate detection of spoofing. In the following, we investigate how far the methodology from Cheng et al. can be extended to filter out spoofed traffic used in DRDoS attacks. In contrast to the original HCF, this process cannot rely solely on TCP handshakes from previous connections by the client, as protocols used in DRDoS attacks, such as NTP or DNS, are connection-less. Simply dropping all packets from any host without a previous TCP connection would render any benign use of UDP-based services moot. Therefore, we investigate with what margin of error TTLs for an alleged sender can be learned by the server to evaluate the efficacy of TTL-based filtering on the Internet.

3.1 Protocol-Based Probing

The most intuitive way for a server to ascertain a TTL value of a client is to receive an unspoofed packet from that host. This can be done after a successful TCP handshake, as an established connection can only occur if the alleged sender actually initiated the connection. Due to its connection-less nature, we cannot rely on such a process for UDP. Instead, we need to prompt the alleged sender for an unspoofed packet. To achieve this, we can rely on ICMP, TCP, or UDP requests to the system in question. The ports we used in our work for

TCP and UDP are derived from the most scanned port discussed by Durumeric et al. [8]. We realize that it might not be feasible to send a plethora of probes to an end host whenever a packet to a UDP-based service is received, as this itself would be an amplification attack. Regardless, we want to investigate how different protocols and techniques might be leveraged to learn the TTL.

One way of compelling the probed system to send a packet is to use ICMP. ICMP *echo* can be used to measure the round trip time of a packet to a given host. The TTL of the probe target can be extracted from the IP header of an echo reply. In addition to the echo command, several operating systems also implement the non-mandated *timestamp* command. This can be used in the same fashion to induce a response from the probed system.

Additionally, the probing server can itself try to establish a TCP connection to the alleged sender. The methodology is independent of the actual application used underneath, since the TCP handshake is conducted by the operating system before handing the socket to the underlying application.

In contrast to TCP, where no application data needs to be sent to the probed host, most UDP-based services require protocol-specific data to be submitted. As an example, DNS and NTP servers only react to datagrams which are conformant to the respective protocol. On the other hand, the UDP-based *chargen* service "simply sends data without regard to the input" [20]. Therefore, we send protocol-conformant packets to DNS and NTP ports, and random data to chargen.

3.2 Interpreting Responses

In any of the cases described above, we may receive a positive or negative response. In the following, we discuss these types of responses and indicate how they can be used to extract the TTL from probed systems.

Positive Responses. When using ICMP, an echo or timestamp reply suffices to extract the TTL value from the encapsulating IP packet. For TCP, if a service listens on the probed port, the operating system will follow the three-way handshake process and respond with a SYN/ACK packet. In the case of UDP, the process differs slightly: when a service is listening on the probed port and the incoming packet adheres to the specification of that service, it sends a response back to the requesting system. Analogously to ICMP, the TTL value can be extracted from TCP and UDP responses by simply examining the IP header.

Negative Responses. In addition to responses which indicate that the host is up or a service is listening on the probed port, we can also leverage negative responses or error messages to learn the TTL. For example, in cases where a TCP port is not open, the host system may respond with a packet which has the RST flag set. Assuming that the packet is usually generated by the probed system (we discuss exceptions to this rule in Sect. 3.4), we can extract the TTL value in the same fashion used for positive responses. For UDP, we leverage ICMP *Port Unreachable* replies.

Next to these protocol-specific errors, we may also receive a message indicating that the host is not reachable. For example, the last router on the path can issue an ICMP *Host Unreachable* message. In this case, given the assumption that only the last router will send such a message, we can use the TTL from the incoming packet and decrease it by one (since the original sender would have had one more hop). ICMP also features a more generic *Destination Unreachable* message; this, however, can be sent by any router on the path and therefore cannot be used to conclusively calculate the TTL value. Next to these, we may receive ICMP *Communication Administratively Prohibited* messages. Such a message can either be sent by a router or the system itself when a packet is rejected by the firewall.

3.3 Horizontal Probing

A probed host may not answer, e.g., because it is firewalled and drops any incoming packets. In these cases, we may still gather valuable information on the path to the host by probing neighboring hosts. A neighbor in this case is a host which is located within the same subnet as the target. Although assuming that each subnet consists of exactly 256 IPs is not correct, this measure can still provide partial insight into the route and give a close estimate of the actual TTL value. Therefore, we probe neighbors by changing the last octet of the IP address ± 1, and use previous knowledge from hosts within the same /24 subnet, as this is the smallest network section generally advertised and accepted via BGP [18].

3.4 Caveats of Active Probing

There are several scenarios which can induce errors in probes. Typically, private customers receive a router for their dial-up account, which uses Network Address Translation (*NAT*) to allow multiple LAN clients access to a single Internet connection. Unless these routers are configured to forward packets to a machine behind the NAT, any response to the previously mentioned probes will be generated by the router. As the router adds an additional hop (and hence decreases the TTL by one) on the way from the NAT client to the server, the TTL values will mismatch in such a case.

For negative responses, additional artefacts may skew the results. Specifically, TCP resets or ICMP error packets may be generated by a firewall located before the intended probe target. In such a case, the firewall itself must spoof the probed IP to send these packets to ensure that the packet is attributed correctly on the system which initiated the connection. Hence, we may assume that negative responses are indeed generated by the probed system. Since we cannot learn the number of hops between the firewall and probed system, using negative responses can yield false results. We discuss the number of false results in Sect. 4.

As outlined before, the initial TTL value depends on the operating system of the sending host. Considering an example in which a Windows client is located behind a NAT router, which is running a Linux system with an initial TTL value of 255. Even though a packet originating from the Windows machine will only have one additional hop on its way to the probing server, the TTL value received by the probing system will greatly differ depending on whether the Windows or Linux host responded to the probing request. To accommodate for this and for horizontal probing, we normalize all TTL values to values between 0 and 63, i.e., $TTL = TTL\%64$. As the maximum TTL of 255 is not divisible by 64, we first increment TTL values above 128 by one to correct this discrepancy.

4 Probing Analysis

To evaluate how well active probing could be used in the wild to enable the use of HCF, we set up two systems. First, we used a regular NTP server not susceptible to DRDoS to attract benign clients. Second, we set up a honeypot system running a vulnerable version of NTP to attract spoofing attackers. In the following, we describe both data sets, discussing for what fraction of hosts we could learn any TTL value, and comparing this to the TTL values of incoming packets. Although we are using NTP servers for our evaluation, it is out of convenience of getting both spoofed and non-spoofed clients for comparison. In contrast, for protocols like chargen, getting benign traffic would have been significantly harder. We end this section with a discussion on the implications of the results of our analysis.

4.1 Benign Traffic

To capture benign traffic, we set up an NTP server that does not implement *monlist* feature at all, and is therefore not susceptible to amplification vectors. To attract NTP clients, we joined the NTP pool project. Note that the term *client* refers to its role in NTP, i.e., such a host could either be an end user's computer or a server synchronizing its clock with us. Within hours, the server was added to the public pool and started to receive NTP requests. We analyzed the incoming traffic for patterns of suspicious behavior (especially dreaded *monlist* requests). Our analysis showed that such requests were only issued in small numbers by scanners (e.g., operated by research groups). As we did not respond to such amplification requests and did not notice any suspicious activity, it is highly unlikely that an attacker would choose our server for his amplification attack. Hence, we deem this data set to consist exclusively of unspoofed traffic.

In total, we gathered data for 48 h, in which we received packets from 543,514 distinct IP addresses. In a first step, we probed each of these hosts immediately after their first contact using the different types of probes outlined in Sect. 3.1. In doing so, we could extract TTL values for 316,012 (58.1 %) for probed systems. The most successful type of probe was ICMP echo, which yielded a result for 257,694 or 47.4 % of the hosts. In comparison, the most successful TCP-based, positive response were SYN/ACKs from TCP port 443 (HTTPS), which accounted for a mere 31,966 (5.9 %) of the hosts. For any UDP-based probes, we only received negligible amounts of positive responses. Among the negative

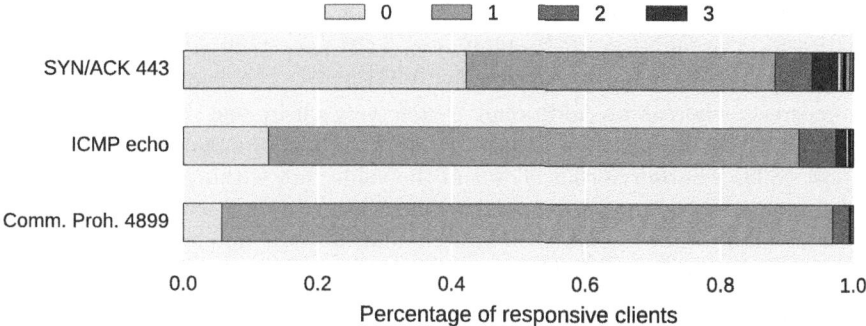

Fig. 1. Deviation differences for selected probe types

responses, ICMP *Communication Prohibited* for TCP port 4899 (Radmin) was the most frequent message (113,058 or 20,8 %).

To find out how accurate these results actually are, we compared the normalized TTL values to the ones from the incoming traffic. As stated before, we assume that the traffic directed to the NTP server is indeed generated by the alleged senders, i.e., the ground truth value for each sending host can be extracted from these incoming packets. Initially, we consider all probes to a specific host for our analysis. In cases where the measured TTL values differ between the probe types, we select the minimum value of any test. The intuition of this is straightforward: whenever a firewall or router answers instead of the probed system, the number of hops between them and our probing server is smaller. Hence, by choosing the minimum TTL value, we ensure that we measure the longest path between us and the host responding to the probe. Therefore, if the probed system answers to one probe whereas all others are responded to by the firewall, we still measure the accurate value for the system in question.

The results of applying this methodology on the data set are shown in Table 1. We observe that, with respect to the total number of responding systems, 26.1 % of the measured TTLs match the ground truth. Moreover, 92.2 % of the values are within a threshold of ± 1, and almost 97 % within ± 2. In the following, we analyze the results for specific tests in more detail, and discuss potential reasons for the observed deviations.

Table 1. Accuracy of measured TTLs (direct probes only)

Deviation	Amount	Fraction	Cumulated fraction
± 0	82,629	26.1 %	26.1 %
± 1	208,891	66.1 %	92.2 %
± 2	14,623	4.6 %	96.9 %
± 3	4,684	1.5 %	98.4 %
More	5,185	1.6 %	100 %

The deviation between the measured and actual values is shown in Fig. 1 for ICMP echo, Communication Prohibited to TCP port 4899, and SYN/ACK for TCP port 443. We can observe that for ICMP echo, 12.8 % of measured TTLs were correct, whereas an additional 78.8 % were off-by-one, i.e., 91.6 % of the measured TTLs were within a threshold of ±1. For *Communication Prohibited* on port 4899, we observe that 96.8 % of the values are within ±1, whereas 91 % are off-by-one. This appears natural to the scenarios we discussed: ICMP echo requests will often be answered by routers and firewalls due to network address translation. Although SYN on TCP port 443 was only responsive on 5.9 % of the hosts, the results are quite interesting. We observe that for 42.2 % of the hosts which responded to such a probe, the TTL value could be correctly measured. In addition, another 45.9 % were off-by-one, resulting in 88 % of the values being within a threshold of ±1. We argue that this is caused by nature of TCP, i.e., we only receive a SYN/ACK in case a service is listening on the probed system. This can either occur if the connection directly reached the probed system, i.e., it is not behind a NAT or the corresponding port is forwarded, or there could be a chance that a public-facing administrative interface is being exposed for service needs [2]. Therefore, it is plausible that such routers may respond to HTTPS requests, explaining the high number of our off-by-one measurements.

Next to probing of the target system itself, we can probe neighboring hosts. More specifically, we probe direct neighbors (IP ±1) and additionally rely on previous measurements aimed towards other hosts within the same /24 network. In doing so, we find that both types of probing increase the coverage. In our experiment, we found that directly probing neighbors increases the number of measurable TTLs by 69,399, resulting in a total coverage of 73.4 %. Taking into account all information from hosts within the same /24 network increases the coverage more drastically (by 168,730 hosts), yielding TTL values for 91.6 % of all hosts. At the same time, the accuracy remains similar, with 27 % of the probed values matching the ground truth. For ±1, we can correctly measure the TTL in 88.9 % of the cases, and 94.3 % of all measurements are within a threshold of ±2. Given these results for coverage and accuracy, we note that combining different types of probing towards a single host with horizontal probing of the system's neighbors allows us measure the TTL within a threshold of ± 2 for 86.4 % of all connecting hosts.

4.2 Spoofed Traffic

Next to the benign data set, for which we can measure the TTL within a small threshold for the majority of the hosts correctly, we wanted to investigate how well HCF would be suited for spoofed traffic. To that end, we set up a honeypot running a vulnerable version of NTP server prone to becoming an amplifier for DRDoS attacks. To avoid unnecessarily harming the spoofed targets while still pretending to be attractive to adversaries, the outgoing bandwidth was limited, i.e., we answered to at most two monlist requests per host per minute. We did not announce the IP address of this machine in any manner and hence assume that no legitimate traffic would be directed to the host. Instead, incoming NTP

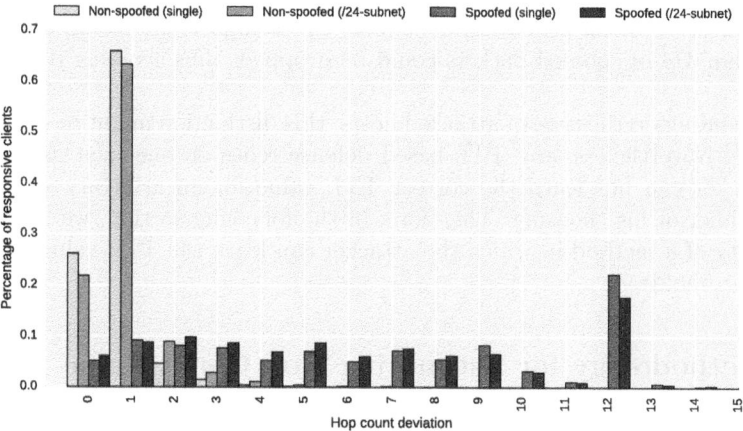

Fig. 2. Deviation difference between spoofed and non-spoofed traffic

requests are either due to scanning, or spoofed packets sent by an attacker. In a time-period of 96 h, we recorded 5,616 distinct alleged sender addresses, for which we could gather direct probe results in 3,983 cases (70.9 %). This slightly higher coverage (compared to the benign data) can be explained by the fact that most attacks are targeting servers, which also are more likely to expose services we actively probe for.

Before conducting any of our measurements, one property of the spoofed traffic became apparent: more than 99 % of all incoming packets had an assumed initial TTL of 255. This specific feature, however, should not be used solely to detect spoofed traffic, since the initial TTL can be changed without much effort by the attacker. Therefore, we normalized the TTL value as outlined before.

Figure 2 shows the comparison between the measured TTL values and the TTL values extracted from incoming packets, for both benign and spoofed data sets. While we can clearly observe that for the majority of benign clients, the TTL can be guessed within a threshold of ±2, we note that no such trend is visible for spoofed traffic.

4.3 Implications

In this section, we outlined the results of our experiments on benign and spoofed data sets to evaluate a feasible margin of error for HCF. With respect to those data sets, we find that distinguishing between benign and spoofed traffic appears to yield useful results when using a threshold of 2. The reasons for the imprecision of the measurements are manifold, e.g., when a client is behind a NAT or incoming traffic to the machine is filtered by a firewall. Therefore, a TTL-based defense mechanism must make a trade-off between false positives and false negatives, respectively. Based on the data sets we analyzed, if a TTL-based defense mechanism was to be deployed to protect a service against becoming an unwilling actor in an attack, over 85 % of the benign traffic could pass, while more than 3/4 of spoofed packets could be dropped, thus avoiding to harm the targets.

Depending on the type of attacked hosts, this distinction might be even easier to make. Nevertheless, any TTL-based defense relies on one tacit assumption: an attacker can not learn the correct TTL value for an arbitrary victim and an amplifier of his choosing. Therefore, in the following section, we discuss the feasibility of a method in which the attacker can learn the TTL value (within a given threshold).

5 Methodology for Estimating Hop Count Value

So far we showed that deploying a TTL-based filtering at the server side would require some tolerance interval to be functional and avoid collateral damage by incorrectly classifying legitimate traffic. In this section, we assess if an attacker can actually bypass the filtering by predicting the correct hop count value between the hosts and properly adjusting the TTL value. That is, we present a methodology for estimating the hop count value between amplifiers and victims.

5.1 Key Idea and Attacker Model

Our key idea lies on the observation that paths between arbitrary locations to a selected destination share (small) segments of the path. We leverage the fact that such path information can be learned by an attacker to estimate the number of hops of a packet sent from one location to another. To learn subpaths, we (i) probabilistically model known paths obtained via traceroutes, and (ii) combine this knowledge with BGP routing information. Figure 3 shows our idea for estimating the distance (number of hops) between an amplifier (M) and a victim (V). For our methodology, we use the common approach for representing the Internet, which is a graph where nodes are the autonomous systems and edges are the peerings (routing links) between them. Additionally, we assign weights to the nodes to denote the hop count number within the individual AS. One way to build such a graph that illustrates the AS-level topology of the Internet is to use available BGP data to discover the connectivity information for the ASes. Nevertheless, studies have shown that BGP data is only available to a limited extent, therefore the Internet AS-level topology is partially hidden [9,16]. However, our methodology does not primarily rely on the available BGP data, but rather on the traceroute information an attacker can obtain. We use the BGP data, when available, as a complement to the traceroute data in order to discover the missing ASes, and to subsequently calculate the number of hops.

Our attacker (A) aims at evading any TTL-based filter or, at least, reduce its effectiveness in mitigating amplification attacks. His main goal is to predict the TTL value as close as possible to the correct one, such that he can craft requests which are deemed to be legitimate to the server, i.e., amplifier. In theory, there are few approaches that the attacker may follow to learn the correct TTL value.

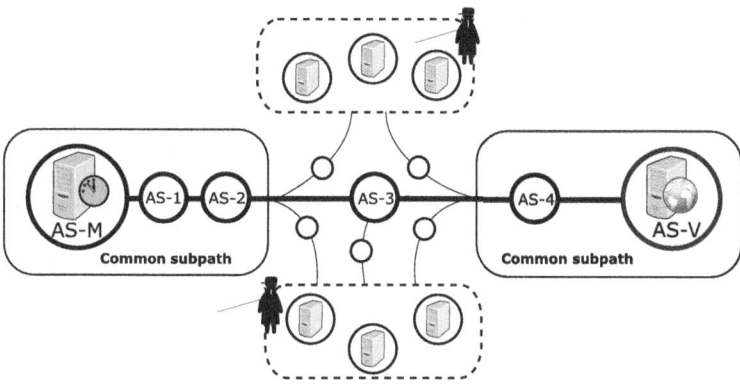

Fig. 3. Approach to estimate the hops between amplifier (M) and victim (V)

First, he may learn the TTL value by actively or passively monitoring traffic anywhere on the route, and then probe the destination in order to calculate the remaining part of the route. This approach is neither realistic nor practical because the attacker has to be present at every route R_i between M_i and the victim V. Second, if the attacker can position a probe either in the network of M or V, he can easily measure the TTL value by tracerouting to the other host.

For a more realistic scenario, we restrict the attacker's capabilities. Figure 3 illustrates this attacker model. Similar to the reverse traceroute method [11], our attacker is capable of probing from random, distributed locations and can use any publicly available online resources to traceroute to the amplifier and to the victim (e.g., RIPE Atlas [3] or looking glass servers). However, he does not have control over the amplifier and not necessarily full control over the probes.

We restrict neither the location of the amplifiers nor the victims, i.e., they can be located at arbitrary network locations. We assume that A can obtain a set of amplifiers (e.g., NTP, DNS), all of which deploy TTL-based filtering and respond to valid requests only[1].

5.2 Methodology

We propose a methodology for estimating the distance between hosts on the internet through an Exploratory Data Analysis (EDA)[2]. Our methodology is comprised of three main components, namely, data collection, data processing, and EDA. Figure 4 illustrates the methodology we propose in this paper.

---

[1] We assume that the amplifiers have deployed HCF to protect against amplification attacks, therefore "valid" protocol requests are those with matching TTL value.
[2] Exploratory Data Analysis is not a method or a technique, but rather a philosophy for data analysis that employs a variety of techniques.

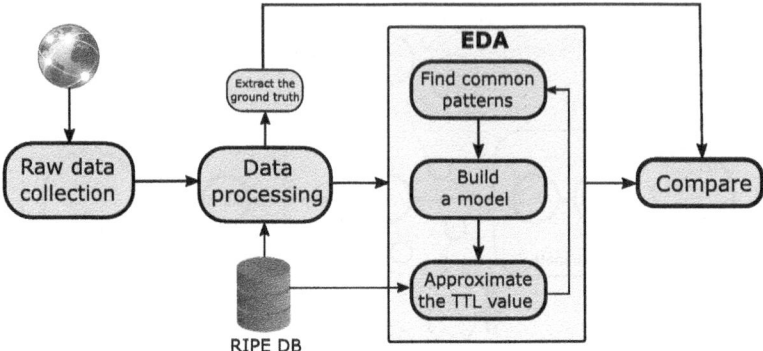

Fig. 4. Workflow of the methodology

Data Collection. First, depicted in the data collection component, the attacker collects traceroute data for the victim and the amplifier(s). The attacker launches traceroutes to the targeted locations from a globally distributed set of hosts on the Internet such as RIPE Atlas [3]. Note that the distribution of the selected hosts is required to be global such that there will be a diversity of the paths, allowing us to predict TTLs for arbitrarily chosen victims.

Data Processing. Second, in the data processing component, we have to ensure that the relevant data collected in the previous stage is complete and usable. In an ideal world, tracerouting returns a complete path including all the IP addresses and ASes on the way up to the destination. In practice, the collected data from the previous phase is usually imperfect, with a plethora of missing connecting hops [13]. Such data can pose difficulties in effective data analysis; therefore, we need to develop certain methods for efficient data scrubbing. First, we discard all the traceroutes that are missing more than a certain percentage (e.g., 50 %) of the intermediate hops. Also, we ignore traceroutes that cannot reach at least the AS of the destination. In the case where the destination address belongs to the same AS as the last replying node, we make an intuitive assumption that this is the last AS in the path, and we supplement the route with the AS number of the last replying node. We then continue filling up the gaps of the unknown ASes due to private IP addresses within the traceroute. Private addressing might occur when a packet passes through someone's internal network with implemented Multiprotocol Label Switching (MPLS) routing [21]. In such cases, we assume that the border AS, the one with a public IP address before the MPLS routing, is the correct one, and we fill in the gaps accordingly. Finally, to fill in the remaining missing hops, we apply a technique that employs the publicly available BGP data. The BGP data assists in the discovering of the neighboring AS[3] and helps us to bridge the gap between two known autonomous

---

[3] A neighbor (or peering) autonomous system is the one that the AS directly interconnect with in order to exchange traffic.

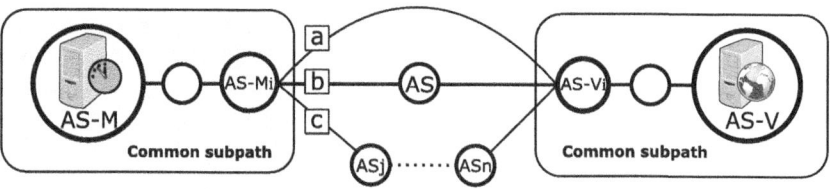

Fig. 5. Connecting border ASes (AS-Mi and AS-Vi)

systems. Note that this technique can only complete the lacking AS numbers, but not the actual hops (and their IP addresses).

Exploratory Data Analysis. Once the data is processed, i.e., prepared for analysis, we dissect the data set using the EDA approach. This stage of the methodology repeats for every victim and it involves three subsequent steps.

Find Common Patterns. Finding common patterns is the first step in the data exploration. This method transforms the paths from detailed traceroutes with IP addresses of the hops to coarse-grained ones with only AS-level paths and their weights, i.e., the number of hops in each AS for a particular traceroute.

Build a Model. This method assists in constructing a probabilistic table that identifies the likelihood of an AS to be part of the route between amplifier and victim. If all collected traceroutes pass through a particular AS, say AS-1, on the way to the target location T, the method denotes the probability of 1 that the AS-1 exist as a hop on the way to T. Moreover, this method also considers the average number of hops within the AS and the distance of the AS from the target. The average number is the AS internal hop count value, and it may vary due to routing-related reasons such as load balancing. To identify the border autonomous systems (in the next step), we need to define the distance as a number of hops that a particular AS is distant from the target AS. For example, the AS the target T belongs to always has a probability of 1 and distance 0.

Approximate the TTL Value. The probabilistic modeling helps in building a partial path between two hosts. Consider the scenario illustrated in Fig. 5. The model identifies with a degree of certainty the common subpaths of the target and the source. Furthermore, it estimates the hop count value of these subpaths. To estimate the final hop count value, we need to bridge these two subpaths with the missing intermediate AS(s). To this end, we apply techniques based on the available BGP data such that the final result is a fully connected AS-level path.

Initially, we identify the border autonomous systems (labeled as AS-Mi and AS-Vi in Fig. 5), i.e., the last certain (most distant) AS in the common subpaths. With respect to the possible missing hops for connecting these two subpaths, we distinguish three different scenarios (marked with a, b and c in Fig. 5):

Direct connection (a) When a direct peering between the border autonomous systems exists, i.e., AS-Mi is in the neighborhood[4] of AS-Vi and vice versa, and the intersection set of the AS-Mi and AS-Vi neighbors is empty; we assume that the border ASes are directly connected (AS-Mi ⟷ AS-Vi).

One-hop connection (b) To identify the single connecting point in between, accordingly, we have to check the neighbors of the border ASes. In the case where only one intersecting AS exists, we assume that this particular AS is the connecting point. If the intersection set contains more than one common AS, we refer to our probability table. We then accordingly choose the AS with the biggest probability to be a part of the route.

N-hop connection (c) A more complex scenario is when two or more intermediate AS are missing. In such a scenario, we build a tree of possible subpaths by examining additional two levels[5] of neighbors. Upon building up the tree of all possible paths, we test every branch over the database of available BGP routes and the pre-computed table of probabilities. In case the branch is present in the BGP routing database, we deem that particular route to be the accurate one.

Once the bridging subpath is identified, we add up the average hop count of the connecting ASes to the sum of the hop count value estimated for the subpaths.

6 Experimental Setup and Results

In the following, we describe the data set used to evaluate our approach. Subsequently, we present and discuss the experimental results of the evaluation.

6.1 Data Set

To evaluate the proposed methodology, we mainly use services provided by the RIPE Atlas network [3], which is the largest Internet measurement network built by RIPE NCC. Moreover, they provide an API for creating different types of measurements and for collecting the data in a structured format. In the following, we list the services and data sources used for our experimental evaluation.

1. RIPE Atlas probes: To attain a global coverage and also to have a possibility to obtain the ground truth, we use the RIPE Atlas network of probes [3] as a basis for our experiments. We observe that this network has around 9,000 active probes, spread across 181 countries and 3,386 ASes [4]. Such a global coverage fulfils the requirements for our experimental evaluation. Moreover, the platform give us the flexibility for requesting custom measurements, in

---

[4] Peering ASes are ASes which directly interconnect with each other. We obtain this information from the available BGP data.
[5] Statistics [3] show that average length of AS-level paths is 4, therefore we bound the subpath examination to 2 levels, i.e., we can examine paths of at least 6 hops.

our case traceroutes, by selecting any of the deployed active probes. This flexibility is of particular importance for our experiments since we can select a subset of nodes with different geographical and logical locations to collect the traceroute data. Additionally, when a probe acts as a victim in our leave-one-out analysis (which we outline in the following), we can easily obtain the ground truth by running traceroute measurement from the probes to the amplifiers.
2. BGP data: When the collected traceroute data is not enough for making the final assessment of the connectivity between the ASes, we utilize available BGP data. In order to infer the AS-level connectivity, we use RIPE Atlas as an accurate source for BGP data. Also the BGP data helps to obtain a ground truth of individual ASes.
3. Amplifiers: To investigate the real-world implications of our attack, we scanned for chargen amplifiers on the Internet. In total, we randomly selected 16 such servers.

6.2 Leave-one-out Evaluation

To evaluate the performance of our methodology, we use a leave-one-out (L-1-O) evaluation approach, in which every probe acts like a victim at a selected time. Informally, for a data set with P probes, we perform P experiments with $P-1$ training cases and one test case. In other words, for every experiment we temporarily remove one probe from the data set and select that particular probe as our victim. Upon fixing the probe P_i as a victim V, the model is rebuilt upon this newly defined set.

Suppose that $P = p_1, \ldots, p_n$ is a set of probes, $M = m_1, \ldots, m_l$ set of amplifiers, and $R = r_{11}, \ldots, r_{nm}$ set of traceroutes where r_{ij} is a traceroute from p_i to m_j. For ease of exposition, we use the notation $p_i \Rightarrow_R M$ to describe a set of all traceroutes from p_i to every member of the set M. Applying the L-1-O approach to the methodology works as follows:

1. Collect the traceroute data $(R \bigcup \{p_i \Rightarrow_R P \backslash \{p_i\} | i = 1, \ldots, n\})$.
2. Process the data and extract the ground truth.
3. Remove probe p_i from P ($P \backslash \{p_i\}$) and set $V = p_i$, where V is the victim.
4. Extract the ground truth for p_i to M i.e., the distance from $p_i \Rightarrow_R M$.
5. Run the EDA using the remaining data.
6. Repeat step 3–5 for $i = 1, \ldots, n$

L-1-O in Practice. We apply the L-1-O method on a set of 40 random RIPE Atlas probes, located in different ASes, and 16 randomly distributed chargen amplifiers. We first collect the required data, namely, we obtain the path from every probe to all of the 16 amplifiers, and also between the probes within the set. We use the RIPE Atlas REST API to create IPv4 traceroutes using ICMP packets and hops limit of 32. In order to get more precise paths and avoid measurements inconsistencies caused by load balancing routers, we employ the Paris traceroute measurement tool [6].

Once the traceroute data is collected and the data set is processed, i.e., cleaned up using the method described in Sect. 5.2, we pass the data through step 3–6 from the L-1-O approach. In such experimental setup, L-1-O theoretically can evaluate 640 TTL predictions, i.e., paths from 16 amplifiers to 40 victims. Unfortunately, because of the incompleteness of the traceroute data as well as instability of some of the probes, the method was able to predict and evaluate around 593 (92.6%) individual paths.

Overall Performance. Table 2 shows the overall performance of our methodology. The experimental results show that using our methodology, an attacker can predict correctly without any deviation roughly 13% of the paths between the amplifiers and the victims, i.e., 13% of the measured hop counts match the ground truth. However, we showed in Sect. 4 that, with a tolerance of ±2, a TTL-based defense could block over 75% of spoofed traffic, while allowing 85% of benign traffic to pass. Therefore, when we take this threshold into consideration, our methodology is effective for 56.3% of the paths.

Table 2. Overall performance of the methodology

	Amount	Fraction	Cumulated fraction
±0	78	13.2%	13.2%
±1	170	28.7%	28.5%
±2	132	22.3%	56.3%
±3	49	8.3%	69.1%
More	164	27.7%	100%

Moreover, we observe that applying our methodology to a set of randomly chosen amplifiers, the attacker can isolate amplifiers for which he can predict the hop count value between the amplifier and any arbitrary victim with higher accuracy. Thus, he can bypass the TTL-based defense running on the amplifier and exploit it for a DRDoS attack. Figure 6 illustrates the average hop count deviation per amplifier and shows that the attacker can, indeed, sample a set of *good* amplifiers. We see several explanations for such a deviation among the amplifiers. The geographical and logical location of the amplifiers and the victims plays an important role. As we discussed before, the limitation of the BGP data makes our methodology not equally precise for all the AS. Also another cause is the inconsistency of the collected data between BGP data and traceroute path caused by Internet Exchange Points and sibling ASes managed by the same institution. However, these results show that even with a low threshold value at the amplifier, by wisely choosing amplifiers to use, an attacker is able to circumvent any TTL-based defense against DRDoS attacks.

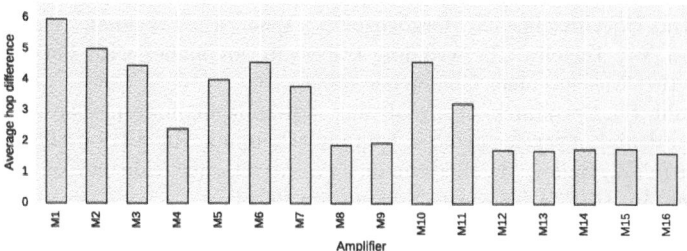

Fig. 6. Average hop deviation per amplifier

7 Conclusion

In this paper, we evaluated the feasibility of using Hop Count Filtering to mitigate DRDoS attacks. To that end, we detailed how a server can use active probing to learn TTLs of alleged packet senders. Based on data sets of benign and spoofed NTP requests, we find that with a tolerance of ± 2, a TTL-based defense could block over 75 % of spoofed traffic, while allowing 85 % of benign traffic to pass. Subsequently, however, we show that an attacker can use a combination of tracerouting and BGP data to build statistical models, which allows him to estimate the TTL for his target within that tolerance level. Hence, by wisely choosing amplifiers to use, he is able to circumvent any TTL-based defense against DRDoS attacks. We therefore argue that any (current or future) defensive system based on TTL values can be bypassed in a similar fashion, and find that future research must be steered towards more fundamental solutions to thwart any kind of IP spoofing attacks.

Acknowledgments. This work was supported by the German Federal Ministry of Education and Research (BMBF) through funding for the Center for IT-Security, Privacy and Accountability (CISPA) as well as through the BMBF grant 01IS14009B ("BDSec").

The authors would like to thank Sven Bugiel for his comments on an earlier version of the paper. Additionally, we are grateful for the feedback from our shepherd Roberto Perdisci as well as those of our anonymous reviewers.

References

1. Default TTL values in TCP/IP. http://www.map.meteoswiss.ch/map-doc/ftp-probleme.htm
2. Functional requirements for broadband residential gateway devices. https://www.broadband-forum.org/technical/download/TR-124.pdf
3. RIPE Atlas: Internet data collection system. https://atlas.ripe.net/
4. RIPE Atlas: Statistics and network coverage. https://atlas.ripe.net/results/maps/network-coverage/
5. Technical details behind a 400Gbps NTP amplification DDoS attack. https://goo.gl/j7zWEp

6. Augustin, B., Cuvellier, X., Orgogozo, B., Viger, F., Friedman, T., Latapy, M., Magnien, C., Teixeira, R.: Avoiding traceroute anomalies with Paris traceroute. In: Internet Measurement Conference (2006)
7. Beitollahi, H., Deconinck, G.: Analyzing well-known countermeasures against distributed denial of service attacks. Comput. Commun. **35**, 1312–1332 (2012)
8. Durumeric, Z., Bailey, M., Halderman, J.A.: An internet-wide view of internet-wide scanning. In: USENIX Security Symposium (2014)
9. Gregori, E., Improta, A., Lenzini, L., Rossi, L., Sani, L.: On the incompleteness of the AS-level graph: a novel methodology for BGP route collector placement. In: Internet Measurement Conference (2012)
10. Jin, C., Wang, H., Shin, K.G.: Hop-count filtering: an effective defense against spoofed DDoS traffic. In: Proceedings of the 10th ACM Conference on Computer and Communications Security. ACM (2003)
11. Katz-Bassett, E., Madhyastha, H.V., Adhikari, V.K., Scott, C., Sherry, J., van Wesep, P., Anderson, T.E., Krishnamurthy, A.: Reverse traceroute. In: USENIX NSDI (2010)
12. Kührer, M., Hupperich, T., Rossow, C., Holz, T.: Exit from hell? Reducing the impact of amplification DDoS attacks. In: USENIX Security Symposium (2014)
13. Mao, Z.M., Rexford, J., Wang, J., Katz, R.H.: Towards an accurate AS-level traceroute tool. In: Conference on Applications, Technologies, Architectures, and Protocols for Computer Communication (2003)
14. Mirkovic, J., Reiher, P.L.: A taxonomy of DDoS attack and DDoS defense mechanisms. Comput. Commun. Rev. **34**, 39–53 (2004)
15. Mukaddam, A., Elhajj, I., Kayssi, A.I., Chehab, A.: IP spoofing detection using modified hop count. In: International Conference on Advanced Information Networking and Applications (2014)
16. Oliveira, R.V., Pei, D., Willinger, W., Zhang, B., Zhang, L.: The (in)completeness of the observed internet AS-level structure. IEEE/ACM Trans. Netw. **18**(1), 109–122 (2010)
17. Paxson, V.: An analysis of using reflectors for distributed denial-of-service attacks. Comput. Commun. Rev. **31**(3), 38–47 (2001)
18. Pepelnjak, I., Durand, J., Doering, G.: BGP operations and security. RFC 7454, RFC Editor (2015). https://tools.ietf.org/html/rfc7454
19. Postel, J.: Internet protocol specification. RFC 791, RFC Editor (1981). https://tools.ietf.org/html/rfc791
20. Postel, J.: Character generator protocol. RFC 864, RFC Editor (1983). https://tools.ietf.org/html/rfc864
21. Rosen, E.C., Viswanathan, A., Callon, R.: Multiprotocol label switching architecture. RFC 3031, RFC Editor, January 2001. http://tools.ietf.org/html/rfc3031
22. Rossow, C.: Amplification hell: revisiting network protocols for DDoS abuse. In: NDSS (2014)
23. Ryba, F.J., Orlinski, M., Wählisch, M., Rossow, C., Schmidt, T.C.: Amplification and DRDoS attack defense-a survey and new perspectives. arXiv preprint arXiv:1505.07892 (2015)
24. Specht, S.M., Lee, R.B.: Distributed denial of service: taxonomies of attacks, tools, and countermeasures. In: International Conference on Parallel and Distributed Computing Systems (2004)

Systematization of Knowledge and Experience Reports

A Look into 30 Years of Malware Development from a Software Metrics Perspective

Alejandro Calleja[1]([✉]), Juan Tapiador[1], and Juan Caballero[2]

[1] Department of Computer Science, Universidad Carlos III de Madrid, Getafe, Spain
{accortin,jestevez}@inf.uc3m.es
[2] IMDEA Software Institute, Madrid, Spain
juan.caballero@imdea.org

Abstract. During the last decades, the problem of malicious and unwanted software (malware) has surged in numbers and sophistication. Malware plays a key role in most of today's cyber attacks and has consolidated as a commodity in the underground economy. In this work, we analyze the evolution of malware since the early 1980s to date from a software engineering perspective. We analyze the source code of 151 malware samples and obtain measures of their size, code quality, and estimates of the development costs (effort, time, and number of people). Our results suggest an exponential increment of nearly one order of magnitude per decade in aspects such as size and estimated effort, with code quality metrics similar to those of regular software. Overall, this supports otherwise confirmed claims about the increasing complexity of malware and its production progressively becoming an industry.

Keywords: Malware · Source code analysis · Software metrics

1 Introduction

The malware industry seems to be in better shape than ever. In their 2015 Internet Security Threat Report [5], Symantec reports that the total number of known malware in 2014 amounted to 1.7 billion, with 317 million (26 %) new samples discovered just in the preceding year. This translates into nearly 1 million new samples created every day. A recent statement by Panda Security [32] provides a proportionally similar aggregate: out of the 304 million malware samples detected by their engines throughout 2015, 84 million (27 %) were new. These impressive figures can be partially explained by the adoption of reuse-oriented development methodologies that make exceedingly easy for malware writers to produce new samples, and also by the increasing use of packers with polymorphic capabilities. Another key reason is the fact that over the last decade malware has become a profitable industry, thereby acquiring the status of a *commodity* [13,20] in the flourishing underground economy of cyber crime [35,37]. From a purely technical point of view, malware has experienced a remarkable evolutionary process since the 1980s, moving from simple file-infection viruses to stand-alone programs with

© Springer International Publishing Switzerland 2016
F. Monrose et al. (Eds.): RAID 2016, LNCS 9854, pp. 325–345, 2016.
DOI: 10.1007/978-3-319-45719-2_15

network propagation capabilities, support for distributed architectures based on rich command and control protocols, and a variety of modules to execute malicious actions in the victim. Malware writers have also rapidly adapted to new platforms as soon as these acquired a substantial user base, such as the recent case of smartphones [36].

The surge in number, sophistication, and repercussion of malware attacks has gone hand in hand with much research, both industrial and academic, on defense and analysis techniques. The majority of such investigations have focused on binary analysis, since most malware samples distribute in this form. Only very rarely researchers have access to the source code and can report insights gained from its inspection. (Notable exceptions include the analysis of the source code of 4 IRC bots by Barford and Yegneswaran [11] and the work of Kotov and Massacci on 30 exploit kits [26].) One consequence of the lack of wide availability of malware source code is a poor understanding of the malware development process, its properties when looked at as a software artifact, and how these properties have changed in the last decades.

In this paper, we present a study of the evolution of malware from a software engineering perspective. Our analysis is based on a dataset composed of the source code of 151 malware samples ranging from 1975 to 2015, including early viruses, worms, trojans, botnets, and remote access trojans (RATs). We make use of several metrics used in software engineering to quantify different aspects of the source code of malware understood as a software artifact. Such metrics are grouped into three main categories: (i) measures of size: number of source lines of code (SLOC), number of source files, number of different programming languages used, and number of function points (FP); (ii) estimates of the cost of developing the sample: effort (man-months), required time, and number of programmers; and (iii) measures of code quality: comment-to-code ratio, complexity of the control flow logic, and maintainability of the code. We also use these metrics to compare malware source code to a selection of benign programs. To the best of our knowledge, our work is the first to explore malware evolution from this perspective. We also believe that our dataset of malware source code is the largest analyzed in the literature. The main findings of our work include:

1. We observe an exponential increase of roughly one order of magnitude per decade in the number of source code files and SLOC and FP counts per sample. Malware samples from the 1980s and 1990s contain just one or a few source code files, are generally programmed in one language and have SLOC counts of a few thousands at most. Contrarily, samples from the late 2000s and later often contain hundreds of source code files spanning various languages, with an overall SLOC count of tens, and even hundreds of thousands.
2. In terms of development costs, our estimates evidence that malware writing has evolved from small projects of just one developer working no more than 1–2 months full time, to larger programming teams investing up to 6–8 months and, in some cases, possibly more.

3. A comparison with selected benign software projects reveals that the largest malware samples in our dataset present software metrics akin to those of products such as Snort or Bash, but are still quite far from larger software solutions.
4. The code quality metrics analyzed do not suggest significant differences between malware and benign software. Malware has slightly higher values of code complexity and also better maintainability, though the differences are not remarkable.

The remaining of this paper is organized as follows. Section 2 provides an overview of the software metrics used in this work. In Sect. 3 we describe our dataset of malware source code. Section 4 contains the core results of this work and Sect. 5 discusses the suitability of our approach, its limitations, and additional conclusions. Finally, Sect. 7 concludes the paper.

2 Software Metrics

This section provides an overview of the software metrics concepts used in this work to quantify various aspects of malware source code. We first introduce the two most widely used measures of software size: lines of source code (SLOC) and function points (FP). We then introduce effort estimation metrics, specifically the Constructive Cost Model (COCOMO), and also measures of source code complexity and maintainability.

2.1 Measuring Software Size

The number of lines in the source code of a program (SLOC) constitutes the most commonly used measure of its size. The number of physical SLOC refers to a count of the number of lines in the source code of a program, excluding comment and blank lines. Contrarily, logical SLOC counts take into account language-specific aspects, such as terminating symbols and style or formatting conventions, to deliver an estimate of the number of executable statements. Both IEEE [23] and the Software Engineering Institute (SEI) [31] had provided definitions and counting guidelines to obtain SLOC measures.

SLOC counts have a number of shortcomings [29] and can be easily misused. Despite this, it has a long-standing tradition as the most popular sizing metric. Furthermore, SLOC is an essential input for many estimation models that aim at predicting the effort required to develop a system, its maintainability, the expected number of bugs/defects, or the productivity of programmers.

Comparing size across different programming languages can give misleading impressions of the actual programming effort: the more expressive the programming language, the lower the size. An alternative metric to using SLOCs as the estimated software size is to use a measure of its functionality. The best known of such measures is the *function-point count*, initially proposed by Albrecht [7] and later refined by Albrecht and Gaffney [8]. The function-point count refers to the overall functionality of the software and is measured by estimating four program features: external inputs and outputs, user interactions, external interfaces, and files used. The overall count also involves various weights that account for the possibly different complexity of each of the above elements. Thus, the so-called unadjusted function-point count (UFC) is computed by simply multiplying each count by the appropriate weight and summing up all values. The UFC can be subsequently adjusted through various factors that are related to the complexity of the whole system.

The expected size in SLOC of a software project can be estimated from function-point counts through a process known as *backfiring* [25]. This consists in the use of existing empirical tables that provide the average number of SLOC per function point in different programming languages. Software Productivity Research (SPR) [24] annually publishes such conversion ratios for the most common programming languages in what is known as Programming Languages Tables (PLT), which are empirically obtained by analyzing thousands of software projects. Table 1 shows the SLOC-to-function-point ratios provided by PLT v8.2 for the languages most commonly observed in malware. Overall, backfiring is useful as SLOC counts are not available early enough in the requirements phase for estimating purposes. Also, the resulting UFC measure is a more normalized measure of the source code size.

Table 1. SLOC to function-point ratios for various programming languages.

Programming language	SLOC/FP	Programming language	SLOC/FP
ASP / ASP.Net	69	Java	53
Assembly	119	Javascript	47
Shell / DOS Batch	128	PHP	67
C	97	Pascal	90
C#	54	Python	24
C++	50	SQL / make	21
HTML / CSS / XML / XSLT	34	Visual Basic	42

2.2 Effort Estimation: The Constructive Cost Model (COCOMO)

One of the core problems in software engineering is to make an accurate estimate of the effort required to develop a software system. This is a complex issue that has attracted much attention since the early 1970s, resulting in various techniques that approach the problem from different perspectives [34]. A prominent class of such techniques are the so-called algorithmic cost modeling methods, which are based on mathematical formulae that provide cost figures using as input various measures of the program's size, organizational practices, and so on.

One of the best known algorithmic software cost estimation methods is the Constructive Cost Model (COCOMO) [12]. COCOMO is an empirical model derived from analyzing data collected from a large number of software projects.

These data were used to find, through basic regression, formulae linking the size of the system, and project and team factors to the effort to develop it. As in most algorithmic cost models, the number of lines of source code (SLOC) in the delivered system is the basic metric used in cost estimation. Thus, the basic COCOMO equation for the effort (in man-months) required to develop a software system is

$$E = a_b(\text{KLOC})^{b_b}, \quad (1)$$

where KLOC is the estimated number of SLOC expressed in thousands. The development time (in months) is obtained from the effort as

$$D = c_b E^{d_b}, \quad (2)$$

and the number of people required is just

$$P = \frac{E}{D}. \quad (3)$$

In the equations above, the coefficients a_b, b_b, c_b, and d_b are empirical estimates dependent on the type of project (see Table 2). COCOMO considers three types of projects: (i) *Organic* projects (small programming team, good experience, and flexible software requirements); *Semi-detached* projects (medium-sized teams, mixed experience, and a combination of rigid and flexible requirements); and (iii) *Embedded* projects (organic or semi-detached projects developed with tight constraints).

Table 2. Basic COCOMO coefficients.

Software project	a_b	b_b	c_b	d_b
Organic	2.4	1.05	2.5	0.38
Semi-detached	3.0	1.12	2.5	0.35
Embedded	3.6	1.20	2.5	0.32

The model described above is commonly known as *Basic COCOMO* and is very convenient to obtain a quick estimate of costs. A further refinement is provided by the so-called *Intermediate COCOMO*. The main difference consists in the addition of various multiplicative modifiers to the effort estimation (E) that account for attributes of both the product and the programming process such as the expected reliability, and the capability and experience of the programmers. Since these are not known for malware, we will restrict ourselves to the Basic COCOMO model.

2.3 Source Code Complexity and Maintainability

Software complexity metrics attempt to capture properties related to the interactions between source code entities. Complexity is generally linked to maintainability, in the sense that higher levels of complexity might translate into a higher risk of introducing unintentional interactions and, therefore, software defects [27].

One of the earliest—and still most widely used—software complexity metric is McCabe's cyclomatic complexity [28], often denoted M. The cyclomatic complexity of a piece of source code is computed from its control flow graph (CFG) and measures the number of linearly independent paths within it; that is, the number of paths that do not contain other paths within themselves. Thus, a piece of code with no control flow statements has $M = 1$. A piece of code with one single-condition IF statement would have $M = 2$, since there would be two paths through the code depending on whether the IF condition evaluates to true or false. Mathematically, the cyclomatic complexity of a program is given by

$$M = E - N + 2P, \qquad (4)$$

where E is the number of edges in the CFG, N the number of nodes, and P the number of connected components. The term "cyclomatic" stems from the connections between this metric and some results in graph theory and algebraic topology, particularly the so-called *cyclomatic number* of a graph, which measures the dimension of the cycle space of a graph [16].

The cyclomatic complexity has various applications in the process of developing and analyzing software products. The most direct one is to limit the complexity of the routines or modules that comprise the system. McCabe recommended that programmers should limit each module to a maximum complexity of 10, splitting it into smaller modules whenever its complexity exceeds this value. The NIST Structured Testing Methodology [38] later adopted this practice and relaxed the figure up to 15, though only occasionally and if there are well grounded reasons to do it. The cyclomatic complexity has also implications in program testing because of its connection with the number of test cases that are necessary to achieve thorough test coverage. Specifically, M is simultaneously: (i) an upper bound for the number of test cases needed to achieve a complete branch coverage (i.e., to execute all edges of the CFG); and (ii) a lower bound for the number of paths through the CFG. Thus, a piece of code with high M would have more pathways through the code and would therefore require higher testing effort.

The cyclomatic complexity is also connected to another code metric called the maintainability index (MI), introduced by Oman and Hagemeister in [30]. The MI is a value between 0 and 100 that measures how maintainable (i.e., easy to understand, support, and change) the source code is, with high values meaning better maintainability. One of the most common definitions of the MI is given by

$$MI = 100 \frac{171 - 5.2\ln\left(\overline{V}\right) - 0.23\overline{M} - 16.2\ln\left(\overline{SLOC}\right)}{171}, \qquad (5)$$

where $\overline{V}$ is Halsteads average volume per module (another classic complexity metric; see [21] for details), $\overline{M}$ is the average cyclomatic complexity per module, and $\overline{SLOC}$ is the average number of source code lines per module. This is, for instance, the definition used by Visual Studio, and does not take into account the comment-to-code ratio as the original one proposed in [30]. As in the case of the COCOMO estimators, Oman and Hagemeister arrived at this formula through statistical regression over a dataset consisting of a large number of software projects tagged with expert opinions. The MI has been included in Visual Studio since 2007, and in the JSComplexity and Radon metrics for Javascript and Python. Although not exempt from criticisms, its use was promoted by the Software Engineering Institute in their "C4 Software Technology Reference Guide" [33] as a potentially good predictor of maintainability. As for its interpretation, there is no agreed upon safe limits. For example, Visual Studio flags as suspicious modules with $MI < 20$.

3 Dataset

Our work is based on a dataset of malware source code collected by the authors over several months in 2015. Collecting malware source code is a challenging endeavor because malware is typically released in binary form. Only occasionally its source code is released or leaked, with its availability being strongly biased towards classical viruses and early specimens. When leaked, the source code may be difficult to access in underground forums. These challenges make it impossible to try to be complete. While we try to collect as many samples as possible, the goal is to acquire representative examples of the malware ecosystem during the last 30+ years, constrained to the limited availability.

Samples were obtained from a variety of sources, including virus collection sites such as *VX Heaven*, code repositories such as *GitHub*, classical e-zines published by historically prominent malware writing groups such as *29A*, various malware exchange forums available in the web, and through various P2P networks. We expanded our list of sources by using a snowballing methodology, exploring previously unknown sources that were referenced in sites under examination.

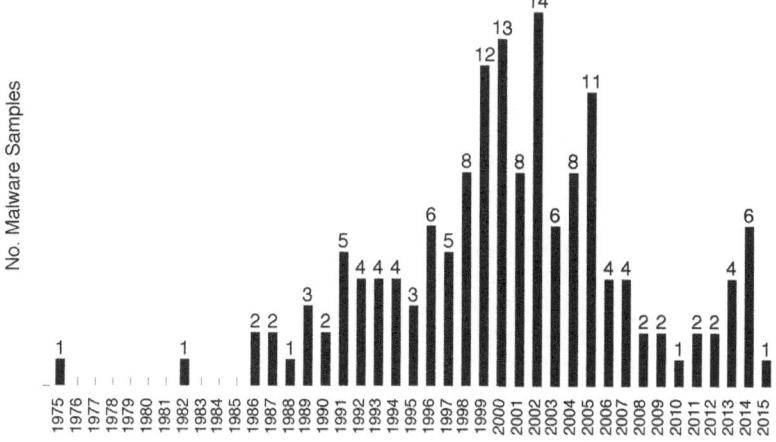

Fig. 1. Distribution of malware source code samples in the dataset.

Our initial collection contained 210 different samples of malware source code. Each sample was first quickly verified through manual inspection and then compiled, executed and, whenever possible, functionally tested. Approximately 30 % of the obtained samples were discarded at this point, either because testing them was unfeasible (e.g., due to nontrivial compilation errors or unavailability of a proper testing environment), or simply because they turned out to be fake.

Table 3. Malware source code samples in the dataset.

Year	Name	Type	Year	Name	Type	Year	Name	Type	Year	Name	Type
1975	ANIMAL	T	1997	CSV	V	2001	Anarxy	W	2005	Egypt	V
1982	ElkCloner	V	1997	Cabanas	V	2001	Ketamine	V	2005	Eternity	V
1986	Rushrour	V	1997	Harrier	V	2001	MW	W	2005	Friendly	V
1986	V11	V	1997	RedTeam	V	2001	Nicole	V	2005	Gripb	V
1987	Bvs	V	1997	V6000	V	2001	OU812	V	2005	Hidan	V
1987	Numberone	V	1998	Anaphylaxis	W	2001	Plexar	V	2005	Kroshkaenot	V
1988	MorrisWorm	W	1998	Ch0lera	W	2001	Rudra	V	2005	Nanomites	V
1989	AIDS	V	1998	Gift	W	2001	Tapakan	V	2005	Spieluhr	T
1989	CIA	V	1998	Marburg	V	2002	DW	V	2005	WRhRage	W
1989	Eddie	V	1998	PGPMorf2	V	2002	Efishnc	V	2006	Gurdof	W
1990	Anthrax	V	1998	Plague2000	W	2002	Gemini	V	2006	Kekule	W
1990	Diamond	V	1998	Shiver	M	2002	Grifin	W	2006	Macbet	W
1991	486	V	1998	Teocatl	M	2002	Junkmail	V	2006	Ston	W
1991	808	V	1999	Babylon	V	2002	Lexotan	V	2007	Antares	V
1991	Badbrains	V	1999	BeGemot	V	2002	Omoikane	V	2007	BO2K	R
1991	Demonhyak	V	1999	Demiurg	V	2002	PieceByPiece	W	2007	GhostRAT	R
1991	Tormentor	V	1999	Fabi2	V	2002	Ramlide	V	2007	Zeus	T
1992	ACME	V	1999	IISW	W	2002	Simile	V	2008	BatzBack	W
1992	Proto-t	V	1999	Melissa	M	2002	Solaris	V	2008	Grum	B
1992	Rat	V	1999	Nemesi	V	2002	Taichi	V	2009	Cairuh	W
1992	Thunderbyte	V	1999	Prizzy	V	2002	Vampiro	V	2009	Hexbot2	T
1993	Asexual	V	1999	Rinim	V	2002	ZMist	V	2010	Carberp	V
1993	Beavis	V	1999	RousSarcoma	V	2003	Blaster	W	2011	KINS	T
1993	DarkApocalypse	V	1999	YLANG	V	2003	Mimail	W	2011	PC-RAT	R
1993	Nakedtruth	V	1999	Yobe	V	2003	Obsidian	W	2012	AndroR	R
1994	Batvir	V	2000	Chainsaw	W	2003	Rainbow	V	2012	Dexter	V
1994	Bluenine	V	2000	Dream	V	2003	Seraph	V	2013	Alina	T
1994	Dichotomy	V	2000	Energy	W	2003	Tahorg	V	2013	Beetle	V
1994	Digitisedparasite	V	2000	Examplo	V	2004	Beagle	B	2013	Pony2	T
1995	242	V	2000	ILOVEYOU	W	2004	Caribe	W	2013	SharpBot	R
1995	Bluelightening	V	2000	Icecubes	W	2004	Jollyroger	V	2014	Dendroid	R
1995	RCE285	V	2000	Milennium	V	2004	Mydoom	W	2014	Gopnik	B
1996	Apocalyptic	V	2000	Rammstein	V	2004	Netsky	W	2014	OmegaRAT	R
1996	Combat	V	2000	Troodon	W	2004	Pilif	W	2014	Rovnix	T
1996	Galicia	V	2000	Tuareg	V	2004	Sasser	W	2014	SpyNet	R
1996	Jupiter	V	2000	W2KInstaller	V	2004	Shrug	V	2014	Tinba	T
1996	Mars	V	2000	XTC	W	2005	Assiral	W	2015	Pupy	R
1996	Staog	V	2000	Zelda	W	2005	Blackhand	V			

The 151 successfully tested samples that comprise our final dataset have been tagged with a year and a loose category. The year corresponds to their development when stated by the source, otherwise with the year they were first spotted in the wild. They are also tagged with a coarse-grained malware type: Virus (V), Worm (W), MacroVirus (M), Trojan (T), Botnet (B), or RAT (R). We are aware that this classification is rather imprecise. For instance, nearly all Botnets and RATs include bots that can be easily considered as Trojans, Backdoors or Spywares and, in some cases, show Worm features too. The same applies to some of the more modern viruses, which also exhibit Worm-like propagation strategies or behave like stand-alone Trojans. We chose not to use a more fine-grained malware type because it is not essential to our study and, furthermore, such classifications are problematic for many modern malware examples that feature multiple capabilities.

Figure 1 shows the distribution by year of the final dataset of 151 samples. Approximately 62 % of the samples (94) correspond to the period 1995–2005, with the remaining equally distributed in the 2006–2015 (27) and 1985–1994 (28) periods, plus two samples from 1975 and 1982, respectively. The largest category is Viruses (92 samples), followed by Worms (33 samples), Trojans (11 samples), RATs (9 samples), MacroViruses (3 samples), and Botnets (3 samples). A full listing of the 151 samples is provided in Table 3.

4 Analysis

This section describes our analysis over the malware source code dataset. It first details source code analytics (Sect. 4.1), then it estimates development cost (Sect. 4.2), next it discusses complexity and maintainability metrics (Sect. 4.3), and finally compares malware to benign code (Sect. 4.4).

4.1 Source Code Analytics

We next discuss various statistics obtained from the source code of the malware samples in our dataset.

Number of Source Code Files. Figure 2a shows the distribution over time of the number of files comprising the source code of the different malware samples. Except for a few exceptions, until the mid 1990s there is a prevalence of malicious code consisting of just one file. Nearly all such samples are viruses written in assembly that, as discussed later, rarely span more than 1,000 lines of code (LOC). This follows a relatively common practice of the 1980s and 1990s when writing short assembly programs.

From the late 1990s to date there is an exponential growth in the number of files per malware sample. The code of viruses and worms developed in the early 2000s is generally distributed across a reduced (<10) number of files, while some Botnets and RATs from 2005 on comprise substantially more. For instance, Back Orifice 2000, GhostRAT, and Zeus, all from 2007, contain 206, 201, and 249 source code files, respectively. After 2010, no sample comprises a single file.

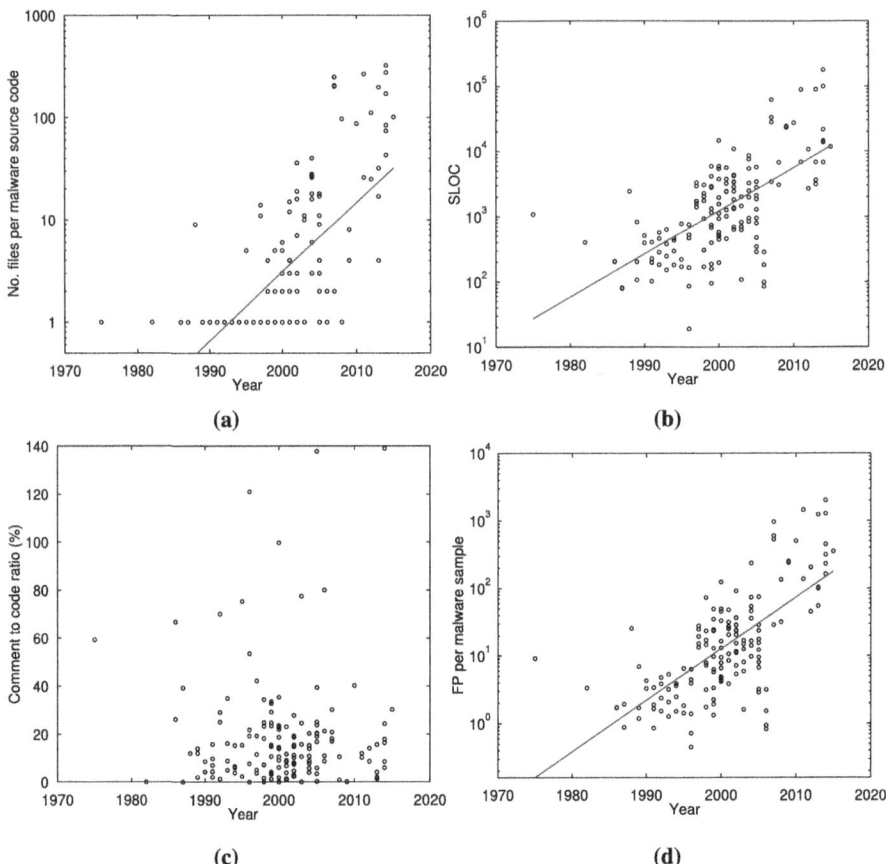

Fig. 2. Source code analytics of the malware samples in our dataset. (a) Number of files. (b) SLOC. (c) Comment-to-code ratios. (d) FP counts. Note that in (a), (b) and (d) the y-axis is shown in logarithmic scale.

Examples of this time period include KINS (2011), Rovnix (2014), and SpyNet (2014), with 267, 276, and 324 files, respectively. This increase reveals a more modular design, which also correlates with the use of higher-level programming languages discussed later.

Simple least squares linear regression over the data points shown in Fig. 2a yields a regression coefficient (slope) of 1.17. (Note that the y-axis is in logarithmic scale and, therefore, such linear regression actually corresponds to an exponential fit.) This means that the number of files has grown at an approximate yearly ratio of 17 %; or, equivalently, that it has doubled every 4.5 years.

Source Code Size. Figure 2d shows the distribution over time of the number of physical source lines of code (SLOC) of all samples in the dataset. For this we used cloc [1], an open-source tool that counts blank lines, comment lines, and SLOC, and reports them broken down by programming language. The data shown in Fig. 2d was obtained by simply aggregating the SLOC counts of all source code files belonging to the same malware sample, irrespective of the programming language in which they were written.

Again, the growth over the last 30 years is clearly exponential. Thus, up to the mid 1990s viruses and early worms rarely exceeded 1,000 SLOC. Between 1997 and 2005 most samples contain several thousands SLOCs, with a few exceptions above that figure, e.g., Troodon (14,729 SLOC) or Simile (10,917 SLOC). The increase in SLOC count during this period correlates positively with the number of source code files and the number of different programming languages used. Finally, a significant number of samples from 2007 on exhibit SLOC counts in the range of tens of thousands. For instance, GhostRAT (33,170), Zeus (61,752), KINS (89,460), Pony2 (89,758), or SpyNet (179,682). Most of such samples correspond to moderately complex malware projects whose output is more than just one binary. Typical examples include Botnets or RATs featuring a web-based C&C server, support libraries, and various types of bots/trojans. There are exceptions, too. For instance, Point-of-Sale (POS) trojans such as Dexter (2012) and Alina (2013) show relatively low SLOC counts (2,701 and 3,143, respectively).

In this case the linear regression coefficient over the data points is 1.16, i.e., the number of SLOCs per malware has increased approximately 16% per year; or, equivalently, the figure doubles every 4.7 years, resulting in an increase of nearly an order of magnitude each decade.

Function Points Estimates. We used the SLOC-to-function-point ratios provided by PLT v8.2 (see Table 1) in an attempt to use a more normalized measure of source code size for the malware samples in our dataset. To do that, we used such ratios in reverse order, i.e., to estimate function-point counts from SLOCs rather than the other way round. In doing so we pursue: (i) to better aggregate the various source code files of the same malware that are written in different languages; and (ii) to provide a fairer comparison among the sizes of the samples.

As expected, there is a clear correlation between FP and SLOC counts and the conclusions in terms of sustained growth are similar. Starting in 1990, there is roughly an increase of one order of magnitude per decade. Thus, in the 1990s most early viruses and worms contain just a few (<10) FPs. From 2000 to 2010 the FP count concentrates between 10 and 100, with Trojans, Botnets, and RATs accounting for the higher counts. Since 2007 on, many samples exhibit FP counts of 1,000 and higher; examples include Rovnix (2014), with FP = 1275.64, KINS (2011), with FP = 1462.86, and SpyNet (2014), with FP = 2021.79. Linear regression over the data points yields a coefficient of 1.19, i.e., FP counts per malware has suffered an approximate growth of 19% per year; or, equivalently, the figure doubles every 4 years.

Density of Comments. Figure 2c shows the comments-to-code ratios for the malware samples in the dataset. This is simply computed as the number of comment lines divided by the SLOC. There is no clear pattern in the data, which exhibit an average of 18.83%, a standard deviation of 23.44%, and a median value of 12.05%. There are a few notable outliers, though. For example, W2KInstaller (2000) and OmegaRAT (2014) show ratios of 99.6% and 139.1%, respectively. Conversely, some samples have an unusually low ratio of comments. We ignore if they were originally developed in this way or, perhaps, comments were cut off before leaking/releasing the code.

Programming Languages. Figure 3a shows the distribution over time of the number of different languages used to develop each malware sample. This includes not only compiled and interpreted languages such as assembly, C/C++, Java, Pascal, PHP, Python, or Javascript, but also others used to construct resources that are part of the final software package (e.g., HTML, XML, CSS) and scripts used to build it (e.g., BAT or make files).

Figure 3b shows the usage of different programming languages to code malware over time extracted from our dataset. The pattern reveals the prevalent use of assembly until the mid 2000s. From 2000 on C/C++ become increasingly popular, as well as other "visual" development environments such as Visual Basic and Delphi (Pascal). Botnets and RATs from 2005 on also make extensive use of web interfaces and include numerous HTML/CSS elements, pieces of Javascript, and also server-side functionality developed in PHP or Python. From 2012 to date the distribution of languages is approximately uniform, revealing the heterogeneity of technologies used to develop modern malware.

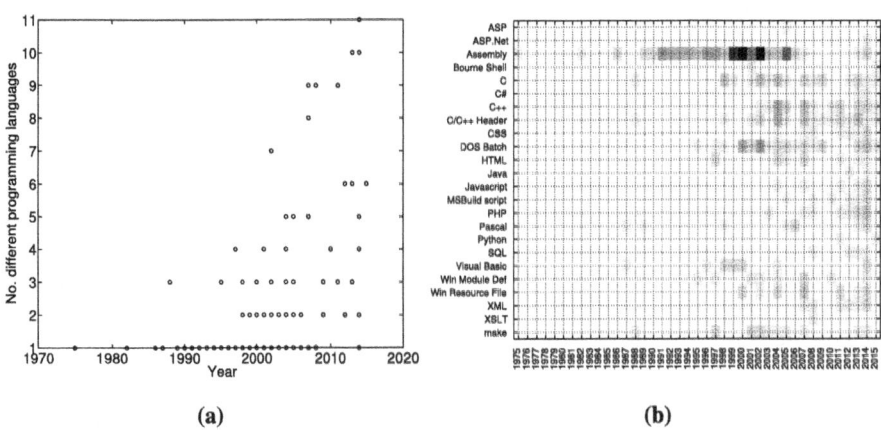

Fig. 3. (a) Number of different programming languages per malware sample in the dataset. (b) Use of programming languages in malware samples. The chart shows the number of samples using a particular language each year, with darker colors representing higher number of samples.

4.2 Cost Estimation

In this section we show the COCOMO estimates for the effort, time, and team size required to develop the malware samples in our dataset. One critical decision

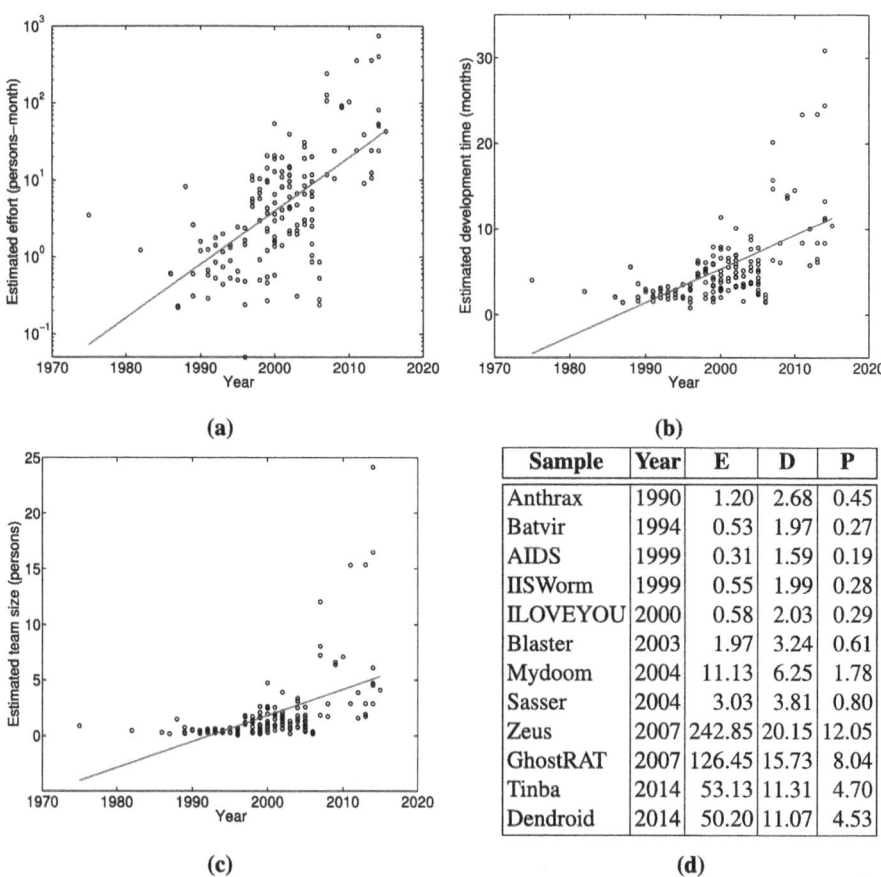

Fig. 4. COCOMO cost estimators for the malware samples in the dataset. (a) Effort (man-months). (b) Development time (months). (c) Team size (number of people). (d) Selected examples with effort (E), development time (D), and number of people (P). Note that in (a) and (b) the y-axis is shown in logarithmic scale.

here is selecting the type of software project (organic, semi-detached, or embedded) for each sample. We decided to consider all samples as organic for two main reasons. First, it is reasonable to assume that, with the exception of a few cases, malware development has been led so far by small teams of experienced programmers. Additionally, we favor a conservative estimate of development efforts which is achieved using the lowest COCOMO coefficients (i.e., those of organic projects) and can thus be seen as a (estimated) lower bound of development efforts.

Figure 4a shows the COCOMO estimation of effort required to develop the malware samples. The evolution over time is clearly exponential, with values roughly growing one order of magnitude each decade. While in the 1990s most samples required approximately 1 man-month, this value rapidly escalates up to 10–20 in the mid 2000s, and to 100s for a few samples of the last few years. Linear regression confirms this, yielding a regression coefficient of 1.17; i.e., the effort growth ratio per year is approximately 17%; or, equivalently, it doubles every 4.5 years.

The estimated time to develop the malware samples (Fig. 4b) experiences a linear increase up to 2010, rising from 2–3 months in the 1900s to 7–10 months in the late 2000s. The linear regression coefficient in this case is 0.395, which translates into an additional month every 2.5 years. Note that a few samples from the last 10 years report a considerable higher number of months, such as Zeus (2007) or SpyNet (2014) with 20.15 and 30.86 months, respectively.

The amount of people required to develop each sample (Fig. 4c) grows similarly. Most early viruses and worms require less than 1 person (full time). From 2000 on, the figure increases to 3–4 persons for some samples. Since 2010, a few samples report person estimates substantially higher. For these data, the linear regression coefficient is 0.234, which roughly translates into an additional team member every 4 years.

Finally, the table in Fig. 4d provides some numerical examples for a selected subset of samples. For additional details, we refer the reader to the full datasets[1] with the raw data used in this paper.

4.3 Complexity and Maintainability

In this section we show the complexity and maintainability metrics obtained for the samples in our dataset. To compute McCabe's cyclomatic complexity, we used the Universal Code Count (UCC) [6], a tool that provides various software metrics from source code. While many other tools exist for measuring cyclomatic complexity (e.g., Jhawk [3], Radon [4], or the metrics plugin for Eclipse [2]), these have a strong bias towards a particular language or a small subset of them. Contrarily, UCC works over C/C++, C#, Java, SQL, Ada, Perl, ASP.NET, JSP, CSS, HTML, XML, JavaScript, VB, PHP, VBScript, Bash, C Shell Script, Fortran, Pascal, Ruby, and Python. Since our dataset contains source code written in different languages, UCC best suits our analysis. Despite UCC's wide support for many languages, obtaining the cyclomatic measurements for each sample was not possible. As suggested by Fig. 3b, a large fraction of our samples contain a substantial amount of assembly code, which UCC does not support. Filtering out samples that contain at least one source file in assembly left 44 samples for analysis, i.e., approximately 33% of the dataset.

Figure 5a shows the average cyclomatic complexity per function for each analyzed sample. Most of the samples have complexities between 2 and 5, with values higher than that being very uncommon. Only DW (2002) exhibits an average cyclomatic complexity of around 7. Two main conclusions can be drawn from Fig. 5a (note that samples are temporarily ordered). First, even if there is no clear evolution over time of the average complexity per function, there is a slight decreasing trend. This might be a consequence of a more modular design,

---

[1] Available at: http://www.seg.inf.uc3m.es/~accortin/RAID_2016.html.

with functions and class methods being designed with less complex control flow logic structures. Second, a closer inspection at the full output of UCC reveals that no function or method in the 44 samples exceeds McCabe's recommended complexity threshold of 10.

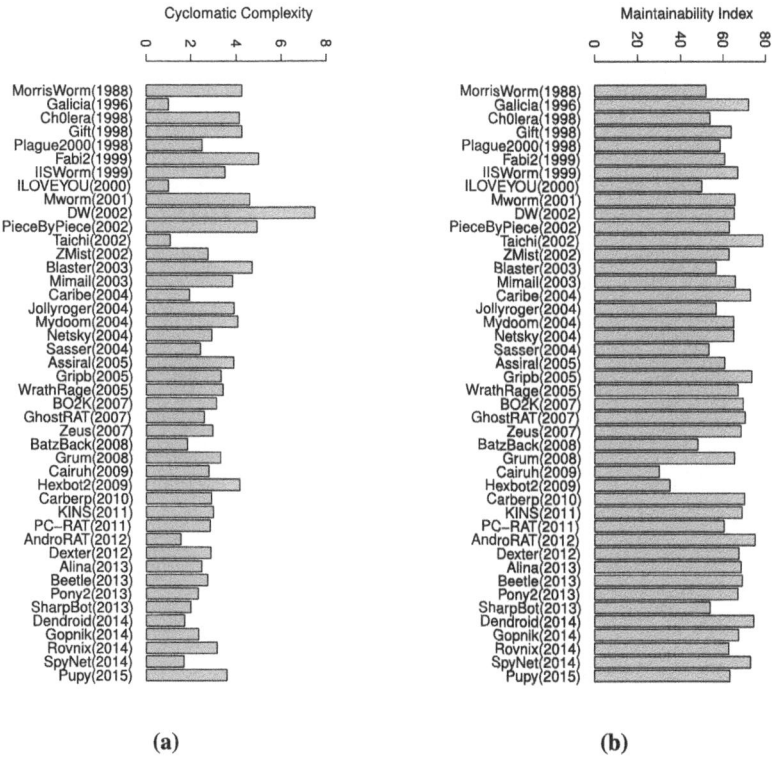

Fig. 5. (a) Average cyclomatic complexity per function and sample sorted by year. (b) Maintainability index per sample sorted by year.

Using the metrics discussed throughout this section, we have also computed an upper bound for the maintainability index MI provided by Eq. (5). Note that we cannot estimate it exactly since we do not have the average Halstead's volume for each sample. Since this is a negative factor in Eq. (5), the actual maintainability index would be lower than our estimates. Nevertheless, note that such a factor contributes the lowest to MI, so we expect our figures to provide a fair comparison among samples. Figure 5b shows the MI values for each sample in the reduced dataset. As in the case of cyclomatic complexities, no clear trend is observed. Values are generally high, with most samples having an MI higher than 50. The most extreme values are those of Cairuh ($MI = 30.05$) and Hexbot2 ($MI = 34.99$) on one side of the spectrum, and Taichi ($MI = 78.77$), AndroRAT

($MI = 75.03$), and Dendroid (74.47) on the other. All in all, these are reasonably high values for MI.

4.4 Comparison with Regular Software

In order to better appreciate the significance of the figures presented throughout this section, we next discuss how they compare to those of a selected number of open source projects whose source code is freely available. To do this we selected 9 software packages belonging to different categories: 3 security products (the IPTables firewall, the Snort IDS, and the ClamAV antivirus); a compiler (gcc); a web server (Apache); a version control tool (Git); a numerical computation suite (Octave); a graphic engine (Cocos2d-x); and a Unix shell (Bash). The code was downloaded from the web page of each project. For each one of them we then computed the metrics discussed above for malware samples. As in the case of malware samples, we use the COCOMO coefficients for organic projects. The results are shown in Table 4 in increasing order of SLOC count.

Table 4. Software metrics for various open source projects. **E**: COCOMO effort; **D**: COCOMO development time; **P**: COCOMO team size; **FP**: function points; **M**: cyclomatic complexity; **CR**: comment-to-code ratio; **MI**: maintainability index.

Software	Version	Year	SLOC	E	D	P	FP	M	CR	MI
Snort	2.9.8.2	2016	46,526	135.30	16.14	8.38	494.24	3.31	10.32	63.27
Bash	4.4 rc-1	2016	160,890	497.81	26.47	18.81	2,265.35	3.40	17.08	52.42
Apache	2.4.19	2016	280,051	890.86	33.03	26.97	4,520.10	3.02	23.42	61.56
IPtables	1.6.0	2015	319,173	1,021.97	34.80	29.37	3,322.05	3.06	27.33	68.88
Git	2.8	2016	378,246	1,221.45	37.24	32.80	4,996.44	3.37	12.15	41.84
Octave	4.0.1	2016	604,398	1,998.02	44.89	44.51	11,365.09	2.52	27.69	52.42
ClamAV	0.99.1	2016	714,085	2,380.39	47.98	49.61	10,669.97	2.79	33.57	63.87
Cocos2d-x	3.10	2016	851,350	2,863.02	51.47	55.63	16,566.78	2.96	17.55	66.60
gcc	5.3	2015	6,378,290	2,3721.97	114.95	206.37	90,278.41	2.10	31.24	50.57

The first natural comparison refers to the size of the source code. Various malware samples from 2007 on (e.g. Zeus, KINS, Pony2, or SpyNet) have SLOC counts larger than those of Snort and Bash. This automatically translates, according to the COCOMO model, into similar or greater development costs. The comparison of function point counts is alike, with cases such as Rovnix and KINS having an FP greater than 1000, or SpyNet, with an FP count comparable to that of Bash. In general, only complex malware projects are comparable in size and effort to these two software packages, and they are still far away from the remaining ones.

In terms of comment-to-code ratio, the figures are very similar and there is no noticeable difference. This seems to be the case for the cyclomatic complexity, too. To further investigate this point, we computed the cyclomatic complexities at the function level; i.e., for all functions of all samples in both datasets. The histograms of the obtained values is shown in Fig. 6. Both distributions are very similar, with a

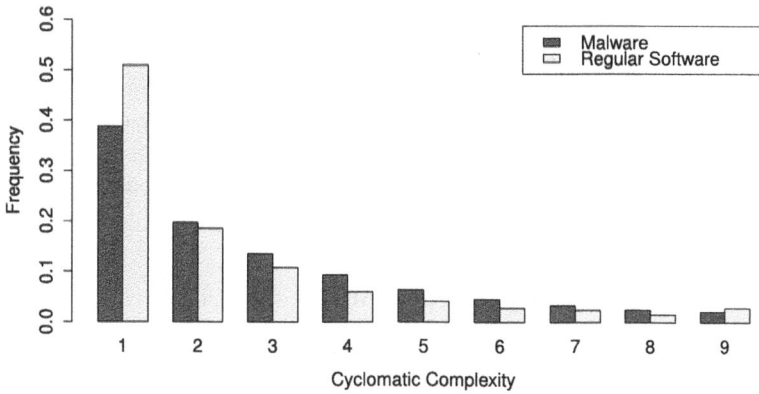

Fig. 6. Histograms of the cyclomatic complexity values computed at the function level for both malware and regular software samples.

clear positive skewness. A Chi-squared and two-sample Kolgomorov-Smirnov tests corroborate their similarity for a significance level of $\alpha = 0.05$.

More differences appear in terms of maintainability. Up to 12 malware samples show MI values higher than the highest one for regular software—IPtables, with $MI = 68.88$. In general, malware samples (particularly the most recent ones) seem to have slightly higher maintainability indexes than regular software. As discussed before, two notable exception are Cairuh and Hexbot2 with surprisingly low values.

5 Discussion

We next discuss some aspects of the suitability of our approach, the potential limitations of our results, and draw some general conclusions.

Suitability of Our Approach. Software metrics have a long-standing tradition in software engineering and have been an important part of the discipline since its early days. Still, they have been subject to much debate, largely because of frequent misinterpretations (e.g., as performance indicators) and misuse (e.g., to drive management) [34]. In this work, our use of certain software metrics pursues a different goal, namely to quantify how different properties of malware as a software artifact have evolved over time. Thus, our focus here is not on the accuracy of the absolute values (e.g., effort estimates given by COCOMO), but rather on the relative comparison of values between malware samples, as well as with benign programs, and the trends that the analysis suggests.

Limitations. Our analysis may suffer from several limitations. Perhaps the most salient is the reduced number of samples in our dataset. However, as discussed in Sect. 3, obtaining source code of malware is hard. Still, we discuss 151 samples, which to the best of our knowledge is the largest dataset of malware source code analyzed in the literature. While the exact coverage of our dataset cannot be known, we believe it is fairly representative in terms of different types of malware (one remarkable exception is ransomware, for which we were not able to find any samples). Another limitation is selection bias. Collection is particularly difficult for newest samples and more sophisticated samples (e.g., those used in targeted attacks) have not become publicly available and thus escape our collection. We believe those samples would emphasize the increasing complexity trends that we observe.

Main Conclusions and Open Questions. In the last 30 years the complexity of malware, considered as a software product, has increased considerably. We observe increments of nearly one order of magnitude per decade in aspects such as the number of source code files, source code lines, and function point counts. One question is whether this trend will hold in time. If so, we could soon see malware specimens with more than 1 million SLOC. On the other hand, evolving into large pieces of software involves a higher amount of vulnerabilities and defects. This has been already observed (and exploited), e.g., in [14,17]. In addition, such evolution requires larger efforts and thus possibly larger development teams. While we observe the trend we have not examined in detail those development teams. For this, we could apply authorship attribution techniques for source code [15,19]. More generally, the results shown in this paper provide a quantified evidence of how the malware development industry has been progressively transforming into a fully fledged engineering.

6 Related Work

While malware typically propagates as binary code, some malware families have distributed themselves as source code. Arce and Levy performed an analysis of the Slapper worm source code [10], which upon compromising a host would upload its source code, compile it using gcc, and run the compiled executable. In 2005, Holz [22] performed an analysis of the botnet landscape that describes how the source code availability of the Agobot and SDBot families lead to numerous variants of those families being created.

Barford and Yegneswaran [11] argue that we should develop a foundational understanding of the mechanisms used by malware and that this can be achieved by analyzing malware source code available on the Internet. They analyze the source code of 4 IRC botnets (Agobot, SDBot, SpyBot, and GTBot) along 7 dimensions: botnet control mechanisms, host control mechanisms, propagation, exploits, delivery mechanisms, obfuscation, and deception mechanisms.

Other works have explored the source code of exploit kits collected from underground forums and markets. Exploit kits are software packages installed on Web servers (called exploit servers) that try to compromise their visitors by exploiting vulnerabilities in Web browsers and their plugins. Different from client malware, exploit kits are distributed as (possibly obfuscated) source code. Kotov and Massacci [26] analyzed the source code of 30 exploit kits collected from underground markets finding that they make use of a limited number of vulnerabilities. They evaluated characteristics such as evasion, traffic statistics, and exploit management. Allodi et al. [9] followed up on this research by building a malware lab to experiment with the exploit kits. Eshete and Venkatakrishnan describe WebWinnow [18] a detector for URLs hosting an exploit kit, which uses features drawn from 40 exploit kits they installed in their lab. Eshete et al. follow up this research line with EKHunter [17] a tool that given an exploit kit finds vulnerabilities it may contain, and tries to automatically synthesize exploits for them. EKHunter finds 180 in 16 exploit kits (out of 30 surveyed), and synthesizes exploits for 6 of them. Exploitation of malicious software was previously demonstrated by Caballero et al. [14] directly on the binary code of malware samples installed in client machines.

7 Conclusion

In this paper, we have presented a study on the evolution of malware source code over the last decades. Our focus on software metrics is an attempt to quantify properties both of the code itself and its development process. The results discussed throughout the paper provide a numerical evidence of the increase in complexity suffered by malicious code in the last years and the unavoidable transformation into an engineering discipline of the malware production process.

Acknowledgments. We are very grateful to the anonymous reviewers for constructive feedback and insightful suggestions. This work was supported by the MINECO grant TIN2013- 46469-R (SPINY: Security and Privacy in the Internet of You), the CAM grant S2013/ICE-3095 (CIBERDINE: Cybersecurity, Data, and Risks), the Regional Government of Madrid through the N-GREENS Software-CM project S2013/ICE-2731 and by the Spanish Government through the Dedetis Grant TIN2015-7013-R.

References

1. CLOC - count lines of code. http://github.com/AlDanial/cloc. Accessed 22 Sep 2015
2. Eclipse metrics plugin. https://marketplace.eclipse.org/content/eclipse-metrics. Accessed 4 Apr 2016
3. Jhawk. http://www.virtualmachinery.com/jhawkprod.htm. Accessed 4 Apr 2016
4. Radon. https://pypi.python.org/pypi/radon. Accessed 4 Apr 2016
5. Symantec's 2015 internet security threat report. https://www.symantec.com/security_response/publications/threatreport.jsp. Accessed 6 Apr 2016
6. Unified code counter. http://csse.usc.edu/ucc_wp/. Accessed 4 Apr 2016
7. Albrecht, A.J.: Measuring Application Development Productivity. In: IBM Application Development Symposium, pp. 83–92. IBM Press, October 1979
8. Albrecht, A.J., Gaffney, J.E.: Software function, source lines of code, and development effort prediction: a software science validation. IEEE Trans. Softw. Eng. 9(6), 639–648 (1983)
9. Allodi, L., Kotov, V., Massacci, F.: MalwareLab: experimentation with cybercrime attack tools. In: USENIX Workshop on Cyber Security Experimentation and Test, Washington D.C., August 2013

10. Arce, I., Levy, E.: An analysis of the slapper worm. IEEE Secur. Priv. **1**(1), 82–87 (2003)
11. Barford, P., Yegneswaran, V.: An Inside Look at Botnets. In: Christodorescu, M., Jha, S., Maughan, D., Song, D., Wang, C. (eds.) Malware Detection. Advances in Information Security, vol. 27, pp. 171–191. Springer, Heidelberg (2007)
12. Boehm, B.W.: Software Engineering Economics. Prentice-Hall, Upper Saddle River (1981)
13. Caballero, J., Grier, C., Kreibich, C., Paxson, V.: Measuring pay-per-install: the commoditization of malware distribution. In: Proceedings of the 20th USENIX Conference on Security, p. 13, SEC 2011. USENIX Association, Berkeley (2011)
14. Caballero, J., Poosankam, P., McCamant, S., Babic, D., Song, D.: Input generation via decomposition and re-stitching: finding bugs in malware. In: ACM Conference on Computer and Communications Security, Chicago, IL, October 2010
15. Caliskan-Islam, A., Harang, R., Liu, A., Narayanan, A., Voss, C., Yamaguchi, F., Greenstadt, R.: De-anonymizing programmers via code stylometry. In: USENIX Security Symposium (2015)
16. Diestel, R.: Graph Theory. Graduate Texts in Mathematics, vol. 173, 4th edn. Springer, New York (2012)
17. Eshete, B., Alhuzali, A., Monshizadeh, M., Porras, P., Venkatakrishnan, V., Yegneswaran, V.: EKHunter: a counter-offensive toolkit for exploit kit infiltration. In: Network and Distributed System Security Symposium, February 2015
18. Eshete, B., Venkatakrishnan, V.N.: WebWinnow: leveraging exploit kit workflows to detect malicious urls. In: ACM Conference on Data and Application Security and Privacy (2014)
19. Frantzeskou, G., MacDonell, S., Stamatatos, E., Gritzalis, S.: Examining the significance of high-level programming features in source code author classification. J. Syst. Softw. **81**(3), 447–460 (2008). http://dx.doi.org/10.1016/j.jss.2007.03.004
20. Grier, C., Ballard, L., Caballero, J., Chachra, N., Dietrich, C.J., Levchenko, K., Mavrommatis, P., McCoy, D., Nappa, A., Pitsillidis, A., Provos, N., Rafique, M.Z., Rajab, M.A., Rossow, C., Thomas, K., Paxson, V., Savage, S., Voelker, G.M.: Manufacturing compromise: the emergence of exploit-as-a-service. In: Proceedings of the 2012 ACM Conference on Computer and Communications Security, pp. 821–832, CCS 2012. ACM, New York (2012)
21. Halstead, M.H.: Elements of Software Science (Operating and Programming Systems Series). Elsevier Science Inc., New York (1977)
22. Holz, T.: A short visit to the bot zoo. IEEE Secur. Priv. **3**(3), 76–79 (2005)
23. IEEE: IEEE standard for software productivity metrics (IEEE std. 1045-1992). Technical report (1992)
24. Jones, C.: Programming Languages Table, Version 8.2. Software Productivity Research, Burlington (1996)
25. Jones, C.: Backfiring: converting lines-of-code to function points. Computer **28**(11), 87–88 (1995)
26. Kotov, V., Massacci, F.: Anatomy of exploit kits. In: Jürjens, J., Livshits, B., Scandariato, R. (eds.) ESSoS 2013. LNCS, vol. 7781, pp. 181–196. Springer, Heidelberg (2013)
27. Lehman, M.M.: Laws of software evolution revisited. In: Montangero, C. (ed.) EWSPT 1996. LNCS, vol. 1149, pp. 108–124. Springer, Heidelberg (1996)
28. McCabe, T.J.: A complexity measure. In: Proceedings of the 2nd International Conference on Software Engineering, ICSE 1976, CA, USA, p. 407. IEEE Computer Society Press, Los Alamitos (1976)

29. Nguyen, V., Deeds-rubin, S., Tan, T., Boehm, B.: A SLOC counting standard. In: COCOMO II Forum 2007 (2007)
30. Oman, P., Hagemeister, J.: Metrics for assessing a software system's maintainability. In: Proceedings of Conference on Software Maintenance, pp. 337–344 (1992)
31. Park, R.E.: Software size measurement: a framework for counting source statements. Technical report CMU/SEI-92-TR- 20, ESC-TR-92-20, Software Engineering Institute, Carnegie Mellon University, Pittsburgh, Pennsylvania 15213, September 1992
32. Security, P.: 27 % of all recorded malware appeared in 2015. http://www.pandasecurity.com/mediacenter/press-releases/all-recorded-malware-appeared-in-2015. Accessed 6 Apr 2016
33. Software Engineering Institute: C4 Software Technology Reference Guide - A Prototype. Technical report CMU/SEI-97-HB-001, January 1997
34. Sommerville, I.: Software Engineering: (Update) (8th Edn.) (International Computer Science). Addison-Wesley Longman Publishing Co. Inc., Boston (2006)
35. Stringhini, G., Hohlfeld, O., Kruegel, C., Vigna, G.: The harvester, the botmaster, and the spammer: n the relations between the different actors in the spam landscape. In: Proceedings of the 9th ACM Symposium on Information, Computer and Communications Security, pp. 353–364. ASIA CCS 2014, NY, USA. ACM, New York (2014)
36. Suarez-Tangil, G., Tapiador, J.E., Peris-Lopez, P., Ribagorda, A.: Evolution, detection and analysis of malware for smart devices. IEEE Commun. Surv. Tutorials **16**(2), 961–987 (2014)
37. Thomas, K., Huang, D., Wang, D., Bursztein, E., Grier, C., Holt, T.J., Kruegel, C., McCoy, D., Savage, S., Vigna, G.: Framing dependencies introduced by underground commoditization. In: Workshop on the Economics of Information Security (2015)
38. Watson, A.H., Mccabe, T.J., Wallace, D.R.: Special publication 500-235, structured testing: a software testing methodology using the cyclomatic complexity metric. In: U.S. Department of Commerce/National Institute of Standards and Technology (1996)

Small Changes, Big Changes: An Updated View on the Android Permission System

Yury Zhauniarovich[1](✉) and Olga Gadyatskaya[2](✉)

[1] Qatar Computing Research Institute, HBKU, Doha, Qatar
yzhauniarovich@qf.org.qa
[2] SnT, University of Luxembourg, Luxembourg City, Luxembourg
olga.gadyatskaya@uni.lu

Abstract. Since the appearance of Android, its permission system was central to many studies of Android security. For a long time, the description of the architecture provided by Enck et al. in [31] was immutably used in various research papers. The introduction of highly anticipated runtime permissions in Android 6.0 forced us to reconsider this model. To our surprise, the permission system evolved with almost every release. After analysis of 16 Android versions, we can confirm that the modifications, especially introduced in Android 6.0, considerably impact the aptness of old conclusions and tools for newer releases. For instance, since Android 6.0 some signature permissions, previously granted only to apps signed with a platform certificate, can be granted to third-party apps even if they are signed with a non-platform certificate; many permissions considered before as threatening are now granted by default. In this paper, we review in detail the updated system, introduced changes, and their security implications. We highlight some bizarre behaviors, which may be of interest for developers and security researchers. We also found a number of bugs during our analysis, and provided patches to AOSP where possible.

Keywords: Android security · Permission system · Runtime permissions · Compatibility challenges

1 Introduction

Nowadays, Android is the dominating smartphone operating system. It occupied more than 80 % of the total smartphone market share in 2015 [20]. Furthermore, Android is truly ubiquitous existing in the Auto, TV, and Wear flavors. Moreover, many other types of devices, e.g., cameras or game consoles, run tweaked Android firmware [17]. Overall, more than 1.4 billion active devices are currently powered by Android [14]. This huge user-base was achieved by Google thanks

---

We thank the anonymous reviewers for their comments that allowed to improve the paper. We are also very grateful to William Enck for shepherding the paper and suggesting many improvements to it. The work of Olga Gadyatskaya was supported by the Luxembourg National Research Fund (C15/IS/10404933/COMMA).

to, among all, frequent updates of the operating system that keep introducing new features and improving performance.

Yet, the wide landscape of device types and platform versions gives rise to compatibility challenges. While the latest devices are relatively well-updated, others can be left behind, or even never updated after the release. For instance, Google reported that 2.6 % of devices that had visited the Google Play Store in March 2016 ran Android 2.3 released in 2011 [13]. At the same time, third-party applications are typically updated frequently, yet some of them are unsupported by the developers after a while. Therefore, there is a high fragmentation of the eco-system, and many problems, including security ones, emerge due to discrepancies in update cycles of the platform and apps.

The Android permission system regulating access of apps to device capabilities and system components, such as telephony, file system, sensors, networks, etc., is a crucial part of the Android security model. Not surprisingly, from the beginning it was, and still is, central to many studies of Android security (it is featured in [23,25,28,31,33,35,41,45,46,49,50,52,53], to mention a few). However, only some of them acknowledged that the permission system was not stable. Among those, an early investigation by Enck, Ongtang and McDaniel [31] reported on the substantial shift introduced to the permission system across the earliest Android releases. Since that time, the vast majority of Android studies still rely on the same understanding introduced in this seminal paper.

The **emergence of runtime permissions in Android 6.0** forced us to take a closer look at the permission system design. In this paper we analyze the changes in the permission system introduced in the last 6 years and provide an updated view on the current architecture of the Android permission system since its description in [31]. We reveal the core changes that need to be considered during the security analysis, the main of which are the following:

– **Runtime permissions.** In Android 6.0, permissions are divided into install-time and runtime. *Normal* and *signature* (with some exceptions) permissions are permanently assigned upon the app installation, while *dangerous* permissions are now granted at runtime, and the user may revoke them at any time.
– **Runtime permissions are granted on the group basis.** If an app requires runtime permissions related to the same permission group, once one of them is granted, others are granted as well. Instead of enabling more fine-grained control of dangerous functionality, Android 6.0 does the opposite.
– **Some *signature* permissions can be obtained by third-party applications.** The Android community is used to consider *signature* permissions to be install-time granted to apps that have the same digital signature as the package declaring the permission. However, several new types of *signature* permissions appeared in Android that can be obtained by third-party apps not conforming to this condition.
– **The *signature|system* protection level is deprecated.** Currently, the *signature|system* protection level is marked as deprecated and should not be used neither for custom (third-party), nor for platform permissions.

– **Some dangerous permissions are now granted without user's consent.** In Android 6.0, 22 permissions, previously considered as sensitive, are granted by default and the user cannot revoke them in any way. For instance, the INTERNET, BLUETOOTH, NFC permissions are now automatically granted at app installation. Previously they had to be approved by the user.

Considering the aforementioned modifications, it is clear that the Android community needs to update its view on the permission system and to evaluate security implications of the changes. To address this need, in this paper we present an updated security architecture of the system and important internal details of its implementation. Furthermore, to assess the compatibility challenges implications, we performed a thorough longitudinal study of the Android permission system that yielded many **interesting findings**, e.g.,:

 – Even though the *signature|system* protection level is deprecated, permissions of this level still exist in the system. Moreover, 9 permissions of this type were added in the Android 6.0 release itself. We have submitted to Google several patches to fix this issue in Android Open Source Project (AOSP), and some of them have already been merged into the master branch.
 – The runtime permissions have backward compatibility issues. Developers that expect their apps to run on older platform versions are still required to make a runtime check for permissions. However, the permissions that did not exist on some platform version are always denied (while they should not be required at all). We have found 8 such permissions, e.g., ADD_VOICEMAIL.
 – Some non-*dangerous* permissions are assigned to permission groups, although there is no reason for this. We found 8 such permissions, e.g., USE_FINGERPRINT. We consider these to be coding nits that could be fixed by Google developers.

Our findings emphasize considerable flaws that emerged due to the high change rates in the permission system design. Considering the aforementioned discrepancies in update cycles of platforms and apps, it is time for the security community to re-evaluate the attack surface of the Android permission system.

Roadmap. Section 2 outlines the established view on the Android permission system. Section 3 incrementally updates this view, while Sect. 4 gives internal details of the permission system implementation. Section 5 presents our quantitative analysis of evolution in the permission system, and Sect. 6 presents the key findings of our qualitative study. Finally, Sect. 7 discusses related work, and Sect. 8 concludes the paper.

2 The Established View on the Permission System

By default, all Android apps are executed as low-privileged processes at the Linux kernel level. Thus, every app has access only to a limited set of system capabilities. At the same time, to be fully-functional an app should be able to interact with other applications and obtain data from various system services (e.g., location or telephony) running in other processes. To enable these interactions, Android provides a special inter-component communication (ICC) protocol called Binder. Certainly, these communications should not be arbitrary, i.e., only approved interactions must be possible within the system. The Android permission system provides such access control mechanism. Permissions, which are unique security labels, are assigned to sensitive resources. Once an app is granted with the permission, it receives access to the corresponding protected object, otherwise interactions with the resource are prohibited.

A permission must be declared by the developer in the `AndroidManifest.xml` file of the app (in the special `permission` tag) and assigned to the protected resource (either in the manifest file or by performing corresponding checks in the code). Once declared, other packages may ask for access to the object by requesting the corresponding permission using the `uses-permission` tag of their own `AndroidManifest.xml` file. *Platform* permissions are declared within the Android operating system itself: either in the Android framework or in the packages supplied with the platform. Third-party app developers may also declare their own *custom* permissions and use them to protect sensitive components of their apps.

Upon declaration, any Android permission is assigned with a *protection level*. It defines what apps can be granted with the corresponding permissions, and how this process occurs. Starting with Android 0.9 [31], permissions were divided into 4 levels: *normal*, *dangerous*, *signature* and *signature|system*. According to the established permission system view, the least sensitive *normal* permissions were granted automatically to any app declaring these permissions, while more sensitive *dangerous* permissions were granted only after user's explicit consent during app installation. If the user wanted to refuse even a single permission, the application would not be installed on the device. *Signature* permissions were granted only if packages declaring the permission and using it are signed with the same certificate. Finally, permissions of the *signature|system* protection level acted like *signature* permissions, but could be additionally granted to apps installed into the system partition. Thus, prior to Android 6.0 all permissions were granted or denied once and for all at the installation time.

A permission can belong to a *permission group* that clusters together security labels according to particular functionality. Permission groups were mainly introduced to simplify the presentation by grouping permissions together. Yet, before Android 6.0 groups were not widely adopted in the "vanilla" Android, although they were used in the Google Play client application.

This vision of the Android permission system migrated for a long time from one research paper to another. In the meanwhile, the system did not stand still, but continuously changed all that time. However, the modifications were not that crucial, and remained mostly unnoticed.

3 New Android Permission System Overview

In Android 6.0, **all permissions are divided into installation and runtime**. Roughly, this division occurs in the following way: *normal*, *signature* and *signature|system* permissions are permanently granted upon the app installation (yet,

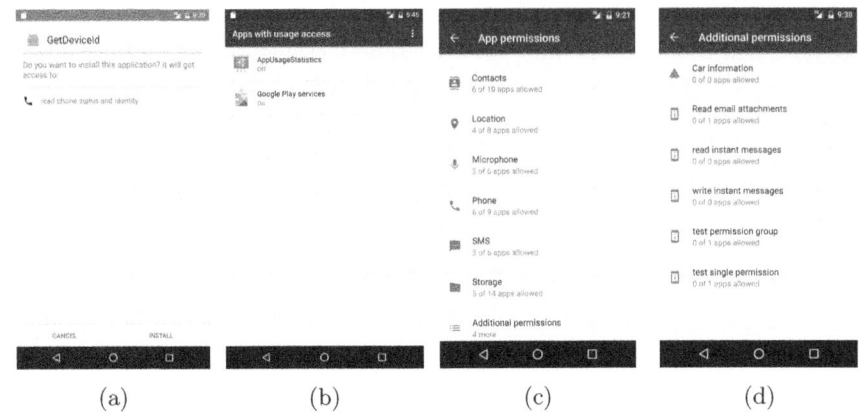

Fig. 1. Screenshots: (a) Permission request during installation of legacy applications in Android 6.0; (b) Screen to grant or revoke "appop" permission; (c) Separate screens are developed for core permission groups to grant and revoke permissions; (d) List of additional permissions.

with some exceptions considered further), while *dangerous* permissions are now checked at runtime. The *signature|system* protection level is **deprecated** starting Android 6.0 and should not be used [12]. However, our analysis of permissions defined in the platform code shows that such permissions are still abundant (see Sects. 5 and 6 for more details).

Previously, *dangerous* permissions were to be approved by the user in the special screen shown during app installation. Once approved, the app could be instantly used and the user did not deal with permissions anymore. In Android 6.0, the screen to grant *runtime* permissions is not shown (for apps targeting API 23 and up). Instead, all *runtime* permissions after installation are in the *disabled* state and must be approved by the user once the app needs access to the protected functionality.

To support runtime permissions, special protected API calls were added to PackageManager allowing to grant and revoke permissions dynamically. Additionally, new APIs were added allowing app developers to check at runtime if permissions are granted and to request them if necessary [19]. Within the *Settings* app, the users are provided with two screens to review, grant and revoke runtime permissions: on the first screen permissions are grouped on per app basis, on the second – per permission group.

Obviously, new applications must be forward compatible with the older Android versions, because only a small fraction of devices runs the newest Android (in April 2016 only 5 % of devices ran Android 6.x [13]). To ensure compatibility, Google provided a special compatibility library that proxies the calls for checking granted permissions (ContextCompat.checkSelfPermission). However, this proxy call must still rely underneath on the permission check functionality available in the previous releases, which, not surprisingly, is based on the `Context.checkPermission` API call. In previous Android versions permissions are granted upon installation, thus, the check will always pass, and new runtime permission request functionality will not be called. However, we found out that this functionality does not always work as expected (see Sect. 6).

Backward compatibility of legacy apps with the new version of Android is provided through the *AppOps* system allowing users to grant and revoke permissions at runtime through a dedicated user interface within the *Settings* system application. It shares the same interface with the runtime permission manager. This hidden app permission manager unofficially appeared in Android 4.3. Unfortunately, access to this component was suppressed in Android 4.4.2 and reappeared only in Android 6.0. However, *AppOps* handles only platform permissions and, thus, cannot enforce custom *dangerous* permissions declared by a developer. Upon installation of a legacy app through the installer on device the user is still presented with the "old" grant permission screen (see Fig. 1(a). The user must agree with the presented permissions, or the app will not be installed. This behavior differs from the one of the apps targeting Android 6.0, what results in some user experience inconsistencies. We describe them in details in Sect. 6.

Runtime permissions are granted per **permission groups**, i.e., if one permission from a group is granted or revoked, the same happens for all permissions in this group. For instance, if an app is granted with the `READ_CONTACTS` permission, it automatically receives `WRITE_CONTACTS` (if requested), because they both belong to the `CONTACTS` permission group. Android 6.0 defines nine permission groups for *dangerous* permissions: `CALENDAR`, `CAMERA`, `CONTACTS`, `LOCATION`, `MICROPHONE`, `PHONE`, `SENSORS`, `SMS`, `STORAGE`. While the app developers still have to declare permissions from these groups individually, the end-users only grant or revoke access per permission groups, and they are oblivious to which individual permissions the app requests.

Before it was assumed that third-party applications cannot obtain any *signature* permission if they are not signed with the same certificate. Yet, in Android 6.0 new permissions called *appop* were added. These *signature* permissions (`PACKAGE_USAGE_STATS`, `WRITE_SETTINGS` and `SYSTEM_ALERT_WINDOW`) can now be granted to third-party apps after an explicit user's consent through *Settings*.

We continue to explore the changes to the Android permission system and their implications for security analysis in Sect. 6.

4 Permission System Implementation Details

The behavior of permissions is controlled through assigning special string values to the attributes (`android:protectionLevel` and `android:permissionFlags`) upon permission declaration in the `AndroidManifest.xml` file. During the installation of a package, these values are parsed influencing on the bits of two 32-bit integer fields (`protectionLevel` and `flags`) of the `PermissionInfo` class. This section reviews how the bits of these two fields affect the permissions behavior.

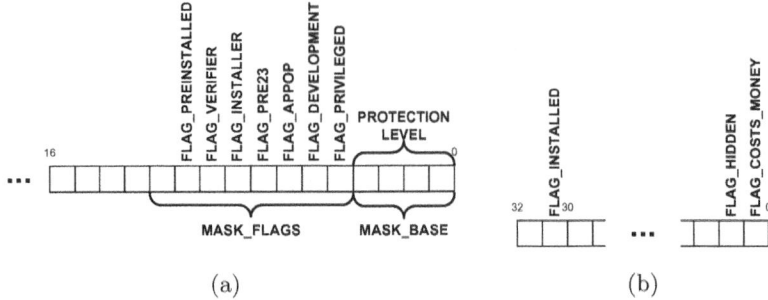

Fig. 2. "Protection Level" (a) and "Additional Flags" (b) field map.

4.1 Protection Level

Figure 2a shows a map of the lower 16 bits of the `protectionLevel` field (the higher 16 bits are currently not in use). The lower 4 bits are used to specify the protection level of a permission. The protection level value is determined by applying bitwise AND operation to the `protectionLevel` field and the `MASK_BASE` constant. Since a permission can only have one protection level, its values have sequential order, where the *normal* protection level is equal to 0, *dangerous* is 1, *signature* – 2, and *signature|system* is equal to 3. Interestingly, although *signature|system* level has a higher protection level value, *signature* permissions are considered as more sensitive. If a permission protection level is not specified in the manifest file, by default, *signature* protection level is used.

Protection level flags can be used only with *signature* permissions. Flags with other protection levels will generate an error at the time of manifest parsing. Protection level flags are masked with the `MASK_FLAGS` constant.

The first flag `FLAG_PRIVILEGED` enforces that only apps either signed with the same certificate or installed into the special location can obtain the permission. Until Android 4.4 all applications installed on the system image were granted with these privileged permissions by default. This means that even unprivileged system apps, e.g., Calculator, were able to obtain such permissions. To reduce the attack surface, system apps were later divided into the *ordinary* and *privileged* ones [9]. The ordinary system apps remain in the `/system/app` directory, but **are not** granted with privileged permissions anymore. To obtain privileged permissions an app must be installed into a separate `/system/priv-app` folder. Besides setting this flag directly, the developer can achieve the same permission behavior by setting the protection level to *signature|system* (deprecated since Android 6.0).

In Android 4.1 [12], the *development* permissions (marked with the flag `FLAG_DEVELOPMENT`) were introduced. These permissions usually protect the functionality required to perform development tasks, e.g., read system logs (`READ_LOGS`). An app can request these permissions, but they will not be automatically granted. At runtime the user can grant and revoke these permissions on demand by using special commands `pm grant` and `pm revoke` of the Android shell [30].

FLAG_APPOP was introduced in Android 5.0 [4], although explicitly it has started to be used only with Android 6.0. This flag was added to allow selective access to certain critical platform operations protected by *signature* permissions to third-party apps, after an explicit approval from the user. As we mentioned, typically, the *signature* protection level ensures that the corresponding platform permission is automatically granted at install time to the apps signed with the same certificate as the system image. Yet, this flag relaxes the requirement that the protected functionality can be used only by the system components. However, upon installation, access to the resources is disabled by default to third-party apps. For every permission of this *appop* type there is a separate configuration screen, where the user may explicitly grant or revoke access to these operations for system and third-party apps. E.g., Fig. 1b shows the screen for the PACKAGE_USAGE_STATS permission. The flag name shows that the enforcement of this type of permissions happens through the *AppOps* system.

FLAG_PRE23, as the name suggests, indicates that the corresponding permission is automatically granted to apps targeting pre-6.0 Android (API levels less than 23) versions [11]. For instance, the permission to draw a window over other apps SYSTEM_ALERT_WINDOW before Android 6.0 had the *dangerous* level, and thus was granted automatically upon installation. In Android 6.0 the protection level of this permission was changed to *signature*. However, apps targeting previous API versions are not aware of this change. Thus, during their execution an invocation of the functionality protected with this permission will generate an error. FLAG_PRE23 permits to overcome this issue by automatically granting the permission with this flag set to apps targeting previous versions of Android.

The flags FLAG_INSTALLER and FLAG_VERIFIER introduced in Android 6.0 [5] indicate that permissions are automatically granted to the packages set as the required installer and verifier (see more in [30]). However, to use these permissions the installer package must be installed on the system image, while the verifier package must be additionally granted with the PACKAGE_VERIFICATION_AGENT permission which has the *signature|privileged* protection level.

Finally, FLAG_PREINSTALLED added in Android 6.0 [8] indicates that the permission can be granted not only to the apps installed into the privileged folder, but to any app installed in the system partition.

4.2 Permission Flags

Permission flags were introduced in Android 4.2 [3]. Internally, permission flags are also represented as an integer 32-bit field which map is shown in Fig. 2b. These flags are controlled through the android:permissionFlags attribute of the permission tag. It should be noted that only the FLAG_COSTS_MONEY and FLAG_HIDDEN flags may be set through this attribute, while FLAG_INSTALLED is not accessible through a permission declaration.

The flag FLAG_COSTS_MONEY introduced in Android 4.1 [3] influences how a permission with this flag set is presented to a user. These permissions are marked with the "coins" sign displayed on the screen shown during app installation (in versions before Android 6.0). Interestingly, there are no restrictions on

Table 1. Versions of the android platform used in our study

API level	Branch	Codename	Release date (mm-dd-yyyy)
23	`android-6.0.0_r1`	Marshmallow	10-05-2015
22	`android-5.1.0_r1`	Lollipop	03-09-2015
21	`android-5.0.1_r1`	Lollipop	12-02-2014
19	`android-4.4_r1`	KitKat	10-31-2013
18	`android-4.3_r1`	Jelly Bean	07-24-2013
17	`android-4.2_r1`	Jelly Bean	11-13-2012
16	`android-4.1.1_r1`	Jelly Bean	07-11-2012
15	`android-4.0.3_r1`	Ice Cream Sandwich	12-16-2011
14	`android-4.0.1_r1`	Ice Cream Sandwich	10-21-2011
10	`android-2.3.3_r1`	Gingerbread	02-09-2011
9	`android-2.3_r1`	Gingerbread	12-06-2010
8	`android-2.2_r1`	Froyo	05-20-2010
7	`android-2.1_r1`	Eclair	01-12-2010
6	`android-2.0.1_r1`	Eclair	12-03-2009
5	`android-2.0_r1`	Eclair	10-26-2009
4	`android-1.6_r1`	Donut	09-15-2009

the usage of this flag, thus, even custom permissions could use it. Similarly, the flag FLAG_HIDDEN added in Android 6.0 [7] also influences presentation, making a permission hidden from the user's sight. This flag is used for the platform permissions that have become deprecated and removed from the system. However, a developer may use this flag to conceal custom dangerous permissions.

The flag FLAG_INSTALLED was introduced in Android 6.0 [10]. It is set by the operating system itself. This flag shows that the permission has been actually installed into the system, and influences presentation of permissions. For instance, if a permission has not been declared by an application but is requested by another app, it will not be shown in the list of requested permissions.

5 Analysis of Permission Changes

To investigate empirically how the Android permission system evolved across platform updates, we retrieved the source code of the Android platform for versions released from 2009 till 2015 that **resulted in the API level change** (the latest release at the time of writing is Android Marshmallow). Table 1 overviews the Android platform releases covered in our study.

We performed the analysis aiming at detection of odds in the permission system. In our study we focus on the Android platform permissions, and we do not cover custom permissions, which are defined by third-party applications to protect access to their resources. We divide platform permissions into 4 categories:

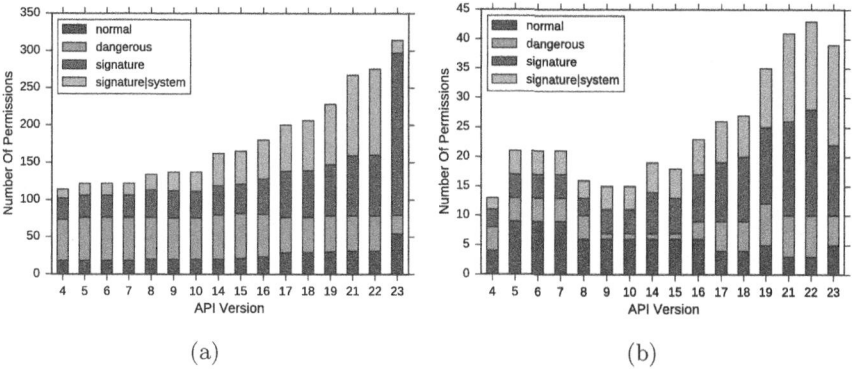

Fig. 3. Number of permissions for every platform release: (a) for *core* permissions; (b) for *package* permissions.

- *sample* – permissions that are declared by the sample apps shipped with the platform source code (appeared from API 21).
- *test* – permissions that are declared in the manifest files of packages developed for testing purposes;
- *package* – permissions that are declared in various packages that complement the framework, and that are not of *test* or *sample* groups;
- *core* – permissions that are declared in the core Android manifest file located in the frameworks/base/core/res folder;

The categories discussed above reflect the basic purposes why permissions are used within AOSP [1]: some permissions (from the categories *core* and *package*) are the "true" permissions used for access control, while others are auxiliary utilized in example applications (*sample*) or for testing (*test*). We focus our study on *core* and *package* permissions, because they are the ones that truly influence the behavior of the operating system.

The study done by Wei et al. in 2012 revealed that the number of permissions steadily increased with each Android release [49]. Our study, as of the beginning of 2016, confirms that finding and shows that **the total amount of permissions declared within the Android platform continues to grow**, reaching 314 in API 23 compared to 165 in API 15 (the last version analyzed by Wei et al. [49]). Figure 3a and b illustrate the growth of the number of permissions for *core* and *package* categories correspondingly. Obviously, the main contributor to the continuous increase are *core* permissions. The amount of the *package* permissions fluctuates, although still showing the overall upward trend. These plots also demonstrate the changes in the amounts of permissions of different protection levels. Table 2 characterizes the changes between consequent API levels. The data confirms that almost every Android API release (besides the API 6, 7, 10) introduced new permissions, as access to the new platform functionality often needs to be guarded.

Table 2. Permission changes in *core* and *package* categories

API level	Amount of permission changes					
	Added	Removed	Type changed	Protection level changed		
				Inc	Dec	Total
5	14	2	0	0	0	0
6	0	0	0	0	0	0
7	0	0	0	0	0	0
8	13	2	1	5	1	6
9	8	6	0	4	0	4
10	0	0	0	1	0	1
14	30	1	0	5	1	6
15	3	1	0	0	0	0
16	20	0	0	6	0	6
17	21	0	0	7	8	15
18	10	1	0	0	0	0
19	28	2	0	2	0	2
21	54	9	0	6	3	9
22	11	3	0	0	0	0
23	46	8	0	7	128	135

Interestingly, while the total amount of permissions increases with every new Android release, the number of permissions with *normal* and *dangerous* levels, which guard the functionality exposed to third-party applications, remains fairly stable. Therefore, from the developer perspective, the cognitive load did not increase much in terms of new permissions (however, the amount of compatibility issues to be handled is still growing due to the fluctuations in permissions). At the same time, security researchers, and platform and system app developers have to cope with more and more permissions.

At the same time, permissions are not only added. Throughout the platform evolution, many permissions were removed or changed their protection level. We analyzed code commits to AOSP [1] and found the following reasons why permissions are removed. Most of the *package* permissions were removed, because either the corresponding packages were deleted from the system, or the functionality of these packages became closed-source. Some permissions became obsolete because the corresponding functionality was either provided to all applications (e.g., the backup functionality protected with the BACKUP_DATA permission was made available to all apps in API 8) or merged with other functionality, as in case of GRANT_REVOKE_PERMISSIONS (removed in API 23) used to protect the runtime granting of *development* permissions. Interestingly, while the permission READ_OWNER_DATA was removed in API 9, more than 5 years ago, the current documentation still contains references to it[1]. Additionally, permissions may be simply renamed (e.g., BROADCAST_SCORE_NETWORKS became BROADCAST_NETWORK_PRIVILEGED). All these perturbations hinder understanding of the permission system and its changes across Android releases.

According to Table 2, there was only 1 case of the category change: the ACCESS_CACHE_FILESYSTEM permission in API 7 was in the *package* category, while in API 8 its declaration was moved to the core Android Manifest file.

As for the protection level changes, Table 2 reports the number of permissions that increased or decreased[2] their protection level.

The overall trend in the table shows that, prior to Android 6.0, permissions had a tendency to increase their protection level with the lapse of time. However, the majority of protection level updates were related to changing the protection level from *signature* to *signature|system*, what is actually not a restriction in control. Although internally *signature|system* permissions are assigned with a higher value, in general the *signature* permissions are more restrictive, because they allow the apps to obtain these permissions only if the declaring and requesting packages are signed with the same certificate. Permissions of the *signature|system* level can be also granted if the app is installed into the special system folder, what allows vendors to use this functionality to vest pre-installed applications with additional capabilities. For instance, the ability to shutdown the system (protected with the SHUTDOWN permission) in API 14 was also given to vendor apps. At the same time, other changes of protection level mostly aimed at limiting the privileges of third-party apps. E.g., in API 16 the READ_LOGS permission allowing to read the system log that may contain sensitive data, changed level from *dangerous* to *signature|system*.

Before API 23 there were not so many cases of decreases in the protection level. These were mostly related to relaxing *dangerous* permissions in order to avoid bothering the end-users with their approval. For instance, the WAKE_LOCK permission allowing an app to prevent the system from going into the sleep mode changed its level from *dangerous* to *normal* in API 17.

There are permissions that changed their protection level several times. E.g., permission BATTERY_STATS initially appeared as *normal*. In API 17 it became *dangerous*, and in API 19 it emerged as a *signature|system* permission. Finally, in API 23 it became a *signature* permission. Thus, during its life BATTERY_STATS has had all possible security levels.

The API level 23 introduced significant changes in protection levels of permissions. Now, there are only a few *dangerous* permissions, as opposed to all previous Android releases. Table 2 shows that the protection level decreased for 128 permissions. The main reason for this change is deprecation of the *signature|system* protection level (104 permissions became *signature*). Moreover, the shift to runtime permissions forced platform developers to reconsider the entries

---

[1] http://developer.android.com/guide/topics/manifest/manifest-intro.html.
[2] For this table we interpret the protection levels *normal*, *dangerous*, *signature* and *signature|system* as an ordered set, where *normal* corresponds to the least critical permissions and *signature|system* – to the most critical.

in the *dangerous* set, leaving only the most critical ones that can be comprehended by users. Consequently, some *dangerous* permissions were transformed into *normal* (22 cases). Section 6 discusses the effects of these changes.

Permission groups show more stable behavior with respect to changes. In Android 1.6 (API 4) there were 11 groups. As permission groups were not widely used, this number remained the same till API 17, when 19 new groups were added. In API 18 one additional group appeared, resulting in 31 total. There is not much information why this reorganization happened in these 2 consecutive releases. However, this may be connected with the Google Play installer app starting to cluster permissions according to their groups [18]. In Android 6.0 permission groups were completely reconsidered once again. There are 4 new groups added, while 26 were removed, resulting in 9 groups total. This radical change happened because *dangerous* permissions are now granted on per-group basis. Thus, the amount of groups was considerably reduced to avoid overwhelming users with lots of permissions.

6 Key Findings

Ideally, the security critical components of a system should remain quite stable to ensure easy security assessment. Unfortunately, this does not hold true in case of the Android operating system. This section reports on our findings and doubts inferred during the analysis of the evolution of the permission system.

6.1 Important Changes in API 23

(1) Runtime permissions. Undoubtedly, from the security perspective one of the biggest changes in Android 6.0 is the introduction of runtime permissions. Such a change requires efforts from both the OS designers and third-party developers to ensure backward compatibility of old apps with the new platform version, and forward compatibility of new apps with older platforms.

Backward compatibility of old apps with the new platform. Although the intention was to make legacy (targeting the Android API levels before 23) and new (API level 23) apps to behave in the same way, the differences are quite substantial. First, during the installation of a legacy app the user must agree with the requested permissions, or it will not be installed (see Fig. 1a), while apps targeting API 23 will be installed silently. Second, after the installation all *dangerous* permissions of legacy apps will be in the granted state, while *runtime* permissions of new apps will be disabled. Third, and most important, in Android 6.0 only *core* permissions can granted and revoked to legacy apps, while if an app targets API 23 it is also possible to adjust custom *dangerous* permissions. Furthermore, some subtle differences require high attention from developers. For instance, developers must ensure that the application, which functionality is called, has been already granted with the permission to access this functionality [43]. Additionally, in order to use an external library, which requires access to the protected functionality, the developers must handle properly runtime permission requests [42].

Forward compatibility of new apps with older platforms. The new runtime permission functionality has not come transparently for the application developers. According to the new guidelines [19], before making an API call protected with a permission, the app should ascertain that the appropriate permission has been granted. If not, the developer must ask for the permission, and the user can allow or deny it. Irrespectively of the user's decision, both cases must be handled by the developer (see Sect. 3). Unfortunately, the check whether the permission has been granted does not always return the correct result. We found out that if a developer runs an app on the older Android version, which has not yet declared the requested permission, the permission check returns that the permission is denied, while actually it is not required. We made a script that automatically identifies the permissions producing this unexpected behavior by extracting the list of *runtime* permissions in Android 6.0, and comparing it with the lists of *dangerous* permissions in the previous versions. We found 8 such permissions added after API 4, namely USE_SIP (added in API 9); ADD_VOICEMAIL (in API 14); WRITE_CALL_LOG, READ_CALL_LOG, READ_CELL_BROADCASTS, READ_EXTERNAL_STORAGE (in API 16); BODY_SENSORS (in API 21[3]); and READ_TV_LISTINGS (in API 23). These peculiarities are not described in the Android documentation, although some developers have started to experience problems[4]. At the same time, there is no bullet-proof solution how to overcome this issue at the operating system level (it is possible to implement the corresponding check in apps themselves [44]). As previous versions of Android are usually not supported (patches for older versions are rarely produced and deployed), it is practically impossible to deploy patches on all devices running older versions of Android. Handling through patching the Android support library is not a solution also, because developers may simply not use it in their apps. Thus, the developers must consider these cases in their applications themselves. In any case, this issue must be at least specified in the documentation.

(2) Runtime permissions are granted per permission groups. Clearly, this decision was made to reduce the amount of interruptions for asking permissions at runtime and to facilitate user's understanding of permissions [36]. At the same time, experienced users are not given any option to control permissions in a more fine-grained manner. Similar functionality introduced for the first time in the Google Play client received negative feedback both from the users and security analysts [18]. Moreover, this architectural decision implies that security researchers have to consider permission groups in their analysis of apps.

We can remark here that for a long time security researchers have asked for better and more fine-grained control over sensitive data and functionality on

---

[3] This permission was added in API 20, which we did not analyze (API 20 was developed for wearable systems).

[4] http://stackoverflow.com/questions/33482474/android-marshmallow-permission-model-on-os-4-0-read-external-storage-permission.

Android (e.g., [32,41,45], to mention just a few). Android 6.0 clearly moves in the opposite direction. Arguably, the users often did not understand the implications of various *dangerous* permissions, and the reduced complexity of permissions could be beneficial for some end-users [36]. Therefore, new evaluations and studies of the system are required from the community.

(3) UID sharing. There was an attempt to change permission granting to on per package basis. It failed, and permissions are still granted per UID [2]. This creates an additional attack possibility for collaborative applications sharing the same UID to access the functionality protected with *runtime* permissions. As we explained in Sect. 3, in Android 6.0 the screen with the required *runtime* permissions is not shown to the user during app installation, but the user's approval for these permissions is requested at the runtime. Thus, the user finds out about the required permissions only once they are requested. If two applications share the same UID, then if a user grants a *runtime* permission to one app, the second will be automatically granted with the same permission, and the user will be unaware of this fact. For instance, the Microsoft Excel [15] and Microsoft PowerPoint [16] apps share the same UID. Thus, if at runtime Microsoft Excel is granted with READ_EXTERNAL_STORAGE permission, the Microsoft PowerPoint app instantly receives the same permission even without user's consent. Additionally, the apps will also receive rights to perform the actions protected with the WRITE_EXTERNAL_STORAGE permission (if it is requested by the apps), because both permissions belong to the same group. This is clearly not the behaviour the user expects. The effort from the OS developers should be put into this direction.

(4) Signature permissions available to third-party apps. Before it was assumed that third-party applications cannot obtain any *signature* permission if they are not signed with the same certificate. However, this is not true anymore, and any new security system for Android needs to take these permissions into account. In our analysis we found 4 groups of exceptions that considerably influence the security analysts. This change especially affects permission maps, which considered before only *dangerous* and *normal* permissions as available for third-party apps [23].

Appop permissions. Introduction of the *appop* permissions (with FLAG_APPOP set) entails quite substantial consequences. First of all, for every set of such permissions a separate activity was added where the user can grant them to an app. Currently, there are 3 different activities responsible for granting such permissions (an example is given in Fig. 1b): to grant the *usage access* (PACKAGE_USAGE_STATS), *draw over other apps* (SYSTEM_ALERT_WINDOW), and *modify system settings* (WRITE_SETTINGS) privileges. Interestingly, these activities are accessed through different configuration screens: the first one is located under the "Security" settings, while the last two are on the "Configure apps" screen. This design decision is inconvenient for the users who must look in different locations to grant these permissions. Moreover, internally these activities are represented as 3 different classes with the corresponding permissions hardcoded within each class. Thus, if any new *appop* permission appears in the future, this will require the OS developers to add a new class processing this permission. In our study, we have also discovered one particular permission CHANGE_NETWORK_STATE, which in Android 6.0 were an *appop* permission. However, with the release 6.0.1 (i.e., still within API 23) its protection level was relaxed to *normal*.

Development permissions. These permissions (with FLAG_DEVELOPMENT set), although being of the *signature* protection level, can be granted to third-party applications by using the `pm grant` shell command. While the code for granting and revoking *development* permissions in Android 6.0 was merged with the one handling *runtime* permissions, these groups are quite different. First, *development* permissions are granted simultaneously to all system users, while *runtime* – only to the current user. Second, they are not displayed in the user interface as *runtime* permissions.

Pre-23 permissions. The permissions with FLAG_PRE23 set are automatically granted to all legacy (whose target API level is below 23) applications requesting them.

Installer and verifier permissions. These *signature* permissions are automatically granted to the apps marked as required installer and verifier.

(5) The deprecated *signature|system* protection level. Although the *signature|system* protection level is now deprecated, Fig. 3a and b show that there are still many permissions using this deprecated value. What is even more confusing, 9 new permissions of this level appeared in API 23. We attribute this inconsistency to the lack of communication among the groups of developers responsible for different modules. We have developed and submitted to AOSP [1] patches to fix these issues. Currently, *out of 9 submitted patches, 2 patches were merged into the master branch, while 3 were verified and 5 were code-reviewed*.

(6) Some dangerous permissions are now normal. In Android 6.0 the amount of *dangerous* permissions was considerably reduced. For 22 *dangerous* permissions the protection level was lowered to *normal*. Thus, the users now do not have any control over functionality protected with these permissions: *normal* permissions are not displayed and are automatically granted upon the installation. At runtime, a user can neither check them nor revoke. For instance, the INTERNET permission controlling the access of apps to the Internet, which was widely used by malware [55] especially in combination with other permissions [32], is now granted automatically.

From the security perspective, this is one of the most controversial changes, because many permissions regarded before as sensitive are now granted automatically. The fact that 22 permissions (including, e.g., NFC, BLUETOOTH, WRITE_PROFILE, MANAGE_ACCOUNTS) have been demoted in the security level emphasizes that the Android security architecture is far from being stable.

6.2 Interesting Findings

(1) Protection level flags. Developers cannot use protection level flags in their third-party apps. An application containing permission declaration with protection level flags will not pass validation checks during the compilation. The developers may only select one of the four main protection levels for their custom permissions: (*normal, dangerous, signature* and *signature|system*). At the same time, the validation check is performed only during application compilation. During installation of an app similar checks are not fired, and it is possible to add a protection level flag through app repackaging, e.g., using apktool[5]. Clearly, the checks in IDEs should conform to the new permission specifications, i.e., the *signature|system* protection flag should be removed, and there should be a possibility for third-party application developers to assign protection level flags to their custom permissions.

In Android 6.0 the protection level flag FLAG_PREINSTALLED was added. Previously, all *signature* permissions were divided into *privileged*, which could be obtained only if a system app was installed in the special folder, and others, which could be obtained by apps signed with the same certificate. FLAG_PREINSTALLED relaxes this strict division, and permits all system apps to receive automatically the permissions with this flag set.

(2) Additional flags. Currently there are no restrictions for a third-party developer on assigning additional flags to custom permissions. For instance, it is possible to declare a permission with FLAG_COSTS_MONEY set. As a result, on older systems you will see the corresponding permission accompanied with a special coins icon. Similarly, the usage of FLAG_HIDDEN is also not restricted. This may be used by a developer to conceal a permission from the list of app's *dangerous* permissions. While we cannot say if this functionality can be used with malicious purposes, these edge cases violate the principle of least privilege.

Moreover, as mentioned in Sect. 4.2, 2 out of 3 flags can be set by a developer, while the third flag FLAG_INSTALLED can be installed only by the operating system. Such behavior is considered as security anti-pattern, when publicly accessible data is combined with private information.

(3) Hard-coded screens for granting permissions. Every permission group defined in the core AndroidManifest.xml file has its own screen, where a user grants and revokes permissions assigned to this group (see Fig. 1c for the entry points to these screens). At the same time, permission groups defined in the system or third-party packages do not have dedicated screens. The "Additional permissions" screen collects all of them. There is no separation between groups and single permissions on this screen. E.g., Fig. 1d shows that the permission group (*test permission group*) and the single permission (*test single permission*) are listed on the same screen along with other groups defined in system packages. As we mentioned, the groups and single permissions will be displayed on this screen only if the corresponding package targets API 23.

---

[5] https://ibotpeaches.github.io/Apktool/.

(4) **Permission groups.** We mentioned that there is no restriction on adding custom permissions to the system permission groups. If a custom permission has the *dangerous* protection level, then, when an app requests this permission at runtime, it is also granted with all permissions from the same group. At the same time, if the protection level of a custom permission is not *dangerous*, the remaining permissions from the group will not be automatically granted. Thus, to our point of view, there is no reason to group permissions beside those with the *dangerous* protection level. We analyzed system non-*dangerous* permissions to detect if there are any assigned to groups. For the API level 23 we found 6 such *package* permissions and 2 *core* permissions. For example, the USE_FINGERPRINT permission assigned to the SENSORS permission group has the *normal* protection level, while ACCESS_IMS_CALL_SERVICE belonging to the PHONE group has the *signature|system* level. We do not see reasons for this assignment and expect these issues to be fixed in the future Android releases.

(5) **Permission declaration duplicates.** During our analysis we found that some permission declarations are duplicated even within AOSP. The most frequent duplicates are declarations of INSTALL_SHORTCUT and UNINSTALL_SHORTCUT permissions. These flags are declared both in the core and package manifest files. Before API 19 there were no declarations of these permissions on the core level, but due to a bug they were added to the core manifest file [6]. Interestingly, these permissions in the core and packages manifest files have different protection levels: *normal* in the former case and *dangerous* in the latter. Additionally, while exploring this issue, we discovered that in API 17 the declarations of two permissions (SET_SCREEN_COMPATIBILITY and CHANGE_CONFIGURATION) were duplicated even within the core file. This shows that some classes and configuration files reached critical complexity within AOSP. It is necessary either to refactor them, or to use extensively static analyzers to prevent these inconsistencies.

7 Related Work

Studies in the literature investigated many aspects of the Android permission system [34,37]. Indeed, the permission system is a cornerstone of the Android security model [31], while permission misuse is a great concern [27,51], and permission request patterns in apps are widely used for pinpointing malicious or dubious behavior (e.g., [21,28,46,52]). At the same time, Android developers require guidance for understanding permissions and using them correctly. For example, [26,35] looked at permission enforcement in Android and have shown that the principle of least privilege was often neglected by developers. Many studies looked into improving the permission system design and proposing more secure or more usable solutions (e.g., [29,41,45,54]), while some researchers argued that finer granularity of permissions could be viable [38]. In absence of a reliable documentation from Google, researchers had also to provide a means of linking permissions to precise platform APIs that are protected with these permissions (a permission map) [23,24,26,35,40,48]. Outside the Android platform, smartphone permission systems were explored in [22,39,47].

Wei et al. [49] have performed an early study of the permission system evolution in Android demonstrating that the permission system has become even more complex over time from the user's perspective (since its introduction in 2008 till the study publication in 2012). [49] revealed that the principle of least privilege was more and more violated with the time (the amount of overprivileged apps had consistently grown). Moreover, the permission system had become more complex: the total number of permissions had increased, and the amount of *dangerous* permissions had grown.

Au et al. [23] performed another longitudinal study of Android permissions with a focus on the sensitive API and permission changes spanning Android versions 2.2 up to Android 4.0. This study showed that the number of documented APIs requiring permissions had grown significantly in Android 4.0, and that many APIs changed their permission requirements over Android versions; this is also consistent with our own findings. The difference of our study with [23] is that we explore the changes in the permission system in the whole, while Au et al. concentrated on relations between permissions and API calls.

The studies by Wei et al. [49] and Au et al. [23] were reported in 2012. Thus, our study incrementally adds to theirs by surveying also more recent platform versions. To the best of our knowledge, the new Android permission system architecture, including runtime permissions, has not yet been extensively studied by the security research community. However, runtime permission requests were previously suggested by security researchers [50], and the effect of dynamic permission revocation on the Android apps has been empirically evaluated [33].

8 Conclusion

In this paper, we conducted a comprehensive study of the Android permission system. Driven by the aspiration to understand new runtime permissions, we discovered that the permission system has considerably evolved after its seminal description in [31]. To help security researchers and Android developers to understand better the new model and its implications, we presented an updated view on the permission system. Besides giving the overview and intrinsic details of the new design, we have shown its main changes during the last 6 years. At the individual permission level we discovered and reported many issues that have implications on the Android security state and research. These findings emphasise the dynamic complexity of the Android permission system that needs to be taken into account by the community.

References

1. Android Open Source Project. http://source.android.com/. Accessed 31 Mar 2016
2. Commit 2af5708: Add per UID control to app ops. https://android.googlesource.com/platform/frameworks/base/+/2af5708

3. Commit 2ca2c87: More adjustments to permissions. https://android.googlesource.com/platform/frameworks/base/+/2ca2c87
4. Commit 33f5ddd: Add permissions associated with app ops. https://android.googlesource.com/platform/frameworks/base/+/33f5ddd
5. Commit 3e7d977: Grant installer and verifier install permissions robustly. https://android.googlesource.com/platform/frameworks/base/+/3e7d977
6. Commit 4516798: Moving launcher permission to framework. https://android.googlesource.com/platform/frameworks/base/+/4516798
7. Commit 6d2c0e5: Remove not needed contacts related permissions. https://android.googlesource.com/platform/frameworks/base/+/6d2c0e5
8. Commit a90c8de: Add new "preinstalled" permission flag. https://android.googlesource.com/platform/frameworks/base/+/a90c8de
9. Commit ccbf84f: Some system apps are more system than others. https://android.googlesource.com/platform/frameworks/base/+/ccbf84f
10. Commit cfbfafe: Additional permissions aren't properly disabled after toggling them off. https://android.googlesource.com/platform/frameworks/base/+/cfbfafe
11. Commit de15eda: Scope WRITE_SETTINGS and SYSTEM_ALERT_WINDOW to an explicit toggle to enable in Settings. https://android.googlesource.com/platform/frameworks/base/+/de15eda
12. Commit e639da7: New development permissions. https://android.googlesource.com/platform/frameworks/base/+/e639da7
13. Dashboards. http://goo.gl/mFciT7. Accessed 31 Mar 2016
14. Google says Android has 1.4 billion active users. http://goo.gl/aUuUNw. Accessed 31 Mar 2016
15. Microsoft Excel. https://play.google.com/store/apps/details?id=com.microsoft.office.excel. Accessed 31 Mar 2016
16. Microsoft PowerPoint. https://play.google.com/store/apps/details?id=com.microsoft.office.powerpoint. Accessed 31 Mar 2016
17. Not just for phones and tablets: what other devices run Android? http://goo.gl/kQ4Pi8. Accessed 31 Mar 2016
18. Play store permissions change opens door to rogue apps. http://goo.gl/nJCwoY. Accessed 31 Mar 2016
19. Requesting permissions at run time. http://developer.android.com/training/permissions/requesting.html
20. Smartphone OS market share, 2015 Q2. http://goo.gl/WQwfZO. Accessed 31 Mar 2016
21. Arp, D., Speizenbarth, M., Hubner, M., Gascon, H., Rieck, K.: DREBIN: effective and explainable detection of Android malware in your pocket. In: Proceedings of NDSS (2014)
22. Au, K., Zhou, Y.F., Huang, Z., Gill, P., Lie, D.: Short paper: a look at smartphone permission models. In: Proceedings of SPSM (2011)
23. Au, K.W.Y., Zhou, Y.F., Huang, Z., Lie, D.: PScout: analyzing the Android permission specification. In: Proceedings of CCS (2012)
24. Backes, M., Bugiel, S., Derr, E., Weisgerber, S., McDaniel, P., Octeau, D.: On demystifying the Android application framework: re-visiting Android permission specification analysis. In: Poster Session of IEEE EuroS&P (2016)
25. Barrera, D., Kayacik, H.G., van Oorschot, P.C., Somayaji, A.: A methodology for empirical analysis of permission-based security models and its application to Android. In: Proceedings of CCS (2010)

26. Bartel, A., Klein, J., Le Traon, Y., Monperrus, M.: Automatically securing permission-based software by reducing the attack surface: an application to Android. In: Proceedings of ASE (2012)
27. Bugiel, S., Davi, L., Dmitrienko, A., Fischer, T., Reza-Sadeghi, A., Shastry, B.: Towards taming privilege-escalation attacks on Android. In: Proceedings of NDSS (2012)
28. Chen, K.Z., Johnson, N., D'Silva, V., Dai, S., MacNamara, K., Magrino, T., Wu, E., Rinard, M., Song, D.: Contextual policy enforcement in Android applications with permission event graphs. In: Proceedings of NDSS (2013)
29. Conti, M., Crispo, B., Fernandes, E., Zhauniarovich, Y.: CRêPE: a system for enforcing fine-grained context-related policies on Android. IEEE Trans. Inf. Forensics Secur. **7**(5), 1426–1438 (2012)
30. Elenkov, N.: Android Security Internals: An In-Depth Guide to Android's Security Architecture, 1st edn. No Starch Press, San Francisco (2014)
31. Enck, W., Ongtang, M., McDaniel, P.: Understanding Android security. IEEE Secur. Priv. Mag. **7**(1), 50–57 (2009)
32. Enck, W., Ongtang, M., McDaniel, P.: On lightweight mobile phone application certification. In: Proceedings of CCS (2009)
33. Fang, Z., Han, W., Li, D., Guo, Z., Guo, D., Wang, X.S., Qian, Z., Chen, H.: revDroid: code analysis of the side effects after dynamic permission revocation of Android apps. In: Proceedings of ASIACCS (2016)
34. Fang, Z., Han, W., Li, Y.: Permission based Android security: issues and countermeasures. Comput. Secur. **43**, 205–218 (2014)
35. Felt, A.P., Chin, E., Hanna, S., Song, D., Wagner, D.: Android permissions demystified. In: Proceedings of CCS (2011)
36. Felt, A.P., Ha, E., Egelman, S., Haney, A., Chin, E., Wagner, D.: Android permissions: user attention, comprehension, and behavior. In: Proceedings of SOUPS (2012)
37. Fragkaki, E., Bauer, L., Jia, L., Swasey, D.: Modeling and enhancing Android's permission system. In: Proceedings of ESORICS (2013)
38. Fratantonio, Y., Bianchi, A., Robertson, W., Egele, M., Kruegel, C., Kirda, E., Vigna, G.: On the security and engineering implications of finer-grained access controls for Android developers and users. In: Almgren, M., Gulisano, V., Maggi, F. (eds.) DIMVA 2015. LNCS, vol. 9148, pp. 282–303. Springer, Heidelberg (2015)
39. Gadyatskaya, O., Massacci, F., Zhauniarovich, Y.: Security in the firefox OS and Tizen mobile platforms. IEEE Comput. **47**(6), 57–63 (2014)
40. Gibler, C., Crussell, J., Erickson, J., Chen, H.: AndroidLeaks: automatically detecting potential privacy leaks in Android applications on a large scale. In: Katzenbeisser, S., Weippl, E., Camp, L.J., Volkamer, M., Reiter, M., Zhang, X. (eds.) Trust 2012. LNCS, vol. 7344, pp. 291–307. Springer, Heidelberg (2012)
41. Jeon, J., Micinski, K.K., Vaughan, J.A., Fogel, A., Reddy, N., Foster, J.S., Millstein, T.: Dr. Android and Mr. Hide: fine-grained permissions in Android applications. In: Proceedings of SPSM (2012)
42. Murphy, M.: Libraries and dangerous permissions. https://goo.gl/NJAjMx. Accessed 25 June 2016
43. Murphy, M.: Runtime permissions, files, and ACTION_SEND. https://goo.gl/slhHoI. Accessed 25 June 2016
44. Murphy, M.: You cannot hold non-existent permissions. https://goo.gl/nyDjUj. Accessed 25 June 2016

45. Nauman, M., Khan, S., Zhang, X.: Apex: extending Android permission model and enforcement with user-defined runtime constraints. In: Proceedings of ASIACCS (2010)
46. Pandita, R., Xiao, X., Wang, W., Enck, W., Xie, T.: WHYPER: towards automating risk assessment of mobile applications. In: Proceedings of USENIX Security (2013)
47. Singh, K.: Practical context-aware permission control for hybrid mobile applications. In: Stolfo, S.J., Stavrou, A., Wright, C.V. (eds.) RAID 2013. LNCS, vol. 8145, pp. 307–327. Springer, Heidelberg (2013)
48. Vidas, T., Christin, N., Cranor, L.F.: Curbing Android permission creep. In: Proceedings of W2SP (2011)
49. Wei, X., Gomez, L., Neamtiu, I., Faloutsos, M.: Permission evolution in the Android ecosystem. In: Proceedings of ACSAC (2012)
50. Wijesekera, P., Baokar, A., Hosseini, A., Egelman, S., Wagner, D., Beznosov, K.: Android permissions remystified: a field study on contextual integrity. In: Proceedings of USENIX Security (2015)
51. Xing, L., Pan, X., Wang, R., Yuan, K., Wang, X.: Upgrading your Android, elevating my malware: privilege escalation through mobile OS updating. In: Proceedings of S&P (2014)
52. Zhang, Y., Yang, M., Xu, B., Yang, Z., Gu, G., Ning, P., Wang, X.S., Zang, B.: Vetting undesirable behaviors in Android apps with permission use analysis. In: Proceedings of CCS (2013)
53. Zhauniarovich, Y., Ahmad, M., Gadyatskaya, O., Crispo, B., Massacci, F.: StaDynA: addressing the problem of dynamic code updates in the security analysis of Android applications. In: Proceedings of CODASPY (2015)
54. Zhauniarovich, Y., Russello, G., Conti, M., Crispo, B., Fernandes, E.: MOSES: supporting and enforcing security profiles on smartphones. IEEE Trans. Dependable Secure Comput. **11**(3), 211–223 (2014)
55. Zhou, Y., Jiang, X.: Dissecting Android malware: characterization and evolution. In: Proceedings of S&P (2012)

Who Gets the Boot? Analyzing Victimization by DDoS-as-a-Service

Arman Noroozian[1]([✉]), Maciej Korczyński[1], Carlos Hernandez Gañan[1], Daisuke Makita[2,3], Katsunari Yoshioka[2], and Michel van Eeten[1]

[1] Delft University of Technology, Delft, Netherlands
a.noroozian@tudelft.nl
[2] Yokohama National University, Yokohama, Japan
[3] National Institute of Information and Communications Technology, Koganei, Japan

Abstract. A lot of research has been devoted to understanding the technical properties of amplification DDoS attacks and the emergence of the DDoS-as-a-service economy, especially the so-called *booters*. Much less is known about the consequences for victimization patterns. We profile victims via data from amplification DDoS honeypots. We develop victimization rates and present explanatory models capturing key determinants of these rates. Our analysis demonstrates that the bulk of the attacks are directed at users in access networks, not at hosting, and even less at enterprise networks. We find that victimization in broadband ISPs is highly proportional to the number of ISP subscribers and that certain countries have significantly higher or lower victim rates which are only partially explained by institutional factors such as ICT development. We also find that victimization rate in hosting networks is proportional to the number of hosted domains and number of routed IP addresses and that content popularity has a minor impact on victimization rates. Finally, we reflect on the implications of these findings for the wider trend of commoditization in cybercrime.

1 Introduction

While Distributed Denial-of-Service (DDoS) attacks have been around for a long time, the use of amplification techniques has transformed the criminal ecosystem. These techniques now make up the bulk of the observed attack traffic [1,2]. This shift is intimately related to another trend: the rise of DDoS-as-a-service, also known as *booters*. Booters are a clear example of the so-called commoditization of cybercrime [3]: criminal service providers bundling all the resources and tools needed for an attack and offering them in an accessible way as a commodity service to anyone willing to pay.

Several in-depth studies have illuminated the supply side of the market for DDoS: the technical resources and techniques deployed by the criminal service providers [2,4,5]. We have also learned quite a bit about the economics of booters from publicly-leaked dumps of several operational databases containing information about revenue and customers [6–8].

What is much less understood, however, is how the abundance and affordability of DDoS-as-a-service has impacted victimization patterns. Who is bearing the brunt of the lowered barriers for DDoS attacks? Existing studies have revealed some basic distributions of victims across countries, Regional Internet Registries (RIRs) and Autonomous Systems (ASes). They have pointed to end hosts, gaming servers and hosting providers [1], but they lack a more in-depth investigation and explanation of victimization patterns.

This paper addresses this knowledge gap and profiles the affected networks and victims. It uses a dataset of 1,115,795 victim IP addresses captured over the past two years (2014–2015) via several amplifier-honeypots [2]. From the IP addresses, we infer certain properties of the victims and identify the factors determining their distributions across networks and countries.

Since the existing work on amplifiers and booters has not focused on the victims, the public understanding of them has been shaped by anecdotal news articles and by industry reports compiled by DDoS mitigation providers. The former focus on the more news-worthy cases, i.e., the attacks against high profile targets. The latter are biased towards their own customer base, i.e., enterprises purchasing DDoS protection services, as that is where the data is being collected. As we demonstrate in this paper, neither provide a good understanding of the ecosystem of commoditized DDoS attacks.

We summarize the main contributions of this paper as follows:

- We show that the bulk of the victims (62%) are users in access networks, rather than in hosting networks (26%). Only a small fraction resides in enterprise networks;
- We demonstrate that the victimization rate in access networks is highly proportional to the number of broadband subscribers in those networks, suggesting that the commoditization of attacks has led to a democratization of victims;
- We find that certain countries have a significantly higher number of victims per subscriber. This rate is weakly related to institutional factors such as information and communication technologies (ICT) development, suggesting geographical network effects among attackers and victims increasing the uptake of DDoS-as-a-service;
- We demonstrate that victimization in hosting networks is proportional to the number of IP addresses and hosted domains, and also influenced by the popularity of the hosted content.
- Where we were able to specifically identify webhosting victims, we find that they have barely any enterprises among them or other valuable targets. The largest victim group are gaming-related sites, most notably around Minecraft, suggesting that the commoditization of DDoS facilitates crime that is mostly not profit driven.

In what follows we first present some background (Sect. 2) and the data collection method (Sect. 3), we then discuss the distribution of victim IP addresses over access, hosting and other networks (Sect. 4). Next we delve deeper into victimization patterns in access networks (Sect. 5) and hosting networks (Sect. 6).

We briefly explore whether attack duration is different across victim populations (Sect. 7). After comparing our findings to related work, we summarize our conclusions on the consequences of DDoS-as-a-service and discuss the implications for the wider issue of the commoditization of cybercrime.

2 Background

DDoS attacks have been associated with a range of motives. They can be profit-driven – as in the case of extortion, disrupting competitors, or using it as a smoke screen for committing financial fraud – or motivated by other objectives, such as political protest, harassment, or gaining advantage in online gaming [1,3].

Amplification DDoS attacks now make up a considerable fraction of network-layer DDoS incidents [9–11]. Attackers send requests to amplifiers – a.k.a. reflectors – and spoof the source IP address, so that the amplifiers responses are directed to the victim. A whole range of protocols can be abused for amplification and millions of machines run these protocols which enables such attacks [12].

Most of the amplification attacks stem from booter services [2,7]. The price for purchasing an amplified DDoS attack can be as low as $1, as the analysis of some leaked booter databases demonstrates [7,13]. A purchase from a booter would typically entail access to the service for a limited amount of time, tied to different pricing tiers. Most attacks are very short, less than 10 min [7].

On the customer side of booter services, leaked databases have shown that most customers of DDoS-as-a-service use it only once to attack a single target [7] and only a small fraction of them hide their tracks via TOR or VPN. This might indicate that their technical skills are limited or that they do not perceive a need to hide. The users that do hide their tracks, tend to return for more and also tend to launch more attacks [6]. The databases have also revealed that gamers make up a specific and important customer group [6]. On the victim side, booter databases contain the targeted IP addresses or URLs, but these sets are limited in scope and volume. The top 100 most attacked sites were mostly game servers and game forums [6].

Besides booter databases, NTP amplification attacks allow victim IPs to be retrieved from the NTP servers. From this data, Czyz et al. [1] point to end hosts and gaming servers to be common victims [1]. Amplification honeypots have also collected victim IP addresses [2]. They have only been superficially analyzed, in terms of the distribution over countries and IP address space. The U.S., China and France were the most attacked countries. In this paper, we significantly extend the analysis of honeypot data.

The only other systematic source of information comes from industry reports by DDoS mitigation providers. Akamai points to gaming, software and the financial industry as the major victims [9], with a small fraction of victims belonging to the telecom industry. Other reports suggest hosting as major victims [14]. These industry reports have specific limitations and biases, which we will return to in Sect. 4.

3 Honeypot Data

The victim data used in this study was gathered via a set of amplifier honeypots – dubbed AmpPots [2] – which have been deployed over the past two years (2014–2015). They run services that are known to be misused for amplification attacks: QotD (17/udp), CharGen (19/udp), DNS (53/udp), NTP (123/udp), SNMP (161/udp) and SSDP (1900/udp). Each AmpPot uses real server software (in 'proxy' mode) to provide the aforementioned services except for SSDP in which an emulated script is used instead. The responses of AmpPots are filtered in order to prevent from contributing to actual attacks. More details of AmpPot can be found in the previous study [2].

Table 1. Overview of deployed AmpPots.

AmpPot ID	Deployed on	IP Changes	Notes
H01	2012-10-07	19	added QOTD, NTP, SNMP, SSDP on 2014-09-25. Discontinued on 2015-10-09
H02	2013-05-13	25	only DNS supported
H03	2014-05-13	9	added SNMP support on 2014-09-17 and SSDP on 2014-10-03 *
H04	2014-05-13	10	added SNMP, SSDP support on 2014-09-17 *
H05	2014-05-10	4	added SNMP, SSDP support on 2014-10-18 *
H06	2014-05-10	6	added SNMP, SSDP support on 2014-10-18 *
H07	2014-05-10	8	added SNMP, SSDP support on 2014-10-18 *
H08	2015-11-09	0	–**

Note:* Deployed with QOTD, CharGen, DNS and NTP support
Note:** Deployed with support for all protocols

In total 8 AmpPots were deployed on the Internet during the measurement period of 2014–2015. Table 1 shows a summary of the operational timeline and supported protocols of these devices. At the start of the measurement period (2014-01-01), two AmpPots were operational and initially only supported the CharGen and DNS protocols. With a sustained effort to monitor more amplification attacks, more devices were gradually added with support for additional abused protocols. At the end of the measurement period (2015-12-31) the deployed AmpPots collectively monitored 6 services except for H02 which only supports DNS. All AmpPots are located at ISPs in Japan and their IP addresses are dynamically assigned. Depending on the ISP, the IP addresses changed every 5–30 weeks, on average.

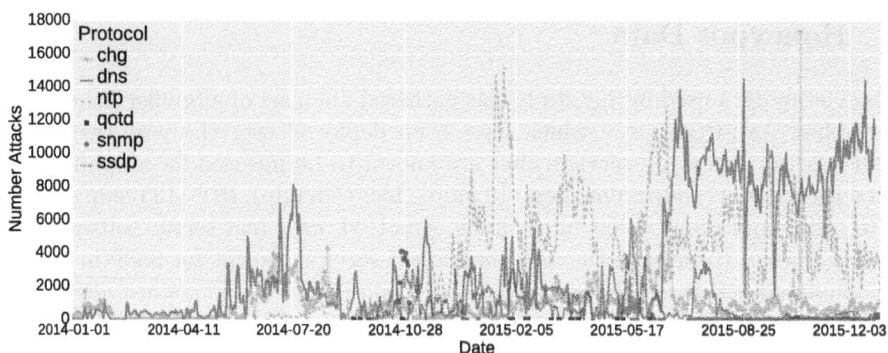

Fig. 1. Number of amplification attacks per protocol

AMPPOTs observe not only amplification attacks, but also scans from researchers or attackers who search for vulnerable devices. To separate actual attacks from scans, attacks are defined as a series of at least 100 consecutive query packets that a single host sent to an AMPPOT, where consecutive means that there was no gap of more than 600 s between two packets. This definition is in concord with the one used in [2]. We did, however, reduce the gap from 3600 s to 600 s, in order to analyze attack duration with a more fine-grained approach.

Collectively, the AMPPOTs have monitored 1,115,795 unique victim IP addresses from 92 countries and 15,044 unique victim ASes. Figure 1 shows the number of attacks per protocol during 2014 and 2015. As the figure demonstrates, the total number of attacks has increased over time and protocols like DNS, NTP and SSDP have been used more often to launch amplification attacks. During the measurement period, the AMPPOTs have monitored 5,726,150 amplification DDoS attacks in total: DNS (41.26%), NTP (38.73%), CharGen (11.32%), SSDP (8.01%), SNMP (0.65%), and QotD (0.01%).

4 Victims of Amplification Attacks

Given our amplification attack data the first question we pursue is: *In which type of networks are victims concentrated?*

To avoid confusion, we first define the main concepts. The term *attack* has been defined and operationalized in the previous section. We use the term *target* to refer to the entity (or entities) that the attacker intended to affect. This may be a person, organization, service or machine. Since the data consists of IP addresses, the attacker's intention is not directly observable. For this reason, we use the term *victim* to refer to the targeted IP addresses and the hosts residing there. As DDoS attacks are also a cost to the networks in which the victims reside, we refer to the Autonomous System (AS) that routes the traffic for the victims as *victim AS* or *victim network*. To answer our question we looked up the ASes of the victims and categorized them into three groups: *broadband ISPs*, *hosting* providers, and *other* networks.

To reliably identify the broadband ISPs, we utilize a previously developed mapping that identifies the ASes of broadband ISPs in 82 countries and that has been used to study botnet mitigation in broadband ISPs [15]. The mapping accurately distinguishes between and provides labels for ASNs which have been manually mapped to broadband ISPs, hosting, governmental, mobile ISP, educational and other types of networks. In total, the mapping contains 2,050 labeled Autonomous Systems. The mapping is organized around ground truth data in the form of a highly accurate commercial database; *TeleGeography Globalcomms* [16], containing the broadband subscriber numbers of 211 countries. Compared to machine learning approaches that map AS types [17], our mapping is more accurate since it manually identifies access networks, and the completeness of the mapping is verified with the Telegeography database.

To identify *hosting* providers, we take all the non-broadband ASes in our data and apply a simple heuristic to them. First, we count the number of unique second-level domains (2LDs) hosted within the ASes. For this we used all observed domains in 2014 and 2015 in DNSDB, a large passive DNS (pDNS) database generously provided to us by Farsight Security [18]. DNSDB is sourced from more than 100 sensors located around the world, in addition to authoritative DNS data from various top-level domain (TLD) zone operators. To illustrate: in 2015 DNSDB observed $287M$ unique 2LDs, which map to 69M distinct IP addresses.

We use the accurate AS labels mentioned above to identify a threshold for the number of hosted domains per AS that most accurately separates the ASes labeled as hosting from other types of ASes which may also host domains. Our approach does mean that CDNs and others networks like Cloudflare also get categorized as hosting. Based on the ROC curve constructed we identify this threshold to be 2700 2LDS. Therefore we define as hosting any AS that has not been previously identified as a broadband ISP and that hosts more than 2,700 2LDs. This corresponds to a false-positive/true-positive rate of 0.17/0.74. This accuracy is far from perfect, but better than available alternatives. We compared it to machine learning approaches, such as CAIDA's classification of ASes [17]. Using CAIDA's **Content** label as an alternative means for classifying the hosting providers results in a 0.04/0.32 false-positive/true-positive rate of classification. This classification has a better false-positive rate, but this comes at the cost of a highly reduced true-positive rate in comparison to our classification. Alternative methods for identifying hosting providers have also been explored in [19]. They are not directly comparable due to their organizational level classification rather than AS level.

Finally, all ASes that have not been classified as broadband ISP or hosting are labeled as *other*. Our labels and manual inspection show that this group contains governmental and educational networks, mobile and cloud providers, enterprises and more.

Having constructed our network classification, we can now examine the distribution of victims over these networks. Figure 2 plots the results.

It clearly shows that the majority of attacks and victim IPs are located in broadband ISPs, even though they only constitute a small fraction of all ASes

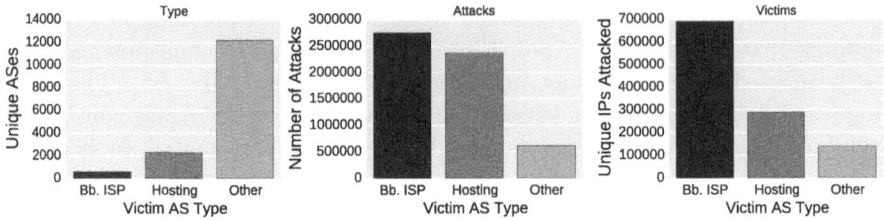

Fig. 2. Distribution of types, attacks and victim IPs

that have been attacked. More precisely, 48% of the attacks and 62% of the victims are in access networks. In total, we observe victim IPs from 92 countries in the attack data. We have detailed information on ISPs from 77 of these 92 countries. All identified ISPs in these 77 countries receive attacks, except for 5 countries (GB, US, JO, KE, LV) where at most 2 smaller ISPs are missing from the attack data. This suggests that the whole global broadband market is victimized by these attacks.

The second largest category is hosting: 41% of attacks and 26% of victims. The remaining victim networks constitute only a small fraction of the attacks and victims (11% and 12%, respectively).

This distribution of victims across broadband and hosting networks is different from earlier work by Czyz et al. [1]. They observed that the top 10 most targeted networks consisted of eight hosting providers and two telecom companies and that access nodes made up around half of all victims. They did observe already a trend that the portion of victims in access networks was increasing, which seems to have continued after their measurement period. Our analysis of the UDP ports used for the attacks largely agrees with that of [1]. The most frequently attacked UDP ports by a large margin include ports 80 and 8080, that are more likely to be open and accessible through firewalls. Other application specific ports are also targeted such as (7000) for BitTorrent trackers and CORBA management agent (1050).

We have triangulated our results with CAIDA's mapping of ASes [17], which classifies them as Content, Enterprise or Transit/Access. While these categories are different from ours, which means we cannot directly compare the exact distributions, the CAIDA mapping also locates most victims in Transit/Access networks, followed by Content and Enterprise. This is consistent with our findings.

Networks are not homogeneous, of course. Broadband networks, for example, can also contain hosting services. To probe deeper into the AS-level pattern, we take a closer look at the IP addresses of victims in access and hosting networks. We checked whether the addresses were associated with any domains in our pDNS data. Domains are used for a variety of hosting services; websites, but also for gaming servers, email servers, basically for any service where a human readable name is more convenient than an IP address. The pDNS data found that 95% of the victims in broadband networks have never been associated with any domains in 2014 and 2015. This suggests that the bulk of the victims in these networks are access nodes. The remaining 5 % host on average 20.8 domains per IP address (The median domain count is 1 and 75 % of these victims host 3 or less domains).

Since this categorization is dependent on the coverage of our pDNS data, we have cross-checked our domain data with the *Bing.com* search engine. We took a random sample of 1000 broadband victim IP addresses and queried Bing ('IP:<x.x.x.x>') to see if any domains were associated with it. For 9 % of the cases, BING reports observing domains where our pDNS data did not observe any. The opposite was true in 2 % of the cases. This suggests that the pDNS data gives a reasonably accurate picture.

In hosting networks, we found that 46.6 % of the victim IPs have been associated with domains. This confirms earlier work that webhosting is just one among many targets. Figure 3 summarizes the breakdown of the victim types and the subsets which we analyze in more detail in subsequent sections.

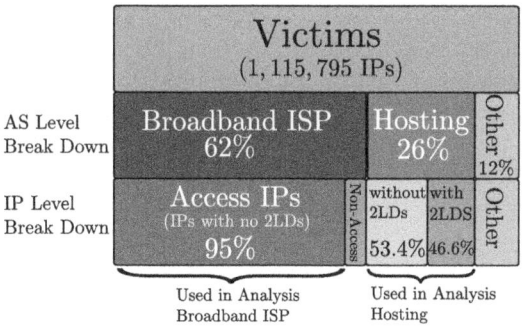

Fig. 3. Breakdown victims

Our results substantially differ from the victimization analysis in the reports of DDoS mitigation providers. There are two types of industry reports: based on traffic data or based on customer surveys. An example of the former is Akamai's State of the Internet report [20]. It identifies the gaming industry as the largest victim of DDoS attacks with 54 % of the attacks, followed by the software and technology industry (23 %) and financial industry (7 %). Only 4 % of attacks map to the Internet and Telecom industry. Another type of industry report is based on surveys among customers of DDoS mitigation providers. A recent example is Arbor Networks' WISR [10], which surveys 287 different organizations of which 24 % are ISPs and 5 % hosting providers. Other industry reports [14] point to hosting as the main victim however, this could be due to a focus on botnet-assisted DDoS attacks.

The mismatch between these reports and our findings is evident. We would argue that when it comes to observing victimization, the industry analyses are more biased than the honeypot data. Industry data is typically collected in the networks of the customers of the DDoS mitigation providers. It is unlikely that users in retail broadband networks are purchasing these kinds of services and thus those victims are severely under-counted by the industry reports. The amplifier data is much less biased towards certain types of victims. This strength does come at the cost of a weakness: missing attacks that are not amplifier-based. Earlier work suggests this is not a significant issue. Czyz et al. compared the data captured by observing NTP amplifiers against industry measurements and victim network data and they found that the patterns observed in the amplifier data were consistent with the industry measurements [1].

The contrast between our findings and industry reports are more than measurement issues. They have significant theoretical implications for our understanding the DDoS ecosystem, a point to which we will return later in the paper. We first turn to a more in-depth look at the victimization patterns in broadband ISPs and hosting.

5 Victims in Broadband Providers

We have now established that the majority of victims reside in broadband providers and that the majority of these victims are access nodes. In other words, home routers are typically the most affected devices. It suggests that the actual target is a regular home user behind that router. This brings us to the next question: *How are victims distributed over broadband networks?*

A simple count of unique victim IP addresses over the whole measurement period, does not give us a decent metric of victimization rates per ISP because of DHCP churn. ISPs re-assign IP addresses to their users at varying rates, where high rates lead to significant over-estimation of the number of victims. One method to reduce the effect of churn is to use short measurement windows [15,21]. For this reason, we count the unique number of IP addresses seen for each day and then average those daily counts to get to victimization rates over larger time frames. This results in a more accurate representation of the relative victimization rate per ISP.

In Fig. 4, we have plotted the average daily number of victims against the number of subscribers of those ISPs. The subscriber data is drawn from the TeleGeography database discussed in the previous section [16]. The database provides accurate worldwide subscriber numbers for ISPs from 77 countries that appear in our attack data. It provides a more precise proxy for the number of users in a network than technical network properties, like the number of advertised IP addresses, can provide.

As we can see, victimization rates differ by several orders of magnitude across ISPs, but these difference are highly correlated with the size of the customer base: $R^2 = 0.60$. As an aside, the correlation with the number of IP addresses advertised by each ISP also shows a firm linear relation, though a bit weaker ($R^2 = 0.56$).

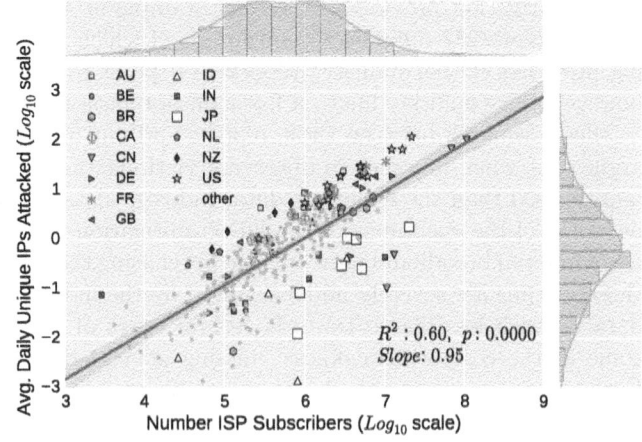

Fig. 4. Correlation access victims with ISP subscribers

In other words, the number of users is a strong predictor for the number of observed victims. This is consistent with the earlier speculation that it is individual users that are being attacked, rather than services or devices. It also means that, to some extent, victimization rates are uniform across ISPs. Whatever motivations attackers may have, it seems they select targets somewhat evenly across broadband networks.

Notwithstanding the effect of the size of the subscriber base, as captured by the regression line, the figure also clearly shows that there is significant variation around that line. That raises a new question: *why do some ISPs have disproportionately more or fewer victims?* We can use the victim rates of ISPs (i.e., the daily average number of victim IP addresses divided by the number of ISP subscribers) to further explain the variance among them. From the size-corrected victim rates we can see that there are several orders of magnitude differences among the most and least attacked ISPs. How can these differences be explained?

In Fig. 4, we have color coded ISPs by the country in which they operate. To better highlight between and within country relations, Fig. 5 plots the distribution of ISP victims per subscriber in relation to the country in which they operate. Two things become apparent. First, in many countries, ISP victimization rates are remarkably clustered, compared to the overall variance across countries. Second, ISPs in some countries are victimized less, according to our metrics. In other words, there seem to be country-level effects at work, in addition to network- and user-level effects. The plot shows that ISPs in New Zealand, Australia, U.S., U.K. and France have disproportionately more victims, while ISPs within countries such as China, Japan and Indonesia have disproportionately fewer. It is important to note that almost all ISPs in the 77 countries are present in the data, so there is no selection bias at work in these patterns.

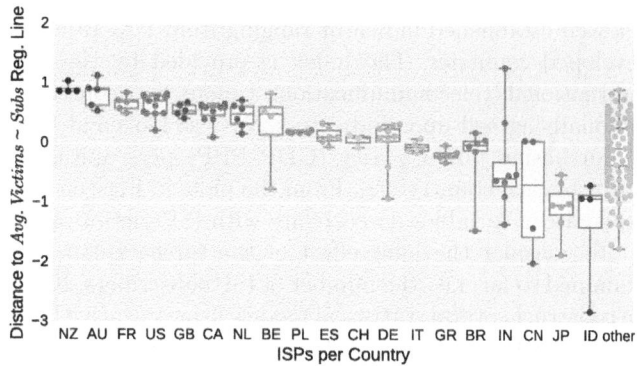

Fig. 5. Between and within country differences among ISPs

The differences between countries might be explained by institutional characteristics of the countries in which the ISPs operate. Two institutional differences that we tested for are: *(i)* the development of the ICT infrastructure of each country and *(ii)* the overall economic status of the country. In both cases we expect to observe more victims in more developed countries, as more online activity and better infrastructure might drive more motives and opportunities

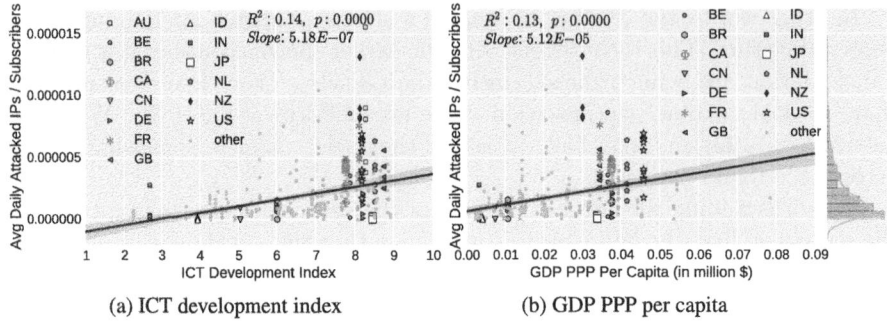

(a) ICT development index (b) GDP PPP per capita

Fig. 6. Correlation of ISP victim rates with country level variables

for attacks – around online gaming, for example. The ICT development index is a well established indicator ranging from 1 to 10 with higher values for more developed countries. The index is provided by the ITU (the United Nations International Telecommunications Union) and constructed from a set of internationally agreed-upon indicators. We also looked at the gross domestic product at purchasing power parity (GDP PPP) per capita, to capture the economic status of each country [22]. From the plots in Figs. 6a and b, it is clear that both explanatory variables do correlate with ISP victim rates, but only weakly.

To consider the joint effect of the three explanatory factors that we have examined so far, i.e., the number of ISP subscribers, ICT and GDP PPP indexes, we construct several statistical models using negative binomial, generalized linear model (GLM) regression. The models predict the number of victims per ISP given a set of explanatory variables. A summary of these statistical models are presented in Table 2.

$Model_1$ only includes the attack surface size, $Model_2$ adds the ICT development index as an additional factor and finally $Model_3$ adds the GDP PPP per capita. As expected, $Model_1$ demonstrates the effect of the size of the subscriber population – i.e., the size of the 'attack surface' – in correspondence with

Table 2. Negative binomial GLM regression models with 'Log_e' link function for number of ISP victims

	Dependent variable:		
	# Victims per ISP		
	(1)	(2)	(3)
Subscribers	2.160***	1.996***	1.977***
(log_{10})	(0.079)	(0.075)	(0.074)
ICT Dev. Index		0.249***	
(2015)		(0.034)	
GDP PPP per Capita			0.030***
(in $1000)			(0.004)
Constant	−5.880***	−6.712***	−5.705***
	(0.454)	(0.468)	(0.430)
Observations	304	300	291
Log Likelihood	−2,255.880	−2,204.260	−2,128.202
θ	0.963*** (0.070)	1.097*** (0.082)	1.143*** (0.087)
Akaike Inf. Crit	4,515.761	4,414.520	4,262.404

Note: *p<0.1; **p<0.05; ***p<0.01

our earlier results (Fig. 4). The other two models demonstrate that in addition to size, the two institutional country variables considerably contribute to the variation in the number of victims per ISP, however their effects are much smaller. We interpret the results of $Model_2$ as an example. While holding everything else constant, increasing the number of subscribers by one unit (equivalent to multiplying the number of subscribers by 10 due to the log_{10} scale of the variable) multiplies the number of victims per ISP by $e^{1.996} = 7.36$. Similarly, increasing the ICT development index by one unit (while other factors are held constant) multiplies the number of victims by $e^{0.249} = 1.28$. $Model_3$ can be interpreted in a similar fashion. Note that due to the correlation of ICT development and GDP we do not include both variables in one model.

We have also examined other factors, such as 'gaming popularity' and 'piracy' which show weak correlations with victimization rates as well. Including these in separate GLM models shows a significant small effect of online gaming as captured by the average number of games owned per country on the Steam online gaming platform. This could be indicative of a possibly weak relation with online gaming and end-host victimization. However, further examination of the variable indicates strong correlations with ICT development and GDP therefore bearing little added information which the other factors did not already include in our models.

Given that the institutional factors have a weak effect, it begs the question of why, in the majority of the countries, ISP victim rates are closely clustered together. More specifically, the ISPs of only 12 of the 77 countries are dispersed by more than one order of magnitude (among them are Brazil, India, and China). Even with quite similar infrastructure and economic conditions, the differences among ISPs are larger between the countries than within them. This pattern suggests that there are specific country-level factors at work, beyond the general factors we examined.

We can only speculate why ISPs in a certain country are so clustered, but one explanation is that attackers and victims are geographically concentrated and that their interaction leads to network-effects. We know from the research on booters that many of the customers are gamers [6]. Other studies have told us that many of the victims are also related to gaming [1]. Combine this with findings from online social network analysis, inside and outside of gaming, which found that these online networks are shaped by geographical vicinity. In other words, users in online networks tend to be friends or familiar with each other in offline networks as well [23,24]. In other words, they are geographically close.

Jointly, these three factors might drive a geographically concentrated network effect: some of the victims become attackers themselves, which is easy because of the booter services. These new attackers, in turn, victimize others, and the cycle continues. This pattern fits with anecdotal evidence from news reports. In the Netherlands, for example, DDoS-ing became such a widespread phenomenon among schoolkids [13], that even those who did not play online games started to use booters, because everyone was doing it. One more technically skilled youngster said he quit DDoS-ing, as "it became too easy" and "even my sister can do it" [25].

Overall, our findings reveal that the number of subscribers of ISPs is a very strong predictor for the number of victims per ISP (see Fig. 4). This result suggests that the chances of being victimized are surprisingly uniform across ISPs. The accessibility of DDoS-as-a-service might have caused a democratization of victims: everywhere there are now regular users deemed worthy of attack. This is a far cry from the highly publicized attacks on high profile targets like governments and enterprises. Those are attacked too, of course, but the bulk is targeted at regular netizens.

That being said, we do see significant variation in terms of victimization rates. The country-level differences are partially explained by institutional factors and partially by specific country-level effects. In the absence of direct evidence, we speculated that the remaining variation might be driven by geographically concentrated network effects.

6 Hosting Providers

In this section we take a closer look at victims located in hosting provider networks. As for ISPs, the main questions at this stage are: *How are victims distributed across different hosting ASes* and *Do some hosting providers have disproportionately more victims than others?*. Unlike broadband victims, we do not expect the dynamic nature of IP allocation to significantly effect or lead to a misrepresentation of the number of victims. Therefore we can examine the distribution of victims over networks by simply counting the number of unique victim IPs that we observe per AS.

As with broadband networks, we expect differences in customer base or network size to correlate with the number of victims. To test this, we need to estimate the size of the hosting providers. One approximation is to use the number of hosted second-level domains (2LDs) per each provider. Recall, however, that we found that only 46.6 % of the hosting victim IPs have been observed to host domains. This implies that the number of domains will not be a very reliable approximation of the attack surface size. We can use the number of routed IP addresses by each hosting provider as a second proxy for size. This metric, however, is less able to account for shared hosting (several 2LDs sharing the same IP address). As we will see below, using both proxies in combination gives the best results.

Figures 7a and b plot the number of unique victim IPs per hosting provider against the number of routed IP addresses and hosted 2LDs of the provider respectively. Both figures demonstrate a moderate effect of attack surface size on the number of victims, but size does not appear to explain a large portion of the variance as indicated by the relatively lower R^2 values. This simply means that only a small part of the variation among hosting ASes is explainable purely through the attack surface size. We can see that some hosting ASes are disproportionately attacked more (data points far above the regression line) or less

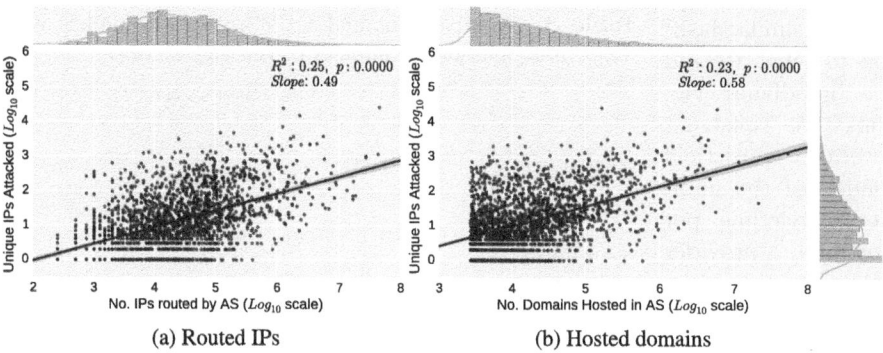

Fig. 7. Correlation hosting victim counts with size estimates.

(data points far below the regression line) in relation to their size. This signals that attacks on hosting providers are also quite strongly driven by other explanatory factors. The question to consider then is *what additional factors can explain the variation that we observe after the size effect has been corrected for?* As before correcting for size effects can be achieved through dividing the number of victims per provider by the size estimate of the provider.

One possible non-size related explanatory factor that we consider is related to the popularity of the hosted content. The expectation here is that more popular content is more likely to be attacked. In our analysis we use the list of top 1 million Alexa ranking domains as a proxy for the popularity of the hosted content [26]. Given the 2LDs that we have identified per hosting provider, we use the median ranking of the subset of top 1M Alexa ranked domains as an indicator of popularity. Note that in our analysis we use reversed rankings: the most popular Alexa domain has the rank of $1,000,000$.

A second possible factor that we consider is the type of hosting service that is offered. We expect that dedicated hosting is more likely to be attacked in comparison to shared hosting and other similar cheaper services offered by hosting providers. We use the number of IP addresses that have been used by the hosting provider to host all of its 2LDs as an indicator of the type of hosting. This indicator combined with size estimates (routed IPs and hosted 2LDs) captures the spread/density of domains per available IP address. A lower density of domains per IP is an indication for more dedicated services to their customers, while higher densities are indicators of shared hosting.

Our analysis of these non size-related factors demonstrates a weak correlation with the number of victims per provider after correcting for size effects. For the sake of brevity we do not include the details and instead move on to consider the joint effect of all explanatory factors.

In a similar fashion to what we did for broadband victims, we construct several statistical models of the number of victims per hosting provider using negative binomial GLM regression. A summary of these models is presented in Table 3. They clearly demonstrate that for larger attack surfaces there are more victims.

$Model_3$ uses all variables to explain the variance in victimization of hosting

Table 3. Negative Binomial GLM regression models with 'Log_e' link function for number of Hosting Victims

	Dependent variable:		
	# Victims per Hosting Provider		
	(1)	(2)	(3)
f_1: Routed IPs	1.198***		0.507
(log_{10})	(0.040)		(0.354)
f_2: Hosted Domains		1.237***	1.050***
(log_{10})		(0.050)	(0.243)
f_3: IPs with Domains			−0.415
(log_{10})			(0.427)
f_4: Median Alexa Rank			0.305***
(log_{10})			(0.075)
$f_1 \times f_2$			−0.338***
(Interaction term)			(0.088)
$f_1 \times f_3$			0.266***
(Interaction term)			(0.044)
$f_2 \times f_3$			0.198**
(Interaction term)			(0.084)
Constant	−1.120***	−0.988***	−3.859***
	(0.177)	(0.215)	(1.093)
Observations	2,203	2,203	2,203
Log Likelihood	−10,594.160	−10,703.310	−10,192.260
θ	0.421*** (0.011)	0.393*** (0.010)	0.546*** (0.014)
Akaike Inf. Crit	21,192.330	21,410.620	20,400.520

Note: *p<0.1; **p<0.05; ***p<0.01

providers. Due to the unavoidable correlations between these variables we include interaction terms which control for the covariance between them. The model demonstrates that when considered jointly, the number of hosted 2LDs and the popularity of content have a significant effect on the number of victims per hosting provider. As expected, the size-related factor has the largest effect while the popularity of content as represented by the median Alexa rank is moderately affecting the victim numbers. It also suggests that there is not enough evidence to support the hypothesis that the density of domains or type of hosting has a significant effect on victim numbers. Due to the inclusion of interaction terms, $Model_3$'s results need to be interpreted in a slightly different manner. The more complex and improved model (as indicated by the improved log likelihood) suggests that while holding all other factors constant, increasing the 'Hosted Domains' variable by one unit (equivalent to multiplying the number of hosted 2LDs by 10 due to the log_{10} scale of the variable) multiplies the number of victims by $e^{1.050−0.338+0.198} = 2.48$. Increasing the 'Median Alexa Rank' variable by one unit (equivalent to multiplying the median Alexa rank of the content by 10 due to the logarithmic scale) multiplies the number of victims by $e^{0.305} = 1.35$. Finally, note that in $Model_3$ the number of routed IPs is not a significantly contributing factor. This does not negate the size effect as observed in $Model_1$ and simply means that when considered jointly with the other factors the number of routed IPs does not add more information to the model that has not been already captured by the other included factors. Based on these results we can conclude that in addition to size factors which have the strongest effect on the number of victims per hosting provider the popularity of content also weakly contributes to this number.

To get a better sense of the actual victims, we have taken a closer look at some of the hosting victims that are associated with domain names. Many IP addresses are associated with multiple domains, obscuring the target and potential motive of the attackers. However, a subset of around 23,855 IP addresses are associated with just a single domain name according to our passive DNS data. We took a random sample of 1 % of this set (238 domains) and checked all of them manually to assess what type of website was being attacked. Of the 238 domains, 107 no longer showed any content. Most of them could no longer be resolved, others ran into connection issues or were replaced by parking pages. Given that the victim data was collected over two years, some degree of 'link rot' is to be expected, though this decay of domains is much higher than those found in other studies (e.g. [27]), suggesting that a lot of the victims had a somewhat fleeting presence on the web, rather than being well-established businesses or organizations.

Of the 132 sites that offered content, 55 sites (42 %) were directly related to gaming. Of these, 27 were associated with a single game: Minecraft (17), followed by Counterstrike (6) and Runescape (4). The remaining 77 sites (58 %) were highly heterogeneous, including but not limited to a few large stores, an airline, two football clubs, two schools, two escort services, one porn site, several hobby forums, a casino, a nature conservancy, and Twitpic, owned by Twitter since late 2014. In short: motives for DDoS attacks are highly varied, though gaming-related feuds are the most dominant of motives. In the Minecraft community specifically, DDoS attacks seem to be part of the culture.

We can summarize our results with respect to hosting providers as follows. Hosting providers constitute the second largest group of victims in the amplification honeypot data. Some providers are attacked disproportionately more than others. This can be partially explained by the size of their attack surface. Furthermore, hosting popular content increases the number of victims. Finally, in agreement to what others have also found we see a large victimization of gaming related resources within the hosting providers.

7 Attack Duration

In previous sections we have examined the question of who gets attacked more, whether that is disproportionate and if some factors can explain the variance among victim counts. We can also approach the question of who gets attacked more from the view point of time. That is, rather than looking at victim counts we can also approach the question as *who gets attacked longer and possibly why?*

To answer these questions, we take all victim IP addresses and measure the intervals under which they were continuously attacked. These intervals are calculated regardless of which AMPPOT or protocol was used to attack the victim IP. The resulting interval lengths are defined as the attack duration. Note that here, we have merged attacks that are closer than 600 s apart and consider them as one continuous attack on the victim. Given these durations, the primary

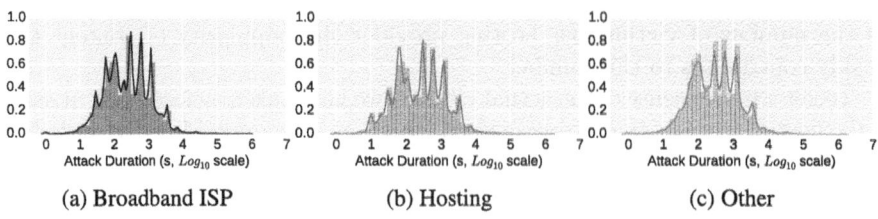

Fig. 8. Distribution of attack durations for various victim types.

question is *whether the distribution of these durations differs per victim type*. These distributions are shown in Fig. 8.

The median attack duration for broadband ISPs, hosting and the other types of victims are 272, 285 and 300 s, respectively. One surprising observation is the frequency of relatively short attack durations. The majority of attacks are shorter than 286 s long. For attacks longer than 300 s, we observe similar distributions of attack durations for all three types of victims. Interestingly, we observe an increased number of attacks that last around 5, 10, 20, 60, or 120 min. The trend suggests that, in general, the attacks are largely originated from booter services and are most possibly driven by attackers' capabilities rather than victim types (see Fig. 8).

To further compare the differences in durations for different victim types, we use a well established statistical technique that is commonly referred to as survival analysis. The technique is used to answer questions about the proportion of a population that will survive past a certain point of time on a measurement timeline and at what rate the individuals 'survive' or 'die'. In our case, the event that we analyze is the '*end of an attack*' on a victim IP. Figure 9 demonstrates our survival analysis results. We use the Kaplan-Meier estimator to approximate the survival function [28], measuring the probability of an attack exceeding a certain duration for various victim types.

A log-rank comparison of the survival probabilities indicates a significant difference at a 0.99 confidence level between attack durations on different victim types. The log-rank chi-square statistic comparison between broadband/hosting, broadband/other and hosting/other are equal to 2,131.8, 3,493.4, and 739.3 respectively. These results indicate a significant difference among the attack durations per victim type, however in terms of magnitude, the differences seem to be quite small (see Fig. 9).

We can also compare the survival rates of each victim type using the Cox proportional hazards model. The Cox model does not depend on distributional assumptions of survival time and allows to estimate the hazard ratio defined as the relative risk based on a comparison of event rates. The hazard ratios show that relative to hosting providers, attacks end 14 % faster for broadband victims while 3 % slower for the other type of victims. While the results demonstrate that attacks are statistically shorter on broadband ISP victims the magnitudes of the differences are not large enough to have significant implications.

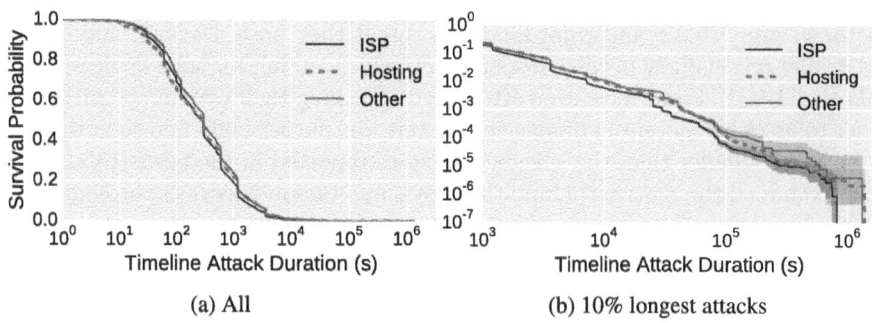

Fig. 9. Survival analysis of attack durations

To conclude, all victim types experience attacks ranging from short lived attacks in the order of several seconds to long attacks which last several days. In other words, there is no significant variance among the duration of attacks on victims of different types.

We have further manually analyzed victim IP addresses of the 100 longest attacks of which 98 lasted more than 24 h. They were launched against 87 unique IP addresses and 46 unique ASes. Interestingly, we do not observe any domains historically hosted on as many as 41 IP addresses (47 attacks). Of these, 6 IP addresses were directly related to gaming, including two victims against which the attacks lasted more than 16 days. Of the remaining 46 unique IP addresses, which were identified to be hosting some content, 17 were mapped to just a single domain name in passive DNS data. Of these, we have identified 6 victim IP addresses that hosted websites which provide torrent files to facilitate P2P file sharing, 4 websites related to gaming, 2 chat websites, one Internet banking website, and one TorGuard VPN website. By manual analysis of 15 IP addresses for which we observed 2 or 3 domains, we have further identified three victim IP addresses that mapped mainly to torrent, gaming, and TorGuard websites, respectively. The remaining 14 victim IP addresses mapped to more than 3 domains; 4 among them appeared to be used for shared web hosting and they mapped to 51, 346, 614, and 931 domains. To conclude, our manual analysis reveals that not only gaming but also torrent sharing-related IP addresses are among long-duration attacked victims.

8 Related Work

Much research has been devoted to analyzing the technical properties of amplification DDoS attacks: which protocols can me misused and how; how large the population of vulnerable reflectors is; how difficult or easy it is to find and misuse these reflectors; and how they could be mitigated [1,12,29,30]. We know for example that many UDP based protocols are prone to be misused (NTP, DNS, SNMP and Chargen) and we know what their amplification factors are [12]. We also know how large the populations of vulnerable devices running these protocols are [1,5,12] and what kind of a threat they pose. Darknet and honeypot traffic reveals how perpetrators are actively scanning for such devices in the wild [1,2,12,31]. Some have even attempted attacking their own infrastructure in order to asses the potential damage of booters and surprisingly find their damage to be much smaller than the spectacular cases reported in the news [13]. Others have examined the motives behind the provision of booter services through interviews [32]. Analysis of trends also reveals how over time specific protocols rise and fall out of popularity among attackers and how remediation and intervention has affected the landscape [1,8].

Earlier work on amplification DDoS attacks have focused less on studying the victims. The most in-depth understanding comes from the special case of NTP attacks, which allows probing the amplifier for victim IP addresses. Czyz et al. [1] provided the most comprehensive overview. The analysis of the smaller subset of victims from leaked booter databases [6,7] also point towards gaming-related victims. We corroborate earlier findings, especially [1,8], that many of the victims are end hosts and gaming-related resources, but we also expand on this and show that the distributions have shifted. Moreover, we provide a wholly novel contribution by developing victimization rates and providing an explanatory analysis of key determinants behind victimization patterns.

Finally, part of what we know about victims is based on industry reports from DDoS mitigation providers [9–11,14]. These mostly provide information on the type of industry that is affected most by DDoS attacks and point to the gaming industry and software industry as main victims. Our results paint a rather different picture, agreeing only with those reports in that many victims are gaming-related. Industry reports seems to be vulnerable to biases related to the fact that data collection often takes place in networks of the customers of DDoS mitigation providers.

9 Discussion and Implications

This study has presented the first in-depth look at victimization patterns of DDoS amplification attacks - and thus of the booter services that drive the bulk of these attacks. We found that broadband networks harbored most of the victims (62%), followed by hosting networks (26%). Educational, governmental and enterprise networks make up just a small fraction of the victim population (12%), contrary to industry reports and news items about high-profile attacks.

The population of victims is predictably distributed across broadband and hosting networks. To a large extent, the size of the user population drives the victimization rate – in broadband around 60% of the variance in victim counts can be explained from just the number of subscribers of the provider. Further explanatory factors are ICT development and GDP per capita. We also see significant differences among countries, however, that are not explained by these institutional factors. Remarkably, within most countries, ISP victimization rates are clustered together. This implies there are specific country-level effects at play, perhaps the result of geographically concentrated network effects among attackers and victims.

In hosting provider networks, the size effect is also visible, though less pronounced. The popularity of content, as measured by Alexa rankings, had a small effect. When we looked at victims IP addresses associated with a single domain, we found that 42 % of the sites we could identify were related to gaming, most notably to Minecraft.

Attack duration did not differ significantly across the victim populations. When we examined the 100 longest attacks, 98 of which lasted more than 24 h, we found, again, mostly gaming-related content rather than high-profile targets.

What do these findings mean for the consequences of the so-called commoditization of DDoS attacks? Rather than going after high-value targets, DDoS-as-s-service has invited attackers to go after regular users. With the commoditization of attacks, victimhood has democratized. And so has criminality, in all likelihood. Assuming that the users are targeted by someone that actually knows them, rather than by a random stranger, our findings imply that the attacker population has also broadened. In short, booters have indeed drawn more attackers into the DDoS ecosystem, as the commoditization theory suggests, and this has led to a an expansion of victims among regular users, who now make up the bulk of all victims.

Overall, the fact that most victims are regular users suggests that profit is not a dominant motive anymore, assuming it ever was. The commoditization provided by booters has enabled attacks for as little as one U.S. dollar. This type of cybercrime is priced in the same range as, or even below, many entertainment products. It is now cost-effective to pursue many more motives than profit, even very frivolous ones – like harassing your schoolmates during Minecraft games or online chats. Many of the new attackers probably do not see themselves as cybercriminals. Everyone is doing it, and they are not making any money from it.

The fact that attack patterns are so proportional to the number of users might seem unsurprising, but it has far-reaching implications. Rather than a phenomenon of motivated attackers with specific objectives and targets, DDoS has become a cultural phenomenon. The closest parallel to the observed pattern seems to be wide-spread use of torrents and file lockers to download copyright-infringing materials. This suggests a new route of action for fighting the DDoS problem: rather than using criminal law to go after motivated attackers, a better approach might be what criminologists call *situational crime prevention* [3]. It shifts the focus from identifying and penalizing attackers to taking away the opportunities that trigger crime. It can draw on a much broader mix of measures, often based on civil rather than criminal law. It can range from soft measures, such as awareness campaigns for youngsters, to harder ones, like the takedown of booter accounts by providers such as PayPal [8].

What are the implications of our findings for the wider commoditization of cybercrime? Should we expect an influx of attackers and an expansion of victims in other criminal markets as well? Not per se. As Florencio and Herley have argued, cybercrime is often harder than it looks and it scales less well than one would assume at first glance [33,34]. Indeed, in many markets, we do not see the rapid expansion of crime that effective commoditization would cause. This can be explained by the fact that many of these service models do not supply complete criminal value chains. Take fraud using banking Trojans for example. It is one thing to buy malware-as-a-service and distribute it via pay-per-install, but that doesn't mean one can successfully execute online banking fraud. There are bottlenecks elsewhere, especially in the use of money mules and other cash-out channels. Mules-as-a-service did not manage to solve this bottleneck yet.

We see the predicted effects of commoditization in DDoS attacks, because here the booter provides the value chain end-to-end. In other forms of cybercrime this seems much harder or even impossible, though some might come close, like ransomware-as-a-service using bitcoin. And indeed, we did recently see an explosion of ransomware attacks. We can only hope that for many other forms of cybercrime, bottlenecks will remain resistant to successful commoditization.

Acknowledgements. This work has been enabled through the support of NWO Pr. Nr. CYBSEC.12.003/628.001.003, SIDN, the Dutch National Cyber Security Center and Beatriu Pinos BP-A-214. We would like to thank Dr. Paul Vixie and Farsight Security for providing our pDNS data. In addition we would like to acknowledge the support of the MEXT (Program for Promoting Reform of National Universities) and PRACTICE (Proactive Response Against Cyber-attacks Through International Collaborative Exchange) programs.

References

1. Czyz, J., Kallitsis, M., Papadopoulos, C., Bailey, M.: Taming the 800 Pound Gorilla: the rise and decline of NTP DDoS attacks. In: Proceedings of ACM IMC, pp. 435–448 (2014)
2. Krämer, L., Krupp, J., Makita, D., Nishizoe, T., Koide, T., Yoshioka, K., Rossow, C.: AmpPot: monitoring and defending against amplification DDoS attacks. In: Bos, H., et al. (eds.) Raid 2015. LNCS, vol. 9404, pp. 615–636. Springer, Heidelberg (2015). doi:10.1007/978-3-319-26362-5_28
3. Thomas, K., Yuxing, D., David, H., Holt, T.J., Kruegel, C., Mccoy, D., Bursztein, E., Grier, C., Savage, S., Vigna, G.: Framing dependencies introduced by underground commoditization. In: WEIS (2015)
4. Santanna, J.J., Sperotto, A.: Characterizing and mitigating the DDoS-as-a-Service phenomenon. In: Sperotto, A., Doyen, G., Latré, S., Charalambides, M., Stiller, B. (eds.) AIMS 2014. LNCS, vol. 8508, pp. 74–78. Springer, Heidelberg (2014)
5. Kuhrer, M., Hupperich, T., Bushart, J., Rossow, C., Holz, T.: Going wild: large-scale classification of open DNS resolvers categories and subject descriptors. In: Proceedings of ACM IMC (2015)
6. Karami, M., Mccoy, D.: Understanding the emerging threat of DDoS-As-a-Service. In: Proceedings of Usenix LEET, pp. 2–5 (2013)
7. Santanna, J.J., Durban, R., Sperotto, A., Pras, A.: Inside booters: an analysis on operational databases. In: Proceedings of IFIP/IEEE IM, pp. 432–440 (2015)
8. Karami, M., Park, Y., McCoy, D.: Stress testing the booters: understanding and undermining the business of DDoS services. In: Proceedings of WWW (2016)
9. Akamai: State of the Internet / Security Q4. Technical report Akamai (2014). https://www.stateoftheinternet.com/
10. Arbor Networks: Worldwide infrastructure security report volume X. Technical report (2015). https://www.arbornetworks.com/insight-into-the-global-threat-landscape

11. Incapsula: DDoS global threat landscape report. Technical report (2015). http://lp.incapsula.com/ddos-report-2015.html
12. Rossow, C.: Amplification Hell: revisiting network protocols for DDoS abuse. In: Proceedings of NDSS, pp. 23–26 (2014)
13. Santanna, J., Van Rijswijk-deij, R., Hofstede, R., Sperotto, A.: Booters - an analysis of DDoS-as-a-Service attacks. In: Proceedings of IFIP/IEEE IM (2015)
14. Kaspersky: Statistics on botnet assisted DDoS attacks (2015). https://securelist.com/blog/research/70071/statistics-on-botnet-assisted-ddos-attacks-in-q1-2015/
15. Asghari, H., van Eeten, M.J.G., Bauer, J.M.: Economics of fighting botnets: lessons from a decade of mitigation. IEEE Secur. Priv. **13**(5), 16–23 (2015)
16. TeleGeography: Telegeography globalcomms data. http://shop.telegeography.com/products/globalcomms-database
17. CAIDA: AS classification. http://www.caida.org/data/as-classification/
18. Farsight Security: DNSDB. https://www.dnsdb.info
19. Tajalizadehkhoob, S., Korczynski, M., Noroozian, A., Ganan, C., van Eeten, M.: Apples, oranges and hosting providers: heterogeneity and security in the hosting market. In: Proceedings of IEEE/IFIP NOMS, pp. 289–297 (2016)
20. Akamai: State of the internet/security Q4. Technical report (2015). https://www.stateoftheinternet.com/downloads/pdfs/q4-2015-securityreport-ddos-stats-trends-analysis-infographic.pdf
21. Asghari, H., Ciere, M., Van Eeten, M.J.G.: Post-Mortem of a Zombie: conficker cleanup after six years. In: USENIX Security (2015)
22. PRB. Population Reference Bureau - Gross Domestic Product. http://www.prb.org/DataFinder/Topic/Rankings.aspx?ind=260
23. Ledbetter, A.M., Kuznekoff, J.H.: More than a game: friendship relational maintenance and attitudes toward Xbox LIVE communication. Commun. Res. **39**(2), 269–290 (2012)
24. Allamanis, M., Scellato, S., Mascolo, C.: Evolution of a location-based online social network. In: Proceedings of ACM IMC, p. 145. ACM Press, New York (2012)
25. Schravese, F., Born, A.: Lekker thuis providers platleggen (2015). http://www.nrc.nl/handelsblad/2015/10/17/lekker-thuis-providers-platleggen-1545974
26. Alexa: Alexa top 1M ranked sites (2015). http://s3.amazonaws.com/alexa-static/top-1m.csv.zip
27. Zittrain, J., Albert, K., Lessig, L.: Perma: scoping and addressing the problem of link and reference rot in legal citations. Legal Inform. Manage. **14**(02), 88–99 (2014)
28. Kaplan, E.L., Meier, P.: Nonparametric estimation from incomplete observations. J. Am. Statist. Assoc. **53**(282), 457–481 (1958)
29. Kuhrer, M., Hupperich, T., Rossow, C., Holz, T.: Exit from Hell? Reducing the impact of amplification DDoS attacks. In: USENIX Security, pp. 111–125 (2014)
30. Kuhrer, M., Hupperich, T., Rossow, C., Thorsten Holz, G.: Horst: Hell of a handshake: abusing TCP for reflective amplification DDoS attacks. In: Proceedings of USENIX WOOT (2014)
31. Durumeric, Z., Bailey, M., Halderman, J.A.: An internet-wide view of internet-wide scanning. In: USENIX Security, pp. 65–78 (2014)
32. Hutchings, A., Clayton, R.: Exploring the provision of online booter services. In: Deviant Behavior, pp. 1–16 (2016)
33. Florencio, D., Herley, C.: Where do all the attacks go? In: Economics of Information Security and Privacy III, pp. 13–33 (2013)
34. Florencio, D., Herley, C.: Is everything we know about password- stealing wrong? IEEE Secur. Priv. Mag. **10**(6), 63–69 (2012)

Web and Mobile Security

Uses and Abuses of Server-Side Requests

Giancarlo Pellegrino[1(✉)], Onur Catakoglu[2], Davide Balzarotti[2], and Christian Rossow[1]

[1] CISPA, Saarland University, Saarland Informatics Campus, Saarbrücken, Germany
{gpellegrino,crossow}@cispa.saarland
[2] Eurecom, Biot, France
{onur.catakoglu,davide.balzarotti}@eurecom.fr

Abstract. More and more web applications rely on server-side requests (SSRs) to fetch resources (such as images or even entire webpages) from user-provided URLs. As for many other web-related technologies, developers were very quick to adopt SSRs, even before their consequences for security were fully understood. In fact, while SSRs are simple to add from an engineering point of view, in this paper we show that—if not properly implemented—this technology can have several subtle consequences for security, posing severe threats to service providers, their users, and the Internet community as a whole.

To shed some light on the risks of this communication pattern, we present the first extensive study of the security implication of SSRs. We propose a classification and four new attack scenarios that describe different ways in which SSRs can be abused to perform malicious activities. We then present an automated scanner we developed to probe web applications to identify possible SSR misuses. Using our tool, we tested 68 popular web applications and find that the majority can be abused to perform malicious activities, ranging from server-side code execution to amplification DoS attacks. Finally, we distill our findings into eight pitfalls and mitigations to help developers to implement SSRs in a more secure way.

1 Introduction

Web applications have evolved from purely client-to-server patterns to an intertwined network of multiple web services. As a consequence, an increasing number of web applications retrieve external resources provided by other web services, often steered by user inputs. For example, social networks regularly fetch pages to display image and video previews of links posted by users, online calendars can import remote iCal data, web mail clients fetch emails from user-provided inboxes, and online image editors retrieve images from user-provided URLs. Such service-to-service communication is also integrated into business web applications and is at the core of several web-based protocols (e.g., OpenID and SAML) and Cashier-as-a-Service web applications (e.g., online stores using PayPal Express Checkout).

To support service-to-service communication, web applications rely on *server-side requests* (SSRs), which are HTTP requests generated by a server towards another web service. SSRs are often used to avoid passing relay messages between different services via the user, or to allow complex services to perform requests outside the boundaries of the same origin policy. Unfortunately, although the communication between web services is not new, we noticed an alarming lack of information and understanding regarding the threats and the security implications of this communication pattern. For example, when a user posts a URL to a social network, the server-side web application automatically fetches the content from the URL to display a visual preview of the page. However, giving the user the freedom to choose the URL means that she can control the destination and potentially also the content of SSRs. This communication pattern is getting more and more common to improve user experience and provide advanced features in a wide range of applications. Unfortunately, as is often the case for emerging web technologies, developers are often too quick to jump on the bandwagon without fully understanding the risks for security. In fact, as we present in this paper, SSRs are difficult to get right and, if not properly implemented, they can be abused to conduct malicious actions against the service itself, its users, or even third-party web applications.

Existing work in this field focuses on *Server-Side Request Forgery* (SSRF), a family of software vulnerabilities that allow an attacker to misuse SSRs to perform port scans [15,27] and buffer overflows [22]. However, this is only the tip of the iceberg of the possible security flaws that affect this communication pattern. Unfortunately, to date, we still lack a complete picture of the threats posed by SSRs.

To shed some light on the risks of this communication pattern, in this paper we present the first extensive assessment of the security implications of SSRs. We first present a classification to propose a common terminology for future research in the field. Our classification groups SSRs according to the level of control the attacker has, the role played by the vulnerable systems, and the potential attack targets. We then apply our classification to introduce four attack scenarios in which seemingly innocuous services can be composed together to form sophisticated attacks. For example, we show how popular services can be abused to distribute links to phishing pages—bypassing existing URL blacklists and reputation services.

In order to understand how widespread the problem is and what the most common mistakes are, we propose a tool called GÜNTHER and use it to analyze 68 web applications that accept user-provided URLs. We found weaknesses and security risks in 52 of them. Finally, to help developers to take more informed decisions and reduce the risks associated with this delicate communication pattern, we distilled our findings in a list of eight security-related recommendations. To summarize, this paper makes the following contributions:

- We propose a new classification to classify SSRs;
- We present four new attack scenarios in which SSRs can be used to mount sophisticated Denial-of-Service (DoS) attacks, deliver malware, and bypass

client-side countermeasures. We show that SSRFs are only one of the possible security flaws introduced by SSRs.
- We discuss the results of the experiments we conducted on 68 web services, 54 of which we found to be affected by at least one security flaw.
- We present a clear set of mitigations to help developers to implement SSRs in a more secure way.

2 Background

In this section, we present the SSR communication pattern, and we elaborate on its use in modern web applications. Then, we present an overview of the threat models, and finally, we present the current understanding of the security risks.

2.1 Server-Side Request Communication Pattern

The SSR pattern is shown in Fig. 1a. It involves three entities: a client C, an SSR service S, and an external server ES. The protocol starts when C sends an HTTP request $req(url_{ES})$ to S containing a user-specified url_{ES}. The position of url_{ES} in the HTTP request is application-specific, e.g., it could be inserted in the query string, in the POST data, or even in the resource field of the HTTP request. S extracts the URL and initiates a connection to fetch the corresponding resource res_{ES} from the remote server ES. Depending on the use of SSR, S can forward the resource res_{ES} back to C (i.e., $res_S = res_{ES}$), or return the result of a transformation (i.e., $res_S = f(res_{ES})$). For instance, S can embed res_{ES} into res_S, or simply return an identifier of the retrieved resource.

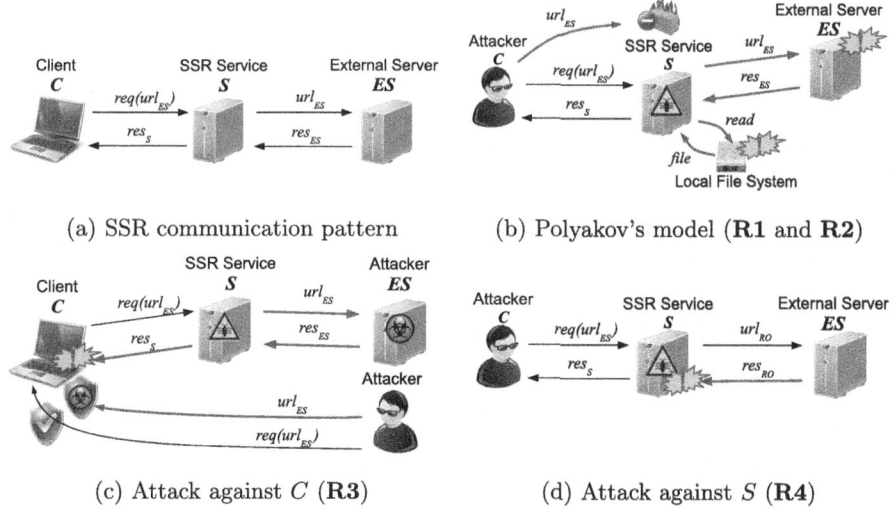

(a) SSR communication pattern (b) Polyakov's model (**R1** and **R2**)

(c) Attack against C (**R3**) (d) Attack against S (**R4**)

Fig. 1. SSR pattern and risks

Use Cases—SSRs are widely used in web applications. For example, social networks use SSRs to retrieve user-provided URLs and share them on the user's page. SSRs are also common in business applications, such as web office suites, in which they are used to include online resources (e.g., pictures) in documents. The list also includes online development tools, news aggregators, and image processing applications. Online development tools help developers, for example, to validate documents such as XML or JSON objects, or allow developers to test their web application with different browsers. SSRs are also at the core of news aggregators, which retrieve news from newspapers or RSS documents. Another use of SSRs is in web-based security protocols, such as the OpenID authentication protocol [8]. In OpenID, a client wants to be authenticated at the service provider (SP) by using her own credentials at the identity provider (IdP). OpenID allows the two providers to communicate either indirectly, i.e., by using the client's browser as a relay agent, or directly via SSRs. In this case, the SP acts as an HTTP client and initiates the connection with the IdP, which in turn acts as an HTTP server. SSRs are also used in other web-based security protocols, such as SAML SSO.

Server- vs. Client-Side Requests—The counterparts of SSRs are client-side requests (CSRs) in which C retrieves a resource at ES and sends it to S. However, replacing SSRs with CSRs may not be practical, secure, or efficient.

Practicality: CSRs can be implemented with cross-origin requests (CORs) in which a resource in the domain of ES is transmitted to S. These requests are subject to the same-origin policy (SOP for CORs) and the cross-origin resource sharing mechanism [26] (CORS). The former forbids accessing resources in a domain (i.e., ES) of a different origin from the request (i.e., S). These requests can be relaxed with CORS; however, CORS assumes a pre-established agreement between two different domain origins to allow requests from one to access resources of the other. This solution is often not practical because each service needs to keep and maintain a whitelist of domains that can access their services, and developers may not be able to modify the whitelist of third-party services. This has spurred the development of techniques to circumvent these obstacles, e.g., to bypass SOP for CORs (often considered to be security flaws, such as JSONP), or using the more flexible SSR paradigm.

Security: In protocols like OpenID, the involved parties do not agree on shared secrets such as cryptographic keys. Instead, they generate or exchange keys during the protocol run. In contrast to SSRs, CSRs may expose keys to attackers, thus endangering the validity of the authentication process.

Efficiency: CSRs may introduce additional costs. For example, social networks and online tools for developers may need to retrieve several resources to create a synthesis of the web page or to analyze its content. For each resource, an SSR service will issue one request and one response. With CSRs, on the other hand, the number of messages can double: The first request-response pair retrieves the resource from ES, while the second pair uploads the resource to S for further processing.

2.2 Security Risks and Threat Models

While SSR is a useful communication pattern which enables service-to-service communication, if not properly implemented it can be abused to perform a wide range of malicious activities, such as:

R1 SSRs can be abused as stepping stones to attack ES, for instance by performing denial-of-service attacks against Internet-facing services. Other attacks can be against services of S's private network.

R1 S may accept untrusted URLs which reference local resources, e.g., files hosted by S. For example, this attack can be used to exfiltrate system configuration files, passwords, and databases.

R2 SSRs introduce a new level of indirection between web browsers and the origin of resources. As a result, browsers may no longer be able to determine the real origin of a page, thus leaving users exposed to malicious content such as malware.

R3 Vulnerabilities in S can be exploited with incoming responses from ES. Responses may be processed to generate res_S for C. An adversarial ES can potentially craft malicious messages res_{ES} with the purpose of exploiting vulnerabilities in S.

These risks are shown in Fig. 1b (for **R1** and **R2**), Fig. 1c (for **R3**), and Fig. 1d (for **R4**). Figure 1b corresponds to the initial threat model proposed by Polyakov et al. [22]. The entities of Polyakov's model are an attacker C, an SSR service S, a service ES, the file system of S, and a firewall. C aims to access ES or the local file system of S. However, ES is protected by a firewall that blocks direct access from the Internet. S is exposed both to the Internet and to the local network. If not carefully implemented, an attacker can abuse SSRs performed by S to access internal servers that are in S's network, i.e., **R1**, or even retrieve files from S (e.g., via the `file://` protocol), i.e., **R2**.

Unfortunately, Polyakov's threat model is not complete as it neglects C as a possible victim (i.e., **R3**) and it considers only a fraction of the attack surface of S, thus ignoring other threats (i.e., **R4**). In this paper, we propose a more complete threat model that also incorporates new attacks in which SSRs are abused to target C (see Fig. 1c) and S (see Fig. 1d). In Fig. 1c, ES hosts malicious content and C is an honest client that adopts URL-based countermeasures to protect the user from malicious content (such as filtering mechanisms like Google Safe Browsing). The attacker targets C by tricking the user into visiting the malicious page ES, possibly abusing an innocent but vulnerable S. While C may believe she is visiting a well-reputed service S, in fact, S may just act as a proxy for malicious content hosted at ES, effectively circumventing any reputation-based mechanisms deployed by C. In Fig. 1d, the attacker is C, whereas ES hosts malicious content. The attacker submits the URL of the malicious content to S, which fetches res_{ES} and processes it. For example, if S implements poor resource validation mechanisms, it may be susceptible to resource exhaustion attacks via specially-crafted resources.

2.3 Awareness of the Security Risks

A closer look in the academic and non-academic literature and developer best practices (e.g., design patterns, coding rules, and API documentation) shows that (i) SSRs have received no attention by academic literature and (ii) existing non-academic works focus exclusively on Polyakov's threat model and thus neglect threats against C and S. In addition, despite the popularity of the attacks in Polyakov's threat model, there is a lack of documentation describing proper ways to implement SSR services and attack countermeasures. As a result, developers may develop vulnerable SSR services that can be abused by attackers.

3 SSR Classification

Despite anecdotal evidence, to date there is no systematic study of the SSR communication pattern. Therefore, we introduce a classification that proposes a common terminology for us and for future researchers. Our classification (Fig. 2) includes and supersedes pre-existing categorizations, classifying SSRs according to four different directions: *flaws*, attacker *control*, S's *behavior*, and *victims*. To the best of our knowledge, this is the most extensive existing classification of SSRs.

The four dimensions of our classification are not mutually exclusive. In fact, services often play multiple roles and may suffer from multiple flaws. For this reason, our classification cannot be considered a *taxonomy*. Furthermore, our classification is based on the current knowledge of SSR abuse which may change. However, while target and control dimensions covers all possible combinations, flaw and behavior dimensions are an enumeration and thus may be incomplete. As the popularity of the SSR pattern increases, new types of vulnerabilities and behaviors can be detected. Nevertheless, new discoveries can be used to extend both flaws and behaviors dimensions. In the rest of this section, we describe each category in more detail.

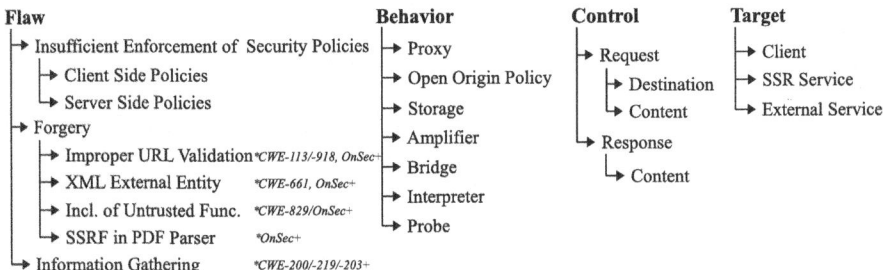

Fig. 2. SSRs classification

3.1 Flaw-Based Classification

The first classification is based on the type of flaw of S. A flaw can occur when S accepts and processes inputs from C, and when S accepts and processes the resource res_{ES}. This classification includes known vulnerabilities, i.e., forgery and information disclosure vulnerabilities of the CWE database and OnSec classification. Additionally, we extend it with a new class of vulnerabilities called *insufficient security policy enforcement*.

Insufficient Security Policy Enforcement—An HTTP conversation between the browser of C and ES can involve different security policies. For example, C may use URL-based reputation lists to avoid visiting malicious pages. Similarly, the server may restrict access to its resources, e.g., by using the Access-Control-Allow-Origin header (ACAO, for short). The problems arise when S acts as an intermediary and it fails to enforce the aforementioned policies. We distinguish two types of this flaw, according to which side of the security policy is not being enforced. However, as SSRs are used to bypass the SOP for CORs, SSR services suffer by design from the server-side variant of this flaw. For this reason, we focus on client-side security policies. While this flaw is not a vulnerability *per se*, as we will see in Sect. 4.1, insufficient client-side security policy enforcement is the root cause of a class of attacks targeting C that we call *Web Origin Laundering* attacks.

Forgery—SSR forgeries occur when S does not properly validate the user input that is used to generate the SSR, e.g., XML documents, PDF files, and URLs. SSR forgeries encompass all the currently known SSRF vulnerabilities. More specifically, this regroups and reorganizes flaws from Common Weaknesses Enumeration (CWE-113, CWE-661, CWE-829) [25], OnSec [16], and Polyakov et al. [22] which were exploited in documented attacks, i.e., against SAP NetWeaver [22], Google+ [1,27], and Facebook [27]. Our classification also includes the TCPDF bug[1]. Besides these vulnerabilities, our classification introduces the class of *improper URL validation vulnerabilities*, which supersedes the improperly-called class of SSRF flaws (CWE-918). This group of flaws occurs when S does not validate user-provided URLs, e.g., rejecting URLs with unexpected URL schemes (e.g., file://), blacklisted domains, or invalid characters. Then, our classification considers two special cases of improper URL validation, i.e., improper enforcement of expected destination and improper neutralization of CRLF in HTTP headers (CWE-113). Improper enforcement of expected destination occurs when S does not sufficiently validate that the URL refers to an expected destination [25]. Improper neutralization of CRLF in HTTP headers occurs when software fails to remove the CR and LF characters from input data, such that an attacker can inject HTTP headers or *smuggle* HTTP requests.

Information Gathering—A service S can unintentionally disclose sensitive information of ES to an attacker. This class of vulnerabilities includes SSR vulnerabilities of the 2xx group of the CWE catalog, i.e., (i) improper neutralization

---

[1] See bug #1005, http://sourceforge.net/projects/tcpdf/files/CHANGELOG.TXT.

of error messages and (ii) side channels. The former type occurs when S reveals information about exceptional behavior of ES in res_S. For example, S may return an error message to C detailing the reasons why ES is not reachable or the target resource is not available. Side channels occur when S unwillingly leaks information about ES. A typical side channel can be caused by a noticeable difference in the response time between $req(url_{ES})$ and res_S or by the variation in the type and size of the responses.

3.2 Behavior-Based Classification

SSRs can also be classified according to the behavior of S. We observed seven distinct behaviors that capture the way a service can be abused. While some of these may seem legitimate in isolation, we will show that their combination can lead to sophisticated attacks.

Proxy—S acts as a proxy when it returns res_{ES} to C. We distinguish proxy services as transparent (when res_{ES} is forwarded to C without any modification) or non-transparent (when, for example, res_{ES} is embedded inside res_S).

Open Origin Policy—An open origin policy service (OOP) always returns the least restrictive ACAO:* header, ignoring the actual value (if any) that is set by ES. OOP services allow bypassing SOP for CORs (if ES did not include the ACAO header) and any cross-origin resource sharing policy.

Storage—A storage service can be used to store and retrieve resources. That is, S fetches res_{ES} from ES and stores the resource locally. Then, S returns an ID to C for the resource that can be later used to retrieve res_{ES}.

Amplifier—An amplifier service can increase the number of SSRs and/or the amount of data sent in SSRs as compared to CSRs. We designate amplifiers as request amplifiers (when they increase the number of requests) or data amplifiers (when they increase the size of each request or response).

Bridge—A bridge service connects different layers of a protocol stack and allows S to send packets to non-HTTP services. With reference to Fig. 1a, when S processes a crafted URL, instead of generating an HTTP request, it opens a TCP connection and sends raw data to ES. This behavior is often the result of forgery vulnerabilities, e.g., improper URL validation.

Interpreter—An interpreter service uses HTTP clients capable of interpreting JavaScript code. For instance, S can be used to control the different parts of a more complex attack, or to perform any computations on the attacker's behalf.

Probe—A probe service can be used to collect information about an external service ES. Information can be leaked to C over side channels. Depending on the information leaked, probe services can be used to perform port scanning, host discovery, or application fingerprinting. This type of service is the result of two flaws: forgery, i.e., accepting custom TCP ports, and information gathering.

3.3 Control-Based Classification

The third SSRs classification is according to the control an attacker has on the content of SSRs and responses generated by S. In particular, we distinguish the control over the *destination* and the *content* of SSRs. The destination consists of the domain or IP address of the server, the HTTP Host header, and the path of the HTTP request, whereas the content of a request covers the request parameters and the body. This classification supersedes Polyakov's classification [22] as we add control over the response. For the response, we consider only the content, i.e., the body of the HTTP response res_S.

3.4 Target-Based Classification

Finally, we examine who can be the target of an SSR-based attack. We distinguish between attacks against the client C, the SSR service S, and the remote service ES. Most of the vulnerabilities discovered by prior work target ES, such as the vulnerabilities on Facebook and Google services [27], the XXE on SAP NetWeaver [22], and the vulnerability of DB4Web (CVE-2002-1484) which all allowed attacks against third-party services. We extend this threat model with attacks against the client, such as the Web Origin Laundering attack. In addition, we define S as a potential target, e.g., of resource exhaustion attacks.

Table 1. Mapping between attacks and the four angles of our classification: flaw, behavior, control, and target.

Attacks		Flaw			Behaviors						Controls			Target
		No Enf.	*Forgery*	*Inf. Gath.*	*Proxy*	*OOP*	*Storage*	*Amplifier*	*Bridge*	*Interpr.*	*Probe*	*Req. Dest.*	*Req. Cont.*	*Resp. Cont.*	
Origin Laundering	Attack 1.1	✗			✗							✗		✗	C
	Attack 1.2	✗			✗							✗		✗	C
Denial of Service	Attack 2.1 (Dom. Blacklist.)	✗			✗							✗		✗	S
	Attack 2.2 (with Data Amplifier)	✗	✗					✗ ✗		✗		✗ ✗	✗		S, ES
	Attack 2.3 (against Data Amplifier)	✗	✗					✗ ✗		✗		✗ ✗	✗		S, ES
Reconnaissance Attacks			✗ ✗								✗	✗			S, ES
Bridging Attacks				✗					✗			✗ ✗			S, ES

4 Attacks

We now instantiate our classification and present seven attacks. Attacks are divided into four categories: browser countermeasure evasions (Sect. 4.1), DoS attacks (Sect. 4.2), reconnaissance (Sect. 4.3), and bridging attacks (Sect. 4.4). Only the last two were previously known. The mapping between attacks and our classification (including the root cause flaw) is shown in Table 1. As opposed to the known exploitations of SSRF [12,15,16,22,27], two out of seven attacks actually target C—an insight that should bring additional attention to SSR abuse.

4.1 Web Origin Laundering

Web browsers implement various URL-based defenses to protect users and data from attacks, such as Google Safe Browsing [9], NoScript [13], or AdBlock [6]. These mechanisms make security decisions based on requested URLs, e.g., limit the scope of JavaScript programs or even deny the JavaScript execution.

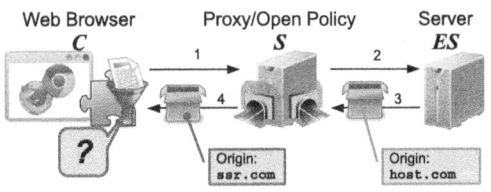

Fig. 3. The *Web Origin Laundering* attack.

Web origin laundering is an attack which hides resource origins, thus bypassing URL-based defenses, leaving users exposed. With reference to our threat model, this is an attack against C, i.e., risk **R3**. First, C requests a resource of ES via S. Note that the victim's browser is not aware of the fact that the request of step 1 contains the URL of a resource of ES. Then, S fetches the resource from ES and returns it to C (steps 2–4). Finally, the web browser verifies the origin of the resource to enforce security mechanisms. Unfortunately, the browser will falsely assume that S is the origin, possibly leading to a wrong decision in the security checks. We now preset two instances of this attack to bypass browser countermeasures.

Attack 1.1—With reference to Fig. 3, the attacker prepares a URL that is distributed to C. For example, the URL refers to a proxy service to fetch malicious content hosted by ES, e.g., http://ssr.com/?url=host.com/mal.html. The attacker sends this URL to C, e.g., via phishing email, or linking it in forums and social networks. The victim clicks on the URL and, as a result, her browser verifies whether the URL is blacklisted. As ssr.com is not blacklisted, C sends message 1 to S. S extracts the URL from the parameter url, and fetches the malicious content at host.com/mal.html. Finally, it returns the malicious content to C. We have successfully performed this attack, bypassing the Google Safe Browsing mechanism as implemented by Google Chrome 43.0.2357.130 and Mozilla Firefox 39.0. In these attacks, we have used two proxy services to relay known phishing pages, drive-by download pages, and other malicious content including malware binaries (i.e., EICAR Standard Anti-Virus Test File and Virus.Win32.Virut).

Researchers have recently found criminals using a similar technique to distribute links to phishing pages. The attacker distributes a Google URL that redirected to the malicious target[2]. However, browser countermeasures can discover the attempt to redirect the user to a malicious domain and then block the attack. Furthermore, this attack is limited only to pages indexed by Google. Our attack does not rely on redirect but instead on SSRs which hide the true origin of the malicious content. Finally, an additional confirmation of the severity of

---

[2] See https://isc.sans.edu/diary/How+Malware+Campaigns+Employ+Google+Redirects+and+Analytics/19843.

this threat was provided in a recent NoScript bypass attack based on a SSRF vulnerability in the content delivery network of Akamai[3].

Attack 1.2 (Escaping Content Dispositions)—Attack 1.1 can be blocked by the Content-Disposition response header of S. This header suggests to a browser not to display the returned resource to the user. We will discuss the use of this header in Sect. 6. However, even in presence of the content disposition header, it is still possible to deliver and display malicious content to the user. Consider the following JavaScript code embedded in a malicious web page hosted by a third-party service:

```
1 var malware = "http://host.com/mal.html";
2 var cor = new XMLHttpRequest();
3 cor.onreadystatechange=function() {
4   var ct = this.getResponseHeader("content-type")
5   window.location = "data:" + ct "," + encodeURIComponent(cor.responseText);
6 }
7 cor.open("GET", "http://ssr.com/?url=" + encodeURIComponent(malware), false);
8 cor.send();
```

The URL of the malicious resource, i.e., url_{ES}, is in the variable malware (Line 1) which is retrieved with an asynchronous request (Lines 2 and 7–8). Note that the URL used in the Ajax request is of the SSR service S (line 7). If the attacker directly used the value in malware (line 8), the attempt to reach a malicious server RE would be detected (e.g., by Google Safe Browsing). Then, once the malicious resource is fetched, the JavaScript program transforms it into a *data URL*. Such URL does not point to a resource, but instead contains the resource within the URL itself. Finally, the browser is directed to the data URL (line 5) and the malicious content is displayed to the user. We have developed proofs of concept of these attacks and bypassed the Google Safe Browsing mechanism of Chrome and Firefox. To this end, we used a proxy service which returned the Content-Disposition response header. Similarly to the previous attack, we used URLs of real phishing pages and binaries of actual malware.

4.2 Denial of Service

We now present three scenarios in which SSR is abused to perform DoS attacks against S. We group these attacks into two categories: *domain blacklisting* and *resource exhaustion*.

Attack 2.1 (DoS via Domain Blacklisting)— As discussed before, browsers prevent users from visiting websites that are known to host malicious content. An attacker may be able to poison these blacklists to block benign sites that expose a proxy behavior by using the web origin laundering technique. To this end, the attacker prepares a URL for the proxy service that contains the URL of a malicious page, and submits it to the blacklist operator (e.g., to Google in the case of Safe Browsing) to initiate a scan. Since the malicious content seems to originate from the proxy service, once the URL is detected as malicious, the proxy itself gets blacklisted. To avoid to disrupt the operations of SSR services,

---

[3] See https://www.blackhat.com/us-15/briefings.html.

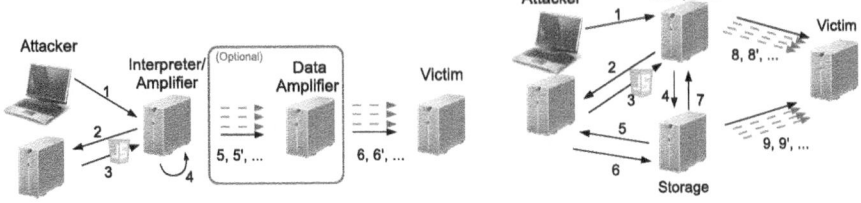

Fig. 4. DoS with data amplier   **Fig. 5.** DoS against data amplifier

we did not test this attack in practice. With reference to our threat model, this is an attack against S, i.e., risk **R4**.

Attack 2.2 (DoS with Data Amplifier): In this second scenario, an attacker can target *any* Internet-facing service and flood it with HTTP requests. The general idea is to use an interpreter service as coordinator to amplify number and size of requests by using data amplifier services via CORs. In order to bypass SOP for CORs, this attack uses the web origin laundering presented in Sect. 4.1 whenever the interpreter needs to send a request towards another service role. Figure 4 shows an example involving the attacker, an interpreter, and an amplifier service. The attacker (C) submits the URL of the JavaScript program to the interpreter service $(S,$ step 1). The interpreter fetches and executes a malicious program (steps 2 and 3) that performs two operations: *enlistment* and *attack*. The enlistment consists in re-submitting the URL of the JavaScript programs to the interpreter service. This will increase the number of instances of JavaScript programs participating in the attack. In the attack phase, the JavaScript code instructs the web service to send many HTTP requests to the victim (ES). Browsers, such as used by S, can generate about 3,000 requests per second using the XMLHttpRequest API [21]. One can further increase the attack impact by using data amplifier services that receive compressed requests and submit the decompressed data to the victim (step 6). Data amplifiers allow about a 1:1000 ratio between the data sent to the amplifier and the data sent to the victim [20].

For ethical reasons we did not perform any resource exhaustion DoS attacks. Instead, we manually verified that the building blocks of this attack are offered by the services involved in the attack. More specifically, we verified that (i) interpreters offer the features needed for the attacks (e.g., XMLHttpRequest API or Image API), (ii) chains and combinations of SSR services can be created, and (iii) the composition of the services can be invoked by interpreters. With reference to our threat model, this is an attack against ES, i.e., risk **R1**.

Attack 2.3 (DoS against Data Amplifier)—A similar setup of Attack 2.2 can also be used to attack the data amplifier, by keeping it busy with decompression tasks (see Fig. 5). In this case, the attack also requires a storage service to store attacker-controlled compressed data. The interpreter, again controlled by a malicious program, will request the storage service to fetch the compressed resource from the web server of the attacker (steps 4–6). Then, the storage service returns an ID of the resource to the interpreter (step 7). Finally, the interpreter will send many compressed requests to the victim that trigger the victim to fetch resources from the storage (step 8, 8', ...). The victim is not only forced to decompress the requests, but it also has to continuously fetch compressed resources from the storage service and decompress them, easily leading to memory exhaustion. Similarly for Attack 2.2, we did not perform the attack but we verified that the building blocks of this attack are offered by the services involved in the attack. With reference to our threat model, this is an attack against S, i.e., risk **R4**.

4.3 Network Reconnaissance

Network reconnaissance is a previously-known family of attacks (i.e., risk **R1**) which entails attacks that gather information about a network, server, or service. We distinguish between *port scanning*, *host discovery*, and *application fingerprinting*. Reconnaissance is the main documented attack exploiting SSRF [15,24].

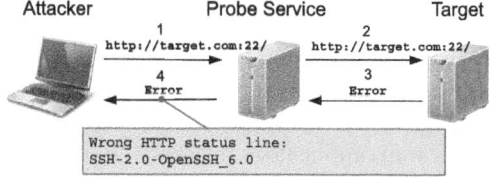

Fig. 6. Port scanning with probe services

While classical attacks require connecting directly to the victim, probe services can be used to offer anonymity and even allow access to private networks across firewall boundaries. Figure 6 shows this attack with a probe service S. The attacker prepares a request for S which contains the URL with the host or service to be scanned. For example, if the attacker would like to probe an SSH service, she can submit the URL http://target.com:22. As a result, S connects to the URL (an SSH server) and responds to the attacker, potentially leaking information about the status of the target service. In our example, S tries to interpret the response of the target as an HTTP response, and returns the reason for the failure (e.g., reporting that a given SSH server banner is not a valid HTTP message). If S does not leak information about the target, as we will show, an attacker can use *side channels* to determine the state of a TCP port, the availability of a resource, or the reachability of a host.

4.4 Protocol Bridging Attacks

Protocol bridging is a previously-known family of attacks. The service S often supports different URL schemes, including `ftp`, `gopher`, and `dict`. In particular, the `gopher` scheme allows the attacker to send arbitrary data over the TCP connection, by using the following URL: gopher://target.com:port/payload. If a service does not properly validate the schemes of user-provided URLs, SSRs can be used to send arbitrary data (i.e., *payload*) over TCP connections to non-HTTP network services—effectively acting as a *bridge* between different protocols. In the past, this technique has been used to connect to remote procedure calls (RPC) services and exploit buffer overflow vulnerabilities [22], but it could be used for many other malicious purposes, such as to send spam messages to an SMTP server. With reference to our threat model, this is an attack against ES, i.e., risk **R1**. A variation of this attack involves the `file` URL scheme to retrieve files in S's filesystem (e.g., by sending `file:///etc/passwd` to a bridge service S). In one incident, such an attack allowed access to system files (e.g., passwd) of Google servers [1]. According to our threat model, this is an attack against local resources of S, i.e., risk **R2**.

5 Case Studies and Analysis

In an attempt to investigate the prevalence of SSR attacks, we analyzed 68 services taken from seven web application classes, i.e., social networks, business web applications (e.g., spreadsheet and calendar web applications), software development tools, online image processing, OpenID service providers, RSS readers, and online web screenshot tools. For each category, we selected the most popular web applications prioritized by Google search ranks. About 60 % of our case studies are among the top 50,000 web sites, including six of the top 10 web sites on Alexa.

Table 2. Mapping between tests and classification.

GÜNTHER *Capabilities*	Flaws			Behavior				
	No Enf.	Forgery	Inf. Gath.	Proxy	OOP Storage	Amplif.	Bridge	Interpr. Probe
(T1) IP Addr. and TCP port	✗							✗
Non-HTTP schemes	✗						✗	
(T2) Transparent Proxying				✗				
Store Resource					✗			
Malicious Content	✗							
(T3) ACAO: *	✗			✗				
HTTP Req/Resp Compr.						✗		
(T4) Image/Ajax API								✗
Web Worker							✗	✗
(T5) Side Channel		✗						✗

The goal of our analysis is to study real SSR services and map them to our classification. To aid our analysis, we developed GÜNTHER, a novel open-source black-box testing tool[4] that reveals SSR flaws and service behaviors. GÜNTHER takes as input a description of $url(req_{ES})$, possibly enriched with session data (i.e., session cookies). Then, GÜNTHER generates a list of requests to probe the service. GÜNTHER consists of a *tester* and a *monitor* component. The tester probes S whereas the monitor dynamically spawns servers to receive SSRs originated by the service. With reference to Fig. 1a, the tester and the monitor play the roles of C and S, respectively. The current version of GÜNTHER supports the tests in Table 2, i.e., **(T1)** URL validation and validation bypass via HTTP 3xx redirection, **(T2)** proxy behavior, **(T3)** response header analysis, **(T4)** HTTP client analysis, and **(T5)** side channel analysis. These tests are mapped to flaws and behaviors as shown in Table 2.

---

[4] The tool is freely available here: https://github.com/tgianko/guenther.

We ran GÜNTHER against the 68 services in our dataset. The experiment results are shown in Table 3. We anonymized each service in Table 3a by replacing its domain name with an identifier (column *ID*) because not all of them have been fixed. To improve readability, we have grouped services with the same flaws and behaviors in the same row. Our experiments revealed at least one service for each flaw and service behavior. In total, 50 out of 68 services suffer from one of the flaws in our classification. All these services are either proxy, open origin policy, probe, or bridge services. One also behaves as an amplifier and four can act as interpreters and therefore can be abused to coordinate other attacks. Then, ten services (14.7%) implement weak forms of URL validation that GÜNTHER successfully bypassed via HTTP 3xx redirections. Finally, only 14 services (20.6%) in our experiments are *not* affected by SSR-based vulnerabilities.

6 Mitigations

After discussing the vast potential and impact of SSRs, we will now discuss eight mitigations and pitfalls. From our experiments on the case studies, and reviewing the state of the art on the mitigation side, we extracted a list of seven mitigations. Finally, as none of the observed ones are sufficient to block Attack 1.2, we propose an additional mitigation to enforce URL-based browser countermeasures.

(M1) Monitoring—Monitoring is a mitigation technique which aims at detecting suspicious activity at service runtime. The owner of S5 reported to us that they rely on a sophisticated monitoring technique to detect the SSR abuse targeting C (**R3** in Fig. 1c). Unfortunately, the use of monitoring to detect this type of abuse has two shortcomings which make it insufficient as a general solution. First, a complex infrastructure and a considerable amount of resources are required to support monitoring, especially for popular services that serve a large number of users. Second, while monitoring SSRs may successfully mitigate large-scale abuses, it is often ineffective for detecting low-volume attacks. For example, the advent of APT-based attacks has changed the distribution from large-scale to a targeted distribution in which only a single user or organization is attacked. For these reasons, we believe that monitoring should be complemented with further preventive guidelines.

(M2) Avoid Acting as a Proxy or Wrap Response—Among our case studies, three services can be abused as transparent proxy to serve malicious content to a client. However, we are not aware of intended use cases for transparent proxies, and thus services should be explicitly designed to avoid this behavior. For example, S can use a JSON envelope to wrap res_{ES}, which prevents a web browser from interpreting the resource res_{ES} and thus blocks the Web Origin Laundering Attack 1.1. Services S12, S59, and S60 use custom JSON data structures to wrap res_{ES}, i.e., they behaved as non-transparent proxies. However, this countermeasure alone is not sufficient to also block Attack 1.2. As this second attack uses malicious JavaScript to retrieve res_{ES}, the JavaScript program

Table 3. Results of our Experimental Analysis

(a) Case studies to flaws/behaviors

ID	No Enf.	Forgery	Inf. Gath.	Proxy	OOP	Storage	Amplif.	Bridge	Interpr.	Probe
Business Applications										
S5	✗		✗	✗	✗		✗			✗
S2	✗				✗					
S1		✗	✗						✗	✗
S3, S7			✗							✗
S4, S6, S8										
Development Tools										
S10			✗	✗						✗
S12		✗	✗					✗		✗
S14		✗						✗		
S9, S11, S13			✗							✗
Image Editing										
S15	✗	✗	✗				✗	✗		✗
S16	✗		✗	✗						✗
S17			✗							✗
S18										
OpenID										
S29			✗	✗						✗
S35		✗	✗					✗		✗
S19-27, S31-34, S36-40			✗							
S28, S30										
RSS Readers										
S41, S46	✗	✗						✗		✗
S43-45, S47			✗							✗
S42										
Screenshot										
S54		✗		✗						✗
S53, S56		✗							✗	✗
S52, S55										
S48-51									✗	
Social Networks										
S64	✗				✗					
S67		✗							✗	✗
S59-60, S62, S65-66		✗								✗
S57-58, S61, S68, S63										
Total	4	8	47	3	4	1	1	8	7	47

(b) URL validation results

Tests		Accept	Reject	Bypass
(T1)	IP address	60	8	2
	Dict scheme	4	64	4
	Goph. scheme	3	65	4
	TCP port	55	13	0

(c) Proxy, header, and client test results

Tests		Serv.	% rel.
(T2)	Transp. Prox.	3	4.41%
	Non-transp. Prox.	6	8.82%
	Store Resource	1	1.47%
	Malicious URL	4	5.88%
(T3)	ACAO:*	4	5.88%
	Decompr. Req.	1	1.47%
	Decompr. Resp.	36	52.94%
(T4)	Image API	7	10.29%
	XMLHTTPReq. API	5	7.35%
	Web Worker	2	2.94%

(d) Side channel analysis

(T5) Tests	Serv.	% rel.
Port Scanning		
Open/closed/filtered	13	19.12%
Open (partially)	40	58.82%
No leak	15	22.06%
Fingerprinting		
Res. exists/does not exist	37	54.41%
Res. exists (partially)	3	4.41%
No leak	24	41.18%
Host Discovery		
On/offline	45	66.18%
Online (partially)	16	23.53%
No leak	7	10.29%

can unpack res_{ES} and then encode it as inline data (i.e., via the data URI scheme). Attack 1.2 can partially be mitigated by enforcing URL-based browser countermeasures, such as Google Safe Browsing, at S (see M8).

(M3) Perform Proper URL Validation—S should validate url_{ES} before fetching the target resource. Table 3b shows how our case studies validate user-provided URLs. The vast majority accept URLs containing an IP address (60 services) and/or a port number (55 services). None of these behaviors can be considered a vulnerability per se. Some applications rejected URLs with IP addresses, probably as an attempt to block attackers who may try to access local machines in the company intranet. However, it is important to understand that this countermeasure is often insufficient, as attackers can still address any IP by pointing an attacker-controlled domain to a local IP address (*DNS rebinding*).

Moreover, we found weak forms of URL validation that can be circumvented. URL validation of ten services can be bypassed with HTTP redirections (last column in Table 3b). This is critical, because it shows how the service developers attempted to mitigate the problem, but were not aware of all the details of this security threat. Worse, while few of the 68 services accept URLs with the Dict (four services) or Gopher schemes (three services), redirection helps to bypass an additional four cases for each scheme. These *bridges* are a severe threat, as they give full control of a TCP socket and enable attackers to communicate with non-HTTP network services.

URL validation that protects against rebinding can be implemented in HTTP libraries. To the best of our knowledge, SafeCurl [14] is the only HTTP library that provides these countermeasures for PHP services. Developers using other programming languages or headless browsers need to implement the above mechanisms on their own.

(**M4**) **Content Disposition**—The content disposition header is used to suggest that a browser should not display a resource inline [7]. This header has been proposed in the past to fix Reflected File Download attacks [11]. An SSR service that uses this header can block the Web Origin Laundering Attack 1.1. In fact, as the resource is not shown to the user inline, phishing attacks are prevented. In our experiments, services S5 and S9 use the content disposition header. While Content-Disposition mitigates Attack 1.1, it does not protect from Attack 1.2. Content-Disposition alone does not solve the root cause of the insufficient security policy enforcement flaw, but instead raises the difficulty for an attacker to abuse SSRs. To mitigate Attack 1.2, see M8.

(**M5**) **Limit Resource Usage**—DoS attacks of Sect. 4.2 are the result of a combination of services: interpreters to orchestrate the attack, amplifiers to amplify the size and number of requests, and OOP services to chain SSRs services. This mitigation targets the first two services (for the OOP services, see instead **M6**). Table 3c shows that 10 % of our case studies use browsers with full JavaScript support, including JavaScript APIs that can be used to orchestrate DoS attacks. In particular, seven services support the Image API, five services support the XMLHttpRequest API, and two services support the Web Worker API. These APIs can be abused to turn a seemingly innocuous web browser into a weaponized HTTP-based bot that can generate thousands of HTTP requests per second [10,21]. To avoid this abuse, interpreter services need to limit the request rate. Another source of resource exhaustion is data compression. With reference to Table 3c, data compression is supported by most tested services, and one also supports HTTP request decompression. Decompressing HTTP requests is not a standardized behavior, but instead is a web server-specific feature [20]. We are not aware of the reasons to support this feature, and we would recommend disabling it. Unlike this particular case, HTTP response compression is standardized and a more common feature. Also in this case, we would recommend disabling data compression. If this is not possible, then developers should verify that their services limit the resources used when decompressing incoming messages (see [20] for guidelines toward a secure implementation of data decompression).

(M6) Remove Open Access Control Policies for CORs—As OOP services can be accessed via CORs from any domain, they can be used by interpreters to chain SSR services in order to mount the attack. Among our case studies, four services use the header `ACAO: *`, which is bad practice in the presence of our threat model. The other 64 services omit ACAO headers, thus effectively blocking cross-origin requests. Another effective countermeasure to block this attack is to limit the access to SSR services to CORs from trusted origins.

(M7) Limit Information Leakage—72 % of the services can be used as probes to perform network reconnaissance. This makes this role the most widespread behavior among the applications we tested. All probe services of Table 3a allow, with different degrees of granularity, network reconnaissance via response time analysis and response code. Information leaks can be solved by making S's behavior independent from the success of the SSR. For example, S can enforce a constant response time (i.e., a fixed delay between C's request and the response sent to C). We observed this behavior for 15 services that do not allow distinguishing the port state, seven services that do not leak information about the host availability, and 24 services that do not disclose the availability of an HTTP resource. However, enforcing a constant time introduces undesired delays, thus making it unsustainable for scenarios in which responsiveness is important. In these cases, S may deploy weaker security measures which can limit network reconnaissance attacks. This can be achieved, for example, by accepting URLs only with selected TCP ports with mitigation M3, or by rate-limiting the requests.

(M8) Enforce URL-Based Browser Countermeasures—None of the mitigations we obseved in the wild (M1-7) can solve Web Origin Laundering Attack 1.2. The root cause of this attack is that S allows one to retrieve and serve malicious content, and hide the true origin of the malicious content with S's domain.

To block Web Origin Laundering Attack 1.2, we propose that SSR services should implement the same countermeasures deployed by browsers in order to block harmful and unwanted content, e.g., Google Safe Browsing. Once the client submits the URL to S, S validates the URL using the Google Safe Browsing protocol. If the URL is malicious, then S refuses to retrieve it. While this approach at least partially mitigates the distribution of malicious content, it does not fix the problem if web browsers implement custom security policies, e.g., NoScript or AdBlock custom domain blacklists. In conclusion, a general solution to Web Origin Laundering Attack 1.2 is still lacking.

7 Developers Feedback

We responsibly disclosed all vulnerabilities to the respective developers. In most of the cases, developers reacted to our first reports. If developers were unresponsive for over a month, we tried a second time and then alerted the US CERT. Our disclosure resulted in a variety of responses from developers, strongly related to the type of flaw of our classification.

Forgery—75 % of such vulnerabilities have been fixed by now. Six vendors (i.e., S1, S14, S15, S35, S46, and S64) patched their services, while two vendors (S12 and S41) were unresponsive. The high number of fixes may be due to a partial awareness of the security risks of forgery vulnerabilities: forgery is the first documented SSR flaw, and developers deploy countermeasures against forgery, i.e., URL validation (e.g., 64 services reject URLs with non-HTTP schemes, 13 with TCP ports, and eight with IPs). However, the fact that countermeasures can be bypassed with HTTP redirections indicates that the complete exploitation space of SSR flaws is not entirely understood.

Information Gathering—The disclosure of these vulnerabilities revealed a more fragmented situation. Five services patched the problem, while the vast majority ignored the issue or did not respond to our report. An interpretation of these results is in the rejected reports. In three cases, developers did not want to modify S as they are using monitoring to prevent abuses (i.e., S3, S5, and S59). The use of monitoring suggests prudence and a general attention to security-related issues. However, the choice of monitoring over a patch in S may indicate that developers rate this risk a low priority. Other developers (S7, S60, and S62) consider this flaw not to be a security risk at all.

Enforcement of Security Policies—Out of four affected services, S15 has been shut down and S2 has partially solved the flaw by adding the content disposition header into the response. Developers of S16 reported having fixed the flaw, but the patch did not solve the problem. Lastly, developers of S5 rejected our report because they use monitoring to prevent abuses. As discussed in Sect. 6, monitoring may work for large-scale abuses, but potentially still misses individual exploitations.

8 Related Work

In this section, we review SSR literature according to four thematic groups. First, we review academic literature with a focus on vulnerability analysis and detection. Then, we review known SSR-based attacks against popular web applications. Third, we present current attempts to classify and categorize existing SSR threats. Finally, we survey existing tools to detect SSR vulnerabilities.

Vulnerability Analyses and Detection—Web vulnerabilities have been extensively studied from different angles, e.g., categorization and prioritization [17,23], impact and trends [18], detection techniques [2,19] and effectiveness [4], and defense mechanisms [3]. While existing works focused largely on classical, yet severe, vulnerabilities, to the best of our knowledge, no scientific work has studied the SSR communication pattern.

Attacks and Classifications—The vast majority of security incidents are described in reports and whitepapers. These attacks are SSR forgery attacks and were brought to the community's attention by Polyakov et al. [22] and Walikar [27]. Polyakov et al. [22] described an XXE vulnerability in SAP NetWeaver whereas Walikar [27] described an insufficient input validation vulnerability in popular social networks. Other exploitations of SSR forgery vulnerabilities were reported by Almroth et al. [1], in which they retrieve local resources in Google services. All these attacks are included in Polyakov's threat model. With respect to the current knowledge about SSR-based attacks, our paper presents five previously-unknown SSR-based attacks, i.e., two Web Origin Laundering attacks and three DoS attacks.

Following the initial incidents, the community started classifying and categorizing known SSR-based vulnerabilities. All efforts focused on SSR forgery (e.g., CWE [25] and OnSec [16]). However, current knowledge on SSR vulnerabilities is sparse, disjoint, and incomplete. While the CWE database includes some SSR-related vulnerabilities, they are mainly isolated entries which are not correlated to each other. As a result, developers cannot identify all possible flaws that can affect an SSR service. Furthermore, as we have shown, there are other attacks targeting C and S which do not rely on forgery but instead abuse improper enforcement of security policies.

Detection Tools—Existing detection tools target only SSRF vulnerabilities. They are available in the form of proof-of-concept scripts (e.g., the SSRF bible [16]) or as testing tools. A proprietary tool that can find SSRF vulnerabilities is Acunetix WVS version 9 with AcuMonitor[5]. However, this tool is not freely available and we were not able to inspect it. Existing public tools offer limited detection power (only SSRF) which make them inapplicable to the purpose of this paper. Ussrfuzzer [28] fuzzes HTTP requests with URLs to detect SSRs, however, it does not perform any security test. In contrast, the OWASP Skanda [5] tool can detect information disclosure flaws, in particular leaks of TCP port status. However, it cannot be used to detect other types of leakage, e.g., web application fingerprint, nor other vulnerabilities or security related features. For all these reasons, we developed GÜNTHER, a first comprehensive SSR testing tool, that we plan to release to the public.

9 Conclusion

To the best of our knowledge, this is the first comprehensive study of the security of SSRs. We presented a classification of SSRs based on the type of flaw, the level of control of the messages, the behavior of the vulnerable services, and the potential attack targets. Furthermore, we unveiled previously-unknown exploitations techniques in which a combination of seemingly innocuous services can be used to mount sophisticated attacks targeting both users and servers on the Internet. We also presented experiments on 68 popular web applications. Our experiments showed that the majority of the web applications can be abused to perform malicious activities, ranging from server-side code execution to DoS

---

[5] See http://www.acunetix.com/vulnerability-scanner/.

attacks. We also presented eight mitigations to help developers to implement SSRs in a more secure way.

Acknowledgments. This work was supported by the German Federal Ministry of Education and Research (BMBF) through funding for the Center for IT-Security, Privacy and Accountability (CISPA) and for the BMBF project 13N13250.

References

1. Almroth, F., Karlsson, M.: How we got read access on Googles production servers. http://blog.detectify.com/post/82370846588/how-we-got-read-access-on-googles-production
2. Balzarotti, D., Cova, M., Felmetsger, V.V., Vigna, G.: Multi-module vulnerability analysis of web-based applications. In: ACM CCS 2007 (2007)
3. Barth, A., Jackson, C., Mitchell, J.C.: Robust defenses for cross-site request forgery. In: ACM CCS 2008 (2008)
4. Bau, J., Bursztein, E., Gupta, D., Mitchell, J.: State of the art:Automated blackbox web application vulnerability testing. In: IEEE S&P 2010 (2010)
5. Chauhan, J.: OWASP SKANDA - SSRF Exploitation framework. http://www.chmag.in/article/may2013/owasp-skanda-%E2%80%93-ssrf-exploitation-framework
6. Eyeo GmbH: Adblock plus. https://adblockplus.org/
7. Fielding, R., Gettys, J., Mogul, J., Frystyk, H., Masinter, L., Leach, P., Berners-Lee, T.: Hypertext Transfer Protocol – HTTP/1.1. In: RFC 2616 (Draft Standard). Request for Comments. Internet Engineering Task Force (1999). http://www.ietf.org/rfc/rfc2616.txt
8. Fitzpatrick, B., Recordon, D., Hardt, D., Hoyt, J.: OpenID authentication 2.0 - Final. http://openid.net/specs/openid-authentication-2_0.html
9. Google Inc.: Safe browsing API. https://developers.google.com/safe%2Dbrowsing/
10. Grossman, J., Johansen, M.: Million browser botnet. https://media.blackhat.com/us%2D13/us%2D13%2DGrossman%2DMillion%2DBrowsed%2DBotnet.pdf
11. Hafif, O.: Reflected file download a new web attack vector. https://drive.google.com/file/d/0B0KLoHg_gR_XQnV4RVhlNl96MHM/view
12. Heiland, D.: Web portals gateway to information or a hole in our perimeter defenses. http://www.shmoocon.org/2008/presentations/Web+portals,+gateway+to+information.ppt
13. InformAction: NoScript. https://noscript.net/
14. Jack Whitton: SafeCurl. https://github.com/fin1te/safecurl
15. Kulkarni, P.: SSRF/XSPA bug in https://www.coinbase.com 06, http://www.prajalkulkarni.com/2013/06/ssrfxspa
16. ONsec Lab: SSRF Bible, Cheatsheet. https://docs.google.com/document/d/1v1TkWZtrhzRLy0bYXBcdLUedXGb9njTNIJXa3u9akHM
17. OWASP: The OWASP top 10 project. https://www.owasp.org/index.php/Category:OWASP_Top_Ten_Project
18. Payet, P., Doupé, A., Kruegel, C., Vigna, G.: Ears in the wild: large-scale analysis of execution after redirect vulnerabilities. In: ACM SAC 2013 (2013)
19. Pellegrino, G., Balzarotti, D.: Toward black-box detection of logic flaws in web applications. In: NDSS 2014 (2014)

20. Pellegrino, G., Balzarotti, D., Winter, S., Suri, N.: In the compression Hornet's Nest: a security study of data compression in network services. In: USENIX Security 2015 (2015)
21. Pellegrino, G., Rossow, C., Ryba, F.J., Schmidt, T.C., Wählisch, M.: Cashing out the great Cannon? On browser-based DDoS attacks and Economics. In: USENIX WOOT 2015 (2015)
22. Polyakov, A., Chastukjin, D., Tyurin, A.: SSRF vs. business-critical applications. Part 1: XXE Tunnelling in SAP NetWeaver. http://erpscan.com/wp%2Dcontent/uploads/2012/08/SSRF%2Dvs%2DBusinness%2Dcritical%2Dapplications%2Dwhitepaper.pdf
23. SANS Institute: Critical security controls for effective cyber defense. https://www.sans.org/media/critical-security-controls/CSC-5.pdf
24. Santese, A.: Yahoo! SSRF/XSPA vulnerability, 06. http://hacksecproject.com/yahoo%2Dssrfxspa%2Dvulnerability/
25. The MITRE Corporation: Common weakness enumeration. http://cwe.mitre.org/
26. van Kesteren, A.: Cross-origin resource sharing - W3C Recommendation, 16 January 2014. http://www.w3.org/TR/cors/
27. Walikar, R.A.: Cross site port attacks - XSPA. http://www.riyazwalikar.com/2012/11/cross%2Dsite%2Dport%2Dattacks%2Dxspa%2Dpart%2D1.html
28. Zaitov, E.: Universal SSRF fuzzer. https://github.com/kyprizel/ussrfuzzer

Identifying Extension-Based Ad Injection via Fine-Grained Web Content Provenance

Sajjad Arshad[✉], Amin Kharraz, and William Robertson

Northeastern University, Boston, USA
{arshad,mkharraz,wkr}@ccs.neu.edu

Abstract. Extensions provide useful additional functionality for web browsers, but are also an increasingly popular vector for attacks. Due to the high degree of privilege extensions can hold, extensions have been abused to inject advertisements into web pages that divert revenue from content publishers and potentially expose users to malware. Users are often unaware of such practices, believing the modifications to the page originate from publishers. Additionally, automated identification of unwanted third-party modifications is fundamentally difficult, as users are the ultimate arbiters of whether content is undesired in the absence of outright malice.

To resolve this dilemma, we present a fine-grained approach to tracking the provenance of web content at the level of individual DOM elements. In conjunction with visual indicators, provenance information can be used to reliably determine the source of content modifications, distinguishing publisher content from content that originates from third parties such as extensions. We describe a prototype implementation of the approach called ORIGINTRACER for Chromium, and evaluate its effectiveness, usability, and performance overhead through a user study and automated experiments. The results demonstrate a statistically significant improvement in the ability of users to identify unwanted third-party content such as injected ads with modest performance overhead.

Keywords: Web security · Ad injection · Browser extension

1 Introduction

Browser extensions enhance browsers with additional useful capabilities that are not necessarily maintained or supported by the browser vendor. Instead, this code is typically written by third parties and can perform a wide range of tasks, from simple changes in the appearance of web pages to sophisticated tasks such as fine-grained filtering of content. To achieve these capabilities, browser extensions possess more privilege than other third-party code that runs in the browser. For instance, extensions can access cross-domain content, and perform network requests that are not subject to the same origin policy. Because these extensive capabilities allow a comparatively greater degree of control over the browser, they provide a unique opportunity to attack users and their data, the underlying system, and even the Internet at large. For this reason, newer browser extension frameworks such as Chromium's have integrated least privilege separation via isolated worlds and a fine-grained permissions system to restrict the capabilities of third-party extensions [7].

However, extension security frameworks are not a panacea. In practice, their effectiveness is degraded by over-privilege and a lack of understanding of the threats posed by highly-privileged extensions on the part of users [18]. Indeed, despite the existence of extension security frameworks, it has recently been shown that extension-based advertisement injection has become a popular and lucrative technique for dishonest parties to monetize user web browsing. These extensions simply inject or replace ads in web pages when users visit a website, thus creating or diverting an existing revenue stream to the third party. Users often are not aware of these incidents and, even if this behavior is noticed, it can be difficult to identify the responsible party.

While ad injection cannot necessarily be categorized as an outright malicious activity on its own, it is highly likely that many users in fact *do not want or expect* browser extensions to inject advertisements or other content into Web pages. Moreover, it can have a significant impact on the security and privacy of both users as well as website publishers. For example, recent studies have shown that ad-injecting extensions not only serve ads from ad networks other than the ones with which the website publishers intended, but they also attempt to trick users into installing malware by inserting rogue elements into the web page [46,48].

To address this problem, several automatic approaches have been proposed to detect malicious behaviors (e.g., ad injection) in browser extensions [26,28,48]. In addition, centralized distribution points such as Chrome Web Store and Mozilla Add-ons are using semi-automated techniques for review of extension behavior to detect misbehaving extensions. However, there is no guarantee that analyzing the extensions for a limited period of time leads to revealing the ad injection behaviors. Finally, a client-side detection methodology has been proposed in [46] that reports any deviation from a legitimate DOM structure as potential ad injections. However, this approach requires a priori knowledge of a legitimate DOM structure as well as cooperation from content publishers.

Although ad injection can therefore potentially pose significant risks, this issue is not as clear-cut as it might first seem. Some users might legitimately want the third-party content injected by the extensions they install, even including injected advertisements. This creates a fundamental dilemma for automated techniques that aim to identify clearly malicious or unwanted content injection, since such techniques cannot intuit user intent and desires in a fully automatic way.

To resolve this dilemma, we present ORIGINTRACER, an in-browser approach to highlight extension-based content modification of web pages. ORIGINTRACER monitors the execution of browser extensions to detect content modifications such as the injection of advertisements. Content modifications are visually highlighted in the context of the web page in order to *(i)* notify users of the presence of modified content, and *(ii)* inform users of the *source* of the modifications. With this information, users can then make an informed decision as to whether they actually want these content modifications from specific extensions, or whether they would rather uninstall the extensions that violate their expectations.

ORIGINTRACER assists users in detecting content injection by distinguishing injected or modified DOM elements from genuine page elements. This is performed by annotating web page DOM elements with a *provenance label set* that indicates the principal(s) responsible for adding or modifying that element, both while the page is loading from the publisher as well as during normal script and extension execution. These annotations serve as trustworthy, fine-grained provenance indicators for web page content. ORIGINTRACER can be easily integrated into any browser in order to inform users of extension-based content modification. Since, ORIGINTRACER identifies all types of content injections, it is able to highlight all injected advertisements regardless of their types (e.g., flash ads, banner ads, and text ads).

We implemented a prototype of ORIGINTRACER as a set of modifications to the Chromium browser, and evaluated its effectiveness by conducting a user study. The user study reveals that ORIGINTRACER produced a significantly greater awareness of third-party content modification, and did not detract from the users' browsing experience. Our results also suggests that ORIGINTRACER can be used as a complementary system to ad blocking systems such as Adblock Plus [2] and Ghostery [4].

To summarize, the main contributions of this paper are:

- We introduce a novel in-browser approach to provenance tracking for web content at the granularity of DOM elements, and present a semantics for provenance propagation due to script and extension execution. The approach leverages a high-fidelity in-browser vantage point that allows it to construct a precise provenance label set for each DOM element introduced into a web page.
- We implement a prototype called ORIGINTRACER that uses content provenance to identify and highlight third-party content injection – e.g., unwanted advertisements – by extensions to notify users of their presence and the originating principal.
- We evaluate the effectiveness, usability, and performance of our prototype, and show that it is able to significantly assist users in identifying ad injection by extensions in the wild without degrading browser performance or the user experience.

2 Background and Motivation

In the following, we introduce background information on browser extensions, present an overview of advertisement injection as a canonical example of questionable content modification, and motivate our approach in this context.

2.1 Browser Extensions

Browser extensions are programs that extend the functionality of a web browser. Today, extensions are typically implemented using a combination of HTML, CSS, and JavaScript written against a browser-specific extension API. These APIs expose the ability to modify the browser user interface in controlled ways, manipulate HTTP headers, and modify web page content through the document object model (DOM) API. An extension ecosystem is provided by almost all major browser vendors; for instance, Google and Mozilla both host centralized repositories of extensions that users can download at the Chrome Web Store and Mozilla Add-ons sites, respectively.

2.2 Advertisement Injection

As web advertising grew in popularity, those in a position to modify web content such as ISPs and browser extension authors realized that profit could be realized by injecting or replacing ads in web pages. For instance, some ISPs began to tamper with HTTP traffic in transit, injecting DOM elements into HTML documents that added ISP's advertisements into pages visited by their customers [10,30]. In a similar fashion, browser extensions started modifying pages to inject DOM elements in order to show ads to users without necessarily obtaining the user's prior consent. Ad injection has evolved to become a common form of unrequested third-party content injection on today's web [37].

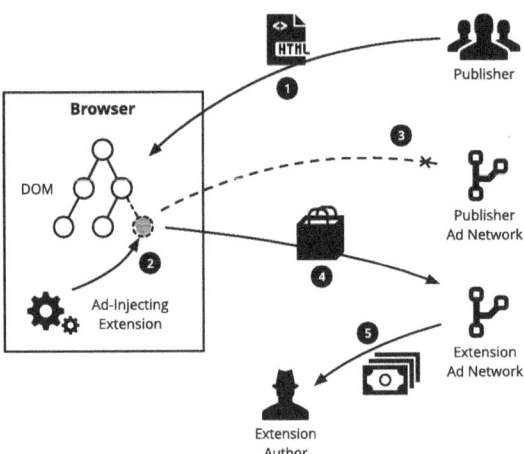

Fig. 1. Overview of advertisement injection. **(1)** The user accesses the publisher's site. **(2)** An ad-injecting browser extension adds DOM elements to display ads to the user, and optionally removes existing ads. **(3)** Ad revenue is diverted from the publisher. **(4)** Ad impressions, clicks, and conversions are instead directed to the extension's ad network. **(5)** Ad revenue flows to the extension author.

These practices have several effects on both publishers and users. On one hand, ad injection diverts revenue from the publisher to the third party responsible for the ad injection. If advertisements are the primary source of income for a publisher, this can have a significant effect on their bottom line. If the injected ads contain or reference undesired content (e.g., adult or political topics), ad injection can also harm the reputation of the publisher from the user's perspective. If the content injection is also malicious in nature, the publisher's reputation can be further harmed in addition to exposing users to security risks due to malware, phishing, and other threats. Prior work has shown that users exposed to ad injection are more likely to be exposed to "malvertising" and traditional malware [46,48]. Figure 1 gives an overview of ad injection's effect on the normal ad delivery process, while Fig. 3 shows an instance of ad injection on amazon.com.

2.3 Motivation

Recently, there have been efforts by browser vendors to remove ad-injecting extensions from their repositories [1]. Although semi-automated central approaches have been successful in identifying ad-injecting extensions, deceptive extensions can simply hide their ad injection behaviors during the short period of analysis time. In addition, finding web pages that trigger ad injection is a non-trivial task, and they can miss some ad-injecting extensions. Moreover, there are extensions that are not provided through the web stores, and users can get them from local marketplaces, which may not examined the extensions properly. Hence, we believe that there is a need for a protection tool to combat ad injection on the client side in addition to centralized examination by browser vendors.

Table 1. Five popular Chrome extensions that modify web pages as part of their benign functionality.

Extension	No. of users	Injected element
Adblock plus	10,000,000+	`<iframe>`
Google translate	6,000,000+	`<div>`
Tampermonkey	5,800,000+	`<img>`
Evernote web clipper	4,300,000+	`<iframe>`
Google dictionary	3,000,000+	`<div>`

Furthermore, automatically determining whether third-party content modification – such as that due to ad injection – should be allowed is not straightforward. Benign extensions extensively modify web pages as part of their normal functionality. To substantiate this, we examined five popular Chrome extensions as of the time of writing; these are listed in Table 1. Each of these extensions are available for all major browsers, and all modify web pages (e.g., inject elements) to implement their functionality. Therefore, automated approaches based on this criterion run a high risk of false positives when attempting to identify malicious or undesirable extensions.

Moreover, it is not enough to identify that advertisements, for instance, have been injected by a third party. This is because some users *might legitimately desire* the content that is being added to web pages by the extensions they install. To wit, it is primarily for this reason that a recent purge of extensions from the Chrome Web Store did not encompass the entirety of the extensions that were identified as suspicious in a previous study, as the third-party content modification could not be clearly considered as malicious [46]. Instead, we claim that *users themselves* are best positioned to make the determination as to whether third-party content modification is desired or not. An approach that proceeds from this observation would provide sufficient, easily comprehensible information to users in order to allow an informed choice as to whether content is desirable or should be blocked. It should be noted that defending against drive-by downloads and general malware is not the focus of this paper. Rather, the goal is to highlight injected ads to increase likelihood that user will make an informed choice to not click on them.

We envision that ORIGINTRACER could be used as a complementary approach to existing techniques such as central approaches used by browser vendors. Also, browser vendors can benefit from using our system in addition to end users to detect the content modifications by extensions in a more precise and reliable way. In the following sections, we present design and implementation of our system.

3 Web Content Provenance

In this section, we describe an in-browser approach for identifying third-party content modifications in web browsers. The approach adds *fine-grained provenance tracking* to the browser, at the level of individual DOM elements. Provenance information is used in two ways: *(i)* to distinguish between content that originates from the web page publisher and content injected by an unassociated third party, and *(ii)* to indicate *which* third party (e.g., extension) is responsible for content modifications using provenance indicators. By integrating the approach directly into the browser, we guarantee the trustworthiness of both the provenance information and the visual indicators. That is, as the browser is already part of the trusted computing base (TCB) in the web security model, we leverage this as the appropriate layer to compute precise, fine-grained provenance information. Similarly, the browser holds sufficient information to ensure that provenance indicators cannot be tampered with or occluded by malicious extensions. While we consider malicious or exploited browser plug-ins such as Flash Player outside our threat model, we note that modern browsers take great pains to isolate plug-ins in least privilege protection domains. We report separately on the implementation of the approach in Sect. 4.

In the following, we present our approach to tracking and propagating content provenance, and then discuss provenance indicators and remediation strategies.

3.1 Content Provenance

Web pages are composed of HTML that references resources such as stylesheets, scripts, images, plug-ins such as Flash objects, or even other web pages loaded inside frames. The document object model (DOM) is a natural structural representation of a web page that can be manipulated through a standard API, and serves as a suitable basis for provenance tracking. In particular, our system tracks the provenance of each element e contained in a DOM. Provenance for a DOM element is recorded as a set of labels $\ell \in \mathcal{P}(L)$, where the set of all labels L corresponds to a generalization of standard web origins to include extensions. That is, instead of the classic origin 3-tuple of $\langle \text{scheme}, \text{host}, \text{port} \rangle$, we record

$$L = \langle S, I, P, X \rangle$$
$$S = \{\text{scheme}\} \cup \{\text{``extension''}\}$$
$$I = \{\text{host}\} \cup \{\text{extension-identifier}\}$$
$$P = \{\text{port}\} \cup \{\text{null}\}$$
$$X = \{0, 1, 2, \ldots\}$$

In other words, a label is a 4-tuple that consists of a normal network scheme or extension, a network host or a unique extension identifier, a port or the special null value, and an index used to impose a global total order on labels as described below. While browsers use different extension identifiers, including randomly-generated identifiers, the exact representation used is unimportant so long as there is a one-to-one mapping between extensions and identifiers and their use is locally consistent within the browser. An overview of provenance tracking is depicted in Fig. 2.

Static Publisher Provenance. Content provenance tracking begins with a web page load. As the DOM is parsed by the browser, each element is labeled with a singleton label set containing the origin of the publisher, $\{l_0\}$. Thus, static provenance tracking is straightforward and equivalent to the standard use of origins as a browser security context.

Dynamic Publisher Provenance. Content provenance becomes more interesting in the presence of dynamic code execution. As JavaScript can add, modify, and remove DOM elements in an arbitrary fashion using the DOM API exposed by the browser, it is necessary to track these modifications in terms of provenance labels.

New provenance labels are created from the publisher's label set $\{l_0\}$ as follows. Whenever an external script is referenced from the initial DOM resulting from the page load, a new label $l_i, i \in \{1, 2, \ldots\}$ is generated from the origin of the script. All subsequent DOM modifications that occur as a result of an external script loaded from the initial DOM are recorded as $\{l_0, l_i\}$. Successive external script loads follow the expected inductive label generation process – i.e., three

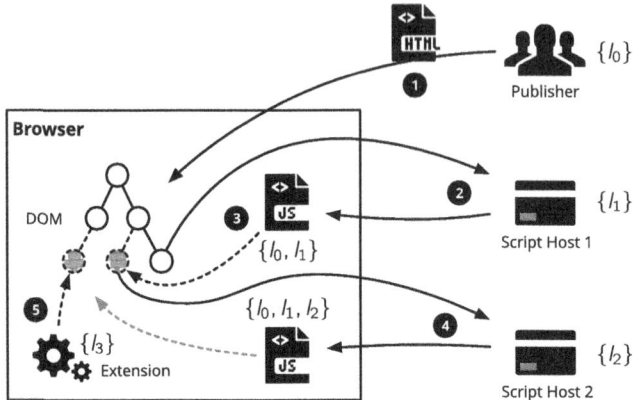

Fig. 2. Element-granularity provenance tracking. (**1**) Content loaded directly from the publisher is labeled with the publisher's origin, l_0. (**2**) An external script reference to origin l_1 is performed. (**3**) DOM modifications from l_1's script are labeled with the label set $\{l_0, l_1\}$. (**4**) Further external script loads and subsequent DOM modifications induce updated label sets – e.g., $\{l_0, l_1, l_2\}$. (**5**) A DOM modification that originates from an extension produces provenance label sets $\{l_0, l_1, l_2, l_3\}$ for the element.

successive external script loads from unique origins will result in a label set $\{l_0, l_i, l_j, l_k\}$. Finally, label sets contain unique elements such that consecutive external script loads from a previously accessed origin are not reflected in the label for subsequent DOM modifications. For instance, if the web page publisher loads a script from the publisher's origin, then any resulting DOM modifications will have a provenance label set of $\{l_0\}$ instead of $\{l_0, l_0\}$. Content provenance is propagated for three generic classes of DOM operations: element insertion, modification, and deletion.

Element insertions produce an updated DOM that contains the new element labeled with the current label set, and potentially generates a new label set if the injected element is a script. Element modifications produce a DOM where the modified element's label set is merged with the current label set. Finally, element deletions simply remove the element from the DOM.

Extension Provenance. The third and final form of provenance tracking concerns content modifications due to DOM manipulations by extensions. In this case, provenance propagation follows the semantics for the above case of dynamic publisher provenance. Where these two cases differ, however, is in the provenance label initialization. While provenance label sets for content that originates, perhaps indirectly, from the web page publisher contains the publisher's origin label l_0, content that originates from an extension is rooted in a label set initialized with the *extension's* label. In particular, content modifications that originate from an extension *are not labeled* by the publisher's origin. An exception to this occurs when the extension, either directly or indirectly, subsequently loads scripts from the publisher, or modifies an existing element that originated from the publisher.

3.2 Content Provenance Indicators

With the fine-grained content provenance scheme described above, identifying the principal responsible for DOM modifications is straightforward. For each element, all that is required is to inspect its label set ℓ to check whether it contains the label of any extension.

A related, but separate, question is how best to relay this information to the user. In this design, several options are possible on a continuum from simply highlighting injected content without specific provenance information to reporting the full ordered provenance chain from the root to the most recent origin. The first option makes no use of the provenance chain, while the other end of the spectrum is likely to overwhelm most users with too much information, degrading the practical usefulness of provenance tracking. We suspect that a reasonable balance between these two extremes is a summarization of the full chain, for instance by reporting only the label of the corresponding extension.

Finally, if a user decides that the third-party content modification is unwanted, another design parameter is how to act upon this decision. Possible actions include blocking specific element modifications, removing the offending extension, or reporting its behavior to a central authority. We report on the specific design choices we made with respect to provenance indicators in the presentation of our implementation in Sect. 4.

4 OriginTracer

In this section, we present ORIGINTRACER, our prototype implementation for identifying and highlighting extension-based web page content modifications. We implemented ORIGINTRACER as a set of modifications to the Chromium browser. In particular, we modified both Blink and the extension engine to track the provenance of content insertion, modification, and removal according to the semantics presented in Sect. 3. These modifications also implement provenance indicators for suspicious content that does not originate from the publisher. In total, our changes consist of approximately 900 SLOC for C++ and several lines of JavaScript[1]. In the following, we provide more detail on the integration of ORIGINTRACER into Chromium.

4.1 Tracking Publisher Provenance

A core component of ORIGINTRACER is responsible for introducing and propagating provenance label sets for DOM elements. In the following, we discuss the implementation of provenance tracking for publisher content.

Tracking Static Elements. As discussed in Sect. 3, provenance label sets for static DOM elements that comprise the HTML document sent by the publisher as part of the initial page load are equivalent to the publisher's web origin – in our notation, l_0. Therefore, minimal modifications to the HTML

---
[1] SLOC were measured using David Wheeler's SLOCCount [5].

parser were necessary to introduce these element annotations, which is performed in an incremental fashion as the page is parsed.

Tracking Dynamic Elements. To track dynamic content modifications, this component of ORIGINTRACER must also monitor JavaScript execution. When a `script` tag is encountered during parsing of a page, Blink creates a new element and attaches it to the DOM. Then, Blink obtains the JavaScript code (fetching it from network in the case of remote script reference), submits the script to the V8 JavaScript engine for execution, and pauses the parsing process until the script execution is finished. During execution of the script, some new elements might be created dynamically and inserted into the DOM. According to the provenance semantics, these new elements inherit the label set of the script. In order to create new elements in JavaScript, one can *(i)* use DOM APIs to create a new element and attach it to the web page's DOM, or *(ii)* write HTML tags directly into the page.

In the first method, to create a new element object, a canonical example is to provide the tag name to the `createElement` function. Then, other attributes of the newly created element are set – e.g., after creating an element object for an a tag, an address must be provided for its `href` attribute. Finally, the new element should be attached to the DOM tree as a child using `appendChild` or `insertBefore` functions. In the second method, HTML is inserted directly into the web page using the functions such as `write` and `writeln`, or by modifying the `innerHTML` attribute. In cases where existing elements are modified (e.g., changing an image's `src` attribute), the element inherits the label set of the currently executing script as well. In order to have a complete mediation of all DOM modifications to Web page, `Node` class in Blink implementation was instrumented in order to assign provenance label sets for newly created or modified elements using the label set applied to the currently executing script.

Handling Events and Timers. An additional consideration for this ORIGINTRACER component is modifications to event handlers and timer registrations, as developers make heavy use of event and timer callbacks in modern JavaScript. For instance, such callbacks are used to handle user interface events such as clicking on elements, hovering over elements, or to schedule code after a time interval has elapsed. In practice, this requires the registration of callback handlers via `addEventListener` API for events, and `setTimeout` and `setInterval` for timers. To mediate callbacks related to the addition and firing of events and timers, we slightly modified the `EventTarget` and `DOMTimer` classes in Blink, respectively. Specifically, we record the mapping between the running scripts and their registered callback functions, and then recover the responsible script for DOM modification during callback execution.

4.2 Tracking Extension Provenance

Chromium's extension engine is responsible for loading extensions, checking their permissions against those declared in the manifest file, injecting content scripts, dispatching background scripts and content scripts to the V8 script engine for execution, and providing a channel for communication between content scripts and background page.

Chromium extensions can manipulate the web page's content by injecting *content scripts* into the web page or using the webRequest API. Content scripts are JavaScript programs that can manipulate the web page using the shared DOM, communicate with external servers via XMLHttpRequest, invoke a limited set of chrome.* APIs, and interact with their owning extension's background pages. By using webRequest, extensions are also able to modify and block HTTP requests and responses in order to change the web page's DOM.

In this work, we only track content modifications by content scripts and leave identifying ad injection by webRequest for future engineering work. Prior work, however, has mentioned that only 5 % of ad injection incidents occurred via webRequest; instead, Chrome extensions mostly rely on content scripts to inject advertisements [46]. Moreover, with modern websites becoming more complex, injecting stealthy advertisement into the page using webRequest is not a trivial task.

Tracking Content Script Injection and Execution. To track elements created or modified during the execution of content scripts, extension engine was modified to hook events corresponding to script injection and execution. Content scripts can be inserted into the web page using different methods. If a content script should be injected into every matched web page, it must be registered in the extension manifest file using the content_scripts field. By providing different options for this field, one can control when and where the content scripts be injected. Another method is programmatic injection, which is useful when content scripts should be injected in response to specific events (e.g., a user clicks the extension's browser action). With programmatic injection, content scripts can be injected using the tabs.executeScript API if the tabs permission is set in the manifest file. Either way, content scripts have a provenance label set initialized with the extension's label upon injection.

Handling Callback Functions. Chromium's extension engine provides a messaging API as a communication channel between background pages and content scripts. Background pages and content scripts can receive messages from each other by providing a callback function for the onMessage or onRequest events, and can send messages by invoking sendMessage or sendRequest. To track the registration and execution of callback functions, the send_request and event modules were slightly modified in the extension engine. Specifically, we added some code to map registered callbacks to their corresponding content scripts in order to find the extension responsible for DOM modification.

4.3 Content Provenance Indicators

Given DOM provenance information, ORIGINTRACER must first *(i)* identify when suspicious content modifications – e.g., extension-based ad injection – has occurred, and additionally *(ii)* communicate this information to the user in an easily comprehensible manner. To implement the first requirement, our prototype monitors for content modifications where a subtree of elements are annotated with label sets that contains a particular extension's label. This check can be performed efficiently by traversing the DOM and inspecting element label sets after a set of changes have been performed on the DOM.

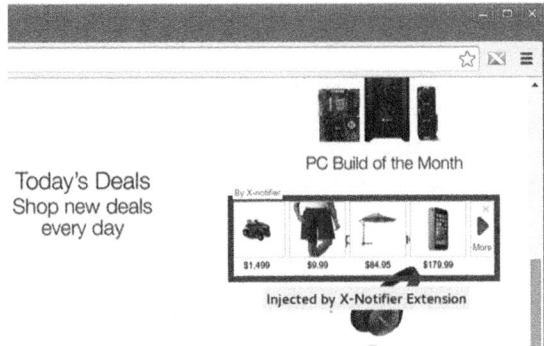

Fig. 3. An example of indicator for an injected advertisement on amazon.com.

There are several possible options to communicate content provenance as mentioned in Sect. 3. In our current prototype, provenance is indicated using a configurable border color of the root element of the suspicious DOM subtree. This border should be chosen to be visually distinct from the existing color palette of the web page. Finally, a tooltip indicating the root label is displayed when the user hovers their mouse over the DOM subtree. An example is shown in Fig. 3. To implement these features, ORIGINTRACER modifies `style` and `title` attributes. In addition, since ORIGINTRACER highlights elements in an online fashion, it must delay the addition of highlighting until the element is attached to the page's DOM and is displayed. Therefore, modifications were made to the `ContainerNode` class that is responsible for attaching new elements to the DOM.

While we did not exhaustively explore the design space of content provenance indicators in this work (e.g., selective blocking of extension-based DOM modifications), we report on the usability of the prototype implementation in our evaluation.

5 Evaluation

In this section, we measure the effectiveness, usability, and performance of content provenance indicators using the ORIGINTRACER prototype. In particular, the questions we aim to answer with this evaluation are:

(Q1) How susceptible are users to injected content such as third-party advertisements? (Sect. 5.1)

(**Q2**) Do provenance indicators lead to a significant, measurable decrease in the likelihood of clicking on third-party content that originates from extensions? (Sect. 5.1)
(**Q3**) Are users likely to use the system during their normal web browsing? (Sect. 5.2)
(**Q4**) Does integration of the provenance tracking system significantly degrade the users' browsing experience and performance of the browser on a representative sample of websites? (Sect. 5.3)

Ethics Statement. As part of the evaluation, we performed two experiments involving users unaffiliated with the project as described below. Due to the potential risk to user confidentiality and privacy, we formulated an experimental protocol that was approved by our university's institutional review board (IRB). This protocol included safeguards designed to prevent exposing sensitive user data such as account names, passwords, personal addresses, and financial information, as well as to protect the anonymity of the study participants with respect to data storage and reporting. While users were not initially told the purpose of some of the experiments, all users were debriefed at the end of each trial as to the true purpose of the study.

5.1 Effectiveness of the Approach

Similar to prior work [13], we performed a user study to measure the effectiveness of content provenance in enabling users to more easily identify unwanted third-party content. However, we performed the user study with a significantly larger group of participants. The study population was composed of 80 students that represent a range of technical sophistication. We conducted an initial briefing prior to the experiments where we made it clear that we were interested in honest answers.

User Susceptibility to Ad Injection. The goal of the first phase of the experiment was to measure whether users were able to detect third-party content that was not intended for inclusion by the publishers of web pages presented to them. Users were divided into two equal sized groups of 40. In each group, users were first presented with three unmodified Chromium browsers, each of which had a separate ad-injecting extension installed: Auto Zoom, Alpha Finder, and X-Notifier for the first group, and Candy Zapper, uTorrent, and Gethoneybadger for the second group. These extensions were chosen because they exhibit a range of ad injection behaviors, from subtle injections that blend into the publisher's web page to very obvious pop-ups that are visually distinct from the publisher's content.

Using each browser, the participants were asked to visit three popular retail websites: Amazon, Walmart, and Alibaba. Each ad-injecting extension monitors for visits to these websites, and each injects three different types of advertisements into these sites. For each website, we asked the participants to examine the page and tell us if they noticed any content in the page that did not belong to the website – in other words, whether any content did not seem to originate from the publisher. For each group, we aggregated the responses and presented the percentage of correctly reported ad injection incidents for each extension in Fig. 4.

The results demonstrate that a significant number of Internet users often do not recognize when ad injection occurs in the wild, even when told to look for foreign content. For example, 34 participants did not recognize *any* injected ads out of the three that were added to Amazon website by Auto Zoom extension. Comparatively more users were able to identify ads injected by Alpha Finder and X-Notifier. We suspect the reason for this is because these extensions make use of pop-up advertisements that are easier to recognize as out-of-place. However, a significant number of users nevertheless failed to note these pop-up ads, and even after prompting stated that they thought these ads were part of the publisher's content. More generally, across all websites and extensions, many participants failed to identify any injected ads whatsoever.

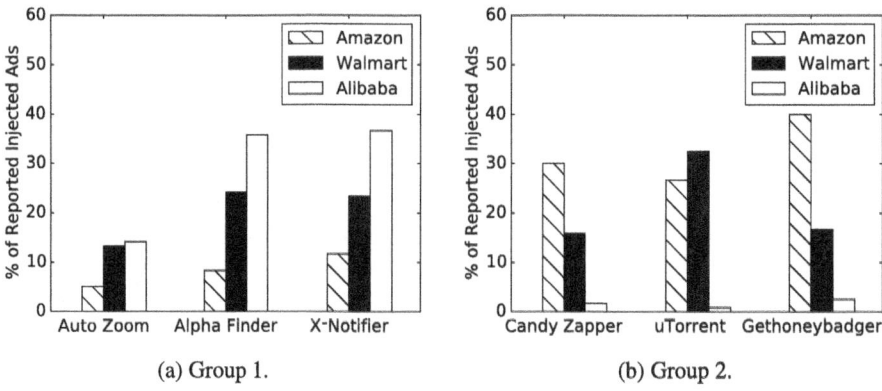

Fig. 4. Percentage of injected ads that are reported correctly by all the participants.

We then asked each participant whether they would click on ads in general to measure the degree of trust that users put into the contents on the publisher's page. Specifically, we asked participants to rate the likelihood of clicking on ads on a scale from one to five, where one means that they would never click on an ad while five means that they would definitely click on an ad. We aggregated the responses and present the results in Fig. 5a.

These results show that a significant number of users, roughly half, *would* click on advertisements that might not originate from the publisher, but that were instead injected by an extension. This demonstrates the effectiveness of ad injection as a mechanism for diverting revenue from publishers to extension authors. It also shows the potential effectiveness of malicious extensions in using content modifications to expose users to traditional malware.

Effectiveness of Content Provenance Indicators. After the first phase of the experiment, we briefly explained the purpose of ORIGINTRACER and content provenance to the participants. Then, for each participant in each group, we

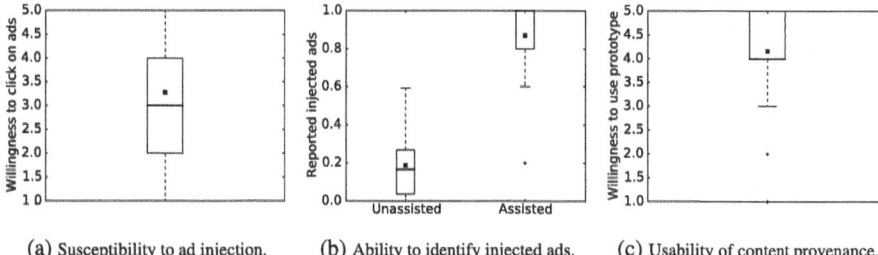

(a) Susceptibility to ad injection. (b) Ability to identify injected ads. (c) Usability of content provenance.

Fig. 5. User study results. For each boxplot, the box represents the boundaries of the first and third quartiles. The band within each box is the median, while the black square is the mean. The whiskers represent 1.5 IQR boundaries, and outliers are represented as a + symbol.

picked one of the three ad-injecting extensions in which, the participant did not detect most of the injected ads and installed it on a Chromium instance equipped with ORIGINTRACER. Then, each participant was asked to visit one of the three retail websites by his choice and identify third-party content modifications – i.e., injected ads – with the help of provenance indicators. The results are shown in Fig. 5b, where unassisted identification is the aggregated number of reported ad injections without any assistance in the presence of three ad-injecting extensions across three retail websites, and assisted identification is the number of reported injected ads with the help of content provenance indicators. Results are normalized to $[0, 1]$.

These results clearly imply that users are more likely to recognize the presence of third-party content modifications using provenance indicators. To confirm statistical significance, we performed a hypothesis test where the null hypothesis is that provenance indicators do not assist in identifying third-party content modifications, while the alternative hypothesis is that provenance indicators do assist in identifying such content. Using a paired t-test, we obtain a p-value of 4.9199×10^{-7}, sufficient to reject the null hypothesis at a 1 % significance level. The outliers in assisted identification are due to the fact that our ad highlighting technique was not identifiable by a small number of participants. We believe that using different visual highlighting techniques would make it easier for users to identify the injected ads.

Finally, we asked each participant how likely they would be to use the content provenance system in their daily web browsing. We asked participants to rate this likelihood on a scale from one to five, where one means they would never use the system and five means that they would always use it. The results are shown in Fig. 5c, and indicate that most users would be willing to use a content provenance system. The reason behind the outliers is because a few of the participants stated that they do not need our system since they would not click on any advertisements. However, we note that it can be difficult to distinguish between advertisements and other legitimate content (e.g., products in retail sites) and, consequently, users might be lured into clicking on ad content injected by extensions.

Summary. From this user study, we draw several conclusions. First, we confirm that in many cases users are unable to distinguish injected third-party content from publisher content. We also show that because users place trust in publishers, they will often click on injected ads, and thus they tend to be susceptible to ad injection. Our data shows that content provenance assists in helping users distinguish between trusted publisher content and injected third-party content that should not be trusted. Finally, we show that many users would be willing to use the system based on their experience in this study.

5.2 Usability

We conducted another experiment on a separate population of users to measure the usability of the ORIGINTRACER prototype. The user population was composed of 13 students with different technical background. We presented the participants with ORIGINTRACER integrated into Chromium 43, and asked them to browse the web for several hours, visiting any websites of their choice. For privacy reasons, however, we asked users to avoid browsing websites that require a login or that involve sensitive subject matter (e.g., adult or financial websites). In addition, for each user, we randomly selected 50 websites from the Alexa Top 500 that satisfy our user privacy constraints and asked the user to visit them. In particular, each participant was asked to browse at least three levels down from the home page and visit external links contained in each site. Finally, to gain some assurance that ORIGINTRACER would not break benign extensions, we configured the browser with the five high-profile extensions list in Table 1.

During the browsing session, the browser was modified to record the number of URLs visited. We also asked participants to record the number of pages in which they encountered one of two types of errors. Type I errors are those where the browser crashed, system error messages were displayed, pages would not load, or the website was completely unusable for some other reason. Type II errors include non-catastrophic errors that impact usability but did not preclude it – e.g., the page took an abnormally long time to load, or the appearance of the page was not as expected. We also asked users to report any broken functionality for the benign extensions described above as well.

Out of close to 2,000 URLs, two catastrophic errors and 27 non-catastrophic errors were encountered. However, we note that the majority of URLs rendered and executed correctly. In addition, none of the participants reported any broken extensions. We therefore conclude that the proposed approach is compatible with modern browsers and benign extensions, and further work would very likely allow the prototype to execute completely free of errors.

5.3 Performance

To measure the performance overhead of ORIGINTRACER, we configured both an unmodified Chromium browser and the prototype to automatically visit the

Alexa Top 1 K. The Alexa Top 1 K covers many popular websites and is weighted towards being representative of the sites that people use most often. By using this test set, we ensured that each browser visited a broad spectrum of websites that include both static and dynamic content, and especially websites that make heavy use of third-party components and advertisements. Moreover, we configured both browser instances with the five benign extensions discussed in Sect. 2 that change the DOM to measure performance in the presence of extensions. A more detailed evaluation would analyze more pages on these websites to garner a more realistic representation, but that is beyond the scope of the current work.

We built a crawler based on Selenium WebDriver [44] to automatically visit the entire list of websites and recorded the total elapsed time from the beginning of the browsing process until the entire list of websites was visited. Specifically, our crawler moves to the next website in the list when the current website is fully loaded, signified by the firing of the onload event. In order to account for fluctuations in browsing time due to network delays and the dynamic nature of advertisements, we repeated the experiment 10 times and measured the average elapsed time. The average elapsed time for browsing the home pages of the Alexa Top 1 K websites measured in this way is 3,457 s for the unmodified browser and 3,821 s for ORIGINTRACER. Therefore, ORIGINTRACER incurred a 10.5 % overhead on browsing time on average. We also measured the delay imposed by ORIGINTRACER on startup time by launching the browser 10 times and measuring the average launch time. ORIGINTRACER did not cause any measurable overhead on startup time.

While this overhead is not insignificant, we note that our user study in Sect. 5.2 indicates that many users would be willing to trade off actual perceived performance overhead against the security benefits provided by the system. Moreover, this prototype is just a proof-of-concept implementation of our system and there is still room for optimizing the implementation to decrease the page load time.

6 Related Work

6.1 Malicious Advertising

Substantial research on malicious advertisements has focused on isolation and containment [3,15,34]. Other approaches have focused on detecting drive-by downloads by employing the properties of HTTP redirections to identify malicious behavior [38,45]. Dynamic analyses have also been used to detect drive-by downloads and web-hosted malware [11,12,36]. Li et al. [31] investigated the advertisement delivery process to detect malvertising by automatically generating detection rules. Web tripwires [43] were proposed to detect in-flight page changes performed by ISPs to inject advertisements.

6.2 Browser Extension Security

Browser extension security has recently become a hot topic. The Chromium extension framework substantially improved the ability of users to limit the amount of privilege conferred upon potentially vulnerable extensions [7], and follow-on work has studied the success of this approach [18,33]. Other work has broadly studied malicious extensions that attempt to exfiltrate sensitive user data [32,35]. For instance, Arjun et al. showed that many extensions in the Chrome Web Store are over-privileged for the actual services they purport to provide [21].

A recent line of work has focused on the problem of ad injection via browser extensions. Thomas et al. [46] proposed a detection methodology in which, they used a priori knowledge of a legitimate DOM structure to report the deviations from that structure as potential ad injections. However, this approach is not purely client-side and requires cooperation from content publishers. Expector [48] inspects a browser extension and determines if it injects advertisements into websites. Hulk [28] is a dynamic analysis system that automatically detects Chrome extensions that perform certain types of malicious behaviors, including ad injection. WebEval [26] is an automatic system that considers an extension's behaviors, code, and author reputation to identify malicious extensions distributed through the Chrome Web Store.

In contrast, our work does not attempt to automatically classify extensions that engage in content modification as malicious or not, but rather focuses on enabling users to make informed decisions as to whether extensions engage in desirable behavior or not.

6.3 Provenance Tracking

A significant amount of work has examined the use of provenance in various contexts. For instance, one line of work has studied the collection of provenance information for generic applications up to entire systems [19,24,42]. However, to our knowledge, no system considers the provenance of fine-grained web content comprising the DOM. Provenance tracking is also related to information flow control (IFC), for which a considerable body of work exists at the operating system level [16,29,49], the language level [9,40], as well as the web [20,25]. In contrast to our work, IFC is focused more on enforcing principled security guarantees for new applications rather than tracking and indicating data provenance for existing ones.

Numerous systems have examined the use of dynamic taint analysis, a related concept to provenance. Some prior work [8,17] focuses on tracking information flow within the browser, Sabre [14] detects whether extensions access sensitive information within the browser, and DSI enforcement [41] defends against XSS attacks by preserving the integrity of document structure in the browser. While there is certainly an overlap between dynamic taint analysis and provenance, taint analysis is most often focused on simple reachability between sources and sinks, while provenance is concerned with precisely tracking principals that influenced data.

Finally, there is a line of work that examines provenance on the web. Some prior work [22,23,39] concerns coarse-grained ontologies for describing the origins of data on the web, and does not consider provenance at a fine-grained scale within the browser. ESCUDO [27] only considers the principals that can be controlled by web applications, and it does not handle plug-ins and browser extensions. LeakTracker [47] performs principal-based tracking on web pages to study privacy violations related to JavaScript libraries, but it only tracks injection of scripts into the page, and does not provide any provenance information for other types of DOM elements. Excision [6] is the closest work to ours, which tracks inclusions of different resources in web pages and blocks inclusion of malicious resources by analyzing inclusion sequences on the page. Although the techniques are similar, they are used for different purposes. Excision discards the injection of DOM elements that do not reference remote content (e.g., `div`), and aside from source attributes, that does not track modifications to DOM elements. However, ORIGINTRACER identifies all types of DOM modification in the page, and instead of blocking content originating from extensions, it highlights them in the context of the web page.

7 Conclusion

In this paper, we introduced fine-grained web content provenance tracking and demonstrated its use for identifying unwanted third-party content such as injected advertisements. We evaluated a prototype implementation, a modified version of Chromium we call ORIGINTRACER, through a user study that demonstrated a statistically significant improvement in the ability of users to identify unwanted third-party content. Our performance evaluation shows a modest overhead on a large representative sample of popular websites, while our user experiments indicate that users are willing to trade off a slight decrease in performance for more insight into the sources of web content that they browse. We also performed a comprehensive study on the content modifications performed by ad-injecting extensions in the wild.

In future work, we plan to explore other uses of provenance on the web. Due to the highly interconnected structure of the web and the oftentimes obscure nature of its trust relationships, we believe that surfacing this information in the form of provenance is a generally useful capability, and can be applied in other novel ways in order to lead to safer and more informed web browsing. Finally, we plan to open source our prototype implementation in the hopes that it will be useful to the wider research community.

References

1. The ad injection economy. http://googleonlinesecurity.blogspot.com/2015/05/new-research-ad-injection-economy.html
2. Adblock Plus. https://adblockplus.org/
3. ADsafe. http://www.adsafe.org/
4. Ghostery. https://www.ghostery.com/en/
5. SLOCCount. http://www.dwheeler.com/sloccount/

6. Arshad, S., Kharraz, A., Robertson, W.: Include me out: in-browser detection of malicious third-party content inclusions. In: Financial Cryptography and Data Security (FC) (2016)
7. Barth, A., Jackson, C., Reis, C.: The security architecture of the chromium browser. Technical report (2008). The Google Chrome Team
8. Bauer, L., Cai, S., Jia, L., Passaro, T., Stroucken, M., Tian, Y.: Run-time monitoring and formal analysis of information flows in Chromium. In: Network and Distributed System Security Symposium (NDSS) (2015)
9. Chong, S., Vikram, K. and Myers, A.C.: SIF: enforcing confidentiality and integrity in web applications. In: USENIX Security Symposium (2007)
10. Coldewey, D.: Marriott puts an end to shady ad injection service (2012). http://techcrunch.com/2012/04/09/marriott-puts-an-end-to-shady-ad-injection-service/
11. Cova, M., Kruegel, C., Vigna, G.: Detection and analysis of drive-by-download attacks and malicious JavaScript code. In: International World Wide Web Conference (WWW) (2010)
12. Dewald, A., Holz, T., Freiling, F.C.: ADSandbox: sandboxing JavaScript to fight malicious websites. In: Symposium on Applied Computing (SAC) (2010)
13. Rachna Dhamija, J.D., Tygar, M.H.: Why phishing works. In: Proceedings of the SIGCHI Conference on Human Factors in Computing Systems (CHI) (2006)
14. Dhawan, M., Ganapathy, V.: Analyzing information flow in JavaScript-based browser extensions. In: Annual Computer Security Applications Conference (ACSAC) (2009)
15. Dong, X., Tran, M., Liang, Z., Jiang, X.: AdSentry: comprehensive and flexible confinement of JavaScript-based advertisements. In: Annual Computer Security Applications Conference (ACSAC) (2011)
16. Efstathopoulos, P., Krohn, M., VanDeBogart, S., Frey, C., Ziegler, D., Kohler, E., Mazieres, D., Kaashoek, F., Morris, R.: Labels and event processes in the Asbestos operating system. In: ACM Symposium on Operating Systems Principles (SOSP) (2005)
17. Egele, M., Kruegel, C., Kirda, E., Yin, H., Song, D.: Dynamic spyware analysis. In: USENIX Annual Technical Conference (ATC) (2007)
18. Felt, A.P., Greenwood, K., Wagner, D.: The effectiveness of application permissions. In: USENIX Conference on Web Application Development (WebApps) (2011)
19. Gehani, A., Tariq, D.: SPADE: support for provenance auditing in distributed environments. In: Narasimhan, P., Triantafillou, P. (eds.) Middleware 2012. LNCS, vol. 7662, pp. 101–120. Springer, Heidelberg (2012)
20. Giffin, D.B., Levy, A., Stefan, D., Terei, D., Mazieres, D., Mitchell, J.C., Russo, A.: Hails: protecting data privacy in untrusted web applications. In: USENIX Symposium on Operating Systems Design and Implementation (OSDI) (2012)
21. Guha, A., Fredrikson, M., Livshits, B., Swamy, N.: Verified security for browser extensions. In: IEEE Symposium on Security and Privacy (Oakland) (2011)
22. Harth, A., Polleres, A., Decker, S.: Towards a social provenance model for the web. In: Workshop on Principles of Provenance (PrOPr) (2007)
23. Hartig, O.: Provenance information in the web of data. In: Workshop on Linked Data on the Web (LDOW) (2009)
24. Hasan, R., Sion, R., Winslett, M.: SPROV 2.0: a highly configurable platform-independent library for secure provenance. In: ACM Conference on Computer and Communications Security (CCS) (2009)

25. Hicks, B., Rueda, S., King, D., Moyer, T., Schiffman, J., Sreenivasan, Y., McDaniel, P., Jaeger, T.: An architecture for enforcing end-to-end access control over web applications. In: ACM Symposium on Access Control Models and Technologies (SACMAT) (2010)
26. Jagpal, N., Dingle, E., Gravel, J.P., Mavrommatis, P., Provos, N., Rajab, M.A., Thomas, K.: Trends and lessons from three years fighting malicious extensions. In: USENIX Security Symposium (2015)
27. Jayaraman, K., Du, W., Rajagopalan, B., Chapin, S.J.: ESCUDO: a fine-grained protection model for web browsers. In: 30th IEEE International Conference on Distributed Computing Systems (ICDCS) (2010)
28. Kapravelos, A., Grier, C., Chachra, N., Kruegel, C., Vigna, G., Paxson, V.: Hulk: eliciting malicious behavior in browser extensions. In: USENIX Security Symposium (2014)
29. Krohn, M., Yip, A., Brodsky, M., Natan Cliffer, M., Kaashoek, F., Kohler, E., Morris, R.: Information flow control for standard os abstractions. In: Symposium on Operating Systems Principles (SOSP) (2007)
30. Kumparak, G.: Real evil: ISP inserted advertising. http://techcrunch.com/2007/06/23/real-evil-isp-inserted-advertising/ (2007)
31. Li, Z., Zhang, K., Xie, Y,. Yu, F., Wang, X.: Knowing your enemy: understanding and detecting malicious web advertising. In: ACM Conference on Computer and Communications Security (CCS) (2012)
32. Li, Z., Wang, X.-F., Choi, J.Y.: SpyShield: preserving privacy from spy add-ons. In: Kruegel, C., Lippmann, R., Clark, A. (eds.) RAID 2007. LNCS, vol. 4637, pp. 296–316. Springer, Heidelberg (2007)
33. Liu, L., Zhang, X., Yan, G., Chen, S.: Chrome extensions: threat analysis and countermeasures. In: Network and Distributed System Security Symposium (NDSS) (2012)
34. Ter Louw, M., Ganesh, K.T., Venkatakrishnan, V.N.: AdJail: practical enforcement of confidentiality and integrity policies on web advertisements. In: USENIX Security Symposium (2010)
35. Ter Louw, M., Lim, J.S., Venkatakrishnan, V.N.: Enhancing web browser security against malware extensions. J. Comput. Virol. 4(3), 179–195 (2008)
36. Lu, L., Yegneswaran, V., Porras, P., Lee, W.: BLADE: An attack-agnostic approach for preventing drive-by malware infections. In: ACM Conference on Computer and Communications Security (CCS) (2010)
37. Marvin, G.: Google study exposes "tangled web" of companies profiting from ad injection (2015). http://marketingland.com/ad-injector-study-google-127738
38. Mekky, H., Torres, R., Zhang, Z.L., Saha, S., Nucci, A.: Detecting malicious HTTP redirections using trees of user browsing activity. In: Annual IEEE International Conference on Computer Communications (INFOCOM) (2014)
39. Moreau, L.: The foundations for provenance on the web. Found. Trends Web Sci. 2(2–3), 99–241 (2010)
40. Myers, A.C.: JFlow: practical mostly-static information flow control. In: Symposium on Principles of Programming Languages (POPL) (1999)
41. Nadji, Y., Saxena, P., Song, D.: Document structure integrity: a robust basis for cross-site scripting defense. In: Network and Distributed System Security Symposium (NDSS) (2009)
42. Pohly, D.J., McLaughlin, S., Butler, K.: Hi-Fi: collecting high-fidelity whole-system provenance. In: Annual Computer Security Applications Conference (ACSAC) (2012)

43. Reis, C., Gribble, S.D., Kohno, T., Weaver, N.C.: Detecting in-flight page changes with web Tripwires. In: USENIX Symposium on Networked Systems Design and Implementation (NSDI) (2008)
44. Selenium Contributors. Selenium: Web browser automation. http://www.seleniumhq.org/
45. Stringhini, G., Kruegel, C., Vigna, G.: Shady paths: leveraging surfing crowds to detect malicious web pages. In: ACM Conference on Computer and Communications Security (CCS) (2013)
46. Thomas, K., Bursztein, E., Grier, C., Ho, G., Jagpal, N., Kapravelos, A., McCoy, D., Nappa, A., Paxson, V., Pearce, P., Provos, N., Rajab, M.A.: Ad injection at scale: assessing deceptive advertisement modifications. In: IEEE Symposium on Security and Privacy. IEEE, Oakland (2015)
47. Tran, M., Dong, X., Liang, Z., Jiang, X.: Tracking the trackers: fast and scalable dynamic analysis of web content for privacy violations. In: Bao, F., Samarati, P., Zhou, J. (eds.) ACNS 2012. LNCS, vol. 7341, pp. 418–435. Springer, Heidelberg (2012)
48. Xing, X., Meng, W., Weinsberg, U., Sheth, A., Lee, B., Perdisci, R., Lee, W.: Unraveling the relationship between ad-injecting browser extensions and malvertising. In: International World Wide Web Conference (WWW) (2015)
49. Zeldovich, N., Boyd-Wickizer, S., Mazieres, D.: Security distributed systems with information flow control. In: USENIX Symposium on Networked Systems Design and Implementation (NSDI) (2008)

Trellis: Privilege Separation for Multi-user Applications Made Easy

Andrea Mambretti[1]([✉]), Kaan Onarlioglu[1], Collin Mulliner[1],
William Robertson[1], Engin Kirda[1], Federico Maggi[2], and Stefano Zanero[2]

[1] Northeastern University, Boston, USA
{mbr,onarliog,wkr,ek}@ccs.neu.edu, collin@mulliner.org
[2] Politecnico di Milano, Milano, Italy
{federico.maggi,stefano.zanero}@polimi.it

Abstract. Operating systems provide a wide variety of resource isolation and access control mechanisms, ranging from traditional user-based security models to fine-grained permission systems as found in modern mobile operating systems. However, comparatively little assistance is available for defining and enforcing access control policies within multi-user applications. These applications, often found in enterprise environments, allow multiple users to operate at different privilege levels in terms of exercising application functionality and accessing data. Developers of such applications bear a heavy burden in ensuring that security policies over code and data in this setting are properly expressed and enforced.

We present Trellis, an approach for expressing hierarchical access control policies in applications and enforcing these policies during execution. The approach enhances the development toolchain to allow programmers to partially annotate code and data with simple privilege level tags, and uses a static analysis to infer suitable tags for the entire application. At runtime, policies are extracted from the resulting binaries and are enforced by a modified operating system kernel. Our evaluation demonstrates that this approach effectively supports the development of secure multi-user applications with modest runtime performance overhead.

1 Introduction

Operating systems provide a wide range of resource isolation and access control mechanisms to realize well-established computer security principles such as privilege separation and assignment of minimal privileges to users and tasks. For instance, UNIX-like systems employ the traditional access control model based on user and group identifiers assigned to resources, Linux uses a *capability* system for fine-grained process permission management, and modern mobile operating systems such as Android and iOS allow users to control application permissions during installation or runtime.

Although these techniques are effective at isolating users of a multi-user system from each other, or controlling access to operating system-owned resources such as hardware devices and the filesystem, they do not address the problem of enforcing access control *within* an application itself. In particular, many complex programs that target enterprise markets (e.g., SAP CRM) support multiple user roles such as administrators and other unprivileged users, each allowed different access levels to sensitive application data.

Due to this lack of standard operating system support for developing applications with multiple privilege levels, the responsibility of implementing an application-specific access control model is relegated to application programmers. However, this can often result in implementation errors, or incorrect use of various application components as access control primitives, exposing the application to privilege escalation attacks. Recent work by Mulliner et al. [21] demonstrates this problem by showing that many enterprise applications rely on selectively hiding GUI elements to naïvely control the access to the respective, sensitive functionalities. This inadequate enforcement scheme was easily be subverted by the authors using existing GUI inspection tools, allowing them to access administrator-only features with an unprivileged user account.

There exists substantial prior work that has explored ways to separate applications into privileged and unprivileged components to contain privilege escalation attacks. For instance, Provos et al. [24] described a methodology to manually split programs into a privileged *monitor* and an unprivileged *slave* that communicate via IPC channels, and Kilpatrick [16] proposed a software library to ease the development of such applications. Brumley and Song [10] use source code annotation and static analysis, and Wu et al. [32] use dynamic analysis to automate parts of this process. However, this work primarily targets system services, and aims to minimize the code run with superuser privileges. They do not address the problem of building applications that support strong separation of multiple users, each with specific code and data access requirements.

In this paper, we introduce an approach called Trellis to develop and enforce secure hierarchical access control models within multi-user applications. Trellis provides a simple annotation mechanism for software developers to specify the required access levels for critical functions and static data, uses static analysis to derive an access control policy for the entire application, and compiles this source code into binary executables that are strongly protected by the operating system. At runtime, the operating system tracks the program control flow and data accesses, including dynamically allocated data, and enforces the statically-derived access control policy. Our prototype implementation implements code and data privilege separation using dynamic adjustment of memory segment permissions. Trellis does not require drastic modifications to the application architecture, making it easy to apply to existing source code. It also does not split applications into multiple components and thus, in contrast to previous work, does not incur IPC overhead during runtime.

To summarize, we make the following contributions in this paper.

- We propose Trellis, a novel operating system-supported application development framework to assist software authors with the development of hierarchical access control policies for multi-user applications. Trellis uses a

combination of source code annotation, static analysis, and dynamic analysis to automatically integrate these policies into applications, and to enforce them at the operating system level.
- We present a prototype implementation of our system based on LLVM/Clang, the GNU C library, and the Linux kernel.
- Our evaluation including micro-benchmarks, and experiments on real-world applications demonstrate that Trellis imposes a low runtime performance overhead, an acceptable tradeoff for its additional security guarantees.

2 Threat Model

The environment we consider for this work is a large, multi-user application that runs on a shared machine. Typical examples of this scenario include kiosk applications, or large enterprise applications (e.g., SAP CRM) with several users (e.g., employees) each having a distinct profile. These users can use the application at different moments in time and each user, depending on her own profile, can access different subsets of the application's functionality and data.

In this setting, the attacker has local or remote access to a computer running such a multi-user application. The attacker further has access to a user account on the application. Note that the attacker could already be an ordinary user of the application; in other words, she may be authorized to legitimately access a subset of the application's features. Alternatively, the attacker could compromise a different user's account in order to gain unauthorized access to the application.

Our threat model includes two attack scenarios. In the first scenario, the attacker's goal is to exercise application features (i.e., execute code) reserved for higher-privileged application users. Likewise, in the second scenario, the attacker aims to gain access to data associated with a different, higher-privileged application user. Both attacks are made possible due to the fact that resources associated with different user accounts are managed in the same address space within the application.

Note that we assume sensitive code and data that could be targeted by an attacker is already protected by traditional operating system protections, and therefore, sensitive disk or memory contents cannot be accessed by the attacker directly. Instead, successfully carrying out one of the described attacks requires the attacker to exploit an application-level vulnerability, and bypass privilege-separation mechanisms provided by the application in question.

The trusted computing base (TCB) we assume for this work includes the software development toolchain (i.e., the compiler and linker), which ensures that an adversary cannot subvert the access control policies specified by developers. The TCB also includes the hardware and software stack up to and including the operating system kernel. This implies that adversaries cannot subvert the enforcement of the developer-specified policies, or tamper with the authentication procedure to transition between privilege levels. Finally, we assume that the adversary cannot tamper with the binary itself, which contains a machine-readable specification of the intended access control policy, nor with the loading

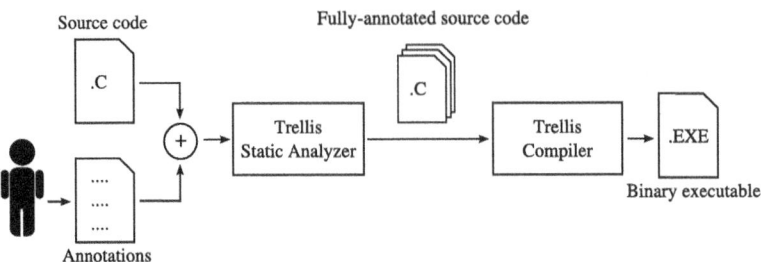

Fig. 1. An overview of compiling applications with Trellis.

of this specification into the kernel. Achieving these guarantees has several solutions, such as relying upon normal operating system-enforced user access control or, alternatively, using trusted computing primitives. The exact mechanism used is considered outside the scope of this work.

3 Design

Trellis spans both the development toolchain and the runtime environment. First, it provides a source code annotation mechanism for software developers to specify the different privilege levels (i.e., roles) required for effective access control in their applications, as well as compilation tools and system libraries capable of building Trellis-aware binaries. Second, it enhances the operating system kernel to monitor execution flows and authorize transitions between privilege levels consistent with specified access control policies.

At a high level, running a Trellis-enhanced application is a two stage process. First, an instrumented binary executable must be built according to the annotated source code. Then, the executable must be loaded with its initial privilege state and run.

An overview of the first stage, the compilation of binary executables, is shown in Fig. 1. The application developer first (partially) annotates the program source code, which involves marking security sensitive code and data with their corresponding privilege levels (often, user roles) required to access them. The partially annotated source code is then inspected by the static analyzer component, which explores the program function call graph and automatically infers privilege level tags for all unmarked code and static data. Finally, the fully-annotated source code is compiled by an augmented tool chain, which instruments the binary according to the specified access control policy and creates an executable file including the necessary Trellis metadata.

The executable can then be loaded and launched. An overview of this process is shown in Fig. 2. Here, Trellis uses an enhanced binary loader that first reads the access control policy metadata stored inside the binary, and communicates this information to the operating system to initialize the application. Once launched, the operating system monitors the application and its memory accesses to enforce

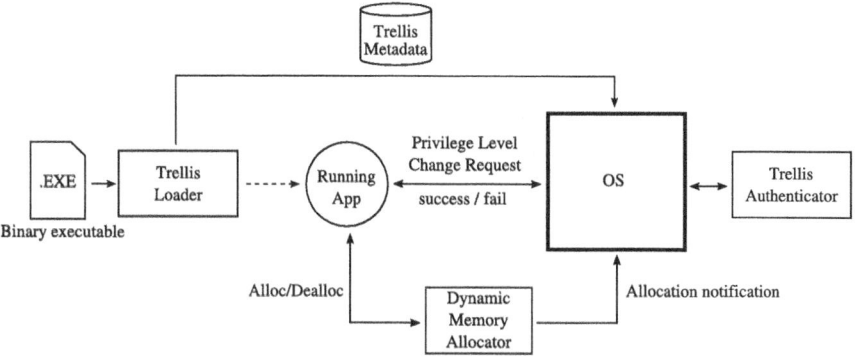

Fig. 2. An overview of running applications with Trellis.

the implemented access control policy. In the case of dynamic memory allocation requests by the application, a modified system memory allocator notifies the operating system of the performed operation. In this way, access control checks can be applied to those memory regions as well. Of course, during runtime, the application might need to change the active privilege level to a more privileged one. In that case, the application issues a privilege level change request to the operating system, and the operating system in turn consults an authentication module to check whether the request should be served. If permission is granted, the system performs the change.

3.1 Access Control Model

The design of Trellis permits a flexible access control model, where developers can tag units of code (e.g., functions) with a set of privilege levels $l \in L$. A partial ordering is defined on L such that the usual notions of reflexivity, antisymmetry, and transitivity are satisfied. More formally, given

$l \in L$ a set of partially-ordered privilege levels,
$(C, l) \in \mathbb{C}$ a set of units of tagged program code,
$(d, l) \in D$ a set of tagged data,
$D \in \mathbb{D}$ a set of all program data,

we define a program state as

$$S = \langle \mathbb{C}, \mathbb{D} \rangle$$

which describes the currently-executing unit of code at level l and the set of data upon which it can (potentially) compute. In the following, we refer to "units of code" as functions, although this need not be the level of granularity implemented in practice.

The developer is responsible for annotating functions with a privilege level according to application-specific requirements. These annotations, however, do not need to be completely specified for each function. Instead, Trellis permits developers to *partially* specify privilege levels, and an inference procedure will propagate privilege levels according to the program call graph. More precisely, given a call relation $(\rightsquigarrow) : C \mapsto C$, the inference process will assign an unannotated function $(C', \cdot)$ the infimum, or greatest lower bound, of all of its callers:

$$(C', l') \text{ s.t. } l' = \inf \bigcup_i (C_i, l_i), C_i \rightsquigarrow C' \forall C_i. \tag{1}$$

Note that the inference procedure might require an iterative fixpoint computation to establish privilege levels for all unannotated functions.

Given an annotated program, we can then define a transition relation

$$(\Rightarrow) : S \times S$$

that specifies *(i)* how transitions between privilege levels can occur during execution, and *(ii)* how data is tagged at runtime.

First, for function invocation, we have:
invoke : $\mathbb{C} \mapsto \{\mathbb{C} \cup \emptyset\}$

$$((C_i, l_i), D_i) \Rightarrow ((C_j, l_j), D_i) \text{ where}$$
$$C_i \rightsquigarrow C_j,$$
$$(l_j \leq l_i) \vee (\text{auth}\,((C_i, l_i), (C_j, l_j)))$$

Here, auth : $\mathbb{C} \times \mathbb{C} \mapsto \{\text{t}, \text{f}\}$ is an authentication predicate that is left as an open parameter of the implementation. The only requirement is that a binary decision is returned to either permit or deny an invocation between functions at given privilege levels. auth is only invoked if transitioning to a higher privilege level; otherwise, the transition is implicitly allowed to occur.

Another important operation we formally specify is data allocation:
alloc : $\mathbb{C} \mapsto \mathbb{D}$

$$((C_i, l_i), D_i) \Rightarrow ((C_i, l_i), D_j) \text{ where}$$
$$\text{alloc}\,((C_i, l_i)) = (d, l_i),$$
$$(d, l_i) \in D_j$$

For this transition rule, we further distinguish between statically-allocated data, stack-allocated data, and heap-allocated data. For statically-allocated data, the developer either provides a privilege level annotation for the system, or one is automatically inferred. Stack-allocated data, on the other hand, is always tagged with the privilege level for the associated function. Finally, heap-allocated data is tagged with the level of the enclosing function of the allocation site.

Finally, we specify the notion of data access, which subsumes both data reads and writes:

$$\text{access}: \mathbb{C} \times D \mapsto \{t, f\}$$
$$((C_i, l_i), D_i) \Rightarrow ((C_i, l_i), D_j) \text{ where}$$
$$\text{access}\,((C_i, l_i), (d_j, l_j)) \equiv l_j \leq l_i,$$
$$(d_j, l_j) \in D_j$$

Here, we simply state that reads or writes of data must only be permitted when the current privilege level is greater than or equal to the data's tag.

4 Implementation

In this section, we present a proof-of-concept implementation of Trellis in detail for Linux. We begin by describing the compile-time annotation and tag propagation procedure, and then discuss the implementation of runtime policy enforcement. Note that while the formal model we describe in Sect. 3.1 defines a partially-ordered set of privileges, our prototype implementation assumes a strict hierarchy of privilege levels for simplicity.

4.1 Compile-Time Component

The compile-time component of Trellis is implemented as a series of transformation passes for the LLVM/Clang compiler suite. As input, this toolchain takes a program that has been partially annotated by the application developers.

Privilege Level Annotations. Privilege level annotations are applied using a custom attribute that allows developers to express the minimum required privilege level to execute a function or access a static variable. At compile time, the new attribute is processed by the Clang compiler front-end, which supports custom attributes by forwarding them to subsequent Clang or LLVM transformation passes alongside the associated function or global variable identifier.

Since we need to keep track of the attribute parameter (e.g., 2 or 6 in Fig. 3's example), we modified Clang to forward the parameter value to LLVM. The attribute is considered valid for both functions and global variable declarations and specifies the privilege level of functions and global variables. For instance, Fig. 3 exemplifies a function fun of privilege level 2 and a global variable dat at privilege level 6. In this example, the developer wants to prevent function fun from accessing the memory area where the variable dat will be stored at runtime.

The attribute value indicates the privilege level of the associated object, which ranges from 0 and a tunable constant NUM_LEVELS, where higher levels indicate higher privileges. The main function is automatically set to 0, the lowest privileve level, by Trellis. If the developer tries to use a level greater than NUM_LEVELS, she receives a compile-time error.

Therefore, the prototype implements a simple access control variant of our proposed model, where privilege levels exist in a strict, linear hierarchy. More flexible variants that can model an arbitrary lattice of privilege levels are possible; however, we consider their implementation an engineering exercise.

```
1 void fun()  __attribute__((trellis_level(2)));
2 int  dat    __attribute__((trellis_level(6)));
```

Fig. 3. Example of function and global variable annotations using custom attributes.

Tag Inference. The first transformation pass implements privilege level tag inference. It analyzes attribute values specified by the developers and propagates them to non-tagged functions and data. Clearly, the developer could tag every function and global variable. However, tag inference improves the ergonomics of the system by allowing for a partial specification to be automatically extended to cover the entire program. Developers can inspect the output of the transformation to identify potential errors in the final policy, or modify it as necessary.

The pass first computes a queue of all annotated functions. Then, operating in a breadth-first fashion, the pass visits callees of the current function. If the callee has been manually annotated by the developer, then its tag is considered immutable and is not changed. If the callee is already tagged, a level is assigned that is the minimum of the new and existing tags (as dictated by Eq. 1). Otherwise, the caller's privilege level is used to tag the callee. In either of the preceding two cases where the callee's tag has been modified, the callee is added to the queue of functions to visit. The pass continues processing the function queue until a fixpoint is reached (i.e., the queue is empty). The search is guaranteed to terminate because privilege levels never increase and there exists a global minimum privilege level.

Transition Instrumentation and Error Handling. Trellis protects code and data tagged with a privilege level that is higher than the current level. However, the application should be able to change levels at runtime. To do so, Trellis leverages a new system call to inform the Linux kernel that the application requests a level transition. This system call, `trellis_switch`, is automatically injected by another transformation pass at every call site of the program when the caller has a lower privilege level than the callee. After the call site, another invocation of `trellis_switch`, is injected to inform the kernel that the application should return to the caller's privilege level. In particular, whenever this transformation pass encounters such a call site, it inserts a code snippet as exemplified in Fig. 4.

In case of failure because the current user is not authorized for the requested level, a wrapper function, `trellis_exit_wrapper`, is called. Through the wrapper, Trellis allows the developer to specify her own custom failure handling, where she can for instance implement recovery from the failure. If nothing is specified by the developer, the system by default will invoke `exit` to safely terminate the application.

Code and Data Reordering. The final transformation involves the reordering of all functions and static data. Every unit of code and static data is, at this point, tagged with a certain level. With a simple LLVM pass, each function and global variable is grouped by privilege level. Each group is then moved to

```
if (trellis_switch(x) != 1) {
    trellis_exit_wrapper();
}

call();
trellis_switch(y);
```

Fig. 4. Example of privilege level transition instrumentation and authentication error handler invocation.

a pair of separate sections of the binary, one for code and the other for data. The section names are created by concatenating the data type and level. For instance, in the case of code, the name will follow the pattern fun_trellis_l for every function that is tagged with level l. An analogous name dat_trellis_l is created for data tagged with level l.

The pass records all the levels used by the program under analysis and generates a custom linker script. The linker script is used to map each of the sections above to a unique program segment. The script also aligns the start address of each segment to a machine page boundary to avoid loader redefinition.

4.2 Run-Time Component

At this point, the binary has been produced and is ready to be run. The next subsections explain the runtime execution phase in detail.

Policy Loading. During normal program execution, the dynamic loader is responsible for several tasks that include mapping any shared libraries as well as mapping program segments from an executable image into memory. Our prototype contains a modified loader that parses the privilege level for each Trellis segment added at compile time, and communicates this information to the kernel with a special system call added for this purpose: trellis_init.

trellis_init copies the program's memory layout from userspace to kernel space, and attaches a list of memory boundaries (see Fig. 5) to the task_struct of the application. The task_struct is the canonical process descriptor for the running application inside the kernel, and contains all information regarding the process (e.g., credentials, memory maps).

trellis_init is executed during dynamic loading before control is passed to the application. Trellis allows this system call to be invoked only once for each process. This prevents an attacker from using a second invocation of this system call during execution to elevate privileges by relaxing the intended access control policy. For the same reason, after the execution of trellis_init, mprotect cannot be invoked by the process.

After dynamic loading has completed and main is ready to be invoked, the process is in a state where *(i)* only code and data at the lowest privilege level is accessible, and *(ii)* all other (higher-privileged) segments are *not* readable, writable, or executable.

```
struct trellis_dyn_t{
    int priv_level;
    int size;
    void *mem;
    struct trellis_dyn_t *next;
};
```

Fig. 5. Memory chunk information element.

Privilege Level Transitions. The second system call added to the Linux kernel is `trellis_switch`. It allows an application to request a transition from the current privilege level to another, specified using the parameter `new_level`.

When transitioning to a higher level, the kernel wakes a daemon that blocks the resumption of the requesting application until authentication has completed; this allows the use of interactive authentication if desired. In the meantime, the process is moved by the operating system into the wait state and will be woken only at the end of the `trellis_switch` system call. If the authentication succeeds, the kernel changes the permissions of the code and data segments for the requested level and returns control to the application. Otherwise, the wrapper for authentication failure is invoked. When transitioning to an equal or lower level, authentication is not required, and therefore the inverse of the above segment re-permissioning procedure is performed automatically. An example of the dynamic memory segment permission process is shown in Fig. 6.

Dynamic Data Tagging. The third system call is `trellis_tracemalloc`, which manages dynamic memory allocations. Typically, applications allocate memory at runtime using standard functions from the `malloc` family, and release it using `free`. These functions are merely the interface to a heap allocator, and underlying this application-level interface are system calls such as `brk` and `mmap` that are used to request additional memory from the operating system.

This presents two main challenges for our protection mechanism. The first challenge is that it is not straightforward to assign privilege levels to heap-allocated data due to the additional indirection imposed by the heap allocator. That is, the page-level permission scheme used for code and static global data does not map cleanly into the variable-sized chunk allocation interface exposed by the heap allocator. The second challenge is that chunk metadata is stored inline with application data. This implies that page-level permissions would potentially restrict access not only to the data but also the chunk metadata that is used by the allocator.

To overcome these challenges, Trellis introduces a multi-heap allocator using `trellis_tracemalloc` that effectively partitions dynamic memory allocation according to privilege levels. This allocator exposes two functions, `trellis_malloc` and `trellis_free`, to allocate and release memory, respectively. This allocator also maintains chunk metadata in a separate area of memory by tracking different lists of pages, where every list of pages corresponds to a separate heap. These structures are shown in Fig. 7. Other standard allocation

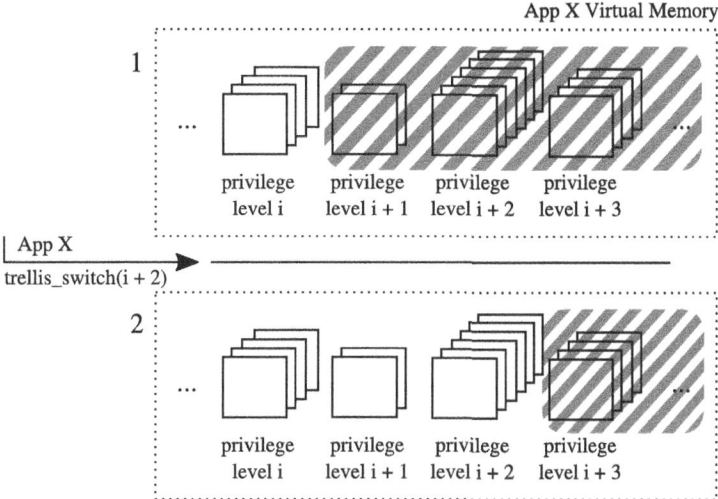

Fig. 6. Example of a dynamic memory segment permission update to transition between permission levels – in this case, from level i to $i+2$. Shaded segments indicate inaccessible code and data regions.

```
1  void *heaps[NUM_LEVELS] = { NULL, };
2
3  /* Memory chunk */
4  struct trellis_chunk {
5      size_t size;
6      struct trellis_chunk *next;
7      struct trellis_chunk *prev;
8      void *ptr;
9  };
10
11 /* Page struct with list of empty and used chunks */
12 struct trellis_page {
13     struct trellis_chunk *free;
14     struct trellis_chunk *used;
15     struct trellis_page *next;
16     struct trellis_page *prev;
17     size_t size;
18 };
```

Fig. 7. Chunk and page list structures for the multi-heap dynamic memory allocator.

routines are implemented in terms of these two basic primitives. The compiler toolchain can optionally replace uses of the traditional allocation functions in a transparent fashion, or the developer can be responsible for doing so.

Authentication and Authorization. Transition authorization is implemented by a userspace daemon, a kernel netlink interface, and `trellis_switch`. Before the application is executed, the netlink interface is activated through a kernel module and the daemon starts. This can be performed either manually or automatically when needed. When the application requests a privilege level transition, `trellis_switch` writes the requested privilege level into the netlink channel where the daemon receives it. The daemon then performs the authentication check and transmits a message over the netlink channel to notify the kernel of an authentication success or failure. The netlink communication channel is secure according to the attacker model defined in Sect. 2.

To implement authentication, the prototype simply forwards the request to the standard Pluggable Authentication Module (PAM) framework. PAM is modular, versatile, supports a variety of authentication mechanisms (e.g., passwords, smart cards, fingerprints), and is well-tested and widely used.

5 Evaluation

In this section, we first describe our experiments to measure the performance overhead introduced when compiling, loading and running applications with Trellis. Specifically, we present *micro-benchmarks* to characterize the cost of the newly introduced Trellis operations, and *end-to-end* performance tests reflecting the overhead of running complete applications with Trellis. Next, we present an empirical evaluation of the developer effort required to adapt an application to work with Trellis, and test the system's security.

All experiments were performed on a machine with an Intel i7-3520M CPU and 4 GB of memory, running Gentoo Linux with a Trellis-patched kernel version 3.9.11 and glibc 2.19. The test binaries were built using LLVM/Clang version 3.5. The results for non-Trellis experiments were obtained on an identical setup running the vanilla versions of the Linux kernel and glibc.

5.1 Micro-benchmarks

Privilege Level Change. In this experiment, we measured the time required to change the privilege level of a running application. We created a benchmark program, and performed measurements at the entry and return points of the function that requests the privilege change. That is, our measurement includes the switch from userspace to kernel space, the call to the corresponding Trellis system call and all subsequent operations, and the switch back to userspace. During this experiment, the authentication module was configured to automatically allow all privilege change requests in order to avoid any human interaction overhead. Note that since a system without Trellis does not contain a corresponding operation, we cannot obtain any baseline to compare these results with. Therefore, here we only report the absolute runtime cost of the tested operation.

Dynamic Memory Allocation. We designed this experiment to characterize the overhead of Trellis's modified `malloc` operation. We created a simple benchmark program that takes measurements before and after a call to `malloc` to compute the elapsed time, and repeated the experiment with the standard, unmodified glibc memory allocator for comparison.

In order to see the effects of allocated chunk size on performance, we repeated this experiment with varying allocation sizes of 1 KB, 2 KB, 4 KB, 1 MB, and 100

MB. We did not observe a significant correlation between chunk size and runtime, and Trellis's overhead remained nearly constant in all experiments. Therefore, we only report the worst-case performance we observed in this section.

Executable Loading. In this experiment, we measured the overhead incurred by the dynamic loader for reading the Trellis metadata associated with a binary executable, and setting up the initial active privilege level inside the kernel prior to launching the application. To this end, we instrumented the executable loader with timing functions, and experimented with launching a test binary executable both with and without Trellis support.

5.2 End-to-End Performance

Because we did not have source code access to an actual commercial multi-user application that would benefit from Trellis's features, we instead opted to follow a different evaluation strategy. First, we ran experiments on an application developed in-house to test Trellis with, which we will call *StoreManager*. Next, we took an existing open-source application, *HomeBank* [2], extended it with multi-user capabilities, and adapted it to work with Trellis.

StoreManager is a store inventory management software that supports three distinct user roles. "Unprivileged users" are ordinary employees that can browse and view details of the items registered in the database, or view aggregate reports about the inventory status. "Managers" have additional privileges to manage the inventory, such as adding, removing, or editing the details of items. Finally, "system administrators" hold the highest level of privileges, and are able to create or delete user accounts on the system, or directly manipulate the inventory.

HomeBank is a popular accounting software that provides account management, analysis, and reporting features. While HomeBank is originally designed for personal use, we extended it support four different user roles. Prior to authentication, the application runs under an "unprivileged user" role, with access to only the basic features. "Analysts" are only able to access analysis and reporting functionalities, but cannot add or modify accounts. "Accountants" have the additional privileges to schedule new transactions on existing accounts. Finally, "managers" hold the highest privileges and are able to access critical features including creating and modifying accounts, transactions, and budgets.

We created two instances of each application. One was built to run on an ordinary Linux system, and access control was enforced by disabling access to the GUI elements that perform privileged operations inside the application. The other's source code was manually annotated by the authors according to the aforementioned access control policy, and built to run with Trellis. All of the following experiments were performed using these applications.

Compilation Time. In this test, we measured the overhead incurred for Trellis-specific code analysis, annotation propagation, and source code instrumentation performed during compilation and linking of the binary executables. We first compiled the two test applications using the unmodified toolchain, and then with Trellis to compare the results.

Table 1. Trellis performance evaluation results. See Sect. 5 for detailed explanations.

Experiments	Baseline	Trellis	Overhead
Privilege level change	-	159.91 μs	-
Dynamic memory allocation	34.04 μs	57.27 μs	68.24 %
Executable loading	108.44 μs	136.45 μs	25.83 %
StoreManager compilation time	850.17 ms	933.29 ms	9.78 %
HomeBank compilation time	28.62 s	28.72 s	0.36 %
StoreManager runtime	14.75 s	15.20 s	3.05 %
HomeBank runtime	14.37 s	14.94 s	4.02 %

Application Performance. As the final part of our evaluation plan, we designed a comprehensive use-case scenario for each of the two test applications that exercises all program features using different user profiles, and measured the end-to-end runtime. For this task, we used the GUI automation tool Linux Desktop Testing Project (LDTP) [3], and configured the Trellis authentication module to automatically allow privilege level change requests—as we are not interested in timing the user interaction. For the StoreManager experiment, our use-case involved viewing numerous inventory items as an ordinary user, creating and deleting items as a store manager, and manipulating user accounts as a system administrator. The HomeBank use-case involved setting up new accounts and budgets as a manager, scheduling transactions as an accountant, and reviewing reports as an analyst. We ran these use-cases with and without Trellis enabled, and computed the overall runtime overhead of our system.

5.3 Experiment Results

We performed the above micro-benchmarks 1000 times, compilation time measurements 50 times, and application runtime measurements 300 times. The average runtimes over all runs are presented in Table 1.

The compilation time experiment shows that building a Trellis-aware executable for StoreManager takes about 10 % longer than compiling an unprotected program. Although this overhead could suggest discernibly longer compilation times for complex applications, we note that this is a one-time performance trade-off for the significant access control enforcement benefits provided by Trellis. Also note that, compared to StoreManager, the compilation time overhead for HomeBank is much lower at only 0.36 %. This is because HomeBank's codebase is considerably larger than StoreManager's, which leads to its normal, lengthy compilation time over-shadowing the overhead imposed by Trellis. Similarly, despite the seemingly large executable loading overhead of about 26 %, we stress that the absolute application launch time difference is only on the order of micro seconds, and is unlikely to be noticed by users.

For the application runtime measurements, even though we do not have a baseline to compare the privilege level change performance against, we expect the overhead to be acceptable since privilege level changes are not expected to be common operations during runtime. Moreover, they are likely to be completely over-shadowed by human response times if an interactive authentication scheme is used. The Trellis dynamic memory allocator, however, is shown to perform significantly worse than the default glibc allocator. This could potentially lead to performance drops in applications that perform heavy dynamic memory allocation in small chunks, and could require optimization techniques such as using pre-allocated memory caches. Despite this potential shortcoming, our final performance tests show that the runtime impact on real-world applications, with typical use-cases, is only around 4%.

5.4 Developer Effort

Unfortunately, systematically quantifying the developer effort required to adapt an existing application to work with Trellis is a non-trivial task, requiring a large-scale study with an extensive corpus of Trellis-enabled software. Therefore, we provide anecdotal results obtained during our modifications to HomeBank.

The development of our multi-user version of HomeBank was carried out by a single developer, one of the authors of this paper. While the developer had over ten years of C programming experience, he had no prior experience with the HomeBank application's codebase. We measured the time taken during all phases of active development, and report the results in the following.

Surprisingly, significant effort before development went into adapting Home-Bank's compilation chain (i.e., autoconf scripts, Makefiles, etc.) that is designed around using GCC, to Trellis's LLVM/Clang environment. We spent around 2 h to be able to compile HomeBank with our system. Next, 4 h were taken to understand the codebase, and identify the relevant points that should be modified to achieve the desired privilege separation. Finally, all Trellis annotations and changes were applied and tested in another 2 h. Overall, with a single developer, and without prior familiarity with the application, HomeBank could be adapted to work with Trellis in under 8 h, which we believe to be a reasonable and acceptable degree of developer effort.

5.5 Security Experiments

Trellis' security properties hold by definition, and there are no heuristics for attack detection or any probabilistic decisions involved in the system. In order to empirically verify the effectiveness of Trellis against concrete, practical attack scenarios, we created a set of exploits following the methodology laid out in [21].

Specifically, in [21], the authors define a novel class of access control vulnerabilities called GUI Element Misuse (GEM), which involves bypassing an application's built-in access control checks through manipulation of its GUI elements (e.g., by un-hiding a hidden button that allows access to privileged functionality). GEM vulnerabilities exemplify a recent, high-impact instance of the type of attacks that Trellis aims to address. Unfortunately, we were not able to use the same set of applications that were exploited in [21] due to them being closed-source Windows applications. Thus, we opted to perform our experiments on StoreManager, and our extended multi-user version of HomeBank.

Following the steps outlined in [21], we first analyzed the test applications using a GUI explorer tool *Parasite* [4], and identified buttons that would trigger privileged functionality. Using the same tool, we then attempted to forcefully enable and interact with these GUI elements with an unprivileged user account, using both the vanilla and Trellis-protected versions of the two test applications.

The vanilla versions of the programs were vulnerable to GEM attacks as we expected, and we were able to execute privileged operations as an unprivileged user. On the contrary, Trellis-enabled versions were protected against our attacks; Trellis blocked our access attempts to privileged code pages, and simply rolled back the applications to a default state that we defined in the corresponding `trellis_exit_wrapper` routines.

6 Discussion and Limitations

A prerequisite for using Trellis is access to the application's source code. As we have discussed in Sect. 7, virtually all previous work also has not explored partitioning of binary executables directly. Given that many commercial multi-user applications that would be suitable targets for privilege-level partitioning are provided on a closed-source model, privilege separation on binary code appears to be a challenging, yet promising future research direction. However, note that Trellis aims to enforce privilege separation and access control over application-specific functionality and data, and therefore, annotating or recompiling third-party libraries used by the target application is not necessary.

Although the Trellis implementation we present in this paper is for applications written in C and C++, the high-level design we propose could be applied to other compiled languages. However, application of our ideas to interpreted or just-in-time-compiled languages requires a significant rethinking of the design. In a similar vein, the Trellis static analyzer can only propagate the privilege level tags up to the statically reachable portion of the call graph (i.e., as seen by the compiler), thus leaving out callbacks or dynamic calls in general. Likewise, our prototype implementation does not currently handle control flow transitions that deviate from normal function calls and returns (e.g., jumps into signal handlers, `longjmp`, C++ exception handlers across multiple levels of functions); however, Trellis could be extended to support these cases in principle. Furthermore, complex applications that use pre-allocated memory pools may necessitate further developer effort to ensure that all dynamic memory regions are annotated correctly according to their appropriate privilege levels.

As evidenced by the dynamic memory allocator experiments in Sect. 5, Trellis may lead to a discernible performance impact when applied to memory allocation intensive applications. Although this problem could be alleviated through manual code optimization techniques such as using memory caching techniques instead of frequent calls to `trellis_malloc`, similar mechanisms could also be built directly inside Trellis's allocator to make the process transparent to application developers. Also note that using the Trellis memory allocator is only required for protecting sensitive application data, and the system's default allocator (or any custom allocator) could still be used for all other, non-sensitive memory allocations to avoid incurring runtime overhead.

One operation that Trellis does not yet support in a flexible, first-class manner is declassification of data to a lower privilege level. This capability can be useful in situations where the application developer can certify that information computed in a higher privileged context can safely be released to a lower privileged context in accordance with the application's security policies.

Since Trellis is an application-level access control mechanism, it is not designed to provide protection against attacks at lower-level system components (e.g., operating system exploits, hardware backdoors, etc.). Likewise, Trellis is designed strictly to support privilege separation; it does not aim to address common memory corruption vulnerabilities that may expose code and data *within the same privilege level* to attacks. These threats are outside the scope of this work, and Trellis should be used in conjunction with established defense mechanisms that support memory integrity such as ASLR [27] and stack canaries [13].

In future work, we plan to investigate extensions of Trellis to address limitations of the current approach. While our prototype implementation assumes a strict ordering of user privileges, it provides the necessary primitives to enable the lattice-based privilege model we describe in Sect. 3.1. One promising research direction is extending Trellis further to allow more complex access control models, to address concerns such as privacy of user profiles sharing the same privilege level. Other potential avenues of research include lifting the guarantees provided by the approach to higher-level languages, removing the need for source code, and reification of declassification within the framework. Finally, the dynamic memory segment permission management component of Trellis could be applied to other settings such as binary attack surface reduction by temporarily disabling access to unneeded portions of an application's address space.

7 Related Work

The principles of least privilege and privilege separation have long been studied as prominent software design principles to minimize trusted code in programs and contain damage in the face of security exploits [24,25]. The architectures of many prevalent programs such as vsftpd [15], Postfix [28], and Sendmail [11] are explicitly designed around these principles.

Prior work most similar to Trellis aims to apply these principles to existing programs. Provos et al. [24] present a design methodology for applying privilege separation to security sensitive system services. Here, applications are separated into a privileged *monitor* and unprivileged *slave* processes that communicate via IPC channels. The authors also demonstrate their approach by discussing its application to OpenSSH. Kilpatrick [16] introduces a reusable framework to ease the implementation of partitioned applications. Bittau et al. [9] propose an application compartmentalization framework that provides a set of operating system primitives to assist developers with partitioning programs. In this approach, developers mark allocated memory regions with tags, and create special compartmentalized threads with specific access rights to the tagged memory.

While the above work lays down the guidelines for manually partitioning applications and provides tools for assistance, later work attempts to automate this process. Brumley and Song [10] use a combination of code annotation and static analysis to automatically separate C code into the aforementioned monitor and slave parts. Wu et al. [32] instead employ a dynamic data dependency analysis, which constructs a data dependency graph over the program's functions, and then partitions this into subgraphs representing least privilege components.

Trellis also uses code annotation and static analysis to perform privilege separation; however, unlike the previous work, it does not partition applications into separate processes. Instead, code and data at different privilege levels are segregated into separate memory pages, and access control is enforced by the operating system. Moreover, our system supports any number of privilege levels, instead of only a privileged and an unprivileged partition.

Other works apply similar application partitioning techniques to different security contexts. Kim and Zeldovich [17] present a Linux kernel module that allows unprivileged system users to utilize Linux security features (e.g., allocating new user IDs, setting up firewall rules, setting up `chroot` environments, etc.) to confine applications and reduce the amount of code running as root. Murray and Hand [22] discuss early ideas of segregating the trusted computing base of an application into small, dynamic libraries. Chong et al. [12] proposes a system that partitions web applications into JavaScript client-side code and Java server-side code according to the specified information-flow policies. Zdancewic et al. [33], and Zheng et al. [35] employ automatic code and data partitioning to address the problem of secure distributed computation. In contrast to the above, Trellis aims to address the problem of enforcing access control on multi-user applications that transitions between different privilege levels during runtime.

Various software security frameworks provide access control features analogous to Trellis for higher-level languages such as Java and Python, where access control enforcement capabilities are provided on top of the corresponding virtual machines or language interpreters. For instance, Apache Shiro [1] and Spring Security [6] allow Java applications to implement a role-based access control model for enterprise applications. In comparison, Trellis is applicable to multi-user programs written in C and C++, and it introduces a novel architecture to enforce hierarchical access control policies at the operating system level.

Trellis has comparable goals to History-Based Access Control (HBAC) [7], a model that assigns privileges to code during runtime based on previous execution history. This model largely relies on a runtime framework such as Java Virtual Machine or Common Language Runtime. In contrast, Trellis allows software developers to define privilege levels statically at compile time, and enforces access control at runtime. Similarly, Trellis shares some of its design principles with Decentralized Information Flow Control (DIFC) (e.g., Asbestos [14], Flume [18],

HiStar [34]), which allows labeling data, and restricting its flow between application and operating system components. Other related program confinement solutions include various operating system mechanisms [5,8,23,30], capability systems [26,31], and software-based fault isolation techniques [19,20,29]. Unlike these, Trellis specifically addresses the problem of enforcing access control *within* an application. In particular, our system protects applications against vulnerabilities resulting from incorrect access control implementations, such as the misuse of GUI elements as access control primitives [21].

8 Conclusion

In this paper, we presented Trellis, a novel approach for specifying and enforcing access control policies in multi-user applications to separate code and data that logically belongs to different privilege levels. Enforcing such policies in multi-user applications is a responsibility that has heretofore been borne by application developers; Trellis automates this critical, error-prone aspect of application security. Our prototype implementation demonstrates that Trellis imposes a low end-to-end runtime performance overhead.

Acknowledgments. We would like to thank our shepherd Vasileios P. Kemerlis for his helpful feedback. This work was supported by the National Science Foundation (NSF) under grant CNS-1409738, and Secure Business Austria.

References

1. Apache Shiro. https://shiro.apache.org/index.html
2. HomeBank. http://homebank.free.fr
3. Linux Desktop Testing Project. http://ldtp.freedesktop.org/
4. Parasite. https://chipx86.github.io/gtkparasite
5. SELinux. http://selinuxproject.org
6. Spring Security. http://projects.spring.io/spring-security
7. Abadí, M., Fournet, C.: Access control based on execution history. In: NDSS (2003)
8. Badger, L., Sterne, D., Sherman, D., Walker, K.M., Haghighat, S.A.: A domain and type enforcement UNIX prototype. In: USENIX Security (1995)
9. Bittau, A., Marchenko, P., Handley, M., Karp, B.: Wedge: splitting applications into reduced-privilege compartments. In: USENIX NSDI (2008)
10. Brumley, D., Song, D.: Privtrans: automatically partitioning programs for privilege separation. In: USENIX Security (2004)
11. Carson, M.E.: Sendmail without the superuser. In: USENIX Security (1993)
12. Chong, S., Liu, J., Myers, A.C., Qi, X., Vikram, K., Zheng, L., Zheng, X.: Secure web applications via automatic partitioning. In: ACM SOSP (2007)
13. Cowan, C., Pu, C., Maier, D., Walpole, J., Bakke, P., Beattie, S., Grier, A., Wagle, P., Zhang, Q., Hinton, H.: StackGuard: automatic adaptive detection and prevention of buffer-overflow attacks. In: USENIX Security (1998)
14. Efstathopoulos, P., Krohn, M., VanDeBogart, S., Frey, C., Ziegler, D., Kohler, E., Mazières, D., Kaashoek, F., Morris, R.: Labels and event processes in the Asbestos operating system. In: ACM SOSP (2005)

15. Evans, C.: Very Secure FTP Daemon. http://security.appspot.com/vsftpd.html
16. Kilpatrick, D.: Privman: a library for partitioning applications. In: USENIX ATC (2003)
17. Kim, T., Zeldovich, N.: Making Linux protection mechanisms egalitarian with UserFS. In: USENIX Security (2010)
18. Krohn, M., Yip, A., Brodsky, M., Cliffer, N., Kaashoek, M.F., Kohler, E., Morris, R.: Information flow control for standard OS abstractions. In: ACM SOSP (2007)
19. McCamant, S., Morrisett, G.: Evaluating SFI for a CISC architecture. In: USENIX Security (2006)
20. Morrisett, G., Tan, G., Tassarotti, J., Tristan, J.B., Gan, E.: RockSalt: better, faster, stronger SFI for the x86. In: ACM PLDI (2012)
21. Mulliner, C., Robertson, W., Kirda, E.: Hidden GEMs: automated discovery of access control vulnerabilities in graphical user interfaces. In: IEEE Security and Privacy (2014)
22. Murray, D.G., Hand, S.: Privilege separation made easy: trusting small libraries not big processes. In: EuroSec (2008)
23. Peterson, D., Bishop, M., Pandey, R.: A flexible containment mechanism for executing untrusted code. In: USENIX Security (2002)
24. Provos, N., Friedl, M., Honeyman, P.: Preventing privilege escalation. In: USENIX Security (2003)
25. Saltzer, J.H.: Protection and the control of information sharing in multics. Commun. ACM **17**(7), 388–402 (1974)
26. Shapiro, J.S., Smith, J.M., Farber, D.J.: EROS: a fast capability system. In: ACM SOSP (1999)
27. The PaX Team: PaX Address Space Layout Randomization (ASLR) (2003). http://pax.grsecurity.net/docs/aslr.txt
28. Venema, W.: The Postfix Homepage. http://www.postfix.org/
29. Wahbe, R., Lucco, S., Anderson, T.E., Graham, S.L.: Efficient software-based fault isolation. In: ACM SOSP (1993)
30. Walker, K.M., Sterne, D.F., Badger, M.L., Petkac, M.J., Sherman, D.L., Oostendorp, K.A.: Confining root programs with domain and type enforcement (DTE). In: USENIX Security (1996)
31. Wilkes, M.V.: The Cambridge CAP Computer and Its Operating System. North-Holland Publishing Co., Amsterdam (1979)
32. Wu, Y., Sun, J., Liu, Y., Dong, J.S.: Automatically partition software into least privilege components using dynamic data dependency analysis. In: IEEE/ACM ASE (2013)
33. Zdancewic, S., Zheng, L., Nystrom, N., Myers, A.C.: Secure program partitioning. ACM Trans. Comput. Syst. **20**(3), 283–328 (2002)
34. Zeldovich, N., Boyd-Wickizer, S., Kohler, E., Mazières, D.: Making information flow explicit in HiStar. In: USENIX OSDI (2006)
35. Zheng, L., Chong, S., Myers, A.C., Zdancewic, S.: Using replication and partitioning to build secure distributed systems. In: IEEE Security and Privacy (2003)

Blender: Self-randomizing Address Space Layout for Android Apps

Mingshen Sun[1(✉)], John C.S. Lui[1], and Yajin Zhou[2]

[1] The Chinese University of Hong Kong, Hong Kong, China
mssun@cse.cuhk.edu.hk
[2] Qihoo 360 Technology Co. Ltd., Beijing, China

Abstract. In this paper, we first demonstrate that the newly introduced Android RunTime (ART) in latest Android versions (Android 5.0 or above) exposes a new attack surface, namely, the "return-to-art" (ret2art) attack. Unlike traditional return-to-library attacks, the ret2art attack abuses Android framework APIs (e.g., the API to send SMS) as payloads to conveniently perform malicious operations. This new attack surface, along with the weakened ASLR implementation in the Android system, makes the successful exploiting of vulnerable apps much easier. To mitigate this threat and provide *self-protection* for Android apps, we propose a user-level solution called BLENDER, which is able to *self-randomize* address space layout for apps. Specifically, for an app using our system, BLENDER randomly rearranges loaded libraries and Android runtime executable code in the app's process, achieving much higher memory entropy compared with the vanilla app. BLENDER requires no changes to the Android framework nor the underlying Linux kernel, thus is a non-invasive and easy-to-deploy solution. Our evaluation shows that BLENDER only incurs around 6 MB memory footprint increase for the app with our system, and does not affect other apps without our system. It increases 0.3 s of app starting delay, and imposes negligible CPU and battery overheads.

Keywords: Android · ROP · ASLR · Blender

1 Introduction

Due to the increasing functionalities of applications (apps for short) on mobile devices, the security and privacy of apps become one major concern. For apps running on the Android system, they are mainly written in Java. However, to enhance compatibility and performance, developers often choose to use the native development kit (NDK) to develop native libraries written in C/C++ and integrate them in their apps. A recent study [14] showed that around 37 % of Android apps contain at least one native library. These native libraries are *not memory safe* and may suffer from memory corruption issues [4,5,8]. What is even worse that the potential vulnerabilities [9] in Android system libraries are loaded into every app's process and further expose more attack surfaces, even if the app itself does not contain any native library. Attackers could exploit vulnerabilities in native libraries and execute arbitrary shellcode on stack or launch ROP attack [39] if the stack is not executable.

To mitigate such threat, Address Space Layout Randomization (ASLR) [47] is a widely adopted solution in modern operating systems. If properly implemented, a system with the ASLR protection will randomize the loaded code and data into different locations. Therefore, attackers cannot infer the memory layout from previous executions or other side channels, raising the bar for successfully exploiting the system.

Android introduced the ASLR protection since version 4.0 and improved the implementation in later versions. However, as indicated by previous research [32], the ASLR support in Android is not complete. First of all, the ASLR protection in earlier Android versions is only effective for system-related processes started at device booting stage, e.g., service management and communication-related processes. Second, the zygote process creation model of Android *indirectly weakens the effectiveness of memory layout randomization.* System libraries in different apps inherit shared (and same) memory regions from the parent zygote process. Thus, attackers can infer the memory layout from other running apps. This memory layout information helps attackers to initiate attacks and execute any arbitrary code on an Android system. For instance, Lee et al. [32] demonstrated the possibilities of remotely exploiting vulnerable apps and easily bypassing the ASLR protection in the Android system to launch an ROP attack (e.g., return-to-library [23,53] and return-to-linker attacks). They further proposed a countermeasure called Morula that changes the Android system to randomize the memory layout for apps. Framework enhancement appears to be a natural solution. However, the need to change the Android framework could strongly impair the practical deployment due to the deep fragmentation of the Android platform.

In this paper, we first demonstrate that the newly introduced Android app RunTime (ART) exposes a new attack surface, namely return-to-art (ret2art for short). This attack surface increases the predictability of the memory layout of executable code regions which are the pool of useful ROP gadgets. Then, it further facilitates the construction of malicious payloads since attackers could return to the pre-compiled framework libraries and leverage the well-defined Android framework APIs to perform malicious operations. For instance, attackers could easily construct the payload to send SMS, get GPS locations on behalf of the vulnerable app if the app has corresponding permissions, without the need to understand the tedious details of the binder IPC mechanism and bridge the semantic gaps between the high level framework APIs and low level system calls. This new attack surface is not just in theory, but it is actually a practical threat. A recent study [36] leveraged a similar attack surface to exploit the Android system.

To mitigate this threat, we then propose a user-level solution called BLENDER. Our system provides the capability of memory layout self-randomization to (sensitive) Android apps with high security requirement, without waiting for the changes of the Android framework nor the underlying Linux kernel. Specifically, BLENDER first randomizes memory layout of loaded system libraries which are inherited from the zygote process. Then, to prevent the ret2art attack, BLENDER also randomizes the ART executable runtime dynamically at startup time. It ensures that the base addresses of libraries and the ART runtime are unpredictable.

We implement a prototype of BLENDER and evaluate its effectiveness and overhead. Our evaluation shows that apps using our system have a much higher memory entropy than vanilla apps. This means attackers have to try many times to successfully bypass the Android ASLR protection, instead of a single attempt. BLENDER incurs an increase of 6 MB memory footprint for an app. Note that, this only affects apps using our system, and does not affect other ones running on the device, an extra advantage compared with the system-wide solution [32]. Our system increases 0.3 s to the app starting time, and incurs no obvious CPU and battery overhead.

To summarize, this paper makes following contributions:

- We first discover a new attack surface called ret2art attack in recent Android versions. This attack surface provides a large pool for useful ROP gadgets, and facilitates the construction of malicious payloads using high-level framework APIs.
- To mitigate the threat of ret2art attack and weakened ASLR implementation in the Android system, we propose a user-level solution which could *self-randomize* address space layout for both native libraries and the ART runtime of a running app, without the need of framework modification.
- We implement a prototype of the BLENDER system and evaluate the effectiveness and performance overheads. Our experiments show that BLENDER can gain high randomization entropy with only 300 ms delay of the app's startup time, without obvious overhead to the CPU and battery resources.

The paper is organized as follows. In Sect. 2, we discuss the background of Android and related attack/defense methods. Section 3 explains the weakened ASLR mechanism in the current Android system, and we also illustrate conventional ROP attacks and propose a novel ret2art attacks on the latest version of Android. Section 4 presents the design and implementation of BLENDER. We present the experimental results which show the effectiveness, performance and battery overheads of BLENDER in Sect. 5. Finally, we discuss possible limitations in Sect. 6, study related work in Sect. 7, and Sect. 8 concludes the paper.

2 Background

In this section, we briefly introduce the new Android runtime (ART runtime) and the ASLR protection on Android.

2.1 Dalvik VM and ART Runtime

An Android app is a zip file packaged with Dalvik executable code (i.e., **dex** file) and other resources. In previous Android versions (before Android 5.0), Android utilizes the Dalivk virtual machine (DVM) to interpret the Dalvik bytecode at runtime. When an app is started, each Dalvik instance is created and system libraries and app bytecode will be loaded into an individual process. However, creating a new process and fully loading dependent libraries is a time-consuming process, especially on resource-limited mobile platforms. Android optimizes this process by creating the `zygote` process and pre-loading all the system libraries into this `zygote` process when the system is booting. Then all other apps are forked from this `zygote` process and inherit the pre-loaded system libraries (and the Dalvik instance) in the `zygote` process. This optimization improves an app's launch-time, however, defeats the ASLR protection in Android since the system libraries in different apps are shared the same memory layout. Figure 1 shows that the system libraries like `libc.so` and `libart.so` are shared between different apps and their addresses could be predicted by attackers. We will illustrate the way of launching corresponding attacks using the knowledge of predicted address space layout in Sect. 3.1.

Since Android 5.0, Google optimizes the Android system by introducing a new Android runtime, i.e., the ART runtime. ART introduces an ahead-of-time (AOT) compilation strategy to compile the Dalvik bytecode into native machine code. Due to this optimization, the framework-level APIs in the format of Dalvik bytecode are now converted into native code, and are shared between different apps. The new executable machine code is internally stored in the `oat` file format, which is nearly same with the traditional `ELF` format.

Figure 2 illustrates the flow of code execution of an app by the ART runtime. This runtime introduces three different memory regions into the app's process space. The first one is the `classes.dex` file, which contains an app's logic. The file name has a legacy extension which was inherited from the Dalvik runtime, but it is actual in the `oat` format. The second region is the `system@framework@boot.oat` file (i.e., "ART boot code" short for `boot.oat`). This region contains the compiled executable code of all Android framework bytecode. The third region is a data area and it does not contain any executable code. It is mapped with the `system@framework@boot.art` file (i.e., "ART boot image" internally and is called `boot.art` for short) which contains all necessary objects for bootstrapping the ART runtime. Basically, it provides a mapping table between a framework function and its real address of the executable code. To invoke a framework function in the app, the code will first (1) query the `boot.art` mapping table, then (2) call the actual code in the text section in `boot.oat`. For the ART runtime, there are class tables and method tables which maintain information of all loaded classes and methods. The runtime can call `Invoke()` of the `ArtMethod` in the method table to execute the compiled code through an invocation assembly code stub.

We found that the introduction of the ART runtime exposes a new attack surface due to two reasons. First, the large chunk of pre-compiled framework native code are shared between different apps, and its memory layout is more predictable than other system libraries. Thus, this increases the pool of libraries that could be used as ROP gadgets. Second, the ART runtime exposes all pre-compiled code of the framework functions at predictable locations. *Attackers can*

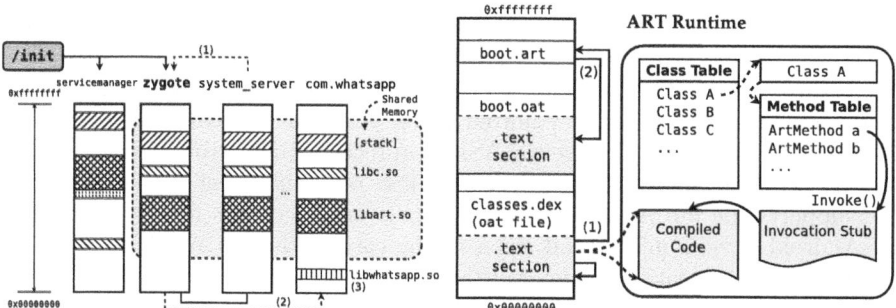

Fig. 1. Android booting and app creation process.

Fig. 2. Android ART runtime and memory structure.

utilize this code as payloads and invoke high-level framework APIs more easily than the previous Dalvik runtime. We will elaborate this form of attack surface in Sect. 3.2.

2.2 DEP/ASLR Protection on Android

Control flow hijacking is a way to exploit vulnerable program and control the program's execution flow. In old days, attackers usually hijacked the control flow to the data area and executed the prepared shellcode on stack. DEP is a security feature which intends to defeat this type of attack, by disallowing the memory page as writable and executable at the same time. This feature is supported in modern hardware and enabled by default in many operating systems, including the Android system.

Then researchers proposed the *return-oriented programming* (ROP) attack to defeat the effectiveness of the DEP protection. It does not need to inject shellcode into the data area and then mark the data area as executable. Instead, it reuses the already loaded code in the process to launch attack. Specifically, the ROP attack hijacks the program's control flow and jumps to existing executable instruction sequences which end with return instructions. These instruction sequences are called "*gadgets*". By chaining gadgets together, attackers can perform arbitrary operations regardless of the DEP protection. There are many kinds of ROP techniques, e.g., return into binary executable, return into shared libraries and return into non-randomized memory. The most widely used technique is the return-into-library technique, due to the fact that libraries such as libc contain functions (or gadgets) for invoking system calls and other functionalities which are useful to attackers.

To defend against ROP attacks, in conjunction with DEP, Address Space Layout Randomization (ASLR) was proposed in a probability manner. The basic idea of ASLR is that addresses of loaded executable, stack, heap and loaded libraries for each new process are randomized. Therefore, attackers cannot easily predict the memory address and jump to a fixed executable address of a gadget for an ROP attack. Although there are several techniques [34] to bypass DEP/ASLR, ASLR indeed makes attacks more difficult and limited.

Android gradually adopted memory layout randomization on stack, library, heap, and dynamic linker in Android 2.3.4, Android 4.0, Android 4.0.3, and Android 5.0 respectively. However, ASLR protection on Android is not as effective as expected due to several reasons. First, only the latest version Android 5.x supports the full ASLR protection, but it only accounts for 12.4 % among all Android devices [6]. Second, even in the case of the full ASLR protection, the zygote app creation model still tampers this protection (Sect. 2.1). Third, the pre-compiled system framework oat files increase the pool for ROP gadgets and facilitate the construction of malicious payloads, and introduce a new attack surface.

3 A New Attack: Ret2art

In this section, we discuss how to circumvent the ASLR protection on Android and present a new attack surface introduced by the ART runtime.

3.1 ASLR Circumvention

What Went Wrong? As discussed in the previous section, all apps are forked from the zygote process. This implies that the memory structures of child apps are identical and duplicated by the parent zygote process. In other words, the base addresses of stacks, common libraries such as libc.so, and the dynamic linker are same in every app. Attackers can now easily predict memory layout information of all apps from one single exploited app. Moreover, even if some system libraries are not used by the app, they are still mapped into the app's process because the zygote process has loaded them. This further increases the possibility of the success of the ROP attack. In summary, the way that Android app is created *defeats the purpose of ASLR mechanism*.

We discover that the loaded libraries of the zygote process provide rich sources of ROP gadgets which every other app will inherit. To quantify the attack surface, we measure the size of text section (or executable section) of system libraries loaded in the zygote process for different Android major versions. Figure 3 shows that the number of loaded libraries increases from 50 to about 100, and the largest size of executable section is about 22 MB. This exposes a large number of vulnerable executable instructions for attackers. We then utilize an automatic ROP gadget search tool [7] to find out possible gadgets (i.e., instruction sequences ended with bx reg, blx reg and pop, pc) in shared libraries of the zygote process. Table 1 shows the number of unique ROP gadgets found by the tool in Android 5.1.1. Two common system libraries libandroid_runtime.so and libc.so (highlighted in the table) contain around a thousand usable gadgets. Because these two libraries provide basic functionalities for other part of the system, they are stable across different Android versions. Attackers could leverage the found ROP gadgets in them to launch the ROP attack.

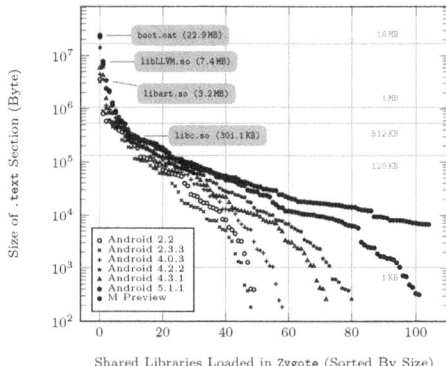

Fig. 3. Increasing .text section sizes of loaded shared libraries in zygote for different Android major versions.

Table 1. Number of unique ROP gadgets of loaded libraries in the zygote process.

Shared Library *	# of ROP Gadgets
libpdfium.so	56 154
libft2.so	7318
...	...
libandroid_runtime.so	1951
libEGL.so	1804
libz.so	1626
libvorbisidec.so	1219
libc.so	1049
...	...
Total	102 311

* Sorted by the number of ROP gadgets.

How to Exploit? To further understand the way to launch the ROP attack on Android, we use an example to illustrate the whole process. Figure 4 shows the flow of this attack. The attack scenario involves two apps. The objective of the first app (App A) is to obtain the current memory layout. This app can be a simple trojan app installed beforehand. Note that one app can access its own memory layout without any privileged permission. By reading the /proc/self/maps file, attackers can easily obtain the memory mapping information including library names, base addresses, and protect permissions, etc. The second app (App B) is the target app for an ROP attack, which has a buffer overflow vulnerability (e.g., popular apps like VLC [13] and Adobe Flash [1] have such vulnerability). Attackers first induce users to install the first app (App A) (step 1) to obtain the current memory layout (step 2). Secondly, attackers can craft a chain of gadgets using common libraries such as libc.so and libart.so, then determine the absolute addresses according to the current memory layout obtained previously. At last, attackers exploit the buffer overflow vulnerability of the legitimate app (App B) to initiate an ROP attack (step 3). By jumping and chaining executable gadgets, attackers can execute arbitrary privileged code for further attacks.

Even though the proposed attack in Fig. 4 leverages the first app (App A) to obtain the memory layout information, this information could be obtained through exploiting vulnerabilities in legitimate apps. For example, several known vulnerabilities of the Chrome Browser [4,5] and Samsung KNOX browser [8] can leak part of the memory information. That means the proposed attack could be launched remotely without the need to install the first app (App A). This conclusion has been demonstrated in the previous research [32] and we will not discuss its details in this paper.

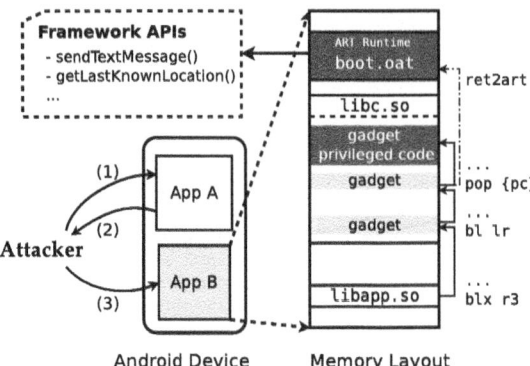

Fig. 4. ROP attack on Android (return-to-library attack and return-to-art attack).

3.2 The New Return-to-ART Attack (ret2art)

When launching the ROP attack, the most complicated part is to design a valuable gadget chain and execute malicious payloads. Traditionally, attackers could leverage particular system calls (e.g., execve()) or existing functions in common libraries (e.g., system() and strcpy() in libc library) for this purpose. However, in the context of the Android system, it is hard for attackers to construct meaningful payloads. For instance, if attackers want to send a text message to subscribe to a premium service to make money, or to steal private information from a local database, they have to bridge the semantic gap between the malicious operations and low level APIs. Though the Android framework provides many useful APIs, it is hard for attackers to invoke them since these APIs are in the format of the Dalvik bytecode and cannot be executed directly. Therefore, it is a non-trivial task to construct malicious payloads on Android.

The ART runtime was introduced since the latest Android version 5.0. We found that the design and implementation of the ART runtime *exposes a new attack surface*, which is called *return-to-ART (ret2art) attack*. It eases the construction of malicious payloads and attackers could initiate more powerful and damaging attacks.

What Went Wrong? Due to the introduction of the ART runtime, the addresses of the pre-compiled native code of the system framework APIs are predictable. First, boot.oat and boot.art files contain the compiled native code and related metadata of Android framework APIs. These two files are generated by phone vendors before shipping the devices to users, and will not change unless there is a new OTA update image. Therefore, these files are same across all devices using the same firmware image. Second, the base address of boot.art is fixed (0x70000000 for the 32-bit ARM architecture) in the AOSP source code (in the /build/core/dex_preopt_libart.mk file [11]). The exact mapping address of the boot.oat file is patched when the device is first booted, and will not change unless a system update is performed. The patch offset

```
1   $ adb shell oatdump -oat-file=/system/framework/arm/boot.oat
2   ...
3   IMAGE PATCH DELTA: -724992 (0xfff4f000)
4   ...
5   40: Landroid/telephony/SmsManager; (offset=0x015d849c) (type_idx=198) (StatusVerified) (
          ↪ OatClassSomeCompiled)
6   ...
7     37: void android.telephony.SmsManager.sendTextMessage(java.lang.String, java.lang.String,
          ↪ java.lang.String, android.app.PendingIntent, android.app.PendingIntent)} (
          ↪ dex_method_idx=844)
8     OatMethodOffsets (offset=0x015d853c)
9       code_offset: 0x02ca944d
10  ...
11    CODE: (code_offset=0x02ca944d size_offset=0x02ca9448 size=324)...
12      0x02ca944c: f5bd5c00   subs    r12, sp, #8192
13  ...
```

Code Snippet 1.1. Example of oatdump for boot.oat file.

of the boot.oat file is fixed between -0x01000000 and 0x01000000 as indicated in /art/build/Android.common_build.mk. For instance, if the patch offset of boot.oat is 0x8000, then boot.oat will be mapped to the fixed address 0x70008000 every time for every app running on the device, until the device updates its firmware image.

The predictable nature of the addresses of loaded oat and art files exposes a new attack surface (the ret2art attack). First, boot.oat is loaded by the zygote process and inherited by all other apps. Therefore, the base address of the boot.oat file is fixed for *every app in each execution*. Second, the boot.oat file is mapped as an executable region in memory. It contains abundant number of compiled native code of all methods in the Android framework, and provides a fertile ground for ROP gadgets. According to Fig. 3, the size of the executable code in this file is around 22.9 MB. Third, the code offsets for each method are fixed and can be easily located from the structured metadata from either the boot.art file or the boot.oat file. Therefore, attackers can craft gadgets and jump to the native code offset of a method in the boot.oat file. Figure 4 illustrates the basic flow of the re2art attack. Similar with the conventional ROP attack, attackers can hijack the control flow to the ART executable code. This way, attackers can invoke framework APIs in the ART runtime, which facilitates the construction of malicious payloads. For instance, attackers can use the getLastKnowLocation() API to obtain any recent geographical location information.

How to Exploit? Suppose attackers want to send a text message to achieve an *unauthorized premium services subscription*. *First*, attackers need to get the offset of the sendTextMessage method in the boot.oat file. This can be achieved by reading the boot.oat of the firmware using the oatdump tool. Note that, since this offset is only related to particular firmware, attackers could get this knowledge in advance by downloading firmwares from Internet and obtain a mapping table of offsets of interested APIs to the firmware fingerprint. The base

Table 2. Parameter description of "Invocation Stub".

Parameter	Description
r0 register	method pointer to the invoke ArtMethod class object
r1 register	argument array or NULL for no argument methods
r2 register	size of argument array in bytes
r3 register	thread pointer
[sp]	address for return value
[sp + 4]	address for shorty character representation of return value

```
1   ENTRY art_quick_invoke_stub
2   ...
3       ldr    r0, [r11]         @ restore method*
4       ldr    r1, [sp, #4]      @ copy arg value for r1
5       ldr    r2, [sp, #8]      @ copy arg value for r2
6       ldr    r3, [sp, #12]     @ copy arg value for r3
7       mov    ip, #0            @ set ip to 0
8       ldr    ip, [r0, #METHOD_QUICK_CODE_OFFSET_32]
9                                @ get pointer to the
                                   code
10      blx    ip                @ call the method
11  ...
12  END art_quick_invoke_stub
```

Code Snippet 1.2: Invocation stub function.

address of the boot.oat file is fixed after the system is first powered, and could be obtained through another trojan app or information leak vulnerabilities in other apps, and even guessed since the base address is around a fixed location 0x70000000. Code snippet 1.1 shows an example of the dumped boot.oat file. We can find that the code offset of the sendTextMessage method is fixed in the boot.oat file at 0x02ca944d (line 11). *Second*, similar to the previous ROP attack, attackers can obtain the base address of boot.oat file locally or remotely. Combing the obtained offset and the base address, attackers now have the absolute address of the method. *Third*, attackers exploit existing or zero-day buffer overflow vulnerabilities of the target app to hijack the control flow for initiating a ret2art attack. Note that attackers cannot directly jump to this address and execute the code, because the framework code should be executed with the support of the ART runtime. Specifically, the ART runtime executes native methods through an invocation stub code, i.e., the art_quick_invoke_stub function defined in the quick_entrypoints_arm.S assembly file [12] for the ARM platform. Before invoking this code, attackers have to prepare several registers for related parameters as shown in Table 2. After passing these registers to the art_quick_invoke_stub function, the function will finally load the compiled code to a register as a branch address. As shown in Code Snippet 1.2, the address is calculated by summing up r0 with an offset METHOD_QUICK_CODE_OFFSET_32 in line 8, that is, the address of entry_point_from_quick_compiled_code_ field in the ArtMethod class. Moreover, r1-r3 are copied from the stack controlled by attackers, which makes the ret2art attack even easier. Therefore, to initiate a ret2art attack, the attacker can branch (e.g., blx reg) to this stub function and invoke the sendTextMessage framework API. If the target app has declared the "SEND_SMS" permission, attackers can use this technique to subscribe to some premium services, or to spread the trojan app via messages.

4 Blender

In this section, we present the design and implementation of BLENDER, a user-level solution to mitigate threats caused by the weakened ASLR implementation on Android and the new ret2art attack.

4.1 High Level System Design

Design Requirements. Our goal is to provide a user-level solution. Accordingly, we follow several design requirements to balance protection strength, performance, and practical system deployment.

Complete Protection: Our system needs to mitigate the threats introduced by both the zygote application creation process and the new ART runtime. This means that our system has to eliminate the predictability of the memory layout for loaded system libraries, and the pre-compiled native code of the framework APIs (the boot.oat file).

Lightweight Protection: It naturally requires that our system should be memory- and energy-efficient. The performance overhead should not affect user experience. Moreover, the overhead introduced should not affect the apps without our protection.

Easy Deployment: Our system should maintain the compatibility of existing apps, and not require any change to the Android framework nor the Linux kernel. Also, the changes made to apps for deploying our system should be minimum.

Threat and Trust Model. As our purpose is to provide a user-level solution to mitigate the threat of weakened ASLR protection on Android, we assume app developers are trusted. However, their apps or libraries that apps are depending on may have security vulnerabilities and could be exploited by attackers both locally and remotely to arbitrarily read, write, and execute code in app's memory. Their apps have higher security requirements, and they want to provide the self-protection capability to their apps. By deploying our solution, the empowered self-protection capability makes the exploitation of the vulnerabilities in their apps much harder.

Design Overview. BLENDER provides protection in two different aspects. First, BLENDER randomizes the addresses of loaded system libraries for apps using our system. This eliminates the possibility that the memory layout of these libraries are predictable. From this perspective, our system provides similar security guarantees as previous work [32], by solely in user space, without making changes to the Android framework. Second, BLENDER deals with the new ret2art attack by randomizing the executable code of the pre-compiled framework APIs (i.e., boot.art and boot.oat files) in the ART runtime. This is a new security guarantee which is not covered by previous research.

Accordingly, BLENDER contains three components: (1) the bootstrap module, (2) BLENDER library randomization module (short for BLENDERLRM), and (3) BLENDER ART randomization module (short for BLENDERART). The bootstrap module takes over the startup stage of an app, and prepares the running environment of our system. Like other user-level solutions [54, 60], this bootstrap module is integrated into the app by simply including a proxy class which extends the Application class. Then the bootstrap module will invoke BLENDERLRM to self-randomize the current loaded libraries. After that, it will invoke BLENDERART to rearrange the ART runtime in the memory. Finally, the original app will be loaded and started. Since the bootstrap module has been extensively discussed in previous research [54,60], in this paper, we will explain BlenderLRM and BlenderART, respectively.

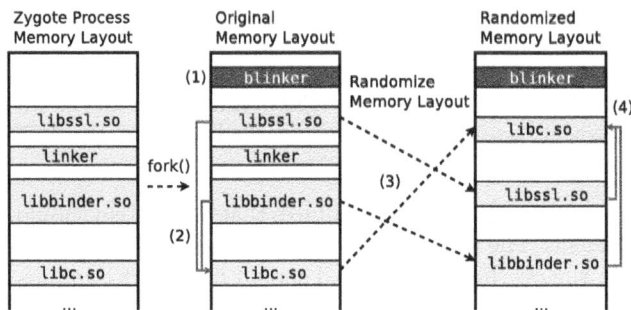

Fig. 5. Overview of Blender library randomization module.

4.2 BlenderLRM

Figure 5 illustrates the overview of BlenderLRM. The main purpose of BlenderLRM is to randomize the addresses of already loaded system libraries inherited from the `zygote` process, and all other app-provided third-party libraries. For this purpose, BlenderLRM leverages a customized dynamic linker (named as `blinker`), which first rearranges the already loaded system libraries and then takes over the process of loading app-provided third-party libraries and randomizes their addresses. Note that all the described operations in this section later are only applied to its own process of the app with our system, and does not affect other processes running on the same device.

Rearrange System Libraries. Rearranging the system libraries looks straightforward, since all system libraries on the Android with ASLR support should be compiled as position independent code (PIC). This means that these libraries could be loaded into any addresses[1]. We can simply copy the loaded libraries from one location to another one to randomize the loaded addresses of them. However, most, if not all, system libraries are dynamically linked. These dynamically linked libraries depend on other libraries, and their dependencies have been resolved when creating the `zygote` process. Simply moving the system libraries from one location to another location will break the resolved dependencies, and crash the app.

---

[1] In early versions of Android without ASLR support, system libraries are pre-loaded into fixed locations.

Algorithm 1. Memory Randomization Algorithm

1: **function** RANDOMIZELIBRARIES(*libraryDependencyGraph*)
2:     *sortedNodes* ← TOPOSORT(*libraryDependencyGraph*)
3:     **for** each $n \in sortedNodes$ **do**
4:         DUPMAP(n)   ▷ Duplicate memory mapping to a random free space.
5:         **for** each node m with an edge from n to m **do**
6:             FIXGOT(m, n)   ▷ Fix symbol resolution in GOT of m.
7:         **end for**
8:         SAVELIBRARYINFORMATION(n)
9:         UNMAP(n)   ▷ Unmap library n from memory mappings.
10:    **end for**
11: **end function**

Before presenting our method to solve this challenge, we will describe the background of dynamic linking first to help readers better understand our proposed method. For each dynamically linked library, there is a Procedure Linkage Table (PLT) section (.plt), which contains several stubs to call external functions. For example, suppose library A uses the `strcpy` function in `libc`, then there is a stub for the `strcpy` function in the PLT section of library A. The functionality of this PLT stub is to load the real address of the `strcpy` (of `libc` in the memory) from the entry of the Global Offset Table (GOT) section, and then jump to it. Each external function used by the library has an entry in GOT, and its real address is resolved by the dynamic linker (i.e., /system/bin/linker in Android) when the library is first loaded into the memory and written in the corresponding GOT entry. Note that the dynamic linker in Android does not adopted the "lazy binding" mechanism [20], which is common in the desktop systems, to speed up the app startup stage.

To solve the challenge of dependencies between system libraries, `blinker` generates a dependency graph on the loaded libraries and fixes the wrong addresses in GOT due to library rearrangement. We say that library A depends on library B if there exists a function call from library B to library A. For instance, `liblog.so` uses the `strcpy()` function in `libc.so`, and we say `libc.so` depends on `liblog.so`. In the dependency graph, there will be an edge from A (e.g., `libc.so`) to B (e.g., `liblog.so`). Correspondingly, the GOT section of `liblog.so` should contain an entry of the `strcpy` function pointing to `libc.so`. Figure 6 illustrates the dependency graph of ten common libraries loaded by `zygote`. From the figure, we can see that there are eight libraries which depend on `libc.so`. Therefore, if BLENDERLRM rearranges `libc.so` library to other address, addresses pointing to `libc.so` in GOTs of its dependent libraries needs to be updated. Note that `blinker` itself is statically linked, otherwise it will depend on other system libraries which will be rearranged and a dead lock will be created between `blinker` and its dependent libraries.

After generating the dependency graph, `blinker` rearranges system libraries according to the method described in Algorithm 1. The algorithm takes a library dependency graph as an input. `blinker` first topologically sorts the dependency graph. For each node in the sorted node list, `blinker` first duplicates it into a

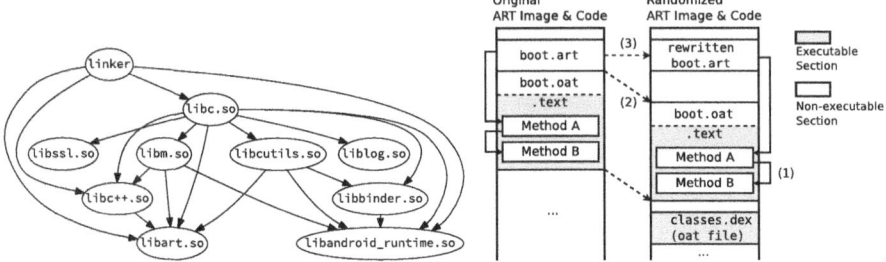

Fig. 6. Dependency graph.　　　**Fig. 7.** Overview of BlenderART.

random free space aligned with the memory page size. Then, **blinker** fixes GOTs of its dependent nodes. Furthermore, **blinker** will store the library information including new base locations, names, dependency information, etc. This information will help **blinker** to link libraries which will be added at later stages. Finally, **blinker** will unmap the original libraries from memory.

Rearrange App-Provided Third-Party Libraries. Besides system libraries, an app may have its own third-party libraries. For instance, the app using the Cocos2d game engine will include the corresponding native libraries in the app. Our system needs to randomize these libraries as well to ensure they have different addresses in different runs. For this purpose, **blinker** takes over the role of the original linker. Specifically, native libraries are loaded into memory by the **dlopen()** function in **libdl.so**. We modify the dynamic linker related function pointers in the GOT section of **libdl.so** to our customized **blinker**. Then, if a new native library is loaded into memory by using the **dlopen()** function, **blinker** will map it into a random address and resolve external function calls.

4.3 BlenderART

As discussed in Sect. 3.2, the newly introduced ART runtime exposes a new attack surface, due to the fact that the pre-compiled **boot.oat** file is in a fixed memory location after the system is first booted and will not change unless an OTA update is performed[2]. Our system needs to rearrange this **boot.oat** to other locations. However, the differences between the **boot.oat** and other system libraries we discussed in Sect. 4.2 pose new challenges, and we cannot directly apply the method proposed in Sect. 4.2 to the **boot.oat** file.

Figure 7 illustrates the workflow of BlenderART. There are three steps to carry out the ART runtime randomization: (1) patch the **boot.oat** file with an offset, (2) load this patched **boot.oat** file into the memory, (3) fix code addresses of the class linker instance in the ART runtime.

---

[2] Actually, the app's bytecode in the file classes.dex is also compiled into the native code. However, this compiled native code is loaded into different places each time the app is started.

Patch and Load Boot.oat. of the boot.oat file, two main components in the boot.oat file should be patched. First, some branch instructions in the boot.oat use *absolute* addresses to jump to the target instruction. For instance, suppose method A invokes method B in the framework as shown in Fig. 7, the branch instruction jumping from method A to method B uses an absolute address in memory. These absolute addresses should be patched if we want to move the boot.oat to another location. Second, the metadata information in the oat file header contains absolute addresses, and need to be patched too.

One natural choice to patch the address is to leverage the binary rewriting tool to disassemble the compiled native code, locate and modify absolute addresses in branch instructions. However, writing a binary rewriting tool from scratch is a tedious and error-prone process. In this work, we take advantage of a convenient interface provided by Google for binary rewriting, which is called the oat_patches. When converting the dex bytecode to native code, the ART compiler first translates the dex bytecode into an intermediate representations (MIR), and then compiles it into the low-level intermediate representation (LIR). During the converting stage from MIR to LIR, the compiler records all literals (including code, method, class, and string literals) which contain absolute addresses and can be modified later (implemented in InstallLiteralPools() methods in the codegen_util.cc file [10] from AOSP). And the literal information will be written into one special ELF section of the final oat file, which is called the oat_patches section. We leverage the oat_patches tool to help us relocate boot.oat and patch the original fixed absolute addresses. In fact, this oat_patches information is also used by Android to patch the boot.oat when the system is first powered on.

BLENDERART first randomly picks a free memory region and calculates the offset (Δ) between the new base address and the original one ($\mathcal{B}$). Algorithm 2 illustrates the procedure to patch the boot.oat file. The patching algorithm takes the oat file and offset number as input, and will go through all patches and add an offset. The FixupOatHeader function is to relocate the metadata of the embedded oat header. The FixupELF function is to rewrite the section header information, dynamic symbol section (dynsym) and the symbol table section (symtab) information. At last, the patched boot.oat will be loaded into the memory. Because we already fixup all relocation based on an offset, the load address should be $\mathcal{B} + \Delta$.

Algorithm 2. ART Runtime (boot.oat) Patching Algorithm

1: **function** PATCHOAT(*oatFile*, *offset*)
2:   **for each** *patch* ∈ *oatFile.oatPatches* **do**
3:     *patchLocation* ← GETLOCATION(*patch*)
4:     ∗*patchLocation* ← *patchLocation* + *offset*
5:   **end for**
6:   FIXUPOATHEADER(*oatFile*, *offset*)
7:   FIXUPELF(*oatFile*, *offset*)
8: **end function**

Fix Class Linker Data Instance. Besides the absolute address in the code area in the boot.oat file, some information in the data area of the ART runtime should be patched too. Class linker (i.e., the ClassLinker class) is a single global instance maintained by the ART runtime. Since the executable code in the boot.oat file has been relocated by our system, several important information maintained by it should be fixed too. For instance, it maintains a class table (the class_table_ field), which contains loaded classes information (i.e., the mirror::Class class). For each class structure, it contains corresponding methods in the method tables. There are two types of methods: direct methods and virtual methods, which are stored in the direct_methods_ table and virtual_methods_ table respectively. The methods in the method table are in the mirror::ArtMethod class. There is a pointer sized field contains four entry point addresses. For example, the entry_point_from_quick_compiled_code_ field of a framework method points to the actual compiled code address of boot.oat in the memory. Since boot.oat has been relocated, this pointer should be fixed to point to the new address. Finally, BLENDERART changes the old memory region of boot.oat to non-executable to ensure data in this file cannot be executed, but can still be accessed by the ART runtime. In theory, we could fully unmap this memory region. However, we then need to fix all the references to this memory region in the ART runtime, which is a time-consuming work. As long as the code area is no-longer executable, it is safe to leave it there since attackers cannot leverage it to construct ROP gadgets.

Optimization. Apps with BLENDERART should perform all the previous steps to achieve the ART runtime randomization. However, patching the boot.oat file introduces an overhead of around 1.6 s which will be shown in Sect. 5. To reduce this overhead, we cache the randomized boot.oat so as to reduce the app's startup time. We design a patched boot.oat pool which contains a set of offline patched boot.oat files with different random patched offsets. For each execution, our system picks up a patched boot.oat file from the pool and loads it into the memory, without patching it online.

4.4 Implementation Details

We prototype our BLENDER system based on Android 5.1 Lollipop (the AOSP tag android-5.1.0_r1) for 32-bit ARM architecture. Since the code base of the ART runtime is stable after Android 5.0, our implementation is generic for Android 5.0 and 6.0 versions. The system contains about two thousand lines of code including C/C++ and Java. For the implementation, we reuse the peer-reviewed code from AOSP as much as possible. This will ensure the stability and security of BLENDER. We use the /dev/random file as the seed for randomization.

There is no official ART support for Android versions less than 5.0[3]. Therefore, the Dalvik virtual machine runtime cannot be exploited by using the

---

[3] There is an experimental implementation of the ART runtime in Android 4.4 but is disabled by default.

ret2art attack technique. Although a researcher discovered interpreter exploitation [16] on the conventional JIT based virtual machine, it is still difficult to initiate attacks on the Dalvik runtime. However, the security issue caused by the `zygote` app creation model still exists. To harden the ASLR for old Android versions (before Android 5.0), we port BLENDERLRM to them so as to self-randomize addresses of system libraries inherited from the `zygote` process. Because BLENDER is a user-level solution and provides self-randomization capability to the apps using our system, rather than modifying the source code of the Android framework, app developers could safely deploy our system and their apps immediately get protected.

5 Evaluation

In this section we evaluate the effectiveness of BLENDER by measuring the app memory entropy, and the performance overhead at apps' startup time, execution, memory, and battery usage. The device used in the evaluation is a Nexus 5 device with Quad-core 2.3 GHz CPU, 2 GB memory and 16 GB internal storage. The test device runs the Google official Android firmware which is Lollipop 5.1 with the build number `LMY47D` and the kernel version 3.4.0.

5.1 Effectiveness

The goal of the BLENDER system is to prevent attackers from predicting address space layout of apps. To evaluate the effectiveness of BLENDER, we first discuss from an app's perspective.

To measure the address space layout randomness of shared system libraries, we use the notion of *entropy*. Entropy is a metric to represent the uncertainty of random variables. We apply entropy to measure memory layout randomness, and the library loading addresses are treated as a random variable. We utilize the space layout entropy metric from [32] to evaluate the application randomness. Specifically, for a shared library or runtime image code m, let X_m be a discrete random variable with base addresses $\{x_1, x_2, \ldots, x_n\}$ and $p(x_i)$ is a probability of $x_m = x_i$. The normalized address space layout entropy can be defined as $H(X_m) = -\sum_{i=1}^{n} p(x_i) \frac{\ln p(x_i)}{\ln n}$, and $0 \leq H(X_m) \leq 1$ because of normalization.

App Randomness. Because BLENDER only randomizes memory of certain apps with the BLENDER protection, we evaluate the entropy on one app for multiple executions. We define $\{x_1, x_2, \ldots, x_n\}$ as base addresses of the library m, and n is the number of executions for one app. For instance, suppose $n = 10$, we execute the app with BLENDER ten times, and the base addresses of library `libart.so` are totally different. Because each base address is uniformly distributed, the output will have a probability of 0.1. At last, the entropy for the `libart.so` library is $H(X_{libart.so}) = 1$. This means, for the ten times execution of this app, `libart.so` is mapped into different addresses. We calculate the average entropy for all loaded libraries in application A. It is defined as $R(A) = \frac{\sum_{m \in M} H(X_m)}{|M|}$. We measure $R(\mathcal{A})$ on a simple app ($\mathcal{A}$) (generated by

Table 3. Entropy analysis results.

Mode	App entropy R(A)
Original App	0.005
BLENDERLRM only	0.981
BLENDERLRM and BLENDERART	0.991

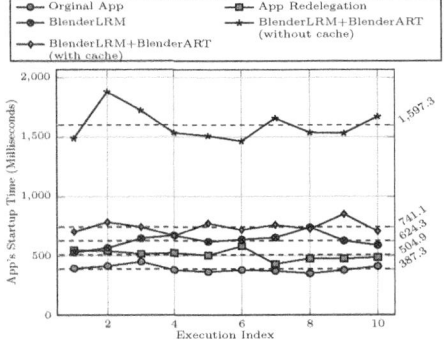

Fig. 8. App's startup time.

Fig. 9. Memory usages at the startup of apps for different setups.

the blank app template of Android Gradle 1.2.3 [2]). App $\mathcal{A}$ contains 109 native libraries at runtime, and 108 of them are shared libraries which are inherited from zygote. We execute the app without and with BLENDER protection ten times respectively, and record the memory layout after the startup stage. Table 3 shows the results of the average entropy. The average entropy of original app, app with BLENDERLRM only, and app with full BLENDER support are 0.005, 0.981, and 0.991 respectively. The average entropy of the original system is quite low, which shows that there is nearly no randomness in the original app. After using BLENDER with library randomization module, the entropy increases significantly. When adding with the ART runtime randomization module, the entropy increases about 0.1. Although the increased entropy of BLENDERART is small, but the security gain is considerably high because of the large range of executable regions.

5.2 Performance

Startup Time. Because BLENDER conducts the library and ART randomization when app is first started, we want to evaluate its overhead in terms of the startup time delay, which is crucial for user experience. To quantify the startup time, we conduct experiments on a simple app. We create the app targeting Android 5.1 with one activity (generated by the app template of Android Gradle 1.2.3 [2]). In the app, we override attachBaseContext methods in the activity

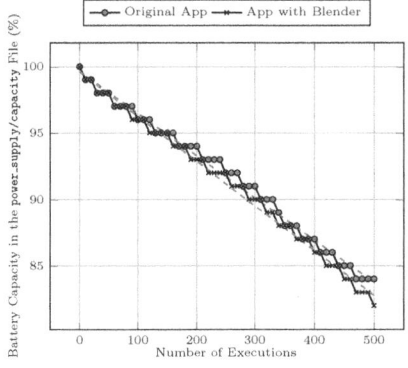

Fig. 10. Battery capacity after multiple executions.

Table 4. Benchmark scores.

	Baseline	BlenderLRM	Full Blender
CPU	35915	36480	35969
Memory	13900	13846	14653
I/O	5874	5893	5900
2D	330	330	298
3D	1967	2019	1981
Total	57986	58568	58801

and log the current time (t_1). To accurately calculate the startup elapsed time, we use a UI/application exerciser (monkey tool) to launch this application and record the time (t_0) by reading the $EPOCHREALTIME value. $t_1 - t_0$ represents the elapsed time from launch time into application context. We measure the startup time of the original app, app only with the bootstrap module (app re-delegation), app with BlenderLRM, app with the whole Blender without BlenderART cache, and finally, app with the optimized Blender with cache. We execute the app for ten times and record the results. Figure 8 illustrates the startup time (in millisecond) for each launch and the average numbers of different setups. First, because app re-delegation needs to load the app at runtime, it introduces about 120 ms overhead. Second, without using the cache, BlenderART needs to execute code patching for each time. The startup time is about 1.5 s, which is noticeable by normal users. For the system with cache, the startup time is about 740 ms and incurs about 360 ms overhead, which is comparable with Morula [32]. It is worth noting that, this overhead only affects at the app's first startup time (cold start), and will not affect the following launching of the app (warm start) if the app is not killed due to low memory. Moreover, unlike Morula [32], this delay only applies to apps with our protection, and does not affect other apps.

Runtime Overheads. Blender provides self-randomization capability to apps and the randomization process happens at the app's startup time, it will not affect the runtime performance. We use the Quadrant Standard Edition v2.1.1 to measure the general purpose benchmark for CPU, memory, I/O, 2D, and 3D graphics. Because we cannot get the source code of the benchmark tool, we use apktools [52] to repackage the app and add the Blender protection for our evaluation. Table 4 illustrates the benchmark results. Because of startup time randomization, the benchmark results are nearly same.

Memory Overheads. We also evaluate the memory usage at runtime for the original app, app with re-delegation, app with BlenderLRM only, and app with BlenderLRM and BlenderART. We create a script to monitor the

/proc/[pid]/status file which contains all memory information at runtime. Figure 9 shows the VmRSS sizes during the start time to 2000 ms. VmRSS (virtual memory resident set size) represents the portion of memory occupied by a process in memory. At the first 250 ms, the VmRSS value increases from a low level and then becomes stable. The VmRSS values of BLENDERLRM only and BLENDERLRM/ART together are nearly same at runtime, and introduces about 5513 kB (11.5 %) overhead. BLENDER incurs less memory overhead compared to previous mitigation solution Morula [32] by patching the Android which introduces 13 MB for each app.

Battery Overheads. Battery consumption is important for mobile devices. Because BLENDER conducts randomization at the startup time of an app, BLENDER will consume more battery than original settings. We conduct the following experiments to measure the battery overhead of the BLENDER system. Firstly, we use a fully charged device (Nexus 5) and set screen as "always on". Then, we launch and close the experiment app (the same app in the performance evaluation experiments) for 500 times with 10 s interval. For each execution, we record the current time and the current battery capacity. For the BLENDER evaluation, we use a fully charged device to execute the experiment app with BLENDER installed and record the battery capacity. For both experiments, we obtain the battery capacity by reading the /sys/class/power_supply/battery/capacity file. Figure 10 illustrates the remaining battery capacities after multiple number of executions for two apps, and we plot their linear fit as two dashed lines. There is only 1 % more power consumption after 500 executions for about 6400 s which is comparable with the Morula system. Therefore, the battery overhead is negligible for normal users.

6 Discussion

Limitations of Caching Patched ART Code. To balance security gain and performance overheads, our design caches patched ART code (i.e., boot.oat) in a pool. Although attackers can try multiple times to guess the offsets of the boot.oat file in the pool, they still cannot obtain the current offset by previous executions or by other side channels. However, this technique decreases the entropy of the randomization. To achieve high entropy randomization, developers can disable utilizing cached code and conduct randomization at runtime. Although this may introduce more startup overhead (less than two seconds), this is still acceptable for apps with high security requirements. Also we may randomize the boot.oat file at runtime, such as when the app is idle in the background, to reduce the startup time delay. However, this may need deep understanding of the app's logic and more involvement from the app developer's side.

Blender on Other Architectures. Because most mobile devices are based on the ARM architecture (99 % according to report [3]), our ret2art attack and BLENDER system are implemented on an ARM-based device. In fact, the latest Android version support other architectures including x86 and MIPS. The only differences are architecture specific source code. Therefore, the weakness of ASLR introduced by zygote process creation model still exists. And one can easily write code to initiate ret2art attack on those platforms. For the BLENDER system, one can port to other architectures by translating architecture specific ARM assembly code to the corresponding architecture.

Randomization within Shared Library. Another limitation of current system is that BLENDER does not randomize the functions inside a library. This means that if there is a memory leak vulnerability, attackers could know the base address and compute offsets of ROP gadgets to launch an ROP attack. To overcome this potential security problem, we can use method proposed as binary stirring [51] to randomly rewrite the binary code blocks of loaded libraries. However, this method requires disassembling, rewriting and assembling all loaded libraries at launch time of an app. This will introduces considerable overheads. Therefore, we leave it as our future work.

7 Related Work

Security problem in memory is one of the oldest issues in computer security. Previous studies [28,46,49] summarize the attack and defense solutions on memory security. Our work focuses on attacking and protecting weakened ASLR mechanism on Android.

Attacks and Defenses of ASLR Mechanism. Because modern operating systems have implemented/deployed ASLR and DEP defense mechanisms by default [24,30,47], attackers try many bypassing techniques from different perspectives. Several works [34,42] focus on bypassing by brute-forcing method. Moreover, leaked pointers, type confusion and use-after-free bugs can be also exploited [40,41]. Furthermore, by repeatedly abuse a memory disclosure, attackers can map an application's memory layout on-the-fly with dynamically discovered gadgets [43]. There are many return oriented programming techniques described in several papers [34,53]. Moreover, some researchers [22,51] proposed to protect memory by introducing high randomization entropy.

Attacks and Defenses on Android. Compared to traditional desktop operating system, mobile OS have their domain-specific architecture design which introduces new attack surfaces. For Android, many researches discuss about security issues on permission mechanism [19,29,31] of Android. In addition, some work exploit underlying system components on Android [15,21,27,35,37,38,48,50,57]. Because there are a number of malware on Android, Zhou et al. [59] provide the characterization and evolution of Android malware. In addition, some systems propose to prevent [45] or detect malware [44]. Moreover, researchers also propose both static analysis systems [26,33,56,58] and dynamic analysis systems [25,55] to assist malware researchers to understand the malicious logic.

Mitigating ASLR on Android. Because of the limitations of mobile system, the design and implementation of ASLR mechanism is rather weak. Retouching [17], Morula [32] and LR^2 [18] are three systems which discuss attacking techniques and provide mitigation solutions. Retouching can randomize prelinked code when deploying Android applications. However, Retouching does not resolve the issue of uniform memory layout introduced by the `zygote` process creation model. Morula proposes a patch for Android source code to randomize all layout of apps after forking from `zygote` and also introduces low overheads. LR^2 proposes a leakage-resilient layout randomization method by introducing transformations as passes on compiler. However, they all have a major deployment issue. Current systems needs to modify Android source code to achieve randomization functionality. Users should replace original firmware with the customized system. Moreover, the system should keep up with the latest Android version with new features and bug fixes. Hence, because of the deployment issues, both users and developers cannot easily adopt this mitigation solution. Our work provides a non-invasive methodology for both developers and users.

8 Conclusion

In this paper, we show that the ASLR protection on Android is weakened due to the `zygote` app creation model. Moreover, we demonstrate a newly discovered attack surface introduced by the ART runtime, and present a novel way to exploit the weakness of the ASLR protection and this new attack surface. Then we propose a non-invasive user-level solution called BLENDER which does not need framework modification. BLENDER *self-randomizes* address space layout for apps, hence raising the bar for successfully bypassing the weakened ASLR protection on Android. We discuss the design, implementation, and present the effectiveness and performance overhead of our system.

References

1. Adobe Flash Use-after-free Vulnerability. http://cve.mitre.org/cgi-bin/cvename.cgi?name=CVE-2015-3108
2. Android plugin for gradle. https://developer.android.com/intl/ru/tools/building/plugin-for-gradle.html
3. Arm designs one of the world's most-used products. http://www.bloomberg.com/bw/articles/2014-02-04/arm-chips-are-the-most-used-consumer-product-dot-where-s-the-money
4. CVE-2013-0912. https://cve.mitre.org/cgi-bin/cvename.cgi?name=CVE-2013-0912
5. CVE-2015-1233. https://cve.mitre.org/cgi-bin/cvename.cgi?name=CVE-2015-1233
6. Distribution of android platform versions. https://developer.android.com/about/dashboards/index.html
7. Ropgadget - gadgets finder and auto-roper. http://shell-storm.org/project/ROPgadget/
8. Samsung galaxy KNOX android browser RCE. https://www.exploit-db.com/exploits/35282/
9. Stagefright (bug). https://en.wikipedia.org/wiki/Stagefright_(bug)

10. codegen_util.cc file in AOSP. https://android.googlesource.com/platform/art/+/android-6.0.0_r26/compiler/dex/quick/codegen_util.cc
11. dex_preopt_libart.mk file in AOSP. https://android.googlesource.com/platform/build/+/android-6.0.0_r26/core/dex_preopt_libart.mk#36
12. quick_entrypoints_arm.S file in AOSP. https://android.googlesource.com/platform/art/+/android-6.0.0_r26/runtime/arch/arm/quick_entrypoints_arm.S
13. VLC media player 2.0.4 suffers from buffer overflow. https://trac.videolan.org/vlc/ticket/7860
14. Afonso, V., Bianchi, A., Fratantonio, Y., Doupé, A., Polino, M., de Geus, P., Kruegel, C., Vigna, G.: Going native: using a large-scale analysis of android apps to create a practical native-code sandboxing policy. In: NDSS (2016)
15. Bianchi, A., Corbetta, J., Invernizzi, L., Fratantonio, Y., Kruegel, C., Vigna, G.: What the app. is that? deception and countermeasures in the Android user interface. In: SP (2015)
16. Blazakis, D.: Interpreter exploitation. In: WOOT (2010)
17. Bojinov, H., Boneh, D., Cannings, R., Malchev, I.: Address space randomization for mobile devices. In: WiSec (2011)
18. Braden, K., Crane, S., Davi, L., Franz, M., Larsen, P., Liebchen, C., Sadeghi, A.-R.: Leakage-resilient layout randomization for mobile devices. In: NDSS (2016)
19. Bugiel, S., Davi, L., Dmitrienko, A., Fischer, T., Sadeghi, A.-R., Shastry, B.: Towards taming privilege-escalation attacks on android. In: NDSS (2012)
20. Chamberlain, S., Taylor, I.L.: The GNU linker (1991)
21. Chen, Q.A., Qian, Z., Mao, Z.M.: Peeking into your App without actually seeing it: UI state inference and novel android attacks. In: USENIX Security (2014)
22. Chen, Y., Wang, Z., Whalley, D., Lu, L.: Remix: on-demand live randomization. In: CODASPY (2016)
23. Solar Designer: return-to-libc attack. Bugtraq, August 1997
24. Durden, T.: Bypassing PaX ASLR protection. Phrack Mag. **59**, 9 (2002)
25. Enck, W., Gilbert, P., Han, S., Tendulkar, V., Chun, B.-G., Cox, L.P., Jung, J., McDaniel, P., Sheth, A.N.: Taintdroid: an information-flow tracking system for realtime privacy monitoring on smartphones. In: TOCS. ACM (2014)
26. Enck, W., Octeau, D., McDaniel, P., Chaudhuri, S.: A study of android application security. In: USENIX Security (2011)
27. Enck, W., Ongtang, M., McDaniel, P.: Understanding Android security. IEEE Secur. Priv. **7**(1), 50–57 (2009)
28. Erlingsson, U.: Low-level software security: attacks and defenses. In: Aldini, A., Gorrieri, R. (eds.) FOSAD 2007. LNCS, vol. 4677, pp. 92–134. Springer, Heidelberg (2007)
29. Felt, A.P., Wang, H.J., Moshchuk, A., Hanna, S., Chin, E.: Permission re-delegation: attacks and defenses. In: USENIX Security (2011)
30. Giuffrida, C., Kuijsten, A., Tanenbaum, A.S.: Enhanced operating system security through efficient and fine-grained address space randomization. In: USENIX Security (2012)
31. Grace, M.C., Zhou, Y., Wang, Z., Jiang, X.: Systematic detection of capability leaks in stock android smartphones. In: NDSS (2012)
32. Lee, B., Lu, L., Wang, T., Kim, T., Lee, W.: From Zygote to Morula: Fortifying weakened ASLR on android. In: SP (2014)
33. Lu, L., Li, Z., Wu, Z., Lee, W., Jiang, G.: CHEX: statically vetting Android apps for component hijacking vulnerabilities. In: CCS (2012)
34. Müller, T.: ASLR smack & laugh reference. In: Advanced Exploitation Techniques (2008)

35. Mulliner, C., Oberheide, J., Robertson, W., Kirda, E.: Patchdroid: scalable third-party security patches for android devices. In: ACSAC (2013)
36. Peles, O., Hay, R.: One class to rule them all: 0-day deserialization vulnerabilities in Android. In: WOOT (2015)
37. Razeen, A., Wu, B., Cheemalapati, S.: Spandex: Secure password tracking for Android. In: USENIX Security (2014)
38. Ren, C., Zhang, Y., Xue, H., Wei, T., Liu, P.: Towards discovering and understanding task hijacking in Android. In: USENIX Security (2015)
39. Roemer, R., Buchanan, E., Shacham, H., Savage, S.: Return-oriented programming: systems, languages, and applications. In: TISSEC. ACM (2012)
40. Roglia, G.F., Martignoni, L., Paleari, R., Bruschi, D.: Surgically returning to randomized lib(c). In: ACSAC (2009)
41. Serna, F.J.: The info leak era on software exploitation. Black Hat USA (2012)
42. Shacham, H., Page, M., Pfaff, B., Goh, E.-J., Modadugu, N., Boneh, D.: On the effectiveness of address-space randomization. In: CCS (2014)
43. Snow, K.Z., Monrose, F., Davi, L., Dmitrienko, A., Liebchen, C., Sadeghi, A.-R.: Just-in-time code reuse: on the effectiveness of fine-grained address space layout randomization. In: SP (2013)
44. Sun, M., Li, M., Lui, J.C.S.: Droideagle: seamless detection of visually similar Android Apps. In: WiSec (2015)
45. Sun, M., Zheng, M., Lui, J.C.S., Jiang, X.: Design and implementation of an Android host-based intrusion prevention system. In: ACSAC (2014)
46. Szekeres, L., Payer, M., Wei, T., Song, D.: Sok: Eternal war in memory. In: SP (2013)
47. Team, P.: Pax address space layout randomization (ASLR) (2003)
48. Thomas, D.R., Beresford, A.R., Rice, A.: Security metrics for the Android ecosystem. In: SPSM (2015)
49. van der Veen, V., dutt-Sharma, N., Cavallaro, L., Bos, H.: Memory errors: the past, the present, and the future. In: Balzarotti, D., Stolfo, S.J., Cova, M. (eds.) RAID 2012. LNCS, vol. 7462, pp. 86–106. Springer, Heidelberg (2012)
50. Vidas, T., Votipka, D., Christin, N.: All your droid are belong to us: a survey of current android attacks. In: WOOT (2011)
51. Wartell, R., Mohan, V., Hamlen, K.W., Lin, Z.: Binary stirring: self-randomizing instruction addresses of legacy x86 binary code. In: ASIACCS (2012)
52. Winsniewski, R.: Android-apktool: a tool for reverse engineering Android apk files (2012)
53. Wojtczuk, R.N.: The advanced return-into-lib(c) exploits: PaX case study. Mag. 0x0b(0x3a) (2001)
54. Xu, R., Saidi, H., Anderson, R.: Aurasium: practical policy enforcement for Android applications. In: USENIX Security (2012)
55. Yan, L.-K., Yin, H.: Droidscope: seamlessly reconstructing the OS and Dalvik semantic views for dynamic Android malware analysis. In: USENIX Security (2012)
56. Zhang, M., Duan, Y., Yin, H., Zhao, Z.: Semantics-aware Android malware classification using weighted contextual API dependency graphs. In: CCS (2014)
57. Zheng, M., Sun, M., Lui, J.: Droidray: a security evaluation system for customized Android firmwares. In: ASIACCS (2014)
58. Zheng, M., Sun, M., Lui, J.C.: Droidanalytics: a signature based analytic system to collect, extract, analyze and associate Android malware. In: TrustCom (2013)
59. Zhou, Y., Jiang, X.: Dissecting Android malware: characterization and evolution. In: SP (2012)
60. Zhou, Y., Patel, K., Wu, L., Wang, Z., Jiang, X.: Hybrid user-level sandboxing of third-party Android Apps. In: ASIACCS (2015)

Author Index

Amira, Rony 143
Antonakakis, Manos 188
Arshad, Sajjad 415
Athanasopoulos, Elias 3

Backes, Michael 165, 303
Bailey, Michael 143
Balzarotti, Davide 24, 393
Ben-Yoash, Adi 143
Berger, Ari 143
Blackthorne, Jeremy 211
Bozzato, Claudio 97
Brengel, Michael 165
Bursztein, Elie 143

Caballero, Juan 230, 325
Calleja, Alejandro 325
Catakoglu, Onur 393
Chen, Yizheng 188
Cheng, Yao 254

Dabrowski, Adrian 279
Dagon, David 188

Focardi, Riccardo 97
Folger, Ori 143
Fu, Yangchun 49, 71

Gadyatskaya, Olga 346
Gañan, Carlos Hernandez 368

Hardon, Amir 143
Holz, Thorsten 303
Hu, Xunchao 254

Inoue, Daisuke 165
Ioannidis, Sotiris 3
Ishii, Kou 165

Jiang, Guofei 71
Joffe, Rodney 188

Kaiser, Benjamin 211
Kasama, Takahiro 165

Kharraz, Amin 415
Kintis, Panagiotis 188
Kirda, Engin 437
Korczyński, Maciej 368
Koromilas, Lazaros 3
Kotzias, Platon 230
Kountouras, Athanasios 188
Kruegel, Christopher 24

Lee, Ruby B. 118
Lever, Chaz 188
Li, Zhichun 71
Lin, Zhiqiang 49, 71
Lui, John C.S. 457

Maggi, Federico 437
Makita, Daisuke 368
Mambretti, Andrea 437
Matsumoto, Tsutomu 165
Muench, Marius 24
Mulliner, Collin 437

Nadji, Yacin 188
Noroozian, Arman 368

Onarlioglu, Kaan 437

Pagani, Fabio 24
Palmarini, Francesco 97
Papa, Yinmin 165
Pellegrino, Giancarlo 393
Petzl, Georg 279
Prakash, Aravind 254

Rhee, Junghwan 71
Rivera, Richard 230
Robertson, William 415, 437
Rossow, Christian 165, 303, 393
Rytilahti, Teemu 303

Sebastián, Marcos 230
Shoshitaishvili, Yan 24
Simeonovski, Milivoj 303
Steel, Graham 97

Stock, Ben 303
Sun, Mingshen 457

Tanabe, Rui 165
Tapiador, Juan 325
Thomas, Kurt 143

van Eeten, Michel 368
Vasiliadis, Giorgos 3
Vigna, Giovanni 24

Wang, Jinghan 254
Weippl, Edgar R. 279

Yener, Bülent 211
Yin, Heng 254
Yokoyama, Akira 165
Yoshioka, Katsunari 165, 368

Zanero, Stefano 437
Zeng, Junyuan 49
Zhang, Hui 71
Zhang, Tianwei 118
Zhang, Yinqian 118
Zhauniarovich, Yury 346
Zhou, Rundong 254
Zhou, Yajin 457

The manufacturer's authorised representative in the EU is Springer Nature Customer Service Centre GmbH, Europaplatz 3, 69115 Heidelberg, Germany. If you have any concerns regarding our products, please contact ProductSafety@springernature.com

Printed and bound by CPI Group (UK) Ltd, Croydon, CR0 4YY

23/03/2026

02076662-0018